Primary Dictionary

Collins

Collins Primary Dictionary

First published 2001

© HarperCollinsPublishers Ltd 2001
10 9 8 7 6 5 4 3 2
ISBN 0 00 316157 9 hardback
ISBN 0 00 316158 7 paperback

A catalogue record for this book is available from the British Library.

Published by Collins
A division of HarperCollinsPublishers Ltd
77-85 Fulham Palace Road
Hammersmith
London W6 8JB

www.**Collins**Education.com
On-line Support for Schools and Colleges

www.**fire**and**water**.com
Visit the book lover's website

Compilers	Ginny Lapage with Marguerite de la Haye and Judith Fisher
Consultant Editor	Evelyn Goldsmith
Literacy consultants	Kay Hiatt, Rosemary Boys
Numeracy consultants	Jan Henley, Karen Pegram, Jayne Spiller
Science consultant	Rona Wyn Davies
Cover designer	Susi Martin
Design	Chi Leung, Wordcraft and DSM Partnership

Illustrators
Tim Archbold, Cy Baker, Simone Boni, Maggie Brand, Tamsin Cook, Joanne Cowne, Luigi Crittone, William Donohoe, Richard Draper, Luigi Gallante, Jeremy Gower, Nick Harris, Christian Hook, Felicity House, Hans Jenssen, Sharon MacCausland, John Mack, Kevin Maddison, Tony Morris, Pat Murray, Chris Orr Associates, Malcolm Porter, Sebastian Quigley, Steve Roberts, Mike Saunders, Peter Scott, Siena Artworks, Hayley Simmons, Gill Thomblin, Phil Weare, Steve Weston, Sarah Wimperis, Ann Winterbotham, Sue Woollatt.

Photos
All commissioned photos by Steve Lumb.

The publishers wish to thank the following for permission to use photographs:
Cover photos by Art Wolfe, Tony Stone Images (tiger) and B. & C. Calhoun, Bruce Coleman Collection (hummingbird).
Andes Press: p.388 toucan, p. 412 waterfall, p. 423 yashmak; **Art Directors & Trip**: p. 14 aircraft, p. 53 cactus, p. 54 canal, p.119 eclipse, p. 152 fur, p. 156 geyser, p. 183 iceberg, p. 192 inlet, p. 203 junk, p. 208 lagoon, p. 216 limpet, p. 226 marble, p. 248 neon, p. 260 otter, p. 293 propeller, p. 297 pyramid, p. 313 reservoir, p. 318 roller coaster, p. 361 stilts, p. 404 valley, p. 418 windmill; **John Birdsall Library**: p. 46 braille; **Bridgeman Art Library**: p. 376 tapestry; **Greg Evans**:

p. 101 desert, p. 160 gondola, p. 241 mosaic, p. 390 tram; **In Character**: p. 206 knight; **Oxford Scientific Films**: p. 22 aqueduct, p. 94 dam, p. 99 delta, p. 181 hurricane, p. 358 stalagmite, p. 395 tuna, p. 409 vulture, p. 423 x-ray; **Panos Pictures**: p. 112 double bass, p. 117 dyke; **Tony Stone**: p. 111 dolphin, p. 154 gargoyle, p. 234 minaret, p. 307 reef, p. 370 surf.

All other photos and illustrations © HarperCollins*Publishers* Ltd, 2001

Acknowledgements
The publishers would like to thank all the teachers, staff and pupils who contributed to this book:

Models
Lauren Carroll	Stacey Cleary	Tom Crane
Katherine Davis	William Davis	Ruby Feroze
Elizabeth Fison	Jesse Johnson	Ismael Khan
Margaret Omoboade	Zina Patel	Dunia Pavlovic
Petra Pavlovic	Milo Petrie-Foxwell	Dexter Sampson
Mauri-Joy Smith	Tom Symonds	Rosie Ward

Schools
Aberhill Primary, Fife; ASDAC, Fife; Canning St Primary, Newcastle upon Tyne; Cowgate Primary, Newcastle upon Tyne; Crombie Primary, Fife; the Literacy Team at Dryden Professional Development Centre, Gateshead; Dunshalt Primary, Fife; Ecton Brook Lower, Northampton; English Martyrs RC Primary, Newcastle upon Tyne; Hotspur Primary, Newcastle upon Tyne; John Betts Primary School, London; Lemington First, Newcastle upon Tyne; LMTC Education Centre, Northumberland, Melcombe Primary, London; Methihill Primary, Fife; Newcastle Literacy Centre, Newcastle upon Tyne; Northampton High, Northampton; Pitcoudie Primary, Fife; Pitreavie Primary, Fife; Ravenswood Primary, Newcastle upon Tyne; St Andrew's CE Primary, London; Simon de Senlis Lower, Northampton; Sinclairtown Primary, Fife; Standens Barn Lower, Northampton; Touch Primary, Fife; Towcester Infants, Northampton; Wooton Primary, Northampton.

Printed in Great Britain by Scotprint Book Printers, Haddington, East Lothian

Contents

Using this dictionary 4

Abbreviations 6

The dictionary 7

The solar system 426

The sky at night 428

Continents 430

A cross-section of the earth 432

Parts of the body 433

Parts of a plant 434

Parts of a flower 434

Parts of an insect 434

Tricky words to spell 435

Words from other languages 435

Parts of speech 436

Singular and plural 437

Question words 437

Prepositions 438

Prefixes 440

Suffixes 441

Synonyms, antonyms and homonyms 442

Punctuation 443

Measures 444

Time 444

Shapes 446

Angles 447

Numbers 448

Using this dictionary

A dictionary helps you to find out what a word means and how to spell it correctly, and also offers you new words to use. The words in a dictionary are arranged in alphabetical order.

How to find a word

An **alphabet line** has been printed at the side of each page, and the letter in the red box tells you which letter the words on that page begin with. This will help you find the word you are looking for. For example, if you want to find the word **infant**, use the alphabet line to look for words beginning with **i**.

You will probably find that there are several words that start with the same letter as your word,

so you will then have to look at the second letter to help you find the right word. You are looking for a word that begins with **in**. Use the **guide word** at the top of the page. The guide word at the top left of the page tells you the *first word* on the page, and the one at the top right tells you the *last word* on the page. On this page the guide word is **indigo**. Does this guide word begin in the same way as the word you are looking for?

When you think you have the right page, look at the **headwords**, which are in alphabetical order. If you look down this page you will see that all the words begin with **in**, so you must look at the third letter to help you find **infant**. Does **inf** come after **ind**? Continue to look until you find the word.

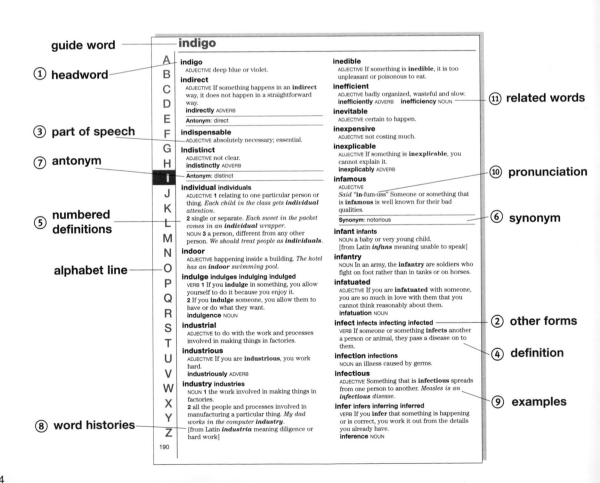

guide word

① headword

③ part of speech

⑦ antonym

⑤ numbered definitions

alphabet line

⑧ word histories

⑪ related words

⑩ pronunciation

⑥ synonym

② other forms

④ definition

⑨ examples

indigo

A B C D E F G H i J K L M N O P Q R S T U V W X Y Z

190

indigo
ADJECTIVE deep blue or violet.

indirect
ADJECTIVE If something happens in an **indirect** way, it does not happen in a straightforward way.
indirectly ADVERB
Antonym: direct

indispensable
ADJECTIVE absolutely necessary; essential.

indistinct
ADJECTIVE not clear.
indistinctly ADVERB
Antonym: distinct

individual individuals
ADJECTIVE 1 relating to one particular person or thing. *Each child in the class gets **individual** attention.*
2 single or separate. *Each sweet in the packet comes in an **individual** wrapper.*
NOUN 3 a person, different from any other person. *We should treat people as **individuals**.*

indoor
ADJECTIVE happening inside a building. *The hotel has an **indoor** swimming pool.*

indulge indulges indulging indulged
VERB 1 If you **indulge** in something, you allow yourself to do it because you enjoy it.
2 If you **indulge** someone, you allow them to have or do what they want.
indulgence NOUN

industrial
ADJECTIVE to do with the work and processes involved in making things in factories.

industrious
ADJECTIVE If you are **industrious**, you work hard.
industriously ADVERB

industry industries
NOUN 1 the work involved in making things in factories.
2 all the people and processes involved in manufacturing a particular thing. *My dad works in the computer **industry**.*
[from Latin *industria* meaning diligence or hard work]

inedible
ADJECTIVE If something is **inedible**, it is too unpleasant or poisonous to eat.

inefficient
ADJECTIVE badly organized, wasteful and slow.
inefficiently ADVERB **inefficiency** NOUN

inevitable
ADJECTIVE certain to happen.

inexpensive
ADJECTIVE not costing much.

inexplicable
ADJECTIVE If something is **inexplicable**, you cannot explain it.
inexplicably ADVERB

infamous
ADJECTIVE
Said "in-fum-uss" Someone or something that is **infamous** is well known for their bad qualities.
Synonym: notorious

infant infants
NOUN a baby or very young child.
[from Latin *infans* meaning unable to speak]

infantry
NOUN In an army, the **infantry** are soldiers who fight on foot rather than in tanks or on horses.

infatuated
ADJECTIVE If you are **infatuated** with someone, you are so much in love with them that you cannot think reasonably about them.
infatuation NOUN

infect infects infecting infected
VERB If someone or something **infects** another person or animal, they pass a disease on to them.

infection infections
NOUN an illness caused by germs.

infectious
ADJECTIVE Something that is **infectious** spreads from one person to another. *Measles is an infectious disease.*

infer infers inferring inferred
VERB If you **infer** that something is happening or is correct, you work it out from the details you already have.
inference NOUN

Finding out about a word

① The **headword** is the word you are looking up.
② On the same line as the headword you will see how to spell **other forms** of a word, such as plural nouns, verb tenses or other adjective forms, called comparatives and superlatives.
③ The **part of speech** tells you what type of word the headword is, such as a noun, verb, adjective, adverb or pronoun.
④ The **definition** tells you what the word means.
⑤ The definitions are **numbered** if there is more than one meaning or use. The part of speech is given if it is different to the part of speech for the previous definition.
⑥ **Synonyms**, or words that you can use instead, are given for some words.
⑦ **Antonyms**, or words that have the opposite meaning, are given for some words.
⑧ **Word histories** tell you more about some words.
⑨ Some words have **examples** in *italics* to show how the word might be used.
⑩ There is help with **pronunciation** for words where the pronunciation is not obvious, or where there are two ways of pronouncing a word that have different meanings.
⑪ **Related words** are given at the end of some entries to tell you, for example, the noun or adverb form of the word.

Other features of this dictionary

● Some headwords and other forms can be spelt in more than one way, so the **alternative spelling** is given as well.

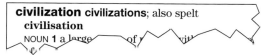

civilization civilizations; also spelt **civilisation**
NOUN **1** a large ...

● Sometimes definitions include a **label**, such as FORMAL, INFORMAL or TRADEMARK. This tells you a little more about the word or how it is used.

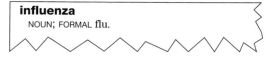

influenza
NOUN; FORMAL flu.

● Sometimes, where it is interesting or helpful, a **photo** or other **illustration** is included.

cog cogs
NOUN a wheel with teeth, which turns another wheel or part of a machine.

● **Usage tips** ✔ provide additional useful information on the spelling, and use of words. For example, it is sometimes hard to tell which of two words that look or sound the same you should use.

continual
ADJECTIVE happening again and again. *Mum had a **continual** stream of phone calls.*
✔ *Continual* and *continuous* are sometimes confused. *Continual* means happening all the time with breaks in between; *continuous* means happening all the time with no break.

● Some definitions tell you where to find **more information**, such as another headword or the pages at the back of the dictionary.

constellation constellations
NOUN a group of stars. *See* pages 428–9.

Topic pages

There are special **topic pages** in this dictionary to support your writing.

● **Picture pages** have labelled illustrations of things such as a plant, an insect, the human body, the earth, the solar system and shapes.

● **Grammar pages** provide information about parts of speech, punctuation, prepositions, prefixes and suffixes.

● **Word banks** and **number banks** provide lists to help you learn and spell difficult words, time words, synonyms and antonyms, abbreviations, measures, numbers and fractions.

Abbreviations

AD	in the year of our Lord (from the Latin *Anno Domini*)
a.m.	before noon (in the morning)
anon.	anonymous
BC	before Christ
°C	degrees Celsius
CD	compact disc (such as a music CD)
CD-ROM	a CD that is played on a computer
cm	centimetre
cm²	square centimetre
DIY	do-it-yourself
Dr	Doctor
DVD	digital video disc *or* digital versatile disc
e.g.	for example (from Latin *exempli gratia*)
etc.	et cetera, which means "and so on" in Latin
EU	European Union
g	gram
GP	general practitioner (a doctor)
ICT	information and communications technology
IT	information technology
kg	kilogram
km	kilometre
l	litre
m	metre
ml	millilitre
MEP	Member of the European Parliament
MP	Member of Parliament
Mr	a title used before a man's name
Mrs	a title used before a married woman's name
Ms	a title used before a woman's name
OAP	old age pensioner
p	pence
p.	page
PC	personal computer *or* police constable *or* politically correct
PE	physical education
p.m.	after noon (in the afternoon or evening)
pp.	pages
PS	PS is written at the end of a letter when an extra note is added (from the Latin *post scriptum*)
PTO	please turn over
RSVP	please reply (from the French *Répondez s'il vous plaît*)
SOS	a Morse code signal for help, said to be an abbreviation of "Save Our Souls"
TV	television
UFO	unidentified flying object
VCR	video cassette recorder
VDU	visual display unit
VIP	very important person
www	World Wide Web

Aa

a an
ADJECTIVE **A** and **an** are used when you talk about one of something. **A** is used when the next sound is a consonant: *a car*, *a dog*. **An** is used when the next sound is a vowel (a, e, i, o or u): *an apple*, *an elephant*.

abacus abacuses
NOUN a frame with beads that slide along rods, used for counting.
[from Greek *abax* meaning board covered with sand for doing sums on]

abandon abandons abandoning abandoned
VERB If you **abandon** someone or something, you leave them or give them up for good. *He abandoned all hope of catching the train on time.*

abbey abbeys
NOUN a church with buildings attached to it in which monks or nuns live.

abbreviation abbreviations
NOUN a short form of a word or phrase. *N is an abbreviation for North.*

abdomen abdomens
NOUN the front part of your body below your chest, containing your stomach and intestines.
abdominal ADJECTIVE

abdomen

ability abilities
NOUN If you have **ability**, you have the intelligence and skill to do things.

able
ADJECTIVE If you are **able** to do something, you can do it.

Antonym: unable

abnormal
ADJECTIVE not normal or usual.
abnormally ADVERB

aboard
PREPOSITION OR ADVERB If you are **aboard** a plane or a ship you are on it.

Aborigine Aborigines
NOUN someone descended from the people who were living in Australia before the European settlers arrived.

about
PREPOSITION OR ADVERB **1** If you talk or write **about** a particular thing, you say things that are to do with that subject: *a book about London.*
2 You say **about** in front of a number to show it is not exact: *about two o'clock.*
PHRASE **3** If you are **about to** do something, you are just going to do it. *He was about to leave.*

above
PREPOSITION OR ADVERB If one thing is above another, it is higher up. *The plane was flying above the clouds.*

Antonym: below

abroad
ADVERB If you go **abroad**, you go to another country.

abscess abscesses
NOUN a painful swelling on the body, which contains pus.

abseil abseils abseiling abseiled
VERB If you **abseil** down a rock face, you use ropes to go down it.

absent
ADJECTIVE If you are **absent** from a place, you are not there.

Antonym: present

absolute
ADJECTIVE **1** total and complete: *absolute darkness.*
2 having total power: *an absolute ruler.*

absolutely
ADVERB If you are **absolutely** sure about something, you are completely sure of it.

absorb absorbs absorbing absorbed
VERB If something **absorbs** liquid or gas, it soaks it up. *Plants* **absorb** *moisture from the soil.*

absorbent
ADJECTIVE If a something is **absorbent**, it soaks up liquids easily.

abstract
ADJECTIVE **1** An **abstract** idea is based on thoughts and ideas rather than on real objects or happenings, for example "bravery" and "happiness".
2 Abstract art uses shapes rather than images of people or objects.
3 In grammar, **abstract** nouns refer to qualities or ideas, rather than physical objects, for example "happiness". *See* **noun**.

absurd
ADJECTIVE Something that is **absurd** is stupid or ridiculous.

abuse abuses abusing abused
Said "ab-**yooss**" NOUN **1** cruel treatment of someone.
2 rude and unkind remarks.
Said "ab-**yooz**" VERB **3** To **abuse** someone is to treat them cruelly.
4 If you **abuse** someone, you speak to them in a rude and insulting way.

abysmal
ADJECTIVE very bad.
abysmally ADVERB

academic academics
ADJECTIVE **1 Academic** work is done in school, college and university.
NOUN **2** someone who teaches or does research in a college or university.

academy academies
NOUN **1** a school or college, usually one that specializes in a particular subject: *The Royal Academy of Arts.*
2 an organization of scientists, writers, artists or musicians.

accelerate accelerates accelerating accelerated
VERB To **accelerate** is to speed up.

Antonym: decelerate

acceleration
NOUN the rate at which the speed of something increases.

accent accents
NOUN a way of pronouncing a language. *She had an Australian* **accent.**

accept accepts accepting accepted
VERB **1** If you **accept** something, you say yes to it or you take it from someone. *She* **accepted** *our invitation to the party.*
2 If you **accept** a situation, you realize that it cannot be changed. *I* **accepted** *that I would have to work hard before my exams.*

acceptable
ADJECTIVE satisfactory.

access
NOUN If you have **access** to a place, you may enter it. If you have **access** to a thing, you may use it.

accessible
ADJECTIVE **1** easy to reach or to see. *The beach was* **accessible** *by a narrow path.*
2 Books that are **accessible** are easy to understand.

accident accidents
NOUN **1** something that happens suddenly or unexpectedly, causing people to be hurt or killed.
PHRASE **2** Something that happens **by accident** has not been planned. *We met* **by accident** *in the supermarket.*

accidental
ADJECTIVE Something that is **accidental** has not been planned.
accidentally ADVERB

accommodation
NOUN a place where you can live, work or sleep.

accompany accompanies accompanying accompanied
VERB **1** If you **accompany** someone, you go with them.
2 If you **accompany** a singer, you play an instrument while they sing.

accomplice accomplices
NOUN a person who helps someone else to commit a crime.

accomplish accomplishes accomplishing accomplished
VERB If you **accomplish** something, you succeed in doing it.

according to
PREPOSITION If something is true **according to** a particular person, that person says that it is true. *According to my grandad, that castle is haunted.*

account accounts accounting accounted
NOUN **1** A written or spoken report of something.
2 Money that you keep at a bank.
PHRASE **3 On account of** means because of. *He couldn't play football, on account of a sore throat.*
VERB **4** To **account for** something is to explain it. *The bad weather accounts for the cancellation of the barbecue.*

accountant accountants
NOUN someone whose job is to look after the financial affairs of people and companies.

accumulate accumulates accumulating accumulated
VERB If things **accumulate**, or if you **accumulate** things, they collect over a period of time. *While they were away, a large pile of letters accumulated on the doormat.*
accumulation NOUN

accurate
ADJECTIVE absolutely correct.
accuracy NOUN

accuse accuses accusing accused
VERB If you **accuse** someone of doing something wrong, you say they have done it.
accusation NOUN

ace aces
NOUN **1** In a pack of cards, the **ace** is a card with a single symbol on it.
2 In tennis, an **ace** is a serve that the other player is unable to return.
ADJECTIVE **3** INFORMAL good or skilful: *an ace squash player.*

ache aches aching ached
NOUN **1** a continuous, dull pain.
VERB **2** If a part of your body **aches**, you feel a continuous, dull pain there.

achieve achieves achieving achieved
VERB If you **achieve** something, you are successful at doing it or at making it happen.
✔ The *i* comes before the *e* in *achieve*.

acid acids
NOUN **1** a chemical substance. Strong **acids** can damage skin, cloth and metal, for example sulphuric **acid**. Other **acids**, such as those found in citrus fruit and vinegar, are harmless.
ADJECTIVE **2** If something has an **acid** taste, it tastes sharp or bitter.
[from Latin *acidus* meaning sour]

Antonym: alkali

acid rain
NOUN rain that has been polluted by the burning of fossil fuels, such as coal and oil.

acknowledge acknowledges acknowledging acknowledged
VERB **1** If you **acknowledge** a fact or a situation, you admit that it is true.
2 If you **acknowledge** someone, you show that you have seen and recognized them, by waving or saying "hello".
3 If you **acknowledge** a message or a letter, you tell the person who sent it that you have received it.

acne
NOUN a skin disease that causes spots on the face and neck. **Acne** is common among teenagers.

acorn acorns
NOUN a nut that grows on oak trees.

acquaintance acquaintances
NOUN someone you know slightly but not well.

acre acres
NOUN a unit for measuring land. One acre is equal to 4840 square yards or about 4047 square metres.

acrobat acrobats
NOUN an entertainer who performs difficult gymnastic acts.
acrobatic ADJECTIVE **acrobatics** PLURAL NOUN
[from Greek *akrobates* meaning someone who walks on tiptoe]

acronym acronyms

NOUN a word made up of the initial letters of a phrase. *NATO is an **acronym**, and stands for North Atlantic Treaty Organization.*

across

PREPOSITION OR ADVERB **1** If you go **across** a place, you go from one side of it to the other. *We walked **across** Hyde Park.*

2 Something that is situated **across** a road or river is on the other side of it.

act acts acting acted

VERB **1** If you **act**, you do something. *We have to **act** quickly in an emergency.*

2 If you **act** in a particular way, you behave in that way. *You're **acting** like a baby.*

3 If you **act** in a play or film, you play a role in it.

NOUN **4** a single thing someone does. *The rescue was a brave **act**.*

5 An **Act** of Parliament is a law passed by the government.

6 Stage plays are divided into parts called **acts**.

action actions

NOUN **1** something you do for a particular purpose.

2 a physical movement, such as jumping.

active

ADJECTIVE **1** Someone who is **active** moves around a lot or does a lot of things.

2 In grammar the **active**, or the **active** voice, is the form of the verb in which the subject of the sentence is the person or thing doing the action, rather than having it done to them. For example, the sentence "The dog bit Ben" is in the **active** voice. In the passive voice the subject is acted upon: "Ben was bitten by the dog".

Antonym: (sense 2) passive

activity activities

NOUN **1** a situation in which a lot of things are happening at the same time. *There was a great deal of **activity** in the hall as we got ready for the school play.*

2 something you do for pleasure, such as gymnastics or music.

actor actors

NOUN a man or woman whose job is performing in plays or films.

actress actresses

NOUN a woman whose profession is acting.

actual

ADJECTIVE real, rather than imaginary or guessed at. *You guessed I was eleven – my **actual** age is twelve.*

✔ Don't use *actual* or *actually* when they don't add anything to the meaning of a sentence. For example, say "it's a fact" rather than "it's an actual fact".

actually ADVERB

acute

ADJECTIVE **1** severe or intense. *She had an **acute** pain in her arm.*

2 In mathematics, an **acute** angle measures less than 90 degrees.

3 Someone who is **acute** is intelligent.

AD

ADJECTIVE You use **AD** in dates to show the number of years after the birth of Jesus Christ. [an abbreviation of the Latin ***Anno Domini*** meaning the year of Our Lord]

adapt adapts adapting adapted

VERB **1** If you **adapt** to something, you get used to it.

2 If you **adapt** something, you change it so that it can be used in a new way.

adaptable

ADJECTIVE If you are **adaptable,** you change easily in a new situation or to suit new circumstances.

add adds adding added

VERB **1** If you **add** something to a number of things, you put it with those things. *Each girl **added** more wood to the pile.*

2 If you **add** numbers together, or **add** them up, you work out the total. *Two and three **added** together are five (2 + 3 = 5).*

adder adders

NOUN a small, poisonous snake.

addiction addictions

NOUN If you have an **addiction** to something, you cannot stop doing it or wanting it.

addition additions

NOUN **1** the process of adding two or more numbers together.
2 something that is added to something else. *The **addition** of sugar would improve the taste of these plums.*

additional

ADJECTIVE extra or more.

additive additives

NOUN something that is added to something else, such as food.

address addresses addressing addressed

NOUN **1** Your **address** is the number of the house where you live, together with the name of the street and the town or village.
VERB **2** If someone **addresses** a letter to you, they write your name and address on it.
3 If you **address** a group of people, you speak to them formally.

adenoids

PLURAL NOUN small lumps of flesh at the back of the throat.

adequate

ADJECTIVE just enough for what is needed.

Synonyms: enough, satisfactory, sufficient

adhesive adhesives

NOUN **1** a substance used to stick things together, such as glue.
ADJECTIVE **2** If something is **adhesive**, it sticks to other things.

adjective adjectives

NOUN a word that adds to the description of a noun. For example, "large" and "old" are both **adjectives**.

adjust adjusts adjusting adjusted

VERB **1** If you **adjust** something, you change its position or alter it in some other way. *She **adjusted** her pillow to make herself more comfortable.*
2 If you **adjust** to a new situation, you get used to it.
adjustment NOUN

administration administrations

NOUN the work of managing and supervising an organization.

admiral admirals

NOUN a senior officer in the navy.

admire admires admiring admired

VERB If you **admire** someone or something, you respect and approve of them.
admirer NOUN

admission admissions

NOUN **1** If you are allowed **admission** to a place, you may go into it.
2 If you make an **admission**, you confess to something or agree that it is true.

admit admits admitting admitted

VERB **1** If you **admit** something, you agree that it is true.
2 If you **admit** to something, you agree that you did something you shouldn't have done.
3 To **admit** someone or something to a place is to allow them to enter it.

admittance

NOUN the right to enter somewhere. *There will be no **admittance** to the party after eight o'clock.*

adolescent adolescents

NOUN a young person who is no longer a child, but is not yet an adult.
adolescence NOUN
[from Latin *adolescere* meaning to grow up]

adopt adopts adopting adopted

VERB If someone **adopts** a child, they take them into their family as their son or daughter by a legal process.
[from Latin *adoptare* meaning to choose for oneself]

adorable

ADJECTIVE loveable and attractive.

adore adores adoring adored

VERB If you **adore** someone, you feel deep love and admiration for them.
adoration NOUN

adult adults

NOUN a mature and fully developed person or animal.

advance advances advancing advanced
VERB **1** To **advance** is to move forward.
NOUN **2** An **advance** is progress in something. *There have been many scientific **advances** in the past century.*
PHRASE **3** If you do something **in advance** of something, you do it beforehand. *We booked our holiday well **in advance**.*

advanced
ADJECTIVE If something is **advanced**, it is at a high level, or ahead in development or progress. *The children in the top group do **advanced** maths exercises.*

advantage advantages
NOUN **1** a benefit, or something that puts you in a better position. *The **advantage** of e-mail is that it is quicker than the post.*
PHRASE **2** If you **take advantage** of someone, you treat them unfairly for your own benefit.
3 If you **take advantage** of something, you make use of it.

adventure adventures
NOUN something that is exciting, and perhaps even dangerous.

adverb adverbs
NOUN a word that tells you how, when, where or why something happens or something is done. For example, she walked *slowly*, he came *yesterday*, they live *here*.
[from Latin *adverbium* meaning added word]

advert
NOUN an abbreviation for *advertisement*.

advertise advertises advertising advertised
VERB If you **advertise** something, you tell people about it in a newspaper, on a poster or on TV.

advertisement advertisements
NOUN a notice in a newspaper, on a poster or on TV about a job or things for sale.

advice
NOUN a suggestion from someone about what you should do.

advisable
ADJECTIVE If it is **advisable** to do something, it is a sensible thing to do and will probably give the results that you want. *It is **advisable** to wear a helmet when cycling.*

advise advises advising advised
VERB If you **advise** someone to do something, you tell them you think they should do it.

aerial aerials
NOUN **1** a piece of wire for receiving television or radio signals.
ADJECTIVE **2** happening in the air. *We watched the **aerial** displays at the RAF airshow.*

aero-
PREFIX to do with the air, for example **aero**plane.
[from Greek *aer* meaning air]

aerobics
NOUN a type of fast physical exercise that increases the oxygen in your blood and strengthens your heart and lungs.
aerobic ADJECTIVE

aeroplane aeroplanes
NOUN a vehicle with wings and engines that enable it to fly.

aerosol aerosols
NOUN a small, metal container in which liquid is kept under pressure so that it can be forced out as a spray.
✔ *Aerosol* starts with *aer* and not with *air*.

affair affairs
NOUN **1** an event or series of events. *The wedding was a happy **affair**.*
2 If something is your own **affair**, then it is your concern only.

affect affects affecting affected
VERB When something **affects** someone or something, it causes them to change. *Computers **affect** our lives in many ways.*

affection
NOUN a feeling of love and fondness for someone.
affectionate ADJECTIVE

affluent
ADJECTIVE People who are **affluent** have a lot of money and possessions.

afford affords affording afforded
VERB **1** If you can **afford** something, you have enough money to pay for it.
2 If you can **afford** to relax, you feel you have done enough work for the moment, and have time to take things easy.

A B C D E F G H I J K L M N O P Q R S T U V W X Y Z

afloat

ADVERB If something or someone is **afloat**, they are floating.

afraid

ADJECTIVE **1** If you are **afraid**, you are frightened.
2 If you are **afraid** something might happen, you worry that it might happen.

Synonym: (sense 1) scared

after

PREPOSITION OR ADVERB **1** later than a particular time, date or event. *She left just **after** breakfast. Soon **after**, he went to work.*
PREPOSITION **2** If you come **after** someone or something, you are behind them and following them. *They ran **after** her.*

afternoon afternoons

NOUN the part of the day between twelve noon and about six o'clock.

afterwards

ADVERB after an event or time. *We went swimming, and **afterwards** we had an ice cream.*

again

ADVERB happening one more time. *The film was so good that we went to see it **again**.*

Synonym: once more

against

PREPOSITION **1** touching and resting on. *He leaned the ladder **against** the wall.*
2 in opposition to. *France played **against** England.*

age ages ageing or aging aged

NOUN **1** The **age** of something or someone is the number of years they have lived or existed.
2 a particular period in history: *the Iron **Age**.*
PLURAL NOUN **3** INFORMAL **Ages** means a very long time. *He's been talking for **ages**.*
VERB **4** To **age** is to grow old or to appear older.
✔ *Ageing* and *aging* are both correct spellings.

agency agencies

NOUN an organization or business that provides special services: *detective **agency**, advertising **agency**.*

agenda agendas

NOUN a list of items to be discussed at a meeting.

agent agents

NOUN **1** someone who does business or arranges things for other people: *a travel **agent**.*
2 someone who works for their country's secret service.

aggravate aggravates aggravating aggravated

VERB **1** If you **aggravate** something, you make it worse.
2 INFORMAL If you **aggravate** someone, you annoy them.
aggravating ADJECTIVE **aggravation** NOUN

aggressive

ADJECTIVE full of hostility and violence. *Some breeds of dog are more **aggressive** than others.*

Synonyms: belligerent, hostile

agile

ADJECTIVE able to move quickly and easily. *He is as **agile** as a cat.*
agilely ADVERB **agility** NOUN

agitated

ADJECTIVE worried and anxious.
agitation NOUN

ago

ADVERB in the past. *She bought her flat three years **ago**.*

agony

NOUN very great physical or mental pain.

Synonyms: suffering, torment

agree agrees agreeing agreed

VERB **1** If you **agree** with someone, you have the same opinion as they do.
2 If you **agree** to do something, you say you will do it.

agreeable

ADJECTIVE **1** pleasant or enjoyable.
2 If you are **agreeable** to something, you are willing to allow it or to do it.
agreeably ADVERB

agreement agreements

NOUN If you reach an **agreement** with one or more people, you make a decision with them or come to an arrangement with them.

agriculture

NOUN farming.

ahead

ADVERB **1** in front. *He looked **ahead** as he cycled down the road.*
2 more advanced than someone or something else. *Some countries are **ahead** of others in space travel.*
3 in the future. *I can't think that far **ahead**.*

aid aids

NOUN **1** money, equipment or services provided for people in need.
2 something that makes a job easier. *The whiteboard is a useful teaching **aid**.*

AIDS

NOUN **AIDS** is an abbreviation for *acquired immune deficiency syndrome*. It is a disease that attacks the body's natural immune system.

ailment ailments

NOUN a minor illness.

aim aims aiming aimed

VERB **1** If you **aim** at something, you point a weapon at it.
2 If you **aim** to do something, you are planning to do it.
NOUN **3** Your **aim** is what you intend to achieve. *The **aim** of the jumble sale is to raise money for charity.*

Synonyms: (sense 2) intend, mean
(sense 3) goal, objective

aimless

ADJECTIVE If you are **aimless,** you have no clear purpose or sense of direction.
aimlessly ADVERB

air

NOUN **1** the mixture of oxygen and other gases that we breathe and that forms the earth's atmosphere.
2 the space around things or above the ground. *The balloons floated up into the **air**.*
3 used to refer to travel in aircraft. *My uncle often travels by **air**.*

air conditioning

NOUN a way of keeping cool, fresh air in a building.

aircraft

NOUN any vehicle that can fly.

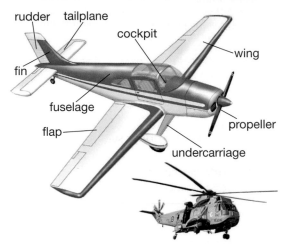

air force air forces

NOUN the part of a country's armed services that fights using aircraft.

airline airlines

NOUN a company that provides air travel.

airmail

NOUN the system of sending letters and parcels by air. *He sent letters from Hong Kong to Britain by **airmail**.*

airport airports

NOUN a place where people go to catch aeroplanes.

airtight

ADJECTIVE If something is **airtight**, no air can get in or out.

aisle aisles

NOUN a long, narrow gap that people can walk along between rows of seats or shelves. *The ticket collector was coming down the **aisle**.*

ajar

ADJECTIVE A door or window that is **ajar** is slightly open.

alarm alarms alarming alarmed
NOUN **1** a feeling of fear and worry. *The cat sprang back in alarm.*
2 an automatic device used to warn people of something. *The burglar alarm went off accidentally.*
VERB **3** If something **alarms** you, it makes you worried and anxious.

album albums
NOUN **1** a CD, cassette or record with a number of songs on it.
2 a book in which you keep a collection of things, such as photographs or stamps.

alcohol
NOUN the name for drinks such as beer, wine and spirits.

alert alerts alerting alerted
ADJECTIVE **1** If you are **alert**, you are paying full attention to what is happening.
VERB **2** If you **alert** someone to a problem or danger, you warn them of it.

Synonyms: (sense 1) vigilant, watchful

algebra
NOUN a branch of mathematics in which symbols and letters are used to represent unknown numbers.

alias aliases
NOUN a false name.

alibi alibis
NOUN If you have an **alibi**, you have evidence proving you were somewhere else when a crime was committed.

alien aliens
NOUN **1** In science fiction, an **alien** is a creature from outer space.
ADJECTIVE **2** Something that is **alien** to you seems strange because it is not part of your normal experience. *The desert is an alien environment to many people.*
[from Latin *alienus* meaning foreign]

alight alights alighting alighted
ADJECTIVE **1** Something that is **alight** is burning.
VERB **2** If something **alights** somewhere, it lands there.
3 If someone **alights** from a vehicle, they get out of it.

alike
ADJECTIVE **1** Things that are **alike** are very similar in some way.
ADVERB **2** If people or things are treated **alike**, they are treated the same.

alive
ADJECTIVE If someone or something is **alive**, they are living.

alkali alkalis
NOUN a chemical substance sometimes used in cleaning materials. **Alkalis** can neutralize acids.
alkaline ADJECTIVE

Antonym: acid

all
ADJECTIVE, NOUN OR ADVERB **1** the whole of something. *She told us all about it. He ate all the chocolate.*
ADVERB **2** also used to show that both sides in a game or contest have the same score. *The final score was three points all.*

Allah
PROPER NOUN the Muslim name for God.

allege alleges alleging alleged
VERB If you **allege** that something is true, you say it's true, but you cannot prove it.

allergy allergies
NOUN If you have an **allergy** to something, it makes you ill to eat or touch it.
allergic ADJECTIVE

alley alleys
NOUN a narrow street or passageway between buildings.

alliance alliances
NOUN a group of countries, organizations or people who have similar aims and who work together to achieve them.

alligator alligators
NOUN a large, scaly reptile, similar to a crocodile.
[from Spanish *el lagarto* meaning lizard]

alliteration
NOUN the use of several words together that begin with the same letter or sound. For example, "the slithery snake slid silently across the sand".

a
b
c
d
e
f
g
h
i
j
k
l
m
n
o
p
q
r
s
t
u
v
w
x
y
z

allotment allotments

NOUN a piece of land that people rent to grow fruit and vegetables on.

allow allows allowing allowed

VERB If someone **allows** you to do something, they let you do it.

all right

ADJECTIVE **1** If something is **all right**, it is satisfactory, but not especially good. *Do you like mushrooms? They're all right.*
2 If someone is **all right**, they are safe and not harmed.
3 You say **all right** if you agree to something. *Will you help? All right.*

ally allies

NOUN a person or a country that helps and supports another.

Synonyms: friend, partner

almond almonds

NOUN an oval edible nut, cream in colour.

almost

ADVERB very nearly. *I have almost as many points as you.*

Synonyms: just about, practically

alone

ADJECTIVE not with other people or things.

along

PREPOSITION **1** moving forward. *We strolled along the road.*
2 from one end of something to the other. *The cupboards stretched along the wall.*

alongside

PREPOSITION OR ADVERB next to something. *We tied our boat alongside the jetty.*

aloud

ADVERB When you read **aloud**, you read so that people can hear you.

alphabet alphabets

NOUN all the letters used to write words in a language. The letters of an **alphabet** are written in a special order.

alphabetical

ADJECTIVE If something is in **alphabetical** order, it is arranged according to the letters of the alphabet.
alphabetically ADVERB

already

ADVERB If you have done something **already**, you did it earlier. *Josh has already gone to bed.*

also

ADVERB in addition to something that has just been mentioned. *I bought an ice cream, and I also bought a drink.*

altar altars

NOUN a holy table in a church or temple.

alter alters altering altered

VERB If something **alters**, or if you **alter** it, it changes.

alternate alternates alternating alternated

Said "ol-**ter**-nut" ADJECTIVE **1** If something happens on **alternate** days, it happens on one in every two days
Said "**ol**-ter-nayt" VERB **2** If two things **alternate**, they regularly happen one after the other.

alternative alternatives

NOUN something you can do or have instead of something else. *Is there an alternative to meat on the menu?*
✔ If there are more than two choices in a situation, you should say there are three *choices* rather than three *alternatives*, because the strict meaning of *alternative* is a choice between two things.

although

CONJUNCTION in spite of the fact that. *He wasn't well-known in America, although he had made a film there.*

altitude altitudes

NOUN height above sea level. *The mountain range reaches an altitude of 1330 metres.*

altogether

ADVERB **1** completely or entirely. *The car got slower, then stopped altogether.*
2 in total – used of amounts. *I have two cats and two dogs. That's four pets altogether.*

aluminium

NOUN a silvery-white lightweight metal.

always

ADVERB **1** all the time. *He's always late.*
2 forever. *I'll always remember this day.*

am

VERB a present tense of *be*.

a.m.

a.m. is used to show times in the morning. [an abbreviation of the Latin *ante meridiem* meaning before noon]

amateur amateurs

NOUN someone who does something without being paid for it. *He began playing football as an amateur, but now he is a professional.*

amaze amazes amazing amazed

VERB If something **amazes** you, it surprises you very much.

amazement NOUN

Synonyms: astonish, astound

---

amazing

ADJECTIVE If something is **amazing,** it is very surprising.

amazingly ADVERB

ambassador ambassadors

NOUN a person sent to a foreign country as the representative of their own government.

amber

NOUN **1** a hard, yellowish-brown substance from trees, used in making jewellery.

NOUN OR ADJECTIVE **2** an orange-brown colour.

ambiguous

ADJECTIVE If something is **ambiguous**, it can have more than one meaning.

ambiguously ADVERB   **ambiguity** NOUN

ambition ambitions

NOUN If you have an **ambition** to do something, you want very much to do it.

amble ambles ambling ambled

VERB If you **amble**, you walk along in a slow, relaxed way.

ambush ambushes ambushing ambushed

NOUN **1** a surprise attack.

VERB **2** If one group of people **ambushes** another, they hide and lie in wait, and then make a surprise attack.

ambulance ambulances

NOUN a vehicle for taking sick and injured people to hospital.

ammonia

NOUN a strong-smelling colourless liquid or gas, often used in cleaning substances.

ammunition

NOUN anything that can be fired from a gun or other weapon, for example bullets and shells.

amoeba amoebas or amoebae

NOUN a tiny living organism that has only one cell. An **amoeba** reproduces by dividing into two.

among or **amongst**

PREPOSITION **1** surrounded by.

2 in the company of. *He was among friends.*

3 between more than two. *The money will be divided among seven charities.*

✔ If there are more than two things, you should use *among(st)*. If there are only two things, you should use *between*. *Amongst* is old-fashioned; *among* is used more often.

amount amounts

NOUN how much there is of something. *You need a large amount of flour for this recipe.*

amphibian amphibians

NOUN a creature that lives partly on land and partly in water, for example a frog or a newt.

amphibious ADJECTIVE

newt   frog

amplify amplifies amplifying amplified

VERB If you **amplify** a sound, you make it louder.

amplifier NOUN

amputate amputates amputating amputated

VERB If a surgeon **amputates** part of the body, such as an arm or a leg, they cut it off.

amputation NOUN

amuse amuses amusing amused

VERB **1** If something **amuses** you, you think it is funny.

2 If you **amuse** yourself, you find things to do that stop you from being bored.

amused ADJECTIVE   **amusing** ADJECTIVE

a
b
c
d
e
f
g
h
i
j
k
l
m
n
o
p
q
r
s
t
u
v
w
x
y
z

amusement amusements

NOUN **1** the feeling you have when you think that something is funny or you have pleasure.
2 a mechanical device used for entertainment, at a fair for example.
3 Amusements are ways of passing the time pleasantly.

an

ADJECTIVE **An** is used instead of "a" in front of words that begin with the vowels a, e, i, o, or u: *an apple*, *an egg*.

anaemia

NOUN a medical condition in which there are too few red cells in the blood. It makes you feel tired and look pale.
anaemic ADJECTIVE

anaesthetic anaesthetics; also spelt **anesthetic**

NOUN a substance that stops you feeling pain. A general **anaesthetic** stops you from feeling pain in the whole of your body by putting you to sleep. A local **anaesthetic** makes just one part of your body go numb.

anagram anagrams

NOUN a word or phrase formed by changing the order of the letters of another word or phrase. For example, "draw" is an **anagram** of "ward" and "dear" is an **anagram** of "read".

analogue

ADJECTIVE An **analogue** watch or clock shows the time with pointers that move round a dial.

Antonym: digital

analogy analogies

NOUN a comparison between two things that are similar in some ways.

analyse analyses analysing analysed

VERB If you **analyse** something, you investigate it carefully to understand it or to find out what it consists of.

anatomy anatomies

NOUN the study of the structure of bodies, both animal and human, to find out how they work.
anatomical ADJECTIVE

ancestor ancestors

NOUN a member of your family who lived many years ago. *He could trace his **ancestors** back 700 years.*
[from Latin ***antecessor*** meaning one who goes before]

anchor anchors anchoring anchored

NOUN **1** a heavy, hooked object at the end of a chain. It is dropped from a boat into the water to keep the boat from floating away.
VERB **2** If you **anchor** something, you hold it down firmly.

ancient

ADJECTIVE Things that are **ancient** existed or happened a very long time ago.

Antonym: modern

and

CONJUNCTION You use **and** to link two or more parts of a sentence together. *Let's go to the cinema **and** then have pizza.*

anecdote anecdotes

NOUN a short, sometimes entertaining story about a person or an event.

angel angels

NOUN a being who, some people believe, lives in heaven and acts as a messenger for God.
[from Greek ***angelos*** meaning messenger]

anger

NOUN the strong feeling you get about something unfair or cruel.

Synonyms: fury, rage, wrath

angle angles

NOUN **1** the distance between two lines at the point where they join together. **Angles** are measured in degrees: *an **angle** of 90 degrees.*
2 the direction from which you look at something. *He painted pictures of the garden from all **angles**.*

angry angrier angriest

ADJECTIVE very annoyed.

Synonyms: furious, cross

anguish

NOUN great suffering. *She was full of **anguish** when her grandfather died.*

animal animals
NOUN any living being that is not a plant.

animation animations
NOUN a way of making films using drawings that appear to move when you watch them.
animated ADJECTIVE

ankle ankles
NOUN the joint that connects your foot to your leg.

annihilate annihilates annihilating annihilated
VERB If someone or something **annihilates** someone or something else, they destroy them completely.
annihilation NOUN

anniversary anniversaries
NOUN a date that is remembered because something special happened on that date in a previous year. *We celebrated Mum and Dad's twelfth wedding* **anniversary**.

announce announces announcing announced
VERB If you **announce** something, you tell people about it publicly or officially. *They* **announced** *the team on Friday morning.*
announcement NOUN

Synonym: make known

annoy annoys annoying annoyed
VERB If someone or something **annoys** you, they make you angry or impatient.
annoyance NOUN

Synonyms: bother, irritate

annual annuals
ADJECTIVE 1 happening once a year. *our* **annual** *sports day.*
NOUN 2 a book that is published once a year for children.

anonymous
ADJECTIVE If something is **anonymous**, nobody knows who is responsible for it. *The charity received an* **anonymous** *donation.*

anorak anoraks
NOUN a warm, waterproof jacket, usually with a hood.
[an Eskimo word]

anorexia
NOUN a psychological illness in which the person refuses to eat because they are frightened of becoming fat.
[from Greek **an** + **orexis** meaning no appetite]

another
ADJECTIVE OR PRONOUN one more person or thing.

answer answers answering answered
VERB 1 If you **answer** someone, you reply to them in speech or writing.
NOUN 2 the reply you give when you answer someone. *I received an* **answer** *to my letter.*
3 a solution to a problem.

ant ants
NOUN **Ants** are small insects that live in large groups.

antagonize antagonizes antagonizing antagonized
VERB If you **antagonize** someone, you upset them and make them feel angry.

Antarctic
NOUN the area around the South Pole.

antelope antelopes
NOUN a hoofed animal, similar to a deer.

antenna antennae or antennas
NOUN 1 one of the two long, thin parts attached to the head of an insect or other animal, which it uses to feel with. The plural is **antennae**.
2 In Australian, New Zealand and American English, an **antenna** is a radio or television aerial. The plural is **antennas**.

anthem anthems
NOUN usually a song of celebration, and sometimes a religious song.

anther anthers
NOUN the part of the stamen in a flower where the pollen matures.

anthology anthologies
NOUN a collection of writings by various authors, published in one book.
[from Greek **anthologia** meaning flower gathering]

anti-
PREFIX against or opposite: *an* **anti**malaria *tablet.*

Antonym: pro-

a b c d e f g h i j k l m n o p q r s t u v w x y z

antibiotic antibiotics

NOUN a drug or chemical used in medicine to kill bacteria and cure infections.

anticipate anticipates anticipating anticipated

VERB If you **anticipate** an event, you are expecting it and are getting prepared for it. **anticipation** NOUN

anticlimax anticlimaxes

NOUN If something is an **anticlimax**, it disappoints you because it is not as exciting as you expected, or because it occurs after something that was more exciting.

anticlockwise

ADJECTIVE OR ADVERB moving in the opposite direction to the hands of a clock.

Antonym: clockwise

antidote antidotes

NOUN a chemical substance that works against the effects of a poison.

antique antiques

NOUN an object from the past that is collected because of its value or beauty.

antiseptic

ADJECTIVE Something that is **antiseptic** can kill some germs.

antler antlers

NOUN **Antlers** are the branched horns on the top of a male deer's head.

antonym antonyms

NOUN a word that means the opposite of another word. *Happy is the **antonym** of sad.* See page 442.

anvil anvils

NOUN a heavy, iron block on which hot metal is beaten into shape.

anxiety anxieties

NOUN nervousness or worry.

anxious

ADJECTIVE **1** If you are **anxious**, you are nervous or worried.

2 If you are **anxious** to do something, you very much want to do it. *She was **anxious** to pass her ballet exam.*

any

ADJECTIVE OR PRONOUN **1** one, some or several. *Have you **any** sausages?*
2 even the smallest amount or even one. *She can't eat nuts of **any** kind.*
3 no matter which or what. *I'm so thirsty, **any** drink will do.*

anybody

PRONOUN any person.

anyhow

ADVERB **1** in any case. *It's still early, but I'm going to bed **anyhow**.*
2 in a careless way. *They were all shoved in **anyhow**.*

anyone

PRONOUN any person. *I won't tell **anyone**.*

anything

PRONOUN any object, event, situation or action. *Can you see **anything**?*

anyway

ADVERB in any case. *It's raining, but I'm going out **anyway**.*

anywhere

ADVERB in, at or to any place. *Can you see him **anywhere**? We haven't got **anywhere** to play.*

apart

ADVERB OR ADJECTIVE **1** When something is **apart** from something else, there is a space or a distance between them. *The gliders landed about seventy metres **apart**.*
ADVERB **2** If you take something **apart**, you separate it into pieces.

apartment apartments

NOUN a set of rooms for living in, usually on one floor of a building.

ape apes aping aped

NOUN **1** a large animal similar to a monkey, but without a tail. **Apes** include chimpanzees and gorillas.
VERB **2** If you **ape** someone's speech or behaviour, you imitate it.

apex apexes or apices

NOUN The **apex** of something is its pointed top: *the **apex** of a triangle.*

apex

Synonym: vertex

apologize apologizes

apologizing apologized; also spelt **apologise**

VERB When you **apologize** to someone, you say you are sorry for something you have said or done.

apology NOUN

apostrophe apostrophes

NOUN **1** a punctuation mark (') used to show that one or more letters have been missed out of a word, for example "he's" for "he is".

2 Apostrophes are also used with *-s* at the end of a noun to show that what follows belongs to or relates to the noun. If the noun already has an *-s* at the end, for example because it is plural, the **apostrophe** comes after the *s*. For example, *my brother's books* (one brother), *my brothers' books* (more than one brother).

apparatus

NOUN the equipment used for a particular task. *The firefighters wore breathing **apparatus**.*

apparent

ADJECTIVE **1** An **apparent** situation seems to exist, although you cannot be certain of it.

2 clear and obvious. *It was **apparent** they would get on well together.*

apparently ADVERB

appeal appeals appealing appealed

VERB **1** If you **appeal** for something, you make an urgent request for it. *The police **appealed** for witnesses to come forward.*

2 If something or someone **appeals** to you, you find them attractive or interesting.

NOUN **3** a formal or serious request: *an **appeal** for funds to help people in need.*

appear appears appearing appeared

VERB **1** When something **appears**, it moves from somewhere you could not see to somewhere you can see it. *The sun **appeared** from behind the clouds.*

2 If something **appears** to be a certain way, it seems or looks that way.

appearance appearances

NOUN **1** Someone's or something's **appearance** is the way they look to other people.

2 If a person makes an **appearance** in a film or a show, they take part in it.

3 The **appearance** of something is the time it begins to exist.

appendicitis

NOUN a painful illness in which a person's appendix becomes infected.

appendix appendices or appendixes

NOUN **1** Your **appendix** is a small, closed tube forming part of your digestive system.

2 extra information that comes at the end of a book.

✔ The plural of the part of the body is *appendixes*. The plural of the extra section in a book is *appendices*.

appetite appetites

NOUN a desire to eat.

[from Latin ***appetere*** meaning to desire]

appetizing

ADJECTIVE When food is **appetizing**, it looks or smells good and you want to eat it.

applause

NOUN the sound of people clapping to show their enjoyment or approval of something.

apple apples

NOUN a round fruit with smooth skin and firm white flesh.

appliance appliances

NOUN any machine in your home that you use to do a job like cleaning or cooking. For example, a toaster is a kitchen **appliance**.

application applications

NOUN If you make an **application** for something, you make a formal request, usually in writing.

apply applies applying applied

VERB **1** If you **apply** for something, you ask for it formally, usually by writing a letter. *My brother is **applying** for jobs.*

2 If you **apply** something to a surface, you put it on or rub it into the surface. *She **applied** sun cream to her face.*

3 If you **apply** yourself to a task, you give it all of your attention.

a
b
c
d
e
f
g
h
i
j
k
l
m
n
o
p
q
r
s
t
u
v
w
x
y
z

B
C
D
E
F
G
H
I
J
K
L
M
N
O
P
Q
R
S
T
U
V
W
X
Y
Z

appoint appoints appointing appointed
VERB If a person **appoints** someone to a job or position, they formally choose them for it. *The teacher **appointed** Sunita as team captain.*

appointment appointments
NOUN an arrangement you have with someone to meet them.

appreciate appreciates appreciating appreciated
VERB If you **appreciate** something that someone has done for you, you are grateful to them for it.

apprehensive
ADJECTIVE If you are **apprehensive** about something, you feel worried and unsure about it.

apprentice apprentices
NOUN someone who works with another person for a length of time to learn that person's job or skill.

approach approaches approaching approached
VERB If you **approach** something, you come near or nearer to it.

appropriate
ADJECTIVE suitable or acceptable for a particular situation.

approval
NOUN If you ask for **approval** for something that you want to do, you ask for agreement with your plans.

approve approves approving approved
VERB 1 If you **approve** of something or someone, you think they are acceptable or good.
2 If someone **approves** a plan or idea, they agree to it. *The council **approved** plans for the new swimming pool.*

Synonyms: (sense 1) favour, like
(sense 2) agree to, permit

approximate
ADJECTIVE near but not exactly right. *What was the **approximate** time you arrived?*

apricot apricots
NOUN a small, soft, yellowish-orange fruit.

April
NOUN the fourth month of the year. **April** has 30 days.

apron aprons
NOUN a piece of clothing worn over the front of normal clothing to protect it.

aquarium aquaria or aquariums
NOUN a glass tank filled with water in which fish and other aquatic animals or plants are kept.

aquatic
ADJECTIVE An **aquatic** animal or plant lives in water.

aqueduct aqueducts
NOUN a bridge with many arches, which carries a water supply over a valley.

arable
ADJECTIVE **Arable** land is used for growing crops.

arc arcs
NOUN 1 a smoothly curving line.
2 In geometry, an **arc** is a section of the circumference of a circle.

arcade arcades
NOUN a covered passageway where there are shops or market stalls.

arch arches arching arched
NOUN 1 a structure that has a curved top, supported on either side by a pillar or wall.
VERB 2 If something **arches**, or if you **arch** it, it forms a curved line or shape. *The cat **arched** its back.*

archaeology or **archeology**
NOUN the study of the past by digging up and examining the remains of things such as buildings, tools, and pots.
[from Greek **arkhaios** meaning ancient]

archbishop archbishops

NOUN a bishop of the highest rank in a Christian Church: *the Archbishop of Canterbury*.

archery

NOUN a sport in which people shoot at a target with a bow and arrow.

architect architects

NOUN a person who designs buildings.

architecture

NOUN the art or practice of designing buildings.

arctic

NOUN 1 The **Arctic** is the region north of the Arctic Circle.

ADJECTIVE 2 very cold indeed. *You need specially warm clothes for arctic conditions*.

are

VERB a present tense of *be*.

area areas

NOUN 1 a particular part of a place, country, or the world: *a built-up area of the city*.
2 the measurement of a flat surface. *The area of the playground is 1500 square metres (1500 m²)*.

Synonyms: (sense 1) district, region, zone

arena arenas

NOUN a place where sports and other public events take place.
[from Latin *harena* meaning sand, because of the sandy centre of an amphitheatre where gladiators fought]

aren't

VERB a contraction of *are not*.

argue argues arguing argued

VERB 1 If you **argue** with someone about something, you disagree with them about it, sometimes in an angry way.
2 If you **argue** that something is true, you give reasons why you think that it is.

argument arguments

NOUN a talk between people who do not agree.

arid

ADJECTIVE **Arid** land is very dry because there has been very little rain.

Antonym: fertile

arise arises arising arose arisen

VERB When something such as an opportunity or a problem **arises**, it begins to exist.

aristocrat aristocrats

NOUN someone whose family has a high social rank, and who has a title such as Lord or Lady.
aristocratic ADJECTIVE   **aristocracy** NOUN

arithmetic

NOUN the part of mathematics that is to do with the addition, subtraction, multiplication and division of numbers.
arithmetical ADJECTIVE   **arithmetically** ADVERB
[from Greek *arithmos* meaning number]

ark

NOUN In the Bible, the **ark** was the boat built by Noah for his family and the animals during the Flood.

arm arms arming armed

NOUN 1 the part of your body between your shoulder and your wrist.
PLURAL NOUN 2 **Arms** are weapons used in a war.
VERB 3 If a country **arms** itself, it prepares for war.

armada armadas

NOUN a large fleet of warships. *The Spanish Armada was the fleet sent to destroy the English in 1588*.

armchair armchairs

NOUN a large chair with a support on each side for your arms.

armistice armistices

NOUN In war, an **armistice** is an agreement to stop fighting.

armour

NOUN 1 In the past, **armour** was metal clothing worn for protection in battle.
2 In modern warfare, tanks are often referred to as **armour**.

army armies

NOUN a large group of soldiers who are trained to fight on land.

aroma aromas

NOUN a strong, pleasant smell.
aromatic ADJECTIVE
[a Greek word meaning spice]

around

PREPOSITION **1** situated at various points in a place or area. *There are several post boxes **around** the town.*
2 from place to place inside an area. *We walked **around** the stalls at the summer fair.*
3 surrounding or encircling a place or object. *We were sitting **around** the table.*
4 at approximately the time or place mentioned. *The jumble sale began **around** noon.*

arrange arranges arranging arranged

VERB **1** If you **arrange** to do something, or **arrange** something for someone, you make plans for it or make it possible. *I **arranged** to meet him later. Dad **arranged** a trip to the circus for us.*
2 If you **arrange** objects, you set them out in a particular way. *We **arranged** the books in alphabetical order.*

array arrays

NOUN **1** a large number of different things displayed together.
2 a mathematical way of grouping. For example, 3×2 is shown as ::: and 2×3 is shown as ::

arrest arrests arresting arrested

VERB **1** If the police **arrest** someone, they take them to a police station because they believe they may have committed a crime.
NOUN **2** An **arrest** is the act of arresting someone.

arrive arrives arriving arrived

VERB **1** When you **arrive** at a place, you reach it at the end of your journey.
2 When you **arrive** at a decision you make up your mind.
arrival NOUN

arrogant

ADJECTIVE **Arrogant** people behave as if they are better than other people.

arrow arrows

NOUN a long, thin weapon with a sharp point at one end, shot from a bow.

arsenal arsenals

NOUN a place where weapons and ammunition are stored or produced.

arsenic

NOUN a strong, dangerous poison that can kill.

arson

NOUN the crime of deliberately setting fire to something, especially a building.

art arts

NOUN **1** the creation of objects, such as paintings and sculptures, that are thought to be beautiful or that express a particular idea. *He wanted to take **art** classes to learn how to draw and paint well.*
2 **Art** is also used to refer to the objects themselves. *We saw lots of interesting paintings and sculptures at the **art** exhibition.*
3 something that needs special skills or ability. *I would like to master the **art** of sewing.*

artery arteries

NOUN the tubes that carry blood from your heart to the rest of your body. *See **vein**.*
arterial ADJECTIVE

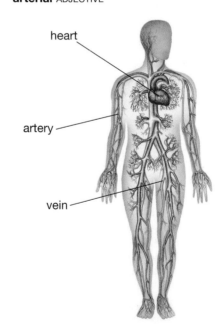

heart

artery

vein

arthritis

NOUN a condition in which the joints in someone's body become painful, and sometimes swollen.
arthritic ADJECTIVE

article articles
NOUN **1** a piece of writing in a newspaper or magazine.
2 a particular item: *an **article** of clothing.*

artificial
ADJECTIVE Something **artificial** is created by people rather than occurring naturally.

Antonym: natural

artillery
NOUN **1 Artillery** consists of large, powerful guns and rockets.
2 The **artillery** is the branch of an army that uses these weapons.

artist artists
NOUN a person who draws or paints or produces other works of art.

as
CONJUNCTION **1** at the same time that. *We watched television **as** we ate our sandwiches.*
2 because. ***As** I like school I get there early.*
PHRASE **3** You use **as if** or **as though** when you are giving an explanation for something. *Shane walked past **as if** he didn't know me.*

ascend ascends ascending ascended
VERB; FORMAL If someone or something **ascends**, they move or lead upwards. *We **ascended** the stairs to the second floor.*

Antonym: descend

ash ashes
NOUN the grey or black powdery remains of anything that has been burnt. *We put the **ashes** from the bonfire on the compost heap.*

ashamed
ADJECTIVE **1** If you are **ashamed**, you feel embarrassed or guilty.
2 If you are **ashamed** of someone, you feel embarrassed to be connected with them.

ashore
ADVERB If someone or something comes **ashore**, they comes on to the land from the sea or a river.

aside
ADVERB If you move something **aside**, you move it to one side. *She closed the book and laid it **aside**.*

ask asks asking asked
VERB **1** If you **ask** someone something, you put a question to them.
2 If you **ask** someone to do something, you tell them you want them to do it. *We **asked** him to do his card trick.*
3 If you **ask** for something, you say you would like to have it. *She **asked** for a drink of water.*
4 If you **ask** someone to come or go somewhere, you invite them there.

asleep
ADJECTIVE If you are **asleep**, your eyes are closed and your whole body is resting.

aspect aspects
NOUN one of many ways of seeing or thinking about something.

aspirin aspirins
NOUN **1** a white drug used to relieve pain, fever and colds.
2 a small white tablet of this drug.

ass asses
NOUN another name for a donkey.

assassinate assassinates assassinating assassinated
VERB If someone **assassinates** an important person, they murder them.
assassination NOUN

assault assaults
NOUN a violent attack on someone.
[from Latin ***assalire*** meaning to leap upon]

assemble assembles assembling assembled
VERB **1** If people **assemble**, they gather together. *We **assembled** in the playground to watch the display.*
2 If you **assemble** something, you fit the parts of it together. *It took us ages to **assemble** the model car.*

assembly assemblies
NOUN a group of people who have gathered together for a meeting.

assess assesses assessing assessed
VERB If you **assess** something, you consider it carefully and make a judgement about it. *She tried to **assess** how much further they had to walk.*

Synonyms: judge, size up

asset assets

NOUN **1** If someone or something is an **asset**, they are useful or helpful. *He's an **asset** to the school.*
2 The **assets** of a person or a company are all the things they own that could be sold to raise money.

assignment assignments

NOUN a job you are given to do.

assist assists assisting assisted

VERB If you **assist** someone, you help them to do something.

assistant assistants

NOUN someone who helps another person to do their job.

associate associates associating associated

VERB **1** If you **associate** with someone, you spend time with them.
2 If you **associate** one thing with another, you make a connection between them.

association associations

NOUN **1** an organization for people who have similar interests, jobs or aims.
2 An **association** between two things is a link you make in your mind between them.

assorted

ADJECTIVE **Assorted** things are a mixture of various sorts of something. They may be different colours, sizes and shapes.

assortment assortments

NOUN a group of similar things that are different sizes, shapes and colours. *There was an amazing **assortment** of toys in the shop.*

assume assumes assuming assumed

VERB **1** If you **assume** that something is true, you believe it, even if you have not thought carefully about it.
2 If you **assume** responsibility for something, you decide to do it. *I **assumed** responsibility for feeding the hamster.*

assure assures assuring assured

VERB If you **assure** someone of something, you say something to make them less worried about it. *I **assured** him that I wouldn't be late.*

asterisk asterisks

NOUN a symbol (*) used in writing and printing to draw attention to something that is explained somewhere else, usually at the bottom of the page.

asteroid asteroids

NOUN one of the large number of very small planets that move around the sun between the orbits of Jupiter and Mars.

asthma

NOUN a disease of the chest that causes wheezing and difficulty in breathing.
asthmatic ADJECTIVE
[from Greek *azein* meaning to breathe hard]

astonish astonishes astonishing astonished

VERB If something **astonishes** you, it surprises you very much.
astonished ADJECTIVE **astonishing** ADJECTIVE
astonishingly ADVERB **astonishment** NOUN

astrology

NOUN the study of the sun, moon and stars in the belief that their movements can influence people's lives.

astronaut astronauts

NOUN a person who operates a spacecraft.
[from Greek *astron* meaning star and *nautes* meaning sailor]

astronomy

NOUN the scientific study of stars and planets.
astronomer NOUN

at

PREPOSITION **1** where someone or something is. *John waited for me **at** the bus stop.*
2 the direction something is going in. *I threw the snowball **at** my brother.*
3 when something happens. *The party starts **at** six o'clock.*

ate

VERB the past tense of *eat*.
✔ Another word that sounds like *ate* is *eight*.

atheist atheists

NOUN someone who does not believe in any form of God.

athlete athletes

NOUN a person who is very good at sport and who takes part in sporting competitions.

athletics
NOUN sporting events such as running, long jump and discus.

Atlantic
NOUN the ocean that separates North and South America from Europe and Africa.

atlas atlases
NOUN a book of maps.
[from the giant *Atlas* in Greek mythology, who supported the sky on his shoulders]

atmosphere atmospheres
NOUN **1** gases that surround a planet.
2 the general mood of a place. *There was a friendly atmosphere at the party.*

atom atoms
NOUN the smallest part of an element that can take part in a chemical reaction.

atrocity atrocities
NOUN an extremely shocking and cruel act.

attach attaches attaching attached
VERB If you **attach** something to something else, you join or fasten the two things together.

attack attacks attacking attacked
VERB **1** If someone **attacks** another person or animal, they use violence in order to hurt or kill them. *The lion attacked the zebra in order to kill it for food.*
2 In a game such as football or hockey, players **attack** to get the ball into a position from which a goal can be scored.
NOUN **3** violent, physical action against someone.

attempt attempts attempting attempted
VERB **1** If you **attempt** to do something, you try to do it.
NOUN **2** the act of trying to do something. *He made a brave attempt to help.*

attend attends attending attended
VERB **1** If you **attend** school, church or hospital, you go there regularly.
2 If you **attend** an event, you are present at it.
attend to VERB **3** If you **attend to** something, you deal with it. *We should attend to our homework before going to the park.*

attendant attendants
NOUN someone whose job is to help people in a place such as a museum or shop.

attention
NOUN the thought or care that you give to someone or something. *I paid a lot of attention to my homework.*

attentive
ADJECTIVE When you are **attentive**, you pay close attention.
attentively ADVERB

attic attics
NOUN a room at the top of a house immediately below the roof.

attitude attitudes
NOUN the way you think about someone or something and behave towards them. *I'm not going in that shop again. I don't like their attitude.*

attract attracts attracting attracted
VERB **1** If something **attracts** people, it interests them and makes them want to go to it.
2 If someone **attracts** you, you like them and are interested in them.
3 When magnetic materials are **attracted** to a magnet, they are pulled towards it.

attraction attractions
NOUN **1** If you feel an **attraction** for someone, you like them very much.
2 somewhere people like to visit for interest or pleasure, such as a fun fair or a stately home.
3 A force of **attraction** pulls magnetic materials towards a magnet.

attractive
ADJECTIVE **1** Someone who is **attractive** is good-looking or has an exciting personality.
2 If something is **attractive**, it is interesting.

aubergine aubergines
NOUN a dark purple, pear-shaped vegetable. It is also called an eggplant.

auburn
ADJECTIVE a red-brown hair colour.

auction auctions auctioning auctioned
NOUN **1** a public sale in which goods are sold to the person who offers the highest price.
VERB **2** to sell something in an auction.

audible
ADJECTIVE If something is **audible**, you can hear it.

audience audiences
NOUN **1** the group of people who are watching or listening to a performance.
2 a private or formal meeting with an important person. *The winners of the bravery awards had an **audience** with the Queen.*

audition auditions
NOUN a short performance by an actor or musician, so that a director can decide whether they are suitable for a part in a play or a film, or for a place in an orchestra.

auditorium auditoriums or auditoria
NOUN the part of a theatre or concert hall where the audience sits.

August
NOUN the eighth month of the year. **August** has 31 days.

aunt aunts
NOUN Your **aunt** is the sister of your mother or father, or the wife of your uncle.

au pair au pairs
NOUN a young person from abroad who comes to live with a family to look after the children, help with the housework and learn the language.
[From a French expression meaning on equal terms]

author authors
NOUN The **author** of a book is the person who wrote it.
✔ Use *author* to talk about both men and women writers.

authority authorities
NOUN **1** the power to tell other people what to do. *The teacher had the **authority** to give me detention.*
2 an organization that controls public interests: *the local health **authority**.*
3 Someone who is an **authority** on something, knows a lot about it.

authorize authorizes authorizing authorized
VERB If someone **authorizes** something, they give official permission for it.
authorization NOUN

auto-
PREFIX **1** self or same: ***auto**biography.*
2 self-propelling: ***auto**matic car.*

autobiography autobiographies
NOUN an account of someone's life that they have written themselves.
autobiographical ADJECTIVE

autograph autographs
NOUN the signature of a famous person.
[from Greek ***auto*** meaning self and ***graphos*** meaning written]

automatic automatics
ADJECTIVE **1** An **automatic** machine is programmed to perform tasks without needing a person to operate it.
NOUN **2** a car in which the gears change automatically as the car's speed changes.

autumn autumns
NOUN the season between summer and winter, when the leaves fall off the trees. *I love the golden colours of the trees in **autumn**.*

available
ADJECTIVE **1** If something is **available**, it is easy to get or to buy.
2 A person who is **available** is ready for work or free to talk to.

avalanche avalanches
NOUN a huge mass of snow and ice that falls down a mountainside.

avenue avenues
NOUN a street, especially one with trees along it.

average averages
NOUN **1** a result obtained by adding several amounts together and then dividing the total by the number of different amounts. *If I shared 36 sweets between four children, the **average** would be nine sweets per child.*
ADJECTIVE **2** standard or usual. *The **average** teenager is interested in pop music.*
PHRASE **3** You say **on average** when mentioning what usually happens in a situation. *Men are, **on average**, taller than women.*

Synonyms: (sense 2) normal, ordinary, typical

aviary aviaries
NOUN a large cage or group of cages in which birds are kept.

aviation
> NOUN the science of flying aircraft.

avocado avocados
> NOUN a pear-shaped fruit with dark green skin, soft greenish-yellow flesh, and a large stone.

avoid avoids avoiding avoided
> VERB **1** If you **avoid** someone or something, you keep away from them. *To* **avoid** *him, she went home the other way.*
> **2** If you **avoid** doing something, you make an effort not to do it.

Synonyms: (sense 2) dodge, shirk

---

awake
> ADJECTIVE Someone who is **awake** is not sleeping.

award awards awarding awarded
> NOUN **1** a prize or certificate for doing something well.
> VERB **2** If someone **awards** you something, they give it to you formally or officially. *He was* **awarded** *the prize for fastest runner.*

aware
> ADJECTIVE **1** If you are **aware** of something, you know about it.
> **2** If you are **aware** of something, you can see, hear, smell or feel it.

away
> ADVERB **1** moving from a place. *I saw them walk* **away** *from the house.*
> **2** at a distance from a place. *The nearest supermarket is 12 kilometres* **away**.
> **3** in its proper place. *He put his CDs* **away**.
> **4** not at home, school or work. *My friend's been* **away** *from school for a week.*

awe
> NOUN; FORMAL a feeling of great respect mixed with amazement, and sometimes slight fear. *Looking up at the mountains, we felt a sense of* **awe**.

awful
> ADJECTIVE very unpleasant or very bad. *Isn't the weather* **awful**?

Synonyms: dreadful, terrible

---

awkward
> ADJECTIVE **1** difficult to deal with: *an* **awkward** *situation.*
> **2** clumsy and uncomfortable. *The large bag was* **awkward** *to carry.*
> [from Old Norse **ofugr** meaning turned the wrong way]

axe axes
> NOUN a tool with a handle and a sharp blade, used for chopping wood.

axis axes
> NOUN **1** an imaginary line through the middle of something, around which it moves. *The earth turns on its* **axis**.
> **2** one of the two sides of a graph.
> ✔ The plural is pronounced "**ax**-eez".

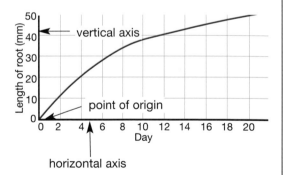

Line graph of seed growth

axle axles
> NOUN the long bar that connects a pair of wheels on a vehicle.

Bb

A B C D E F G H I J K L M N O P Q R S T U V W X Y Z

babble babbles babbling babbled
VERB If someone **babbles**, they talk in a quick and confused way that is difficult to understand.

baboon baboons
NOUN an African monkey with a pointed face, large teeth and a long tail.

baby babies
NOUN a child in the first year or two of its life.

baby-sit baby-sits baby-sitting baby-sat
VERB If you **baby-sit** for someone, you look after their children while they are out.

bachelor bachelors
NOUN a man who has never been married.

back backs backing backed
ADVERB **1** When people or things move **back**, they move in the opposite direction to the one they are facing.
2 When you go **back** to a place or situation, you return to it. *She went **back** to sleep.*
NOUN **3** the rear part of your body.
ADJECTIVE **4** The **back** parts of something are the ones at the rear: *the dog's **back** legs.*
VERB **5** If a building **backs** on to something, the back of it faces in that direction.

backbone backbones
NOUN the column of linked bones along the middle of the back of a human and other vertebrates.

background backgrounds
NOUN **1** the things in a picture or scene that are less noticeable than the main things.
2 the kind of home you come from, and your education and experience.

backstroke
NOUN a style of swimming movement on your back.

backward
ADJECTIVE If you take a **backward** look, you look behind you.

backwards
ADVERB **1** If you move **backwards**, you move to a place behind you.

2 If you do something **backwards**, you do it opposite to the usual way. *He told them to count **backwards** from 20 to 5.*

bacon
NOUN meat from the back or sides of a pig, which has been salted or smoked.

bacteria
PLURAL NOUN very tiny organisms that can cause disease.
bacterial ADJECTIVE
[from Greek **bakterion** meaning little rod; some bacteria are rod-shaped]

bad worse worst
ADJECTIVE **1 Bad** things are harmful or upsetting. *I have some **bad** news.*
2 not enough or of poor quality. *The food was **worse** than usual.*
3 Bad food is not fresh.

Synonyms: (sense 1) distressing, grave, terrible
(sense 3) rotten, decayed
---

badge badges
NOUN a piece of plastic or metal with a design or message on it that you can pin to your clothes.

badger badgers badgering badgered
NOUN **1** a nocturnal mammal that has a white head with two black stripes on it.
VERB **2** If you **badger** someone, you keep asking them questions or pestering them to do something.

badminton
NOUN a game in which two or four players use rackets to hit a feathered object, called a shuttlecock, over a high net.

bag bags
NOUN a container for carrying things in.
[From Old Norse **baggi** meaning bundle]

baggage
NOUN Your **baggage** is all the suitcases, holdalls and bags that you take with you when you travel.

bagpipes
PLURAL NOUN a musical instrument played by squeezing air out of a leather bag and through pipes.

baguette baguettes

NOUN a long, thin French loaf of bread.

bail bails

NOUN **1** In cricket, the **bails** are the two small pieces of wood placed on top of the stumps to form the wicket.

2 a sum of money paid to a court to allow an accused person to go free until the time of the trial. *The accused man was released on **bail**.*

bait baits baiting baited

NOUN **1** a small amount of food placed on a hook, or in a trap, to attract and catch a fish or wild animal.

VERB **2** If you **bait** a hook or a trap, you put some food on it to catch a fish or wild animal.

bake bakes baking baked

VERB **1** When you **bake** food, you cook it in an oven without using extra liquid or fat.

2 If you **bake** earth or clay, you heat it until it becomes hard.

baker bakers

NOUN a person who makes and sells bread and cakes.

balance balances balancing balanced

VERB **1** When someone or something **balances**, they remain steady and do not fall over.

2 used in maths when weighing and comparing two weights. If two weights are equal, they **balance**.

NOUN **3** the state of being upright and steady. *She lost her **balance** and fell.*

4 the amount of money in someone's bank account.

balcony balconies

NOUN **1** a platform on the outside of a building, with a wall or railing round it.

2 an area of upstairs seats in a theatre or cinema.

bald balder baldest

ADJECTIVE A **bald** person has little or no hair on their head.

[from Middle English **ballede** meaning having a white patch]

bale bales baling baled

NOUN **1** a large bundle of something, such as paper or hay, tied tightly.

VERB **2** If you **bale** water from a boat, you remove it using a container; also spelt **bail**.

ball balls

NOUN **1** a round object used in games such as tennis, soccer, and hockey.

2 The **ball** of your foot or thumb is the rounded part where your toes join your foot or your thumb joins your hand.

ballad ballads

NOUN **1** a long song or poem that tells a story.

2 a slow, romantic pop song.

ballerina ballerinas

NOUN a female ballet dancer.

ballet

NOUN a type of artistic dancing based on precise steps.

[from Italian **balletto** meaning little dance]

balloon balloons

NOUN **1** a small bag made of thin rubber that you blow into until it becomes larger. **Balloons** are often used as party decorations.

2 a large, strong bag filled with gas or hot air, that travels through the air carrying passengers in a basket underneath it. *They went on a hot air **balloon** flight over the city.*

ballpoint ballpoints

NOUN a pen with a small, metal ball at the writing point.

bamboo

NOUN a tall tropical grass with hard, hollow stems used for making furniture.

ban bans banning banned

VERB **1** If you **ban** something, you forbid it to be done.

NOUN **2** If there is a **ban** on something, it is not allowed.

Synonyms: (sense 1) forbid, prohibit

banana bananas

NOUN a long, curved fruit with a yellow skin.

band bands

NOUN **1** a group of musicians who play jazz or pop music together.

2 a group of people who share a common purpose.

3 a narrow strip of something used to hold things together. *She tied her hair back with an elastic **band**.*

bandage bandages
NOUN a strip of cloth wrapped round a wound to protect it.

bang bangs banging banged
NOUN **1** a sudden, short, loud noise.
2 a hard, painful bump against something.
VERB **3** If you **bang** something, you hit it or put it down violently so that it makes a loud noise.
4 If you **bang** a part of your body against something, you accidentally bump it.

banish banishes banishing banished
VERB **1** If someone is **banished**, they are sent away and never allowed to return.
2 If you **banish** something from your thoughts, you try not to think about it.
banishment NOUN

banister banisters
NOUN a rail supported by posts up the side of a staircase.

banjo banjos or banjoes
NOUN a musical instrument, like a small guitar with a round body.

bank banks banking banked
NOUN **1** a business that looks after people's money.
2 the raised ground along the edge of a river or lake.
VERB **3** If you **bank on** something happening, you rely on it. *I know we said we'd go swimming, but don't **bank on** it.*

banner banners
NOUN **1** a long strip of cloth with a message or slogan on it. *We saw **banners** advertising the fair.*
ADJECTIVE **2** A **banner** headline is a headline printed right across the page of a newspaper.

banquet banquets
NOUN a grand, formal dinner, often followed by speeches.
[from Old French **banquet**, originally meaning little bench]

baptism baptisms
NOUN the ceremony in which someone has water sprinkled on them, or they are immersed in water, as a sign that they have become a Christian.

baptize baptizes baptizing baptized; also spelt **baptised**
VERB When a church official **baptizes** someone, they sprinkle water on them, or immerse them in water, as a sign that they have become a Christian.

bar bars barring barred
NOUN **1** a long, straight piece of metal.
VERB **2** If you **bar** someone's way, you stop them going somewhere by standing in front of them.
NOUN **3** a counter or room where alcoholic drinks are served.
4 a piece of something made in a rectangular shape: *a **bar** of soap.*

barbecue barbecues
NOUN **1** a grill with a charcoal fire on which you cook food, usually outdoors.
2 an outdoor party where you eat food cooked on a **barbecue**.
[from a Caribbean word meaning framework]

barber barbers
NOUN a man who cuts men's hair.

bar chart bar charts
NOUN a kind of graph where the information is shown in rows or bars.

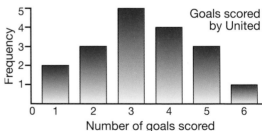

bar code bar codes
NOUN a pattern of lines and numbers on something that is for sale, so that the price can be read by a machine.

bare barer barest
ADJECTIVE **1** If a part of your body is **bare**, it is not covered by any clothing: ***bare** feet.*
2 If something is **bare**, it is not covered or decorated with anything: ***bare** wooden floors.*
3 The **bare** minimum, or the **bare** essentials, means the very least that is needed.

Synonyms: (sense 1) naked, uncovered

barely

ADVERB If you **barely** manage to do something, you only just succeed in doing it.

bargain bargains bargaining bargained

NOUN **1** an agreement in which two people or groups discuss and agree what each will do, pay or receive.
2 something that is sold at a low price and that is good value. *The apples are a **bargain** at this price.*
VERB **3** When people **bargain** with each other, they discuss and agree terms about what each will do, pay or receive.

barge barges barging barged

NOUN **1** a boat with a flat bottom used for carrying heavy loads, especially on canals.
VERB **2** INFORMAL If you **barge** into a place, you push into it in a rough or rude way.

bark barks barking barked

VERB **1** When a dog **barks**, it makes a short, loud noise, once or several times.
NOUN **2** the tough material that covers the outside of a tree.

barley

NOUN a cereal that is grown for food and is also used for making beer and whisky.

bar mitzvah

NOUN A Jewish boy's **bar mitzvah** is a ceremony that takes place on his 13th birthday, after which he is regarded as an adult.

barn barns

NOUN a large farm building used for storing crops or animal food.
[from Old English ***beren*** meaning barley room]

barnacle barnacles

NOUN a small shellfish that fixes itself to rocks and to the bottom of boats.

barometer barometers

NOUN an instrument that measures air pressure and shows when the weather is changing.

barrel barrels

NOUN **1** a wooden container with rounded sides and flat ends.
2 The **barrel** of a gun is the long tube through which the bullet is fired.

barricade barricades barricading barricaded

NOUN **1** a temporary barrier put up to stop people getting past.
VERB **2** If you **barricade** yourself inside a room or building, you put something heavy against the door to stop people getting in.
[from Old French ***barriquer*** meaning to block with barrels]

barrier barriers

NOUN a fence or wall that prevents people or animals getting from one area to another.

barrister barristers

NOUN a lawyer who is qualified to represent people in the higher courts.

barrow barrows

NOUN **1** the same as a wheelbarrow.
2 a large cart from which fruit or other goods are sold in the street.

base bases basing based

NOUN **1** the lowest part of something. *The waves crashed at the **base** of the cliffs.*
2 The **base** of a triangle or a square-shaped pyramid is the bottom.
3 a place where part of an army, navy or air force works from.
VERB **4** If you **base** one thing is on another, you develop from it. *She **based** the film on a true story.*
5 If you are **based** somewhere, you live there or work from there. *My dad is **based** in Cardiff, but spends a lot of time abroad.*

baseball

NOUN a team game played with a bat and a ball. It is popular in the USA.

basement basements

NOUN a room or set of rooms below the level of the street. *My aunt lives in the **basement** of our house.*

basic

ADJECTIVE **1** The **basic** aspects of something are the most necessary ones. *The **basic** ingredients of bread are flour, yeast and water.*
2 having only the essentials, and no extras or luxuries.
basically ADVERB

basin basins

NOUN **1** a round, wide container which is open at the top.

2 A river **basin** is a bowl of land from which water runs into the river.

basis bases

NOUN If something is the **basis** of something else, it is the main principle on which it is based, and from which other points and ideas can be developed.

✔ the plural is pronounced "**bay**-seez".

bask basks basking basked

VERB If you **bask** in hot weather, you lie in the sun and enjoy the warmth.

basket baskets

NOUN a container made of thin strips of wood or metal woven together: *a shopping **basket***.

basketball

NOUN a game in which two teams try to score goals by throwing a large ball through one of two circular nets that are suspended high up at each end of the **basketball** court.

bass basses

NOUN **1** a man with a very deep singing voice.

ADJECTIVE **2** a musical instrument that produces a very deep sound: *a **bass** guitar*.

bassoon bassoons

NOUN a large woodwind instrument.

bat bats batting batted

NOUN **1** a specially shaped piece of wood with a handle, used for hitting a ball in games such as table tennis or cricket.

2 a small animal like a mouse with leathery wings. **Bats** fly at night and sleep hanging upside down.

VERB **3** If you are **batting** in cricket, baseball or rounders, it is your turn to hit the ball.

batch batches

NOUN A **batch** of things is a group of things that are all the same or are being dealt with at the same time. *They delivered the first **batch** of books at the start of term.*

bath baths

NOUN a long container that you fill with water and sit in to wash yourself.

bathe bathes bathing bathed

VERB When you **bathe** in a sea, river or lake, you swim or play there.

bathroom bathrooms

NOUN a room with a bath or shower, a washbasin and often a toilet in it.

baton batons

NOUN **1** a light, thin stick that a conductor uses to direct an orchestra or choir.

2 a short stick passed from one runner to another at the changeover in a relay race.

battalion battalions

NOUN an army unit consisting of three or more companies.

batter batters battering battered

NOUN **1** a mixture of flour, eggs and milk, used to make pancakes, or to coat food before frying it.

VERB **2** When someone or something **batters** someone or something, they hit them many times. *The waves **battered** the sides of the ship.*

battery batteries

NOUN a device for storing energy and producing electricity, for example in a torch or a car.

battle battles

NOUN a fight between armed forces, or a struggle between two people or groups with different aims.

battlefield battlefields

NOUN a place where a battle has been fought or is being fought.

battlements

PLURAL NOUN the top part of a castle where there are openings through which arrows or guns could be fired.

battleship battleships

NOUN a large fighting ship carrying powerful guns.

bawl bawls bawling bawled
VERB If someone **bawls**, they shout or cry loudly.

bay bays baying bayed
NOUN **1** part of the coastline where the land curves.
2 a space or an area used for a particular purpose: *a loading* **bay**.
3 a tree with dark green leaves. The leaves are used for flavouring food.
VERB **4** When a dog or a wolf **bays**, it makes a deep, howling sound.
PHRASE **5** If you keep something **at bay**, you stop it hurting you. *Try eating an orange to keep a cold* **at bay**.

bayonet bayonets
NOUN a sharp blade that can be fixed to the end of a rifle.

bazaar bazaars
NOUN **1** an area with many small shops and stalls, especially in Eastern countries.
2 a sale to raise money for charity: *a Christmas* **bazaar**.
[from Persian **bazar** meaning market]

BC
ADJECTIVE You use **BC** to show the dates before the birth of Jesus Christ. It is an abbreviation for *before Christ*.

be am is are; being; was were; been
VERB **1** You can use **be** with the present participle of other verbs. *Look! I* **am** *riding on my own!*
2 You can also use **be** to say that something will happen. *I will* **be** *nine in November.*
3 You use **be** to say more about something or somebody. *His name* **is** *Tom*

beach beaches
NOUN an area of sand or pebbles beside the sea.

beacon beacons
NOUN In the past, a **beacon** was a light or fire on a hill, which acted as a signal or warning.

bead beads
NOUN **1** a small, shaped piece of glass, stone or wood with a hole through the middle. **Beads** are strung together with others to make necklaces or bracelets.

2 a drop of liquid: **beads** *of perspiration*.

beak beaks
NOUN the hard part of a bird's mouth that sticks out. It is used for pecking up food and for carrying things such as twigs.

beam beams beaming beamed
NOUN **1** a long, thick bar of wood or metal, especially one that supports a roof.
2 a band of light that shines from something such as a torch or the sun.
VERB **3** If you **beam**, you smile broadly.

bean beans
NOUN the seed or pod of a plant, eaten as a vegetable or used for other purposes: *runner* **beans**, *coffee* **beans**, *soya* **beans**.

bear bears bearing bore borne
NOUN **1** a large, strong, wild mammal with thick fur and sharp claws: *polar* **bear**, *grizzly* **bear**.
VERB **2** If someone or something **bears** something, they carry it or support its weight. *The ice wasn't thick enough to* **bear** *their weight.*
3 If something **bears** a mark or typical feature, it has it. *The room* **bore** *all the signs of a violent struggle.*
4 If you **bear** something difficult, you accept it and are able to deal with it. *He* **bore** *the death of his gerbil bravely.*

beard beards
NOUN the hair that grows on the lower part of a man's face.

beast beasts
NOUN **1** an old-fashioned word for a large, wild animal.
2 INFORMAL If you call someone a **beast**, you mean that they are cruel or spiteful.

beat beats beating beat beaten
VERB **1** If someone or something **beats** someone or something else, they hit them hard and repeatedly. *The rain was* **beating** *against the window.*
2 If you **beat** someone in a race or game, you defeat them or do better than them.
3 When your heart **beats**, it pumps blood with a regular rhythm.
NOUN **4** the main rhythm of a piece of music or poetry.

A
B
C
D
E
F
G
H
I
J
K
L
M
N
O
P
Q
R
S
T
U
V
W
X
Y
Z

beautiful
ADJECTIVE very attractive or pleasing.

Synonym: lovely

beauty beauties
NOUN **1** the quality of being beautiful: *the beauty of the stars on a clear night.*
2 The **beauty** of an idea or a plan is what makes it attractive or worth doing. *The beauty of going in September is that the sea will be warmer for swimming.*

beaver beavers
NOUN a mammal with a big, flat tail and webbed hind feet. **Beavers** build dams.

because
CONJUNCTION **1 Because** is used with other words to give the reason for something. *I went home because I was tired.*
PHRASE **2 Because of** is used with a noun that gives the reason for something. *I had to stay late because of detention.*

beckon beckons beckoning beckoned
VERB If you **beckon** to someone, you make a sign to them with your hand, asking them to come to you.

become becomes becoming became become
VERB If someone or something **becomes** something else, they start feeling or being that thing. *I became more and more angry.*
[from Old English *becuman* meaning to happen]

bed beds
NOUN **1** a piece of furniture that you lie on when you sleep.
2 an area of ground in a garden which has been dug and prepared for planting.
3 The **bed** of the sea or a river is the bottom of it.

bedraggled
ADJECTIVE If a person or animal is **bedraggled**, they are wet, dirty and messy.

bedroom bedrooms
NOUN a room for sleeping in.

bedtime bedtimes
NOUN the time when you go to bed.

bee bees
NOUN a winged insect that makes honey. Many types of **bee** live in large groups.

beech beeches
NOUN a tree with a smooth, grey trunk and shiny leaves.

beef
NOUN the meat of a cow, bull or ox.

beehive beehives
NOUN a specially designed structure in which bees are kept so that their honey can be collected.

been
VERB the past participle of *be*.

beer beers
NOUN an alcoholic drink made from malt and flavoured with hops.

beetle beetles
NOUN a flying insect with hard wings that cover its body when it is not flying.
[from Old English *bitan* meaning to bite]

beetroot beetroots
NOUN a round, dark red root vegetable.

before
ADVERB, PREPOSITION, OR CONJUNCTION If something happens **before**, it happens earlier than something else. *Can I see you before you go?*

Antonym: after

beg begs begging begged
VERB **1** When people **beg**, they ask for food or money, because they are very poor.
2 If you **beg** someone to do something, you ask them very anxiously to do it. *David begged his dad to take him to the cinema.*

began
VERB the past tense of *begin*.

begin begins beginning began begun
VERB If you **begin** something, you start it.

beginner beginners
NOUN someone who has just started to learn something.

Synonym: learner

beginning beginnings

NOUN The **beginning** of something is when or where it starts.

begun

VERB the past participle of *begin*.

behalf

PHRASE If you do something **on behalf of** someone or something, you do it for them or in their name. *We did the sponsored swim **on behalf of** various charities.*

behave behaves behaving behaved

VERB **1** If you **behave** in a particular way, you act in that way. *He knew that he'd **behaved** badly.*
2 If you **behave** yourself, you act correctly or properly.

behind

PREPOSITION **1** at the back of. *The moon disappeared **behind** a cloud.*
2 supporting someone. *The whole school was **behind** him in the competition.*
ADVERB **3** If you stay **behind**, you remain after other people have gone.
4 If you leave something **behind**, you do not take it with you.

beige

ADJECTIVE a cream-brown colour.

being

VERB the present participle of *be*.

belch belches belching belched

VERB **1** If you **belch**, you make a sudden noise in your throat because air has risen up from your stomach.
2 If something **belches** smoke or fire, it sends it out in large amounts. *Smoke **belched** from the factory chimneys.*
NOUN **3** the noise you make when you belch.

belief beliefs

NOUN If you have a **belief** in something, you are certain that it is right or true.

believe believes believing believed

VERB **1** If you **believe** that something is true, you think that it is true.
2 If you **believe** someone, you accept that they are telling the truth.

bell bells

NOUN **1** a cup-shaped metal object with a piece inside it called a clapper that hits the side and makes a ringing sound.
2 an electrical device that you can ring or buzz to get attention.

bellow bellows bellowing bellowed

VERB If a human or other animal **bellows**, they shout very loudly or make a very loud, deep noise like a roar.

belly bellies

NOUN the part of your body, especially your stomach, that holds and digests food.

belong belongs belonging belonged

VERB **1** If something **belongs** to you, it is yours and you own it.
2 If you **belong** to a group, you are a member of it.
3 If something **belongs** in a particular place, that is where it should be. *That book **belongs** on the top shelf.*

belongings

PLURAL NOUN Your **belongings** are all the things that you own.

below

PREPOSITION OR ADVERB **1** If something is **below** something else, it is in a lower position. *We could hear music coming up from the flat two floors **below**.*
2 If something is **below** a particular amount or level, it is less than it: ***below** average rainfall*.

Antonym: above

belt belts

NOUN a strip of leather or cloth that you fasten round your waist to hold your trousers or skirt up.

bench benches

NOUN a long seat that two or more people can sit on.

bend bends bending bent

VERB **1** When you **bend** something, you use force to make it curved or angular.
2 When you **bend**, you move your head and shoulders forwards and downwards. *I **bent** over to pick up my glasses.*
NOUN **3** a curved part of something: *a **bend** in the road*.

beneath
PREPOSITION AND ADVERB; FORMAL underneath.

benefit benefits benefiting benefited
NOUN **1** the advantage that something brings to people: *the **benefit** of a good education.*
VERB **2** If you **benefit** from something, it helps you. *He'll **benefit** from some extra tuition.*
[from Latin ***benefactum*** meaning good deed]

bent
ADJECTIVE curved or twisted out of shape.

bereaved
ADJECTIVE; FORMAL You say that someone is **bereaved** when a close relative of theirs has recently died.
bereavement NOUN

berry berries
NOUN a small, round fruit that grows on bushes or trees.

berserk
ADVERB If somebody goes **berserk**, they lose control of themselves and become extremely violent.
[from Icelandic ***berserkr*** meaning a Viking who wore a shirt made from the skin of a bear and who worked himself into a mad frenzy before going into battle]

berth berths
NOUN **1** a space in a harbour where a ship stays when it is being loaded or unloaded.
2 In a boat or caravan, a **berth** is a bed.
PHRASE **3** If you give someone or something **a wide berth**, you avoid them because they are unpleasant or dangerous.

beside
PREPOSITION If one thing is **beside** another thing, it is next to it.

besides
ADVERB also or in addition to.

best
ADJECTIVE **1** the superlative of *good* and *well*. *That was one of the **best** films I've ever seen.*
ADVERB **2** The thing that you like **best** is the thing that you prefer to everything else.

Antonym: (sense 1) worst

bet bets betting bet
VERB If you **bet** on the result of an event, you will win money if what you bet on happens and lose money if it does not.

betray betrays betraying betrayed
VERB If you **betray** someone who trusts you, you tell people something secret about them.

better
ADJECTIVE **1** the comparative of *good* and *well*. *I am feeling **better** today.*
2 If you are **better** after an illness, you are no longer ill.

Synonym: (sense 2) cured

between
PREPOSITION OR ADVERB **1** If something is **between** two other things, it is situated or happens in the space or time that separates them. *He was head teacher **between** 1989 and 2000.*
2 A relationship or a difference **between** two people or two things is one that involves them both: *the difference **between** frogs and toads.*
✔ If there are two things you should use *between*. If there are more than two things you should use *among*.

beware
VERB If you tell someone to **beware** of something, you are warning them that it might be dangerous or harmful.

bewilder bewilders bewildering bewildered
VERB If something **bewilders** you, it confuses and muddles you so that you can't understand.
bewilderment NOUN

beyond
PREPOSITION **1** If something is **beyond** a certain place, it is on the other side of it. ***Beyond** the mountains was the secret valley.*
2 If something is **beyond** you, you cannot do it or understand it.

bi-
PREFIX added to a word to mean two or twice. For example, someone who is **bi**lingual can speak two languages.

bib bibs
NOUN a piece of cloth or plastic put under a baby's chin to protect its clothes from stains.

Bible Bibles

NOUN the sacred book of the Christian religion. *I read about Noah and the Ark in the **Bible**.*

bibliography bibliographies

NOUN a list of books or articles.

bicycle bicycles

NOUN a two-wheeled vehicle that you ride by pushing two pedals with your feet.

bid bids bidding bid

VERB If you **bid** for something, you offer to buy it for a certain sum of money. *He **bid** for an old bike at the auction.*

big bigger biggest

ADJECTIVE large or important.

Antonyms: small, tiny, little

bike bikes

NOUN an abbreviation for *bicycle*.

bikini bikinis

NOUN a small, two-piece swimming costume worn by women.

bilingual

ADJECTIVE involving or using two languages: ***bilingual** street signs.*
[from Latin ***bis*** meaning two and ***lingua*** meaning tongue]

bill bills

NOUN **1** a written statement of how much is owed for goods or services: *a phone **bill**.*
2 a formal statement of a proposed new law that is discussed and then voted on in Parliament.
3 A **bill** can be a piece of paper money: *a dollar **bill**.*
4 A bird's **bill** is its beak.

billiards

NOUN a game in which a long stick called a cue is used to move balls on a table.

billion billions

NOUN a thousand million. *You can write one **billion** like this: 1,000,000,000.*

billow billows billowing billowed

VERB **1** When things made of cloth **billow**, they swell out and flap slowly in the wind.
2 When smoke or cloud **billows**, it spreads upwards and outwards.
NOUN **3** a large wave.

billy goat billy goats

NOUN a male goat.

bin bins

NOUN a container, especially one that you put rubbish in.

binary

ADJECTIVE The **binary** system is a number system used when working with computers. It uses only two digits, 0 and 1.

bind binds binding bound

VERB **1** If you **bind** something, you tie rope or string round it so that it is held firmly.
2 If you **bind** a wound, you wrap bandages round it.
3 When a book is **bound**, the pages are joined together and a cover is put on.

bingo

NOUN a game in which players aim to match the numbers that someone calls out with the numbers on the card they have been given.

binoculars

PLURAL NOUN an instrument with lenses for both eyes, which you look through in order to see objects far away. *They used **binoculars** for bird watching.*

biodegradable

ADJECTIVE **Biodegradable** materials can be broken down naturally, and so they are not dangerous to the environment.

biography biographies

NOUN the history of someone's life, written by someone else.

biology

NOUN the study of living things.
[from Greek ***bios*** + ***logos*** meaning life study]

birch birches

NOUN a tall, deciduous tree with thin branches and thin bark.

bird birds

NOUN an egg-laying animal with feathers, two wings, two legs and a beak.

birth births

NOUN Your **birth** was when you were born.

birthday birthdays

NOUN Your **birthday** is the anniversary of the date on which you were born.

birthmark birthmarks
NOUN a mark on your skin that has been there since you were born.

biscuit biscuits
NOUN a small, flat cake that is crisp and usually sweet.

bisect bisects bisecting bisected
VERB to divide a line or an area in half.

bishop bishops
NOUN a high-ranking clergyman in some Christian Churches.

bison
NOUN a large, hairy animal, related to cattle, with a large head and shoulders. **Bison** used to be very common on the prairies in North America, but they are now almost extinct.

bit bits
VERB **1** the past tense of *bite*. *She **bit** into the toast.*
NOUN **2** A **bit** of something is a small amount of it.
PHRASE **3** INFORMAL **A bit** means slightly or to a small extent. *That's **a bit** difficult.*

bitch bitches
NOUN a female dog.

bite bites biting bit bitten
VERB If you **bite** something, you cut into it with your teeth.

bitter bitterest
ADJECTIVE **1** A **bitter** taste is sharp and unpleasant.
2 A **bitter** wind is extremely cold.
3 If you are **bitter** about something, you feel angry and resentful.

bizarre
ADJECTIVE very strange and weird.

Synonyms: odd, peculiar

black blacker blackest
NOUN OR ADJECTIVE the darkest possible colour, like the sky at night when there is no light.

blackberry blackberries
NOUN a small, soft black fruit that grows on brambles.

blackbird blackbirds
NOUN a common European bird, the male of which has black feathers and a yellow beak.

blackboard blackboards
NOUN a dark-coloured board in a classroom, which teachers write on using chalk.

blackcurrant blackcurrants
NOUN **Blackcurrants** are very small, dark, purple fruits that grow in bunches on bushes.

black hole black holes
NOUN the empty space made by the collapse of a star.

blacksmith blacksmiths
NOUN A **blacksmith** works with metals to make things like horseshoes.

bladder bladders
NOUN the part of your body where urine is held until it leaves your body.

blade blades
NOUN **1** the sharp part of a knife, axe or saw.
2 a single piece of grass.

blame blames blaming blamed
VERB If someone **blames** a person for something bad that has happened, they believe that person caused it.

Synonym: accuse

blank blanker blankest
ADJECTIVE **1** Something that is **blank** has nothing on it: *a **blank** sheet of paper*.
2 If you look **blank**, your face shows no feeling or interest.

blanket blankets
NOUN a large rectangle of thick cloth that is put on a bed to keep people warm.
[from Old French ***blancquete*** meaning little white thing]

blare blares blaring blared
VERB to make a loud, unpleasant noise. *The radio **blared** from the flat below.*

blast blasts blasting blasted
VERB 1 When people **blast** a hole in something, they make a hole with an explosion. *They're using dynamite to **blast** away rocks.*
NOUN 2 a big explosion, especially one caused by a bomb.

blaze blazes blazing blazed
NOUN 1 a large, hot fire.
VERB 2 If something **blazes**, it burns or shines brightly. *The fire **blazed** in the fireplace.*

blazer blazers
NOUN a kind of jacket, often in the colours of a school or sports team.

bleach bleaches bleaching bleached
NOUN 1 a chemical that is used to make material white or to clean thoroughly and kill germs.
VERB 2 If you **bleach** material or hair, you make it white, usually by using a chemical.

bleak bleaker bleakest
ADJECTIVE 1 If a place is **bleak**, it is cold, bare and exposed to the wind: *a **bleak** mountain top.*
2 If a situation is **bleak**, it is bad and seems unlikely to improve.

bleat bleats bleating bleated
VERB When sheep or goats **bleat**, they make a high-pitched cry.

bleed bleeds bleeding bled
VERB When you **bleed**, you lose blood as a result of an injury. *My hand **bled** a lot after I cut it.*

blend blends blending blended
VERB 1 When you **blend** substances, you mix them together to form a single substance. ***Blend** the butter with the sugar.*
2 When colours or sounds **blend**, they combine in a pleasing way.

bless blesses blessing blessed or blest
VERB When a priest **blesses** people or things, he or she asks God to give his protection to them. [from Old English ***bloedsian*** meaning to sprinkle with sacrificial blood]

blew
VERB the past tense of *blow*.

blind blinds blinding blinded
ADJECTIVE 1 Someone who is **blind** cannot see.
VERB 2 If something **blinds** you, it stops you seeing, either for a short time or permanently.
NOUN 3 a roll of cloth or paper that you pull down over a window to keep out the light.

blindfold blindfolds
NOUN a strip of cloth tied over someone's eyes to stop them seeing.

blink blinks blinking blinked
VERB When you **blink**, you close your eyes quickly for a moment.

bliss
NOUN a state of complete happiness.
blissful ADJECTIVE   **blissfully** ADVERB

blister blisters
NOUN a small bubble on your skin containing watery liquid, caused by a burn or rubbing.

blizzard blizzards
NOUN a heavy snowstorm with strong winds.

bloated
ADJECTIVE Something that is **bloated** is much larger than normal, often because there is a lot of liquid or gas inside it.

block blocks blocking blocked
NOUN 1 a large building containing flats or offices.
2 In a town, a **block** is an area of land with streets on all its sides.
3 a large, rectangular, three-dimensional piece of something.
VERB 4 If someone or something **blocks** a road or channel, they put something across it so that nothing can get through.

Synonym: (sense 4) obstruct

block capitals
PLURAL NOUN large upper-case letters.

THESE ARE BLOCK CAPITALS.

block graph block graphs
NOUN *See* **bar chart**.

blonde blondes

ADJECTIVE **1 Blonde** hair is pale yellow in colour. The spelling **blond** is used when referring to men.

NOUN **2** A **blonde** or **blond** is a person with pale yellow hair.

blood

NOUN the red liquid that is pumped by the heart round the bodies of human beings and other vertebrates.

bloodstream

NOUN the flow of blood through your body.

bloodthirsty

ADJECTIVE Someone who is **bloodthirsty** enjoys using or watching violence.

bloom blooms blooming bloomed

NOUN **1** a flower on a plant.

VERB **2** When a plant **blooms**, it produces flowers.

blossom blossoms blossoming blossomed

NOUN **1** all the flowers that appear on a tree before the fruit.

VERB **2** When a tree **blossoms**, it produces flowers.

blot blots

NOUN a mark made by a drop of liquid, especially ink.

blouse blouses

NOUN a light shirt, worn by a girl or a woman.

blow blows blowing blew blown

VERB **1** When the wind **blows**, the air moves.

2 If you **blow**, you send a stream of air from your mouth.

3 If you **blow** your nose, you force air out of it through your nostrils in order to clear it.

NOUN **4** If you receive a **blow**, someone or something hits you.

blow up VERB **5** If something **blows up**, it is destroyed by an explosion.

6 If you **blow up** a balloon or a tyre, you fill it with air.

blubber

NOUN the layer of fat beneath the skin of animals such as whales and seals that protects them from the cold.

blue bluer bluest

ADJECTIVE OR NOUN the colour of the sky on a clear, sunny day.

bluebell bluebells

NOUN a woodland plant with blue, bell-shaped flowers.

bluff bluffs bluffing bluffed

NOUN **1** an attempt to make someone believe that you will do something when you do not really intend to do it.

VERB **2** If you are **bluffing**, you are trying to make someone believe that you are in a strong position when you are not.

[from Dutch **bluffen** meaning to boast]

blunder blunders blundering blundered

NOUN **1** a silly mistake.

VERB **2** If you **blunder**, you make a silly mistake.

blunt blunter bluntest

ADJECTIVE **1** A **blunt** object has a rounded point or edge, rather than a sharp one. *My pencil was blunt so I could not write with it.*

2 If you are **blunt**, you say exactly what you think, without trying to be polite.

Synonyms: (sense 2) outspoken, straightforward

blur

NOUN If something is a **blur**, you can't see it clearly. *The mountain was a blur through the mist.*

blurb blurbs

NOUN the description of a book printed on the back cover.

blurt out blurts out blurting out blurted out

VERB If you **blurt out** something, you say it suddenly, after trying to keep it a secret.

blush blushes blushing blushed

VERB If you **blush**, your face becomes red, because you are embarrassed or ashamed.

[from Old English **blyscan** meaning to glow]

boa boas

NOUN a large snake that kills its prey by coiling round it and crushing it.

boar boars

NOUN **1** a male wild pig.

2 a male domestic pig used for breeding.

board boards boarding boarded

NOUN **1** a long, flat piece of wood.
2 a flat piece of wood, plastic or cardboard, which is used for a particular purpose: *a chessboard, a surfboard.*
3 the group of people who control a company or organization. *My mum is on the board of governors.*
4 the meals provided when you stay in a hotel or guesthouse. *The price includes full board.*
VERB **5** If you **board** a ship or aircraft, you get on it or in it.
PHRASE **6** If you are **on board** a ship or aircraft, you are on it or in it.

boarder boarders

NOUN **1** a pupil who lives at school during term.
2 a lodger.

boast boasts boasting boasted

VERB If you **boast**, you talk proudly about what you have or what you can do.

Synonym: brag

boat boats

NOUN a small vehicle for travelling across water.

body bodies

NOUN **1** Your **body** is all of you, from your head to your feet.
2 you can say **body** when you mean just the main part of a human or other animal, not counting head, arms and legs.

bodyguard bodyguards

NOUN a person employed to protect someone.

bog bogs

NOUN an area of wet, spongy ground.

boil boils boiling boiled

VERB **1** When a hot liquid **boils**, or when you **boil** it, it starts to bubble and to give off steam.
2 When you **boil** food, you cook it in boiling water.

boiler boilers

NOUN a piece of equipment that burns fuel to provide hot water.

boisterous

ADJECTIVE Someone who is **boisterous** is noisy and lively.
boisterously ADVERB

Synonyms: loud, rowdy

bold bolder boldest

ADJECTIVE **1** brave or confident. *He was bold enough to ask for her autograph.*
2 clear and noticeable. *The sign was painted in bold colours.*
[from Old Norse *ballr* meaning dangerous or terrible]

bollard bollards

NOUN a short, thick post used to stop vehicles from entering a road.

bolt bolts bolting bolted

NOUN **1** a metal object that screws into a nut and is used to fasten things together.
VERB **2** If you **bolt** one thing to another, you fasten them together using a bolt. *They bolted the chair to the floor.*
3 If you **bolt** a door or window, you slide a metal bar across in order to fasten it.

bomb bombs bombing bombed

NOUN **1** a container filled with material that explodes when it hits something or when it is set off by a timer.
VERB **2** If you **bomb** something, you attack it with a bomb.
[from Greek *bombos* meaning a booming sound]

bond bonds

NOUN a close relationship between people: *the bond between mothers and babies.*

bone bones

NOUN the hard parts that form the framework of a person's or animal's body.

bonfire bonfires

NOUN a large fire made outdoors, to burn rubbish or to celebrate something.
[from *bone* + *fire* – bones were used as fuel in the Middle Ages]

bonnet bonnets

NOUN **1** the metal cover over a car's engine.
2 a baby's or woman's hat tied under the chin.

bonus bonuses

NOUN **1** an amount of money added to a person's usual pay.
2 a good thing that you get in addition to something else.

a
b
c
d
e
f
g
h
i
j
k
l
m
n
o
p
q
r
s
t
u
v
w
x
y
z

bony bonier boniest

ADJECTIVE **Bony** people or animals are very thin, with not much flesh covering their bones.

book books booking booked

NOUN **1** a number of pages held together inside a cover.

VERB **2** When you **book** something, you arrange to have it or use it at a particular time. *Mum booked two rooms at the hotel.*

bookcase bookcases

NOUN a piece of furniture where you keep books.

booklet booklets

NOUN a small book with a paper cover.

boom booms booming boomed

NOUN **1** a deep, echoing sound.

2 a fast increase in something. *There has been a boom in the sale of sun cream this summer.*

VERB **3** If something **booms**, it makes a loud booming sound. *We heard the foghorn boom in the distance.*

boomerang boomerangs

NOUN a curved, wooden missile that can be thrown so that it returns to the thrower. **Boomerangs** were traditionally used as weapons by Australian Aborigines.

boost boosts boosting boosted

VERB If someone **boosts** something, they improve or increase it. *The teacher boosted Juliet's confidence when she praised her story.*

boot boots

NOUN **1** strong shoes that come up over your ankle, and sometimes your calf.

2 the covered space in a car, usually at the back, for carrying things in.

booth booths

NOUN **1** a small, partly-enclosed area: *a telephone booth.*

2 a stall where you can buy things, for example at a market or a fair.

border borders

NOUN **1** the dividing line between two countries.

2 a strip or band round the edge of something.

3 flower beds round the edges of a garden.

borderline borderlines

NOUN If someone or something is on the **borderline**, they are on the division between two different categories.

bore bores boring bored

VERB **1** If something **bores** you, you find it dull and uninteresting.

2 If you **bore** a hole in something, you make it using a tool such as a drill.

3 the past tense of *bear*.

NOUN **4** someone or something that bores you.

bored

ADJECTIVE If you are **bored**, you are miserable because you have nothing interesting to do.

boring

ADJECTIVE dull and uninteresting.

Antonym: interesting

born

VERB When an animal such as a human baby is **born**, it comes out of its mother's body and starts to live.

borrow borrows borrowing borrowed

VERB If you **borrow** something that belongs to someone else, they let you have it for a period of time. *I borrowed a book from my friend.*

boss bosses bossing bossed

NOUN **1** Someone's **boss** is the person in charge of the place where they work.

VERB **2** If someone **bosses** you, they keep telling you what to do.

bossy bossier bossiest

ADJECTIVE If you are **bossy**, you like to order other people around.

botany

NOUN the study and classification of plants.

both

ADJECTIVE OR PRONOUN **Both** is used when saying something about two things or two people. *You can both come to my party.*

bother bothers bothering bothered

VERB **1** If you don't **bother** to do something, you don't do it because it takes too much effort or it's not important.
2 If something **bothers** you, you are worried about it.
3 If you are not **bothered** about something, you don't care about it.
4 If you **bother** someone, you interrupt them when they are busy.
NOUN **5** trouble, fuss or difficulty. *Mum's having a bit of bother with the car.*

bottle bottles bottling bottled

NOUN **1** a glass or plastic container for keeping liquids in.
VERB **2** If you **bottle** something, you put it in a bottle to store it.

bottom bottoms

NOUN **1** the lowest part of something. *It sank to the bottom of the pond.*
2 Your **bottom** is the part of your body that you sit on.

bottomless

ADJECTIVE If something is **bottomless**, it has no bottom or it is very deep.

bough boughs

Rhymes with "cow" NOUN a large branch of a tree.

bought

VERB the past tense and past participle of *buy*.
✔ Do not confuse *bought* and *brought*. *Bought* comes from *buy*, and *brought* comes from *bring*.

boulder boulders

NOUN a large, rounded rock.

bounce bounces bouncing bounced

VERB When an object **bounces**, it springs back from something after hitting it. *The ball bounced high off the ground.*

bound bounds bounding bounded

ADJECTIVE **1** If you say that something is **bound** to happen, you mean that it is certain to happen. *He's bound to find out.*
NOUN **2** a large leap.
VERB **3** When humans or other animals **bound**, they move quickly with large leaps.

boundary boundaries

NOUN the limit of an area.

bouquet bouquets

NOUN an attractively arranged bunch of flowers.

bout bouts

NOUN **1** something that lasts for a short period of time. *I had a bout of flu.*
2 a boxing or wrestling match.

boutique boutiques

NOUN a small shop that sells fashionable clothes.

bow bows bowing bowed

Rhymes with "now" VERB **1** When you **bow**, you bend your body or lower your head as a sign of respect or greeting.
NOUN **2** the movement you make when you **bow**.
3 the front part of a ship
Rhymes with "low" NOUN **4** a knot with two loops and two loose ends. *The ribbon was tied in a bow.*
5 a long, thin piece of wood with horsehair strings stretched along it, used to play some stringed instruments, such as the violin and the cello.
6 a long, flexible piece of wood used for shooting arrows.
✔ Another word that sounds like *bow* (senses 1, 2 and 3) is *bough*.

bowel bowels

NOUN the tubes leading from your stomach, through which waste passes before it leaves your body.
[from Latin **botellus** meaning little sausage]

bowl bowls bowling bowled

NOUN **1** a round container with a wide, uncovered top, used for holding liquid or for serving food: *a bowl of soup.*
2 the hollow, rounded part of something: *a toilet bowl.*
VERB **3** When you **bowl** in cricket and rounders, you throw the ball towards the batsman.

bowling

NOUN a game in which you roll a heavy ball down a narrow track towards a set of wooden objects called pins, and try to knock them down.

bowls

NOUN a game in which the players try to roll large wooden balls as near as possible to a small ball.

box boxes boxing boxed

NOUN **1** a container with a firm base and sides, and usually a lid.

VERB **2** If someone **boxes**, they fight according to special rules.

boxer boxers

NOUN **1** a person who boxes.

2 a medium-sized, smooth-haired dog with a flat face.

Boxing Day

NOUN the day after Christmas Day.

boy boys

NOUN a male child.

boyfriend boyfriends

NOUN Someone's **boyfriend** is the man or boy with whom they are having a romantic relationship.

bra bras

NOUN a piece of underwear worn by a woman to support her breasts.

brace braces bracing braced

NOUN **1** an object fixed to something to straighten or support it. *I wore a **brace** on my teeth for two years.*

PLURAL NOUN **2 Braces** are elastic straps worn over the shoulders to hold trousers up.

VERB **3** If you **brace** yourself, you stiffen your body to steady yourself. *We **braced** ourselves as the bus went round the corner.*

4 If you **brace** yourself for something unpleasant, you prepare yourself to deal with it.

bracelet bracelets

NOUN a chain or band worn around someone's wrist as an ornament.

[from Old French ***bracel*** meaning little arm]

bracken

NOUN a plant like a large fern that grows on hills and in woods.

bracket brackets

NOUN a pair of written marks, ( ), { } or [ ], placed round a word or sentence that is not part of the main text, or to show that the items inside the **brackets** belong together.

brag brags bragging bragged

VERB If you **brag**, you boast about something.

Braille

NOUN a system of printing for blind people in which letters are represented by raised dots that can be felt with the fingers.

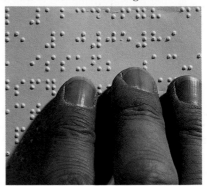

brain brains

NOUN the organ inside your head that controls your body and enables you to think and feel. *See* page 433.

brainstorm brainstorms

NOUN **1** a clever idea that you think of suddenly.

2 If you have a **brainstorm**, you become confused and cannot think clearly.

brainy brainier brainiest

ADJECTIVE clever and good at learning things.

brake brakes braking braked

NOUN **1** a device for making a vehicle stop or slow down.

VERB **2** When drivers **brake**, they make a vehicle stop or slow down by using its brakes.

bramble brambles

NOUN a wild, trailing bush with thorns, which produces blackberries.

branch branches branching branched

NOUN **1** part of a tree that grows out from the trunk.

2 A **branch** of a business or organization is one of its offices or shops.

VERB **3** A road that **branches** off from another road splits off from it to lead in a different direction.

brand brands

NOUN a particular kind or make of something.

brandy

NOUN a strong, alcoholic drink, often drunk after a meal.

[from Dutch *brandewijn* meaning burnt wine]

brass

NOUN OR ADJECTIVE **1** a yellow-coloured metal made from copper and zinc.

2 In an orchestra, the **brass** section consists of instruments such as trumpets and trombones.

brave braver bravest; braves braving braved

ADJECTIVE **1** A **brave** person is willing to do dangerous things and does not show any fear.

VERB **2** If you **brave** an unpleasant or dangerous situation, you face up to it in order to do something. *We braved the snow to go to the party.*

[from Italian *bravo* meaning courageous or wild]

Synonyms: (sense 1) courageous, daring

brawl brawls brawling brawled

NOUN **1** a rough fight.

VERB **2** When people **brawl**, they take part in a rough fight.

bread

NOUN a very common food made from flour, and baked in an oven.

breadth breadths

NOUN the distance between two sides of something. *I can swim the breadth of the pool. See width.*

break breaks breaking broke broken

VERB **1** When an object **breaks**, or when you **break** it, it becomes damaged or separates into pieces.

2 If you **break** a rule or promise, you fail to keep it.

3 To **break** a record means to do better than the previous recorded best. *She broke the record for the long jump.*

NOUN **4** a short period during which you rest or do something different.

break down VERB **5** When a machine or a vehicle **breaks down**, it stops working.

break up VERB **6** When schools **break up**, the term ends. *We break up on Thursday.*

breakable

ADJECTIVE easy to break.

breakdown breakdowns

NOUN If there is a **breakdown** in a system, it stops working.

breaker breakers

NOUN a big sea wave.

breakfast breakfasts

NOUN the first meal of the day.

breast breasts

NOUN one of the two soft, fleshy parts on a woman's chest, which produce milk after she has had a baby.

breath breaths

NOUN **1** the air you take into your lungs and let out again when you breathe. *He took a deep breath before jumping into the pool.*

PHRASE **2** If you are **out of breath**, you are breathing with difficulty after doing something energetic.

breathe breathes breathing breathed

VERB When you **breathe**, you take air into your lungs and let it out again.

breathless

ADJECTIVE If you are **breathless**, you are breathing very fast or with difficulty. *I was breathless after running to catch the bus.*

breathlessly ADVERB   **breathlessness** NOUN

breed breeds breeding bred

NOUN **1** a particular type of animal. For example, an Alsatian is a **breed** of dog.

VERB **2** Someone who **breeds** animals or plants keeps them in order to produce more animals or plants with particular qualities. *He used to breed dogs for the police.*

3 When animals **breed**, they produce young.

Synonym: (sense 3) reproduce

breeze breezes

NOUN a gentle wind.

breezy ADJECTIVE

brewery breweries

NOUN a place where beer is made, or a company that makes beer.

bribe bribes bribing bribed

NOUN **1** a gift or money given to an official to persuade them to allow you to do something.

VERB **2** If someone **bribes** someone else, they give them a bribe.

brick bricks
NOUN a rectangular block of baked clay used in building.

bride brides
NOUN a woman who is getting married or who has just got married.

bridegroom bridegrooms
NOUN a man on or near his wedding day.

bridesmaid bridesmaids
NOUN a woman or girl who helps a bride on her wedding day.

bridge bridges
NOUN **1** a structure built over a river, road or railway so that vehicles and people can cross.
2 a card game for four players.

bridle bridles
NOUN a set of straps round a horse's head and mouth, which the rider uses to control the horse.

brief briefer briefest; briefs briefing briefed
ADJECTIVE **1** Something that is **brief** lasts only a short time. *We only had time for a **brief** visit.*
VERB **2** When you **brief** someone on a task, you give them all the necessary instructions or information about it.

briefcase briefcases
NOUN a small, flat case for carrying papers.

bright brighter brightest
ADJECTIVE **1** strong and startling: *a **bright** light.*
2 clever. *That's a **bright** idea.*

Synonyms: (sense 1) brilliant, dazzling
   (sense 2) intelligent, quick

---

brighten brightens brightening brightened
VERB **1** If something **brightens**, it becomes brighter.
brighten up VERB **2** If you **brighten up** something, you make it look brighter and more attractive.

brilliant
ADJECTIVE **1** A **brilliant** person is extremely clever.
2 INFORMAL Something that is **brilliant** is extremely good or enjoyable.
3 A **brilliant** colour or light is extremely bright.

brim brims
NOUN **1** the wide part of a hat that sticks outwards from the head.
2 If a container is filled to the **brim**, it is filled right to the top.

bring brings bringing brought
VERB **1** If you **bring** something or someone with you when you go to a place, you take them with you.
bring up VERB **2** When someone **brings up** children, they look after them while they grow up.

brink
NOUN **1** the edge of a deep hole, cliff or ravine.
PHRASE **2** If you are **on the brink** of something, you are about to do it. *They were **on the brink** of discovering a cure for the common cold.*

brisk brisker briskest
ADJECTIVE **1** quick and energetic: *a **brisk** walk.*
2 If someone's manner is **brisk**, it shows that they want to get things done quickly and efficiently.
briskly ADVERB   **briskness** NOUN

bristle bristles bristling bristled
NOUN **1** **Bristles** are strong animal hairs used to make brushes.
VERB **2** If the hairs on an animal's body **bristle**, they rise up because it is frightened.
bristly ADJECTIVE

brittle
ADJECTIVE An object that is **brittle** is hard but breaks easily.

broad broader broadest
ADJECTIVE **1** A **broad** river is wide.
2 The **broad** outline of a story gives the main points, but no details.

broadcast broadcasts broadcasting broadcast
NOUN **1** a programme or announcement on radio or television.
VERB **2** When someone **broadcasts** something, they send it out by radio waves, so that it can be seen on television or heard on radio.

broccoli
NOUN a vegetable with green stalks and green or purple flower buds.

brochure brochures

NOUN a booklet that gives information about a product or a service: *holiday* **brochure**.

broke

VERB **1** the past tense of *break*.

ADJECTIVE **2** If you are **broke**, you have no money.

broken

ADJECTIVE A **broken** object is damaged in some way.

bronchitis

NOUN an illness in which the tubes connecting your windpipe to your lungs become infected, making you cough.

brontosaurus brontosauruses

NOUN a very large, plant-eating dinosaur.

bronze

NOUN a yellowish-brown metal that is a mixture of copper and tin.

brooch brooches

NOUN a piece of jewellery with a pin at the back for attaching to clothes.

brood broods brooding brooded

NOUN **1** a family of baby birds.

VERB **2** If you **brood** about something, you are worried about it and can't stop thinking about it.

brook brooks

NOUN a stream.

broom brooms

NOUN a long-handled brush.

brother brothers

NOUN Your **brother** is a boy or man who has the same parents as you.

brother-in-law brothers-in-law

NOUN Someone's **brother-in-law** is the brother of their husband or wife, or their sister's husband.

brought

VERB the past tense and past participle of *bring*.

✔ Do not confuse *brought* and *bought*. *Brought* comes from *bring* and *bought* comes from *buy*.

brown browner brownest

ADJECTIVE OR NOUN the colour of earth or wood.

Brownie Brownies

NOUN a junior member of the Girl Guides.

bruise bruises bruising bruised

NOUN **1** a purple mark that appears on your skin after something has hit it.

VERB **2** If something **bruises** you, it hits you so that a bruise appears on your skin.

brunette brunettes

NOUN a girl or a woman with dark brown hair.

brush brushes brushing brushed

NOUN **1** an object with bristles. There are **brushes** for cleaning things, painting or tidying your hair.

VERB **2** If you **brush** something, you clean it or tidy it with a brush.

paintbrush

floor brush or broom

toothbrush

brutal

ADJECTIVE **Brutal** behaviour is violent and cruel.
brutally ADVERB   **brutality** NOUN

Brussels sprout Brussels sprouts

NOUN a vegetable that looks like a tiny cabbage.

bubble bubbles bubbling bubbled

NOUN **1** a ball of air in a liquid.

VERB **2** When a liquid **bubbles**, bubbles form in it.

buck bucks bucking bucked

NOUN **1** the male of various animals, including deer and rabbits.

VERB **2** If a horse **bucks**, it jumps into the air with all four feet off the ground.

bucket buckets

NOUN a deep, round container with an open top and a handle.

buckle buckles buckling buckled

NOUN **1** a fastening on the end of a belt or strap.

VERB **2** If you **buckle** a belt or strap, you fasten it.

3 If metal **buckles**, it crumples up.

bud buds

NOUN a small, tight swelling on a tree or plant, which develops into a flower or leaf.

a
b
c
d
e
f
g
h
i
j
k
l
m
n
o
p
q
r
s
t
u
v
w
x
y
z

Buddhist

NOUN someone who follows the religious teachings of Buddha, who taught in India in the fifth century. **Buddhists** believe that the way to end suffering is by overcoming our desires. **Buddhism** NOUN

A statue of Buddha

budgerigar budgerigars

NOUN a small, brightly-coloured pet bird. **Budgerigars** originated in Australia. [an Australian Aboriginal name, from *budgeri* + *gar* meaning good cockatoo]

budget budgets budgeting budgeted

NOUN **1** a plan showing how much money will be available and how it will be spent. VERB **2** If you **budget** for something, you plan how you use your money carefully, so as to be able to afford what you want.

buffalo buffaloes

NOUN **1** a wild animal like a large cow with long curved horns.
2 another name for the American bison.

buffet buffets

NOUN **1** a café at a station or on a train.
2 a meal at which people serve themselves.

bug bugs bugging bugged

NOUN **1** a small insect, especially one that causes damage.
2 an infection or virus that makes you ill.
3 a small error in a computer programme that stops it working properly.
VERB **4** If a place is **bugged**, tiny microphones are hidden there to pick up what people are saying.

build builds building built

VERB If you **build** something, you make it from all its parts.

builder builders

NOUN a person whose job is to build buildings.

building buildings

NOUN a structure with walls and a roof.

bulb bulbs

NOUN **1** the glass part of an electric lamp.
2 an onion-shaped root from which a flower or plant grows. Tulips and daffodils are grown from **bulbs**. [from Greek *bolbos* meaning onion]

bulge bulges bulging bulged

VERB **1** If something **bulges**, it swells out.
NOUN **2** a lump on a normally flat surface.

bulk bulks

NOUN **1** a large mass of something.
PHRASE **2** If you buy something **in bulk**, you buy it in large quantities.

bulky bulkier bulkiest

ADJECTIVE Something that is **bulky** is large and heavy and sometimes difficult to move.

bull bulls

NOUN the male of some animal species including cattle, elephants and whales.

bulldozer bulldozers

NOUN a powerful tractor with a broad blade in front, which is used for moving earth or knocking things down.

bullet bullets

NOUN a small piece of metal fired from a gun.

bulletin bulletins

NOUN a short news report on radio or television.

bullion

NOUN gold or silver bars.

bullock bullocks

NOUN a young male bull that is castrated and reared for meat.

bully bullies bullying bullied

NOUN **1** someone who uses their strength or power to hurt or frighten other people.
VERB **2** If someone **bullies** you into doing something, they make you do it by using force or threats.
[a sixteenth-century word meaning fine fellow or hired ruffian]

bump bumps bumping bumped

VERB **1** If you **bump** into something, you knock into it accidentally.

NOUN **2** a soft noise made by something knocking into something else.

3 a raised, uneven part of a surface.

Synonyms: (sense 3) bulge, lump

bumper bumpers

NOUN a bar on the front or back of a vehicle that protects it if it bumps into something.

bumpy bumpier bumpiest

ADJECTIVE Something that is **bumpy** has a rough, uneven surface: *a **bumpy** road*.

bun buns

NOUN a small, round bread roll or cake.

bunch bunches

NOUN a group of things together: *a **bunch** of flowers*.

bundle bundles bundling bundled

NOUN **1** a number of things tied together or wrapped up in a cloth.

VERB **2** If you **bundle** someone or something somewhere, you push them there quickly and roughly.

bungalow bungalows

NOUN a one-storey house.

[from Hindi ***bangla*** meaning house]

bunk bunks

NOUN a bed fixed to a wall in a ship or caravan.

bunk beds

PLURAL NOUN two beds fixed together, one above the other.

buoy buoys

NOUN a floating object anchored to the bottom of the sea, marking a channel or warning of danger.

buoyancy

NOUN Something that has **buoyancy** is able to float in liquid or in the air.

buoyant

ADJECTIVE **1** Something that is **buoyant** is able to float.

2 Someone who is **buoyant** is lively and cheerful.

burden burdens

NOUN a heavy load.

burger burgers

NOUN a flat fried cake of meat, vegetables or cheese, served in a bread roll.

burglar burglars

NOUN someone who breaks into buildings and steals things.

burgle VERB

burn burns burning burned or burnt

VERB **1** If something is **burning**, it is on fire.

2 To **burn** something means to damage or destroy it with fire.

3 People often **burn** fuel, such as coal, to keep warm.

NOUN **4** A **burn** is an injury caused by fire or by something hot.

✔ You can write either *burned* or *burnt* as the past form of *burn*.

burrow burrows burrowing burrowed

NOUN **1** a tunnel or hole in the ground dug by a small animal.

VERB **2** When an animal **burrows**, it digs a burrow.

burst bursts bursting burst

VERB **1** When something **bursts**, or when you **burst** it, it splits open suddenly.

2 When you **burst** into a room, you enter suddenly and with force.

NOUN **3** A **burst** of something is a sudden short period of it: *a **burst** of applause*.

bury buries burying buried

VERB **1** If you **bury** something, you put it in a hole in the ground and cover it with earth.

2 If something is **buried** under something, it is covered by it. *My trainers were **buried** under a pile of clothes.*

bus buses

NOUN a large motor vehicle that carries passengers.

[from Latin ***omnibus*** meaning for all]

bush bushes

NOUN **1** a large plant, smaller than a tree and with a lot of woody branches.

2 In Australia and South Africa, an uncultivated area outside a town or city is called the **bush**.

3 In New Zealand, the **bush** is land covered by rainforest.

bushy bushier bushiest

ADJECTIVE **Bushy** hair or fur grows very thickly. *My dad has **bushy** eyebrows.*

business businesses

NOUN **1** work relating to the buying and selling of goods and services.
2 an organization that produces or sells goods, or provides a service.

Synonyms: (sense 2) company, firm, organization

busker buskers

NOUN someone who sings or plays music in public places for money.

bus stop bus stops

NOUN a place where the bus stops regularly for passengers to get on or off, usually marked with a sign.

busy busier busiest

ADJECTIVE **1** If you are **busy**, you are doing something and are not free to do anything else. *She was too **busy** to come to the cinema with us.*
2 A **busy** place is full of people doing things or moving about.

but

CONJUNCTION **1** used to introduce an idea that is opposite to what has gone before. *I love cooking, **but** I hate washing up afterwards.*
2 used when you apologize for something. *Sorry, **but** I can't come to play tomorrow.*
PREPOSITION **3** except. *There was nothing to eat **but** potatoes.*

butcher butchers

NOUN a shopkeeper who prepares and sells meat.

butter

NOUN a soft, fatty food made from cream, which is spread on bread and used in cooking.

buttercup buttercups

NOUN a wild plant with bright yellow flowers.

butterfly butterflies

NOUN a type of insect with large, colourful wings. **Butterflies** develop from caterpillars.

buttocks

PLURAL NOUN Your **buttocks** are the part of your body that you sit on.
[from Old English **buttuc** meaning rounded slope]

button buttons buttoning buttoned

NOUN **1** a small, hard round object sewn on to clothing such as shirts. *My new jeans fasten with **buttons** instead of a zip.*
2 a small object on a piece of equipment that you press to make it work. *You must push the **button** down to switch the video on.*
VERB **3** If you **button** a garment, you fasten it using its buttons.

buy buys buying bought

VERB If you **buy** something, you get it by paying money for it.

buzz buzzes buzzing buzzed

VERB If something **buzzes**, it makes a humming sound, like a bee.

buzzer buzzers

NOUN a device that makes a buzzing sound. **Buzzers** are used to attract attention. *I pressed the door **buzzer** but nobody was home.*

by

PREPOSITION **1** used to show who or what has done something. *The announcement was made **by** the head teacher.*
2 used to show how something is done. *He cheered us up **by** taking us to the cinema.*
3 next to or near to. *They live **by** the park.*
4 before a particular time. *We should finish **by** tea time.*
PREPOSITION OR ADVERB **5** going past. *We drove **by** her house.*

bypass bypasses

NOUN a road that takes traffic around the edge of a town instead of through the middle. *The centre of town is much quieter since they built the **bypass**.*

byte bytes

NOUN a unit of storage in a computer.

Cc

cab cabs
NOUN **1** a taxi.
2 The **cab** is where the driver sits in a lorry, bus or train.

cabbage cabbages
NOUN a large, green, leafy vegetable.

cabin cabins
NOUN **1** a room in a ship where a passenger sleeps.
2 a small wooden house, usually in the country.

cabinet cabinets
NOUN **1** a small cupboard: *a medicine **cabinet***.
2 The **cabinet** in a government is a group of ministers who advise the leader and decide policies.

cable cables
NOUN **1** a strong, thick rope or chain.
2 a bundle of wires with a rubber covering, which carries electricity.

cable television
NOUN a television service that comes through underground wires.

cactus cacti or cactuses
NOUN a thick, fleshy plant that grows in deserts. **Cactuses** are usually covered in spikes.

cadet cadets
NOUN a young person being trained in the armed forces or police.

café cafés
NOUN a place where you can buy light meals and drinks.
[from the French *café* meaning coffee or coffee house]

caffeine or **caffein**
NOUN a chemical in coffee and tea that makes you more active.

cage cages
NOUN a box or room made with bars, in which birds or animals are kept.
caged ADJECTIVE

cake cakes caking caked
NOUN **1** a sweet food made from eggs, flour, butter and sugar.
2 a block of a hard substance such as soap.
VERB **3** If something is **caked**, it becomes covered with a solid layer of something else. *My shoes were **caked** in mud.*

calamity calamities
NOUN something terrible that happens, causing destruction and misery. *The earthquake was a terrible **calamity**.*

Synonyms: disaster, catastrophe

calcium
Said "**kal**-see-um" NOUN a soft white mineral found in bones and teeth and in some foods. Milk and cheese are good sources of **calcium**.

calculate calculates calculating calculated
VERB If you **calculate** something, you work it out, usually by doing some arithmetic. *We **calculated** how much money we had raised from the sponsored walk.*
[from Latin *calculus* meaning stone or pebble, which the Romans used for counting]

calculation calculations
NOUN something that you think about carefully and work out mathematically, or that you do on a machine such as a calculator.

calculator calculators
NOUN a small electronic machine used for doing mathematical calculations.

calendar calendars
NOUN a chart, usually organized month by month, showing the date of each day in a particular year. *We marked the end of term on the **calendar** in red.*

calf calves
NOUN **1** a young cow.
2 Your **calves** are the backs of your legs between your knees and ankles.

call calls calling called

VERB **1** If you **call** someone or something a particular name, that is their name. *I will call my dog Spot. That type of machine is called a combine harvester.*

2 If you **call** someone, you telephone them.

3 If you **call** someone, you shout their name loudly.

NOUN **4** A **call** is a shout or a cry. *We heard a call for help.*

call off VERB **5** If something is **called off** it is cancelled. *The party was called off.*

VERB **6** If you **call on** someone, you pay them a short visit.

calm calmer calmest

ADJECTIVE **1** Someone who is **calm** is quiet and does not show any worry or excitement.

2 If the sea is **calm**, the water is not moving very much.

calorie calories

NOUN The amount of energy that food gives you is measured in **calories**.

calypso calypsos

NOUN a popular West Indian song with a rhythmic beat.

came

VERB the past tense of *come*.

camel camels

NOUN a large mammal with either one or two humps on its back. **Camels** live in hot desert areas and are used for carrying people and things.

camera cameras

NOUN a piece of equipment used for taking photographs or for filming.

camouflage camouflages camouflaging camouflaged

NOUN **1** a way of avoiding being seen by having the same colour or appearance as the surroundings.

VERB **2** To **camouflage** something is to hide it by giving it the same colour or appearance as its surroundings.

camp camps camping camped

NOUN **1** a place where people live in tents or stay in tents for a holiday.

VERB **2** If you **camp**, you stay in a tent.

NOUN **3** a collection of buildings for soldiers or prisoners.

camper NOUN

campaign campaigns campaigning campaigned

VERB When people **campaign**, they take action in order to achieve something. *She campaigned against the export of live animals.*

campaign NOUN

can could; cans

VERB **1** If someone says you **can** do something, you are allowed to do it.

2 If you **can** do something, you are able to do it. *I can say "hello" in French.*

NOUN **3** a metal container, often sealed, with food or drink inside.

canal canals

NOUN a long, narrow, man-made stretch of water.

A canal in Amsterdam

canary canaries

NOUN a yellow songbird.

cancel cancels cancelling cancelled

VERB If you **cancel** something that has been arranged, you stop it from happening. *They cancelled the school trip.*

cancer cancers

NOUN a serious disease in which abnormal cells in a part of the body increase rapidly, causing growths.

candidate candidates

NOUN a person who is being considered for a job.

candle candles

NOUN a stick of hard wax with a piece of string called a wick through the middle. You light the wick to produce a flame.

cane canes

NOUN **1** the long, hollow stem of a plant such as bamboo.

2 strips of **cane** used for weaving baskets and other containers.

3 a long narrow stick used to support plants.

canine canines

ADJECTIVE **1** relating to dogs.

NOUN **2** a **canine** is one of the pointed teeth near the front of the mouth in humans and some animals.

cannibal cannibals

NOUN a person who eats human flesh.

cannon cannons or cannon

NOUN a large gun, usually on wheels, which fires heavy iron balls.

cannot

VERB the same as **can not**.

canoe canoes

NOUN a small, narrow boat that you row using a paddle.

canoeing NOUN   **canoeist** NOUN

can't

VERB a contraction of *cannot*.

canteen canteens

NOUN a place to eat in a school or workplace.

canvas canvases

NOUN **1** strong, heavy cloth used for making things such as sails and tents.

2 a piece of **canvas** on which an artist does a painting.

canyon canyons

NOUN a narrow river valley with steep sides.

cap caps

NOUN **1** a soft, flat hat, often with a peak at the front.

2 a bottle top.

3 a small explosive used in toy guns.

capable

ADJECTIVE **1** If you are **capable** of doing something, you are able to do it.

2 Someone who is **capable** is able to do something well.

capacity capacities

NOUN the maximum amount that something can hold or produce. *The arena has a seating capacity of two thousand.*

capital capitals

NOUN **1** The **capital** of a country is the city where the government meets. *Paris is the capital of France.*

2 A **capital**, or a **capital** letter, is a larger, upper-case letter used at the beginning of a sentence or a name: Carol, Tim.

capsize capsizes capsizing capsized

VERB If a boat **capsizes**, it turns upside down.

capsule capsules

NOUN **1** a small container with medicine inside, which you swallow.

2 the part of a spacecraft in which astronauts travel.

[from Latin *capsula* meaning little box]

captain captains

NOUN **1** the officer in charge of a ship or aeroplane.

2 the leader of a sports team.

caption captions

NOUN a title printed underneath a picture or a photograph.

captive captives

NOUN someone who is locked up and kept prisoner.

capture captures capturing captured

VERB If someone **captures** someone or something, they take them prisoner.

car cars

NOUN **1** a four-wheeled road vehicle with an engine and room to carry a few passengers.

2 a railway carriage used for a particular purpose: *the buffet car.*

caravan caravans

NOUN **1** a vehicle pulled by a car in which people live or spend their holidays.

2 a group of people and animals travelling together, usually across a desert.

carbohydrate carbohydrates

NOUN a substance that gives you energy. It is found in foods like sugar and bread.

carbon

NOUN a chemical found in coal, diamonds and graphite. All living things contain **carbon**.

carbon dioxide

NOUN the gas that human beings and other animals breathe out.

a b c d e f g h i j k l m n o p q r s t u v w x y z

A B **C** D E F G H I J K L M N O P Q R S T U V W X Y Z

card cards

NOUN **1** a piece of stiff paper or plastic with a message or information on it: *birthday* **card**, *credit* **card**.
2 When you play **cards**, you play a game using special playing **cards**.
3 strong, stiff paper.

cardboard

NOUN thick, stiff paper, which is stronger than card.

cardigan cardigans

NOUN a knitted jacket that fastens up the front.

care cares caring cared

VERB **1** If you **care** about something or someone, you are concerned about them and interested in them.
2 If you **care** for a person or an animal, you look after them.
NOUN **3** worry or trouble. *She didn't have a care in the world.*
4 If you do something with **care**, you concentrate very hard on it so that you don't make mistakes. *He wrote the telephone number down with great* **care**.
PHRASE **5** If you **take care of** a person or an animal, you look after them. *Shakira said she would* **take care of** *the hamsters while we were on holiday.*

career careers

NOUN Your **career** is the series of jobs you have in life, often in the same occupation: *a teaching career*.

careful

ADJECTIVE acting sensibly and with care.
carefully ADVERB

Antonym: careless

careless

ADJECTIVE not paying attention to what you are doing.
carelessly ADVERB   **carelessness** NOUN

Synonyms: slapdash, sloppy

caretaker caretakers

NOUN a person who looks after a large building such as a school.

cargo cargoes

NOUN goods carried on a ship or plane.

Caribbean

Said "carib-**ee**-un" NOUN **1** short for the **Caribbean** Sea, which lies between the West Indies and South America.
ADJECTIVE **2** to do with the **Caribbean** Sea or the islands in it. *I love* **Caribbean** *food.*

carnation carnations

NOUN a plant with thin leaves and scented white, pink or red flowers.

carnival carnivals

NOUN a public festival with music, processions and dancing.

carnivore carnivores

NOUN an animal that eats meat.
carnivorous ADJECTIVE

carol carols

NOUN a religious song sung at Christmas time.

carpenter carpenters

NOUN a person who makes and repairs wooden things.
carpentry NOUN

carpet carpets

NOUN a thick floor covering usually made of material like wool.

carriage carriages

NOUN **1** one of the separate sections of a passenger train.
2 an old-fashioned vehicle for carrying passengers, usually pulled by horses.

Carroll diagram Carroll diagrams

NOUN a way of sorting and displaying information in the form of a grid.

	Walk	Do not walk	
Travel less than 1km	**3** Fiona Sophie Poppy	**3** John Gavin Anita	
Travel 1km or more	**4** Kay Rabi Aaran Hal	**4** Azul Mark George Bao Bao	

How Class 4 travel to school

carrot carrots

NOUN a long, thin, orange-coloured root vegetable.

carry carries carrying carried

VERB **1** If you **carry** something, you hold it and take it somewhere.

2 When a vehicle **carries** people, they travel in it.

3 If people or animals **carry** a germ or a disease, they can pass it on to others.

4 If a sound **carries** it can be heard a long way off. *Their voices **carried** across the valley.*

cart carts

NOUN a vehicle with wheels, used for carrying things and usually pulled by horses or cattle.

carton cartons

NOUN a cardboard or plastic container.

cartoon cartoons

NOUN **1** a humorous drawing in a newspaper, comic or magazine.

2 a film in which all the characters and scenes are drawn.

cartridge cartridges

NOUN **1** a tube containing a bullet and an explosive substance, used in guns.

2 a small plastic container filled with ink that you put in a pen or a printer.

cartwheel cartwheels

NOUN an acrobatic movement in which you lift both arms in the air then throw yourself sideways on to one hand, swinging your body around in a circle with your legs straight until you land on your feet again.

carve carves carving carved

VERB If you **carve** something, you shape it or slice it with a knife.

cascade cascades cascading cascaded

NOUN **1** a small waterfall or group of waterfalls flowing down a rocky hillside.

VERB **2** When water **cascades**, it flows very fast down a hillside or over rocks.

case cases

NOUN **1** a box for keeping or carrying things in.

2 a particular situation or event: *a bad **case** of measles.*

3 A crime that the police are investigating is called a **case**.

cash

NOUN money in notes and coins.

cashier cashiers

NOUN the person who deals with money in a place such as a shop or a bank.

casserole casseroles

NOUN **1** a stew made with meat, vegetables or fish that is baked in the oven.

2 a dish with a lid, which is used for cooking.

cassette cassettes

NOUN a small flat container with magnetic tape inside, which is used for recording and playing back sounds. *My brother bought a **cassette** of classic Beatles' songs.*

cast casts casting cast

NOUN **1** all the people who act in a play or film.

2 an object made by pouring a liquid such as plaster into a container and leaving it to harden.

VERB **3** If an object **casts** a shadow on to a place, it makes a shadow fall there.

castaway castaways

NOUN someone who has been shipwrecked but manages to survive on a lonely shore or an island.

castle castles

NOUN a large building with walls or ditches round it to protect it from attack.

[from Latin ***castellum*** meaning small fort]

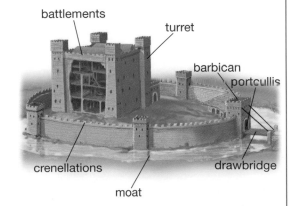

battlements • turret • barbican • portcullis • crenellations • drawbridge • moat

castrate castrates castrating castrated
VERB If a male animal is **castrated**, it has its testicles removed so that it cannot produce sperm.

casual
ADJECTIVE **1** happening by chance and without planning. *I made a casual remark.*
2 Casual clothes are suitable for informal occasions.

casualty casualties
NOUN a person killed or injured in an accident or a war. *There were many casualties after the motorway crash.*

cat cats
NOUN a small, furry mammal with whiskers, a tail and sharp claws, often kept as a pet.

catalogue catalogues
NOUN a list of things, such as the goods you can buy from a company, the objects in a museum, or the books in a library. *I ordered my trainers from a mail order catalogue.*

catapult catapults
NOUN a small weapon made from a forked stick and a piece of elastic, which shoots small stones.

catastrophe catastrophes
NOUN a terrible disaster.
catastrophic ADJECTIVE

catch catches catching caught
VERB **1** If you **catch** an object that is moving through the air, you grasp it with your hands.
2 If you **catch** a person or animal, you capture them. *The police caught the thief.*
3 If you **catch** a bus, train or plane, you get on it and travel somewhere.
4 If you **catch** a cold or a disease, you become ill with it.
NOUN **5** a hook that fastens or locks a door or window.

catching
ADJECTIVE If a disease or illness is **catching** it spreads very quickly. *Measles is catching.*

catchy catchier catchiest
ADJECTIVE Something that is **catchy**, such as a tune, is pleasant and easy to remember.

category categories
NOUN a group of things that have something in common.

caterpillar caterpillars
NOUN the larva of a butterfly or moth. **Caterpillars** look like small, coloured worms and feed on plants.

cathedral cathedrals
NOUN an important church with a bishop in charge of it: *Canterbury Cathedral.*

Catholic Catholics
ADJECTIVE OR NOUN a Roman **Catholic**, or belonging to that religion.

cattle
PLURAL NOUN cows and bulls kept by farmers.

caught
VERB the past tense of *catch.*

cauldron cauldrons
NOUN a large, round metal cooking pot, especially one that sits over a fire.
[from Latin *caldarium* meaning hot bath]

cauliflower cauliflowers
NOUN a large, round, white vegetable surrounded by green leaves.

cause causes
NOUN The **cause** of something is the thing that makes it happen. *The cause of the explosion was a gas leak.*

cautious
ADJECTIVE Someone who is **cautious** acts carefully in order to avoid danger or disappointment.

cavalry
NOUN The **cavalry** is the part of an army that fights on horseback or in armoured vehicles such as tanks.

cave caves caving caved
NOUN **1** a large hole in the side of a cliff or under the ground.
cave in VERB **2** If a roof **caves in**, it collapses inwards.

caveman cavemen
NOUN **Cavemen** were people who lived in caves in prehistoric times.

cavity cavities
NOUN a small hole in something solid. *There were cavities in his back teeth.*

CD
NOUN an abbreviation for *compact disc.*

CD-ROM
NOUN a way of storing video, sound or text on a compact disc that can be played on a computer. **CD-ROM** is an abbreviation for *compact disc read-only memory*.

cease ceases ceasing ceased
VERB **1** If something **ceases**, it stops.
2 If you **cease** doing something, you stop doing it.

ceiling ceilings
NOUN the roof inside a room.

celebrate celebrates celebrating celebrated
VERB If you **celebrate** something, you do something special and enjoyable because of it. *We felt like **celebrating** the end of exams.*
celebration NOUN

celebrity celebrities
NOUN a famous person.

celery
NOUN a vegetable with long, pale green stalks.

cell cells
NOUN **1** In biology, a **cell** is the smallest part of an animal or plant that can exist by itself. Humans, animals and plants are made up of millions of **cells**.
2 a small room in a prison or police station where a prisoner is locked up.

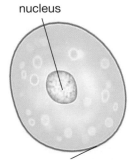

nucleus

cell membrane

cellar cellars
NOUN a room underneath a building.

cello cellos
Said "**chel**-oh" NOUN a large, stringed musical instrument that you play sitting down.
cellist NOUN

Celsius
NOUN a scale for measuring temperature in which water freezes at 0 degrees (0 °C) and boils at 100 degrees (100 °C).
[named after Anders *Celsius* (1701–1744) who invented it]

cement
NOUN a grey powder that is mixed with sand and water to make concrete.

cemetery cemeteries
NOUN an area of land where dead people are buried.

census censuses
NOUN an official survey of the population of a country.

cent cents
NOUN In some countries a **cent** is a unit of currency.

centenary centenaries
NOUN the hundredth anniversary of something.

centigrade
NOUN another name for Celsius.

centimetre centimetres
NOUN a unit of length (cm). One **centimetre** is equal to ten millimetres (mm).

centipede centipedes
NOUN a long, thin insect with many pairs of legs.
[from Latin *centum* + *pedes* meaning a hundred feet]

central
ADJECTIVE **1** Something **central** is in the middle.
2 An idea that is **central** is the main idea.

central heating
NOUN a heating system in which water or air is heated and passed round a building through pipes and radiators.

centre centres
NOUN **1** the middle of an object or area.
2 a building where people go for activities, meetings, or help. *We played badminton at the sports **centre**.*

century centuries
NOUN a period of one hundred years.

ceramic ceramics
Said "ser-**ram**-ic" NOUN **1** a hard material made by baking clay at very high temperatures.
PLURAL NOUN **2 Ceramics** is the art of making objects out of clay.

cereal

cereal cereals
NOUN **1** a food made from grain, often eaten with milk for breakfast.
2 a plant that produces edible grain, such as wheat, oats, barley and rye.

ceremony ceremonies
NOUN a formal event such as a wedding or prizegiving.

certain
ADJECTIVE **1** If you are **certain** about something, you are sure it is true. *She is **certain** she wants to be a vet.*
2 You use **certain** to refer to a particular person, place or thing. *I like **certain** animals, for example cats and dogs.*

certainly
ADVERB without any doubt. *"Will you be at the party?" "I **certainly** will.".*

certificate certificates
NOUN an official piece of paper that proves that something took place: *a birth **certificate**.*

chaffinch chaffinches
NOUN a small European bird with black and white wings.

chain chains
NOUN **1** a number of metal rings linked together in a line.
2 a number of things in a series or connected to each other: *a **chain** of shops, a **chain** of events.*

chair chairs
NOUN a seat for one person to sit on, with a back and four legs.

chalet chalets
NOUN a small wooden house with a sloping roof, especially found in mountain areas or holiday camps.

chalk
NOUN a soft, white rock. Small sticks of **chalk** are used for writing or drawing on a blackboard.
chalky ADJECTIVE

challenge challenges challenging challenged
NOUN **1** something new and exciting that needs a lot of effort. *Learning how to cook is a new **challenge** for me.*
VERB **2** If someone **challenges** you, they suggest that you compete with them. *She **challenged** me to a game of table tennis.*
ADJECTIVE **3** If you find something **challenging**, you find it quite difficult.

chameleon chameleons
NOUN a lizard that is able to change the colour of its skin to match the colour of its surroundings.
[from Greek **khamai** + **leon** meaning ground lion]

champagne champagnes
NOUN a sparkling white wine made in France.

champion champions
NOUN a person who wins a competition.

championship championships
NOUN a competition to find the best player or players of a particular sport.

chance chances
NOUN **1** how possible or likely something is. *I think we've got a good **chance** of winning.*
2 an opportunity to do something.
3 a possibility that something dangerous or unpleasant may happen.
PHRASE **4** Something that happens **by chance** happens unexpectedly, without being planned.

chancellor chancellors
NOUN the head of government in some European countries.

Chancellor of the Exchequer
NOUN the government minister in charge of finance and taxes in Britain.

change changes changing changed
NOUN **1** money you get back when you pay for something with more money than it costs.
VERB **2** When something **changes**, or you **change** it, it becomes different. *The wind **changed** direction.*

channel channels
NOUN **1** a wavelength on which television programmes are broadcast. It can also be the television station itself.
2 a passage for water or other liquid.
3 The **Channel**, or the English **Channel**, is the stretch of sea between England and France.

60

chaos

NOUN a state of complete disorder. *The demonstration ended in* **chaos**.
chaotic ADJECTIVE

chapel chapels

NOUN **1** a section of a church or cathedral with its own altar.
2 a type of small church.

chapter chapters

NOUN one of the parts into which a book is divided.

character characters

NOUN **1** all the qualities that make a person or a place special. *She has a gentle* **character**.
2 The **characters** in a film, play or book are the people in it.

characteristic characteristics

NOUN **1** a special quality about a person, place or thing.
ADJECTIVE **2** typical of a place or person. *Noise and traffic fumes are* **characteristic** *of cities.*

charades

NOUN a party game where one team guesses what the other team is acting out.

charcoal

NOUN burnt wood used as a fuel. **Charcoal** is also used for drawing.

charge charges charging charged

VERB **1** If someone **charges** you money, they ask you to pay for something you have bought or received.
2 rush forward. *She* **charged** *into the room.*
PHRASE **3** If you are **in charge of** someone or something, you are responsible for them. *I left him* **in charge of** *the shop while I went out.*

chariot chariots

NOUN a two-wheeled open vehicle pulled by horses in ancient times.

charity charities

NOUN **1** an organization that raises money to help people in need.
2 money or other help given to people in need.

charm charms charming charmed

NOUN **1** something you wear for good luck.
2 the quality of being attractive and pleasant.
VERB **3** If you **charm** someone, you use your charm to please them.

chart charts

NOUN a diagram or table showing information.

chase chases chasing chased

VERB If you **chase** someone, you run after them or follow them in order to catch them or make them leave a place.

chat chats chatting chatted

NOUN **1** a friendly talk with someone.
VERB **2** When people **chat**, they talk to each other in a friendly way about things that are not very important.
chatty ADJECTIVE

chatter chatters chattering chattered

VERB **1** When people **chatter**, they talk about unimportant things.
2 If your teeth **chatter**, they knock together and make a clicking noise because you are cold.

chauffeur chauffeurs

NOUN a person whose job is to drive another person's car. *He had a* **chauffeur** *to drive him everywhere.*

cheap cheaper cheapest

ADJECTIVE **1** Something that is **cheap** costs very little money.
2 **Cheap** sometimes means of poor quality.
cheaply ADVERB

cheat cheats cheating cheated

VERB If someone **cheats** in a game or exam, they break the rules in order to do better.

check checks checking checked

VERB **1** If you **check** something, you examine it to make sure that everything is all right. *Check your work carefully when you finish.*
NOUN **2** an inspection to make sure that everything is all right.
3 **Checks** are different coloured squares that form a pattern.

checkout checkouts

NOUN the place in a supermarket where you pay for your goods.

cheek cheeks

NOUN **1** Your **cheeks** are the sides of your face below your eyes.
2 speech or behaviour that is rude and disrespectful. *Their grandparents won't stand any* **cheek** *from them.*
cheeky ADJECTIVE   **cheekily** ADVERB

cheer cheers cheering cheered
VERB When people **cheer**, they shout loudly and happily. *We **cheered** our team when they won.*

cheerful
ADJECTIVE A **cheerful** person is happy.
cheerfully ADVERB

cheese cheeses
NOUN a solid savoury food made from milk.

cheetah cheetahs
NOUN a wild mammal like a large cat with black spots, mainly found in Africa.
[from Sanskrit *citra* + *kaya* meaning speckled body]

chef chefs
NOUN a head cook in a restaurant or hotel.
[from French *chef* meaning head]

chemical chemicals
NOUN 1 a substance made by the use of chemistry. *Dangerous **chemicals** should be handled carefully.*
ADJECTIVE 2 involved in chemistry or using chemicals: *a **chemical** reaction.*

chemist chemists
NOUN a shop that sells medicines and cosmetics.

chemistry
NOUN the scientific study of substances and the ways in which they change when they are combined.

cheque cheques
NOUN a printed piece of paper that people can use to pay for things.

cherry cherries
NOUN a small, juicy fruit with a red, yellow or black skin and a hard stone in the centre.

chess
NOUN a game played on a board with 64 squares. Each player has 16 pieces.

chest chests
NOUN 1 the front part of your body between your shoulders and your waist.
2 a large wooden box used for storing things.

chestnut chestnuts
NOUN 1 a reddish-brown nut that grows inside a prickly, green outer covering.
2 the tree that produces these nuts.
ADJECTIVE 3 Something that is **chestnut** is reddish-brown in colour.

chew chews chewing chewed
VERB When you **chew** something, you use your teeth to break it up in your mouth before swallowing it.

chewing gum
NOUN a kind of sweet that you chew for a long time, but which you do not swallow.

chick chicks
NOUN a young bird.

chicken chickens
NOUN a bird kept on a farm for its eggs and meat; also the meat of this bird.

chickenpox
NOUN an illness that causes a fever and blister-like spots to appear on the skin.

chief chiefs
NOUN 1 the leader of a group or organization.
ADJECTIVE 2 main or most important.

chilblain chilblains
NOUN a sore, itchy swelling on a finger or toe, which causes discomfort in cold weather.

child children
NOUN 1 a young person who is not yet an adult.
2 Someone's **child** is their son or daughter.

Synonyms: (sense 1) kid, youngster

childhood childhoods
NOUN Your **childhood** is the time when you are a child.

childish
ADJECTIVE If someone is **childish**, they are not acting in an adult way.
childishly ADVERB

Antonym: adult

childminder childminders
NOUN a person who is paid to look after children while their parents are at work.

children

PLURAL NOUN the plural of *child*.

chill chills chilling chilled

VERB **1** When you **chill** something, you make it cold. *Chill the orange juice before you drink it.*
NOUN **2** a feverish cold.
3 a feeling of cold: *the chill of early morning.*

chilli chillies

NOUN the red or green seed pod of a type of pepper that has a very hot, spicy taste.

chilly chillier chilliest

ADJECTIVE **1 Chilly** weather is rather cold.
2 If people behave in a **chilly** way, they are not very friendly.

chime chimes chiming chimed

VERB **1** When a bell **chimes**, it makes a clear ringing sound.
NOUN **2 Chimes** are a set of bells or other objects that make ringing sounds.

chimney chimneys

NOUN a pipe above a fireplace or furnace through which smoke from the fire can escape.

chimpanzee chimpanzees

NOUN a small ape with dark fur that lives in forests in Africa.

chin chins

NOUN the part of your face below your mouth.

china

NOUN plates, cups, saucers and other dishes that are made from fine clay.

chink chinks

NOUN **1** a small, narrow opening: *a chink in the fence.*
2 a small ringing sound, like glasses touching each other.

chip chips chipping chipped

NOUN **1** thin strips of fried potato.
2 a tiny piece of silicon inside a computer, which is used to form electronic circuits: *computer chips.*
VERB **3** If you **chip** an object, you break a small piece off it.

chirp chirps chirping chirped

VERB When a bird **chirps**, it makes a short, high-pitched sound.

chisel chisels chiselling chiselled

NOUN **1** a tool with a long metal blade and a sharp edge at the end. **Chisels** are used for cutting and shaping wood, stone or metal.
VERB **2** If you **chisel** wood, stone or metal, you cut or shape it using a chisel.

chlorine

NOUN a poisonous greenish-yellow gas with a strong, unpleasant smell. It is used to disinfect water and to make bleach.

chocolate chocolates

NOUN a sweet food made from cocoa beans. [from Aztec *xococ* + *atl* meaning bitter water]

choice choices

NOUN **1** a range of different things that are available to choose from.
2 something that you choose. *You made a good choice when you bought this book.*

Synonyms: (sense 1) range, variety

choir choirs

NOUN a group of singers, for example in a church.

choke chokes choking choked

VERB If you **choke** on something, it prevents you from breathing properly. *He choked on a fish bone.*

cholesterol

NOUN a substance found in all animal fats, tissues and blood.

choose chooses choosing chose chosen

VERB If you **choose** something, you to decide to have it or do it.

Synonyms: pick, select

chop chops chopping chopped

VERB **1** If you **chop** something, you cut it with quick, heavy strokes using an axe or a knife. *Mum chopped the logs for firewood.*
NOUN **2** a small piece of pork or lamb that contains a bone. *We had chops and broccoli for dinner.*

a b **c** d e f g h i j k l m n o p q r s t u v w x y z

A
B
C
D
E
F
G
H
I
J
K
L
M
N
O
P
Q
R
S
T
U
V
W
X
Y
Z

choppy
ADJECTIVE When the sea or a stretch of water is **choppy**, there are a lot of waves on it because it is windy.

chopstick chopsticks
NOUN **Chopsticks** are a pair of thin sticks used for eating Chinese and Japanese food.

choral
Said "kor-al" ADJECTIVE for a choir.

chord chords
NOUN a group of three or more musical notes played together.

chore chores
NOUN an uninteresting job that has to be done.

chorus choruses
NOUN 1 a part of a song that is repeated after each verse.
2 a large group of singers.

chose
VERB the past tense of *choose*.

chosen
VERB 1 the past participle of *choose*.
2 When you are **chosen**, you are picked to do something. *I was **chosen** for the volleyball team.*

christen christens christening christened
VERB When a priest **christens** someone, they name them in a ceremony where water is poured over their head as a sign that they are a member of the Christian church.
christening NOUN

Christian Christians
NOUN a person who believes in Jesus Christ and his teachings.
Christianity NOUN

Christmas Christmases
NOUN a Christian festival held on December 25th to celebrate the birth of Jesus Christ.

chrome
Said "**krome**" NOUN metal plated with chromium, a hard, silver-grey metal.

chromosome chromosomes
Said "**krome**-uh-soam" NOUN the part of a cell in living things that contains the genes that determine what characteristics the animal or plant will have.

chronic
ADJECTIVE lasting a very long time or never stopping. *He suffers from **chronic** hay fever.*

chronological
ADJECTIVE arranged in the order in which things happened. *Tell me the whole story in **chronological** order.*
chronologically ADVERB

chrysalis chrysalises
NOUN a butterfly or moth when it is developing from being a caterpillar to being a fully grown adult.

chrysanthemum chrysanthemums
NOUN a plant with large, brightly-coloured flowers.

chuckle chuckles chuckling chuckled
VERB When you **chuckle**, you laugh quietly.

chunk chunks
NOUN a thick piece of something.

Synonyms: hunk, lump, piece

church churches
NOUN a building where Christians go for religious services and worship.

churchyard churchyards
NOUN an area of land around a church, often used as a graveyard.

churn churns churning churned
NOUN 1 a container used for making milk or cream into butter.
VERB 2 When you **churn** something, you stir it vigorously, for example when making milk into butter.
churn out VERB 3 If you **churn out** something, you produce it quickly in large numbers. *They **churned out** hundreds of leaflets advertising the dance.*

chutney
NOUN a strong-tasting thick sauce made from fruit, vinegar and spices.

cider
NOUN an alcoholic drink made from apples.

cigar cigars
NOUN a roll of dried tobacco leaves, which people smoke.

cigarette cigarettes
NOUN a thin tube of paper containing tobacco, which people smoke.

cinder cinders
NOUN **Cinders** are small pieces of burnt material left after something such as wood or coal has burned.

cinema cinemas
NOUN a place where people go to watch films.

circle circles circling circled
NOUN **1** a regular, two-dimensional round shape. Every point on the edge is the same distance from the centre.
VERB **2** to move around in a circle. *Seagulls circled overhead.*
circular ADJECTIVE

circuit circuits
NOUN **1** the path of an electric current.
2 a racecourse.
3 A training **circuit** is a course of activities.

circulation circulations
NOUN **1** the movement of blood around a body.
2 the number of copies of a newspaper or magazine that are sold each time it is issued.

circumference circumferences
NOUN **1** the outer line or edge of a circle.
2 the length of this line is also called the **circumference**.

circumference

circumstance circumstances
NOUN The **circumstances** of a situation or event are the conditions that affect what happens. *He did well under difficult circumstances.*

circus circuses
NOUN a travelling show performed in a large tent, with performers such as clowns and acrobats.

cistern cisterns
NOUN a tank in which water is stored, such as in the roof of a house, or above a toilet.

citizen citizens
NOUN The **citizens** of a country or city are the people who live in it or belong to it.

citrus fruit citrus fruits
NOUN **Citrus fruits** are juicy, sharp-tasting fruits such as oranges, lemons and grapefruit.

city cities
NOUN a large town where many people live and work.

civil
ADJECTIVE **1** relating to the citizens of a place.
2 Someone who is **civil** is polite.

civilian civilians
NOUN a person who is not in the armed forces.

civilization civilizations; also spelt civilisation
NOUN **1** a large group of people with a high level of organization and culture. *We're learning about the ancient civilizations of Greece, Rome and Egypt.*
2 a highly developed and organized way of life.

civilized or **civilised**
ADJECTIVE **1** A **civilized** society is one with a highly developed social organization and a comfortable way of life.
2 A **civilized** person is polite and reasonable.

civil war civil wars
NOUN a war between groups of people who live in the same country.

claim claims claiming claimed
VERB **1** If you **claim** that something is the case, you say that it is so.
2 If you **claim** something, you ask for it because you believe you have a right to it.

clamber clambers clambering clambered
VERB If you **clamber** somewhere, you climb there with difficulty. *We clambered over the rocks to get to the beach.*

clammy clammier clammiest
ADJECTIVE unpleasantly damp and sticky. *The weather was very clammy.*

clamp clamps clamping clamped
NOUN **1** a device that holds something firmly in place.
VERB **2** When you **clamp** one thing to another, you fasten them together with a clamp.

clan clans
NOUN a group of families related to each other by being descended from the same ancestor.

A
B
C
D
E
F
G
H
I
J
K
L
M
N
O
P
Q
R
S
T
U
V
W
X
Y
Z

clang clangs clanging clanged
VERB When something made of metal **clangs**, or when you **clang** it, it makes a loud, ringing sound.

clank clanks clanking clanked
VERB When something **clanks**, it makes a loud, metallic sound.

clap claps clapping clapped
VERB 1 When you **clap**, you hit your hands together loudly to show that you have enjoyed something or that you approve of something.
NOUN 2 a sudden loud noise of thunder.

clarify clarifies clarifying clarified
VERB If you **clarify** something, you make it clear and easier to understand.
clarification NOUN

clarinet clarinets
NOUN a woodwind instrument with a straight tube and a single reed in its mouthpiece.

clarity
NOUN The **clarity** of something is its clearness. *The **clarity** of the water made me think it was very clean.*

clash clashes clashing clashed
VERB 1 Colours or ideas that **clash** are so different that they do not go together. *Debbie's red shirt **clashed** with her green shorts.*
2 If one event **clashes** with another, they happen at the same time, so you cannot go to both.
3 If people **clash** with each other, they fight or argue.

clasp clasps clasping clasped
VERB 1 If you **clasp** something, you hold it tightly.
NOUN 2 a fastening such as a hook or a catch.

class classes
NOUN 1 a group of pupils or students taught together, or a lesson that they have together.
2 A **class** of people or things is a group of them of a particular type. *Beetles and ants belong to different **classes** of insect.*

Synonyms: (sense 2) group, kind, type

classic
ADJECTIVE Something described as **classic** is considered a high quality example of something. *He has a **classic** car.*

classical
ADJECTIVE 1 traditional in style and content: *classical ballet.*
2 **Classical** music is serious music thought to be of lasting value.

classify classifies classifying classified
VERB to arrange things into groups with something in common. *We **classified** the foods into three groups: fruits, vegetables and meats.*
classification NOUN

classroom classrooms
NOUN a room in a school where lessons take place.

clatter clatters clattering clattered
VERB 1 When things **clatter**, they hit each other with a loud, rattling noise.
NOUN 2 a loud noise made by hard things hitting against each other. *There was a great **clatter** when the waitress dropped the tray.*

clause clauses
NOUN In grammar, a **clause** is a group of words with a subject and a verb, which may be a complete sentence or part of a sentence.

claw claws clawing clawed
NOUN 1 An animal's **claws** are the hard, curved nails at the end of its feet.
2 The **claws** of a crab or a lobster are the two jointed parts at the end of the leg, used for holding things.

claw

VERB 3 If an animal **claws** something, it digs its claws into it.

clay
NOUN a type of earth that is soft and sticky when wet and hard when baked dry. It is used to make pottery and bricks.

clean cleaner cleanest; cleans cleaning cleaned

ADJECTIVE **1** free from dirt or unwanted marks.
VERB **2** to remove dirt from something.

clear clearer clearest; clears clearing cleared

ADJECTIVE **1** easy to understand, see or hear. *The instructions on the packet were very clear.*
2 easy to see through: *a clear liquid.*
VERB **3** To **clear** unwanted things from a place is to remove them. *We cleared the dirty dishes from the table.*
4 If you **clear** a fence or other obstacle, you jump over it without touching it.
clear up VERB **5** When you **clear up** a place, you tidy it and put things away.
clearly ADVERB

clench clenches clenching clenched

VERB **1** When you **clench** your fist, you curl your fingers up tightly.
2 When you **clench** your teeth, you squeeze them together tightly, either in pain or in anger.

clerk clerks

NOUN a person who keeps records or accounts in an office, bank or law court.

clever cleverer cleverest

ADJECTIVE **1** intelligent and quick to understand things.
2 very effective or skilful. *We came up with a clever plan.*

Synonyms: (sense 1) bright, intelligent, smart

cliché clichés

NOUN an idea or phrase that is no longer effective because it has been used so much. For example, "in this day and age" and "over the moon".

click clicks clicking clicked

VERB **1** When something **clicks** or when you **click** it, it makes a short snapping sound.
NOUN **2** a sound of something clicking.

client clients

NOUN someone who pays a professional person or company for a service.

cliff cliffs

NOUN a high area of land with a very steep side, usually next to the sea.

cliffhanger cliffhangers

NOUN a very exciting or frightening situation, usually in a television or radio serial, where you are left not knowing what is going to happen next.

climate climates

NOUN the general weather conditions that are typical of a place.

climax climaxes

NOUN the most exciting moment of something, usually near the end.

climb climbs climbing climbed

VERB **1** If you **climb** something, such as a tree, mountain or ladder, you move towards the top of it.
2 If you **climb** somewhere, you move there with difficulty. *We climbed over the high wall.*
NOUN **3** a movement upwards. *I was tired after the long climb to the top of the hill.*
climber NOUN

cling clings clinging clung

VERB If you **cling** to something, you hold on to it tightly.

clinic clinics

NOUN a place where people go for medical advice or treatment.

clip clips clipping clipped

NOUN **1** a small metal or plastic object used for holding things together.
2 a short piece of a film shown by itself.
VERB **3** If you **clip** something, you cut bits from it to shape it.

clipboard clipboards

NOUN a stiff piece of board or plastic, with a clip at the top to keep papers in place.

clippers

PLURAL NOUN a tool used for cutting: *hedge clippers.*

cloak cloaks cloaking cloaked

NOUN **1** a wide, loose coat without sleeves.
VERB **2** If something **cloaks** something else, it covers or hides it. *The mist cloaked the land.*

cloakroom cloakrooms

NOUN **1** a room where you can leave coats and luggage for a while.
2 a room with toilets and washbasins in a public building.

a
b
c
d
e
f
g
h
i
j
k
l
m
n
o
p
q
r
s
t
u
v
w
x
y
z

clock clocks

NOUN an instrument that measures and shows the time.

clockwise

ADVERB in the same direction as the hands on a clock.

clockwork

NOUN **1** Toys that move by **clockwork** are wound up with a key.

PHRASE **2** If something goes **like clockwork,** it happens with no problems or delays.

clog clogs clogging clogged

VERB **1** When something is **clogged**, or when you **clog** something up, it becomes blocked and doesn't work properly or doesn't allow things to move freely. *The traffic was **clogging** the roads.*

NOUN **2** a shoe made entirely of wood, originally from the Netherlands.

clone clones

NOUN an animal or plant that is an identical copy of another animal or plant.

close closes closing closed; closer closest

Said "klohz" VERB **1** If you **close** something, you move it so that it is no longer open. *He **closed** the door behind him.*

2 If a shop or other building **closes** at a certain time, it does not do business after that time. *Said* "klohss" ADJECTIVE **3** Something that is **close** to something else is near to it.

4 People who are **close** are very friendly with each other and know each other well.

5 If the weather is **close**, it is uncomfortably warm and stuffy.

NOUN **6** a street that is closed at one end. *We live in Park **Close**.*

closely ADVERB

Synonyms: (sense 3) near, nearby

close-up close-ups

Said "klohss-up" NOUN A **close-up** in a film or a photograph is taken at very close range and shows things in great detail.

cloth cloths

NOUN **1** fabric made by a process such as weaving.

2 a piece of material used for wiping or protecting things.

clothes

PLURAL NOUN things people wear on their bodies.

cloud clouds

NOUN **1** a mass of water vapour that is seen as a white or grey patch in the sky.

2 A **cloud** of smoke or dust is a mass of it floating in the air.

cloudy cloudier cloudiest

ADJECTIVE **1** full of clouds. *The sky was **cloudy**.*

2 difficult to see through: *a **cloudy** liquid.*

Synonyms: (sense 1) dull, overcast
  (sense 2) murky

clover

NOUN a small plant with leaves made up of three similar parts.

clown clowns

NOUN a circus performer who wears funny clothes and make-up and does silly things to make people laugh.

club clubs

NOUN **1** a group of people with similar interests, who meet regularly. The place where they meet is also called a **club**: *a youth **club**.*

2 a team that competes in sports competitions.

clue clues

NOUN something that helps solve a problem or mystery. *Police have found **clues** to the robbery.*

clueless

ADJECTIVE; INFORMAL If you say that someone is **clueless**, you think they are stupid and not able to do things properly.

clump clumps

NOUN a small group of things growing or standing close together: *a **clump** of trees.*

clumsy clumsier clumsiest

ADJECTIVE moving awkwardly and carelessly.
clumsily ADVERB

Synonyms: awkward, ungainly

clung

VERB the past tense and past participle of *cling.*

cluster clusters clustering clustered

NOUN **1** a group of things together. *There is a* **cluster** *of houses by the lake.*

VERB **2** If people **cluster** together, they stay together in a close group.

[from Old English *clyster* meaning bunch of grapes]

clutch clutches clutching clutched

VERB If you **clutch** something, you hold it tightly or seize it.

clutter clutters cluttering cluttered

NOUN **1** an untidy mess.

VERB **2** Things that **clutter** a place fill it and make it untidy.

coach coaches coaching coached

NOUN **1** a large bus that takes passengers on long journeys.

2 a section of a train that carries passengers.

VERB **3** If someone **coaches** you, they help you to get better at a sport or a subject.

NOUN **4** someone who coaches a person or sports team.

Synonyms: (sense 3) instruct, train

coal

NOUN a hard, black rock taken from under the ground and burned as a fuel.

coarse coarser coarsest

ADJECTIVE **1** Something that is **coarse** is rough in texture.

2 Someone who is **coarse** talks or behaves in a rude, offensive way.

coarsely ADVERB   **coarseness** NOUN

coast coasts coasting coasted

NOUN **1** the edge of the land where it meets the sea.

VERB **2** If a vehicle **coasts** somewhere, it moves there with the engine switched off. *The car* **coasted** *quietly down the hill.*

coastal ADJECTIVE

coastguard coastguards

NOUN an official who watches the sea near a coast to get help for sailors when they need it.

coat coats coating coated

NOUN **1** a piece of outdoor clothing with sleeves, which you wear over other clothes.

2 An animal's **coat** is the fur or hair on its body.

3 A **coat** of paint or varnish is a layer of it.

VERB **4** If you **coat** something, you cover it with a thin layer of something. *We* **coated** *the biscuits with chocolate.*

coating coatings

NOUN a thin layer of something spread over a surface.

coat of arms coats of arms

NOUN a special symbol, usually in the form of a patterned shield, used to represent high-ranking families, towns or organizations.

coax coaxes coaxing coaxed

VERB If you **coax** someone to do something, you persuade them gently to do it.

cobble cobbles

NOUN **Cobbles** or cobblestones are stones with a rounded surface that were used in the past for making roads.

cobra cobras

NOUN a type of large poisonous snake from Africa and Asia.

cobweb cobwebs

NOUN the very thin net that a spider spins to catch insects.

cock cocks

NOUN an adult male chicken, or any other male bird.

cockerel cockerels

NOUN a young cock.

cockle cockles

NOUN a type of small edible shellfish.

Cockney Cockneys

NOUN someone who was born in the East End of London.

cockpit cockpits

NOUN **1** the area in a plane where the pilot sits in control.

2 the driver's compartment in a racing car.

cockroach cockroaches

NOUN a large, dark-coloured insect often found in dirty rooms.

[from Spanish *cucaracha*]

cocky cockier cockiest

ADJECTIVE; INFORMAL If you are **cocky**, you are sure of yourself and sometimes rather cheeky.

cocoa

NOUN **1** a brown powder made from the seeds of a tropical tree and used for making chocolate. **2** a hot drink made from this powder.

coconut coconuts

NOUN a very large nut with white flesh, milky juice, and a hard hairy shell.

cocoon cocoons

NOUN a silky covering over the larvae of moths and some other insects.

cod

NOUN a large, edible fish.
✔ The plural of *cod* is also *cod*.

code codes

NOUN **1** a system of replacing the letters or words in a message with other letters or words, so that nobody can understand the message unless they know the system. *They wrote messages in* **code**.
2 a group of numbers and letters used to identify something: *the telephone* **code** *for Falmouth*.

coeducation

NOUN **Coeducation** is a system where girls and boys are taught together at the same school.
coeducational ADJECTIVE

coffee

NOUN **1** a powder made by roasting and grinding the beans of the **coffee** plant.
2 a hot drink made from **coffee**.

coffin coffins

NOUN a box in which a dead body is buried or cremated.

cog cogs

NOUN a wheel with teeth, which turns another wheel or part of a machine.

coil coils coiling coiled

NOUN **1** a length of rope or wire wound into a series of loops.

2 A single loop is also called a **coil**.
VERB **3** If something **coils**, or if you **coil** it, it winds into a series of loops. *The snake* **coiled** *around the branch*.

coin coins coining coined

NOUN **1** a small metal disc used as money.
VERB **2** If you **coin** a word or a phrase, you invent it.

coinage

NOUN the coins that are used in a particular country.

coincide coincides coinciding coincided

VERB When two things **coincide**, they happen at the same time. *Auntie's visit* **coincided** *with my birthday*.

coincidence coincidences

NOUN what happens when two or more things occur at the same time by chance.

coke

NOUN a grey fuel produced from coal.

cola colas

NOUN a sweet, brown fizzy drink, like Coca-Cola.

colander colanders

NOUN a bowl-shaped container with holes in it, used for washing or draining food.

cold colder coldest; colds

ADJECTIVE **1** If something is **cold**, it has a very low temperature.
2 If the weather is **cold**, the air temperature is very low.
NOUN **3** a minor illness that makes you sneeze and cough, and sometimes gives you a sore throat.

cold-blooded

ADJECTIVE **1** A **cold-blooded** animal has a body temperature that changes according to the surrounding temperature.
2 Someone who is **cold-blooded** does not show any pity.
cold-bloodedly ADVERB

coleslaw

NOUN a salad of chopped cabbage and other vegetables in mayonnaise.

collaborate collaborates collaborating
collaborated
VERB When people **collaborate**, they work
together to produce something. *The two schools*
collaborated to produce a play.
collaboration NOUN   **collaborator** NOUN

collage collages
NOUN a picture made by sticking pieces of paper
or cloth on to a surface.

collapse collapses collapsing collapsed
VERB **1** If something such as a building
collapses, it falls down suddenly.
2 If a person **collapses**, they fall down
suddenly because they are ill.

collapsible
ADJECTIVE A **collapsible** object can be folded
flat when it is not in use: *collapsible chairs*.

collar collars
NOUN **1** the part around the neck of something,
such as a coat or shirt.
2 a leather band round the neck of a dog or cat.

colleague colleagues
NOUN A person's **colleagues** are the people they
work with.

collect collects collecting collected
VERB **1** If you **collect** things, you gather them
together for a special purpose or as a hobby.
2 If you **collect** someone or something from a
place, you call there and take them away. *We*
collected Ali from school.
3 When things **collect** in a place, they gather
there over a period of time. *Dust collects in*
corners.

collection collections
NOUN **1** a group of things you have gathered
over a period of time: *a stamp collection.*
2 the organized collecting of money, for
example for charity, or the money collected.

collective noun collective nouns
NOUN a noun that refers to a group of people or
things. For example, a flock, a herd, and a shoal
are all **collective nouns**.

college colleges
NOUN a place where students study after they
have left school.

collide collides colliding collided
VERB If a moving object **collides** with
something, it hits it. *They collided with each*
other as they rushed through the door.

collision collisions
NOUN A **collision** is when a moving object hits
something.

Synonym: crash

colon colons
NOUN **1** the punctuation mark (:). It is used to
introduce a list, a quotation or an explanation
of a statement. *We need to buy several things:*
bread, milk, fruit and toothpaste.
2 part of your intestine.

colonel colonels
NOUN an army officer with a fairly high rank.

colony colonies
NOUN **1** a country that is controlled by another
country.
2 a group of people or animals living together.

colossal
ADJECTIVE very large indeed.
[from Greek **kolossos** meaning huge statue]

colour colours
NOUN the appearance something has as a result
of reflecting light. *Red, blue and yellow are the*
primary colours.

colour blind
ADJECTIVE Someone who is **colour blind** is not
able to see the difference between certain
colours.

colourful
ADJECTIVE **1** Something that is **colourful** has a
lot of different colours or bright colours.
2 A **colourful** story is very exciting and
interesting.

Antonyms: (sense 1) dull, colourless
(sense 2) dull, boring

colourless
ADJECTIVE **1** without colour.
2 dull and uninteresting.

colt colts
NOUN a young male horse.

a
b
c
d
e
f
g
h
i
j
k
l
m
n
o
p
q
r
s
t
u
v
w
x
y
z

A
B
C
D
E
F
G
H
I
J
K
L
M
N
O
P
Q
R
S
T
U
V
W
X
Y
Z

column columns

NOUN **1** a tall, solid, upright cylinder, especially one supporting part of a building.
2 In a newspaper or magazine, a **column** is a vertical section of writing.
3 a group of people or vehicles moving in a long line.

coma comas

NOUN a state of deep unconsciousness.

comb combs combing combed

NOUN **1** a flat object with long, thin, pointed parts, which you use for tidying your hair.
VERB **2** When you **comb** your hair, you tidy it with a comb.

combat combats combating combated

NOUN **1** fighting. *In the Falklands War many soldiers had to take part in armed* ***combat***.
VERB **2** If someone **combats** something, they try to stop it happening. *We need new ways to* ***combat*** *crime.*

combination combinations

NOUN **1** a mixture of things. *Fatima won the competition through a* ***combination*** *of skill and determination.*
2 a series of numbers or letters used to open a special lock.

combine combines combining combined

VERB If you **combine** things, you mix them together. ***Combine*** *the butter and sugar, then add the eggs. The book* ***combines*** *adventure and mystery.*

combine harvester combine harvesters

NOUN a large machine used on farms to cut, sort and clean grain.

combustion

NOUN the process of burning.

come comes coming came

VERB **1** If you **come** to a place, you move or arrive there.
2 If something **comes** to a particular point, it reaches that point. *The water* ***came*** *up to her waist.*
3 When a particular time **comes**, it happens. *Spring* ***came*** *early this year.*

comedian comedians

NOUN an entertainer whose job is to make people laugh.

comedy comedies

NOUN a play, film, or television programme that is intended to make people laugh.

comet comets

NOUN an object that travels around the sun leaving a bright trail behind it.
[from Greek ***kometes*** meaning long-haired]

comfort comforts comforting comforted

NOUN **1** the state of being pleasantly relaxed.
2 a feeling of relief from worry or unhappiness. *It's a* ***comfort*** *to me to know that they are safe.*
VERB **3** If you **comfort** someone, you make them less worried or unhappy.

comfortable

ADJECTIVE **1** If you are **comfortable**, you are at ease and relaxed.
2 Something that is **comfortable** makes you feel relaxed: *a* ***comfortable*** *chair.*
comfortably ADVERB

comic comics

NOUN **1** a magazine that contains stories told in pictures.
ADJECTIVE **2** funny: *a* ***comic*** *song.*

comma commas

NOUN the punctuation mark (,). It can show a short pause, or it can separate items in a list or words in speech marks from the rest of the sentence.

command commands commanding commanded

NOUN **1** an order to do something.
VERB **2** If you **command** someone to do something, you order them to do it.

commemorate commemorates commemorating commemorated

VERB If you **commemorate** something, you do something special to show that you remember it. *On Remembrance Day we* ***commemorate*** *all the people who died in the two World Wars.*

comment comments commenting commented

NOUN **1** a remark about something.
VERB **2** If you **comment** on something, you make a remark about it.

commentary commentaries

NOUN a description of an event that is broadcast on radio or television while the event is happening. *The **commentary** on the match was on the radio.*

commentator commentators

NOUN someone who gives a radio or television commentary.

commerce

NOUN the buying and selling of goods.

commercial commercials

NOUN **1** an advertisement on television or radio.
ADJECTIVE **2 Commercial** activities involve producing large amounts of goods to sell and make money.

commit commits committing committed

VERB When someone **commits** a crime or sin, they do it. *The police know who **committed** the burglary.*

committee committees

NOUN a group of people who make decisions on behalf of a larger group.

common commoner commonest; commons

ADJECTIVE **1** Something that is **common** exists in large numbers or happens often.
NOUN **2** an area of grassy land where everyone can go.
ADJECTIVE **3** If something is **common** to two or more people, they all have it or use it. *We had a **common** interest in butterflies.*
PHRASE **4** If two things or people have something **in common**, they both have it. *Sarah and I have a lot **in common**.*

common noun common nouns

NOUN **Common nouns** name things in general. They begin with lower case letters: *girl, boy, animal, picture*. See **noun**.

common sense

NOUN knowing how to behave sensibly in any situation.

Commonwealth

NOUN The **Commonwealth** is a group of countries that used to be ruled by Britain.

commotion

NOUN a lot of noise and excitement.

communal

ADJECTIVE shared by a group of people. *The shop had **communal** changing rooms.*

communicate communicates communicating communicated

VERB When people **communicate**, they exchange information, usually by talking or writing to each other.

communication communications

NOUN **1** the act of exchanging information, usually by talking, writing or, in the case of animals, making sounds: *the **communication** of ideas.*
PLURAL NOUN **2 Communications** are electrical or radio systems that allow people to broadcast or communicate information.

communion

NOUN **1** a Christian religious service in which people share holy bread and wine.
2 the sharing of thoughts and feelings.

community communities

NOUN all the people living in a particular area.

commuter commuters

NOUN a person who has to travel a long way to work every day.

compact

ADJECTIVE Something that is **compact** takes up very little space, or no more space than is necessary.

compact disc
compact discs

NOUN a music or video recording in the form of a small plastic disc.

companion companions

NOUN someone you travel or spend time with.

company companies

NOUN **1** a business that sells goods or provides a service.
2 If you have **company**, you have a friend or visitor with you.
PHRASE **3** If you **keep someone company**, you spend time with them.

comparative comparatives

ADJECTIVE **1** You use **comparative** to show that something is true only when compared with something else.

NOUN **2** In grammar, the **comparative** is the form of an adjective or adverb that shows an increase in size, quality or amount. It is usually formed by adding "-er" to a word, for example, *bigger, faster*, or by putting "more" before the word, for example, *more difficult*.

compare compares comparing compared

VERB When you **compare** things, you see in what ways they are different or similar. *We compared our hair to see whose was longest.*

comparison comparisons

NOUN When you make a **comparison**, you consider two things together and decide in what ways they are different or similar.

compartment compartments

NOUN **1** a section of a railway carriage.
2 one of the separate sections of something such as a bag or a box.

compass compasses

NOUN **1** an instrument with a magnetic needle that always points north. You use a **compass** to find your way.

PLURAL NOUN **2** **Compasses** are a hinged instrument for drawing circles.

compassion

NOUN pity and sympathy for someone who is suffering.

compassionate ADJECTIVE

compass point compass points

NOUN one of the 32 marks on the dial of a compass that show direction. *North, south, east and west are **compass points**.*

compel compels compelling compelled

VERB **1** If you **compel** someone to do something, you force them to do it.

ADJECTIVE **2** A **compelling** story or event is extremely interesting.

3 A **compelling** argument or reason makes you believe that something is true.

compensate compensates compensating compensated

VERB **1** To **compensate** someone means to give them money to replace something that has been lost or damaged.

2 If one thing **compensates** for another, it cancels out the bad effects of it. *The trip to Disneyland **compensated** for her long illness.*

compete competes competing competed

VERB **1** If you **compete** in a contest or game, you take part in it.
2 If you **compete**, you try to do better than others.

competent

ADJECTIVE Someone who is **competent** at something can do it satisfactorily. *He is a **competent** nurse.*

competition competitions

NOUN an event in which people take part to find out who is the best at something.

compile compiles compiling compiled

VERB When you **compile** information, you collect it and put it together.

complain complains complaining complained

VERB **1** If you **complain**, you say that you are not happy about something. *The neighbours **complained** about the noise.*
2 If you **complain** of pain or illness, you say that you have it.
complaint NOUN

complement complements complementing complemented

VERB **1** If one thing **complements** another, the two things go well together. *Her piano music **complements** the poem.*

NOUN **2** In grammar, a **complement** is a word or phrase that gives information about the subject or object of a sentence. For example, in the sentence "Rover is a dog", "is a dog" is the **complement**.

✔ Do not confuse *complement* with *compliment*.

complete completes completing completed

VERB **1** If you **complete** something, you finish it. *She has just **completed** her third short story.*
ADJECTIVE **2** If something is **complete**, none of it is missing.

completely

ADVERB totally.

Synonym: utterly

complex complexes

ADJECTIVE **1 Complex** things have many different parts and are hard to understand.
NOUN **2** a group of buildings used for a particular purpose, such a sports **complex**.

complexion complexions

NOUN the quality of the skin on your face.

complicated

ADJECTIVE Something that is **complicated** is hard to understand.

complication complications

NOUN something that makes a situation more difficult to deal with.

compliment compliments

NOUN If you pay someone a **compliment**, you tell them you admire or like something about them.
✔ Do not confuse *compliment* with *complement*.

component components

NOUN The **components** of something are the parts it is made of.

compose composes composing composed

VERB **1** If you **compose** a piece of music, a letter, or a speech, you write it.
2 If something is **composed** of particular things or people, it is made up of them.

composer composers

NOUN someone who writes music.

composition compositions

NOUN **1** a piece of music or writing.
2 the things that something is made up of.

compost

NOUN a mixture of rotted plants and manure that gardeners add to the soil to help plants grow.

compound word compound words

NOUN a word with a single meaning, but made up of two or more words. For example, gingerbread, housework and teapot are all **compound words**.

comprehend comprehends comprehending comprehended

VERB If you **comprehend** something, you understand it.

comprehensive comprehensives

ADJECTIVE **1** Something that is **comprehensive** includes everything that you need to know.
NOUN **2** a school where children of all abilities are taught together.
comprehensively ADVERB

compress compresses compressing compressed

VERB If you **compress** something, you squeeze it or shorten it. *She **compressed** her story into one page.*

compromise compromises compromising compromised

NOUN **1** an agreement in which people accept less than they really wanted.
VERB **2** When people **compromise**, they settle for less than they really wanted.

compulsory

ADJECTIVE If something is **compulsory**, you have to do it.

computer computers

NOUN an electronic machine that stores information and makes calculations.

computerize computerizes computerizing computerized; also spelt **computerise**

VERB When a system or process is **computerized**, such as train timetables or bank accounts, the work is done by computers.

comrade comrades

NOUN companions, especially in battle.

con cons conning conned

VERB **1** If someone **cons** you, or you are **conned**, you are tricked into doing something. *He **conned** me into buying the tickets.*
NOUN **2** a trick that makes you believe or do something that you would not normally believe or do.

concave

ADJECTIVE A **concave** surface curves inwards, rather than being level or bulging outwards.

Antonym: convex

convex   concave

conceal conceals concealing concealed
VERB If you **conceal** something, you hide it.

conceited
ADJECTIVE Someone who is **conceited** is too proud of their appearance or abilities.

Synonyms: bigheaded, self-important

conceive conceives conceiving conceived
VERB 1 If you can't **conceive** of something, you can't imagine it or believe it. *He couldn't conceive of anything more fun than surfing.*
2 If you **conceive** something such as a plan, you think of it and work out how it could be done. *Alex conceived the idea while eating his lunch.*
3 When a woman **conceives**, she becomes pregnant.

concentrate concentrates concentrating concentrated
VERB 1 If you **concentrate** on something, you give it all your attention. *I need to concentrate on my homework.*
2 When something is **concentrated** in one place, it is all there rather than in several places. *The shops were concentrated in the town centre.*

concentrated
ADJECTIVE A **concentrated** liquid has been made stronger by having water removed from it: *concentrated orange juice.*

concentration concentrations
NOUN 1 the ability to give your full attention to something you do or hear.
2 A **concentration** of something is a large amount of it in one place.

concept concepts
NOUN an abstract or general idea.

conception conceptions
NOUN the idea you have of something.

concern concerns concerning concerned
NOUN 1 worry about something or someone.
2 If something is your **concern**, it is your duty or responsibility.
VERB 3 If something **concerns** you or if you are **concerned** about it, it worries you.
concerned ADJECTIVE

concerning
PREPOSITION You use **concerning** to show what something is about: *an article concerning fox hunting.*

concert concerts
NOUN a public performance by musicians.

concession concessions
NOUN If you make a **concession**, you agree to let someone have or do something.

concise
ADJECTIVE giving all the necessary information using as few words as possible: *a concise explanation.*
concisely ADVERB

Synonyms: brief, short

conclude concludes concluding concluded
VERB 1 If you **conclude** something, you examine the facts and decide what your opinion is. *We concluded that the letter was a fake.*
2 When you **conclude** something, you finish it.

conclusion conclusions
NOUN 1 the end of something.
2 a final decision about something. *We wanted to go for a swim in the sea, but we came to the conclusion that it was too cold.*

concrete
NOUN 1 a building material made by mixing cement, sand and water.
ADJECTIVE 2 real and physical, rather than abstract. *He had no concrete evidence.*

concussion
NOUN damage to the brain caused by a blow or a fall, which causes confusion, sickness or unconsciousness.
concussed ADJECTIVE

condemn condemns condemning condemned
VERB 1 If you **condemn** something, you say it is bad and unacceptable.
2 If someone is **condemned** to a punishment, they are given it. *The burglar was condemned to five years in prison.*

condensation
NOUN a coating of tiny drops of liquid formed on a cold surface by steam or vapour.

condense condenses condensing condensed

VERB **1** If you **condense** a piece of writing or a speech, you shorten it.
2 When a gas or vapour **condenses**, it changes into a liquid.

condition conditions

NOUN **1** the state someone or something is in. *The antique clock was still in good condition.*
2 something that must happen in order for something else to be possible. *I can go swimming on Saturday on the condition that I do my homework first.*

condom condoms

NOUN a rubber sheath worn on a man's penis or in a woman's vagina during intercourse to prevent pregnancy or infection.

conduct conducts conducting conducted

Said "**kon**-duct" NOUN **1** behaviour
Said "kon-**duct**" VERB **2** When you **conduct** an activity, you carry it out.
3 When someone **conducts** an orchestra, a band or a choir, they direct it in a piece of music.
4 If something **conducts** heat or electricity, heat or electricity can pass along it. *Copper conducts electricity well.*

conductor conductors

NOUN **1** someone who conducts an orchestra or choir.
2 someone who moves round a bus or train selling and checking tickets.
3 a substance that conducts heat or electricity.

cone cones

NOUN **1** a regular three-dimensional shape with a circular base and a point at the top.
2 the fruit of a fir or pine tree.

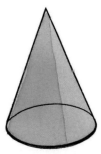

conference conferences

NOUN a meeting at which formal discussions take place.

confess confesses confessing confessed

VERB If you **confess** to something, you admit that you did it.

confession confessions

NOUN **1** If you make a **confession**, you admit that you have done something wrong.
2 the act of confessing something, especially as a religious act, where people confess their sins to a priest.

Synonyms: (sense 1) admission

confetti

NOUN small pieces of coloured paper thrown over the bride and groom at a wedding. [from Italian *confetto* meaning a sweet]

confide confides confiding confided

VERB If you **confide** in or to someone, you tell them a secret.

confidence

NOUN **1** If you have **confidence** in someone, you feel you can trust them.
2 Someone who has **confidence** is sure of their own abilities or qualities.

confident

ADJECTIVE **1** If you are **confident** about something, you are sure it will happen the way you want it to.
2 Someone who is **confident** is very sure of themselves and their own abilities.
confidently ADVERB

confidential

ADJECTIVE **Confidential** information is meant to be kept secret.

confine confines confining confined

VERB **1** If someone **confines** you to a place, you can't leave it. *The doctor confined Debbie to bed for two weeks as she had pneumonia.*
2 If you **confine** yourself to doing something, you do only that thing. *On their trip abroad, they confined themselves to drinking bottled water.*

confirm confirms confirming confirmed

VERB **1** If you **confirm** something, you say or show that it is true. *The teacher confirmed that we had all passed our spelling test.*
2 If you **confirm** an arrangement or appointment, you say it is definite. *Dad confirmed our holiday booking.*

a
b
c
d
e
f
g
h
i
j
k
l
m
n
o
p
q
r
s
t
u
v
w
x
y
z

confiscate confiscates confiscating confiscated

VERB If someone **confiscates** something, they take it away from someone as a punishment. **confiscation** NOUN

[from Latin *confiscare* meaning to seize for the public treasury]

conflict conflicts conflicting conflicted

NOUN **1** disagreement and argument.

2 a war or battle.

VERB **3** When two ideas or interests **conflict**, they are different and it seems impossible for them both to be true.

conform conforms conforming conformed

VERB **1** If you **conform**, you behave the way people expect you to.

2 If something **conforms** to a law or to someone's wishes, it does what is required or wanted.

conformist NOUN OR ADJECTIVE

confront confronts confronting confronted

VERB **1** If you are **confronted** with a problem or task, you have to deal with it.

2 If you **confront** someone, you meet them face to face, especially when you are going to fight or argue with them.

confrontation confrontations

NOUN a serious dispute between two people or groups of people who come face to face.

confuse confuses confusing confused

VERB **1** If you **confuse** two people or things, you mix them up and are not sure which is which.

2 If you **confuse** someone, you make them uncertain about what is happening or what to do.

confusion NOUN

congested

ADJECTIVE **1** When a road is **congested**, it is so full of traffic that normal movement is impossible.

2 If your nose is **congested**, it is blocked and you cannot breathe properly.

congestion NOUN

congratulate congratulates congratulating congratulated

VERB If you **congratulate** someone, you say that you're pleased about something good that has happened to them, or praise them for

something they have done. *He congratulated us on winning the competition.*

congratulations NOUN

congregation congregations

NOUN the people attending a service in a church.

congruent

ADJECTIVE In mathematics, things that are **congruent** are exactly the same size and shape, and would fit exactly on top of each other: *congruent triangles*.

conifer conifers

NOUN any type of evergreen tree that produces cones.

coniferous ADJECTIVE

conjunction conjunctions

NOUN In grammar, a **conjunction** is a word that links two other words or two clauses, such as "and", "but", "or", "while" and "that". For example: "I love bacon *and* eggs." "I'm happy, *but* my brother is not".

conjurer conjurers

NOUN someone who entertains people by doing magic tricks.

conker conkers

NOUN a brown nut from a horse chestnut tree.

connect connects connecting connected

VERB **1** If you **connect** two things, you join them together.

2 If one thing or person is **connected** with another, there is a link between them.

connection connections

NOUN **1** the point where two things are joined together.

2 If you make a **connection** at a station or airport, you continue your journey by catching another train, bus or plane. *Our train was late, so we missed our connection*.

connective connectives

NOUN a word that connects phrases, clauses or words together. *See* **conjunction**.

conquer conquers conquering conquered

VERB **1** If you **conquer** something difficult or dangerous, you succeed in controlling it. *She conquered her fear of spiders.*

2 to take control of a country by force.

conqueror NOUN

conscience
NOUN the part of your mind that tells you what is right or wrong.

conscientious
ADJECTIVE Someone who is **conscientious** takes great care over their work.
conscientiously ADVERB

conscious
ADJECTIVE 1 Someone who is **conscious** is awake, rather than asleep or unconscious.
2 If you are **conscious** of something, you are aware of it.
3 A **conscious** action or effort is done deliberately.

consecutive
ADJECTIVE 1 **Consecutive** events or periods of time happen one after the other. *We had eight consecutive days of rain.*
2 **Consecutive** numbers follow each other in order. For example, 1, 2, 3, 4 are **consecutive** numbers.
consecutively ADVERB

consent consents consenting consented
NOUN 1 permission to do something.
2 agreement between two or more people. *By common consent we went to France for the holiday.*
VERB 3 If you **consent** to something, you agree to do it or allow it to happen.

consequence consequences
NOUN result or effect.

conservation
NOUN the preservation of the environment.
conservationist NOUN OR ADJECTIVE

conservative conservatives
NOUN 1 a member or supporter of the **Conservative** Party in Britain.
ADJECTIVE 2 Someone who is **conservative** does not like change or new ideas.
3 A **conservative** estimate or guess is a cautious or moderate one.

conservatory conservatories
NOUN a room with glass walls and a glass roof in which plants are kept.

conserve conserves conserving conserved
VERB 1 If you **conserve** a supply of something, you make it last as long as possible. *I switched off my torch to conserve the battery.*

2 If you **conserve** something, you keep it as it is and do not change it. *We should conserve this old building.*

consider considers considering considered
VERB If you **consider** something, you think about it carefully.

considerable
ADJECTIVE A **considerable** amount of something is a lot of it.

considerate
ADJECTIVE Someone who is **considerate** thinks of other people's needs and feelings.

consideration considerations
NOUN 1 careful thought about something.
2 something that should be thought about when you are planning or deciding something.
3 Someone who shows **consideration** pays attention to the needs and feelings of other people.

consist consists consisting consisted
VERB Something that **consists** of certain things is made up of them. *This bread consists of flour, yeast and water.*

consistent
ADJECTIVE Something that is **consistent** does not change.

console consoles consoling consoled
Said "kon-**sole**" VERB 1 If you **console** someone who is unhappy, you comfort them and cheer them up
Said "**kon**-sole" NOUN 2 a panel with switches or knobs for operating a machine.

consonant consonants
NOUN all the letters of the alphabet that are not vowels.

conspicuous
ADJECTIVE If something is **conspicuous**, you can see or notice it very easily.

conspiracy conspiracies
NOUN an illegal plan made in secret by a group of people.

constable constables
NOUN a police officer of the lowest rank.

constant

ADJECTIVE **1** Something that is **constant** happens all the time or is always there. *We could hear the constant sound of the waves pounding the shore.*
2 If an amount or level is **constant**, it stays the same.

constellation constellations

NOUN a group of stars. *See* pages 428–9.

constipated

ADJECTIVE Someone who is **constipated** finds it difficult to empty their bowels.
constipation NOUN
[from Latin *constipare* meaning to press together]

constitution constitutions

NOUN **1** The **constitution** of a country is the system of laws and principles by which it is governed.
2 Your **constitution** is your health.

construct constructs constructing constructed

VERB If you **construct** something, you build or make it.

construction constructions

NOUN **1** the process of building or making something.
2 something built or made.

constructive

ADJECTIVE helpful. *The tennis coach made some constructive comments about my backhand.*

consult consults consulting consulted

VERB **1** If you **consult** someone, you ask for their opinion or advice.
2 If you **consult** a book or map, you look at it for information.
consultation NOUN

consultant consultants

NOUN an experienced doctor who specializes in one type of medicine: *a consultant heart surgeon.*

consume consumes consuming consumed

VERB **1** If you **consume** something, you eat or drink it.
2 To **consume** fuel or energy is to use it up.

consumer consumers

NOUN someone who buys things or uses services: *magazines aimed at teenage consumers*.

consumption

NOUN The **consumption** of fuel or food is the using of it, or the amount used. *The consumption of ice cream rises in hot weather.*

contact contacts contacting contacted

NOUN **1** If you are in **contact** with someone, you talk or write to them regularly. *I am in contact with a pen pal in France.*
2 When things are in **contact**, they are touching each other.
VERB **3** If you **contact** someone, you telephone them or write to them.

contact lens contact lenses

NOUN small plastic lenses that you put in your eyes instead of wearing glasses, to help you see better.

contagious

ADJECTIVE A **contagious** disease can be caught by touching people or things infected with it. *Measles is contagious.*

contain contains containing contained

VERB **1** If a substance **contains** something, that thing is a part of it.
2 The things a box or room **contains** are the things inside it.

container containers

NOUN something that you keep things in, such as a box or a jar.

contaminate contaminates contaminating contaminated

VERB If dirt, chemicals or radiation **contaminate** something, they make it impure and harmful.
contamination NOUN

contemplate contemplates contemplating contemplated

VERB **1** If you **contemplate**, you think very carefully about something. *She contemplated what she would do at the weekend.*
2 If you **contemplate** something, you look at it for a long time.

contemporary

ADJECTIVE **1** produced or happening now.
2 A **contemporary** work is one that was written at the time of the events it describes.

contempt

NOUN If you treat someone with **contempt**, you show no respect for them at all.

content

Said "kon-**tent**" ADJECTIVE **1** If you are **content**, you are happy and satisfied with your life.
2 If you are **content** to do something, you are willing to do it.

contents

Said "**kon**-tents" PLURAL NOUN **1** The **contents** of something like a box or a cake are the things in it.
2 The **contents** page of a book tells you what is in it.

contest contests

NOUN a competition or game.

contestant contestants

NOUN someone who takes part in a competition.

Synonyms: competitor, player

context contexts

NOUN The **context** of a word or sentence is the words or sentences that come before and after it, which help to make the meaning clear.

continent continents

NOUN **1** a very large area of land, such as Africa or Asia.
2 In Britain, the mainland of Europe is sometimes called the **Continent**.
See pages 430–31.
[from Latin *terra continens* meaning continuous land]

continental

ADJECTIVE In Britain, **continental** means on, belonging to or typical of the mainland of Europe: *continental breakfast*.

continual

ADJECTIVE happening again and again. *Mum had a continual stream of phone calls* .
✔ *Continual* and *continuous* are sometimes confused. *Continual* means happening all the time with breaks in between; *continuous* means happening all the time with no break.

continue continues continuing continued

VERB **1** If you **continue** to do something, you keep doing it.
2 If something **continues**, it does not stop.
3 You say something **continues** when it starts again after stopping. *She paused for a moment, then continued*.

continuous

ADJECTIVE happening all the time without stopping. *The television made a continuous buzzing noise.*
✔ *Continual* and *continuous* are sometimes confused. *Continuous* means happening all the time with no break; *continual* means happening all the time with breaks in between.

contour contours

NOUN **1** The **contour** of something is its general shape or outline.
2 On a map, a **contour** is a line joining points of equal height.

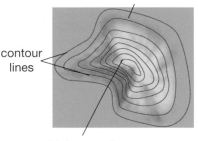

low ground

contour lines

high ground

contraceptive contraceptives

NOUN a device or pill for preventing pregnancy.

contract contracts contracting contracted

Said "**con**-trakt" NOUN **1** a legal agreement about the sale of something or work done for money. *He was given a two-year contract*.
Said "con-**trakt**" VERB **2** When something **contracts**, it gets smaller or shorter. *Metals contract with cold and expand with heat.*

Antonym: (sense 2) expand

contraction contractions

NOUN a shortened form of a word or words, often marked by an apostrophe. *"I've" is a contraction of "I have"*.

a
b
c
d
e
f
g
h
i
j
k
l
m
n
o
p
q
r
s
t
u
v
w
x
y
z

contradict contradicts contradicting contradicted
VERB If you **contradict** someone, you say that what they have just said is wrong.
contradiction NOUN

contrary
ADJECTIVE 1 **Contrary** ideas, opinions or attitudes are completely different from each other.
PHRASE 2 **On the contrary** is used to contradict something that has just been said.

contrast contrasts contrasting contrasted
NOUN 1 a great difference between things: *the contrast between town and country*.
VERB 2 If you **contrast** things, you describe or emphasize the differences between them.

contribute contributes contributing contributed
VERB 1 If you **contribute** to something, you do something to make it successful. *Everyone contributed to the class project.*
2 If you **contribute** money to something, you help to pay for it. *We contributed some money to the appeal for the homeless.*
contribution NOUN

Synonyms: (sense 2) donate, give

control controls controlling controlled
NOUN 1 If you have **control** over something, you are able to make it work the way you want to.
2 The **controls** on a machine are the knobs or other devices used to work it.
VERB 3 If someone **controls** a country or an organization, they make the decisions about how it is run.
4 If someone **controls** something such as a machine, they make it work the way they want it to.
PHRASE 5 If something is **out of control**, nobody has any power over it. *The fire was out of control.*

controversial
ADJECTIVE Something that is **controversial** causes a lot of discussion and argument, because many people disapprove of it. *The film was controversial.*

convalescent convalescents
NOUN someone who is resting while recovering from an illness.

convenient
ADJECTIVE If something is **convenient**, it is easy to use or it makes something easy to do. *It's convenient living close to the bus stop.*
convenience NOUN

convent convents
NOUN 1 a building where nuns live.
2 a school run by nuns.

conventional
ADJECTIVE Someone who is **conventional** thinks or behaves in an ordinary and accepted way.

converge converges converging converged
VERB When things meet or join at a particular place, they **converge**. *The roads converge after three kilometres.*
convergence NOUN

conversation conversations
NOUN When people have a **conversation**, they talk to each other.

convert converts converting converted
VERB 1 If you **convert** something, it changes from one thing to another. *Dad converted the loft into a workshop.*
2 If someone **converts** you, they persuade you to change your religious or political beliefs.
3 In maths, **convert** means to change a number from one form to another. These are equal to each other. For example, you can **convert** a fraction to a decimal ($\frac{1}{2}$ = 0·5).

convex
ADJECTIVE A **convex** surface bulges outwards, rather than being level or curving inwards. *See* **concave**.

Antonym: concave

convey conveys conveying conveyed
VERB 1 If someone **conveys** people or things to a place, they take them there.
2 If you **convey** information, ideas or feelings, you tell people about them.

conveyor belt conveyor belts
NOUN a moving strip used in factories for moving objects along.

convict convicts convicting convicted
Said "kon-**vikt**" VERB **1** If a law court **convicts** someone of a crime, it says they are guilty of it.
Said "**kon**-vikt" NOUN **2** someone serving a prison sentence.

convince convinces convincing convinced
VERB If you **convince** someone of something, you persuade them to do it or that it is true. *I convinced mum and dad to let me go on the school trip.*

convoy convoys
NOUN a group of ships or vehicles travelling together.

cook cooks cooking cooked
VERB **1** When you **cook**, you prepare food for eating by boiling, baking or frying it.
NOUN **2** a person whose job is to prepare food.

cooker cookers
NOUN an apparatus for cooking food.

cookery
NOUN the art of preparing and cooking food.

cool cooler coolest; cools cooling cooled
ADJECTIVE **1** Something **cool** has a low temperature but is not cold.
2 If you are **cool** in a difficult situation, you stay calm.
VERB **3** When something **cools**, it becomes less warm.

cooperate cooperates cooperating cooperated
VERB **1** When people **cooperate**, they work or act together.
2 If you **cooperate**, you do what someone asks you to do.

cooperative cooperatives
ADJECTIVE **1** A **cooperative** person does what they are asked to do willingly and cheerfully.
NOUN **2** a business or organization run by the people who work for it, and who share its profits.

coordinates
PLURAL NOUN a pair of numbers or letters that tell you exactly where a point is on a grid, map or graph.

cop cops
NOUN; INFORMAL a policeman.

cope copes coping coped
VERB If you **cope**, you are able to do something even if the circumstances are difficult. *I managed to cope with my homework and with looking after my little brother at the same time.*

copper
NOUN a soft, reddish-brown metal.

copy copies copying copied
NOUN **1** something made to look like something else: *a copy of a famous painting.*
2 A **copy** of a book, newspaper or record is one of many identical ones produced at the same time: *a copy of today's newspaper.*
VERB **3** If you **copy** what someone does, you do the same thing.
4 If you **copy** something, you make a copy of it.

copyright copyrights
NOUN If someone has the **copyright** on a piece of writing or music, it cannot be copied or performed without their permission.

coral corals
NOUN a hard substance that forms in the sea from the skeletons of tiny animals called **corals**.

cord cords
NOUN **1** strong, thick string.
2 electrical wire covered in rubber or plastic.

corduroy
NOUN heavy, ribbed cloth made of cotton.

core cores
NOUN the most central part of an object or place: *an apple core, the earth's core.*

cork corks
NOUN **1** a soft, light substance that forms the bark of a Mediterranean tree.
2 a piece of **cork** pushed into the end of a bottle to close it.

corkscrew corkscrews
NOUN a device for pulling corks out of bottles.

corn
NOUN **1** crops such as wheat and barley.
2 the seeds of these crops.

corner corners cornering cornered
NOUN **1** the point where two sides or edges of something meet. *The TV was in the **corner** of the room. See* **vertex**.
VERB **2** If someone **corners** a person or animal, they get them into a place they can't escape from. *The police **cornered** the thief.*

cornet cornets
NOUN a small, brass instrument used in brass and military bands.

coronation coronations
NOUN the ceremony at which a king or queen is crowned.

coroner coroners
NOUN an official who investigates the deaths of people who have died in a violent or unusual way.

corporal corporals
NOUN an officer of low rank in the army or air force.

corporal punishment
NOUN punishing of people by beating them.

corps
Said "kor" NOUN part of an army with special duties: *the Medical **Corps***.

corpse corpses
NOUN a dead body.

correct corrects correcting corrected
ADJECTIVE **1** If something is **correct**, there are no mistakes in it.
VERB **2** If you **correct** something that is wrong, you make it right. *She **corrected** my maths homework.*
correction NOUN

correspond corresponds corresponding corresponded
VERB **1** If one thing **corresponds** with another, it is similar to it or it matches it in some way.
2 If numbers or amounts **correspond**, they are the same.
3 When people **correspond**, they write to each other.

correspondence
NOUN **1** letters or the writing of letters.
2 If there is a **correspondence** between two things, there is a similarity between them.

correspondent correspondents
NOUN a newspaper, radio or television reporter.

corridor corridors
NOUN a passage in a building or train.
[from Old Italian *corridore* meaning place for running]

corrode corrodes corroding corroded
VERB When something **corrodes**, it is eaten away. When iron and steel are **corroded**, rust is formed.
corrosion NOUN   **corrosive** ADJECTIVE

corrugated
ADJECTIVE **Corrugated** metal or cardboard has parallel folds to make it stronger.

corrupt corrupts corrupting corrupted
ADJECTIVE **1** People who are **corrupt** act dishonestly or illegally in return for money or power.
VERB **2** If you **corrupt** someone, you make them dishonest.
3 If a bug in a computer spoils files, it **corrupts** them.
corruption NOUN

Synonym: (sense 1) dishonest

cosmetics
PLURAL NOUN lipstick, face powder and other make-up.

cosmic
ADJECTIVE belonging to or relating to the whole universe.

cosmos
NOUN the universe.

cost costs costing cost
NOUN **1** the amount of money needed to buy, do or make something.
VERB **2** You use **cost** to talk about the amount of money you have to pay for things. *You can't have that – it **costs** too much.*

costume costumes
NOUN **1** a set of clothes worn by an actor.
2 the clothing worn in a particular place or during a particular period.

cosy cosier cosiest
ADJECTIVE warm and comfortable.

cot cots
NOUN a small bed for a baby, with bars or panels round it to stop the baby falling out.

cottage cottages
NOUN a small house, especially in the country.

cotton
NOUN **1** cloth made from the soft fibres of the **cotton** plant: *a cotton shirt*.
2 thread used for sewing: *a needle and cotton*.

couch couches
NOUN a long, soft piece of furniture for sitting or lying on.

cough coughs coughing coughed
VERB When you **cough**, you force air out of your throat with a sudden harsh noise.

could
VERB **1** the past tense of *can*.
2 You use **could** to say that something might happen or might be true. *It could rain later.*
3 You use **could** when you are asking for something politely. *Could you tell me the way to the station, please?*

couldn't
VERB a contraction of *could not*.

council councils
NOUN a group of people elected to look after something, especially the affairs of a town, district or county.

counsel counsels counselling counselled
NOUN **1** advice.
VERB **2** If someone **counsels** people, they give them advice about their problems.

count counts counting counted
VERB **1** When you **count**, you say all the numbers in order up to a particular number.
2 If you **count**, or **count** up, all the things in a group, you add them up to see how many there are.
3 If you can **count** on someone or something, you can rely on them. *You can count on me to help.*
PHRASE **4** If you **keep count** of something, you keep a record of how often it happens. *Who's keeping count of the score?*

5 If you **lose count** of something, you cannot remember how often it has happened.

counter counters
NOUN **1** a long, flat surface in a shop, over which goods are sold.
2 a small, flat, round object used in board games.

counterfeit counterfeits counterfeiting counterfeited
Said "**kown**-ter-fit" ADJECTIVE **1 Counterfeit** things are not genuine, but have been made to look genuine in order to deceive people: *counterfeit money*.
VERB **2** If someone **counterfeits** something, they make an exact copy of it in order to trick people.

countless
ADJECTIVE too many to count.

country countries
NOUN **1** one of the political areas the world is divided into.
2 land away from towns and cities. *It is peaceful living in the country.*

countryside
NOUN land away from towns and cities.

county counties
NOUN a region with its own local government. *The county of Lincolnshire is in the east of England.*

couple couples
NOUN **1** two people who are married or who have a very close relationship.
2 A **couple** of things or people means two of them, or not very many.

couplet couplets
NOUN two lines of poetry together that usually rhyme.

coupon coupons
NOUN **1** a piece of printed paper that entitles you to pay less than usual for something.
2 a form you fill in to ask for information or to enter a competition.

courage
NOUN the quality shown by people who do things that they know are dangerous or difficult. *She showed great courage in her efforts to save them from the burning house.*
courageous ADJECTIVE **courageously** ADVERB

courgette courgettes

NOUN a vegetable that looks like a small green marrow.

courier couriers

NOUN **1** someone employed by a travel company to look after people on holiday.
2 someone employed to deliver letters and parcels quickly.

course courses

NOUN **1** a series of lessons or lectures.
2 a piece of land where races take place or golf is played.
3 the route something such as a ship or a river takes. *The captain changed course to avoid the storm.*
4 one of the parts of a meal. *The first course was soup.*
PHRASE **5** If you say *of course*, you are showing that you are absolutely sure about something. *Of course she wouldn't do a thing like that.*

court courts

NOUN **1** a place where legal matters are decided by a judge and jury or a magistrate. The judge and jury or magistrate can also be referred to as the **court**. *He is due to appear in court next week. The court awarded him ten thousand pounds in compensation.*
2 a place where a game such as tennis or badminton is played.
3 the place where a king or queen lives and works.

courteous

ADJECTIVE **Courteous** behaviour is polite and considerate.
courteously ADVERB

courtyard courtyards

NOUN a flat area of ground surrounded by buildings or walls.

cousin cousins

NOUN Your **cousin** is the child of your uncle or aunt.

cove coves

NOUN a small bay on the coast.

cover covers covering covered

VERB **1** If you **cover** something, you put something else over it to protect it or hide it.
2 If something **covers** something else, it forms a layer over it.

3 If you **cover** a particular distance, you travel that distance.
4 If you **cover** a subject, you discuss it in a lesson, course or book. *We covered the Vikings in today's lesson.*
NOUN **5** something put over an object to protect it or keep it warm.
6 The **cover** of a book or magazine is its outside.
7 Cover is trees, rocks or other places where you can shelter or hide. *When it started raining they ran for cover.*

coverage

NOUN The **coverage** of something in the news is the reporting of it. *There was complete coverage of the Wimbledon finals on television.*

cow cows

NOUN a large female mammal kept on farms for its milk and meat.

coward cowards

NOUN a person who is easily frightened and avoids dangerous situations.
cowardly ADJECTIVE   **cowardice** NOUN

cowboy cowboys

NOUN a man employed to look after cattle in America.

coy coyer coyest

ADJECTIVE If someone behaves in a **coy** way, they pretend to be shy and modest.

crab crabs

NOUN a crustacean with four pairs of legs, two claws, and a flat, round body covered by a shell.

crack cracks cracking cracked

VERB **1** If something **cracks**, or if something **cracks** it, it becomes damaged, with lines appearing on its surface.
2 If you **crack** a joke, you tell it.
3 If you **crack** a problem or code, you solve it.
NOUN **4** one of the lines appearing on something when it cracks.
5 a narrow gap. *My ring fell into a crack in the pavement.*

cracker crackers

NOUN **1** a thin, crisp biscuit that is often eaten with cheese.
2 a paper-covered tube that pulls apart with a bang, and usually has a toy and paper hat inside.

crackle crackles crackling crackled

VERB **1** something **crackles**, it makes a series of short sharp sounds. *The bonfire started to crackle as the flames grew higher.*
NOUN **2** a short sharp sound.

cradle cradles cradling cradled

NOUN **1** a box-shaped bed for a baby.
VERB **2** If you **cradle** something in your arms or hands, you hold it there carefully.

craft crafts

NOUN **1** an activity that needs skill with the hands, such as weaving, carving or pottery.
2 a boat, plane or spacecraft.

craftsman/craftswoman
craftsmen/craftswomen

NOUN a person who makes things skilfully with their hands.
craftsmanship NOUN

crafty craftier craftiest

ADJECTIVE **Crafty** people get what they want by tricking other people in a clever way.

Synonyms: cunning, wily

crag crags

NOUN a steep, rugged rock or peak.

cram crams cramming crammed

VERB If you **cram** people or things into a place, you put more in than there is room for. *I crammed my dirty washing into the washing machine.*

cramp cramps

NOUN pain caused when muscles contract.

cramped

ADJECTIVE If a room or a building is **cramped**, it is not big enough for the people or things in it.

crane cranes craning craned

NOUN **1** a machine that moves heavy things by lifting them in the air.
2 a large bird with a long neck and long legs.
VERB **3** If you **crane** your neck, you extend your head in a particular direction to see or hear something better.

crash crashes crashing crashed

NOUN **1** an accident in which a moving vehicle hits something and is damaged.
2 a sudden, loud noise.
VERB **3** If a vehicle **crashes**, it hits something and is badly damaged.

crate crates

NOUN a large box used for transporting or storing things.

crater craters

NOUN a wide hole in the ground caused by something hitting it or by an explosion. *The surface of the moon has many craters.*
[from Greek *krater* meaning mixing-bowl]

crave craves craving craved

VERB If you **crave** something, you want it very much. *I craved a bar of chocolate.*
craving NOUN

crawl crawls crawling crawled

VERB **1** When you **crawl**, you move forward on your hands and knees.
2 When an insect or vehicle **crawls** somewhere, it moves there very slowly.

crayon crayons

NOUN a coloured pencil or a stick of coloured wax.

craze crazes

NOUN something that is very popular for a short time.

crazy crazier craziest

ADJECTIVE; INFORMAL **1** very strange or foolish.
2 If you are **crazy** about something or someone, you like them very much.

creak creaks creaking creaked

VERB **1** If something **creaks**, it makes a harsh sound when it moves or when you stand on it.
NOUN **2** a harsh, squeaking noise.
creaky ADJECTIVE

cream creams

NOUN **1** a thick, yellowish-white liquid taken from the top of milk.
2 a substance that you can rub into your skin to make it soft or protect it.
ADJECTIVE **3** a yellowish-white colour.

crease creases creasing creased

NOUN **1** an irregular line that appears on cloth or paper when it is crumpled.

2 a straight line on something that has been pressed or folded neatly. *Dad ironed a sharp crease in his best trousers.*

VERB **3** If you **crease** something, you make lines appear on it.

create creates creating created

VERB If someone **creates** something, they cause it to happen or exist.
creation NOUN

creative

ADJECTIVE **Creative** people are good at inventing and developing new ideas.

creature creatures

NOUN any living thing that is not a plant.

crèche crèches

NOUN a place where small children are looked after while their parents are working.
[from old French *crèche* meaning crib or manger]

credit credits

NOUN **1** a system where you pay for something in small amounts, regularly over a period of time.

2 praise given to you for good work.

PLURAL NOUN **3 Credits** are the list of people who helped make a film, record or television programme.

PHRASE **4** If your bank account is **in credit**, you have money in it.

credit card credit cards

NOUN a plastic card that allows someone to buy goods on credit rather than paying with cash.

creek creeks

NOUN a narrow inlet where the sea comes a long way into the land.

creep creeps creeping crept

VERB If you **creep** somewhere, you move there quietly and slowly.

creepy creepier creepiest

ADJECTIVE strange and frightening. *The film was creepy.*

Synonyms: eerie, spooky

cremate cremates cremating cremated

VERB If someone is **cremated** when they die, their body is burned instead of buried.

crematorium crematoriums or crematoria

NOUN a building in which people are cremated.

crescent crescents

NOUN a curved shape that is wider in the middle than at the ends, like a new moon.

cress

NOUN a plant with small, strong-tasting leaves, used in salads.

crest crests

NOUN **1** the highest part of a hill or wave.

2 a tuft of feathers on top of a bird's head.

3 a special sign of something, such as a school or other organization.

crevice crevices

NOUN a narrow crack or gap in rock.

crew crews

NOUN The **crew** of a ship, aeroplane or spacecraft are the people who operate it.

cricket crickets

NOUN **1** an outdoor game played by two teams, who take turns at scoring runs by hitting a ball with a bat.

2 a small, jumping insect that produces sounds by rubbing its wings together.

cried

VERB the past tense and past participle of *cry*.

crime crimes

NOUN an action for which you can be punished by law.

criminal criminals

NOUN **1** someone who has committed a crime.
ADJECTIVE **2** involving or related to crime.

crimson

NOUN OR ADJECTIVE dark, purplish-red.

crinkle crinkles crinkling crinkled

VERB **1** If something **crinkles**, it becomes slightly creased or folded.
NOUN **2** a small crease or fold.

cripple cripples crippling crippled

VERB If someone is **crippled** by something, they are injured so severely that they can never move properly again.
crippling ADJECTIVE

crisis crises

NOUN a serious or dangerous situation. *The food crisis was caused by drought.*

crisp crisper crispest; crisps

ADJECTIVE **1** pleasantly fresh and firm: *crisp lettuce leaves.*
NOUN **2** a thin slice of potato that has been fried until it is hard and crunchy.

critic critics

NOUN **1** someone who writes reviews of books, films, plays or musical performances for newspapers or magazines.
2 a person who criticizes someone or something publicly.

critical

ADJECTIVE **1** A **critical** time or situation is a very important and serious one when things must be done correctly.
2 If the state of a sick or injured person is **critical**, they are in danger of dying.
3 Someone who is **critical** judges people and things very severely.

criticism criticisms

NOUN **1** spoken or written disapproval of someone or something.
2 A **criticism** of a book, film or play is an examination of its good and bad points.

criticize criticizes criticizing criticized; also spelt **criticise**

VERB If you **criticize** someone or something, you say what you think is wrong with them.

croak croaks croaking croaked

VERB **1** When animals and birds **croak**, they make harsh, low sounds.
NOUN **2** a harsh, low sound.
croaky ADJECTIVE

crochet crochets crotcheting crotcheted

Said "**kroh**-shay" NOUN **1** a kind of knitting done with a hooked needle and cotton or wool.
VERB **2** If you **crochet**, you use a hooked needle and wool or cotton to make lacy material for things such as clothes and shawls.

crockery

NOUN things you use for eating and drinking, such as plates, cups, bowls and saucers.

crocodile crocodiles

NOUN a large, scaly, meat-eating reptile that lives in tropical rivers.
[from Greek **krokodeilos** meaning lizard]

crocus crocuses

NOUN **Crocuses** are yellow, purple or white flowers that grow in early spring.

crook crooks

NOUN **1** a criminal.
2 The **crook** of your arm or leg is the soft inside part of your elbow or your knee.
3 a long stick with a hooked end used by shepherds.

crooked

ADJECTIVE **1** bent or twisted.
2 dishonest.

crop crops cropping cropped

NOUN **1** plants such as wheat and potatoes that are grown for food.
2 the plants collected at harvest time. *They gather two crops of rice a year.*
VERB **3** If you **crop** something such as your hair, you cut it very short.

cross crosses crossing crossed; crosser crossest

VERB **1** If you **cross** something, such as a room or a road, you go to the other side of it.
2 Lines or roads that **cross** meet and go across each other.
3 If you **cross** your arms, legs or fingers, you put one on top of the other.
NOUN **4** a mark or a shape like + or ✕.
ADJECTIVE **5** Someone who is **cross** is rather angry.
cross out VERB **6** If you **cross out** words on a page, you draw a line through them.

cross-country

NOUN the sport of running across open countryside, rather than on roads or a track.

crossing crossings

NOUN **1** a place where you can cross the road, a railway or a river.
2 a journey by ship to a place across the sea.

crossroads

NOUN a place where two roads meet and cross each other.

cross-section cross-sections

NOUN **1** the flat part of something that you see when you cut straight through it to see inside. *We looked at **cross-sections** of kiwi fruit and oranges.*

2 a typical sample of people or things. *We interviewed a **cross-section** of teenagers.*

crossword crosswords

NOUN a word puzzle in which you work out answers to clues and write them in a grid.

crouch crouches crouching crouched

VERB If you **crouch**, you lower your body with your knees bent.

crow crows crowing crowed

NOUN **1** a large black bird that makes a loud, harsh sound.
VERB **2** When a cock **crows**, it makes a series of loud sounds, usually early in the morning.

crowbar crowbars

NOUN a heavy, iron bar used as a lever or for forcing things open.

crowd crowds crowding crowded

NOUN **1** a large group of people gathered together.
VERB **2** When people **crowd** around someone or something, they gather closely together around them.

crown crowns crowning crowned

NOUN **1** a circular ornament made of gold or jewels, which a king or queen wears on their head.
VERB **2** When a king or queen is **crowned**, a crown is put on their head and they are officially made king or queen.

crucial

ADJECTIVE Something that is **crucial** is very important.

crucify crucifies crucifying crucified

VERB When a person is **crucified** they are tied or nailed to a cross and left there to die.
crucifixion NOUN

crude cruder crudest

ADJECTIVE **1** rough and simple: *a **crude** shelter made of old boxes.*
2 rude and vulgar.

cruel crueller cruellest

ADJECTIVE **Cruel** people deliberately cause pain or distress to other people or to animals.
cruelly ADVERB   **cruelty** NOUN

Synonyms: brutal, unkind

cruise cruises cruising cruised

NOUN **1** a holiday in which you travel on a ship and visit places.
VERB **2** When a vehicle **cruises**, it moves at a constant, moderate speed.

crumb crumbs

NOUN a very small piece of bread or cake.

crumble crumbles crumbling crumbled

VERB When something **crumbles**, or when you **crumble** it, it breaks into small pieces.

crumple crumples crumpling crumpled

VERB If you **crumple** paper or cloth, you squash it so that it is full of creases and folds.

crunch crunches crunching crunched

VERB If you **crunch** something, you crush it noisily, for example between your teeth or under your feet.

crusade crusades

NOUN **1** In the Middle Ages, the **Crusades** were a number of expeditions to Palestine by Christians who were attempting to recapture the Holy Land from the Muslims.
2 a long and determined attempt to achieve something.
crusader NOUN
[from Spanish ***cruzar*** meaning to take up the cross]

crush crushes crushing crushed

VERB **1** If you **crush** something, you squeeze it hard until its shape is destroyed. *He **crushed** the empty can.*
2 If you **crush** against someone or something, you press hard against them. *We **crushed** against each other in the crowded bus.*

crust crusts

NOUN **1** the hard outside part of a loaf.
2 a hard layer on top of something: *the earth's **crust**.*

crustacean crustaceans

Said "krus-**tay**-shun" NOUN an animal with a hard outer shell and several pairs of legs, which usually lives in water. *Crabs, lobsters and shrimps are* **crustaceans**.

crutch crutches

NOUN a support like a long stick that you lean on if you have injured your leg or foot. *I was on* **crutches** *while my ankle healed.*

cry cries crying cried

VERB **1** When you **cry**, tears come from your eyes because you are unhappy or hurt.
2 If you **cry** something, you shout it or say it loudly.
NOUN **3** a shout or other loud sound made with your voice.

crypt crypts

NOUN an underground room beneath a church, usually used as a burial place.

crystal crystals

NOUN **1** a piece of a mineral that has formed naturally into a regular shape.
2 a type of transparent rock, used in jewellery.
3 a type of very high quality glass.
crystalline ADJECTIVE

cub cubs

NOUN **1** the young of some wild animals: *a fox cub*, *a lion cub*.
2 The **Cubs** is an organization for young boys before they join the Scouts.

cube cubes

NOUN a solid shape with six square faces that are all the same size.

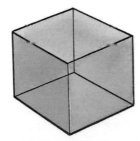

cubic

ADJECTIVE **1** shaped like a cube.
2 used to describe volume when you measure height, width and depth: *a cubic metre*.

cubicle cubicles

NOUN a small enclosed area in a place such as a sports centre or a shop, where you can dress and undress.

cuboid cuboids

NOUN a rectangular, three-dimensional box shape. A **cuboid** has six faces, all of which are rectangles.

cuckoo cuckoos

NOUN a grey bird with a two-note call. **Cuckoos** lay their eggs in other birds' nests.

cucumber cucumbers

NOUN a long, thin, green vegetable that is eaten raw.

cud

NOUN food that has been chewed and digested more than once by cows, sheep or other animals that have more than one stomach.

cuddle cuddles cuddling cuddled

VERB **1** If you **cuddle** someone, you hold them closely in your arms as a way of showing your affection.
NOUN **2** If you give someone a **cuddle**, you cuddle them.
cuddly ADJECTIVE

cuff cuffs

NOUN the end part of a sleeve, especially a shirt sleeve.

cul-de-sac cul-de-sacs

NOUN a road that does not lead to any other roads because one end is blocked off.
[from French **cul** + **de** + **sac** meaning bottom of the bag]

culprit culprits

NOUN someone who has done something harmful or wrong.

cult cults

NOUN **1** a small religious group, especially one that is considered strange.
ADJECTIVE **2** very popular or fashionable among a particular group of people. *It became a* **cult** *film.*

cultivate cultivates cultivating cultivated

VERB When someone **cultivates** land, they grow crops on it.
cultivation NOUN

a
b
c
d
e
f
g
h
i
j
k
l
m
n
o
p
q
r
s
t
u
v
w
x
y
z

culture cultures

NOUN the ideas, customs and art of a particular society.

cunning

ADJECTIVE A **cunning** person or plan achieves things in a clever way, often by deceiving people.

Synonyms: crafty, sly, wily

cup cups cupping cupped

NOUN **1** a small, round container with a handle, which you drink from.

2 a large metal container with two handles, which is given as a prize.

VERB **3** If you **cup** your hands, you put them together to make a shape like a cup.

cupboard cupboards

NOUN **1** a piece of furniture with doors and shelves.

2 a very small room for storing things in. *The broom is in the cupboard under the stairs.*

curator curators

NOUN the person in a museum or art gallery in charge of its contents.

curb curbs curbing curbed

VERB If you **curb** something, you keep it within limits. *You must curb your spending on comics.*

curdle curdles curdling curdled

VERB When milk **curdles**, it turns sour.

cure cures curing cured

VERB **1** If a doctor **cures** someone of an illness, they help them get better.

NOUN **2** something that heals or helps someone to get better.

VERB **3** If someone **cures** meat or fish, they smoke it to give it flavour and preserve it.

curfew curfews

NOUN a rule or a law stating that people must stay indoors between particular times at night.

curiosity curiosities

NOUN **1** the desire to know something or about many things.

2 something unusual and interesting.

curious

ADJECTIVE **1** Someone who is **curious** wants to know more about something.

2 Something that is **curious** is unusual or difficult to understand.

Synonyms: (sense 1) inquisitive, nosy
(sense 2) strange, peculiar

curl curls curling curled

NOUN **1** **Curls** are lengths of hair shaped in tight curves and circles.

2 a curved or spiral shape. *A curl of smoke rose from the chimney.*

VERB **3** If something **curls**, it moves in a curve or spiral. *Smoke curled up the chimney.*

curly ADJECTIVE

currant currants

NOUN a small, dried grape. **Currants** are often used in cakes and puddings.

currency currencies

NOUN A country's **currency** is its coins and banknotes.

current currents

NOUN **1** a steady continuous flowing movement of water or air.

NOUN **2** An electric **current** is a flow of electricity through a wire or circuit.

ADJECTIVE **3** Something that is **current** is happening now: *current fashion trends.*

curriculum curriculums or curricula

NOUN the different courses taught at a school or university.

curry curries

NOUN an Indian dish made with hot spices.

curse curses cursing cursed

NOUN **1** an evil spell. *She said the old house had a curse on it.*

VERB **2** If you **curse**, you swear because you are angry.

cursor cursors

NOUN a sign on a computer monitor that shows where the next letter or symbol is.

curtain curtains

NOUN a hanging piece of material that can be pulled across a window.

curtsy curtsies curtsying curtsied

NOUN **1** a little bobbing bow to show respect. *I made a little curtsy to the Queen.*

VERB **2** the action of making a curtsy.

curve curves curving curved

NOUN **1** a smooth, gradually bending line.

VERB **2** When something **curves**, it moves in a curve or has the shape of a curve. *The lane curved to the right.*

curved ADJECTIVE

cushion cushions cushioning cushioned

NOUN **1** a soft object that you put on a seat to make it more comfortable.

VERB **2** When something **cushions** something else, it reduces its effect. *The pile of leaves cushioned his fall.*

custard

NOUN a sweet, yellow sauce made from milk and eggs.

custody

NOUN **1** If someone has **custody** of a child, they have the legal right to keep it and look after it.

PHRASE **2** Someone who is **in custody** is being kept in prison until they can be tried in a court.

custodial ADJECTIVE

[from Latin *custos* meaning a guard]

custom customs

NOUN something that people usually do: *the custom of decorating the house for Christmas.*

customary

ADJECTIVE usual.

customer customers

NOUN a person who buys things from a shop or firm.

customs

NOUN the place at a border, airport or harbour where you declare any goods that you are bringing into the country.

cut cuts cutting cut

VERB **1** If you **cut** something, you use a pair of scissors, a knife or another sharp tool to mark it or remove parts of it.

2 If you **cut** yourself, you injure yourself with a sharp object.

NOUN **3** a mark made with a knife or a sharp tool.

4 a reduction in something. *There were lots of price cuts during the sales.*

cutlery

NOUN knives, forks and spoons.

cutlet cutlets

NOUN a small portion of meat that you fry or grill.

cycle cycles cycling cycled

NOUN **1** a bicycle.

2 a series of events that is repeated again and again: *the cycle of the seasons.*

VERB **3** When you **cycle**, you ride a bicycle.

cyclist NOUN

cyclone cyclones

NOUN a violent wind that blows in a spiral like a corkscrew.

cygnet cygnets

NOUN a young swan.

cylinder cylinders

NOUN **1** a hollow or solid shape with straight sides and equal circular faces. See **prism**.

2 the part of an engine that the piston moves in.

cylindrical ADJECTIVE

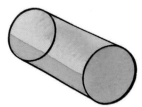

cymbal cymbals

NOUN a circular brass plate used as a percussion instrument. **Cymbals** are clashed together or hit with a stick. See **percussion**.

Dd

dabble dabbles dabbling dabbled
VERB If you **dabble** in something, you work or play at it without being seriously involved in it.

dad or daddy dads or daddies
NOUN; INFORMAL Your **dad** or your **daddy** is your father.

daffodil daffodils
NOUN a plant with yellow trumpet-shaped flowers that blooms in spring.

daft dafter daftest
ADJECTIVE silly and not very sensible.

dagger daggers
NOUN a weapon like a short knife.

daily
ADJECTIVE occurring every day.

dainty daintier daintiest
ADJECTIVE very delicate and pretty.

dairy dairies
NOUN 1 a shop or company that supplies milk and milk products.
2 In New Zealand, a **dairy** is a small shop selling groceries.
ADJECTIVE 3 **Dairy** products are foods made from milk, such as butter, cheese, cream and yogurt.

daisy daisies
NOUN a small, wild flower with a yellow centre and small, white petals.
[from Old English *deagesege* meaning day's eye, because the daisy opens in the daytime and closes at night]

Dalmatian Dalmatians
NOUN a large, smooth-haired white dog with black or brown spots.

dam dams
NOUN a barrier built across a river to hold back water.

damage damages damaging damaged
VERB If you **damage** something, you harm or spoil it.

damp damper dampest
ADJECTIVE slightly wet.
dampness NOUN

damson damsons
NOUN 1 a small, blue-black plum.
2 the tree that damsons grow on.

dance dances dancing danced
VERB 1 When you **dance**, you move around in time to music.
NOUN 2 a series of rhythmic movements that you do in time to music.
3 a social event where people dance with each other.

dandelion dandelions
NOUN a wild plant with yellow flowers that form a ball of fluffy seeds.
[from Old French *dent de lion* meaning lion's tooth, referring to the shape of the leaves]

dandruff
NOUN small, loose scales of dead skin in someone's hair.

danger dangers
NOUN the possibility that someone may be harmed or killed.

Synonyms: peril, risk

dangerous
ADJECTIVE If something is **dangerous**, it is likely to cause hurt or harm. *It is **dangerous** to walk close to the edge of the cliff.*
dangerously ADVERB

Synonyms: unsafe, hazardous

dangle dangles dangling dangled
VERB When something **dangles**, or when you **dangle** it, it swings or hangs loosely. *We sat by the pool and **dangled** our legs in the water.*

dappled
ADJECTIVE marked with patches of a different or darker shade. *The lawn was **dappled** with the shadows of the leafy trees.*

dare dares daring dared

VERB **1** If you **dare** to do something, you have the courage to do it.

2 If you **dare** someone to do something, you challenge them to do it. *I **dare** you to ask him his name.*

✔ When *dare* is used in a question or with a negative, it does not adds an *s*: *Dare* she come? He *dare* not come.

[from Old English ***durran*** meaning to venture or to be bold]

daredevil daredevils

NOUN a person who enjoys doing dangerous things.

daring

ADJECTIVE **1** bold and willing to take risks.

NOUN **2** the courage required to do things that are dangerous.

daringly ADVERB

dark darker darkest

ADJECTIVE **1** If it is **dark**, there is not enough light to see properly.

2 **Dark** colours have a lot of black, grey or brown tones in them.

dark NOUN

darken darkens darkening darkened

VERB If something **darkens**, it becomes darker than it was before. *The sky **darkened** as the storm approached.*

darkness

NOUN being dark.

darling darlings

NOUN You call someone **darling** if you love them or like them very much.

darn darns darning darned

VERB **1** When you **darn** a hole in a garment, you mend it with crossing stitches.

NOUN **2** A **darn** is the part of a garment that has been darned.

dart darts darting darted

NOUN **1** a small, pointed arrow.

2 **Darts** is a game in which the players throw **darts** at a round board divided into numbered sections.

VERB **3** If you **dart** somewhere, you move there quickly and suddenly.

dash dashes dashing dashed

VERB **1** If you **dash** somewhere, you rush there.

NOUN **2** the punctuation mark (–) which may be used instead of brackets.

dashboard dashboards

NOUN the instrument panel in a car.

data

NOUN information, usually in the form of facts or statistics.

✔ *Data* is really a plural word, but it is usually used as a singular.

database databases

NOUN a collection of information stored in a computer.

date dates

NOUN **1** a particular day or year that can be named. *What is your **date** of birth?*

2 If you have a **date**, you have an appointment to meet someone.

3 a small, brown, sticky fruit with a stone inside. **Dates** grow on palm trees.

daughter daughters

NOUN Someone's **daughter** is their female child.

dawdle dawdles dawdling dawdled

VERB If you **dawdle**, you are slow about doing something or going somewhere. *Don't **dawdle**, we have to be there in ten minutes.*

dawn dawns

NOUN the time in the morning when light first appears in the sky.

day days

NOUN **1** the time taken between one midnight and the next. There are 24 hours in one **day**.

2 the period of light between sunrise and sunset.

daydream daydreams daydreaming daydreamed

NOUN **1** pleasant thoughts about things that you would like to happen.

VERB **2** When you **daydream**, you drift off into a daydream.

daylight

NOUN the part of the day when it is light.

daytime

NOUN the part of the day when it is light.

daze

PHRASE If you are **in a daze**, you are confused and bewildered.

dazzle dazzles dazzling dazzled

VERB If a bright light **dazzles** you, it blinds you for a moment.
dazzling ADJECTIVE

de-

PREFIX added to some words to mean removal or reversal of something. *She* **de***bugged the computer program. We had to* **de***frost the windscreen before leaving.*

dead

ADJECTIVE **1** no longer living.
2 no longer functioning. *The phone went* **dead**.
ADVERB **3** precisely or exactly. *We arrived* **dead** *on eight o'clock.*

deadly deadlier deadliest

ADJECTIVE **1** likely or able to cause death: *a* **deadly** *disease.*
ADVERB OR ADJECTIVE **2** used to emphasize how serious or unpleasant something is: **deadly** *dangerous,* **deadly** *serious.*

deaf deafer deafest

ADJECTIVE **Deaf** people are unable to hear anything or unable to hear well.

deafening

ADJECTIVE A **deafening** sound is so loud that you cannot hear anything else.

deal deals dealing dealt

NOUN **1** an agreement or arrangement, especially in business.
VERB **2** If you **deal** with something, you do what is necessary to sort it out.
3 When you **deal** cards, you give them out to the players.
PHRASE **4** **A good deal** or **a great deal** of something is a lot of it.

dear dearer dearest

NOUN **1** You call someone **dear** as a sign of affection.
ADJECTIVE **2** Something that is **dear** is very expensive.
3 You use **dear** at the beginning of a letter, with the name of the person you are writing to. *Dear Sunita.*

death deaths

NOUN the end of the life of a human being or other animal or plant.

debate debates debating debated

NOUN **1** argument or discussion.
2 a formal discussion in which opposing views are expressed.
VERB **3** When people **debate** something, they discuss it in a formal way.

debris

NOUN fragments or rubble left after something has been destroyed. *After the eruption, volcanic* **debris** *was found scattered for miles.*

debt debts

NOUN a sum of money that someone owes.

début débuts

NOUN a performer's first public appearance.

decade decades

NOUN a period of ten years.

decaffeinated

ADJECTIVE coffee or tea that has had most of the caffeine removed.

decathlon decathlons

NOUN an athletic competition in which competitors take part in ten different events.

decay decays decaying decayed

VERB When things **decay**, they rot or go bad.

deceased

ADJECTIVE; FORMAL A **deceased** person is someone who has recently died.

deceit

NOUN behaviour that makes people believe something to be true that is not true.

deceive deceives deceiving deceived

VERB If you **deceive** someone, you make them believe something that is not true.

December

NOUN the twelfth month of the year. **December** has 31 days.

decent

ADJECTIVE honest and respectable.

deception deceptions

NOUN **1** something that is intended to trick or deceive someone.
2 the act of deceiving someone.

deceptive

ADJECTIVE likely to make people believe that something is true when it is not.

decide decides deciding decided

VERB If you **decide** to do something, you choose to do it, usually after thinking about it carefully. **decision** NOUN

Synonym: make up one's mind

deciduous

ADJECTIVE **Deciduous** trees lose their leaves in the autumn every year.

decimal decimals

ADJECTIVE 1 A **decimal** system involves counting in units of ten.
NOUN 2 A **decimal**, or **decimal** fraction, is a fraction in which a dot, called a decimal point, separates the whole numbers on the left from tenths, hundredths and thousandths on the right. For example, 0·5 represents $\frac{5}{10}$ (or $\frac{1}{2}$); 0·05 represents $\frac{5}{100}$ (or $\frac{1}{20}$).

decipher deciphers deciphering deciphered

VERB If you **decipher** a piece of writing or a message, you work out what it means even if it is hard to understand. *The spy **deciphered** the secret message.*

decision decisions

NOUN a choice or judgement that is made about something.

decisive

ADJECTIVE 1 A **decisive** person is able to make decisions quickly.
2 having an important influence on the result of something. *The first goal was a **decisive** moment in the match.*

deck decks

NOUN a downstairs or upstairs area on a bus or ship.

declare declares declaring declared

VERB 1 If you **declare** something, you say it firmly and forcefully.
2 FORMAL If something is **declared**, it is announced publicly. *War was **declared** in 1939.*

Synonyms: (sense 1) announce, proclaim, state

decline declines declining declined

VERB 1 If something **declines**, it becomes smaller or weaker. *The number of students has **declined** this year.*
2 If you **decline** something, you politely refuse to accept it or do it.

decode decodes decoding decoded

VERB If you **decode** a coded message, you convert it into ordinary language.

decompose decomposes decomposing decomposed

VERB If something **decomposes**, it rots after it dies.

decorate decorates decorating decorated

VERB 1 If you **decorate** something, you make it more attractive by adding things to it.
2 If you **decorate** a room or building, you paint or wallpaper it.

decoy decoys

NOUN something used to lead a person or animal into a trap.

decrease decreases decreasing decreased

VERB If something **decreases**, or if you **decrease** it, it becomes less. *The number of children in the class **decreased** rapidly.*

decree decrees decreeing decreed

NOUN an official order by the government, church or the rulers of a country.
VERB If someone **decrees** something, they announce formally that it will happen.

dedicate dedicates dedicating dedicated

VERB 1 If you **dedicate** yourself to something, you give your time and energy to it.
2 If you **dedicate** a book or piece of music to someone, you say that it is written for them.

deduct deducts deducting deducted

VERB If you **deduct** an amount from a total, you take it away.

deed deeds

NOUN 1 something that is done: *a good **deed***.
2 an important piece of paper or document that an agreement is written on.

deep deeper deepest

ADJECTIVE 1 going a long way down from the surface: *a **deep** hole*.
2 great or intense: *deep affection*.
3 a low sound: *a **deep** voice*.

deer

NOUN a large, fast-running, graceful mammal with hooves, that lives wild in parts of Britain and other countries. Male **deer** have antlers.

deface defaces defacing defaced

VERB If you **deface** something, you damage its appearance in some way. *The gang defaced the walls with spray paint.*

defeat defeats defeating defeated

VERB **1** If you **defeat** someone or something, you win a victory over them, or cause them to fail.
NOUN **2** the state of being beaten or of failing. *The team was downhearted after its defeat.*

defect defects defecting defected

NOUN **1** a fault or flaw in something.
VERB **2** If someone **defects**, they leave their own country or organization and join an opposing one.
defection NOUN   **defector** NOUN

defective

ADJECTIVE Something that is **defective** is not perfect or has something wrong with it.

defence defences

NOUN **1** something that protects you against attack. *She carried an alarm as a defence against muggers.*
2 A country's **defences** are its armed forces and its weapons.

defend defends defending defended

VERB **1** If you **defend** someone or something, you protect them from harm or danger.
2 If you **defend** a person or their ideas, you argue in support of them.

defendant defendants a person in a court of law who is accused of a crime.

defer defers deferring deferred

VERB If you **defer** something, you put off doing it until later.

defiant

ADJECTIVE If you are **defiant**, you behave in a way that shows you are not willing to obey someone.
defiance NOUN   **defiantly** ADVERB

deficient

ADJECTIVE lacking in something.
deficiency NOUN

define defines defining defined

VERB If you **define** something, you say what it is or what it means.

definite

ADJECTIVE **1** clear and unlikely to be changed. *We must arrange a definite date for the party.*
2 true rather than being someone's guess or opinion.

definitely

ADJECTIVE AND INTERJECTION certainly; without doubt. *I am definitely going on holiday next week.*

definition definitions

NOUN a statement explaining the meaning of a word or an idea.

deflate deflates deflating deflated

VERB If you **deflate** something, such as a tyre or balloon, you let all the air or gas out of it.

Antonyms: inflate, blow up

deforestation

NOUN the cutting down or the destruction of all the trees in an area.

deformed

ADJECTIVE disfigured or abnormally shaped.

defrost defrosts defrosting defrosted

VERB **1** If you **defrost** frozen food, you let it thaw out.
2 If you **defrost** a freezer or refrigerator, you remove the ice from it.

defuse defuses defusing defused

VERB **1** If someone **defuses** a bomb, they remove its fuse or detonator so that it cannot explode.
2 If you **defuse** a dangerous or tense situation, you make it less dangerous or tense.

defy defies defying defied

VERB If you **defy** a person or a law, you openly refuse to obey.

degree degrees

NOUN **1** a unit of measurement for temperatures, angles, and longitude and latitude, written as ° after a number. *The temperature was 20 °C. A right angle is a ninety-degree angle.*
2 an amount of a feeling or quality. *As captain you have a high degree of responsibility.*
3 a university qualification gained after completing a course of study there.

dehydrated
ADJECTIVE If someone is **dehydrated**, they are weak or ill because they have lost too much water from their body.

deity deities
NOUN a god or goddess.

dejected
ADJECTIVE If you are **dejected**, you are sad and gloomy.
dejection NOUN

delay delays delaying delayed
VERB **1** If you **delay** doing something, you put it off until later.
2 If something **delays** you, it makes you late or slows you down.
NOUN **3** If there is a **delay**, something does not happen until later than planned or expected.

Synonym: (sense 1) postpone

delete deletes deleting deleted
VERB If you **delete** something written, you cross it out or remove it.

deliberate
ADJECTIVE **1** done on purpose or planned in advance.
2 slow and careful in speech and action: *deliberate movements.*
deliberately ADVERB

delicate
ADJECTIVE **1** light and attractive: *a delicate perfume.*
2 fragile and needing to be handled carefully: *a delicate china cup.*
3 precise or sensitive: *delicate instruments.*
delicately ADVERB

delicatessen delicatessens
NOUN a shop selling unusual or imported foods.

delicious
ADJECTIVE **Delicious** food or drink has an extremely pleasant taste.

Synonyms: delectable, scrumptious

delight delights delighting delighted
NOUN **1** great pleasure or joy.
VERB **2** If something **delights** you, or if you are **delighted** by it, it gives you a lot of pleasure.
delighted ADJECTIVE

delinquent delinquents
NOUN a young person who commits minor crimes.
delinquency NOUN

delirious
ADJECTIVE **1** unable to speak or act in a rational way because of illness or fever.
2 wildly excited and happy.
deliriously ADVERB

deliver delivers delivering delivered
VERB **1** If you **deliver** something to someone, you take it and give it to them.
2 If someone **delivers** a baby, they help the woman who is giving birth.

delta deltas
NOUN a triangular piece of land at the mouth of a river where it divides into separate streams.

deluge deluges
NOUN a sudden, heavy downpour of rain.

demand demands demanding demanded
VERB **1** If you **demand** something, you ask for it forcefully.
NOUN **2** If there is **demand** for something, a lot of people want to buy it or have it.

democracy democracies
NOUN a system of government in which the people choose their leaders by voting for them in elections.
democratic ADJECTIVE

demolish demolishes demolishing demolished
VERB If someone **demolishes** a building, they knock it down.
demolition NOUN

a
b
c
d
e
f
g
h
i
j
k
l
m
n
o
p
q
r
s
t
u
v
w
x
y
z

demon demons
NOUN a devil or an evil spirit.

demonstrate demonstrates demonstrating demonstrated
VERB **1** If you **demonstrate** something to somebody, you show them how to do it or how it works.
2 If people **demonstrate**, they march or gather together to show that they oppose or support something.

demonstration demonstrations
NOUN **1** If someone gives a **demonstration**, they show how to do something or how something works.
2 a march or a gathering of people to show publicly what they think about something.

den dens
NOUN **1** a home or hiding place of a wild animal.
2 a special place where you can do what you want without being disturbed.

denial denials
NOUN **1** A **denial** of something is a statement that it is untrue.
2 The **denial** of a request is the refusal to grant it.

denim denims
NOUN strong cotton cloth used for making clothes, especially jeans.
[from French *serge de Nîmes*, meaning serge (a type of cloth) from Nîmes]

denominator denominators
NOUN In mathematics, the **denominator** is the bottom number of a fraction.

dense denser densest
ADJECTIVE **1** Something that is **dense** contains a lot of things or people in a small area. *We cut our way through the **dense** forest.*
2 difficult to see through. *The **dense** fog prevented us from enjoying the view over the hills.*
densely ADVERB

density densities
NOUN **1** thickness.
2 the proportion of mass to volume.

dent dents denting dented
VERB **1** If you **dent** something, you damage its surface by hitting it.
NOUN **2** a hollow in the surface of something.

dental
ADJECTIVE to do with teeth.

dentist dentists
NOUN a person who is qualified to treat people's teeth.

dentures
PLURAL NOUN false teeth.

deny denies denying denied
VERB **1** If you **deny** something, you say that it is not true.
2 If you are **denied** something, you are refused it.

deodorant deodorants
NOUN a substance used to hide or prevent the smell of sweat on your body.

depart departs departing departed
VERB When you **depart**, you leave.
departure NOUN

department departments
NOUN one of the sections into which a large shop or an organization is divided.

department store department stores
NOUN a very large shop divided into departments, each selling different types of goods.

depend depends depending depended
VERB **1** If one thing **depends** on another, it is influenced by it. *The cooking time **depends** on the size of the potato.*
2 If you **depend** on someone or something, you trust them and rely on them.

dependable
ADJECTIVE If someone is **dependable**, you can trust them to be helpful, sensible and reliable.

depict depicts depicting depicted
VERB If you **depict** someone or something, you paint, draw or describe them.

deport deports deporting deported
VERB If someone is **deported** from a country they are sent out of it, either because they have no right to be there, because they have done something wrong or because they did not ask permission to be there.

deposit deposits depositing deposited
VERB **1** If you **deposit** something, you put it down or leave it somewhere.
NOUN **2** a sum of money given in part payment for goods or services.

depot depots
NOUN **1** a place where supplies of food or equipment are stored until they are needed.
2 A bus **depot** is a bus station.

depressed
ADJECTIVE sad and gloomy.

depression depressions
NOUN **1** a state of mind in which someone feels unhappy and has no energy or enthusiasm for anything.
2 a hollow in the ground or on any other surface.
3 a time when there is a lot of unemployment and poverty.

deprive deprives depriving deprived
VERB If you **deprive** someone of something, you take it away from them or prevent them from having it.

depth depths
NOUN **1** the measurement or distance between the top and bottom of something, or the back and front of something. *The **depth** of the swimming pool at the deep end is 1·5 m.*
PHRASE **2** **In depth** means thoroughly. *We studied the poem **in depth**.*

deputy deputies
NOUN a person who helps someone in their job and acts on their behalf when they are away.

derail derails derailed derailing
VERB If a train is **derailed**, it comes off the railway tracks.

derivation derivations
NOUN The **derivation** of something is where it has come from.

derive derives deriving derived
VERB **1** FORMAL If you **derive** something from someone or something, you get it from them. *He **derives** great pleasure from music.*
2 If something is **derived** from something else, it comes from that thing. *His name is **derived** from a Greek word.*

descant descants
NOUN **1** The **descant** to a tune is another tune played at the same time but at a higher pitch.
ADJECTIVE **2** A **descant** musical instrument plays the highest notes in a range of instruments: *a **descant** recorder.*

descend descends descending descended
VERB If someone or something **descends**, they move downwards. *We **descended** to the basement in the lift.*

Antonym: ascend

---

descendant descendants
NOUN A person's **descendants** are all the people in later generations who are related to them.

describe describes describing described
VERB If you **describe** someone or something, you say what they are like.

desert deserts deserting deserted
Said "**dez**-ert" NOUN **1** an area of land, usually in a hot region, that has almost no water, rain, trees or plants: *the Sahara **Desert**.*

The Sahara Desert

Said "de-**zert**" VERB **2** If someone **deserts** you, they leave you and no longer help or support you.

deserted
ADJECTIVE A **deserted** building or place is one that people have left and never come back to.

deserve deserves deserving deserved
VERB If you **deserve** something, you earn it or have a right to it.

design designs designing designed

VERB **1** If you **design** something new, you plan what it should be like.

NOUN **2** a drawing from which something can be built or made.

3 a decorative pattern of lines or shapes.

desire desires desiring desired

VERB **1** If you **desire** something, you want it.

NOUN **2** a strong feeling of wanting something.

Synonyms: (sense 2) longing, want, wish

desk desks

NOUN a piece of furniture with a flat or sloping top, which you sit at to write, read or work.

desktop

ADJECTIVE small enough to be used at a desk: *a desktop computer.*

desolate

ADJECTIVE **1** deserted and bleak: *a desolate mountain top.*

2 lonely, very sad, and without hope.

desolation NOUN

despair despairs despairing despaired

NOUN **1** a total loss of hope.

VERB **2** If you **despair**, you lose hope.

desperate

ADJECTIVE **1** If you are **desperate**, you are in such a bad situation that you will try anything to change it.

2 A **desperate** situation is extremely dangerous or serious.

despicable

ADJECTIVE Something that is **despicable** is nasty, cruel or evil.

despise despises despising despised

VERB If you **despise** someone or something, you have a very low opinion of them.

despite

PREPOSITION If you do something **despite** some difficulty, you manage to do it anyway.

dessert desserts

NOUN a sweet food that you eat at the end of a meal.

destination destinations

NOUN the place you are going to.

destined

ADJECTIVE meant to happen. *They were destined to meet.*

destiny destinies

NOUN Your **destiny** is your fate: the things that will happen to you in the future.

destitute

ADJECTIVE without money or possessions, and therefore in great need.

destitution NOUN

destroy destroys destroying destroyed

VERB If you **destroy** something, you damage it so much that it is completely ruined.

destruction NOUN

Synonyms: demolish, ruin, wreck

destructive

ADJECTIVE Something that is **destructive** can cause great damage, harm or injury.

Synonym: damaging

detach detaches detaching detached

VERB If you **detach** something, you remove or unfasten it.

detachable ADJECTIVE

detached

ADJECTIVE separate or standing apart. *It was a detached house, standing alone at the top of the hill.*

detain detains detaining detained

VERB If you **detain** someone, you keep them from going somewhere or doing something.

detail details

NOUN **1** an individual fact or feature of something. *I remember every detail of that film.*

PLURAL NOUN **2 Details** about something are information about it. For example, your **details** might be your name and address.

detect detects detecting detected

VERB If you **detect** something, you notice or find it. *X-rays can detect broken bones.*

detective detectives

NOUN a person, usually a police officer, whose job is to investigate crimes.

detector detectors

NOUN an instrument used to detect the presence of something: *a metal detector.*

detention

NOUN **1** a form of punishment in which a pupil is made to stay in school for extra time when other children do not have to.
2 arrest or imprisonment.

deter deters deterring deterred

VERB If you **deter** someone from doing something, you persuade them not to do it or try to stop them in some way.

detergent detergents

NOUN a chemical substance used for washing or cleaning things.

deteriorate deteriorates deteriorating deteriorated

VERB If something **deteriorates**, it gets worse.
deterioration NOUN

determination

NOUN a great strength and will to do something.

determined

ADJECTIVE having your mind firmly made up. *She was **determined** to pass her exams.*

deterrent deterrents

NOUN something that prevents people from doing something, usually by making them afraid to do it. *We have a car alarm as a **deterrent** to car thieves.*

detest detests detesting detested

VERB If you **detest** someone or something, you dislike them intensely.
detestable ADJECTIVE
[from Latin ***detestari*** meaning to curse]

detonate detonates detonating detonated

VERB If someone **detonates** a bomb or mine, they cause it to explode.
detonation NOUN   **detonator** NOUN

detour detours

NOUN If you make a **detour** on a journey, you go by a longer or less direct route.

devastate devastates devastating devastated

VERB A place that has been **devastated** has been severely damaged or destroyed.
devastation NOUN

develop develops developing developed

VERB **1** When something **develops**, it grows or becomes more advanced.

2 If you **develop** photographs or film, you produce a visible image from them.

development developments

NOUN gradual growth or progress. *There have been great **developments** in technology over the past fifty years.*

device devices

NOUN a machine or tool that is used for a particular purpose.

devil devils

NOUN an evil spirit.

devious

ADJECTIVE **Devious** people behave in an underhand, nasty and secretive way.

devise devises devising devised

VERB If you **devise** something, you invent it or design it.

devoted

ADJECTIVE very loving and loyal.

devour devours devouring devoured

VERB **1** If you **devour** food, you eat it quickly and greedily.
2 If one creature **devours** another, it eats it.
3 If you **devour** a book, you read it very quickly.

devout

ADJECTIVE very deeply religious.

dew

NOUN drops of moisture that form on the ground and other cool surfaces at night.

diabetes

NOUN a condition in which a person has too much sugar in their blood.
diabetic NOUN OR ADJECTIVE

diagnose diagnoses diagnosing diagnosed

VERB If someone **diagnoses** an illness or problem, they identify what is wrong.

diagonal diagonals

NOUN **1** a straight line that slopes from one corner of a shape to another.
ADJECTIVE **2** in a slanting direction: *a **diagonal** line.*
[from Greek ***diagonios*** meaning from angle to angle]

a
b
c
d
e
f
g
h
i
j
k
l
m
n
o
p
q
r
s
t
u
v
w
x
y
z

diagram diagrams

> NOUN a drawing that shows or explains something: *Carroll or Venn diagram*.

dial dials dialling dialled

> NOUN **1** the part of a clock or meter where the time or a measurement is shown.
> VERB **2** If you **dial** a telephone number, you press the buttons to select the number you want.

dialect dialects

> NOUN the form of a language spoken in a particular area.

dialogue dialogues

> NOUN In a novel, play or film, **dialogue** is conversation.

diameter diameters

> NOUN the length of a straight line drawn across a circle through its centre.

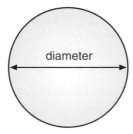
diameter

diamond diamonds

> NOUN **1** a precious stone made of pure carbon.
> **2** a shape with four straight sides of equal length that are not at right angles to each other. *See* **rhombus**.

diarrhoea

> NOUN an illness that attacks your bowels so that you can't stop going to the lavatory.

diary diaries

> NOUN a notebook with a separate space or page for each day of the year.

dice dices dicing diced

> NOUN **1** a small cube with dots on each of its six faces.
> VERB **2** If you **dice** food, you cut it into small cubes.

dictate dictates dictating dictated

> VERB **1** If you **dictate** something, you say it or read it aloud for someone else to write down.
> **2** If you **dictate** to someone, you give them orders in a bossy way.
> **dictation** NOUN

dictionary dictionaries

> NOUN a book in which words are listed alphabetically and their meanings explained.

did

> VERB the past tense of *do*.

didgeridoo didgeridoos

> NOUN an Australian wind instrument made from a long, hollowed-out piece of wood.

didn't

> VERB a contraction of *did not*.

die dies dying died

> VERB **1** When humans, other animals or plants **die**, they stop living.
> **2** When something **dies**, **dies away** or **dies down**, it becomes less intense and disappears. *The wind died down*.

diesel diesels

> NOUN **1** a heavy fuel used in trains, buses and lorries.
> **2** a vehicle with a diesel engine.

diet diets

> NOUN **1** the food you usually eat.
> **2** If you are on a **diet**, you eat only certain foods for health reasons or to lose weight.

difference differences

> NOUN **1** the way in which things are unlike each other.
> **2** the amount by which one number is less than another.
> **3** a change in someone or something.

different

> ADJECTIVE If one thing is **different** from another, it is not like it.
> ✔ One thing is *different from* another thing. Some people think that *different to* is incorrect. *Different than* is American.

difficult

> ADJECTIVE **1** **Difficult** things are not easy to do, understand or solve.
> **2** Someone who is **difficult** behaves in an unreasonable way.

difficulty difficulties

> NOUN a problem.

dig digs digging dug

> VERB **1** If you **dig**, you make a hole in earth or sand, especially with a spade.
> **2** If you **dig** something, you poke it.

digest digests digesting digested
VERB To **digest** food means to break it down in the gut so that it can be easily absorbed and used by the body.
digestible ADJECTIVE

digit digits
Said "**dij**-it" NOUN **1** a written symbol for any of the numbers from zero (0) to nine (9). *A two-**digit** number: 46.*
2 a finger or toe.

digital
ADJECTIVE **Digital** instruments, such as watches, have changing numbers instead of a dial with hands.

Antonym: analogue

dignified
ADJECTIVE **Dignified** people are calm, and behave in a way that other people admire and respect.

dilemma dilemmas
NOUN a situation where you have to choose between two alternatives that are equally difficult or unpleasant.

diligent
ADJECTIVE hard-working and showing care.
diligently ADVERB   **diligence** NOUN

dilute dilutes diluting diluted
VERB If you **dilute** a liquid, you add water or another liquid to it to make it weaker.

dim dimmer dimmest; dims dimming dimmed
ADJECTIVE **1** lacking in brightness and badly lit.
VERB **2** If lights **dim**, or are **dimmed**, they become less bright.

dimension dimensions
NOUN The **dimensions** of something are its measurements or its size.

diminish diminishes diminishing diminished
VERB If something **diminishes**, or you **diminish** it, it reduces in size or importance.

diminutive diminutives
ADJECTIVE **1** very small.
NOUN **2** You can make **diminutives** by adding the suffixes "-kin", "-let" or "-ette" to other words. For example "lambkin", "piglet", "diskette".

dimple dimples
NOUN a small hollow in someone's cheek or chin.

din
NOUN a very loud and unpleasant noise.

dine dines dining dined
VERB; FORMAL When you **dine**, you eat dinner in the evening.

dinghy dinghies
NOUN a small boat that is rowed, sailed or powered by an outboard motor.

dingo dingoes
NOUN an Australian wild dog.

dingy dingier dingiest
ADJECTIVE shabby and dirty to look at.

dinner dinners
NOUN the main meal of the day, eaten either in the evening or in the middle of the day.

dinosaur dinosaurs
NOUN a large reptile that lived in prehistoric times.
[from Greek ***deinos*** + ***sauros*** meaning fearful lizard]

Triceratops

dip dips dipping dipped
VERB **1** If you **dip** something into a liquid, you lower it in and take it out again quickly.
2 If something **dips**, it slopes downwards or goes below a certain level. *The road **dipped** suddenly.*
NOUN **3** a downward slope or hollow. *There was a **dip** in the road.*
4 a quick swim.
5 a savoury mixture for eating, in which you dip crisps, crackers or vegetables.

diploma diplomas

NOUN a certificate that is awarded to a student who has successfully completed a course of study.

diplomat diplomats

NOUN an official who negotiates with another country on behalf of his or her own country.

diplomatic

ADJECTIVE If you are **diplomatic**, you are tactful and say and do things without offending people.

direct directs directing directed

ADVERB **1** If you go **direct** to a place, you go straight there. *This train goes **direct** to Paris.*
ADJECTIVE **2** If someone's speech or behaviour is **direct**, they are honest and say what they mean.
VERB **3** If you **direct** someone to a place, you show them how to get there.
4 Someone who **directs** a film or play decides the way it is made and performed.

Synonyms: (sense 2) frank, open, straightforward

direction directions

NOUN **1** the way that someone or something is moving or pointing.
PLURAL NOUN **2** instructions that tell you how to do something or how to get somewhere.

director directors

NOUN **1** a senior manager of a company.
2 the person who decides how a film or play is made and performed.

directory directories

NOUN a book that gives lists of information, such as people's names, addresses and telephone numbers.

dirt

NOUN **1** any unclean substance such as mud, dust or stains.
2 earth or soil.

dirty dirtier dirtiest

ADJECTIVE **1** marked or covered with dirt.
2 unfair or dishonest.

Synonyms: (sense 1) filthy, grubby, mucky

dis-

PREFIX added to some words to make them mean the opposite. For example, **dis**contented means not content.

disability disabilities

NOUN a condition or illness that limits the way in which someone can use their body.

disabled

ADJECTIVE **Disabled** people have an illness or injury that can restrict their way of life.
disable VERB

disadvantage disadvantages

NOUN something that makes things difficult.

disagree disagrees disagreeing disagreed

VERB **1** If you **disagree** with someone, you have a different opinion or view from them.
2 If you **disagree** with an action or proposal, you believe it is wrong.

disagreeable

ADJECTIVE unpleasant or unhelpful and unfriendly. *The woman was very **disagreeable** and did not even offer to help.*

disappear disappears disappearing disappeared

VERB **1** If someone or something **disappears**, they go where they cannot be seen or found.
2 If something **disappears**, it stops existing or happening.

disappoint disappoints disappointing disappointed

VERB If someone or something **disappoints** you, they fail to live up to what you expected.

disapprove disapproves disapproving disapproved

VERB If you **disapprove** of something or someone, you believe they are wrong or bad.
disapproval NOUN   **disapproving** ADJECTIVE

disaster disasters

NOUN **1** a very bad accident, such as an earthquake or a plane crash.
2 a complete failure. *The party was a **disaster**.*

Synonyms: (sense 1) calamity, catastrophe

disc discs; also spelt **disk**

NOUN **1** anything with a flat, circular shape, such as a compact **disc**.

2 a storage device used in computers. *We backed up our files on a floppy **disc**.*

discard discards discarding discarded

VERB If you **discard** something, you throw it away because it is of no use to you anymore.

discharge discharges discharging discharged

VERB **1** If a doctor **discharges** someone from hospital, they allow them to leave.

2 If something **discharges** or is **discharged**, it is given or sent out. *Cars **discharge** exhaust fumes into the atmosphere.*

disciple disciples

NOUN a follower of someone or something. [from Latin ***discipulus*** meaning pupil]

discipline disciplines disciplining disciplined

NOUN **1** making people obey rules, by training them and by punishing them when they break the rules.

2 the ability to behave and work in a controlled way.

VERB **3** If a parent **disciplines** a child, they punish them.

disc jockey disc jockeys

NOUN someone who introduces and plays pop records on the radio or at a night club.

disco discos

NOUN a party or a club where people go to dance to pop music.

discomfort

NOUN slight pain or worry.

disconnect disconnects disconnecting disconnected

VERB If you **disconnect** something, you detach it from something else or break its connection.

discontinue discontinues discontinuing discontinued

VERB If you **discontinue** something, you stop doing it.

discount discounts

NOUN a reduction in the price of something.

discourage discourages discouraging discouraged

VERB **1** If you **discourage** someone, you take away their enthusiasm for doing something.

2 If you **discourage** someone from doing something, you try to persuade them not to do it.

discouraging ADJECTIVE
discouragement NOUN

discover discovers discovering discovered

VERB If you **discover** something, you find it or learn about it for the first time. *She **discovered** that they'd escaped.*

discreet

ADJECTIVE If you are **discreet**, you keep private things to yourself and can be trusted with a secret.

discretion NOUN

discriminate discriminates discriminating discriminated

VERB **1** If you **discriminate** between people, you treat them differently – often unfairly – because of their race, religion or sex.

2 If you are **discriminating**, you can recognise differences between things and use your judgement to make choices.

discrimination NOUN

discus discuses

NOUN a flat circular weight that athletes throw in a competition.

discuss discusses discussing discussed

VERB When people **discuss** something, they talk about it in detail.

discussion NOUN

disease diseases

NOUN an illness that affects human beings, other animals or plants.

disgrace disgraces disgracing disgraced

NOUN **1** something unacceptable. *Tidy your room – it's a **disgrace**.*

VERB **2** If you **disgrace** yourself, you do something that others disapprove of.

disgruntled

ADJECTIVE If you are **disgruntled**, you are cross and discontented about something.

disguise disguises disguising disguised

VERB **1** If you **disguise** yourself, you change your appearance so that people will not recognize you.

NOUN **2** something you wear or a change you make to your appearance so that people will not recognize you.

disgust disgusts disgusting disgusted

NOUN **1** a very strong feeling of dislike and loathing.

VERB **2** If you **disgust** someone, you make them feel a strong sense of dislike and disapproval.

disgusting ADJECTIVE

dish dishes

NOUN **1** a shallow container for cooking or serving food.

2 a particular kind of food, or food cooked in a particular way: *a vegetarian* **dish**.

disheartened

ADJECTIVE If you are **disheartened**, you feel disappointed.

dishonest

ADJECTIVE not truthful or fit to be trusted.

dishonestly ADVERB

dishwasher dishwashers

NOUN a machine that washes crockery, cutlery, pots and pans.

disinfectant disinfectants

NOUN a chemical substance that kills germs.

disintegrate disintegrates disintegrating disintegrated

VERB If an object **disintegrates**, it breaks into many pieces and so is destroyed.

disintegration NOUN

disk another spelling of *disc*.

dislike dislikes disliking disliked

VERB If you **dislike** something or someone, you think they are unpleasant.

dislocate dislocates dislocating dislocated

VERB If you **dislocate** a bone in your body, you put it out of its usual position by accident.

disloyal

ADJECTIVE not loyal.

dismal

ADJECTIVE depressing and bleak. *It was a* **dismal** *day, with rain pouring down and cold winds blowing.*

dismantle dismantles dismantling dismantled

VERB If you **dismantle** something, you take it apart.

dismay dismays dismaying dismayed

VERB **1** If something **dismays** you, it worries and alarms you.

NOUN **2** a feeling of fear and worry.

dismiss dismisses dismissing dismissed

VERB **1** If you **dismiss** something, you decide that it is not important enough for you to think about.

2 If someone is **dismissed**, they are told to leave a place or leave their job. *She* **dismissed** *the class.*

dismount dismounts dismounting dismounted

VERB to get off a horse or a bicycle.

disobey disobeys disobeying disobeyed

VERB If you **disobey** the rules, you break them. If you **disobey** a person, you refuse to do as they say.

disobedience NOUN　**disobedient** ADJECTIVE

disorder disorders

NOUN **1** a state of untidiness.

2 lack of organization.

3 an illness: *a stomach* **disorder**.

disorderly ADJECTIVE

disorganized or disorganised

ADJECTIVE Someone or something that is **disorganized** is muddled, confused or badly prepared.

dispatch dispatches dispatching dispatched

VERB **1** If you **dispatch** someone or something to a particular place, you send them there for a particular reason.

NOUN **2** an official message.

dispensary dispensaries

NOUN a place where medicines are prepared and given out.

dispersal

NOUN The **dispersal** of something is its spreading or scattering out in many directions.

disperse disperses dispersing dispersed

VERB If someone **disperses** people, they send them away.

display displays displaying displayed
NOUN **1** an arrangement of things designed to attract people's attention: *a firework* **display**.
VERB **2** If you **display** something, you put it on show.
3 If you **display** an emotion, you behave in a way that shows how you feel.

disposable
ADJECTIVE **Disposable** things are designed to be thrown away after they have been used.

dispose disposes disposing disposed
VERB If you **dispose** of something, you get rid of it. *We* **disposed** *of our litter carefully.*

disprove disproves disproving disproved
VERB If you **disprove** something, you show that it is not true.

dispute disputes disputing disputed
NOUN **1** an argument.
VERB **2** If you **dispute** a fact or theory, you say that it is incorrect or untrue.

disqualify disqualifies disqualifying disqualified
VERB If someone **disqualifies** someone from a competition or activity, they officially stop them from taking part in it. *The team was* **disqualified** *from the competition for cheating.*

disregard disregards disregarding disregarded
VERB **1** If you **disregard** someone or something, you take no notice of them.
NOUN **2** If you show **disregard** for something, you show that you do not care for it.

disrespect
NOUN contempt or lack of respect.
disrespectful ADJECTIVE

disrupt disrupts disrupting disrupted
VERB If you **disrupt** something, you break it up or throw it into confusion. *Rain* **disrupted** *the school's sports day.*
disruption NOUN   **disruptive** ADJECTIVE
[from Latin **dirumpere** meaning to smash to pieces]

dissatisfied
ADJECTIVE not pleased or contented.
dissatisfaction NOUN

dissect dissects dissecting dissected
VERB When you **dissect** a plant or part of the body of an animal, you cut it up carefully so that you can examine it closely.

dissolve dissolves dissolving dissolved
VERB If you **dissolve** something, or if something **dissolves** in a liquid, it mixes with the liquid and becomes part of it.

distance distances
NOUN **1** The **distance** between two points is the amount of space between them.
2 the fact of being far away. *My friend's house is a great* **distance** *from mine.*

distant
ADJECTIVE far away in space or time: *a* **distant** *planet.*

distil distils distilling distilled
VERB When you **distil** a liquid, you purify it by boiling it and condensing the vapour.

distinct
ADJECTIVE **1** If one thing is **distinct** from another, there is an important difference between them. *The word "chest" has two* **distinct** *meanings.*
2 If something is **distinct**, you can hear, smell, see or sense it clearly.

distinction distinctions
NOUN **1** a difference between two things.
2 a quality of excellence and superiority: *a woman of* **distinction**.
3 the highest level of achievement in an examination.

distinctive
ADJECTIVE a special quality that makes something recognisable. *Peppermint has a* **distinctive** *smell.*

distinguish distinguishes distinguishing distinguished
VERB **1** If you can **distinguish** one thing from another, you can see or understand the difference between them.
2 If you can **distinguish** something, you can see, hear or taste it. *I heard shouting but couldn't* **distinguish** *the words.*

distort distorts distorting distorted

VERB **1** If you **distort** something, you twist it out of shape.

2 If you **distort** an argument or the truth, you alter the facts to suit yourself.

distract distracts distracting distracted

VERB If you **distract** someone, you take their attention away from what they are doing.

distraction NOUN

distress distresses distressing distressed

NOUN **1** **Distress** is suffering caused by pain or sorrow.

VERB **2** If something **distresses** you, it causes you to be upset or worried.

PHRASE **3** If someone or something is **in distress**, they are in danger and need help.

distribute distributes distributing distributed

VERB **1** If you **distribute** things, you hand them out or deliver them.

2 If you **distribute** something, you share it among a number of people.

district districts

NOUN an area of a town or country.

distrust distrusts distrusting distrusted

VERB **1** If you **distrust** someone, you are suspicious of them because you are not sure whether they are honest.

NOUN **2** suspicion.

distrustful ADJECTIVE   **distrustfully** ADVERB

disturb disturbs disturbing disturbed

VERB If you **disturb** someone, you interrupt their peace or privacy.

disturbance NOUN

disturbance disturbances

NOUN something that disturbs someone or something.

disused

ADJECTIVE If something is **disused**, it is neglected or no longer used.

disuse NOUN

ditch ditches

NOUN a channel cut into the ground at the side of a road or field.

dive dives diving dived

VERB **1** If you **dive**, you plunge head first into deep water.

2 If something or someone **dives**, they move suddenly and quickly. *The birds* ***dived*** *to catch the insects.*

diver divers

NOUN **1** a person who uses breathing apparatus to swim or work under water.

2 a person who takes part in diving competitions.

3 a bird that catches its food by diving into water.

diverse

ADJECTIVE If things are **diverse**, they show a wide range of differences. *There was a* ***diverse*** *collection of paintings in the gallery.*

diversion diversions

NOUN **1** an alternative road you can use if the main one is blocked.

2 something that takes your attention away from what you are doing.

divert VERB

divide divides dividing divided

VERB **1** When you **divide** something, or when it divides, it separates into two or more parts. *We* ***divided*** *the cake into six equal slices.*

2 If something **divides** two areas, it forms a barrier between them. *A tall hedge* ***divided*** *the two gardens.*

3 If you **divide** a larger number by a smaller number, or into a smaller number, you calculate how many times the larger number contains the smaller number. *Thirty-five* ***divided*** *by five is seven* ($35 \div 5 = 7$). *Six* ***divided*** *into three is two.*

Antonym: multiply

divine

ADJECTIVE having the qualities of a god or goddess.

divisible

ADJECTIVE A number that is **divisible** can be divided by another number. *8, 20, 46 and 166 are all* ***divisible*** *exactly by two.*

division

NOUN the process of dividing numbers or things.

divorce divorces divorcing divorced

VERB When married couples **divorce**, they end their marriage legally.

Diwali
NOUN a Hindu festival of light, celebrated in the autumn.

DIY
NOUN the activity of making or repairing things yourself. **DIY** is an abbreviation for *do-it-yourself*.

dizzy dizzier dizziest
ADJECTIVE If you feel **dizzy**, you feel that you are losing your balance and are about to fall.

do does doing did done
VERB **1** If you **do** something, you get on and finish it. *I've done my homework.*
2 You can use **do** with other verbs. *Do you like ice cream?*
3 If you ask people what they **do**, you want to know what their job is.

docile
ADJECTIVE A **docile** person or other animal is calm and unlikely to cause any trouble.

dock docks
NOUN an enclosed space in a harbour where ships go to be loaded, unloaded or repaired.

doctor doctors
NOUN a person who is qualified in medicine and treats people who are ill.

document documents documenting documented
NOUN **1** a piece of paper that provides an official record of something.
VERB **2** If you **document** something, you make a detailed record of it.

documentary documentaries
NOUN a radio or television programme, or a film, that gives information about real events.

dodge dodges dodging dodged
VERB If you **dodge** something, you move suddenly to avoid being seen, hit or caught.

dodgy
ADJECTIVE; INFORMAL dangerous, risky or unreliable.

doe does
NOUN a female deer, rabbit or hare.

does
VERB a present tense of *do*.

doesn't
VERB a contraction of *does not*.

dog dogs
NOUN a mammal that is often kept as a pet or used to guard or hunt things.

dole doles doling doled
VERB If you **dole** something out, you give a certain amount of it to each individual in a group.

doll dolls
NOUN a toy that looks like a baby or a person.

dollar dollars
NOUN a unit of money in the USA, Australia, Canada, New Zealand and some other countries. A **dollar** is worth 100 cents.

dolphin dolphins
NOUN a mammal that lives in the sea.

dome domes
NOUN a rounded roof.

domestic
ADJECTIVE involving or concerned with the home and family. *Dogs and cats are often kept as domestic pets.*

dominant
ADJECTIVE most powerful or important.

dominate dominates dominating dominated
VERB **1** If someone or something **dominates** a situation or an event, they are the most powerful or important thing in it.
2 If one person **dominates** another, they have power and control over them.
[from Latin ***dominari*** meaning to be lord over]

domino dominoes
NOUN a small, rectangular block marked with two groups of spots on one side, used for playing the game called **dominoes**.

donate

donate donates donating donated
VERB If you **donate** something, you give it, especially to a charity.

done
VERB the past participle of *do*.

donkey donkeys
NOUN an animal like a horse, but smaller and with longer ears.

donor donors
NOUN someone who donates something, such as a blood **donor** or someone who gives to charity.

don't
VERB a contraction of *do not*.

doodle doodles doodling doodled
NOUN **1** a drawing done when you are thinking about something else or when you are bored.
VERB **2** When you **doodle**, you draw doodles.

doomed
ADJECTIVE If someone or something is **doomed** to an unhappy or unpleasant experience, they are certain to suffer it.

door doors
NOUN a swinging or sliding panel for opening or closing the entrance to something.

dormitory dormitories
NOUN a large bedroom where several people sleep.

dormouse dormice
NOUN a mammal, like a large mouse, with a furry tail.

dose doses
NOUN a measured amount of a medicine or drug.

dot dots dotting dotted
NOUN **1** a very small, round mark, such as a full stop or a decimal point.
VERB **2** When things **dot** a place or an area they are scattered all over it. *The hillside was dotted with trees.*
PHRASE **3** If you arrive somewhere **on the dot**, you arrive at exactly the right time.

double doubles doubling doubled
ADJECTIVE **1** twice the usual size.
2 consisting of two parts.
VERB **3** If something **doubles**, or if you **double** it, it becomes twice as large. *The number of pupils has **doubled** over the last year.*

NOUN **4** Your **double** is someone who looks exactly like you.

double bass double basses
NOUN a very large stringed instrument. *My brother plays the **double bass** in a jazz band.*

doubt doubts doubting doubted
VERB If you **doubt** something, you think that it is probably not true or possible. *I **doubt** if I'll be allowed to go to the party.*

doubtful
ADJECTIVE uncertain or unlikely.

doubtless
ADVERB certainly; without any doubt.

dough
NOUN a mixture of flour and water used to make bread, pastry or biscuits.

doughnut doughnuts
NOUN a ring of sweet dough cooked in hot fat.

dove doves
NOUN a bird of the pigeon family that makes a soft, cooing sound.

down
PREPOSITION OR ADVERB **1** towards the ground, towards a lower level, or in a lower place.
ADVERB **2** If you put something **down**, you place it on a surface.
3 If an amount of something goes **down**, it decreases. *The water level in the river has gone **down**.*
NOUN **4** the tiny, soft feathers on baby birds.

downcast
ADJECTIVE If you are **downcast**, you feel sad and without hope.

downhill
ADVERB down a slope.

download downloads downloading downloaded

VERB When you **download** a program from a disk or from the Internet, you move it into a file on your own computer.

downpour downpours

NOUN a very heavy shower of rain.

downstairs

ADVERB 1 If you go **downstairs**, you go towards the ground floor.

ADJECTIVE 2 on a lower floor.

doze dozes dozing dozed

VERB When you **doze**, you sleep lightly for a short period.

dozen dozens

NOUN A **dozen** things are twelve of them.

Dr

NOUN an abbreviation for *Doctor*.

drab

ADJECTIVE plain, dull and unattractive.

draft drafts

NOUN an early plan for a story, a book, a letter or a speech that you are going to write.

drag drags dragging dragged

VERB If you **drag** a heavy object somewhere, you pull it there slowly and with difficulty.

dragon dragons

NOUN In stories and legends, **dragons** are large, fire-breathing, lizard-like creatures with claws and leathery wings.

dragonfly dragonflies

NOUN a colourful insect that is often found near water.

drain drains draining drained

NOUN 1 a pipe that carries water or sewage away from a place, or an opening in a surface that leads to the pipe.

VERB 2 If you **drain** something, or if it **drains**, liquid flows out of it or off it.

drake drakes

NOUN a male duck.

drama dramas

NOUN 1 a serious play for the theatre, television or radio.

2 You can refer to the exciting aspects of a situation as **drama**.

dramatic

ADJECTIVE Something **dramatic** is very exciting, interesting and impressive.

drank

VERB the past tense of *drink*.

drape drapes draping draped

VERB If you **drape** a piece of material over something, you hang it loosely.

drastic

ADJECTIVE A **drastic** course of action is very severe and is usually taken urgently.

draught draughts

Said "**draft**" NOUN 1 a current of cold air.

PLURAL NOUN 2 **Draughts** is a game for two people, played on a chessboard with round pieces.

✔ In American English, the game of *draughts* is called *checkers*.

draughty ADJECTIVE

draw draws drawing drew drawn

VERB 1 When you **draw** something, you use a pen or pencil to make a picture of it.

2 If you **draw** the curtains, you pull them so that they cover or uncover the window.

NOUN 3 the result of a game or competition in which both sides have the same score, so nobody wins.

draw lots VERB 4 If you **draw lots**, you decide who will do something by a method that depends on chance, such as taking names out of a hat.

drawback drawbacks

NOUN a problem that upsets a plan. *One **drawback** of eating too much chocolate is that you feel sick.*

drawbridge drawbridges

NOUN a bridge that can be pulled up or lowered.

drawer drawers

NOUN part of a desk or other piece of furniture that is shaped like a box and slides in and out.

a
b
c
d
e
f
g
h
i
j
k
l
m
n
o
p
q
r
s
t
u
v
w
x
y
z

drawing drawings

NOUN a picture made with a pencil, pen or crayon.

drawing pin drawing pins

NOUN a short nail with a broad flat top. You pin papers to a board by pressing a **drawing pin** through them with your thumb.

dread dreads dreading dreaded

VERB If you **dread** something, you feel very worried and frightened about it.

dreadful

ADJECTIVE very bad or unpleasant. *The weather has been **dreadful** this week.*

Synonyms: atrocious, awful, terrible

dreadlocks

PLURAL NOUN a hairstyle where the hair is grown long and twisted into tightly curled strands.

dream dreams dreaming dreamed or **dreamt**

NOUN 1 a series of events that you experience in your mind while asleep.
2 a hope or ambition that you often think about because you would very much like it to happen.
VERB 3 When you **dream**, you see events in your mind while you are asleep.

dreary drearier dreariest

ADJECTIVE extremely dull and boring.

drenched

ADJECTIVE soaking wet.

dress dresses dressing dressed

NOUN 1 a piece of clothing worn by women and girls, made up of a top and skirt joined together.

2 **Dress** is used to describe clothing or costumes in general, such as national **dress** or fancy **dress**.
VERB 3 When you **dress**, you put on your clothes.
4 When you **dress** a wound, you clean it and treat it.
dress up VERB 5 When you **dress up**, you put on clothes that make you look like something else. *Let's **dress up** as witches for the party.*

dressing dressings

NOUN 1 a bandage or plaster to put on a wound.
2 a mixture of oils and spices that can be added to salads and other dishes to heighten the flavour.

dressing gown dressing gowns

NOUN a long, warm garment, usually worn over night clothes.

drew

VERB the past tense of *draw*.

dribble dribbles dribbling dribbled

VERB 1 If a person or animal **dribbles**, saliva trickles from their mouth.
2 In sport, when you **dribble** a ball, you move it along by repeatedly tapping it with your foot or a stick.

drift drifts drifting drifted

VERB 1 When something **drifts**, it is carried along by the wind or by water.
2 When people **drift**, they move aimlessly from one place or one activity to another.
NOUN 3 snow or sand piled up by the wind.
4 INFORMAL the general meaning of something.

drill drills drilling drilled

NOUN 1 a tool for making holes.
2 a routine exercise or routine training.
VERB 3 If you **drill** a hole, you make a hole using a drill.

drink drinks drinking drank drunk

VERB 1 When you **drink** a liquid, you take it into your mouth and swallow it.
NOUN 2 A **drink** is an amount of liquid for drinking.

drip drips dripping dripped

VERB 1 When liquid **drips**, it falls in small drops.
2 When an object **drips**, drops of liquid fall from it. *Stop that tap **dripping**.*
NOUN 3 a drop of liquid that is falling.

drive drives driving drove driven

VERB **1** When someone **drives** a vehicle, they operate it and control its movements.
2 If something **drives** a machine, it supplies the power that makes it work.
NOUN **3** a journey in a vehicle.
4 a private road that leads from a public road to a person's house.

drizzle

NOUN light rain.

drone drones droning droned

VERB **1** If something **drones**, it makes a low, continuous humming noise.
NOUN **2** a continuous, low, dull sound.
3 a male bee.

drool drools drooling drooled

VERB If someone **drools**, saliva drips from their mouth continuously.

droop droops drooping drooped

VERB If something **droops**, it hangs or sags downwards with no strength or firmness.

drop drops dropping dropped

VERB **1** If you **drop** something, you let it fall.
2 If something **drops**, it falls straight down.
3 If the level or the amount of something **drops**, it becomes less.
NOUN **4** a very small, round quantity of liquid.
5 the distance between the top and the bottom of something. *There was a fifty-metre **drop** to the river below.*

drought droughts

NOUN a long period during which there is no rain.

drove

VERB the past tense of *drive*.

drown drowns drowning drowned

VERB When someone **drowns**, or when they are **drowned**, they die because they have gone under water and cannot breathe.

drowsy drowsier drowsiest

ADJECTIVE feeling sleepy.

drug drugs

NOUN **1** a chemical used by the medical profession to treat people with illnesses or diseases.

2 a substance that some people smell, smoke, inject or swallow because of its stimulating or calming effects. **Drugs** can be harmful to health and may be illegal.

drum drums

NOUN **1** a musical instrument consisting of a skin stretched tightly over a round frame.
2 an object or container shaped like a **drum**: *an oil **drum**.*

drunk drunker drunkest

VERB **1** the past participle of *drink*.
ADJECTIVE **2** If someone is **drunk**, they have consumed too much alcohol.

dry drier or dryer driest; dries drying dried

ADJECTIVE **1** Something that is **dry** is not wet, and contains no water or liquid.
VERB **2** When you **dry** something, or when it **dries**, liquid is removed from it.

dual

ADJECTIVE having two parts, functions or aspects. *This is a **dual**-purpose room – it is both the office and the spare bedroom.*

dual carriageway dual carriageways

NOUN a road with several lanes in each direction.

dubious

ADJECTIVE **1** not entirely honest, safe or reliable.
2 doubtful. *I felt **dubious** about the idea.*
dubiously ADVERB

duchess duchesses

NOUN a woman who has the same rank as a duke, or who is a duke's wife or widow.

duck ducks ducking ducked

NOUN **1** a bird that lives in water and has webbed feet and a large flat bill.
VERB **2** If you **duck**, you move your head quickly downwards in order to avoid being hit by something.
3 If you **duck** someone, you push them under water for a very short time.

duckling ducklings

NOUN a young duck.

due

ADJECTIVE expected to happen or arrive. *The train is **due** at eight o'clock.*

duel duels
NOUN a fight arranged between two people.

duet duets
NOUN a piece of music sung or played by two people.

dug
VERB the past tense of *dig*.

duke dukes
NOUN a nobleman with a rank just below that of a prince.

dull duller dullest
ADJECTIVE **1** not interesting. *I thought the story was rather dull.*
2 not bright, sharp or clear: *a dull day.*

dumb dumber dumbest
ADJECTIVE **1** unable to speak. *She was so shocked that she was momentarily struck dumb.*
2 INFORMAL stupid.

dumbfounded
ADJECTIVE If you are **dumbfounded**, you are so shocked or surprised about something that you cannot speak.

dummy dummies
NOUN **1** a rubber or plastic teat given to a baby to suck to keep it happy.
2 an imitation or model of something that is used for display. *I first saw the jacket on a dummy in a shop window.*

dump dumps dumping dumped
VERB **1** If you **dump** something somewhere, you put it there in a careless way.
NOUN **2** a place where rubbish is left.
3 INFORMAL You refer to a place as a **dump** when it is unattractive and unpleasant to live in.

dune dunes
NOUN a hill of sand near the sea or in the desert.

dung
NOUN body waste excreted by large animals.

dungarees
PLURAL NOUN trousers that have a bib covering the chest and straps over the shoulders.
[named after *Dungri* in India, where dungaree material was first made]

dungeon dungeons
NOUN an underground prison.

dunk dunks dunking dunked
VERB If you **dunk** something, you dip it into water or some other liquid for a short time.

duo duos
NOUN any two people who do something together, especially a pair of musical performers.

duplicate duplicates duplicating duplicated
Said "**dyoo**-pli-kayt" VERB **1** If someone **duplicates** something, they make an exact copy of it
Said "**dyoo**-pli-kut" NOUN **2** something that is identical to something else, or an exact copy. **duplication** NOUN

durable
ADJECTIVE Things that are **durable** are very strong and last a long time.

duration
NOUN the length of time during which something happens or exists.

during
PREPOSITION happening throughout a particular time or while something else is going on. *We had an ice cream during the interval.*

dusk
NOUN the time just before nightfall when it is not completely dark.

dust dusts dusting dusted
NOUN **1** dry, fine, powdery material such as particles of earth, dirt or pollen.
VERB **2** When you **dust** furniture or other objects, you remove dust from them using a duster.
3 If you **dust** a surface with something powdery, you cover it lightly with that substance. *Dust the top of the cake with icing sugar.*

dustbin dustbins
NOUN a large container for rubbish.

duster dusters
NOUN a cloth for dusting things.

dustpan dustpans
NOUN a pan for collecting dust with a brush.

dusty dustier dustiest
ADJECTIVE covered with dust.

A B C D E F G H I J K L M N O P Q R S T U V W X Y Z

duty duties

NOUN **1** Your **duty** is what you should do because it is part of your job or because it is expected of you.

PHRASE **2** When workers are **on duty**, they are at work.

duvet duvets

NOUN a large bed cover filled with feathers or similar material, which you use instead of sheets and blankets.

dwarf dwarfs dwarfing dwarfed

NOUN **1** a person or thing that is smaller than average.

VERB **2** If one thing **dwarfs** another, it is so much bigger that it makes it look very small. *The mountains **dwarfed** the village.*

dwindle dwindles dwindling dwindled

VERB If something **dwindles**, it becomes smaller or weaker. *Their supplies of firewood **dwindled**. As it got later the light **dwindled**.*

dye dyes dyeing dyed

VERB **1** If you **dye** something, you change its colour by soaking it in a special liquid.

NOUN **2** a substance used to change the colour of something such as cloth or hair.

dying

VERB the present participle of *die*.

dyke dykes; also spelt **dike**

NOUN a thick wall that prevents a river or the sea from flooding the land.

A dyke in Holland

dynamic

ADJECTIVE A **dynamic** person is full of energy, ambition and new ideas.

dynamite

NOUN a powerful explosive.

dynamo dynamos

NOUN a device that uses movement to produce electricity. A **dynamo** can be used for lighting bicycle lamps.

dynasty dynasties

NOUN a series of rulers of a country, all belonging to the same family.

dyslexia

NOUN a certain type of difficulty with reading and writing.

dyslexic ADJECTIVE OR NOUN

a
b
c
d
e
f
g
h
i
j
k
l
m
n
o
p
q
r
s
t
u
v
w
x
y
z

Ee

each
ADJECTIVE OR PRONOUN every one of a group.

eager
ADJECTIVE If you are **eager**, you are keen to do something.
eagerly ADVERB

Synonym: enthusiastic

eagle eagles
NOUN a large bird of prey.

ear ears
NOUN Your **ears** are the parts of your body on either side of your head, with which you hear sounds.

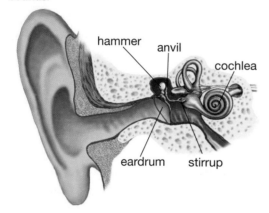

hammer
anvil
cochlea
eardrum
stirrup

earache
NOUN a pain in your ear.

early earlier earliest
ADJECTIVE OR ADVERB **1** before the arranged or expected time.
ADJECTIVE **2** near the beginning of something. *I like to go for a walk in the **early** morning.*

earn earns earning earned
VERB **1** If you **earn** money, you receive it in return for work that you do.
2 If you **earn** something such as praise, you receive it because you deserve it.

earnest
ADJECTIVE If you are **earnest** about something, you are very serious about it.
earnestly ADVERB

earnings
PLURAL NOUN the money or payment that you receive for working.

earring earrings
NOUN a piece of jewellery that you wear on your ear.

earth
NOUN **1** The **earth** is the planet we live on.
2 another word for soil.

earthquake earthquakes
NOUN a violent shaking of the ground caused by movement of the earth's crust.

earthworm earthworms
NOUN a worm that lives in the soil.

earwig earwigs
NOUN a small, brown insect with pincers at the tail end of its body.

ease eases easing eased
VERB **1** When something **eases**, it becomes less difficult or intense. *The rain **eased** as the dark clouds were blown away.*
NOUN **2** a lack of difficulty or trouble. *She finished her homework with **ease**.*
VERB **3** If you **ease** something, you move it gently and slowly. *He **eased** himself into the chair.*

easel easels
NOUN an upright frame that supports a picture that someone is painting.

easily
ADVERB If you do something **easily**, you do it without difficulty.

east
NOUN one of the four main points of the compass. The sun rises in the **east**, and the abbreviation is E.

Easter
NOUN a Christian religious festival celebrating Christ's return to life after his death.
[from Old English ***Eostre***, a goddess whose festival was at the spring equinox]

eastern
ADJECTIVE from or to do with the east, or in the east of a place.

easy easier easiest
ADJECTIVE If something is **easy**, you can do it without difficulty.

eat eats eating ate eaten
VERB When you **eat** food, you chew it and swallow it.

ebb ebbs ebbing ebbed
VERB When the sea or the tide **ebbs**, it goes out.

ebony
NOUN a hard, dark-coloured wood.

eccentric
ADJECTIVE Someone **eccentric** has habits or opinions that other people think are odd or peculiar.
eccentricity NOUN   **eccentrically** ADVERB

echo echoes echoing echoed
NOUN **1** the repeat of a sound caused by the sound being reflected off a surface.
VERB **2** When a sound **echoes**, it is reflected off a surface so that it can be heard again. *Their cries echoed back from the mountain.*

eclipse eclipses
NOUN An **eclipse** of the sun happens when the moon passes between the sun and the earth and part or all of the sun is hidden from view.

ecology
NOUN the relationship between living things and their environment, or the study of this relationship.
ecological ADJECTIVE   **ecologically** ADVERB
ecologist NOUN

economical
ADJECTIVE If you are **economical**, you are not wasteful with money or things.
economically ADVERB

economics
NOUN the system of organizing the money, production, and trade of a country, region or group.

economy economies
NOUN The **economy** of a country or region is the way in which the industries, banks and businesses are organized to make money.
economist NOUN

ecosystem ecosystems
NOUN the relationship between plants and animals and their environment.

eczema
NOUN a skin disease that makes the skin rough and itchy.

edge edges
NOUN the part along the side or end of something.

edible
ADJECTIVE Things that are **edible** are safe to eat.

edit edits editing edited
VERB **1** If you **edit** a piece of writing, you correct it.
2 If you **edit** a film or a television programme, you select different parts of it and arrange them in a particular order.

edition editions
NOUN An **edition** of a book or newspaper is one or all of the copies printed at one time.

editor editors
NOUN **1** someone who is responsible for the contents of a newspaper or magazine.
2 someone who edits a piece of writing, a film or a television programme.

editorial editorials
NOUN an article in a newspaper or magazine which expresses the opinion of the editor.

educate educates educating educated
VERB If you **educate** someone about something, you teach them so that they learn about it.

education
NOUN When you receive an **education**, you gain knowledge and understanding through learning.
educational ADJECTIVE   **educationally** ADVERB

eel eels
NOUN a long thin fish shaped like a snake.

eerie eerier eeriest
ADJECTIVE strange and frightening. *There was an eerie silence after the thunderstorm.*

effect effects
NOUN **1** something that happens as a result of something else. *The effects of global warming are now becoming clear.*
2 the impression something makes. *The effect of the moonlight in the mist was eerie.*

effective

ADJECTIVE If something is **effective**, it works well and gives the results that were intended.
effectively ADVERB

efficient

ADJECTIVE capable of doing something well, without wasting time or energy.
efficiently ADVERB   **efficiency** NOUN

effort efforts

NOUN the physical or mental energy needed to do something.

effortless

ADJECTIVE done easily and without much effort.
effortlessly ADVERB

eg or e.g.

Eg means "for example".

egg eggs

NOUN **1** a rounded object produced by female birds, reptiles, fish and insects. The young animal develops in the **egg** until it is ready to hatch.
2 a hen's **egg** used as food.

either

ADJECTIVE, PRONOUN OR CONJUNCTION **1** You use **either** to refer to each of two possible alternatives. *You can **either** come with me or stay here.*
ADJECTIVE **2** You use **either** to refer to both of two things. *There were fields on **either** side of the road.*

eject ejects ejecting ejected

VERB If you **eject** someone or something, you push or send them out of something with force. *They **ejected** the children from the cinema because they were making too much noise.*
ejection NOUN

elaborate

ADJECTIVE having many different parts, often very detailed or complicated.
elaborately ADVERB   **elaboration** NOUN

elastic

NOUN rubber material that stretches when you pull it, and returns to its original shape when you let it go.

elated

ADJECTIVE very happy or excited.

elbow elbows

NOUN the joint where your arm bends in the middle.

elder

ADJECTIVE Your **elder** brother or sister is older than you.

elderly

ADJECTIVE Someone who is **elderly** is old.

eldest

ADJECTIVE If you are the **eldest** in a family, you are the oldest.

elect elects electing elected

VERB If you **elect** someone, you choose them as your representative by voting for them.

election elections

NOUN When there is an **election**, people choose someone to represent them by voting for them.
[from Latin *eligere* meaning to select]

electric

ADJECTIVE powered or produced by electricity.
electrical ADJECTIVE

electrician electricians

NOUN a person whose job it is to install and repair electrical equipment.

electricity

NOUN a form of energy that provides power for heating, lighting and machines.
[from Greek *elektron* meaning amber. In early experiments, scientists rubbed amber in order to get an electrical charge]

electrocute electrocutes electrocuting electrocuted

VERB If someone **electrocutes** themselves, they accidentally kill themselves or injure themselves badly by touching a strong electric current.
electrocution NOUN

electronic

ADJECTIVE An **electronic** device contains transistors or silicon chips that control an electric current. *Computers and televisions are examples of **electronic** devices.*
electronically ADVERB

elegant

ADJECTIVE attractive and graceful.
elegantly ADVERB   **elegance** NOUN

element elements

NOUN **1** a part of something that combines with others to make a whole.
2 In chemistry, an **element** is a substance that is made up of only one atom.
3 The **elements** are the weather, especially when it is bad.

elephant elephants

NOUN a very large mammal with a long trunk, large ears, thick skin and ivory tusks.

elf elves

NOUN a small, mischievous creature in fairy stories.

eligible

ADJECTIVE If you are **eligible** for something, you are suitable or have the right qualifications. *You are eligible to enter the under-twelves competition.*
eligibility NOUN

eliminate eliminates eliminating eliminated

VERB If you **eliminate** something or someone, you get rid of them.

ellipse ellipses

NOUN a regular oval shape.

elm elms

NOUN a tall tree with broad leaves.

else

ADJECTIVE **1** besides or as well as. *What else do you see?*
PHRASE **2** Or else means otherwise. *You'd better hurry, or else you'll miss the bus.*

elsewhere

ADVERB If you do something **elsewhere**, you do it in another place.

e-mail e-mails; also spelt email

NOUN the short form for electronic mail. When you send an **e-mail** you send a message from one computer to another.

embankment embankments

NOUN a wide wall of earth that stops a river from overflowing, or that carries a road or railway over low ground.

embark embarks embarking embarked

VERB **1** When you **embark**, you go on to a ship at the start of your journey.
2 When you **embark** on a project, you start it.

embarrass embarrasses embarrassing embarrassed

VERB If you **embarrass** someone, you make them feel ashamed or awkward.
embarrassed ADJECTIVE
embarrassing ADJECTIVE
embarrassment NOUN

embassy embassies

NOUN the building in which an ambassador and his or her staff work.

emblem emblems

NOUN an object or a design representing an organization or a country.

embrace embraces embracing embraced

VERB If you **embrace** someone, you put your arms round them to show your affection for them.

embroider embroiders embroidering embroidered

VERB If you **embroider** fabric, you sew a decorative design on to it.
embroidery NOUN

embryo embryos

NOUN an unborn animal, such as a human being, in the very early stages of development.

emerald emeralds

NOUN **1** a bright-green precious stone.
NOUN OR ADJECTIVE **2** bright green.

emerge emerges emerging emerged

VERB If you **emerge** from somewhere, you come out from it.
emergence NOUN

emergency emergencies

NOUN an unexpected and serious situation that must be dealt with quickly.

emigrate emigrates emigrating emigrated

VERB If you **emigrate**, you leave your native country and go to live permanently in another one.
emigration NOUN

Antonym: immigrate

eminent

ADJECTIVE If someone is **eminent**, they are well known and respected for what they do.
eminently ADVERB

emit emits emitting emitted

VERB If something **emits** light, sound, heat or smell, it produces it or lets it out.
emission NOUN

emotion emotions

NOUN a strong feeling, such as love or fear.
emotional ADJECTIVE

emperor emperors

NOUN a male ruler of an empire.

emphasis emphases

NOUN the special importance or stress put on something. *When you read out the poem, you must put **emphasis** on the important words.*

emphasize emphasizes emphasizing emphasized; also spelt **emphasise**

VERB If you **emphasize** something, you make it look or sound more important than the things around it. *He **emphasized** the word by underlining it.*

empire empires

NOUN a group of countries controlled by one ruler. *The Roman **Empire** covered many lands.*
[from Latin ***imperium*** meaning rule]

employ employs employing employed

VERB If you **employ** someone, you pay them to work for you.

employee employees

NOUN someone who works for someone else.

employer employers

NOUN the person or company that someone works for.

employment

NOUN the state of having a paid job.

empty emptier emptiest; empties emptying emptied

ADJECTIVE **1** having nothing or nobody inside.
VERB **2** If you **empty** something, you remove the contents.
emptiness NOUN

emu emus

NOUN a large, Australian bird that can run fast but cannot fly.

enable enables enabling enabled

VERB If you **enable** something to happen, you make it possible. *The ramp **enables** people in wheelchairs to use the library.*

enchanted

ADJECTIVE If you are **enchanted** by something or someone, you are fascinated or charmed by them. *The audience were **enchanted** by her dancing.*

encircle encircles encircling encircled

VERB If you **encircle** someone or something, you surround them completely.

enclose encloses enclosing enclosed

VERB **1** If you **enclose** something with a letter, you put it in the same envelope.
2 If you **enclose** an object or area, you surround it with something solid. *They **enclosed** the garden with a strong fence.*
enclosed ADJECTIVE

encore encores

NOUN an extra item at the end of a performance, when the audience asks for more.
[from French ***encore*** meaning again]

encounter encounters encountering encountered

VERB **1** If you **encounter** someone or something, you meet them or are faced with them. *Did you **encounter** any problems?*
NOUN **2** a meeting, especially when it is difficult or unexpected.

encourage encourages encouraging encouraged

VERB If you **encourage** someone, you give them the confidence to do something.
encouraging ADJECTIVE
encouragement NOUN

encyclopedia encyclopedias; also spelt **encyclopaedia**

NOUN a book or set of books that gives information about a number of different subjects.

end ends ending ended

NOUN **1** The **end** of something is the furthest point of it.
2 The **end** of an event is the last part of it.
VERB **3** When something **ends** it finishes.

endanger endangers endangering endangered

VERB If someone **endangers** something, they cause it to be in a dangerous or harmful situation.
endangered ADJECTIVE

endeavour endeavours endeavouring endeavoured
VERB If you **endeavour** to do something, you try very hard to do it.

ending endings
NOUN The **ending** of something is when it finishes.

endless
ADJECTIVE Something that is **endless** has, or seems to have, no end. *His **endless** chatter was very boring.*
endlessly ADVERB

endure endures enduring endured
VERB **1** If you **endure** someone or something unpleasant, you put up with them.
2 If something **endures**, it continues or lasts.
enduring ADJECTIVE

enemy enemies
NOUN Your **enemy** is someone who is very much against you and may wish to harm you.

energetic
ADJECTIVE full of energy.

Synonyms: active, lively

energy energies
NOUN **1** the physical strength needed to do active things. *He is saving his **energy** for next week's race.*
2 the power that makes things move, light up, make a sound or get hotter: *electrical **energy**, nuclear **energy**.*

engage engages engaging engaged
VERB **1** If you **engage** in an activity, you take part in it.
2 If you **engage** someone to do something, you pay them to do it.

engaged
ADJECTIVE **1** If two people are **engaged**, they have agreed to marry each other.
2 If someone or something is **engaged**, they are busy. *Every time I tried to telephone you, your number was **engaged**.*

engine engines
NOUN **1** the part of a vehicle that produces the power to make it move.
2 the large vehicle that pulls a railway train.

engineer engineers
NOUN a person trained in designing and building machinery and electrical devices, or roads and bridges.

engineering
NOUN the job of designing and building machinery and electrical devices.

engrave engraves engraving engraved
VERB If you **engrave**, you cut letters or designs into a hard surface with a tool. *He **engraved** the stone with an unusual design.*
engraving NOUN

enjoy enjoys enjoying enjoyed
VERB **1** If you **enjoy** something, it gives you pleasure.
PHRASE **2** If you **enjoy yourself**, you are happy and have fun.
enjoyable ADJECTIVE   **enjoyment** NOUN

enlarge enlarges enlarging enlarged
VERB When you **enlarge** something, you make it bigger.
enlargement NOUN

enormous
ADJECTIVE very large in size or amount.

Synonyms: vast, huge, massive

enough
ADJECTIVE OR ADVERB as much or as many as is necessary. *Do you have **enough** money to buy that?*

enquire enquires enquiring enquired
VERB If you **enquire** about something or someone, you ask for information about them.

enrol enrols enrolling enrolled
VERB If you **enrol** for something, such as a course or a society, you register to join or become a member of it.

ensure ensures ensuring ensured
VERB If you **ensure** that something happens, you make certain that it happens. *I will **ensure** that I arrive on time.*

enter enters entering entered
VERB **1** To **enter** a place means to go into it.
2 If you **enter** a competition, you take part in it.
3 If you **enter** something in a diary or a list, you write it down.

A
B
C
D
E
F
G
H
I
J
K
L
M
N
O
P
Q
R
S
T
U
V
W
X
Y
Z

enterprise enterprises

NOUN **1** something new and exciting that you try to do.
2 a large business or company.
enterprising ADJECTIVE

entertain entertains entertaining entertained

VERB If you **entertain** someone, you do something to amuse them.

enthusiasm

NOUN If you show **enthusiasm** for something, you show much interest and excitement.

enthusiastic

ADJECTIVE If you are **enthusiastic** about something, you are very keen on it and talk or behave in an excited and eager way that shows how much you like it.
enthusiastically ADVERB

entire

ADJECTIVE all of something. *The entire class went on the trip.*

entirely

ADVERB wholly and completely. *My sister and I are entirely different.*

entrance entrances

NOUN the doorway or gate to a building or area.

entry entries

NOUN **1** the act of entering a place. *No entry after 11 p.m.*
2 something you write in order to take part in a competition. *Send your entry to the address below.*
3 something written in a diary or list: *the entry for March 23 in her diary.*

envelope envelopes

NOUN the paper cover in which you put a letter.

envious

ADJECTIVE If you are **envious**, you wish you could have what someone else has.
enviously ADVERB

environment environments

NOUN **1** Your **environment** is your surroundings, especially the conditions in which you live or work.

2 the natural world around us. *Many people are keen to preserve the environment.*
✔ There is an *n* before the *m* in *environment.*

envy envies envying envied

VERB If you **envy** someone, you wish that you had what they have.

epidemic epidemics

NOUN an outbreak of a disease that takes place in one area, spreading quickly and affecting many people.

epilepsy

NOUN a condition of the brain that causes fits and periods of unconsciousness.
epileptic NOUN OR ADJECTIVE

episode episodes

NOUN **1** one of the programmes in a serial on television or radio.
2 an event or period of time, especially one that is important or unusual.

epitaph epitaphs

NOUN words about a person who has died, usually found on their gravestone.

equal equals equalling equalled

ADJECTIVE **1** being the same in size, number or amount.
VERB **2** In maths, the symbol (=) stands for **equals**. The numbers before it equal the numbers after it. For example, $3 + 3 = 6$.

equally

ADVERB to the same extent or in the same amounts. *We shared the sweets equally between the three of us.*

equation equations

NOUN a mathematical number sentence stating that two amounts or values are the same: $3 + 6 = 9$ *is an equation because what is on the left equals what is on the right.*

equator

NOUN an imaginary line drawn round the middle of the earth, lying halfway between the north and south poles. *See* **tropic**.
equatorial ADJECTIVE

equilateral

ADJECTIVE An **equilateral** triangle has sides that are all the same length, and angles that are all the same size.

equinox equinoxes

NOUN one of the two days in the year when the day and night are of equal length. The spring **equinox** occurs in March and the autumn **equinox** in September.
[from Latin *aequinoctium* meaning equal night]

equip equips equipping equipped

VERB If you **equip** yourself, you collect together everything that you need to do a particular thing.

equipment

NOUN all the things that are needed or used for a particular job or activity: *camping equipment*.

sleeping bag

tent

torch

cooking equipment

equivalent equivalents

ADJECTIVE **1** equal in use, size, value or effect.
2 in maths, of equal value. Fractions can be **equivalent** if they are of equal value, for example $\frac{2}{4} = \frac{1}{2}$. Different forms can be **equivalent**, for example $0·5 = \frac{1}{2} = 50\%$.
NOUN **3** Something that has the same use, size, value or effect as something else. *One metre is the* **equivalent** *of 1·094 yards. An example of* **equivalent** *fractions is* $\frac{2}{4} = \frac{1}{2}$.

erase erases erasing erased

VERB If you **erase** writing, you rub it out.

erect erects erecting erected

VERB If you **erect** something, you put it up or construct it. *They* **erected** *the tent in the garden.*

errand errands

NOUN If you run an **errand** for someone, you go a short distance to do a job for them, such as taking a message or fetching something.

erratic

ADJECTIVE not following a regular pattern. *His attendance at school was* **erratic**.
erratically ADVERB

error errors

NOUN a mistake, or something that is wrong.

erupt erupts erupting erupted

VERB **1** When a volcano **erupts**, it throws out a lot of hot lava and ash.
2 When a situation **erupts**, it begins suddenly and violently. *A family row* **erupted**.

escalator escalators

NOUN a mechanical, moving staircase.

escape escapes escaping escaped

VERB **1** If you **escape** from someone or something, you succeed in getting away from them.
2 If you **escape** something unpleasant or difficult, you succeed in avoiding it. *She was lucky to* **escape** *serious injury.*
NOUN **3** If you make an **escape** from somewhere, you manage to get away.

escort escorts escorting escorted

NOUN **1** a person or vehicle that travels with another in order to protect or guide them.
VERB **2** If you **escort** someone, you go with them somewhere, especially in order to protect or guide them. *I will* **escort** *you round the new buildings.*

Eskimo Eskimos

NOUN a member of a group of people who live in North America, Greenland and eastern Siberia. Eskimos who come from North America and parts of Greenland are called Inuits.

especially

ADVERB You say **especially** to show that something applies more to one thing, person or situation than to others. *It is always cold at the top of the mountain,* **especially** *when the wind is blowing.*

espionage

NOUN the act of spying to get secret information, especially to find out military or political secrets.
[from French *espionner* meaning to spy]

a
b
c
d
e
f
g
h
i
j
k
l
m
n
o
p
q
r
s
t
u
v
w
x
y
z

essay essays

NOUN a short piece of writing on a particular subject, especially one written as an exercise by a student.

essential essentials

ADJECTIVE **1** Something that is **essential** is absolutely necessary.

NOUN **2** something that is very important or necessary.

establish establishes establishing **established**

VERB **1** If you **establish** something, you set it up and keep it going.

2 If you **establish** a fact, you confirm that it is definitely correct.

established ADJECTIVE   **establishment** NOUN

estate estates

NOUN **1** a large area of land in the country, owned by one person or organization.

2 an area of land that has been developed for housing or industry: *a housing estate*.

estate agent estate agents

NOUN a person who works for a company that sells houses and land.

estimate estimates estimating estimated

Said "**ess**-ti-mayt" VERB **1** If you **estimate** an amount or quantity, you calculate it approximately. *They estimated that the trip would take around three hours.*

Said "**ess**-ti-mut" NOUN **2** an approximate calculation of an amount or quantity. *The final cost was twice the original estimate.*

estuary estuaries

NOUN the wide part of a river near where it joins the sea, and where fresh water mixes with salt water.

etc.

a written abbreviation for *et cetera*.

et cetera

Et cetera means "and so on" or "and similar things".

[from Latin, meaning and others]

eternal

ADJECTIVE lasting forever, or seeming to last forever.

eternally ADVERB

Synonyms: endless, everlasting, perpetual

ethnic

ADJECTIVE connected with a particular racial group of people. *There were many different ethnic groups in the school.*

[from Greek *ethnos* meaning race]

ethnically ADVERB

EU

NOUN an abbreviation for *European Union*.

euthanasia

NOUN causing someone to die painlessly and gently, so that they do not suffer during an incurable illness.

[from Greek *eu* meaning well and *thanatos* meaning death]

evacuate evacuates evacuating evacuated

VERB If people **evacuate**, or are **evacuated**, they move from somewhere dangerous to a place of safety. *The police evacuated shoppers from a store after a bomb scare.*

evacuee NOUN

evaluate evaluates evaluating evaluated

VERB If you **evaluate** something, you assess its quality or value.

evaluation NOUN

evaporate evaporates evaporating **evaporated**

VERB When a liquid **evaporates**, it gradually changes from a liquid into a gas or vapour.

evaporation NOUN

[from Latin *vapor* meaning steam]

even

ADJECTIVE **1** An **even** number is one that can be divided into two equal halves, such as two, four and six.

2 An **even** surface is level, smooth and flat.

3 An **even** measurement or rate stays at about the same level. *Keep the cooker at an even temperature.*

ADVERB **4 Even** is used to say that something is greater in degree than something else. *He was speaking even more slowly than usual.*

PHRASE **5 Even if** or **even though** are used to introduce something that is surprising in relation to the rest of the sentence. *She did not say anything, even though she had been left out again.*

Antonym: (sense 1) odd

evening evenings

NOUN the part of the day between the end of the afternoon and the time you go to bed.

event events

NOUN **1** something that happens, especially when it is unusual or important.
2 an organized activity, such as a sports match or a concert.

Synonyms: (sense 1) happening, incident, occurrence

eventually

ADVERB in the end. *It was a long way, but we got there* ***eventually***.

ever

ADVERB at any time in the past or future. *That's the biggest dog I've* ***ever*** *seen.*

evergreen evergreens

NOUN An **evergreen** is a plant that does not lose its leaves in the winter.

every

ADJECTIVE **1 Every** is used to refer to all the members of a group or all the parts of something. *Every shop in the town was closed.*
2 Every is also used to indicate that something happens at regular intervals. *The clock strikes* ***every*** *hour.*
PHRASE **3** If something happens **every other** day or week, it happens on alternate days or weeks. *Practice sessions are held* ***every other*** *week.*

everybody

PRONOUN every person.

everyone

PRONOUN all the people in a group.

everything

PRONOUN all or the whole of something.

everywhere

ADVERB in many or most places.

evict evicts evicting evicted

VERB To **evict** someone means to officially force them to leave a place they are occupying.
eviction NOUN

evidence

NOUN **1** anything that causes you to believe that something is true or exists.
2 the information used in a court of law to try to prove something.

evident

ADJECTIVE If something is **evident**, it is clear and obvious.
evidently ADVERB

evil evils

NOUN **1 Evil** is used to refer to all the wicked or bad things that happen in the world.
ADJECTIVE **2** Someone or something **evil** is very bad and causes harm to people.

evolution

NOUN a process that takes place over many generations. During this time, living things slowly change as they adapt to different environments.
evolutionary ADJECTIVE

evolve evolves evolving evolved

VERB When living things **evolve**, they gradually change and develop into different forms. *Many people believe that man* ***evolved*** *from apes.*

ewe ewes

NOUN a female sheep.

ex-

PREFIX former: *the* ***ex****-prime minister.*

exact

ADJECTIVE If something is **exact**, it is accurately measured or made.
exactly ADJECTIVE

exaggerate exaggerates exaggerating exaggerated

VERB If you **exaggerate**, you make something seem better, worse, bigger or more important than it really is.
exaggeration NOUN

examination examinations

NOUN **1** If you take an **examination**, you take a test to find out how much you know about a subject.
2 If someone makes an **examination** of something, they look at it very carefully.

examine examines examining examined
VERB **1** If you **examine** something, you inspect it carefully.
2 If a doctor **examines** you, he or she checks your body to find out how healthy you are.
examiner NOUN

example examples
NOUN **1** something that is typical of a particular group of things.
2 Someone who is an **example** to others is worth imitating.
PHRASE **3** You use **for example** to give an example of something you are talking about: *large mammals*, **for example** *whales*.
[from Latin **exemplum** meaning pattern]

Synonyms: (sense 1) sample, specimen

exasperate exasperates exasperating exasperated
VERB If someone or something **exasperates** you, they annoy and frustrate you.
exasperating ADJECTIVE   **exasperation** NOUN

excavate excavates excavating excavated
VERB When someone **excavates**, they remove earth from the ground by digging. When archaeologists **excavate** objects, they carefully uncover remains in the ground to discover information about the past. *They found some interesting Roman artefacts while they were excavating.*
excavation NOUN   **excavator** NOUN

exceed exceeds exceeding exceeded
VERB If something **exceeds** a particular amount, it is greater than that amount.

excel excels excelling excelled
VERB If someone **excels** in something, they are very good at doing it.

excellent
ADJECTIVE very good indeed.
excellence NOUN

Synonyms: first-rate, outstanding, superb

except
PREPOSITION apart from or not including someone or something. *Everyone laughed except Ben.*

exception exceptions
NOUN somebody or something that is not included in a general rule. *All my family are musicians, with the exception of my father.*

exceptional
ADJECTIVE If someone or something is **exceptional**, they are unusual or remarkable in some way. For example, they may be very clever or have special talents.
exceptionally ADVERB

excerpt excerpts
NOUN a short piece of writing, music or film that is taken from a longer piece.

excess excesses
NOUN too much of something.

excessive
ADJECTIVE more than is needed or allowed.
excessively ADVERB

exchange exchanges exchanging exchanged
VERB If you **exchange** something for something else, you replace it with something. *I took the shoes back to the shop and exchanged them for another pair.*

excite excites exciting excited
VERB If something **excites** you, it makes you feel very happy and enthusiastic.
excited ADJECTIVE   **excitedly** ADVERB
exciting ADJECTIVE   **excitement** NOUN

exclaim exclaims exclaiming exclaimed
VERB When you **exclaim**, you cry out suddenly or loudly because you are excited or shocked.
exclamation NOUN

exclamation mark exclamation marks
NOUN a punctuation mark (!) used in writing to show a strong feeling.

exclude excludes excluding excluded
VERB If you **exclude** someone from a place or activity, you prevent them from entering or taking part.
exclusion NOUN

Antonym: include

exclusive
ADJECTIVE 1 available to a small group of rich or privileged people.
2 belonging to a particular person or group only. *Our group will have **exclusive** use of the pool.*
exclusively ADVERB

excrete excretes excreting excreted
VERB If you **excrete** waste matter from your body, you pass it out by sweating or going to the toilet.
excretion NOUN

excruciating
ADJECTIVE extremely painful.
excruciatingly ADVERB

excursion excursions
NOUN a short journey or outing.

excuse excuses excusing excused
Said "ex-**kyooss**" NOUN 1 a reason you give to explain why something has been done, has not been done, or will not be done.
Said "ex-**kyooz**" VERB 2 If you **excuse** someone's behaviour, you give reasons for why they behaved in that way.
PHRASE 3 You say **excuse me** to try to catch somebody's attention or to apologize for an interruption.

execute executes executing executed
VERB To **execute** somebody means to kill them as a punishment for a crime.
execution NOUN

executive executives
NOUN a person who works at a senior level in a company.

exercise exercises exercising exercised
NOUN 1 any activity that you do in order to get fit or stay healthy.
2 a piece of work that you do for practice.
VERB 3 When you **exercise**, you do activities that help you to get fit and stay healthy.

exert exerts exerting exerted
VERB If you **exert** yourself, you make a great deal of effort to do something.

exhale exhales exhaling exhaled
VERB When you **exhale**, you breathe out.

Antonym: inhale

exhaust exhausts exhausting exhausted
VERB 1 If something **exhausts** you, it makes you very tired.
NOUN 2 the pipe that carries the gas or steam out of the engine of a vehicle.
exhaustion NOUN

exhausted
ADJECTIVE If you are **exhausted**, you are very tired.

exhibit exhibits exhibiting exhibited
VERB 1 If someone **exhibits** something, they put it on show for others to see, especially in a gallery or museum.
NOUN 2 something that is put on show for others to see, especially in a gallery or museum.

exhibition exhibitions
NOUN a public display of works of art, products or skills.

exile exiles exiling exiled
NOUN 1 a person who is not allowed to live in their own country.
VERB 2 If someone is **exiled**, they are sent away from their own country, usually as a punishment.

exist exists existing existed
VERB If something **exists**, it is in the world as a real thing.
existence NOUN

exit exits exiting exited
NOUN 1 a doorway through which you can leave a public place.
2 If you make an **exit**, you leave a place.
VERB 3 If you **exit** a place, you leave it.

Antonym: (senses 1 and 2) entrance

a
b
c
d
e
f
g
h
i
j
k
l
m
n
o
p
q
r
s
t
u
v
w
x
y
z

exotic

ADJECTIVE something unusual and interesting, usually because it comes from another country.

expand expands expanding expanded

VERB If something **expands**, or if you **expand** it, it becomes larger.

expansion NOUN

expanse expanses

NOUN a large area of something such as the sky or land.

expect expects expecting expected

VERB **1** If you **expect** something to happen, you believe that it will happen.

2 If you are **expecting** someone, you are waiting for them to arrive.

3 If you **expect** something, you believe that you ought to get it or have it. *I'm expecting you to help me.*

expectation NOUN

expedition expeditions

NOUN **1** an organized journey made for a special purpose, often to explore.

2 the party of people who go on an expedition. *The expedition set out through the rainforest.*

expel expels expelling expelled

VERB **1** If someone **expels** a person from a school or club, they tell them officially to leave because they have behaved badly.

2 If a gas or liquid is **expelled** from a place, it is forced out of it.

expulsion NOUN

expense expenses

NOUN the amount of money it costs to do something or buy something. *They could not afford the expense of the school trip.*

expensive

ADJECTIVE If something is **expensive** it costs a lot of money.

expensively ADVERB

experience experiences experiencing experienced

NOUN **1** all the things that you have done or that have happened to you.

2 something that you do or something that happens to you, especially something new or unusual.

VERB **3** If you **experience** something, it happens to you or you are affected by it. *We had never experienced this kind of holiday before.*

experiment experiments experimenting experimented

NOUN **1** a scientific test that aims to prove or discover something.

VERB **2** If you **experiment** with something or on something, you do a scientific test to prove or discover something about it.

experimentation NOUN
experimental ADJECTIVE
experimentally ADVERB

expert experts

NOUN a person who is very skilled at something or who knows a lot about a particular subject.

expertly ADVERB

Synonyms: authority, specialist

expire expires expiring expired

VERB **1** If something **expires**, it comes to an end and you can no longer use it.

2 If a person or animal **expires**, they die.

explain explains explaining explained

VERB If you **explain** something, you give information about it or reasons for it so that it can be understood.

explanatory ADJECTIVE

Synonyms: clarify, make clear

explanation explanations

NOUN An **explanation** explains something.

explode explodes exploding exploded

VERB If something such as a bomb **explodes**, it bursts with great force.

explosion NOUN   **explosive** ADJECTIVE

exploit exploits exploiting exploited

VERB **1** If somebody **exploits** a person or a situation, they take advantage of it for their own ends.

NOUN **2** something daring or interesting that somebody has done.

explore explores exploring explored

VERB If you **explore** a place, you travel around it to discover what it is like.

exploration NOUN   **exploratory** ADJECTIVE
explorer NOUN

A B C D E F G H I J K L M N O P Q R S T U V W X Y Z

explosive explosives

ADJECTIVE **1** If something is **explosive**, it is likely to explode.

NOUN **2** something that can cause an explosion.

export exports exporting exported

VERB **1** If someone **exports** goods, they sell them to another country.

NOUN **2** **Exports** are goods that are sold to another country.

expose exposes exposing exposed

VERB **1** If you **expose** something, you uncover it so that it can be seen.

2 If a person is **exposed** to something dangerous, they are put in a situation that might harm them. *The patients were isolated so that no one else would be* **exposed** *to the disease.*

exposure exposures

NOUN **1** the harmful effect of the weather on the body if a person is outside too long without any protection.

2 a single photograph on a film.

express expresses expressing expressed

VERB **1** When you **express** an idea or feeling, you show what you think or feel by saying or doing something. *She* **expressed** *her gratitude by giving me a hug.*

ADJECTIVE **2** very fast: *an* **express** *train.*

expression expressions

NOUN **1** Your **expression** is the look on your face that shows what you are thinking or feeling.

2 The **expression** of ideas or feelings is the act of showing them through words, actions or art.

3 An **expression** is a phrase with a special meaning, such as "nosy parker".

expressive ADJECTIVE

exquisite

ADJECTIVE Something that is **exquisite** is extremely beautiful and pleasing.

extend extends extending extended

VERB If you **extend** something, you make it longer or bigger.

extension extensions

NOUN **1** a room or building that is added on to an existing building.

2 an additional telephone connected to the same line as another telephone.

extensive

ADJECTIVE **1** covering a large area. *The gardens are* **extensive**.

2 very great in effect. *After the storm the house required* **extensive** *repairs.*

extensively ADVERB

extent extents

NOUN The **extent** of something is its length or the area it covers.

exterior exteriors

NOUN the outside of something.

exterminate exterminates exterminating exterminated

VERB To **exterminate** people or animals means to kill them deliberately.

extermination NOUN

external

ADJECTIVE existing or happening on the outside of something. *The* **external** *walls of the house need painting.*

extinct

ADJECTIVE **1** An **extinct** species of animal or plant is no longer in existence.

2 An **extinct** volcano is no longer likely to erupt.

extinction NOUN

extinguish extinguishes extinguishing extinguished

VERB If you **extinguish** a light or fire, you put it out.

extra

ADJECTIVE OR ADVERB more than is usual, necessary or expected.

Synonyms: added, additional, further

extract extracts extracting extracted

Said "ex-**trakt**" VERB **1** If you **extract** something from a place you get it out, often by force. *The dentist had to* **extract** *my loose tooth.*

Said "ex-**trakt**" NOUN **2** a small section taken from a book or a piece of music.

extraordinary

ADJECTIVE very unusual or surprising.

extraordinarily ADVERB

Synonyms: exceptional, remarkable

a
b
c
d
e
f
g
h
i
j
k
l
m
n
o
p
q
r
s
t
u
v
w
x
y
z

extraterrestrial

ADJECTIVE something that happens or exists beyond the earth's atmosphere.

extravagant

ADJECTIVE spending or costing more money than is reasonable or affordable.
extravagantly ADVERB   **extravagance** NOUN

extreme extremes

ADJECTIVE **1** very great in degree or intensity: *extreme cold.*
NOUN **2** the furthest point or edge of something. **3** the highest or furthest degree of something. *You experience **extremes** of temperature in the desert, where it is very cold at night and very hot during the day.*
extremely ADVERB

eye eyes eyeing or eying eyed

NOUN **1** the parts of your body with which you see.
VERB **2** To **eye** something means to look at it. *They **eyed** each other's new shoes with interest.*

eyebrow eyebrows

NOUN Your **eyebrows** are the lines of hair that grow on the ridges of bone above your eyes. *She raised her **eyebrows** in surprise when she saw her dad's new hat.*

eyelash eyelashes

NOUN Your **eyelashes** are the hairs that grow on the edges of your eyelids.

eyelid eyelids

NOUN Your **eyelids** are the folds of skin that cover your eyes when they are closed. *I was so tired that my **eyelids** started to droop.*

eyesight

NOUN the ability to see. *His **eyesight** is not very good, so he wears glasses.*

eyewitness eyewitnesses

NOUN someone who has seen something happen and can describe it, especially an accident or a crime. *The police appealed for any **eyewitnesses** to the crash to come forward.*

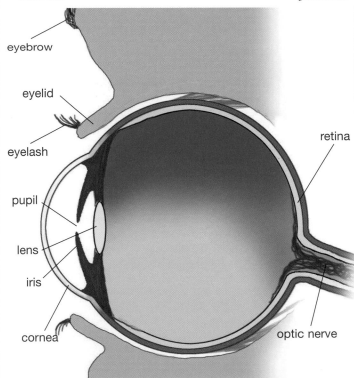

eyebrow

eyelid

eyelash

pupil

lens

iris

cornea

retina

optic nerve

The **pupil** is a hole that changes size to control the amount of light that enters the eye. When it is light the pupil is small and when it is dark the pupil is large.

The **iris** is the coloured part of the eye.

The **cornea** is a clear, tough covering over the iris and pupil that helps protect the eye and begins focusing the light.

The **lens** bends the rays of light coming into the eye so that they fall on the back of the eye.

The back of the eye is called the **retina**, and this is where the light rays are focused.

The **optic nerve** connects the retina to the brain.

A B C D E F G H I J K L M N O P Q R S T U V W X Y Z

Ff

fable fables
NOUN a story intended to teach a moral lesson: *the fable of the tortoise and the hare.*

fabric fabrics
NOUN cloth. *Silk is a delicate fabric.*

fabulous
ADJECTIVE **1** wonderful or very impressive.
2 Fabulous creatures are only found in legends or fairytales.

face faces facing faced
NOUN **1** the front part of your head, from your chin to your forehead.
2 a surface or side of something. *We could see the north face of the mountain.*
VERB **3** If you **face** something or someone, you are opposite them and look in their direction.
4 If you **face** in a certain direction, you look there.

facility facilities
NOUN a piece of equipment or a service that is provided for a particular purpose. *The school has excellent sports facilities.*

fact facts
NOUN **1** a piece of information that is true, or something that has actually happened.
PHRASE **2 In fact** and **as a matter of fact** mean "actually" or "really" and are used for emphasis. *As a matter of fact, I do like the idea.*
factual ADJECTIVE   **factually** ADVERB

factor factors
NOUN **1** something that affects an event or situation. *One of the main factors in our success was our strong team.*
2 The **factors** of a number are the whole numbers that will divide exactly into it. *Two and five are factors of 10: $2 \times 5 = 10$, $10 \div 5 = 2$, $10 \div 2 = 5$.*

Synonyms: (sense 1) element, part

---

factory factories
NOUN a building or group of buildings where goods are made in large quantities.

factual
ADJECTIVE If something is **factual**, it has actually happened.
factually ADVERB

fade fades fading faded
VERB When something **fades**, it slowly becomes less bright or less loud. *The colour has faded from my favourite T-shirt.*

Fahrenheit
Said "fa-ren-hite" NOUN the temperature scale that has the freezing point for water at 32 °F and the boiling point at 212 °F. *See* **Celsius**.

fail fails failing failed
VERB **1** If you **fail** to do something, you do not succeed in doing it.
2 If you **fail** an exam, your marks are too low and you do not pass.
3 If someone or something **fails** to do something that they should have done, they do not do it. *The bomb failed to explode.*
PHRASE **4 Without fail** means definitely or regularly. *He plays football every Sunday without fail.*

Antonym: (sense 1) succeed

---

failure failures
NOUN **1** a lack of success in doing something. *Her attempt to win the race ended in failure.*
2 an unsuccessful person, thing or action.

faint fainter faintest; faints fainting fainted
ADJECTIVE **1** A sound, colour or feeling that is **faint** is not strong or intense. *Their voices grew fainter as they moved away.*
2 If you feel **faint**, you feel dizzy and unsteady. *I was feeling faint, so I sat down.*
VERB **3** If you **faint**, you lose consciousness for a short time.
faintly ADVERB

fair fairer fairest; fairs
ADJECTIVE **1** Something that is **fair** seems reasonable to most people.
2 If the weather is **fair** it is fine.
3 quite good or moderate. *I think I have a fair chance of passing my exams.*
4 People who are **fair** have light-coloured hair.
NOUN **5** a form of entertainment that takes place outside, with stalls, games and rides.
fairly ADVERB   **fairness** NOUN

fairground fairgrounds

NOUN an open piece of ground where fairs are held.

fairly

ADVERB quite or rather. *My room's **fairly** small.*

fairy fairies

NOUN In stories, **fairies** are small, supernatural creatures with magical powers.

fairy tale fairy tales

NOUN a story of magical events.

faith faiths

NOUN **1** If you have **faith** in someone, you trust them.
2 a religious belief.

faithful

ADJECTIVE If you are **faithful** to someone or something, you are loyal and continue to support them. *He is one of my most **faithful** friends.*
faithfully ADVERB

fake fakes faking faked

NOUN **1** an imitation of something, made to trick people into thinking that it is genuine.
ADJECTIVE **2** imitation and not genuine. *The coat was made of **fake** fur.*
VERB **3** If you **fake** a feeling, you pretend that you are experiencing it. *I **faked** illness to avoid the games lesson.*

fall falls falling fell fallen

VERB **1** If someone or something **falls**, or **falls** over, or **falls** down, they drop towards the ground. *The snow **fell** all day, covering the fields and trees.*
2 becoming lower or less. *The temperature usually **falls** at night.*
3 If you **fall ill**, you become ill.
4 If you **fall asleep**, you begin to sleep.
5 If you **fall in love**, you begin to love someone.
6 If you **fall out** with someone, you disagree and quarrel with them.
NOUN **7** If you have a **fall**, you fall over.
✔ In American English, *fall* is autumn.

false

ADJECTIVE **1** untrue or incorrect.
2 not real or genuine, but intended to seem real. *Grandad has **false** teeth.*
falsely ADVERB

fame

NOUN the state of being very well known.

familiar

ADJECTIVE **1** well-known or easy to recognize. *The room was full of **familiar** faces.*
2 If you are **familiar with** something, you know it or understand it well. *He was very **familiar with** the local area.*

Antonym: unfamiliar

family families

NOUN a group of people who are related to each other, especially parents and their children.

family tree family trees

NOUN a diagram that shows how different members of a family are related to each other.

famine famines

NOUN a serious shortage of food that may cause many deaths.
[from Latin ***fames*** meaning hunger]

famished

ADJECTIVE very hungry.

famous

ADJECTIVE very well-known.
famously ADVERB

fan fans fanning fanned

NOUN **1** If you are a **fan** of something or someone famous, you like them very much.
2 a hand-held or mechanical device that moves air to make it cooler.
VERB **3** If you **fan** yourself, you cool the air around you with a fan.

fancy fancies fancying fancied; fancier fanciest

VERB If you **fancy** something, you want to have it.
ADJECTIVE highly decorated and special.

fancy dress

NOUN clothing worn for a party at which people dress up to look like a particular character or animal.

fanfare fanfares

NOUN a short, loud piece of music often played by trumpets on a special occasion.

fang fangs

NOUN a long, sharp tooth.

fantastic

ADJECTIVE **1** wonderful and very pleasing.
2 strange or unusual, like a fantasy.
fantastically ADVERB
[from Greek *phantasia* meaning imagination]

Synonym: (sense 1) marvellous

fantasy fantasies

NOUN an imaginative story that is unlikely to happen in real life.

far farther or further farthest or furthest

ADVERB **1** a long distance away.
ADJECTIVE **2** You can use **far** to ask questions about distance. *How far is the nearest supermarket?*
✔ When you are talking about a physical distance you can use *farther* and *farthest* or *further* and *furthest*. If you are talking about extra effort or time, you should use *further* and *furthest*, e.g. *further* delays are expected because of snow.

Antonyms: near, close

fare fares

NOUN the amount that you pay to travel on a bus, train or plane.

farewell

INTERJECTION goodbye.

far-fetched

ADJECTIVE unlikely to be true.

farm farms farming farmed

NOUN **1** an area of land and buildings, used for growing crops or raising animals.
VERB **2** If someone **farms** land, they plant crops or keep animals there.
farming NOUN

farmer farmers

NOUN someone who looks after a farm.

fascinate fascinates fascinating fascinated

VERB If something **fascinates** you, it interests and attracts you.
fascinating ADJECTIVE

fashion fashions

NOUN a style of dress or way of behaving that is popular at a particular time.
fashionable ADJECTIVE   **fashionably** ADVERB

fast faster fastest; fasts fasting fasted

ADJECTIVE OR ADVERB **1** If something is **fast**, or is happening **fast**, it is happening quickly or with great speed. *Our car is very fast*.
2 If a clock is **fast**, it shows a time that is ahead of the real time.
PHRASE **3** If you are **fast asleep**, you are in a deep sleep.
VERB **4** If you **fast**, you eat no food for a period of time, usually for religious reasons.

fasten fastens fastening fastened

VERB If you **fasten** something, you close it or attach it firmly to something else.
fastener NOUN   **fastening** NOUN

fat fatter fattest

ADJECTIVE **1** having a lot of flesh on the body.
NOUN **2** the greasy, white substance that animals and humans have under their skin. It is used to store energy and helps to keep them warm.
3 the greasy or oily substance from animals and plants that is used in cooking.

fatal

ADJECTIVE A **fatal** accident or illness causes someone's death.
fatally ADVERB

fate fates

NOUN **1** a power that some people believe controls events.
2 Someone's **fate** is what becomes of them.

father fathers

NOUN a male parent.

father-in-law fathers-in-law

NOUN the father of someone's husband or wife.

fatigue

NOUN extreme tiredness.

fault faults faulting faulted

NOUN **1** a mistake or something wrong with the way something is made.
2 If something bad is your **fault**, you are to blame for it.
VERB **3** If you **fault** someone or something, you find something wrong with them. *You can't fault his piano playing.*
faultless ADJECTIVE

faulty

ADJECTIVE If something is **faulty**, there is something wrong with it.

a
b
c
d
e
f
g
h
i
j
k
l
m
n
o
p
q
r
s
t
u
v
w
x
y
z

favour favours favouring favoured

NOUN **1** If you do someone a **favour**, you do something to help them.
VERB **2** If you **favour** someone or something, you prefer them to others.

favourite favourites

ADJECTIVE **1** Your **favourite** person or thing is the one you like best. *Peaches are my favourite fruit.*
NOUN **2** Someone's **favourite** is the person or thing they like best. *I like all sports, but soccer is my favourite.*

fawn fawns

NOUN **1** a young deer.
NOUN OR ADJECTIVE **2** a light-brown colour.

fax faxes faxing faxed

NOUN **1** a machine that sends and receives documents electronically along a telephone line.
2 a document sent in this way.
VERB **3** If you **fax** a document, you send it electronically along a telephone line.

fear fears fearing feared

NOUN **1** the feeling of worry you have when you think that you are in danger or that something bad might happen.
VERB **2** If you **fear** someone or something, you are afraid of them.

fearful

ADJECTIVE If you are **fearful** of someone or something, you are afraid of them.
fearfully ADVERB

fearless

ADJECTIVE If you are **fearless**, you are brave and have no fear.
fearlessly ADVERB

fearsome

ADJECTIVE frightening or terrible.

feast feasts

NOUN a large and special meal for many people.

feat feats

NOUN a difficult and impressive achievement.

feather feathers

NOUN A bird's **feathers** are the light, soft growths covering its body.

feature features

NOUN **1** a particular part or characteristic of something that is interesting or important.
PLURAL NOUN **2** Your **features** are your eyes, nose, mouth and other parts of your face. *Your features are similar to your mother's.*

February

NOUN the second month of the year. **February** usually has 28 days, but has 29 days in a leap year.

fed

VERB the past participle of *feed*.

fed up

ADJECTIVE; INFORMAL unhappy or bored. *I'm fed up with this rainy weather.*

fee fees

NOUN a charge or payment for a job, service or activity.

feeble feebler feeblest

ADJECTIVE weak, with no strength or power.

feed feeds feeding fed

VERB **1** If you **feed** a person or animal, you give them food. *She feeds the pigeons every day.*
2 When an animal or baby **feeds**, it eats. *These insects feed on wood.*
3 If you **feed** something into a machine, you put it in there. *They fed the information into a computer.*

feel feels feeling felt

VERB **1** If you **feel** an emotion or sensation, you experience it. *I felt very happy on my birthday.*
2 If you **feel** something, you touch it. *The doctor felt my forehead.*
PHRASE **3** If you **feel like** doing something, you want to do it.

feeler feelers

NOUN long, thin antennae on the heads of some insects, used to sense things around them.

feeling feelings

NOUN **1** an emotion. *Finishing my homework gave me a feeling of satisfaction.*
2 a physical sensation. *I had a feeling of pins and needles in my foot.*
3 Your **feelings** about something are your general attitudes or thoughts about it.

feet
NOUN the plural of *foot*.

feline
ADJECTIVE relating to the cat family, or cat like. *The dancer moved with **feline** grace.*

felt
VERB **1** past tense and past participle of *feel*.
NOUN **2** a thick cloth made by pressing short threads together.

female females
NOUN **1** a person or animal that belongs to the sex that can have babies or young.
ADJECTIVE **2** concerning or relating to females. [from Latin *femina* meaning woman]

feminine
ADJECTIVE relating to women or considered to be typical of women.

fen fens
NOUN a low, flat area of ground that is very wet.

fence fences
NOUN a wooden or wire barrier between two areas of land.

ferment ferments fermenting fermented
VERB When beer, wine or fruit **ferments**, a chemical change takes place and alcohol is often produced.

fern ferns
NOUN a plant with long, feathery leaves and no flowers.

bracken

wall rue

ferocious
ADJECTIVE violent and fierce.
ferociously ADVERB **ferocity** NOUN

ferret ferrets
NOUN a small mammal that can be trained to hunt rabbits or rats.

ferry ferries ferrying ferried
NOUN **1** a boat that carries people and vehicles across short stretches of water. *We took the **ferry** across to France.*
VERB **2** If someone **ferries** people or goods somewhere, they transport them there, usually on a short, regular journey. *A fleet of buses **ferried** people to the concert.*

fertile
ADJECTIVE **1** If soil is **fertile** it can produce strong, healthy plants.
2 If a human or other animal is **fertile**, they are able to have babies or young.
fertility NOUN

fertilize fertilizes fertilizing fertilized; also spelt **fertilise**
VERB **1** When an egg is **fertilized**, the process of reproduction has begun. *Pollen **fertilizes** the female part of a plant.*
2 When you **fertilize** land, you put manure or chemicals on to it to help the growth of plants.
fertilizer or **fertiliser** NOUN

festival festivals
NOUN **1** an organized series of events and performances. *The film **festival** at Cannes in France is very famous.*
2 a time when something special is celebrated. *Harvest **festival** is in the autumn.*

fetch fetches fetching fetched
VERB If you **fetch** something, you go to where it is and bring it back. *She **fetched** a towel from the bathroom.*

fête fêtes; also spelt **fete**
Said "fayt" NOUN an outdoor event with games, displays and goods for sale. *The school **fête** was a big success.*
[from the French *feste* meaning feast]
✔ Another word that sounds like *fête* is fate.

feud feuds feuding feuded
Said "fyood" NOUN **1** a long-running and bitter quarrel, especially between families.
VERB **2** When people **feud**, they quarrel over a long period of time.

fever fevers

NOUN If you have a **fever**, your temperature is higher than usual because you are ill.

feverish

ADJECTIVE If you are **feverish**, you have a higher body temperature than usual.

feverishly ADVERB

few fewer fewest

ADJECTIVE OR NOUN not many or a small number of things or people. *I saw him a **few** moments ago.*

✔ You use *fewer* to talk about things that can be counted. When you are talking about amounts that can't be counted you should use *less*.

fiancé fiancés

Said "fee-**on**-say" NOUN A woman's **fiancé** is the man to whom she is engaged to be married. [from Old French *fiancer* meaning to promise or betroth]

fiancée fiancées

Said "fee-**on**-say" NOUN A man's **fiancée** is the woman to whom he is engaged to be married. [from Old French *fiancer* meaning to promise or betroth]

fiasco fiascos

Said "fee-**ass**-koh" NOUN When something is a **fiasco**, it fails completely, especially in a ridiculous or disorganized way.

fib fibs fibbing fibbed

VERB If you **fib** about something, you tell a small lie about it.

fibre fibres

NOUN **1** a thin thread of a substance used to make cloth. *Many fabrics today are made from artificial **fibres**.*
2 a part of plants that can be eaten but not digested by your body. ***Fibre** is good for your digestive system.*

fickle

ADJECTIVE If you are **fickle**, you keep changing your mind about what you want.

fiction

NOUN stories about imaginary people and events.

fictional ADJECTIVE

Antonym: non-fiction

fiddle fiddles fiddling fiddled

VERB **1** If you **fiddle** with something, you keep touching it and playing with it in a restless way.
NOUN **2** another word for a violin.

fidget fidgets fidgeting fidgeted

VERB If you **fidget**, you keep changing your position or making small restless movements because you are nervous or bored.

fidgety ADJECTIVE

field fields

NOUN **1** an area of land where crops are grown or animals are kept.
2 an area of land where sports are played: *a football **field***.
3 a particular subject or area of interest.

fiend fiends

Said "**feend**" NOUN **1** a devil or evil spirit.
2 a very wicked or cruel person.

fierce fiercer fiercest

ADJECTIVE very aggressive or intense: *a **fierce** dog, a **fierce** competition*.

fiercely ADVERB

fiery fierier fieriest

ADJECTIVE If you are **fiery**, you show great anger, energy or passion in what you do.

fig figs

NOUN a very sweet fruit that is full of seeds and can be eaten dried.

fight fights fighting fought

VERB **1** When people **fight**, they take part in a battle, a boxing match, or in some other attempt to hurt or kill someone.
2 If you **fight** something, or if you fight against it, you try in a determined way to stop it happening. *I've **fought** all my life against cruelty to animals.*
NOUN **3** a situation in which people hit or try to hurt each other.

Synonyms: (sense 3) battle, conflict

figurative

ADJECTIVE If you use a word or expression in a **figurative** sense, you use it for effect, with a more abstract or imaginative meaning than its usual one. For example, you could write about a person as if he or she was a bird: *he flew down the stairs; she perched on a chair.*

figure figures

NOUN **1** a written number. *He wrote the figures down and then added them up.*
2 Your **figure** is the shape of your body.
3 a diagram or table in a book or a magazine.

figure of speech figures of speech

NOUN an expression, such as a metaphor or a simile, where the words should not be taken literally. *She was as cold as ice* (simile). *The road was a ribbon of moonlight* (metaphor).

file files filing filed

NOUN **1** a box or folder in which papers are kept.
2 In computing, a **file** is a set of related data with its own name. *He copied the file on to a floppy disk.*
3 a tool with rough surfaces, used for smoothing and shaping hard materials.
VERB **4** When someone **files** something, they put it in its correct place with others that are similar. *They filed the students' papers alphabetically.*
5 When a group of people **file** somewhere, they walk one behind the other in a line. *The children filed out of the school.*
PHRASE **6** If people walk **in single file**, they walk one behind the other.

fill fills filling filled

VERB **1** If you **fill** something, or if it **fills** up, it becomes full. *The arena soon began to fill up.*
2 If something **fills** a space, there is very little room left. *The water filled the jug.*
fill in VERB **3** If you **fill in** a form, you write information in the spaces on it.

filling fillings

NOUN **1** the mixture inside a sandwich, cake or pie.
2 a small amount of metal or plastic that a dentist puts into a hole in a tooth.

film films filming filmed

NOUN **1** a series of moving pictures that can be shown in a cinema or on television.
2 a strip of thin plastic that you use in a camera to take photographs.
3 a very thin layer of powder or liquid. *A film of dust covered every surface.*
VERB **4** If you **film** someone or something, you use a camera to take moving pictures of them.

filter filters filtering filtered

NOUN **1** a device that allows some substances, lights or sounds to pass through it, but not others. *The suntan cream acted as a filter against the harmful rays of the sun.*
VERB **2** If you **filter** something, you pass it through a filter to remove tiny particles from it.
filtration NOUN

filthy filthier filthiest

ADJECTIVE very dirty.

fin fins

NOUN a flat object on the body of a fish that helps it to swim and keep its balance. *See* **fish**.

final finals

ADJECTIVE **1** The **final** thing in a series is the last one, or the one that happens at the end: *the final chapter of a book.*
2 A decision that is **final** cannot be changed or questioned. *The judges' decision is final.*
NOUN **3** The **final** is the last game or contest in a series, that decides the overall winner.

finalist finalists

NOUN someone who takes part in the final of a competition.

finally

ADVERB **1** If something **finally** happens, it happens after a long delay. *Finally, he answered the phone.*
2 You use **finally** to introduce the last point or topic. *Finally, I would like to thank everyone for coming.*

Synonyms: (sense 1) at last, eventually
(sense 2) in conclusion, lastly

finance finances financing financed

NOUN **1** **Finance** describes affairs to do with money.
VERB **2** If someone **finances** something, they provide the money for it.

find finds finding found

VERB **1** If you **find** someone or something, you see them or discover where they are. *He eventually found the book under his bed.*
2 If you **find** something, you know it from experience. *I find that air travel tires me.*
find out VERB **3** If you **find out** something, you learn or discover something. *He wants to find out what really happened.*

fine

fine finer finest; fines

ADJECTIVE **1** Something that is **fine** is very good or very beautiful.
2 If something is **fine** it is satisfactory or suitable. *That outfit is fine for the party.*
3 If you are **fine**, you are well and happy.
4 Fine sand or powder is made up of very small particles.
5 When the weather is **fine**, it is bright and sunny.
NOUN **6** a sum of money that must be paid as a punishment.

finger fingers

NOUN one of the four long structures at the end of your hands that you use to feel and hold things.

fingernail fingernails

NOUN the hard coverings at the ends of your fingers.

fingerprint fingerprints

NOUN the unique marks made by the tip of your fingers when you touch something.

finish finishes finishing finished

VERB **1** When you **finish** something, you do the last part of it and complete it.
2 When something **finishes**, it ends. *The film finished at eight o'clock.*
NOUN **3** The **finish** of something is the last part of it. *There was a very exciting finish to the match.*

Synonyms: (sense 3) close, conclusion, end

fir firs

NOUN an evergreen tree with thin, needle-like leaves and cones.

fire fires firing fired

NOUN **1** the flames produced when something burns.
2 a mass of burning material. *We lit a fire on the beach.*
3 a device that uses electricity, coal, gas or wood to heat a room.
VERB **4** If someone **fires** a gun, they shoot a bullet. *He fired the gun into the air.*
5 INFORMAL If an employer **fires** someone, that person loses their job.
PHRASE **6** If something is **on fire**, it is burning.

fire brigade fire brigades

NOUN the organization that has the job of putting out fires.

fire engine fire engines

NOUN a vehicle used by firefighters to help them put out fires.

fire escape fire escapes

NOUN an emergency exit or staircase for use if there is a fire.

fire extinguisher fire extinguishers

NOUN a device that contains water or foam that is sprayed on to fires to put them out.

firefighter firefighters

NOUN a person whose job is to put out fires.

fireplace fireplaces

NOUN the opening beneath a chimney where a fire can be lit.

fireproof

ADJECTIVE If something is **fireproof**, it is resistant to fire.

firework fireworks

NOUN a small object that produces coloured sparks or smoke when lit.

firm firmer firmest; firms

ADJECTIVE **1** Something that is **firm** is fairly hard and does not change shape very much when it is pressed. *I like sleeping on a firm mattress.*
2 A **firm** grasp or push is strong or controlled. *His handshake was firm and confident.*
3 Someone who is **firm** behaves in a fairly strict way and will not change their mind.
NOUN **4** a business that sells or produces something: *an engineering firm.*

first

ADJECTIVE OR ADVERB **1** happening, coming or done before all others. *Andrea came first in the 100 metres race.*
ADJECTIVE **2** the most important. *Her painting won first prize.*
ADVERB **3** for the first time. *They first met in 1995.*
PHRASE **4** You use **at first** to refer to what happens to start with, or what happens at the beginning of something.

first aid

NOUN simple treatment given as soon as possible to a person who is injured or who suddenly becomes ill.

first class

ADJECTIVE Something that is **first class** is of the highest quality or standard.

first person

NOUN In grammar, the **first person** refers to yourself when you are speaking or writing. It is expressed as I or me. *William wrote his story in the **first person**.*

fish fishes fishing fished

NOUN **1** an animal with a tail and fins that lives in water.

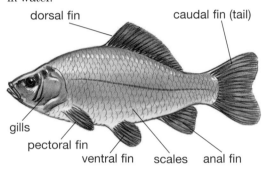

dorsal fin

caudal fin (tail)

gills

pectoral fin

ventral fin   scales   anal fin

VERB **2** If you **fish**, you try to catch fish.
✔ The plural of the noun *fish* can be either *fish* or *fishes*, but *fish* is more common.
fishing NOUN

fisherman fishermen

NOUN someone who catches fish for a living or as a sport.

fishmonger fishmongers

NOUN someone who sells fish in a shop or a market.

fist fists

NOUN a hand with the fingers curled tightly towards the palm.

fit fits fitting fitted; fitter fittest

VERB **1** If something **fits**, it is the right shape or size for a particular person or position. *There is now a computer that **fits** into your pocket.*
2 If you **fit** something, you put it securely in place. *We need to **fit** a new pane of glass in the broken window.*

3 If something **fits** a particular situation, person or thing, it is suitable or appropriate.
NOUN **4** A **fit** of laughter, coughing, rage, or panic is a sudden, uncontrolled outburst of it. *They collapsed in a **fit** of laughter.*
5 If someone has a **fit**, they lose consciousness and their body makes uncontrollable movements: *epileptic **fit**.*
ADJECTIVE **6** Someone who is **fit** is healthy and physically strong.
fitness NOUN

fix fixes fixing fixed

VERB **1** If you **fix** something somewhere, you attach it there securely. *He **fixed** the clock to the wall.*
2 If you **fix** something that is broken, you repair it.

Synonym: (sense 2) mend

fixture fixtures

NOUN **1** a sports event that takes place on a particular date.
2 an object such as a cupboard or a bath that is fixed in position in a building.

fizz fizzes fizzing fizzed

VERB When something **fizzes** it makes a hissing or bubbling sound.

fizzy fizzier fizziest

ADJECTIVE A **fizzy** drink has a gas called carbon dioxide in it to make it bubbly.

flag flags

NOUN a piece of cloth that has a particular colour or design, and is used as the symbol of a country or as a signal.

flake flakes flaking flaked

NOUN **1** a small, thin piece of something. *Flakes of rust came off the old bicycle.*
VERB **2** When something such as paint **flakes**, small, thin pieces of it come off.
flaky ADJECTIVE   **flaked** ADJECTIVE

flame flames

NOUN a hot, bright stream of burning gas. *The **flames** of the fire flickered.*

flamingo flamingos or flamingoes

NOUN a long-legged wading bird with pink feathers and a long neck.

flammable

ADJECTIVE likely to catch fire and burn easily.

✔ Although *flammable* and *inflammable* both mean "likely to catch fire", *flammable* is used more often as people sometimes think that *inflammable* means "not likely to catch fire".

flan flans

NOUN a flat, open tart that can be sweet or savoury.

flannel flannels

NOUN **1** a small square of towelling, used for washing yourself. In Australian English it is called a *washer*.

2 a lightweight woollen fabric.

flap flaps flapping flapped

VERB **1** If something **flaps**, or if you **flap** it, it moves quickly up and down or from side to side. *The flag was **flapping** in the wind.*

NOUN **2** a loose piece of something, such as cloth or plastic, that is attached at one edge: *a cat **flap**.*

flare flares flaring flared

NOUN **1** a device that produces a brightly coloured flame, used especially as an emergency signal.

VERB **2** If a fire **flares**, it suddenly burns much more vigorously.

flash flashes flashing flashed

NOUN **1** a sudden, short burst of light. *There was a **flash** of lightning in the middle of the storm.*

VERB **2** If a light **flashes**, or if you **flash** it, it shines suddenly and briefly. *The light from the lighthouse **flashed** in the night.*

3 If something **flashes**, it moves or happens very quickly. *A car **flashed** past the window.*

flask flasks

NOUN a special bottle used for keeping drinks hot or cold, and for carrying around with you. It is an abbreviation for *vacuum **flask*** or *Thermos **flask**.*

flat flats; flatter flattest

NOUN **1** a set of rooms for living in. A **flat** is part of a larger building. *We live in a block of **flats**.*

ADJECTIVE **2** Something that is **flat** is level and smooth.

3 A **flat** tyre or ball has not got enough air in it.

4 A **flat** battery has lost its electrical charge.

flatten flattens flattening flattened

VERB If you **flatten** something, you make it flat or flatter.

flatter flatters flattering flattered

VERB If you **flatter** someone, you praise them in an exaggerated way, either to please them or to persuade them to do something. *When she **flatters** me I know she wants me to do something for her.*

flattering ADJECTIVE   **flattery** NOUN

flaunt flaunts flaunting flaunted

VERB If you **flaunt** something, you show it off to others.

flavour flavours flavouring flavoured

NOUN **1** the taste of food and drink. *This cheese has a very strong **flavour**.*

VERB **2** If you **flavour** food, you add something to it to give it a particular taste. *You can **flavour** the pasta sauce with herbs.*

flaw flaws

NOUN a fault or weakness in something.

flawed ADJECTIVE   **flawless** ADJECTIVE

flax

NOUN a plant that is used for making rope and cloth.

flea fleas

NOUN a small, wingless, jumping insect that feeds on blood.

fleece fleeces

NOUN A sheep's **fleece** is its coat of wool.

fleet fleets

NOUN a group of ships or vehicles owned by the same organization, or travelling together.

flesh

NOUN the soft part of your body between the bones and the skin.

fleshy ADJECTIVE

flew

VERB the past tense of *fly*.

flex flexes flexing flexed

NOUN **1** a length of wire covered in plastic, that carries electricity to an appliance.

VERB **2** If you **flex** your muscles, you bend and stretch them.

flexible

ADJECTIVE Something that is **flexible** can be bent easily without breaking.

flexibility NOUN

flick flicks flicking flicked

VERB **1** If you **flick** something, you move it sharply with your finger. *He flicked through the pages of the book to find where he was up to.*

NOUN **2** a sudden, quick movement or sharp touch with the finger. *The cat gave a sudden flick of its tail.*

flicker flickers flickering flickered

VERB If a light or a flame **flickers**, its brightness comes and goes.

flies

PLURAL NOUN the plural of *fly*.

flight flights

NOUN **1** a journey made by aeroplane.
2 the action of flying or the ability to fly.
3 A **flight** of stairs or steps is a row of them.
4 the action of running away. *The girl took flight when she saw the big dog.*

flight attendant flight attendants

NOUN a person who looks after the passengers on an aeroplane.

flimsy flimsier flimsiest

ADJECTIVE made of something very thin and easily damaged. *The shelter they made in the garden was very flimsy.*

flinch flinches flinching flinched

VERB If you **flinch,** you make a sudden, small movement in fear or pain. *She flinched when the dentist's drill started.*

Synonyms: cringe, wince

fling flings flinging flung

VERB If you **fling** something somewhere, you throw it there using a lot of force. *He flung his shoes into the corner.*

flint flints

NOUN a very hard, grey-black stone used for building.

flip flips flipping flipped

VERB If you **flip** something, you turn it over quickly. *He flipped open the book to start his homework.*

flipper flippers

NOUN one of the flat limbs of an animal like a penguin or seal that they use for swimming.

float floats floating floated

VERB **1** Something that **floats** is supported by liquid. *A branch floated down the river.*
2 If something **floats** in the air, it hangs in the air or moves slowly through it. *A leaf floated on the breeze.*

NOUN **3** an object attached to a fishing line to keep the hook floating in the water.
4 an amount of money that a shop or stall keeps for change.

flock flocks flocking flocked

NOUN **1** a group of birds, sheep or goats.
VERB **2** If people **flock** somewhere, they go there in large numbers.

flood floods flooding flooded

NOUN **1** If there is a **flood**, a large amount of water covers an area that is usually dry.
2 A **flood** of something is a large amount of it occurring suddenly. *There was a flood of letters after the programme.*
VERB **3** If water **floods** an area that is usually dry, or if the area **floods**, it becomes covered with water. *He left the tap running and flooded the kitchen.*

floodlight floodlights

NOUN a very powerful outdoor light that is used to illuminate sports fields and public buildings.

floor floors

NOUN **1** the part of a room that you walk on.
2 one of the levels in a building. *Our flat is on the fifth floor of the building.*

flop flops flopping flopped

VERB **1** If someone or something **flops**, they fall loosely and heavily. *He flopped down on to the sofa when he got home.*
2 INFORMAL If something **flops**, it fails. *The play flopped after it had some bad reviews.*

floppy disk floppy disks; also spelt **floppy disc**

NOUN a small, magnetic disk on which computer data is stored.

florist florists

NOUN a person or shop selling flowers.

flour

NOUN a white or brown powder made by grinding grain. It is used for making bread, cakes and pastry.

flourish flourishes flourishing flourished

VERB Something that **flourishes** develops or grows successfully or healthily.
[from Latin *florere* meaning to flower]

flow flows flowing flowed

VERB **1** If something **flows** somewhere, it moves there in a steady and continuous manner. *The river flows south from the town.*
NOUN **2** A **flow** of something is a steady, continuous movement of it. *There is a constant flow of traffic down the main road.*

flow chart flow charts

NOUN a diagram that shows the sequence of steps and choices that lead to various results and courses of action.

flower flowers flowering flowered

NOUN **1** the part of a plant that grows at the end of a stem. It carries the reproductive parts of the plant from which the fruit and seeds develop.
VERB **2** When a plant **flowers**, its flowers open.

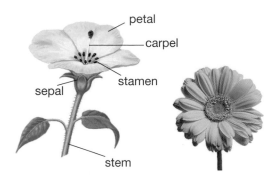

petal

carpel

stamen

sepal

stem

flown

VERB the past participle of *fly*.

flu

NOUN an abbreviation of *influenza*. **Flu** is an illness similar to a bad cold, but more serious.

fluent

ADJECTIVE Someone who is **fluent** in a foreign language can speak it correctly and without hesitation.
fluently ADVERB

fluff

NOUN soft, light, woolly threads or fibres bunched together.

fluffy fluffier fluffiest

ADJECTIVE soft and woolly.

fluid fluids

NOUN a liquid. *Drink plenty of fluids in hot weather.*

fluke flukes

NOUN an accidental success. *It must be a fluke that I did so well in my exams.*

fluorescent

ADJECTIVE **1** When something is **fluorescent**, it gives out its own light when another light is shone on it.
2 A **fluorescent** light is in the form of a tube that shines with a harsh, bright light.

fluoride

NOUN a chemical mixture that is often added to drinking water and to toothpaste because it is thought to prevent tooth decay.

flush flushes flushing flushed

VERB **1** If you **flush**, your face goes red.
2 If you **flush** a toilet or something such as a pipe, you force water through it to clean it.

flute flutes

NOUN a musical wind instrument in the shape of a long tube with holes along it. You play it by blowing over a hole near one end while holding it sideways to your mouth.

flutter flutters fluttering fluttered

VERB If something **flutters**, it flaps or waves with small, quick movements. *I felt the bird flutter in my hands.*

fly flies flying flew flown

NOUN **1** an insect with two pairs of wings.
VERB **2** When a bird, insect or aircraft **flies**, it moves through the air. *The bird flew away.*
3 If you **fly** somewhere, you travel there in an aircraft.
flying ADJECTIVE OR NOUN   **flyer** NOUN

flyover flyovers

NOUN a bridge that takes one road over the top of another one.

foal foals

NOUN a young horse.

foam foams foaming foamed

NOUN **1** a mass of tiny bubbles. *The bubble bath produced a lot of foam*.

VERB **2** When something **foams**, it forms a mass of small bubbles. *The powder foamed in the washing machine*.

focus focuses or focusses focusing or focussing focused or focussed

VERB **1** If you **focus** your eyes or a camera on something, you adjust your eyes or the camera so that the image is clear. *She focused her eyes on the ball*.

2 If you **focus** on a particular topic, you concentrate on it.

PHRASE **3** If an image is **in focus**, the edges of the image are clear and sharp. If it is **out of focus**, the edges are blurred.

[from Latin *focus* meaning hearth, which was seen as the centre of a Roman home]

✔ When you add the verb endings to *focus*, you can either add them straight to *focus* (*focuses, focusing, focused*) or you can put another *s* at the end of *focus* before adding the endings (*focusses, focussing, focussed*). Either way is correct, but the first way is much more common.

fodder

NOUN food given to horses and cattle.

foe foes

NOUN If someone is your **foe**, they are your enemy.

foetus foetuses; also spelt fetus

NOUN A **foetus** is an unborn child or other animal in the womb.

fog

NOUN a thick mist caused by tiny drops of water in the air.

foil foils foiling foiled

VERB **1** If you **foil** someone's attempt at something, you prevent it from succeeding. *The policeman foiled the robbery*.

NOUN **2** thin, paper-like sheets of metal used to wrap food.

fold folds folding folded

VERB **1** If you **fold** something, you bend it so that one part lies over another. *He folded the letter and put it back in the envelope*.

NOUN **2** a crease or bend in paper or cloth.

folder folders

NOUN a thin piece of folded cardboard used for keeping papers together.

foliage

NOUN the leaves of plants.

folk

PLURAL NOUN **1** people. *These are the folk I was telling you about*.

ADJECTIVE **2** **Folk** music and art are traditional or typical of the people of a particular area. *My dad likes Irish folk music*.

folklore

NOUN the traditional stories and beliefs of a community.

follow follows following followed

VERB **1** If you **follow** someone or something, you move along behind them. *We followed him up the steps*.

2 If you **follow** a path or a sign, you go somewhere using the path or sign to direct you. *I followed the signs to the dining room*.

3 If you **follow** instructions or advice, you do what you are told.

4 If you **follow** an explanation or the plot of a story, you understand each stage of it.

follower NOUN

fond fonder fondest

ADJECTIVE If you are **fond** of someone or something, you like them.

font fonts

NOUN **1** a large, stone bowl in a church that holds the water for baptisms.

2 a style of printed writing. There are many **fonts** to choose from, such as: Helvetica; Times; Courier; or Frutiger.

food foods

NOUN what people and other animals eat.

food chain food chains

NOUN a series of living things that are linked together because each one feeds on another in the chain.

fool fools fooling fooled

NOUN **1** someone who is silly and is not sensible.

VERB **2** If you **fool** someone, you deceive or trick them. *Don't be fooled by his appearance*.

foolish

ADJECTIVE stupid or silly.

foolproof

ADJECTIVE If something is **foolproof**, it cannot fail.

foot feet

NOUN **1** the part of your body at the end of your leg.

2 the part of something that is farthest from the top. *The hotel was at the foot of the mountain.*

3 a unit of length equal to 12 inches or about 30·5 centimetres.

football footballs

NOUN **1** a game such as soccer and American **football**, in which the ball can be kicked and two teams try to score goals.

2 a ball used in these games.

foothold footholds

NOUN a place where you can put your foot when climbing.

footpath footpaths

NOUN a path for people to walk on, especially in the countryside.

footprint footprints

NOUN the mark made by a foot on the ground.

footstep footsteps

NOUN the sound made by someone's feet when they are walking. *They heard footsteps in the corridor.*

for

PREPOSITION **1** to be used by or given to a particular person. *I bought a present for my brother.*

2 **For** is used when explaining the reason, cause or purpose of something. *I'm going shopping for a pair of shoes.*

3 You use **for** to show a distance, time or quantity. *I have been waiting here for ages.*

4 If you are **for** something, you support it. *My parents are all for the new school.*

Antonym: (sense 4) against

forbid forbids forbidding forbade forbidden

VERB If someone **forbids** you to do something, they order you not to do it.

forbidden ADJECTIVE

force forces forcing forced

VERB **1** If you **force** someone to do something, you make them do it.

NOUN **2** violence or great strength. *He used a lot of force to pull the wall down.*

3 an organized group of people, especially soldiers or police. *The police force helped to maintain order at the football match.*

4 a push or pull. **Forces** are measured in newtons.

forceful ADJECTIVE   **forcefully** ADVERB

forecast forecasts forecasting forecast or forecasted

NOUN **1** A **forecast** says what is likely to happen: *the weather forecast.*

VERB **2** If you **forecast** an event, you say what is likely to happen. *We forecast that we would win the game.*

foreground foregrounds

NOUN In a picture, the **foreground** is the part that seems nearest to you.

forehead foreheads

NOUN the area at the front of your head, above your eyebrows and below your hair.

foreign

ADJECTIVE belonging to or involving a country that is not your own. *It is useful to learn a foreign language.*

foreigner NOUN

forest forests

NOUN a large area of trees growing close together.

forever

ADVERB permanently or continually.

forfeit forfeits forfeiting forfeited

VERB If you **forfeit** something, you have to give it up as a penalty.

forgave

VERB the past tense of *forgive.*

forge forges forging forged

NOUN **1** a place where a blacksmith works making metal goods by hand.

VERB **2** If someone **forges** metal, they hammer and bend it into shape while it is hot.

3 Someone who **forges** money, documents or paintings makes illegal copies of them.

forgery forgeries

NOUN **1** the crime of making false copies of something.

2 an illegal false copy of something.

forget forgets forgetting forgot forgotten
VERB If you **forget** something, you do not remember it.
forgetful ADJECTIVE

forgive forgives forgiving forgave forgiven
VERB If you **forgive** someone who has done something wrong, you stop being angry with them.

fork forks
NOUN **1** an instrument with prongs on the end of a handle, used for eating food or for digging earth.
2 If there is a **fork** in a road or river, it divides into two or more parts.

forlorn
ADJECTIVE If you are **forlorn**, you are unhappy and lonely.

form forms forming formed
NOUN **1** a particular type or kind of something. *Running is a form of exercise.*
2 the shape or pattern of something. *Cut out your paper in the form of a star.*
3 a class in school.
4 a piece of paper with questions and spaces where you fill in your answers.
VERB **5** If you **form** something, you make it or give it a particular shape. *Please all stand up and form a circle.*
6 If something **forms**, it develops or comes into existence. *The puddles formed on the pavement after the rain.*

formal
ADJECTIVE **1 Formal** speech, writing or behaviour is correct and serious, rather than relaxed and friendly. *At the prizegiving everyone wore formal clothes.*
2 A **formal** action or event is an official one that follows accepted rules.
formally ADVERB

Antonym: informal

format formats
NOUN the way something is arranged and presented. *The format of the book is easy to follow.*

formation formations
NOUN **1** the start or creation of something.
2 the pattern or shape of something.

former
ADJECTIVE **1** happening or existing before now, or in the past. *The former tennis champion presented the trophy to the new champion.*
2 Former refers to the first of two things mentioned. *Exams and coursework are both important, but the former must take priority this term.*
formerly ADVERB

formula formulae or formulas
NOUN a group of letters, numbers or symbols that stand for a mathematical or scientific rule.

fort forts
NOUN a strong, fortified building built for defence.

fortify fortifies fortifying fortified
VERB If someone **fortifies** a building, they make it stronger against attack.

fortnight fortnights
NOUN a period of two weeks.

fortress fortresses
NOUN a very strong and well-protected castle or town.

fortunate
ADJECTIVE lucky.
fortunately ADVERB

fortune fortunes
NOUN **1** luck.
2 a lot of money.

forward forwards
ADVERB **1** If you move something **forward**, you move it towards the front.
NOUN **2** In a game like hockey or football, a **forward** is someone in an attacking position.

fossil fossils
NOUN the remains or impression of an animal or plant from a previous age, which has been preserved in rock.
fossilize VERB

foster fosters fostering fostered
VERB If someone **fosters** a child, they look after the child for a period in their home, but do not become his or her legal parent.
foster child NOUN **foster home** NOUN
foster parent NOUN

A B C D E

F

G H I J K L M N O P Q R S T U V W X Y Z

fought
VERB the past tense of *fight*.

foul fouler foulest; fouls
ADJECTIVE **1** very unpleasant, especially because it is dirty or obscene. *There was a **foul** smell coming from the drains.*
NOUN **2** In sport, a **foul** is an action that breaks the rules.

found founds founding founded
VERB **1** the past tense and past participle of *find*.
2 If someone **founds** an organization or company, they create it. *He **founded** the charity ten years ago.*

foundation foundations
NOUN **1** the basic ideas on which something is based. *A good education is the **foundation** for a successful life.*
PLURAL NOUN **2** The **foundations** of a building are the layer of concrete or bricks below the ground on which it is built.
NOUN **3** the founding of something.

fountain fountains
NOUN an ornamental structure in which a jet of water is forced into the air by a pump.

fountain pen fountain pens
NOUN a pen that has a nib which is supplied with ink from a container inside the pen.

fowl fowls
NOUN a bird, such as chicken or duck, that is kept or hunted for its meat or eggs.

fox foxes
NOUN a wild mammal that looks like a dog and has reddish-brown fur and a thick tail.

foyer foyers
Said "**foy**-ay" NOUN a large entrance hall just inside the main doors of a cinema, hotel or public building.

fraction fractions
NOUN **1** In mathematics, a **fraction** is a part of a whole number.
2 a tiny proportion or amount of something.

fracture fractures fracturing fractured
NOUN **1** a crack or break in something, especially a bone.
VERB **2** If something **fractures**, or if you **fracture** it, it breaks. *She **fractured** her arm while playing netball.*

fragile
ADJECTIVE easily broken or damaged.
fragility NOUN

fragment fragments
NOUN a small piece or part of something. *There were **fragments** of glass on the floor after I dropped the vase.*
fragmentation NOUN   **fragmented** ADJECTIVE

fragrant
ADJECTIVE Something that is **fragrant** smells sweet or pleasant.

frail frailer frailest
ADJECTIVE weak or fragile.
frailty NOUN

frame frames framing framed
NOUN **1** the structure surrounding a door, window or picture.
VERB **2** If you **frame** a picture, you make a frame for it.

framework frameworks
NOUN a structure that forms a support or frame for something: *wooden shelves on a steel **framework**.*

frantic
ADJECTIVE If you are **frantic**, you behave in a wild, desperate way because you are anxious or frightened.
frantically ADVERB

fraud frauds
NOUN the crime of getting money by deceit.

fraught
ADJECTIVE **1** If a situation is **fraught**, it is full of potential problems or difficulties.
2 If someone is **fraught**, they are tense and upset.

frayed
ADJECTIVE If material is **frayed**, the edges are worn and ragged.

freak freaks
NOUN **1** A **freak** is someone whose appearance or behaviour is very unusual.
ADJECTIVE **2** A **freak** event is very unusual. *We had a **freak** storm in the middle of the summer.*

freckle freckles

NOUN a small, light-brown spot on someone's skin, especially their face.

freckled ADJECTIVE

free freer freest; frees freeing freed

ADJECTIVE **1** If something is **free**, you can have it without paying for it.

2 Someone who is **free** is no longer a prisoner.

3 If someone is **free**, they are not busy. *Are you free on Saturday afternoon?*

VERB **4** If you **free** someone or something that is trapped, you release them.

freedom

NOUN If you have the **freedom** to do something, you are free to do it.

free verse

NOUN poetry that does not use patterns of rhyme or rhythm.

freeway freeways

NOUN In Australia, South Africa and the United States, a **freeway** is a road for fast-moving traffic.

freeze freezes freezing froze frozen

VERB **1** When a liquid **freezes**, or when something **freezes** it, it becomes solid because it is very cold.

2 If you **freeze** food, you make it very cold to preserve it.

3 If you **freeze**, you suddenly stop moving because there is danger.

ADJECTIVE **4** You say you are **freezing** when you are very cold.

freezer freezers

NOUN a refrigerator in which you can store food for a long time at very low temperatures.

freight

NOUN goods moved by lorries, ships or other transport.

frenzy frenzies

NOUN If someone is in a **frenzy**, their behaviour is wild and uncontrolled.

frenzied ADJECTIVE

frequency frequencies

NOUN **1** The **frequency** of an event is how often it happens.

2 The **frequency** of a sound or radio wave is the rate at which it vibrates.

frequency table frequency tables

NOUN a chart where you write down how often something happens.

frequent

ADJECTIVE If something happens at **frequent** intervals, it happens often.

frequently ADVERB

fresh fresher freshest

ADJECTIVE **1** Something that is not old or used. *We put fresh towels out for the guests.*

2 **Fresh** food has been made or picked recently, and is not tinned or frozen.

3 **Fresh** water is water that is not salty. *The water in a river or lake is fresh water.*

freshwater

ADJECTIVE A **freshwater** animal lives in a river, lake or pool and not in the sea.

fret frets fretting fretted

VERB **1** If you **fret** about something, you worry about it.

NOUN **2** The **frets** on a stringed instrument, such as a guitar, are the metal ridges across its neck.

friction

NOUN **1** the force that slows things down and can stop them from moving.

2 **Friction** between people is disagreement and quarrels. *There was a lot of friction between the two families.*

Friday Fridays

NOUN the sixth day of the week, coming between Thursday and Saturday. [from Old English *Frigedoeg* meaning Freya's day, the Norse goddess of love]

fridge fridges

NOUN a short form of *refrigerator*.

friend friends

NOUN someone you know well and like, but who is not related to you.

friendly friendlier friendliest

ADJECTIVE A **friendly** person is kind and pleasant to others.

friendship friendships

NOUN the state of being friends with someone. *Her friendship means a lot to me.*

A
B
C
D
E
F
G
H
I
J
K
L
M
N
O
P
Q
R
S
T
U
V
W
X
Y
Z

fright
NOUN a sudden feeling of fear.

frighten frightens frightening frightened
VERB If something or someone **frightens** you, they make you afraid.
frightened ADJECTIVE   **frightening** ADJECTIVE

frill frills
NOUN a strip of material with a lot of folds in it, that is attached to something as decoration.

fringe fringes
NOUN **1** the hair that hangs over a person's forehead. *She had a long fringe that almost covered her eyes.*
2 a decoration on clothes and other objects, consisting of a row of hanging threads. *There is a fringe along the bottom of the curtains.*
fringed ADJECTIVE

frivolous
ADJECTIVE Someone who is **frivolous** behaves in a silly or light-hearted way, especially when they should be serious or sensible.
frivolously ADVERB   **frivolity** NOUN

frizzy frizzier frizziest
ADJECTIVE **Frizzy** hair has tight, wiry curls.

frog frogs
NOUN a small, amphibious animal with long back legs.

frolic frolics frolicking frolicked
VERB When children and other young animals **frolic**, they run around and play in a lively way. *In the spring, the lambs frolic in the fields.*

from
PREPOSITION **1** **From** tells you where someone or something started. *The river flows from the north.*
2 If you take something **from** an amount, you reduce the amount by that much. *If you take five from 20 you are left with 15.*
3 You use **from** to state the range of something. *Lunchtime is from 12 o'clock to 1 o'clock.*

front fronts
NOUN **1** the part of something that faces forward: *a jacket with buttons down the front.*
ADJECTIVE **2** the part of something that is furthest forward. *I like to sit in the front seats of the cinema.*

NOUN **3** In a war, the **front** is the place where two armies are fighting.
4 At the seaside, the **front** is the road or promenade that runs alongside the beach.

frontier frontiers
NOUN a border between two countries. *Their passports were checked at the frontier.*

frost frosts
NOUN powdery white ice that forms on the ground when the temperature outside falls below freezing.

frosty frostier frostiest
ADJECTIVE When it is **frosty**, the temperature outside falls below freezing and powdery white ice forms on the ground.

froth froths frothing frothed
NOUN **1** a mass of small bubbles on the surface of a liquid.
VERB **2** If a liquid **froths**, small bubbles appear on its surface.
frothy ADJECTIVE

frown frowns frowning frowned
VERB **1** If you **frown**, you move your eyebrows closer together and wrinkle your forehead, usually because you are annoyed, worried or puzzled.
NOUN **2** an expression on the face of someone who is frowning.

froze
VERB the past tense of *freeze*.

frozen
VERB **1** the past participle of *freeze*.
ADJECTIVE **2** If you say you are **frozen**, you mean you have become very cold.

fruit fruits
NOUN the part of a plant that develops after the flower has been fertilized, that contains the seeds. Apples, oranges and bananas are all **fruit**.
[from Latin *fructus* meaning produce or benefit]

frustrate frustrates frustrating frustrated

VERB **1** If something **frustrates** you, it prevents you doing what you want and makes you upset. **2** If you **frustrate** something, such as a plan, you prevent it. *They deliberately frustrated my attempts to do my homework.*
frustrated ADJECTIVE **frustrating** ADJECTIVE **frustration** NOUN

fry fries frying fried

VERB When you **fry** food, you cook it in a pan containing hot fat.

fudge

NOUN a soft, brown sweet made from butter, milk and sugar.

fuel fuels

NOUN a substance such as coal, gas, oil or wood that is burned to provide heat or power.

fugitive fugitives

NOUN someone who is running away or hiding, especially from the police.

fulfil fulfils fulfilling fulfilled

VERB **1** If you **fulfil** a promise, you keep it. **2** If something **fulfils** you, it gives you satisfaction.
fulfilling ADJECTIVE **fulfilment** NOUN

full fuller fullest

ADJECTIVE **1** Something that is **full** contains as much as it is possible to hold. *The bus was full so we had to wait for the next one.*
2 to the greatest possible extent. *The radio was playing at full volume.*
3 complete or whole. *I will tell you the full story later.*
ADVERB **4** completely or wholly. *Turn the taps full on.*
fullness NOUN **fully** ADVERB

Antonym: (sense 1) empty

---

full stop full stops

NOUN the punctuation mark (.) used at the end of a sentence and after an abbreviation or initial.

full-time

ADJECTIVE If you have a **full-time** job, you work for the whole of each normal working week.

fumble fumbles fumbling fumbled

VERB If you **fumble**, you feel or handle something clumsily. *I fumbled with the door handle because it was so dark.*

fume fumes fuming fumed

PLURAL NOUN **1 Fumes** are unpleasant-smelling gases and smoke that are sometimes poisonous, and are produced by burning and by some chemicals.
VERB **2** If something **fumes**, it produces smoke or gas.
3 If you **fume**, you are very angry.

fun

NOUN **1** pleasant, enjoyable and light-hearted activity. *Let's have some fun!*
ADJECTIVE **2** If someone or something is **fun**, you enjoy being with them or you enjoy doing it. *She is always fun to be with.*
PHRASE **3** If you **make fun** of someone or something, you tease them or make jokes about them.

function functions functioning functioned

VERB **1** If a thing **functions**, it works as it should.
NOUN **2** The **function** of someone or something is their purpose or the work they are supposed to do.
functional ADJECTIVE

fund funds

NOUN an amount of money that is collected for a particular purpose.

fundamental

ADJECTIVE If something is **fundamental**, it is basic and necessary. *You must understand the fundamental rules of the game before you can progress.*

funeral funerals

NOUN a ceremony for the burial or cremation of someone who has died.

fungus fungi or funguses

NOUN an organism, such as a mushroom or mould, that does not have flowers or leaves.
fungal ADJECTIVE

funnel funnels

NOUN **1** an open cone that narrows to a tube, and is used to pour substances into containers.
2 a metal chimney on a ship or steam engine.

funny funnier funniest

ADJECTIVE **1** causing amusement or laughter. *He told us a **funny** story.*
2 strange or puzzling. *We could hear a **funny** noise.*

Synonyms: (sense 1) amusing, comical, humorous
(sense 2) odd, peculiar

fur

NOUN the thick hair that grows on the bodies of many animals. *Polar bears have white **fur**.*
furry ADJECTIVE

furious

ADJECTIVE extremely angry.
furiously ADVERB

furnace furnaces

NOUN a very large, hot oven used for heating glass and melting metal.

furnish furnishes furnishing furnished

VERB If you **furnish** a house or a room, you put furniture into it.

furniture

NOUN movable objects such as tables, chairs and wardrobes that you need inside a building: *bedroom **furniture**.*

furrow furrows

NOUN a shallow, straight channel dug into the earth by a plough.

further furthest

ADJECTIVE OR ADVERB another word for *farther*.
*See **far**.*

furtive

ADJECTIVE secretive, sly and cautious.
furtively ADVERB

fury

NOUN violent or extreme anger.
[from Latin ***furia*** meaning madness]

fuse fuses fusing fused

NOUN **1** a safety device in an electrical plug or appliance, consisting of a piece of wire that melts to stop the electric current if a fault occurs.
VERB **2** When an electrical appliance **fuses**, it stops working because the fuse has melted to protect it.

fuss fusses fussing fussed

NOUN **1** unnecessarily anxious or excited behaviour.
VERB **2** If someone **fusses**, they behave with unnecessary anxiety and concern for unimportant things.

fussy fussier fussiest

ADJECTIVE If you are **fussy**, you worry too much about unnecessary details.

future futures

NOUN **1** the period of time after the present. *He is already making plans for his **future**.*
ADJECTIVE **2** relating to or occurring at a time after the present.
PHRASE **3** In **future** means from now on. *Be more careful **in future**.*

fuzzy fuzzier fuzziest

ADJECTIVE **1** soft and fluffy.
2 If a picture is **fuzzy**, it is not clear.

Gg

gadget gadgets
NOUN a small mechanical device or tool.

gain gains gaining gained
VERB **1** If you **gain** something, you get more of it or get something you didn't have before. *She was pleased when she began to **gain** better marks.*
2 If a clock or watch **gains** time, it starts telling a later time than it is. *I think my watch has **gained** five minutes. It says five past one and the clock says one o'clock.*

gala galas
NOUN a special, public celebration or performance: *a swimming **gala**.*

galaxy galaxies
NOUN a huge group of stars that extends over millions of kilometres.

Our galaxy, the Milky Way

We are about here

gale gales
NOUN an extremely strong wind.

gallant
ADJECTIVE brave and honourable.
gallantly ADVERB   **gallantry** NOUN

galleon galleons
NOUN a large Spanish sailing ship in the sixteenth and seventeenth centuries.

gallery galleries
NOUN a building where paintings and other works of art are shown.

galley galleys
NOUN a ship, powered by oars, used in ancient and medieval times.

gallon gallons
NOUN a measure of liquid that is equal to eight pints or 4·55 litres.

gallop gallops galloping galloped
VERB When a horse **gallops**, it runs very fast, so that during each stride all four feet are off the ground at the same time.

gallows
NOUN a framework on which criminals used to be hanged.

gamble gambles gambling gambled
VERB When someone **gambles**, they bet money on the result of a contest or race.

game games
NOUN **1** an activity with a set of rules that is played by individuals or teams against each other.
2 a term for wild birds and animals that are hunted for food or sport, such as pheasant or boar.

gammon
NOUN cured meat from a pig, similar to bacon but usually in thicker and larger slices.

gander ganders
NOUN a male goose.

gang gangs ganging ganged
NOUN **1** a group of people who join together for some purpose, for example to commit a crime.
VERB **2** INFORMAL If people **gang up** on you, they join together to oppose you. *The children finally **ganged up** on the bully.*

gangster gangsters
NOUN a violent criminal who is a member of a gang.

gangway gangways
NOUN **1** a space left between rows of seats, for example in a train or cinema, for people to walk through.
2 a movable passenger bridge between a ship and the shore.

gaol
NOUN another spelling of *jail*.

A
B
C
D
E
F
G
H
I
J
K
L
M
N
O
P
Q
R
S
T
U
V
W
X
Y
Z

gap gaps

NOUN a space between two things or a hole in something solid. *He was just able to squeeze through the **gap** in the hedge.*

gape gapes gaping gaped

VERB **1** If you **gape**, you stare with your mouth wide open.
2 If something **gapes**, it is wide open.

garage garages

NOUN **1** a building in which you can keep a car.
2 a place where cars are repaired or where petrol is sold.

garbage

NOUN In American English, **garbage** is rubbish, especially waste from a kitchen.

garden gardens

NOUN an area of land next to a house, with plants, trees and grass.

gardener gardeners

NOUN a person who looks after a garden as a job or as a hobby.

gargle gargles gargling gargled

VERB When you **gargle**, you rinse the back of your throat by putting some liquid in your mouth and making a bubbling sound without swallowing the liquid.

gargoyle gargoyles

NOUN a stone carving below the roof of an old building, in the shape of an ugly person or animal.

garlic

NOUN the small, white bulb of an onion-like plant that has a strong taste and smell and is used in cooking.

garment garments

NOUN an item of clothing.

gas gases

NOUN a substance that is not a liquid or a solid. Air is a mixture of **gases**. The bubbles in fizzy lemonade contain a **gas** called carbon dioxide.

gasp gasps gasping gasped

VERB If you **gasp**, you quickly draw in your breath through your mouth because you are surprised or in pain.

gate gates

NOUN a barrier that can be opened or shut and is used to close off the entrance to a field, garden or path.

gateau gateaux

NOUN a rich, layered cake with cream in it. [from French **gâteau** meaning cake]

gather gathers gathering gathered

VERB **1** If you **gather** things, you collect or pick them. *I **gathered** some flowers from the garden.*
2 When people **gather**, they come together in a group. *We **gathered** at my house before we went to the party.*
3 If you **gather** information, you learn it, often from hearing or reading about it. *I **gather** you passed your exams.*

gathering gatherings

NOUN a meeting of people who gather together for a particular purpose.

gauge gauges gauging gauged

VERB **1** If you **gauge** something, you estimate or work out how much of it there is or how much is required.
NOUN **2** an instrument used for measuring. *The fuel **gauge** shows that we need more petrol.*

gauze

NOUN a thin, cotton cloth, often used for bandages.

gave

VERB the past tense of *give*.

gay gays

ADJECTIVE **1** Someone who is **gay** is homosexual.
2 OLD-FASHIONED lively and full of fun.
NOUN **3** a homosexual person.

gaze gazes gazing gazed

VERB If you **gaze** at something, you look steadily at it for a long time. *We **gazed** up at the stars.*

gazelle gazelles

NOUN a small antelope found in Africa and Asia.

gear gears

NOUN **1** The **gears** in a car or on a bicycle are a set of cogs that work together to send power to the wheels.
2 the clothes or equipment that you need for an activity: *climbing* **gear**.

geese

PLURAL NOUN the plural of *goose*.

gel gels

NOUN a smooth, soft, jelly-like substance: *hair* **gel**.

gem gems

NOUN a jewel or precious stone.

gender genders

NOUN the sex of a person or animal.

gene genes

*Said "***jeen***"* NOUN one of the parts of the chromosomes found inside the cells of an organism. Offspring inherit **genes** from their parents.
genetic ADJECTIVE   **genetically** ADVERB

general generals

ADJECTIVE **1** relating to the whole of something or to most things in a group. *There has been a* **general** *improvement in your work.*
2 including or involving a range of different things. *There was a* **general** *knowledge quiz at the end of term.*
NOUN **3** an army officer of very high rank.
PHRASE **4 In general** is used to indicate that a statement is true in most cases, or that it applies to most people or things. ***In general,*** *people take their holidays over the summer.*
generally ADVERB

general election general elections

NOUN an election in which people vote for who they want to represent them in the national parliament.

generate generates generating generated

VERB If someone or something **generates** something else, they produce or create it. *They built a new power station to* **generate** *more electricity.*

generation generations

NOUN **1** all the people of a similar age: *the younger* **generation**.

2 the length of time that it takes for children to grow up and have children of their own. *The next* **generation** *will see a lot more changes.*

generator generators

NOUN a machine that produces electricity from another form of energy, such as wind or water power.

generous

ADJECTIVE A **generous** person gives or shares what they have, especially time or money.
generously ADVERB

genie genies

NOUN a magical being that obeys the wishes of the person who controls it. *Aladdin rubbed his magic lamp and the* **genie** *appeared.*
[from Arabic ***jinni*** meaning demon]

genitals

PLURAL NOUN the sex organs on the outside of the body.

genius geniuses

NOUN a highly intelligent, creative or talented person: *a mathematical* **genius**.

gentle gentler gentlest

ADJECTIVE Someone or something that is **gentle** is mild and calm. *A* **gentle** *breeze blew across the field.*

Antonyms: violent, rough

gentleman gentlemen

NOUN **1** a man who is polite and well-educated.
2 a polite way of referring to any man.

genuine

ADJECTIVE real and exactly what it appears to be. *It's a* **genuine** *diamond.*

geography

NOUN the study of the physical features of the earth, its countries, climate and people.
geographical ADJECTIVE

geology

NOUN the study of the earth's structure, especially the layers of rock and soil that make up the surface of the earth.
geological ADJECTIVE   **geologist** NOUN

geometry

NOUN that part of mathematics that deals with lines, angles, curves and shapes.

A
B
C
D
E
F
G
H
I
J
K
L
M
N
O
P
Q
R
S
T
U
V
W
X
Y
Z

geranium geraniums

NOUN a plant with bright red, pink or white flowers.

gerbil gerbils

NOUN a small rodent with long back legs that is often kept as a pet.

germ germs

NOUN a very small organism that can cause disease.

germinate germinates germinating germinated

VERB When a seed **germinates**, it starts to grow.
germination NOUN

gesture gestures gesturing gestured

NOUN **1** a movement of your hands or head that suggests a message or feeling. *She made an angry **gesture** with her fist.*
VERB **2** If you **gesture**, you move your hands or head in order to communicate a message or feeling. *She **gestured** to me to come over.*

get gets getting got

VERB **1** If you **get** something, you fetch it or receive it. *He **got** his report on the last day of term.*
2 If you **get** a bus, you travel on it.
3 If you **get** a meal ready, you prepare it.
4 If you **get** someone to do something for you, you persuade them.
5 If you **get** a joke, you understand it.
6 If you **get** ill, you become ill.
7 If you **get** to a place, you arrive there.

geyser geysers

NOUN a natural spring out of which hot water and steam gush in spurts. There are many geysers in Iceland and New Zealand.
[from Old Norse *geysa* meaning to gush]

ghastly ghastlier ghastliest

ADJECTIVE extremely horrible and unpleasant.

ghost ghosts

NOUN the spirit of a dead person that appears to someone who is still alive. *She believes she saw a **ghost** in the old house.*

giant giants

NOUN **1** a huge person in a myth or legend.
ADJECTIVE **2** much larger than other similar things. *There was a **giant** Christmas tree in the town centre.*

giddy giddier giddiest

ADJECTIVE If you feel **giddy**, you feel unsteady on your feet, usually because you are ill.
giddily ADVERB   **giddiness** NOUN

gift gifts

NOUN **1** something that you give someone as a present.
2 a natural skill or ability. *He has a **gift** for acting.*

gifted

ADJECTIVE If you are **gifted**, you have special talents. *She is a **gifted** musician.*

gigantic

ADJECTIVE extremely large. *She was keen to ride on the **gigantic** big wheel.*

Synonyms: huge, massive, enormous

giggle giggles giggling giggled

VERB If you **giggle**, you laugh in a nervous, quiet way.

gill gills

NOUN the organs on the sides of a fish that it uses for breathing.

gimmick gimmicks

NOUN something that is not really necessary, but is unusual and used to attract interest. *The new shop needed a **gimmick** to attract customers.*
gimmicky ADJECTIVE

gin

NOUN a strong, colourless alcoholic drink made from grain and juniper berries.

ginger

NOUN **1** a plant root with a hot, spicy flavour, used in cooking.
ADJECTIVE **2** bright orangey-brown.

gipsy gipsies.
See **Gypsy**.

giraffe giraffes
NOUN a large African mammal with a very long neck, long legs and yellowish skin with dark patches.

girder girders
NOUN a strong metal or concrete beam used in building.

girl girls
NOUN a female child.

girlfriend girlfriends
NOUN Someone's **girlfriend** is the woman or girl with whom they are having a close or romantic relationship.

give gives giving gave given
VERB 1 If you **give** something to someone, you hand it to them or provide it for them. *Please would you **give** me back the book I lent to you?*
2 If you **give** a party, you host it.
3 **Give** can be used to express an action: ***give** a speech*, ***give** the door a push*.
PHRASE 4 If something **gives way**, it collapses.

glacier glaciers
NOUN a huge, frozen river of slow-moving ice.

glad gladder gladdest
ADJECTIVE happy or pleased.

gladiator gladiators
NOUN In ancient Rome, **gladiators** were slaves trained to fight in arenas to provide entertainment.

glance glances glancing glanced
VERB 1 If you **glance** at something, you look at it quickly. *He **glanced** at his watch.*
NOUN 2 a quick look.

gland glands
NOUN an organ in your body which produces and releases special chemicals. Some **glands** help to get rid of waste products from your body. Sweat **glands** are small **glands** in your skin that produce sweat.
glandular ADJECTIVE

glare glares glaring glared
VERB 1 If you **glare** at someone, you look at them angrily.
NOUN 2 a hard, angry look.

glass glasses
NOUN 1 the hard, transparent substance that windows and bottles are made of.
2 a container made of glass, from which you can drink: *a **glass** of water.*

glasses
PLURAL NOUN two lenses in a frame, that some people wear over their eyes to improve their eyesight.

glaze glazes glazing glazed
NOUN 1 a smooth, shiny surface on pottery or food.
VERB 2 If you **glaze** pottery or food, you cover it with a glaze.
3 If someone **glazes** a window, they fit a sheet of glass into the window frame.

gleam gleams gleaming gleamed
VERB 1 If something **gleams**, it shines and reflects light. *He polished the silver teapot until it **gleamed.***
NOUN 2 a pale, shining light. *There was a **gleam** of light at the end of the dark tunnel.*

glide glides gliding glided
VERB 1 If you **glide**, you move smoothly. *The skater **glided** across the ice.*
2 When birds or aeroplanes **glide**, they float on air currents.

glider gliders
NOUN an aeroplane without an engine, that flies by floating on air currents.

glimmer glimmers glimmering glimmered
NOUN 1 a faint, unsteady light. *There was a **glimmer** of light ahead.*
VERB 2 If something **glimmers**, it produces a faint, unsteady light.

glimpse glimpses glimpsing glimpsed
NOUN 1 a brief sight of something.
VERB 2 If you **glimpse** something, you see it briefly. *They **glimpsed** a rare bird through the trees.*

glisten glistens glistening glistened
VERB If something **glistens**, it shines or sparkles. *The frost **glistened** in the moonlight.*

glitter glitters glittering glittered
VERB 1 If something **glitters**, it shines in a sparkling way. *The diamond **glittered** in the sunlight.*
NOUN 2 sparkling light.

gloat gloats gloating gloated
VERB If you **gloat**, you cruelly show how pleased you are about your own success or someone else's failure.

global
ADJECTIVE to do with the whole world. *Pollution of the atmosphere is a **global** concern.*

global warming
NOUN an increase in the world's overall temperature, believed to be caused by a thinning of the ozone layer.

globe globes
NOUN **1** the earth, the planet you live on. **2** a sphere fixed to a stand, with a map of the world on it.
global ADJECTIVE

gloom
NOUN **1** darkness or dimness. *I could not see in the **gloom** of the forest.*
2 a feeling of unhappiness or despair.

gloomy gloomier gloomiest
ADJECTIVE **1** Something that is **gloomy** is dull and dark, and sometimes depressing. *It was a **gloomy** winter day.*
2 If you are **gloomy**, you are unhappy.
gloomily ADVERB

glorious
ADJECTIVE beautiful and splendid. *We were lucky to have **glorious** weather while we were on holiday.*

glory glories
NOUN something considered splendid or admirable. *They enjoyed the **glory** of their son's success.*

gloss
NOUN a bright shine on a smooth surface.

glossary glossaries
NOUN a list of explanations of specialist words, usually found at the back of a book.

glossy glossier glossiest
ADJECTIVE smooth and shiny. *This new shampoo makes my hair **glossy**.*

glove gloves
NOUN **Gloves** cover your hands and keep them warm or give them protection.

glow glows glowing glowed
VERB **1** If something **glows**, it shines with a dull, steady light.
NOUN **2** a dull, steady light.
3 a strong feeling of pleasure or happiness.

glucose
NOUN a natural sugar found in plants and produced in the bodies of animals, including humans, to give them energy.

glue glues gluing or glueing glued
NOUN **1** a substance used for sticking things together.
VERB **2** If you **glue** one object to another, you stick them together using glue. *She **glued** the picture into her book.*

glutton gluttons
NOUN a person who eats too much.
gluttony NOUN

gnarled
ADJECTIVE If something is **gnarled** it is old, twisted and rough. *There is a big, **gnarled** tree in the churchyard.*

gnash gnashes gnashing gnashed
VERB If you **gnash** your teeth, you make a noise with them by grinding them together because you are angry or upset.

gnat gnats
NOUN a tiny flying insect that bites.

gnaw gnaws gnawing gnawed
VERB If someone or something **gnaws** at something, they chew and bite at it repeatedly. *The hamster **gnawed** at the bars of its cage.*

gnome gnomes
NOUN a tiny old man in fairy stories, who usually lives underground.

go goes going went gone

VERB **1** If you **go** somewhere, you walk, move or travel there.

2 If something **goes** well, it is a success.

3 If you **go**, you start to move. *When you hear the whistle, **go** as fast as you can.*

4 If something **goes** somewhere, it leads there. *This road **goes** to the centre of town.*

5 If something **goes**, it works properly. *My watch doesn't **go** any more.*

6 become. *This fruit has **gone** bad.*

NOUN **7** an attempt or a turn at doing something.

VERB **8** disappear. *The mist has **gone**.*

9 If you are **going** to do something, you will do it.

go down VERB **10** If you **go down** with an illness, you catch it.

11 If something **goes down** well, people like it. If it **goes down** badly, they do not like it.

go off VERB **12** If you **go off** someone or something, you stop liking them.

13 If a bomb **goes off**, it explodes.

14 If food **goes off**, it becomes unsafe and has begun to decompose.

go on VERB **15** If you **go on** doing something, you continue to do it.

16 If you **go on** about something, you keep talking about it in a rather boring way.

17 If something is **going on**, it is happening.

go through VERB **18** If you **go through** an unpleasant event, you experience it.

goal goals

NOUN **1** In games like football and hockey, the **goal** is the space into which the players try to get the ball to score a point.

2 In games like football and hockey, if a player scores a **goal**, they get the ball into the **goal**.

3 something that you hope to achieve. *Our **goal** is to raise as much money as possible for charity.*

goat goats

NOUN an animal similar to a sheep, with shaggy hair, a beard and horns.

gobble gobbles gobbling gobbled

VERB **1** If you **gobble** food, you eat it very quickly.

2 When a turkey **gobbles**, it makes a loud gurgling sound.

goblet goblets

NOUN a kind of drinking cup or glass.

goblin goblins

NOUN a small, ugly and mischievous creature found in fairy stories.

god gods

PROPER NOUN **1** God is the being worshipped by Christians, Jews and Muslims as the creator and ruler of the world.

NOUN **2** any of the beings that are believed in many religions to have power over an aspect of the world. *Mars was the Roman **god** of war.*

goddess goddesses

NOUN a female god.

godparent godparents

NOUN someone who agrees, at a child's christening, to be responsible for their religious upbringing.

goggles

PLURAL NOUN special glasses that fit closely round your eyes to protect them. *I usually wear **goggles** when I go swimming.*

go-kart go-karts

NOUN a small motorized vehicle that can be raced.

gold

NOUN **1** a valuable, yellow-coloured metal, used for making jewellery and as an international currency.

ADJECTIVE **2** made of gold: *a **gold** necklace.*

golden

ADJECTIVE gold in colour or made of gold.

goldfish

NOUN a small, orange fish, often kept as a pet in a bowl or pond.

A
B
C
D
E
F
G
H
I
J
K
L
M
N
O
P
Q
R
S
T
U
V
W
X
Y
Z

golf
NOUN a game in which players use special clubs to hit a ball into holes that are spread out over a large area of grassy land.

gondola gondolas
NOUN a long, narrow boat used on the canals in Venice. **Gondolas** are propelled by using a long pole.

gone
VERB the past participle of *go*.

gong gongs
NOUN a flat, circular piece of metal that is hit with a hammer to make a loud sound, often as a signal for something. *They sounded the **gong** for dinner.*

good better best
ADJECTIVE **1** pleasant or enjoyable. *The weather turned out to be **good**.*
2 of a high quality. *The food was very **good**.*
3 sensible or valid. *The rain gives me a **good** reason for staying at home.*
4 well-behaved. *Have the children been **good**?*
PHRASE **5 For good** means forever.

goodbye
GREETING You say **goodbye** when you are leaving someone or ending a telephone conversation.

goodness
NOUN the quality of being good and kind.

good night
GREETING You say **good night** to someone when you are leaving them at night.

goods
PLURAL NOUN things that are bought and sold in a shop or warehouse.

goose geese
NOUN a fairly large bird, with webbed feet and a long neck.

gooseberry gooseberries
NOUN a round, green berry that grows on a bush and has a sharp taste.

gore gores goring gored
NOUN **1** the blood from a wound.
VERB **2** If an animal **gores** someone, it wounds them by sticking a horn or tusk into them.

gorge gorges gorging gorged
NOUN **1** a deep, narrow valley.
VERB **2** If you **gorge** yourself, you eat a lot of food greedily.

gorgeous
ADJECTIVE extremely pleasant or attractive: *a **gorgeous** dress*.

gorilla gorillas
NOUN a very strong, large ape, that lives in family groups.

gory gorier goriest
ADJECTIVE involving a lot of blood and violence: *a **gory** film.*

gosling goslings
NOUN a young goose.

gospel gospels
NOUN one of the four books in the New Testament that describe the life and teachings of Jesus Christ.

gossip gossips gossiping gossiped
NOUN **1** informal conversation, often about people's private affairs.
VERB **2** If you **gossip**, you talk informally with someone, especially about other people.

got
VERB the past tense of *get*.

gouge gouges gouging gouged
VERB If you **gouge** something out, you scoop it out forcefully with a pointed object. *She **gouged** a hole in the apple with a knife.*

govern governs governing governed
VERB When someone **governs** something, they rule or control it, especially a country or state.

government governments
NOUN The **government** is the group of people who officially control a country.
[from Latin ***gubernare*** meaning to steer or to direct]

governor governors

NOUN **1** someone who controls or helps to run a state or organization.
2 In Australia, New Zealand and other commonwealth countries the **Governor** represents the British King or Queen.

GP GPs

NOUN an abbreviation of *general practitioner*. A **GP** is a doctor who treats all kinds of illnesses, and sends people to a specialist if necessary.

grab grabs grabbing grabbed

VERB If you **grab** something, you take it or pick it up quickly and roughly. *He grabbed a sandwich before running for the bus.*

grace graces

NOUN **1** an elegant and attractive way of moving.
2 a short prayer before or after a meal.
3 a pleasant and kind way of behaving.

graceful

ADJECTIVE If you are **graceful**, you move in a smooth and elegant way.
gracefully ADVERB

gracious

ADJECTIVE kind, polite and pleasant. *He always acts in a gracious and thoughtful manner.*
graciously ADVERB

grade grades grading graded

VERB **1** If someone **grades** things, they judge them according to their quality.
NOUN **2** the mark that you get in an exam.

gradient gradients

NOUN a slope or the steepness of a slope. *The gradient of this hill means it will be difficult to climb.*

gradual

ADJECTIVE happening or changing slowly over a long period of time. *Her spelling showed gradual improvement.*
gradually ADVERB

graduate graduates

NOUN someone who has a degree from a university or college.

graffiti

NOUN slogans or drawings scribbled on walls.

grain grains

NOUN **1** a cereal plant, such as wheat, that is grown and harvested for food.
2 a seed from a cereal plant such as wheat or rice.
3 a tiny, hard particle of something. *I have got grains of sand in my shoes from walking on the beach.*
4 the natural pattern of lines in a piece of wood, made by the fibres in it.

gram grams

NOUN a unit of mass and weight (g). There are one thousand **grams** in a kilogram (kg).

grammar

NOUN the rules of a language that state how words can be combined to form sentences.

granary granaries

NOUN a building for storing grain.

grand grander grandest

ADJECTIVE splendid or impressive.

grandad grandads

NOUN; INFORMAL grandfather.

grandchild grandchildren

NOUN Someone's **grandchildren** are the children of their son or daughter.

granddaughter granddaughters

NOUN Someone's **granddaughter** is the daughter of their son or daughter.

grandfather grandfathers

NOUN Your **grandfather** is your father's father or your mother's father.

grandmother grandmothers

NOUN Your **grandmother** is your father's mother or your mother's mother.

grandparent grandparents

NOUN Your **grandparents** are the parents of your father or mother.

grandson grandsons

NOUN Someone's **grandson** is the son of their son or daughter.

granite

NOUN a very strong, hard rock often used in building.

granny grannies

NOUN; INFORMAL grandmother.

a b c d e f **g** h i j k l m n o p q r s t u v w x y z

grant

grant grants granting granted

NOUN **1** an amount of money that an official body gives to someone for a particular purpose. *He was given a **grant** to go to university.*

VERB **2** If you **grant** something to someone, you allow them to have it. *I will **grant** you a wish.*

grape grapes

NOUN a small, green or purple fruit that grows in bunches on vines. **Grapes** are eaten raw or used to make wine.

grapefruit grapefruits

NOUN a large, round, yellow citrus fruit.

graph graphs

NOUN a diagram that gives information about how two sets of numbers and measurements are related.

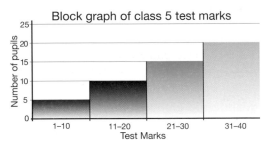

Block graph of class 5 test marks

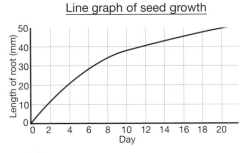

Line graph of seed growth

graphic graphics

ADJECTIVE **1** A **graphic** description is very detailed and clear.

PLURAL NOUN **2 Graphics** are drawings, designs and diagrams: *computer **graphics**.*

grasp grasps grasping grasped

VERB **1** If you **grasp** something, you hold it firmly. *He **grasped** both my hands.*
2 If you **grasp** an idea, you understand it. *She finally **grasped** the answer.*

grass grasses

NOUN the common green plant that grows on lawns and in parks.

grasshopper grasshoppers

NOUN an insect with long back legs that it uses for jumping and making a high-pitched sound.

grate grates grating grated

VERB **1** If you **grate** food, you shred it into small pieces by rubbing it against a tool called a grater.

NOUN **2** a framework of metal bars in a fireplace for holding coal or wood. *A wood fire burned in the **grate**.*

✔ Another word that sounds like *grate* is *great*.

grateful

ADJECTIVE If you are **grateful** for something, you feel thankful for it. *I'm **grateful** to you for your help.*

gratefully ADVERB

Synonym: appreciative

gratitude

NOUN If you show **gratitude** to someone for something, you are thankful.

Synonyms: thankfulness, appreciation

grave graves; graver gravest

NOUN **1** a place where a dead person is buried.
ADJECTIVE **2** FORMAL very serious. *We are in **grave** danger.*

gravel

NOUN small stones used for making roads and paths.

graveyard graveyards

NOUN a place where people are buried, usually in a churchyard.

gravity

NOUN the force that pulls things down towards the earth.

gravy

NOUN a brown sauce made from meat juices.

graze grazes grazing grazed

VERB **1** When animals **graze**, they eat grass that is growing. *The cows **grazed** in the field.*
2 If something **grazes** a part of your body, it scrapes against it, injuring you slightly.
NOUN **3** a slight injury caused by something scraping against your skin.

grease greases greasing greased
NOUN **1** a substance used for oiling machines.
2 animal fat used in cooking.
VERB **3** If you **grease** something, you put grease on it. *Lightly **grease** a baking tray.*

great greater greatest
ADJECTIVE **1** very large in size, amount or degree. *She had **great** difficulty in staying awake.*
2 very important: *a **great** artist.*
3 very good. *That's a **great** idea.*
✔ Another word that sounds like *great* is *grate*.

greedy greedier greediest
ADJECTIVE Someone who is **greedy** wants more of something than is necessary or fair.
greedily ADVERB

green greener greenest; greens
ADJECTIVE OR NOUN **1** a colour between yellow and blue on the spectrum. Grass and leaves are usually **green**.
NOUN **2** a smooth, flat area of grass. *We played cricket on the village **green**.*

greengrocer greengrocers
NOUN a shopkeeper who sells fruit and vegetables.

greenhouse greenhouses
NOUN a glass building in which people grow plants that need to be kept warm.

greenhouse effect
NOUN the gradual increase in the temperature of the earth's atmosphere because the heat absorbed from the sun is not able to escape.

greet greets greeting greeted
VERB If you **greet** someone, you say something friendly and welcoming to them when you meet them.

greeting greetings
NOUN the words or actions that you use when you meet someone.

grenade grenades
NOUN a small bomb that can be thrown by hand. [from Spanish ***granada*** meaning pomegranate, which is a similar shape to a grenade]

grew
VERB the past tense of *grow*.

grey greyer greyest
ADJECTIVE OR NOUN the colour of ashes or of clouds on a rainy day.

grid grids
NOUN a pattern of lines crossing each other to form squares.

grief
NOUN extreme sadness.

grieve grieves grieving grieved
VERB If you **grieve** you are very sad, especially because someone has died.

grill grills grilling grilled
NOUN **1** the part of a cooker where food is cooked by heat from above. *Place the fish under a hot **grill**.*
VERB **2** If you **grill** food, you cook it under or over direct heat. *We **grilled** the chicken on the barbecue.*

grim grimmer grimmest
ADJECTIVE If a situation or piece of news is **grim**, it is very unpleasant and worrying.
grimly ADVERB

grimace grimaces
NOUN a twisted facial expression that shows disgust or pain.

grime
NOUN thick dirt that gathers on the surface of something.
grimy ADJECTIVE

grin grins grinning grinned
VERB **1** If you **grin**, you have a broad smile.
NOUN **2** a broad smile.

grind grinds grinding ground
VERB **1** If you **grind** something, you crush it into a fine powder. *He **ground** the mud into the carpet.*
2 If you **grind** your teeth, you rub your upper and lower teeth together.
PHRASE **3** If something **grinds to a halt**, it slows down and stops.

grip grips gripping gripped; grips
VERB **1** If you **grip** something, you hold it firmly. *He **gripped** his mother's hand tightly.*
NOUN **2** a handle on a bat or racket. *The **grip** on his tennis racket needed repairing.*

gristle

NOUN the tough, rubbery part of meat that is difficult to eat.

groan groans groaning groaned

VERB 1 If you **groan**, you make a long, low sound of pain, unhappiness or disapproval.
NOUN 2 the sound you make when you groan.

grocer grocers

NOUN a person who runs a shop that sells all kinds of food and household supplies.

groceries

PLURAL NOUN the goods that you buy in a grocer's shop.

groove grooves

NOUN a deep line cut into a surface.
grooved ADJECTIVE

grope gropes groping groped

VERB If you **grope** for something, you feel for it with your hands because you cannot see it.

gross grosser grossest

ADJECTIVE 1 extremely bad. *I made a **gross** error on my exam paper.*
2 **Gross** language or behaviour is very rude.
3 The **gross** amount of something is its total, without anything taken away. For example, the **gross** weight of something is the total weight, including the weight of its container.
4 unpleasantly fat or ugly.

grotesque

ADJECTIVE 1 exaggerated and absurd.
2 very strange and ugly.
grotesquely ADVERB

grotto grottoes or grottos

NOUN a small cave that people visit because it is attractive.

ground grounds

NOUN 1 the surface of the land. *They sat on the ground.*
2 an area of land, especially land that is used for a particular purpose: *a football **ground**.*
PLURAL NOUN 3 The **grounds** of a large building are the garden or area of land that surrounds it. *We camped in the **grounds** of the stately home.*
4 FORMAL The **grounds** for something are the reason for it. *I had **grounds** to believe that he was telling the truth.*

VERB 5 the past tense and past participle of *grind.*

group groups grouping grouped

NOUN 1 a number of things or people that are linked in some way: *a small **group** of friends.*
VERB 2 When things or people **group** together, they are linked in some way. *We **grouped** together for the school photograph.*

grovel grovels grovelling grovelled

VERB If you **grovel**, you behave in an unpleasantly humble way towards someone you think is important.
[from Middle English **on grufe** meaning lying on your belly]

grow grows growing grew grown

VERB 1 When someone or something **grows**, it gets bigger or increases. *Children **grow** at different rates.*
2 When people **grow** plants, they plant them and look after them.
3 You use **grow** to say that someone or something gradually changes into a different state. *He's **growing** old.*
grow up VERB 4 When a child **grows up**, they become an adult.

growl growls growling growled

VERB 1 When an animal **growls**, it makes a low rumbling sound, usually because it is angry.
NOUN 2 the sound an animal makes when it growls.

grown-up grown-ups

NOUN an adult.

growth

NOUN The process by which something develops to its full size.

grub grubs

NOUN 1 a worm-like creature that is the young of some insects, after it has hatched but before it becomes an adult.
2 INFORMAL food.

grubby grubbier grubbiest

ADJECTIVE rather dirty. *That shirt looks a bit **grubby**.*

grudge grudges

NOUN If you have a **grudge** against someone, you resent them because they have harmed or upset you in the past.

gruelling

ADJECTIVE difficult and exhausting. *It was a long and gruelling race.*

gruesome

ADJECTIVE shocking and horrible. *The film was unsuitable for the children because it was so gruesome.*

gruff gruffer gruffest

ADJECTIVE If someone's voice is **gruff**, it sounds rough and unfriendly.
gruffly ADVERB

grumble grumbles grumbling grumbled

VERB 1 If you **grumble**, you complain in a bad-tempered way.
NOUN 2 a bad-tempered complaint.

grumpy grumpier grumpiest

ADJECTIVE bad-tempered and fed-up. *She is often grumpy in the morning.*
grumpily ADVERB

grunt grunts grunting grunted

VERB 1 If a person or a pig **grunts**, they make a short, low, gruff sound.
NOUN 2 the sound a person or a pig makes when they grunt.

guarantee guarantees guaranteeing guaranteed

NOUN 1 a promise by a company to do something, especially to replace or repair a product free of charge within a given time period if it develops a fault. *This television has a five-year guarantee.*
VERB 2 If something or someone **guarantees** something, they promise that it will happen. *I guarantee that after all your hard work the day will be a success.*

guard guards guarding guarded

VERB 1 If you **guard** a person or object, you watch them carefully, either to protect them or to stop them from escaping.
NOUN 2 a person whose job is to guard a person, object or place.

guardian guardians

NOUN someone who has been legally appointed to look after a child, but is not the child's parent.

guerrilla guerrillas; also spelt **guerilla**

NOUN a member of a small, unofficial army fighting an official army.

guess guesses guessing guessed

VERB 1 If you **guess** something, you form an opinion about it without knowing all the relevant facts. *She guessed that he was probably older than her.*
NOUN 2 an attempt to give an answer or opinion about something without knowing all the relevant facts. *If you don't know the answer, have a guess.*

guest guests

NOUN someone who has been invited to stay at your home or attend an event.

guide guides guiding guided

NOUN 1 someone who shows you round places, or leads the way through difficult country.
VERB 2 If you **guide** someone somewhere, you lead them there.

guidebook guidebooks

NOUN a book that gives information about a place.

guillotine guillotines

NOUN 1 In the past, the **guillotine** was a machine used for beheading people, especially in France.
2 a piece of equipment with a long, sharp blade, used for cutting paper.
[named after Joseph-Ignace *Guillotin*, who first recommended the guillotine as a way of executing people]

guilt

NOUN 1 the unhappy feeling of having done something wrong.
2 Someone's **guilt** is the fact that they have done something wrong. *After hearing the evidence, the jury felt that his guilt was clear.*

guilty guiltier guiltiest

ADJECTIVE If you are **guilty** of doing something wrong, you did it.
guiltily ADVERB

guinea pig guinea pigs

NOUN 1 a small, furry mammal without a tail, often kept as a pet.
2 a person used to try something out. *You will be a guinea pig in this experiment.*

guitar guitars
NOUN a musical instrument with six strings and a long neck.

gulf gulfs
NOUN a very large bay.

gull gulls
NOUN a sea bird with long wings, white and grey or black feathers, and webbed feet.

gullible
ADJECTIVE If someone is **gullible**, they are easily tricked.

gulp gulps gulping gulped
VERB **1** If you **gulp** food or drink, you swallow large quantities of it quickly and noisily.
NOUN **2** a large quantity of food or drink swallowed quickly and noisily.

gum gums
NOUN **1** Your **gums** are the firm flesh in which your teeth are set.
2 a soft, flavoured substance that people chew but do not swallow.
3 glue.

gumboot gumboots
NOUN a wellington boot.

gumtree gumtrees
NOUN a eucalyptus or other tree that produces gum.

gun guns
NOUN a weapon that fires bullets or shells.

gunpowder
NOUN a powder that explodes when it is lit. It is used for making things such as fireworks.

gust gusts
NOUN a sudden rush of wind. *A **gust** of wind blew his hat off.*

gutter gutters
NOUN the edge of a road next to the pavement, where rain collects and flows away.

gym gyms
NOUN a hall or room for sports and exercise. It is short for *gymnasium*.

gymkhana gymkhanas
Said "jim-**kah**-na" NOUN a competition in which people take part in horse-riding contests.

gymnasium gymnasiums
NOUN a room with special equipment for physical exercises.

gymnastics
NOUN physical exercises, especially ones using equipment such as bars and ropes.

Gypsy Gypsies; also spelt Gipsy
NOUN a member of an ethnic group scattered across most countries of Europe, the Middle East and the Americas. They migrated from north-west India in the 9th century and still have a nomadic lifestyle, although some are settled on sites and in houses. The **Gypsy** language is Romani.
[from *Egyptian* because in the 16th century they were thought to have come from Egypt]

Hh

habit habits

NOUN something that you do often or regularly.

habitat habitats

NOUN the natural home of a plant or animal.

hack hacks hacking hacked

VERB If you **hack** at something, you cut it using rough strokes.

had

VERB past participle of *have*.

haddock

NOUN an edible sea fish.

hadn't

VERB a contraction of *had not*.

haggard

ADJECTIVE A person who is **haggard** looks very tired and ill.

haggis haggises

NOUN a Scottish dish made of the minced internal organs of a sheep, boiled together with oatmeal and spices in a skin.

haggle haggles haggling haggled

VERB If you **haggle** with someone, you argue with them about the price of something.

haiku haiku

NOUN a short, Japanese verse form in 17 syllables.

hail hails hailing hailed

NOUN **1** frozen rain.
VERB **2** When it is **hailing**, frozen rain is falling.

hailstone hailstones

NOUN a drop of frozen rain.

hair hairs

NOUN one of the large number of fine threads that grow on your head and body. **Hair** grows on the bodies of some other animals.

haircut haircuts

NOUN the cutting of someone's hair and the style into which it is cut.

hairdresser hairdressers

NOUN a person who is trained to cut and style hair.

hairstyle hairstyles

NOUN the way in which your hair is arranged or cut.

hairy hairier hairiest

ADJECTIVE covered in a lot of hair.

hajj

NOUN the pilgrimage to Mecca that every Muslim must make at least once in their life, if they are healthy and wealthy enough to do so. [from Arabic *hajj* meaning pilgrimage]

halal or **hallal**

NOUN meat from animals that have been killed according to Muslim law.

half halves

NOUN OR adjective **1** one of two equal parts that make up a whole. It can be written as $\frac{1}{2}$: *the second **half** of the match. My cup is only **half** full.*
ADVERB **2** You can use **half** to say that something is only partly true. *I **half** expected to see the teacher walk in.*
PHRASE **3 Half past** refers to a time that is thirty minutes after a particular hour: *half past twelve.*

halfway

ADVERB If something is **halfway** between two points or two times, it is at the middle point between them.

hall halls

NOUN **1** the room just inside the front entrance of a house that leads into the other rooms.
2 a large room or building for public events: *a school **hall**.*

Halloween

NOUN **Halloween** is October 31st. In the past people thought that ghosts and witches would be about on this night, and it is now celebrated by children dressing up, often as ghosts and witches.

hallucinate hallucinates hallucinating hallucinated

VERB If someone **hallucinates**, they imagine that they see strange things because they are ill or taking drugs.

halo haloes or halos

NOUN a circle of light around something, especially the head of a holy person in a picture.

halt halts halting halted

VERB **1** When someone or something **halts**, they stop. *They **halted** a short distance from the house.*

PHRASE **2** When something **comes to a halt**, it stops.

halter halters

NOUN a strap fastened round a horse's head so that it can be led easily.

halve halves halving halved

VERB If you **halve** something, you divide it into two equal parts.

ham

NOUN meat from the hind leg of a pig.

hamburger hamburgers

NOUN a flat disc of minced meat, fried and eaten in a bread roll.

[named after *Hamburg* in Germany, the city where they were first made]

hammer hammers hammering hammered

NOUN **1** a tool consisting of a heavy piece of metal at the end of a handle, used for hitting nails into things.

VERB **2** If you **hammer** something, you hit it repeatedly with a hammer.

hammock hammocks

NOUN a piece of net or canvas hung between two supports and used as a bed.

hamper hampers hampering hampered

NOUN **1** a large basket with a lid, used for carrying food.

VERB **2** If something **hampers** you, it makes it difficult for you to do what you are trying to do. *The bad weather **hampered** their expedition.*

hamster hamsters

NOUN a small, furry rodent, often kept as a pet.

hand hands handing handed

NOUN **1** the part of your body at the end of your arm, below the wrist.

2 The **hands** of a clock or watch are the pointers that indicate what time it is.

3 In a game of cards, a **hand** is the set of cards dealt to each player.

VERB **4** If you **hand** something to someone, you pass it to them.

PHRASE **5** If you **give a hand**, you help someone to do something.

6 If you do something **by hand**, you do it using your hands rather than a machine.

7 If something gets **out of hand**, it becomes beyond your control.

handbag handbags

NOUN a small bag, usually carried by a woman.

handcuffs

PLURAL NOUN two strong metal rings joined by chains that are locked round a prisoner's wrists.

handful handfuls

NOUN **1** A **handful** of something is the amount of it you can hold in your hand.

2 a small number or quantity of something. *Only a **handful** of people were invited to the party.*

handicap handicaps

NOUN **1** a physical or mental disability.

2 a disadvantage, or anything that makes it more difficult to do something.

handicapped ADJECTIVE

handicraft handicrafts

NOUN an activity that involves making things with your hands, such as pottery or knitting.

handkerchief handkerchiefs

NOUN a small square of fabric used for blowing your nose.

handle handles handling handled

NOUN **1** the part of a tool, bag, cup or other object that you hold in order to pick it up or use it: *door **handle**.*

VERB **2** If you **handle** an object, you hold it or touch it with your hands.

3 If you **handle** something, you deal with it successfully. *She **handled** the stress of the examination very well.*

handlebars

PLURAL NOUN the bars with handles that are used to steer a bicycle.

handset handsets

NOUN The **handset** of a telephone is the part that you speak into and listen with.

handsome

ADJECTIVE very attractive in appearance.

handstand handstands

NOUN the act of balancing upside down on your hands, with your feet in the air.

handwriting

NOUN Someone's **handwriting** is their style of writing with a pen or pencil.

handy handier handiest

ADJECTIVE If something is **handy**, it is useful or conveniently near.

hang hangs hanging hung or hanged

VERB 1 If you **hang** something on a hook, nail or line, or if it **hangs** there, it is attached so that it does not touch the ground. *His jacket* **hung** *from a hook on the door.*

2 To **hang** someone means to kill them by suspending them by a rope around the neck.

hang about or **hang around** VERB 3 INFORMAL If you **hang about** or **hang around** somewhere, you stay or wait there. *Although he had left, he still* **hung around** *outside his old school.*

hang on VERB 4 If you **hang on** to something, you hold it tightly or keep it.

5 INFORMAL If you **hang on**, you wait.

hang up VERB 6 If you **hang up** when you are speaking on the phone, you put down the receiver and end the call.

✔ When *hang* means to kill someone by suspending them by a rope (sense 2), the past tense and past participle are **hanged**.

hangar hangars

NOUN a large building where aircraft are kept.

hanger hangers

NOUN a piece of shaped wood, plastic or wire for hanging up clothes.

hang-glider hang-gliders

NOUN a glider that is made for one or two people who hang below the frame in a harness.

Hanukkah or **Chanukah**

NOUN an eight-day Jewish festival of lights.

haphazard

ADJECTIVE not organized or planned. *He piled the books up in a* **haphazard** *way.*
haphazardly ADVERB

happen happens happening happened

VERB 1 When something **happens**, it occurs or takes place.

2 If you **happen** to do something, you do it by chance. *I* **happened** *to notice he'd dropped his glove.*

happiness

NOUN a feeling of great contentment or pleasure.

happy happier happiest

ADJECTIVE 1 full of contentment or joy.

2 If you are **happy** with something, you are satisfied with it.

3 If you are **happy** to do something, you are willing to do it.
happily ADVERB

Antonyms: (sense 1) miserable, sad
  (sense 2) dissatisfied
  (sense 3) reluctant

---

harass harasses harassing harassed

VERB If someone **harasses** you, they annoy or trouble you continually.
harassed ADJECTIVE

harbour harbours

NOUN a protected area of deep water where boats can be moored.

hard harder hardest

ADJECTIVE OR ADVERB 1 requiring a lot of effort. *The sponsored walk was* **hard** *work.*

2 with a lot of force. *I kicked the ball very* **hard**.

ADJECTIVE 3 difficult.

4 not easy to bend or break.

hard disk hard disks

NOUN a part of a computer that holds a large amount of information.

harden hardens hardening hardened

VERB If something **hardens** it becomes hard or gets harder. *The glue took a long time to* **harden**.

hardly

ADVERB only just. *I could* **hardly** *believe it.*

hardship

NOUN a time or situation of suffering and difficulty.

hardware

NOUN **1** tools and equipment for use in the home and garden.
2 computer machinery rather than computer programs.

hardy hardier hardiest

ADJECTIVE tough and able to bear cold and difficult conditions.

hare hares

NOUN an animal like a large rabbit, but with longer ears and legs.

harm harms harming harmed

VERB **1** If someone **harms** someone or something, they injure or damage them.
NOUN **2** injury or damage.

Synonym: (senses 1 and 2) hurt

harmful

ADJECTIVE having a bad effect on something. *Too much sun can be harmful to your skin.*
harmfully ADVERB

harmless

ADJECTIVE safe to use or be near.
harmlessly ADVERB

harmonica harmonicas

NOUN a small musical instrument played by moving it across the lips and blowing and sucking air through it. Also called a mouth organ.

harmony harmonies

NOUN **1** a state of peaceful agreement and cooperation. *The neighbours lived in harmony.*
2 In music, **harmony** is the pleasant combination of two or more notes played at the same time.

harness harnesses harnessing harnessed

NOUN **1** a set of straps fastened round an animal to control it or attach it to something, such as a horse to a cart.
VERB **2** If you **harness** an animal, you put a harness on it.
3 If someone **harnesses** something, they control it so that they can use it. *The windmills harnessed the power of the wind.*

harp harps

NOUN a musical instrument consisting of a triangular frame with vertical strings that you pluck with your fingers.
harpist NOUN

harpoon harpoons

NOUN a barbed spear attached to a rope, thrown or fired from a gun and used for catching whales or large fish.

harsh harsher harshest

ADJECTIVE **1 Harsh** living conditions or climates are rough and unpleasant.
2 Harsh actions or remarks are unkind and show no sympathy.
harshly ADVERB   **harshness** NOUN

Synonyms: (sense 1) hard, severe, tough

harvest harvests

NOUN the act of gathering a crop, or the time when this is done.
[from Old German *herbist* meaning autumn]

has

VERB part of the verb *have*.

hasn't

VERB a contraction of *has not*.

hassle hassles hassling hassled

NOUN **1** INFORMAL Something that is a **hassle** is difficult or causes trouble. *Organizing the school trip is always a hassle.*
VERB **2** If you **hassle** someone, you annoy them by repeatedly asking them to do something.

hasty hastier hastiest

ADJECTIVE done quickly and without preparation. *Do not give a hasty answer.*

hat hats

NOUN a covering for the head.

hatch hatches hatching hatched

VERB **1** When an egg **hatches**, or when a bird or a reptile **hatches** from an egg, the shell breaks open and the young bird or reptile comes out.
NOUN **2** an opening in a wall where food can be passed through.

hatchback hatchbacks

NOUN a car with a door at the back that opens upwards.

hatchet hatchets
NOUN a small axe.

hate hates hating hated
VERB If you **hate** someone or something, you dislike them very much.

hateful
ADJECTIVE very nasty and detestable.

hatred
NOUN an extremely strong feeling of dislike.

haul hauls hauling hauled
VERB If you **haul** something somewhere, you pull it with great effort.

haunt haunts haunting haunted
VERB If a ghost **haunts** a place, it is seen or heard there regularly.
haunting ADJECTIVE

haunted
ADJECTIVE Somewhere that is **haunted** is visited often by a ghost. *People believe that the house on the hill is **haunted**.*

have has having had
VERB **1** If you **have** something, it belongs to you or you possess it.
2 If you **have** something such as a cold or an accident, you feel or experience it.
3 If you **have** something such as lunch or a letter, you take or get it.
4 If you **have** something such as a haircut, you cause it to be done.
PHRASE **5** If you **have to** do something, you must do it. *I **have to** clean my room before I go out.*
VERB **6 Have** can be used with other verbs to form the past tense. *I **have** already read that book.*

haven't
VERB a contraction of *have not.*

havoc
NOUN disorder and confusion. *The bad weather played **havoc** with our plans.*

hawk hawks
NOUN a bird of prey with short, rounded wings and a long tail.

hay
NOUN grass that has been cut and dried and is used to feed animals.

hay fever
NOUN an allergy to pollen and grass, causing sneezing and watering eyes.

haystack haystacks
NOUN a large, firmly-built pile of hay, usually covered and left out in the open.

hazard hazards
NOUN something that could be dangerous to you. *The pollution in the city centre is a health **hazard**.*

haze
NOUN If there is a **haze**, it is difficult to see clearly because there is moisture or smoke in the air.

hazel hazels
NOUN **1** a small tree with edible nuts.
ADJECTIVE **2** a green-brown colour. *He has **hazel** eyes.*

hazy hazier haziest
ADJECTIVE dim or vague: ***hazy** sunshine, a **hazy** memory.*

he
PRONOUN **He** is used to refer to a man, boy or male animal that has already been mentioned.

head heads heading headed
NOUN **1** the part of your body that has your eyes, brain and mouth in it.
2 the top or front of something, or the most important end of it. *We went to the **head** of the queue.*
3 When you toss a coin, the side called **heads** is the one with the **head** on it.
4 In an organization or group of people, the **head** is the main person in charge.
VERB **5** If you **head** something, you lead it. *She **headed** the expedition to the North Pole.*
6 If you **head** somewhere, you go in that direction or towards something. *We **headed** to the canteen for lunch.*
7 If you **head** a ball, you hit it with your head. *He **headed** the ball into the goal.*

headache headaches
NOUN a pain in your head.

heading headings
NOUN a piece of writing that is written or printed at the top of a page.

headlight headlights

NOUN the large, powerful lights on the front of a motor vehicle.

headline headlines

NOUN The **headline** of a newspaper is the heading printed in big, bold letters on the front page at the top of an article.

headphones

NOUN a pair of small speakers that you wear over your ears to listen to a radio, a television or a stereo without other people hearing.

headquarters

NOUN the main place from which an organization is run.

head teacher head teachers

NOUN the teacher who is in charge of a school.

heal heals healing healed

VERB If a cut or a wound **heals**, it gets better. *The cut on my leg **healed** quickly.*

health

NOUN the condition of someone's body and mind. *I felt in very good **health** after our holiday.*

healthy healthier healthiest

ADJECTIVE **1** Someone who is **healthy** is fit and well, and is not suffering from any illness. *She goes to the gym to stay **healthy**.*
2 Something that is **healthy** is good for you. *You should try and eat a **healthy** diet.*

heap heaps heaping heaped

NOUN **1** an untidy pile of things.
VERB **2** If you **heap** things, you pile them up.

hear hears hearing heard

VERB **1** When you **hear** sounds, you are aware of them because they reach your ears. *We could **hear** the waves crashing on the beach.*
2 When you **hear** from someone, they write to you or phone you.

hearing

NOUN **1** the ability to hear.
2 If someone gives you a **hearing**, they let you give your point of view and listen to you.

hearse hearses

NOUN a large car that carries the coffin at a funeral.

heart hearts

NOUN **1** the organ in your chest that pumps the blood around your body. *See* page 433.

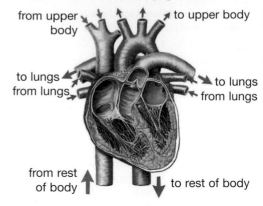

from upper body — to upper body
to lungs — to lungs
from lungs — from lungs
from rest of body — to rest of body

2 Your **heart** is also thought of as the centre of your emotions and feelings. *When his hamster died it broke his **heart**.*
3 the most central or important part of something. *It is always busy in the **heart** of the city.*
4 courage.
5 a curved shape like this ❤, or a playing card with this shape on it.
PHRASE **6** If you learn something **by heart**, you learn it so that you know it from memory.

heart attack heart attacks

NOUN a serious medical condition in which someone's heart suddenly beats irregularly or stops completely.

hearth hearths

*Said "**harth**"* NOUN the floor of a fireplace.

heat heats heating heated

NOUN **1** warmth or the quality of being hot: *the fierce **heat** of the sun.*
2 a contest or race in a competition that decides who will compete in the final.
VERB **3** When you **heat** something, you warm it.

heater heaters

NOUN a device used to produce heat in order to warm a place, such as a room or a car.

heath

NOUN a large open area of land covered in rough grass or heather, with very few trees.

heather
NOUN a plant with small purple or white flowers that grows wild on hills and moorland.

heave heaves heaving heaved
VERB If you **heave** something, you lift, push or throw it with a lot of effort.

heaven
NOUN In some religions, **heaven** is the place where God lives and where good people go when they die.

heavy heavier heaviest
ADJECTIVE 1 Something that is **heavy** weighs a lot.
2 You use **heavy** to talk about how much something weighs. *How **heavy** is the baby?*

Hebrew
Said "**hee**-broo" NOUN an ancient language that is now spoken in Israel by the Jewish people.

hectare hectares
NOUN a unit for measuring an area of land, equal to 10,000 square metres or about 2·471 acres.

hectic
ADJECTIVE involving a lot of rushed activity. *She leads a very **hectic** life.*

he'd
a contraction of *he had*.

hedge hedges
NOUN a row of bushes along the edge of a garden, field or road.

hedgehog hedgehogs
NOUN a small, brown mammal with sharp spikes covering its back.

heel heels
NOUN 1 the back part of your foot, below your ankle.
2 the part on the bottom at the back of a shoe or sock.

heifer heifers
NOUN a young cow that has not yet had calves.

height heights
NOUN 1 a measurement from the bottom to the top of someone or something.
2 a high position or place. *He's afraid of **heights**.*
3 the highest or most important part of something. *He's at the **height** of his success.*

heir heirs
NOUN the person who is entitled to inherit someone's property or title: *the **heir** to the throne.*

held
VERB the past tense of *hold*.

helicopter helicopters
NOUN an aircraft with rotating blades instead of wings, that enable it to take off vertically.

helium
NOUN a gas that is lighter than air. It is sometimes used to fill party balloons.

hell
NOUN 1 In some religions, **hell** is the place where the Devil lives and where wicked people are sent to be punished when they die.
2 INFORMAL In you say that something is **hell**, you mean that it is very unpleasant.

he'll
a contraction of *he will*.

hello
INTERJECTION OR GREETING You say **hello** when you meet someone or answer the telephone.

helmet helmets
NOUN a hard hat that you wear to protect your head.

help helps helping helped
VERB 1 If you **help** someone, you make something easier or better for them.
NOUN 2 assistance. *Thanks for your **help**.*

helpful
ADJECTIVE If you are **helpful**, you cooperate with others and support them.
helpfully ADVERB

helping helpings
NOUN a portion of food at a meal.

helpless
ADJECTIVE If you are **helpless**, you are unable to protect yourself or do anything useful.
helplessly ADVERB

hem hems hemming hemmed
NOUN 1 The **hem** of a garment is the edge of it that has been folded up and stitched in place.
VERB 2 If you **hem** a garment, you make a hem on it.

hemisphere hemispheres
NOUN one half of the earth or a sphere.

hen hens
NOUN 1 a female chicken.
2 any female bird.

heptagon heptagons
NOUN a flat shape with seven flat sides.

her
PRONOUN OR ADJECTIVE 1 refers to a woman, girl or female animal that has already been mentioned. *I like Amy. I often play with her.*
2 shows that something belongs to a particular female. *Mum is going to wear her blue jumper.*

heraldry
NOUN the study of coats of arms.

herb herbs
NOUN a plant whose leaves are used as a medicine or to flavour food.

herbivore herbivores
NOUN an animal that eats only plants.
herbivorous ADJECTIVE

herd herds herding herded
NOUN 1 a large group of animals grazing together: *a herd of cattle.*
VERB 2 If you **herd** animals or people, you make them move together as a group. *The teachers herded the children on to the bus.*

here
ADVERB at, to or in the place where you are.

hereditary
ADJECTIVE passed on to a child from a parent.

heritage
NOUN The **heritage** of a country is all its traditions, customs and art that have been passed from one generation to another.

hermit hermits
NOUN someone who prefers to live a simple life alone and far from other people, often for religious reasons.

hero heroes
NOUN 1 the main, male character in a book, film or play.
2 a person who is admired because they have done something brave or good.

heroine heroines
NOUN the main female character in a book, play or film.

heron herons
NOUN a wading bird with very long legs and a long beak and neck.

herring herrings
NOUN a silvery fish that lives in large shoals in northern seas.

hers
PRONOUN refers to something that belongs or relates to a woman, girl or other female animal.

herself
PRONOUN refers to the same woman, girl or female animal who does an action and is affected by it. *She pulled herself up.*

he's
a contraction of *he is.*

hesitate hesitates hesitating hesitated
VERB If you **hesitate**, you pause or show uncertainty.

heterosexual heterosexuals
NOUN a person who is sexually attracted to people of the opposite sex.

Antonym: homosexual

hexagon hexagons
NOUN a flat shape with six straight sides.
hexagonal ADJECTIVE

hibernate hibernates hibernating hibernated
VERB Animals that **hibernate** spend the winter in a state like a deep sleep.
hibernation NOUN

hiccup hiccups hiccupping hiccupped; also spelt **hiccough**
NOUN 1 short, uncontrolled sounds in your throat.
VERB 2 When you **hiccup**, you suffer from hiccups.

hide hides hiding hid hidden
VERB 1 If you **hide** something, you put it where it cannot be seen, or prevent it from being discovered. *He hid his disappointment.*
2 If you **hide**, you go somewhere where you cannot be seen or found easily.

hideous

ADJECTIVE extremely ugly or unpleasant.
hideously ADVERB

hieroglyphyics

Said "hy-ro-**gliff**-iks" PLURAL NOUN ancient Egyptian writing that uses pictures instead of words. It involves over 700 picture signs.

high higher highest

ADJECTIVE **1 High** refers to how much something measures from the bottom to the top. *The statue was three metres **high**.*
ADJECTIVE OR ADVERB **2** a long way above the ground. *He jumped **high** into the air.*
3 great in degree, quantity or intensity. *There were **high** winds before the storm.*

highlight highlights highlighting highlighted

NOUN **1** the most interesting part of something. *The **highlight** of the week was our trip to the cinema.*
VERB **2** If you **highlight** a point or a problem, you emphasize it.

high-rise

ADJECTIVE **High-rise** buildings are very tall.

highway highways

NOUN a main road,

hijack hijacks hijacking hijacked

VERB If someone **hijacks** a plane or other vehicle, they take control of it unlawfully and by force.
hijacker NOUN

hike hikes hiking hiked

VERB **1** If you **hike**, you go for a long walk across country.
NOUN **2** a long and demanding walk.

hilarious

ADJECTIVE very funny.

hill hills

NOUN a high, rounded piece of ground.

hilt hilts

NOUN the handle of a knife or sword.

him

PRONOUN refers to a man, boy or male animal that has already been mentioned. *Let's invite Ben. I really like **him**.*

himself

PRONOUN refers to the same man, boy or male animal that does an action and is affected by it. *He pushed **himself** to the front of the crowd.*

hind hinds

NOUN **1** a female deer.
ADJECTIVE **2** The **hind** legs of an animal are its back legs.

hinder hinders hindering hindered

VERB If you **hinder** someone or something, you get in their way and make it difficult for them to do what they want to do.

Hindu Hindus

NOUN a person who believes in Hinduism, an Indian religion that has many gods and involves the belief that people have another life on earth after death.

hinge hinges

NOUN the movable joint that attaches a door or window to its frame.

hint hints hinting hinted

NOUN **1** an indirect suggestion. *He dropped **hints** about his birthday present.*
2 a helpful piece of advice.
VERB **3** If you **hint** that something is true, you suggest it indirectly. *The teacher **hinted** that they had all done well in the tests.*

hip hips

NOUN Your **hips** are the joints and the bony parts at the top of your thigh and below your waist.

hippopotamus hippopotamuses or hippopotami

NOUN a large, African mammal with thick, wrinkled skin and short legs, that lives near rivers.

hire hires hiring hired

VERB **1** If you **hire** something, you pay money to use it for a period of time.

PHRASE **2** Something that is **for hire** is available for people to hire. *There are bicycles for hire down by the beach.*

his

PRONOUN refers to something that belongs or relates to a man, boy or other male animal.

hiss hisses hissing hissed

VERB If someone or something **hisses**, they make a long "s" sound.

historic

ADJECTIVE important in the past, or likely to be seen as important in the future.

historical

ADJECTIVE occurring in the past, or relating to the study of the past.

history histories

NOUN **1** the study of the past.

2 the set of facts that are known about a place or subject. *There was a leaflet on the history of the stately home.*

[from Greek *historein* meaning to narrate a story]

hit hits hitting hit

VERB **1** If you **hit** someone or something, you strike or knock them with force.

2 If something **hits** you, it affects you suddenly and forcefully. *The answer suddenly hit me.*

NOUN **3** If someone or something is a big **hit**, they are a great success.

4 the action of hitting something.

hitch hitches hitching hitched

VERB **1** If you **hitch** something, you tie it up using a loop.

2 INFORMAL If you **hitch** somewhere, you travel by getting lifts from passing vehicles.

NOUN **3** a slight problem of difficulty. *Their plans went ahead without a hitch.*

hitchhike hitchhikes hitchhiking hitchhiked

VERB to travel by getting lifts from passing vehicles.

HIV

NOUN a virus that weakens people's resistance to illness and can cause AIDS. **HIV** is an abbreviation for *human immunodeficiency virus.*

hive hives

NOUN **1** a beehive.

2 A place that is a **hive** of activity is very busy.

hoard hoards hoarding hoarded

VERB **1** If you **hoard** things, you save them even though they may no longer be useful.

NOUN **2** a store of things that has been saved or hidden.

✔ Do not confuse *hoard* with *horde*.

hoarse hoarser hoarsest

ADJECTIVE A **hoarse** voice sounds rough and unclear.

hoarsely ADVERB

hoax hoaxes

NOUN a trick or an attempt to deceive someone. *The bomb scare was a hoax.*

hobble hobbles hobbling hobbled

VERB If you **hobble**, you walk awkwardly because of pain or injury.

hobby hobbies

NOUN something that you do for enjoyment in your spare time.

hockey

NOUN a game in which two teams use long sticks with curved ends to try to hit a small ball into the other team's goal.

A hockey stick

hoe hoes

NOUN a long-handled gardening tool with a small, square blade, used to remove weeds and break up the soil.

Hogmanay

NOUN New Year's Eve and its celebrations in Scotland.

hoist hoists hoisting hoisted

VERB If someone **hoists** something, they lift it, especially using ropes and pulleys, a crane or other machinery.

hold holds holding held

VERB **1** If you **hold** something, you carry it or keep it in place, usually with your hands or arms.

2 If you **hold** a meeting or a party, you arrange it and cause it to happen.

3 If you **hold** someone responsible for something, you decide that they did it.

4 If something **holds** a certain amount, it can contain that amount. *This jug **holds** a litre of water.*

5 If you **hold** something, you possess it. *She **holds** the world long jump record.*

NOUN **6** the part of a ship or aircraft where cargo or luggage is stored.

7 If someone has a **hold** over you, they have power over you.

8 If you keep a **hold** on something, you hold it securely.

hole holes

NOUN an opening or hollow space in something.

Holi

NOUN a Hindu festival celebrated in spring.

holiday holidays

NOUN **1** a period of time spent away from home for enjoyment.

2 a day when people do not go to work or school because of a national festival. *In Britain, Christmas Day is always a **holiday**.*

hollow hollows hollowing hollowed

ADJECTIVE **1** Something that is **hollow** has a hole or space inside it.

NOUN **2** a small valley or sunken place.

VERB **3** If you **hollow** something out, you make it hollow. *We **hollowed** out the pumpkin to make a lantern for Halloween.*

Antonym: (sense 1) solid

holly

NOUN an evergreen tree or shrub with spiky leaves. It often has red berries in winter.

hologram holograms

NOUN a three-dimensional picture made by laser beams.

holster holsters

NOUN a holder for a hand gun, worn at the side of the body or under the arm.

holy holier holiest

ADJECTIVE Something that is **holy** relates to God or to a particular religion.

home homes

NOUN **1** the building or place in which you live.

2 A nursing **home** is a building in which elderly or ill people live and are looked after.

3 the place where you feel you belong.

homeless

ADJECTIVE Someone who is **homeless** has nowhere to live.

homelessness NOUN

homesick

ADJECTIVE If you are **homesick**, you are unhappy because you are away from your home and family. *I enjoyed my exchange trip to Germany, but I did feel **homesick** sometimes.*

homework

NOUN school work given to pupils to be done at home.

homograph homographs

NOUN one of a group of words spelt in the same way but with different meanings, such as *saw* (meaning a tool for cutting) and *saw* (the past tense of "see").

homonym homonyms

NOUN one of a group of words that are pronounced or spelt in the same way but have different meanings. For example *eight* and *ate*, or *bank* (meaning a slope) and *bank* (meaning a place where you keep your money).

homophone homophones

NOUN one of a group of words with different meanings that are pronounced in the same way but spelt differently. *Write* and *right* are **homophones**.

homosexual homosexuals

NOUN a person who is sexually attracted to someone of the same sex.

Antonym: heterosexual

honest

NOUN If you are **honest**, you can be trusted to tell the truth.

honestly ADVERB

Synonyms: trustworthy, truthful

a
b
c
d
e
f
g
h
i
j
k
l
m
n
o
p
q
r
s
t
u
v
w
x
y
z

honey
NOUN a sweet, edible, sticky substance made by bees.

honeycomb honeycombs
NOUN a wax structure made with six-sided cells by bees for storing honey.

honeymoon honeymoons
NOUN a holiday for a newly married couple after their wedding.

honour honours honouring honoured
NOUN **1** An **honour** is an award given to someone for something they have done.
2 If you feel that it is an **honour** to do something, you feel proud or privileged to do it.
VERB **3** If you **honour** someone, you give them special praise or attention, or an award.

hood hoods
NOUN **1** a loose covering for the head, usually part of a coat or jacket.
2 In American English, the **hood** of a car is the cover over the engine at the front.

hoof hooves or hoofs
NOUN the hard, bony part of the feet of horses, cattle and deer.

hook hooks hooking hooked
NOUN **1** a curved piece of metal or plastic that is used for catching things or for holding things up.
VERB **2** If you **hook** one thing on to another, you attach it there using a hook. *He hooked the caravan to the car.*

hooligan hooligans
NOUN a destructive and violent young person.
hooliganism NOUN

hoop hoops
NOUN a large wooden, metal or plastic ring.

hoot hoots hooting hooted
VERB **1** If a car horn **hoots**, it makes a makes a loud, honking noise.
2 If someone **hoots**, they make a long "oo" sound like an owl or a car horn. *We all hooted with laughter at his joke.*

hop hops hopping hopped
VERB **1** If you **hop**, you jump on one foot.
2 When animals such as kangaroos, birds or insects **hop**, they jump with two or more feet together.

hope hopes hoping hoped
VERB **1** If you **hope** that something will happen, you want or expect it to happen.
NOUN **2** the wish or expectation that things will go well in the future.

hopeful
ADJECTIVE If you are **hopeful** about something, you hope it will turn out well.
hopefully ADVERB

hopeless
ADJECTIVE **1** You say something is **hopeless** when it is very bad and you do not feel it can get any better.
2 unable to do something well. *I'm hopeless at art.*
hopelessly ADVERB

horde hordes
NOUN a large group or number of people or other animals.
✔ Do not confuse *horde* with *hoard*.

horizon horizons
NOUN the distant line where the sky seems to touch the land or sea.

horizontal
ADJECTIVE flat and level with, or parallel to the ground.
horizontally ADVERB

horn horns
NOUN **1** a warning device on a vehicle that makes a loud noise.
2 one of the hard, pointed things that grow from the head of a cow or goat.

hornet hornets
NOUN **1** a type of very large wasp.
PHRASE **2** A situation described as **a hornet's nest** is very difficult to deal with and likely to cause trouble.

horoscope horoscopes
NOUN a prediction about what is going to happen to someone, based on the position of the stars when they were born.

horrible

ADJECTIVE disagreeable and unpleasant.

horrific

ADJECTIVE If something is **horrific**, it horrifies people.

horrify horrifies horrifying horrified

VERB If someone or something **horrifies** you, they make you feel disgusted and shocked.

horror

NOUN a strong feeling of alarm caused by something very unpleasant.

horse horses

NOUN a large mammal with a mane and tail, that people can ride.

horse chestnut horse chestnuts

NOUN a large tree with flowers and shiny brown nuts known as conkers.

horsepower

NOUN a unit used for measuring how powerful an engine is.

horseshoe horseshoes

NOUN a U-shaped piece of iron that is nailed to the bottom of a horse's hoof to protect it.

hose hoses

NOUN a long, flexible tube through which liquid or gas can be passed: *a garden* **hose**.

hospitable

ADJECTIVE If you are **hospitable**, you are friendly, welcoming and generous to others.

hospital hospitals

NOUN a place where sick people are looked after by doctors and nurses.

host hosts hosting hosted

NOUN **1** the person who gives a party or organizes an event, and who welcomes and looks after the guests.
2 a large number of things. *There was a* **host** *of things to do at the fair.*
VERB **3** If you **host** an event, you organize it and act as the host.

hostage hostages

NOUN a person who is illegally held prisoner and threatened with injury or death unless certain demands are met by other people.

hostel hostels

NOUN a large house where people can stay cheaply for a short time: *a youth* **hostel**.

hostile

ADJECTIVE If someone is **hostile** to you, they behave in an unfriendly aggressive way towards you.

hot hotter hottest

ADJECTIVE **1** having a high temperature.
2 having a burning taste caused by spices.

hotel hotels

NOUN a building where people stay, paying for their room and meals.

hound hounds

NOUN a dog, especially one used for hunting or racing.

hour hours

NOUN a period of 60 minutes.
[from Greek **hora** meaning season or time of day]

house houses

NOUN a building where people live.

household households

NOUN **1** all the people who live as a group in a house or flat.
PHRASE **2** Someone who is **a household name** is very well known.
householder NOUN

housewife housewives

NOUN a married woman who does not have a paid job, but instead looks after her home and children.

housework

NOUN all the work done in the home, like the cleaning and cooking.

hover hovers hovering hovered

VERB When a bird, insect or aircraft **hovers**, it stays in the same position in the air.

hovercraft hovercraft or hovercrafts

NOUN a vehicle that can travel over water or land supported by a cushion of air.

how

ADVERB used to ask about, explain or refer to the way something is done. *How did you get so dirty?*

however

ADVERB **1** You use **however** when you are adding a comment that contrasts with what has just been said. *He is very chatty and seems confident.* ***However**, he is quite shy.*
2 You use **however** to say that something makes no difference to a situation. ***However** hard she tried, nothing seemed to work.*

howl howls howling howled

VERB **1** If someone or something **howls**, they make a long, loud wailing noise such as that made by a dog or a baby when it is upset.
NOUN **2** a long, loud wailing noise.

hub hubs

NOUN **1** the centre part of a wheel.
2 the most important or active part of a place or organization.

huddle huddles huddling huddled

VERB **1** If you **huddle** up, or are **huddled**, you are curled up with your arms and legs close to your body.
2 When people or animals **huddle** together, they sit or stand close to each other, often for warmth.

hug hugs hugging hugged

VERB If you **hug** someone, you put your arms round them and hold them close to you, usually to comfort them or to show affection.

huge

ADJECTIVE extremely large in amount, size or degree. *The party was a **huge** success.*

Synonyms: enormous, gigantic, vast

hull hulls

NOUN The **hull** of a ship is the main part of its body that sits in the water.

hum hums humming hummed

VERB **1** If something **hums**, it makes a continuous, low noise.
2 If you **hum**, you sing with your lips closed.
NOUN **3** a continuous, low noise.

human humans

ADJECTIVE **1** relating to or concerning people. *We are all part of the **human** race.*
NOUN **2** a person.
[from Latin ***homo*** meaning man]

human being human beings

NOUN a person.

humane

ADJECTIVE showing kindness and sympathy towards others.
humaneness NOUN   **humanely** ADVERB

humanity

NOUN **1** the human race.
2 Someone who shows **humanity** is kind and sympathetic.

humble humbler humblest

ADJECTIVE A **humble** person is modest and thinks that they have very little value.
humbly ADVERB

humid

ADJECTIVE If the weather is **humid**, the air feels damp, heavy and warm.
humidity NOUN

humiliate humiliates humiliating humiliated

VERB If you **humiliate** someone, you make them feel ashamed or appear stupid to other people.
humiliation NOUN

humour humours humouring humoured

NOUN **1** the quality of being funny.
2 the ability to be amused by certain things. *She's got a peculiar sense of **humour**.*
VERB **3** If you **humour** someone, you try to please them, so that they will not become upset.

hump humps

NOUN a small, rounded lump or mound: *a camel's **hump**.*

hump

hunch hunches hunching hunched

VERB **1** If you **hunch** your shoulders, you raise them and push them forward, bending forward slightly.
2 If you have a **hunch** about something, you have an idea that something will happen.

hundred

NOUN the number 100.

hung

VERB the past tense and participle of *hang*.

hunger

NOUN the need or desire to eat.

hungry hungrier hungriest

ADJECTIVE If you are **hungry**, you need or want food.

hungrily ADVERB

hunt hunts hunting hunted

VERB **1** If you **hunt** for something, you search for it.

2 When people **hunt**, they chase and kill wild animals for food or sport.

NOUN **3** the act of searching for something. *The neighbours joined in the **hunt** for the missing cat.*

hurdle hurdles

NOUN **1** one of the frames or barriers that you jump over in an athletics race called **hurdles**. *She knocked over the last **hurdle**, but still managed to win the race.*

2 a problem or difficulty. *Several **hurdles** had to be overcome before the school play could go ahead.*

hurl hurls hurling hurled

VERB If you **hurl** something, you throw it with great force.

hurricane hurricanes

NOUN a very violent storm with strong winds.

hurry hurries hurrying hurried

VERB **1** If you **hurry** somewhere, you go there quickly.

2 If you **hurry** someone or something, or if you tell someone to **hurry** up, you try to make something happen more quickly.

PHRASE **3** If you are **in a hurry** to do something, you want to do it quickly. If you do something **in a hurry**, you do it quickly.

hurt hurts hurting hurt

VERB **1** If you **hurt** yourself or someone else, you injure or cause physical pain to yourself or someone else.

2 If a part of your body **hurts**, you feel pain there.

3 If you **hurt** someone, or **hurt** their feelings, you upset them by being unkind towards them.

ADJECTIVE **4** If you are **hurt**, you are injured.

5 If you feel **hurt**, you are upset because of someone's unkindness towards you. *She was **hurt** that they did not invite her to the party.* [from Old French **hurter** meaning to knock against]

hurtle hurtles hurtling hurtled

VERB If someone or something **hurtles**, they move along very fast in an uncontrolled way. *The car **hurtled** along the bumpy road.*

husband husbands

NOUN A woman's **husband** is the man she is married to.

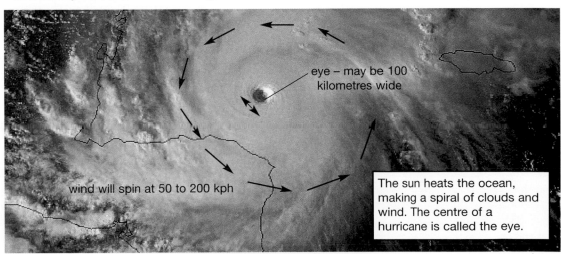

eye – may be 100 kilometres wide

wind will spin at 50 to 200 kph

The sun heats the ocean, making a spiral of clouds and wind. The centre of a hurricane is called the eye.

A satellite image of a hurricane

hustle hustles hustling hustled
VERB **1** If you **hustle** someone, you make them move by pushing and jostling them.
2 hurry.

hut huts
NOUN a small house or shelter.

hutch hutches
NOUN a wooden box with wire mesh at one side, in which small pets can be kept.

hydrant hydrants
NOUN a pipe connected to the main water supply of a town and used for emergencies.

hydraulic
ADJECTIVE operated by water or other fluid that is under pressure.

hydroelectric
ADJECTIVE **Hydroelectric** power is electricity produced from the energy of moving water.

hydrogen
NOUN a colourless gas that is the lightest and most common element in the world.
Hydrogen-filled balloons explode because this gas is very flammable.

hyena hyenas; also spelt **hyaena**
Said "high-**ee**-na" NOUN a wild, dog-like animal found in Africa and Asia, that hunts in packs.
[from Greek *huaina* meaning hog]

hygiene
Said "**hy**-jeen" NOUN the state of being clean and free of germs.

hymn hymns
NOUN a Christian song in praise of God.

hyphen hyphens
NOUN a punctuation mark (-) used to join together words or parts of words, as in *left-handed*.

hypocrite hypocrites
NOUN someone who pretends to have certain views and beliefs that are different from their actual views and beliefs.
hypocritical ADJECTIVE   **hypocrisy** NOUN

hypothermia
NOUN a condition in which a person is very ill because their body has been extremely cold for a long time. *After spending the night stuck on the mountain, the climbers had **hypothermia**.*

Ii

I

PRONOUN A speaker or writer uses **I** to refer to themselves.

ice

NOUN water that has frozen solid.

iceberg icebergs

NOUN a large mass of ice floating in the sea.
[from Dutch *ijsberg* meaning ice mountain]

ice cream ice creams

NOUN a very cold, sweet, creamy food.

ice skate ice skates ice skating ice skated;
also spelt **ice-skate**

NOUN **1** a boot with a metal blade on the bottom, that you wear to move around on ice.
VERB **2** When you **ice-skate**, you move about on the ice wearing ice skates.

icicle icicles

NOUN a piece of ice shaped like a pointed stick, that hangs down from a surface.

icing

NOUN a sweet covering for a cake or biscuits.

ICT

NOUN an abbreviation of Information and Communication Technology. **ICT** is the use of computers, telephones, television and radio to store, organize and give out information.

icy icier iciest

ADJECTIVE **1** Something that is **icy** is very cold.
*We tried to shelter from the **icy** wind.*
2 An **icy** road has ice on it.
icily ADVERB

I'd

a contraction of *I had* and *I would*.

idea ideas

NOUN **1** a plan or possible course of action.
2 an opinion or belief.
3 If you have an **idea** of something, you have a general but not a detailed knowledge of it.
*Could you give me an **idea** of the cost?*

ideal

ADJECTIVE The **ideal** person or thing for a particular purpose is the best possible one.

identical

ADJECTIVE exactly the same. *They are **identical** twins.*

identification

NOUN a document, such as a driver's licence or passport, that states who you are.

identify identifies identifying identified

VERB If you **identify** someone or something, you recognise and name them.
identifiable ADJECTIVE

identity identities

NOUN the things that make you who you are.

idiom idioms

NOUN a group of words that, when used together, mean something different from when the words are used individually. For example, "It rained cats and dogs".

idiot idiots

NOUN someone who is stupid or foolish.

idiotic

ADJECTIVE very stupid.
idiotically ADVERB

idle idler idlest

ADJECTIVE **1** If you are **idle**, you are doing nothing.
2 Machines or factories that are **idle** are not being used.
3 lazy.
idleness NOUN   **idly** ADVERB

idol idols

NOUN a famous person who is loved and admired by fans.

i.e.

i.e. means "that is". *Please meet me in three days' time, **i.e.** on Sunday.*
[from Latin *id est* meaning that is]

A
B
C
D
E
F
G
H
I
J
K
L
M
N
O
P
Q
R
S
T
U
V
W
X
Y
Z

if

CONJUNCTION **1** on condition that. *You can watch TV **if** you do your homework first.* **2** whether. *I asked him **if** he could come to the party.*

igloo igloos

NOUN a dome-shaped house built out of blocks of snow by the Inuit or Eskimo people.
[from ***igdlu***, an Inuit word meaning house]

ignite ignites igniting ignited

VERB If you **ignite** something, or it **ignites**, you set it on fire or it catches fire.
[from Latin ***ignis*** meaning fire]

ignorant

ADJECTIVE If you are **ignorant** of something, you do not know about it.

ignore ignores ignoring ignored

VERB If you **ignore** someone or something, you do not take any notice of them.

iguana iguanas

NOUN a large, tropical lizard.

il-

PREFIX You add **il-** to the beginning of a word to mean that it is not something. For example, **il**legal means not legal, and **il**legible means not legible.

I'll

a contraction of *I will.*

ill

ADJECTIVE unhealthy or sick.
[from Norse ***illr*** meaning bad]

Synonym: unwell

illegal

ADJECTIVE If something is **illegal** it is forbidden by the law.
illegally ADVERB

Synonyms: criminal, unlawful

illegible

ADJECTIVE Writing that is **illegible** is unclear and very difficult to read.
illegibly ADVERB

Antonym: legible

illegitimate

ADJECTIVE Someone who is **illegitimate** is born to two people who are not married to each other.
illegitimacy NOUN

illiterate

ADJECTIVE unable to read or write.

Antonym: literate

illness illnesses

NOUN **1** the state or experience of being ill. **2** a particular disease. *Flu is a common **illness** during the winter months.*

illogical

ADJECTIVE An **illogical** feeling or action is not reasonable or sensible.
illogically ADVERB

Antonym: logical

illuminate illuminates illuminating illuminated

VERB If you **illuminate** something, you shine light on to it so that it is easier to see, or you decorate it with lights.

illumination illuminations

NOUN one of the coloured lights put up to decorate a town, especially at Christmas.

illusion illusions

NOUN **1** an idea that you think is true, but is not. *We were under the **illusion** that this was going to be an easy project.* **2** something that seems to be there but does not really exist.

illustrate illustrates illustrating illustrated

VERB **1** If you **illustrate** a book, you help to explain its meaning by putting in pictures and diagrams. **2** If you **illustrate** a point when you are speaking, you make its meaning clearer, often by giving examples.

illustration illustrations

NOUN a picture or a diagram that helps to explain something.

illustrator illustrators

NOUN someone who produces the pictures that go into books.

im-

PREFIX You add **im-** to the beginning of a word to mean not something. For example, something that is **im**movable cannot be moved, and something that is **im**perfect is not perfect.

I'm

a contraction of *I am*.

image images

NOUN a picture or photograph.

imagery

NOUN The **imagery** of a poem or book is the words that are used to produce a picture in the mind of the reader.

imaginary

ADJECTIVE Something that is **imaginary** exists only in your mind, not in real life.

Antonym: real

imagination imaginations

NOUN If you show **imagination**, you have the ability to form ideas and pictures in your mind.

imaginative

ADJECTIVE If you are **imaginative,** you find it easy to create new and exciting ideas in your mind.

imaginatively ADVERB

Antonym: unimaginative

imagine imagines imagining imagined

VERB If you **imagine** something or someone, you create a picture of them in your mind.

imam

NOUN a person who leads a group in prayer in a mosque.

imitate imitates imitating imitated

VERB If you **imitate** someone or something, you copy them.

Synonym: mimic

imitation imitations

NOUN a copy of something else.

immature

ADJECTIVE **1** Something that is **immature** is not fully grown or developed.

2 An **immature** person does not behave in a sensible way.

immaturely ADVERB   **immaturity** NOUN

Antonym: mature

immediately

ADVERB If something happens **immediately**, it happens at once.

immense

ADJECTIVE very large.

immensely ADVERB   **immensity** NOUN

Synonyms: huge, vast

immerse immerses immersing immersed

VERB **1** If you **immmerse** something, you cover it completely with liquid.

2 If you **immerse** yourself in an activity, you become completely occupied with it.

immersion NOUN

immigrant immigrants

NOUN someone who has come to live in a country from another country.

immigrate immigrates immigrating immigrated

VERB If someone **immigrates**, they come to live permanently in a country that is not their own.

Antonym: emigrate

immobile

ADJECTIVE If something or someone is **immobile**, they are not moving.

immobility NOUN

immoral

ADJECTIVE If someone is **immoral**, they do not follow most people's standards of acceptable behaviour.

immorality NOUN

immortal

ADJECTIVE **1** Someone or something that is **immortal** is famous and will be remembered for a long time.

2 Something that is **immortal** will last forever.

immortality NOUN

immune
ADJECTIVE If you are **immune** to a particular disease, you cannot catch it.
immunity NOUN

immunize immunizes immunizing immunized
VERB If a doctor **immunizes** you against a disease, he gives you an injection so that you are protected from the disease.
immunization NOUN

impact impacts
NOUN **1** The **impact** of one object on another is the force with which it hits it.
2 If something has an **impact** on a situation or person, it has a strong effect on them.
[from Latin *impactus* meaning pushed against]

impartial
ADJECTIVE If you are **impartial** about something, you are fair and unbiased.
impartially ADVERB

Antonym: partial

impatient
ADJECTIVE If you are **impatient**, you become annoyed easily because you do not want to wait for someone or something.
impatiently ADVERB   **impatience** NOUN

Antonym: patient

imperfect
ADJECTIVE Something that is **imperfect** has faults.
imperfectly ADVERB   **imperfection** NOUN

imperial
ADJECTIVE **1** related to an empire, emperor or empress.
2 The **imperial** system of measurement is a system that uses inches, feet and yards, ounces and pounds, and pints and gallons.

impersonal
ADJECTIVE Something that is **impersonal** makes you feel that individuals and their feelings do not matter.
impersonally ADVERB

impersonate impersonates impersonating impersonated
VERB If you **impersonate** someone, you pretend to be that person.
impersonation NOUN   **impersonator** NOUN

impertinent
ADJECTIVE If you are **impertinent**, you are disrespectful and rude to someone.

import imports importing imported
VERB **1** If someone **imports** something, they buy it or bring it in from another country.
NOUN **2 Imports** are goods brought into one country from another country.

Antonym: export

important
ADJECTIVE **1** Something that is **important** is very valuable, necessary or significant.
2 An **important** person has a lot of influence or power.

impose imposes imposing imposed
VERB If someone **imposes** something on someone, they force it on them.

imposing
ADJECTIVE If someone or something is **imposing**, they look impressive and important.

impossible
ADJECTIVE Something that is **impossible** cannot happen or cannot be done.
impossibly ADVERB   **impossibility** NOUN

imposter imposters
NOUN An **imposter** is someone who pretends to be someone else, usually for devious reasons.

impractical
ADJECTIVE If someone or something is **impractical**, they are not sensible or realistic.
*It is **impractical** to camp in this wet weather.*

Antonym: practical

impress impresses impressing impressed
VERB **1** If you **impress** someone, you cause them to admire or respect you.
2 If you **impress** something on someone, you make sure that they understand it and remember it.

impression impressions
NOUN **1** An **impression** of someone or something is a vague idea or feeling that you have about them. *I have the **impression** that I've met you before.*
2 a mark made by pressing. *You leave an **impression** when you press a coin into Plasticine then take it away.*
3 an imitation of a person, animal or thing.

impressive
ADJECTIVE If someone or something is **impressive**, it causes you to admire or respect it.
impressively ADVERB

imprison imprisons imprisoning imprisoned
VERB If someone **imprisons** another person, they put them in prison or lock them up somewhere.
imprisonment NOUN

improbable
ADJECTIVE not probable or likely to happen.
improbably ADVERB   **improbability** NOUN

Antonym: probable

improve improves improving improved
VERB If something **improves**, or if you **improve** it, it gets better.
improvement NOUN

improvise improvises improvising improvised
VERB 1 If you **improvise** something, you make or do something without planning it in advance, and with whatever materials are available. *In order to save money the children **improvised** their costumes for the school play.*
2 When musicians or actors **improvise**, they make up the music or words as they go along.
improvised ADJECTIVE   **improvisation** NOUN

impudent
ADJECTIVE If you are **impudent**, you are rude and insolent.
impudently ADVERB   **impudence** NOUN

impulse impulses
NOUN If you have an **impulse** to do something, you have a strong urge to do it immediately.
impulsive ADJECTIVE

in
PREPOSITION OR ADVERB 1 at or inside. *The cow was **in** the field.*
2 into. *They went **in** the house.*
3 during. *It snows **in** winter.*

in-
PREFIX You add **in-** to the beginning of a word to mean not something. For example, **in**accurate means not accurate, and **in**accessible means not accessible.

inability inabilities
NOUN If you have an **inability** to do something, you cannot do it.

Antonym: ability

inaccessible
ADJECTIVE If something is **inaccessible**, it is very difficult or impossible to reach.

Antonym: accessible

inaccurate
ADJECTIVE If something is **inaccurate**, it is incorrect.

Antonym: accurate

inadequate
ADJECTIVE If something is **inadequate**, there is not enough of it, or it is not good enough for a particular purpose.

Antonym: adequate

inanimate
ADJECTIVE not alive. For example, rocks and furniture are **inanimate**.

inaudible
ADJECTIVE If something is **inaudible**, it cannot be heard.

Antonym: audible

incapable
ADJECTIVE Someone who is **incapable** of doing something is not able to do it.

Antonym: capable

incendiary
ADJECTIVE An **incendiary** device is designed to set fire to things.

incense
NOUN a spicy substance that gives off a sweet smell when it is burned.

incessant
ADJECTIVE If something is **incessant**, it continues without stopping. *The sound of the rain on the windows was **incessant**.*
incessantly ADVERB

inch inches
NOUN a unit of length equal to about 2·54 centimetres.
[from Latin ***uncia*** meaning twelfth part; there are twelve inches in a foot]

incident incidents
NOUN an event or occurrence, especially an unusual one.

incidentally
ADVERB If something happens **incidentally**, it happens along with something else, as a minor part of it.

incinerate incinerates incinerating incinerated
VERB If you **incinerate** something, you burn it until only ashes are left.
incineration NOUN

incisor incisors
NOUN Your **incisors** are the sharp teeth at the front of your mouth, used for biting and cutting food.

inclination inclinations
NOUN If you have an **inclination** to do something, you want to do it.

incline inclines inclining inclined
Said "in-**klyn**" VERB **1** If you are **inclined** to do something, you often do it or you would like to do it
Said "in-klyn" NOUN **2** a slope.

include includes including included
VERB If one thing **includes** another, the second thing is part of the first thing. *Meals are included in the price at this hotel.*

Antonym: exclude

inclusive
ADJECTIVE When something is **inclusive**, it includes everything and nothing is left out. *The price for the meal was inclusive, so Gran had nothing extra to pay for our milkshakes.*

incognito
ADVERB If someone is **incognito**, they are in disguise.
[from Latin *in* + *cognitus* meaning not known]

income incomes
NOUN the money a person earns.

incomplete
ADJECTIVE Something that is **incomplete** is not complete or finished.

Antonym: complete

incongruous
ADJECTIVE If something is **incongruous** in a particular place or situation, it seems unsuitable and out of place.
incongruously ADVERB

inconsiderate
ADJECTIVE If you are **inconsiderate**, you do not consider the needs or feelings of others.

Antonym: considerate

inconspicuous
ADJECTIVE If someone or something is **inconspicuous**, they are not noticeable or obvious, and cannot easily be seen.
inconspicuously ADVERB

Antonym: conspicuous

inconvenient
ADJECTIVE If something is **inconvenient**, it is awkward and causes difficulties: *an inconvenient time to call.*
inconveniently ADVERB

Antonym: convenient

incorporate incorporates incorporating incorporated
VERB If someone **incorporates** one thing into another thing, they include the first thing so that it becomes part of the second.

incorrect
ADJECTIVE Something that is **incorrect** is wrong or untrue.

Antonym: correct

increase increases increasing increased
VERB **1** If something **increases**, or if you **increase** it, it becomes larger in number, level or amount. *Her dad increased her pocket money.*
NOUN **2** a rise in the number, level or amount of something. *There has been an increase in the number of children walking to school.*

Antonym: decrease

incredible
ADJECTIVE totally amazing or impossible to believe.

Synonym: unbelievable

incubate incubates incubating incubated

Said "**in**-kyoo-bayt" VERB When eggs **incubate**, or a bird **incubates** them, they are kept warm until they hatch.

incubator incubators

NOUN a piece of hospital equipment in which sick or weak newborn babies are kept warm and safe.

incurable

ADJECTIVE If someone has an **incurable** disease, they cannot be cured.

Antonym: curable

indebted

ADJECTIVE If you are **indebted** to someone, you are very grateful to them.

indecent

ADJECTIVE Something that is **indecent** is shocking or rude.

indecently ADVERB   **indecency** NOUN

Antonym: decent

indecisive

ADJECTIVE If someone is **indecisive**, they find it difficult to make up their mind.

Antonym: decisive

indeed

ADVERB **1** You use **indeed** to emphasize a point that you are making. *The cake was very good indeed.*
2 You use **indeed** to show that you agree with something: *"Are you going to the party?" "Indeed I am.".*

indefinite

ADJECTIVE If something is **indefinite**, it is vague and unclear.

Antonym: definite

indefinitely

ADVERB If something goes on **indefinitely**, there is no clear time when it will finish and it can go on for an unlimited time.

indent indents indenting indented

VERB If you **indent** a paragraph when you write, you start the first line further to the right, away from the margin.

independent

ADJECTIVE **1** If you are **independent**, you are able to do things yourself and do not need help from other people.
2 free and not controlled by anyone.

independently ADVERB   **independence** NOUN

indestructible

ADJECTIVE If something is **indestructible**, it cannot be destroyed.

indicate indicates indicating indicated

VERB **1** If you **indicate** something to someone, you point it out or show it to them.
2 If the driver of a vehicle **indicates**, they give a signal to show which way they are going to move or turn. *The cyclist indicated that he was turning right.*

indicator indicators

NOUN **1** something that tells you what something is like or what is happening.
2 A car's **indicators** are the lights at the front and back that are used to show when it is turning left or right.

indifferent

ADJECTIVE If you are **indifferent** to something, you have no interest in it.

indifferently ADVERB   **indifference** NOUN

indigestion

NOUN a pain you get when you have difficulty digesting food.

indignant

ADJECTIVE If you are **indignant** about something, you are angry about it because you think it is unfair.

indignantly ADVERB

indigo
ADJECTIVE deep blue or violet.

indirect
ADJECTIVE If something happens in an **indirect** way, it does not happen in a straightforward way.
indirectly ADVERB

Antonym: direct

indispensable
ADJECTIVE absolutely necessary; essential.

indistinct
ADJECTIVE not clear.
indistinctly ADVERB

Antonym: distinct

individual individuals
ADJECTIVE **1** relating to one particular person or thing. *Each child in the class gets **individual** attention.*
2 single or separate. *Each sweet in the packet comes in an **individual** wrapper.*
NOUN **3** a person, different from any other person. *We should treat people as **individuals**.*

indoor
ADJECTIVE happening inside a building. *The hotel has an **indoor** swimming pool.*

indulge indulges indulging indulged
VERB **1** If you **indulge** in something, you allow yourself to do it because you enjoy it.
2 If you **indulge** someone, you allow them to have or do what they want.
indulgence NOUN

industrial
ADJECTIVE to do with the work and processes involved in making things in factories.

industrious
ADJECTIVE If you are **industrious**, you work hard.
industriously ADVERB

industry industries
NOUN **1** the work involved in making things in factories.
2 all the people and processes involved in manufacturing a particular thing. *My dad works in the computer **industry**.*
[from Latin ***industria*** meaning diligence or hard work]

inedible
ADJECTIVE If something is **inedible**, it is too unpleasant or poisonous to eat.

inefficient
ADJECTIVE badly organized, wasteful and slow.
inefficiently ADVERB   **inefficiency** NOUN

inevitable
ADJECTIVE certain to happen.

inexpensive
ADJECTIVE not costing much.

inexplicable
ADJECTIVE If something is **inexplicable**, you cannot explain it.
inexplicably ADVERB

infamous
ADJECTIVE
Said "**in**-fum-uss" Someone or something that is **infamous** is well known for their bad qualities.

Synonym: notorious

infant infants
NOUN a baby or very young child.
[from Latin ***infans*** meaning unable to speak]

infantry
NOUN In an army, the **infantry** are soldiers who fight on foot rather than in tanks or on horses.

infatuated
ADJECTIVE If you are **infatuated** with someone, you are so much in love with them that you cannot think reasonably about them.
infatuation NOUN

infect infects infecting infected
VERB If someone or something **infects** another a person or animal, they pass a disease on to them.

infection infections
NOUN an illness caused by germs.

infectious
ADJECTIVE Something that is **infectious** spreads from one person to another. *Measles is an **infectious** disease.*

infer infers inferring inferred
VERB If you **infer** that something is happening or is correct, you work it out from the details you already have.
inference NOUN

inferior

ADJECTIVE Something that is **inferior** is not as good as something else of a similar kind. *The trainers were of **inferior** quality.*
inferiority NOUN

inferno infernos

NOUN a huge and fierce fire.

infertile

ADJECTIVE **1 Infertile** soil is of poor quality and plants cannot grow well in it.
2 A person, animal or plant that is **infertile** is unable to reproduce.

infested

ADJECTIVE If something is **infested**, it is full of pests, like insects, rats or fleas.

infinite

ADJECTIVE If something is **infinite**, it is endless and without limits.
infinitely ADVERB

infinitive infinitives

NOUN the base form of a verb. An **infinitive** often has "to" in front of it, for example "to be" or "to see".

infirm

ADJECTIVE If someone is **infirm**, they are weak because they are ill or old.
infirmity NOUN

infirmary infirmaries

NOUN a hospital.

inflammable

ADJECTIVE An **inflammable** material burns easily.
✔ Although *inflammable* and *flammable* both mean "likely to catch fire", *flammable* is used more often as people sometimes think that *inflammable* means "not likely to catch fire".

inflammation

NOUN painful redness or swelling of a part of the body.

inflate inflates inflating inflated

VERB If you **inflate** something, you put air or a gas such as helium into it to make it swell.
inflatable ADJECTIVE

inflation

NOUN a general increase in the price of goods and services in a country.

inflexible

ADJECTIVE If someone or something is **inflexible**, they cannot be bent or altered.

inflict inflicts inflicting inflicted

VERB If you **inflict** something unpleasant on someone, you make them suffer it.

influence influences influencing influenced

VERB If you **influence** someone or something, you have an effect on what they do or what happens.

influential

ADJECTIVE Someone who is **influential** is important and can influence people or events. [from Latin *influentia* meaning power flowing from the stars]

influenza

NOUN; FORMAL flu.

inform informs informing informed

VERB If you **inform** somebody about something, you let them know about it.

informal

ADJECTIVE relaxed and casual.
informally ADVERB

information

NOUN knowledge about something. *He used the encyclopedia to find more **information**.*

information technology

NOUN the storage and communication of information using computers.

informative

ADJECTIVE Something that is **informative** gives you information.

infuriate infuriates infuriating infuriated

VERB If someone or something **infuriates** you, they make you very angry.
infuriating ADJECTIVE

ingenious

Said "in-**jeen**-yuss" ADJECTIVE Something that is **ingenious** is clever and involves new ideas.
ingeniously ADVERB

ingratitude

NOUN If you show **ingratitude**, you show a lack of care or thanks for something that has been done for you.

Antonym: gratitude

ingredient ingredients

NOUN the things that something is made from, especially in cookery.

inhabit inhabits inhabiting inhabited

VERB If you **inhabit** a place, you live there.

inhabitant inhabitants

NOUN If you are an **inhabitant** of a place, you live there.

inhale inhales inhaling inhaled

VERB When you **inhale** something, you breathe it in.

inhalation NOUN

inherit inherits inheriting inherited

VERB **1** If you **inherit** money or property, you receive it from someone who has died.
2 If you **inherit** a feature or quality from a parent or ancestor, you are born with it. *Her children have **inherited** her love of sport.*
inheritance NOUN   **inheritor** NOUN

inhospitable

ADJECTIVE **1** If you are **inhospitable**, you are unwelcoming to people who visit you.
2 An **inhospitable** place is an unpleasant and difficult place to live.

inhuman

ADJECTIVE **1** not human or not behaving like a human.
2 extremely cruel.

initial initials

Said "in-**nish**-ul" NOUN **1** one of the capital letters that begin each word of a name.
ADJECTIVE **2** first or at the beginning.
initially ADVERB

initiative

Said "in-**nish**-ut-iv" NOUN If you show **initiative**, you have the ability to see what needs to be done and do it, without relying on others.

inject injects injecting injected

VERB If a doctor or nurse **injects** you, they use a needle and syringe to put medicine into your body.
[from Latin *in* + *jacere* meaning to throw into]

injure injures injuring injured

VERB If you **injure** someone, you hurt or harm them in some way.

injury injuries

NOUN damage to part of a person's or animal's body.

injustice

NOUN If someone suffers **injustice**, they are treated unfairly.

ink

NOUN the coloured liquid used for writing or printing.

inland

ADJECTIVE OR ADVERB If a place is **inland**, it is away from the coast.

inlet inlets

NOUN a narrow bay or channel of water that goes inland from the sea, a lake or a river.

inmate inmates

NOUN someone who lives in an institution, such as a prison.

inn inns

NOUN a small, old country pub or hotel.

inner

ADJECTIVE contained inside a place or object. *The **inner** tube of my front tyre has a puncture.*

innings

NOUN In cricket, an **innings** is a period of time when a particular team is batting.

innocent

ADJECTIVE not guilty of a crime or of doing something wrong.
innocently ADVERB   **innocence** NOUN

Antonym: guilty

innovation innovations

NOUN a completely new idea, product or way of doing things.

inoculate inoculates inoculating inoculated
VERB If a doctor or nurse **inoculates** you, they give you an injection to protect you from catching a particular disease.
inoculation NOUN

input inputs inputting input
NOUN 1 Your **input** is your contribution and what you put into something. *The class project requires input from everyone.*
2 In computing, **input** is information that is fed into a computer.
VERB 3 To **input** information into a computer means to feed it in.

inquest inquests
NOUN an official inquiry to find out what caused a person's death.

inquire inquires inquired inquiring; also spelt **enquire**
VERB If you **inquire** about something, you ask for information about it.

inquiry inquiries
NOUN 1 an official investigation.
2 a question or a request for information.

inquisitive
ADJECTIVE Someone who is **inquisitive** is keen to find out about things.
inquisitively ADVERB   **inquisitiveness** NOUN

insane
ADJECTIVE Someone or something **insane** is mad.
insanely ADVERB   **insanity** NOUN

inscription inscriptions
NOUN the words that are carved or engraved on something such as a monument, gravestone or coin, or written in the front of a book.

insect insects
NOUN a small animal with six legs and no backbone, with its skeleton on the outside. **Insects** often have wings, for example beetles, butterflies and grasshoppers. *See* page 434.
[from Latin ***insectum*** meaning animal that has been cut into, because the bodies of many insects are divided into parts]

insecticide insecticides
NOUN a poisonous chemical used to kill insects.

insecure
ADJECTIVE 1 If you feel **insecure**, you lack confidence and feel worried.
2 If something is **insecure**, it is not fixed properly.
insecurity NOUN

inseparable
ADJECTIVE 1 If people are **inseparable**, they are always together. *The three of them are such good friends, they're inseparable.*
2 If things are **inseparable**, they cannot be parted.

insert inserts inserting inserted
VERB If you **insert** an object into something, you put it inside. *He inserted the key into the lock.*

inside insides
ADVERB, PREPOSITION, OR ADJECTIVE 1 **Inside** means in something: *an inside pocket. I waited inside the house.*
NOUN 2 The **inside** of something is the part that is surrounded by the main part, and is often hidden. *I painted the inside of the shed.*
PHRASE 3 **Inside out** means with the inside part facing outwards. *Her umbrella blew inside out.*
PLURAL NOUN 4 Your **insides** are the parts within your body that cannot be seen.

Antonym: (senses 1 and 2) outside

insight insights
NOUN If you show **insight** into a problem, you show a deep and accurate understanding of it.

insignificant
ADJECTIVE small and unimportant.
insignificantly ADVERB   **insignificance** NOUN

insist insists insisting insisted
VERB If you **insist** on something, you demand it forcefully. *As it was already dark, she insisted on giving us a lift home.*

insistent
ADJECTIVE If you are **insistent**, you insist on having or doing something.
insistence NOUN

insolent
ADJECTIVE very rude and showing no respect.
insolently ADVERB   **insolence** NOUN

insoluble
ADJECTIVE **1** impossible to solve.
2 unable to dissolve.

insomnia
NOUN difficulty in sleeping.
insomniac NOUN

inspect inspects inspecting inspected
VERB If you **inspect** something, you examine or check it carefully.

inspector inspectors
NOUN **1** someone in authority whose job it is to inspect things.
2 a rank of police officer.

inspire inspires inspiring inspired
VERB If someone or something **inspires** you, they give you new ideas, confidence and enthusiasm.
inspired ADJECTIVE   **inspiration** NOUN

install installs installing installed
VERB If you **install** something, you put it in place so that it is ready to be used.
installation NOUN

instalment instalments
NOUN **1** If you pay for something in **instalments,** you pay small amounts of money regularly over a period of time.
2 one of the parts of a story or television series.

instance instances
NOUN **1** a particular example or occurrence of something.
PHRASE **2** You use **for instance** to give an example of something you are talking about. *In some countries, **for instance** in Spain, many shops are closed at lunchtime.*

instant instants
NOUN **1** a moment or short period of time.
ADJECTIVE **2** immediate and without delay. *The book was an **instant** success.*
instantly ADVERB

instead
ADVERB If you do one thing **instead** of another, you do the first thing and not the second thing. *They took the stairs **instead** of the lift.*

instinct instincts
NOUN a natural tendency to do something in a particular way. *Her **instincts** told her to run away as quickly as possible.*

institute institutes
NOUN an organization set up for a purpose, such as teaching or research.

institution institutions
NOUN a large, important organization, such as a university or bank.

instruct instructs instructing instructed
VERB **1** If you **instruct** someone to do something, you tell them to do it.
2 If someone **instructs** you in a subject or skill, they teach you about it.
instructor NOUN   **instructive** ADJECTIVE

instruction instructions
NOUN If you follow an **instruction**, you do what someone tells you to do.

instrument instruments
NOUN **1** a tool that is used to do a particular job.
2 an object, such as a piano or guitar, that you play to make music.

insufficient
ADJECTIVE not enough for a particular purpose. *There is **insufficient** flour to make two cakes.*

insulate insulates insulating insulated
VERB If you **insulate** something, you cover it with materials such as foam or plastic to stop heat or electricity passing out of it.
insulation NOUN   **insulator** NOUN

insulin
NOUN a substance that controls the level of sugar in your blood.

insult insults insulting insulted
Said "**in**-sult" VERB **1** If you **insult** someone, you offend them by being rude to them.
Said "**in**-sult" NOUN **2** a rude remark that offends someone.
insulting ADJECTIVE

insurance
NOUN an amount of money paid on a regular basis to a company that, in return, will pay you money if you have an accident or need medical treatment.

intact
ADJECTIVE If something is **intact**, it is complete and undamaged.

integer integers

NOUN a whole number. For example, 2 is an **integer** but $2\frac{1}{2}$ is not.

integrate integrates integrating integrated

VERB If a person **integrates** into a group, they become a part of it.

integrity

NOUN the quality of being honest and trustworthy.

intellectual

ADJECTIVE involving thought, ideas and understanding: *an **intellectual** exercise, like learning French.*

intelligence

NOUN Your **intelligence** is your ability to understand and learn things.

intelligent

ADJECTIVE clever and able to understand things easily.
intelligently ADVERB

intend intends intending intended

VERB If you **intend** to do something, you decide or plan to do it.

intense

ADJECTIVE very great in strength or amount: *intense heat.*
intensely ADVERB   **intensity** NOUN

intensive

ADJECTIVE If something is **intensive**, it involves a lot of energy or effort over a short time.
intensively ADVERB

intention intentions

NOUN an idea or a plan of what you mean to do. *He had every **intention** of working hard that day.*

intentional

ADJECTIVE If something is **intentional**, it is done on purpose.
intentionally ADVERB

inter-

PREFIX You add **inter-** to a word to mean between or among two or more people or things: ***inter**-school competitions, **inter**national travel.*

interactive

ADJECTIVE If a computer is **interactive**, it allows two-way communication between itself and the person using it, so that information can pass in both directions.

intercept intercepts intercepting intercepted

VERB If you **intercept** someone or something as they move from one place to another, you stop them reaching their destination.
interception NOUN

intercom intercoms

NOUN a device that people use to communicate with each other if they are in different rooms.

interest interests interesting interested

NOUN **1** a thing you enjoy doing.
2 Interest is an extra payment that you receive if you have invested money, or an extra payment that you make if you have borrowed money.
VERB **3** If something **interests** you, you want to know more about it.

interfere interferes interfering interfered

VERB **1** If you **interfere** in a situation, you try to influence it, although it does not concern you.
2 If you **interfere** with a plan, you get in the way of it.

interior interiors

NOUN **1** the inside part of something: *the interior of the building.*
ADJECTIVE **2** inside: *the **interior** walls.*

interjection interjections

NOUN a word or phrase spoken suddenly to expresses an emotion, such as surprise, excitement or anger. For example, "Help!" is an **interjection**.

intermediate

ADJECTIVE An **intermediate** stage occurs in the middle, between two others. *This dance class is for beginners. The next one is at **intermediate** level.*

internal

ADJECTIVE happening on, or part of, the inside of something. *Your lungs are **internal** organs.*

international

ADJECTIVE involving different countries. *This is an important **international** match.*

a
b
c
d
e
f
g
h
i
j
k
l
m
n
o
p
q
r
s
t
u
v
w
x
y
z

Internet

NOUN a worldwide system where people communicate using computers.

interpret interprets interpreting interpreted

VERB **1** If you **interpret** something, you decide what it means. *I tried to **interpret** his painting.*

2 If you **interpret** what someone is saying, you immediately translate it into another language.
interpretation NOUN   **interpreter** NOUN

interrogate interrogates interrogating interrogated

VERB If you **interrogate** someone, you question them in great detail.
interrogation NOUN   **interrogator** NOUN

interrupt interrupts interrupting interrupted

VERB If you **interrupt** someone, you start talking while they are talking.
interruption NOUN

intersect intersects intersecting intersected

VERB When two roads **intersect**, they cross each other.

intersection intersections

NOUN **1** a point where two roads cross over each other.
2 the point where lines, arcs or sets cross each other.

point of intersection

interval intervals

NOUN a short break during a play, concert or performance.

intervene intervenes intervening intervened

VERB If you **intervene** in a situation, you step in, usually to sort out an argument or quarrel.
intervention NOUN

interview interviews interviewing interviewed

NOUN **1** a formal meeting where someone is asked questions.
VERB **2** When someone **interviews** you, they ask you questions, usually in order to find out if you are suitable for something in particular.

intestine intestines

NOUN the part of your digestive system that carries food from your stomach. Your **intestines** are long tubes folded up inside your abdomen.
See page 433.
intestinal ADJECTIVE

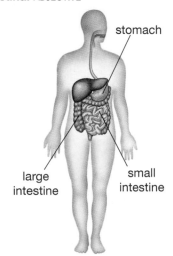

stomach

large intestine

small intestine

intimate

ADJECTIVE **1** If you are **intimate** with someone, you are very friendly with them.
2 Intimate details or thoughts are personal or private.

intimidate intimidates intimidating intimidated

VERB If you **intimidate** someone, you frighten them in a threatening way.
intimidated ADJECTIVE   **intimidating** ADJECTIVE
intimidation NOUN
[from Latin *timidus* meaning fearful]

into

PREPOSITION **1** If you go **into** something, you go inside it. *Come **into** the house.*
2 If you bump or crash **into** something, you bump or crash against it.

intrepid

ADJECTIVE brave and fearless.
intrepidly ADVERB

intricate

ADJECTIVE detailed and complicated.
intricately ADVERB

intrigue intrigues intriguing intrigued
VERB If something **intrigues** you, you are fascinated by it and curious about it.
intrigue NOUN   **intriguing** ADJECTIVE

introduce introduces introducing introduced
VERB **1** If you **introduce** one person to another, you tell them each other's name so that they can get to know each other.
2 If you **introduce** someone to something, they learn about it for the first time from you. *My friend introduced me to water-skiing on holiday.*

introduction introductions
NOUN a piece of writing at the beginning of a book, that tells you what the book is about.
introductory ADJECTIVE

intrude intrudes intruding intruded
VERB If you **intrude** on someone or something, you disturb them.
intrusion NOUN   **intrusive** ADJECTIVE

intruder intruders
NOUN a person who forces their way into someone else's property without their consent. *The security guard caught an intruder last night.*

intuition intuitions
NOUN the ability to know about something without thinking about it or being able to explain it.
intuitive ADJECTIVE   **intuitively** ADVERB

Inuit Inuits
NOUN an Eskimo who comes from North America or Greenland.

invade invades invading invaded
VERB If an army **invades** a country, it enters it by force.

invalid invalids
Said "**in**-va-lid" NOUN **1** someone who is so ill that they need to be looked after by someone else
Said "in-**val**-id" ADJECTIVE **2** If something is **invalid**, it cannot be accepted because there is something wrong with it. *Your ticket is invalid for this train service.*

invaluable
ADJECTIVE extremely useful.

invasion invasions
NOUN the forceful entering or attacking of a place. *At the end of the match, there was an invasion of the pitch by fans.*

invent invents inventing invented
VERB **1** If you **invent** something, you are the first person to think of it or make it.
2 If you **invent** a story or an excuse, you make it up.
inventor NOUN   **invention** NOUN
inventive ADJECTIVE   **inventiveness** NOUN

inverse
NOUN; FORMAL In mathematics, if you turn something upside down or back to front, you have its **inverse**. *The inverse of 23 is 32.*

invert inverts inverting inverted
VERB **1** If you **invert** something, you turn it upside down.
2 If you **invert** a fraction, the top number changes places with the bottom number.

invertebrate invertebrates
NOUN an animal without a backbone.

inverted commas
NOUN punctuation marks (" ") are used to show where speech begins and ends: *"Good morning!" she cried.*

invest invests investing invested
VERB If you **invest** money in something, you try to increase its value, for example by putting it into a bank or building society so that it will gain interest.
investor NOUN   **investment** NOUN

investigate investigates investigating investigated
VERB If someone **investigates** something, they try to find out all the facts about it. *Police are still investigating the accident.*
investigator NOUN

Synonyms: examine, look into, study

investigation investigations
NOUN If you conduct an **investigation** into something, you examine it carefully and try to find out the facts about it. *The disappearance of the money was under investigation.*

invincible
ADJECTIVE If something is **invincible**, it cannot be defeated.
invincibly ADVERB   **invincibility** NOUN

invisible
ADJECTIVE If something is **invisible**, you cannot see it.
invisibly ADVERB   **invisibility** NOUN

invitation invitations
NOUN a request for someone to come to something, such as a party.

invite invites inviting invited
VERB If you **invite** someone to an event, you ask them to come to it.

involve involves involving involved
VERB **1** If a situation or activity **involves** something, that thing is a necessary part of it. *Being president involves a lot of responsibility.*
2 If you **involve** yourself in something, you take part in it. *I'm involved in the production of the school play.*

ir-
PREFIX a variation of in-, meaning not. For example, **ir**relevant means not relevant, and **ir**replaceable means not replaceable.

irate
ADJECTIVE very angry.
irately ADVERB

iris irises
NOUN the coloured part of your eye.
[from Greek *iris* meaning rainbow or coloured circle]

iron irons ironing ironed
NOUN **1** a hard, dark metal used to make steel.
2 an appliance you heat up and press on clothes to remove creases.
VERB **3** If you **iron** clothes, you use a hot iron to remove creases from them.
ironing NOUN

irony
NOUN When you use **irony**, you use words, often in a humorous way, to say the opposite of what you really mean.
ironic ADJECTIVE   **ironically** ADVERB

irrational
ADJECTIVE If you act in an **irrational** way, you show no reason or logic in what you do.
irrationally ADVERB

irregular
ADJECTIVE **1** Something that is **irregular** is not smooth or straight, or does not make a regular pattern.
2 **Irregular** verbs do not follow the usual rules.
irregularly ADVERB   **irregularity** NOUN

irrelevant
ADJECTIVE If something is **irrelevant**, it has nothing to do with what is being said or discussed.
irrelevance NOUN

irresistible
ADJECTIVE **1** If something is **irresistible**, it cannot be controlled. *I had an irresistible urge to laugh.*
2 If someone is **irresistible**, they are very attractive.

irresponsible
ADJECTIVE If you do something in an **irresponsible** way, you act thoughtlessly and carelessly.
irresponsibly ADVERB   **irresponsibility** NOUN

Synonyms: careless, thoughtless

irreversible
ADJECTIVE If something is **irreversible**, it cannot be reversed or changed back to the way it was before.
irreversibly ADVERB

irrigate irrigates irrigating irrigated
VERB To **irrigate** land is to supply it with water brought through pipes or ditches. *In hot, dry countries the land is irrigated.*
irrigated ADJECTIVE   **irrigation** NOUN
[from Latin *rigare* meaning to moisten]

irritable
ADJECTIVE If you are **irritable**, you are easily annoyed.
irritably ADVERB

irritate irritates irritating irritated
VERB If something **irritates** you, it annoys you.
irritation NOUN

is

VERB a present tense of *be*.

Islam

NOUN the Muslim religion, which teaches that there is only one God, Allah, and Mohammed is his prophet.

island islands

NOUN a piece of land surrounded by water.

isle isles

NOUN a literary word for an island.

isn't

VERB a contraction of *is not*.

isolate isolates isolating isolated

VERB **1** If you **isolate** yourself, you separate yourself from other people. *I isolated myself in my room.*
2 To **isolate** a sick person or animal means to keep them away from others so that the disease does not spread.
isolated ADJECTIVE   **isolation** NOUN

isosceles

ADJECTIVE An **isosceles** triangle has two sides of the same length and two equal angles.

issue issues

NOUN **1** an important subject that people are talking about. *The issue of homeless people is important to many people.*
2 a particular newspaper or magazine: *this week's issue of the local paper.*

IT

NOUN an abbreviation of *Information Technology*.

it

PRONOUN **1** used to refer to something that has already been mentioned. **It** can also refer to babies or other animals whose sex is not known. *I like that dog. It is very friendly.*
2 You use **it** to talk about the weather, time or date. *It's been raining all day.*

italics

PLURAL NOUN letters printed in a particular sloping way. They are often used for emphasis. *This writing is in italics.*

itch itches itching itched

VERB **1** When a part of your body **itches**, you have an unpleasant feeling that makes you want to scratch it.
NOUN **2** an unpleasant feeling on your skin that makes you want to scratch it.

item items

NOUN one of a collection or list of objects. *Milk is the most important item on my shopping list.*

itinerary itineraries

NOUN The **itinerary** of a journey is a detailed plan of where to go and what to see along the route.

its

ADJECTIVE OR PRONOUN **Its** is used to refer to something belonging to things, children or animals that have already been mentioned. *The cat won't eat. Its bowl needs cleaning.*

it's

a contraction of *it is*.

I've

a contraction of *I have*.

ivory

NOUN **1** the valuable, creamy white bone that forms the tusk of an elephant. It is used to make ornaments.
NOUN OR ADJECTIVE **2** creamy-white.

ivy

NOUN an evergreen plant that creeps along the ground and up walls.

Jj

A B C D E F G H I **J** K L M N O P Q R S T U V W X Y Z

jack jacks

NOUN **1** a piece of equipment for lifting heavy objects, especially for lifting a car when changing a wheel.
2 In a pack of cards, a **jack** is a card whose value is between a ten and a queen.

jackal jackals

NOUN a wild animal related to the dog.

jacket jackets

NOUN **1** a short coat.
2 the paper cover of a book.

jackpot jackpots

NOUN the top prize in a gambling game. *He was excited to hear he had won the **jackpot** in the lottery.*

jagged

ADJECTIVE A **jagged** rock has a rough, uneven shape with sharp edges.

jail jails jailing jailed

NOUN **1** a building where people convicted of a crime are locked up.
VERB **2** To **jail** someone means to lock them up in a jail.

jam jams jamming jammed

NOUN **1** a food made by boiling fruit with sugar.
2 a situation where there are so many people or things that it is difficult to move. *There is often a traffic **jam** at that junction.*
VERB **3** If you **jam** something into a place, you squeeze it in. *He **jammed** his clothes into the suitcase.*
4 If you **jam** something, or if it **jams**, it becomes stuck. *The coin was **jammed** in the slot.*

jamboree jamborees

NOUN a party or celebration where large numbers of people gather to enjoy themselves with much noise and excitement.

January

NOUN the first month of the year. **January** has 31 days.

jar jars jarring jarred

NOUN **1** a glass container used for storing food.
VERB **2** If something **jars**, you find it unpleasant or annoying.

jargon

NOUN language containing lots of technical words, used by particular groups of people. *Doctors often use **jargon**.*

jaundice

NOUN an illness of the liver, where the skin and the whites of the eyes become yellow.

javelin javelins

NOUN a long spear that is thrown in sports competitions.

jaw jaws

NOUN **1** the bone in which teeth are set.
2 the mouth and teeth of a person or animal.

jazz

NOUN a style of popular music with a strong rhythm.

jealous

ADJECTIVE If you are **jealous**, you feel envious of others, wanting to have what they have or wanting to be like them.
jealously ADVERB   **jealousy** NOUN

jeans

PLURAL NOUN cotton trousers, often made of denim.

jeep jeeps

NOUN; TRADEMARK a four-wheeled motor vehicle designed for driving over rough ground.

jeer jeers jeering jeered

VERB **1** If you **jeer** at someone, you insult them in a loud, unpleasant way.
NOUN **2 Jeers** are rude and insulting remarks.
jeering ADJECTIVE

jelly jellies

NOUN **1** a clear, sweet food eaten as a dessert.
2 a type of clear, set jam. *I like mint **jelly** with lamb.*

jellyfish jellyfishes

NOUN a sea animal with a clear, soft body and tentacles that may sting.

jerk jerks jerking jerked
VERB **1** If you **jerk** something, you give it a sudden, sharp pull.
2 If something **jerks**, it moves suddenly and sharply.

jersey jerseys
NOUN a knitted garment for the upper half of the body.

jet jets
NOUN **1** an aeroplane that can fly very fast.
2 a rush of air, steam or liquid that is forced out under pressure.

jetty jetties
NOUN a wide stone wall or wooden platform at the edge of the sea or a river, where boats can be moored.

Jew Jews
NOUN a person who practises the religion of Judaism or who is of Hebrew descent.
Jewish ADJECTIVE

jewel jewels
NOUN a precious stone, often used to decorate valuable items such as rings or necklaces.
jewelled ADJECTIVE

jeweller jewellers
NOUN a person who makes or sells jewellery.

jewellery
NOUN the ornaments that people wear, like rings and necklaces.

jigsaw jigsaws
NOUN a puzzle that is made up of odd-shaped pieces that must be fitted together to make a picture.

jingle jingles
NOUN **1** a short, catchy phrase or rhyme with music, used to advertise something on radio or television.
2 a gentle ringing sound.

job jobs
NOUN **1** the work that someone does to earn money.
2 anything that has to be done.

jockey jockeys
NOUN someone who rides a horse in a race.

joey joeys
NOUN a young kangaroo.

jog jogs jogging jogged
VERB **1** If you **jog**, you run slowly, often for exercise.
2 If you **jog** something, you knock it slightly so that it shakes or moves. *My pen slipped when he jogged my arm.*
jogger NOUN   **jogging** NOUN

join joins joining joined
VERB **1** If you **join** a club, you become a member of it.
2 When two things **join**, or when one thing **joins** another, they come together. *The two streams join and form a river.*
join in VERB **3** If you **join in** an activity, you take part in it.

Synonyms: (sense 2) connect, link

joiner joiners
NOUN a person who makes wooden window frames, doors and furniture.

joint joints
ADJECTIVE **1** shared by or belonging to two or more people. *The project was a joint effort.*
NOUN **2** a part of your body, such as your elbow or knee, where two bones meet and are able to move together.

joke jokes joking joked
NOUN **1** something that you say to make people laugh.
VERB **2** If you **joke**, you say something amusing or tell a funny story.

jolly jollier jolliest
ADJECTIVE If you are **jolly**, you are happy and cheerful.

jolt jolts jolting jolted
VERB **1** If something **jolts**, it moves or shakes roughly and violently. *The bus jolted along the bumpy road.*
2 If something or someone **jolts** you, they bump into you clumsily.
NOUN **3** a sudden, jerky movement.
4 an unpleasant shock or surprise.

jostle jostles jostling jostled
VERB If people or animals **jostle**, they push and bump into each other roughly, usually because they are in a crowd.

jot jots jotting jotted
VERB If you **jot** something down, you write a quick, brief note.

journal journals
NOUN **1** a magazine that deals with a particular interest.
2 a diary where you write what happens each day.

journalist journalists
NOUN a person whose job is to gather news and write about it for a newspaper or magazine, or present it on television or radio.

journey journeys
NOUN the act of travelling from one place to another.

joust jousts
NOUN In medieval times, a **joust** was a competition between knights fighting on horseback, using lances.

joy joys
NOUN **1** a feeling of great happiness or pleasure.
2 something that makes you happy or gives you pleasure. *It was a joy to see my friend again.*

joystick joysticks
NOUN **1** a lever in a plane that the pilot uses to control height and direction.
2 a lever that controls the cursor on a computer screen, especially in computer games.

jubilee jubilees
NOUN a special anniversary of an event such as a coronation. *Queen Elizabeth's Silver Jubilee was in 1977.*
[from Hebrew *yobhel* meaning ram's horn, blown during festivals and celebrations to mark the freedom of Hebrew slaves each 50th year, known as the jubilee]

Judaism
NOUN the religion of the Jewish people. It is based on a belief in one God, and draws its laws from the Old Testament.
Judaic ADJECTIVE

judge judges judging judged
NOUN **1** the person in a law court who decides how criminals should be punished according to the law.
2 the person who chooses the winner of a competition.

VERB **3** If a person **judges** someone or something, they act as a judge.
4 If you **judge** someone or something, you decide what they are like.

judgment judgments; also spelt judgement
NOUN an opinion that you have after thinking carefully about something.

judo
NOUN a sport in which two people try to force each other to the ground using special throwing techniques. It originated in Japan as a form of self-defence.
[from Japanese *ju do* meaning gentleness art]

jug jugs
NOUN a container with a handle and a lip, used for holding and pouring liquids.

juggernaut juggernauts
NOUN a large, heavy lorry.
[from Hindi *Jagannath*, the name of a huge idol of the god Krishna, which is wheeled through the streets of Puri in India every year]

juggle juggles juggling juggled
VERB When someone **juggles** they throw different objects into the air, keeping more than one object in the air at the same time without dropping them.
juggler NOUN

juice juices
NOUN the liquid that can be obtained from fruit, vegetables and other food: *orange juice*.

juicy juicier juiciest
ADJECTIVE having a great deal of juice. *The orange was very juicy.*

jukebox jukeboxes
NOUN a machine that plays a chosen record when coins are inserted.

July
NOUN the seventh month of the year. **July** has 31 days.

jumble jumbles jumbling jumbled
NOUN **1** an untidy muddle of things.
2 articles for a **jumble** sale.
VERB **3** If you **jumble** things, you mix them up untidily.

jumble sale jumble sales
NOUN an event where second-hand items are sold to cheaply raise money, often for charity.

jump jumps jumping jumped

VERB **1** When you **jump**, you spring off the ground using the muscles in your legs.
2 If someone **jumps**, they make a sudden, sharp movement because they are surprised.

jumper jumpers

NOUN a warm piece of clothing that covers the top part of your body.

junction junctions

NOUN a place where roads or railway lines meet or cross.

June

NOUN the sixth month of the year. **June** has 30 days.

jungle jungles

NOUN a dense, tropical forest where many trees and other plants grow close together. [from Hindi *jangal* meaning wasteland]

junior

ADJECTIVE **1** A **junior** official or employee holds a lower position in an organization. *She will be a junior doctor after finishing her training.*
2 younger. *He is the junior of the two brothers.*

junk junks

NOUN **1** old, unwanted or worthless things that are sold cheaply or thrown away.
2 a Chinese sailing boat that has a flat bottom and wide sails.

junk food

NOUN food that is easy and quick to prepare, or bought ready to eat, but is not always very good for you.

jury juries

NOUN a group of people in a court of law who are chosen to listen to the facts about a crime and then decide whether the accused person is guilty or not.

just

ADJECTIVE **1** Someone who is **just** is fair.
ADVERB **2** If something has **just** happened, it happened a very short time ago.
3 If you **just** do something, you almost don't do it. *He just managed to climb the fence.*
4 If something is **just** what you want, it is exactly what you want.

justice

NOUN **1** fairness in the way that people are treated.
2 the system of laws created by a community.

justify justifies justifying justified

VERB If you **justify** what you are doing or saying, you prove or explain why it is reasonable or necessary.
justification NOUN **justifiable** ADJECTIVE

jut juts jutting jutted

VERB If something **juts** out, it sticks out beyond a surface or an edge. *The pier jutted out into the sea.*

juvenile juveniles

ADJECTIVE **1** suitable for or to do with young people.
2 childish and rather silly.
NOUN **3** a young person not old enough to be considered an adult.

A
B
C
D
E
F
G
H
I
J
K
L
M
N
O
P
Q
R
S
T
U
V
W
X
Y
Z

Kk

kaleidoscope kaleidoscopes

NOUN a toy made of a tube with a hole at one end. When you look through the hole and twist the other end of the tube, you can see a changing pattern of colours.

kangaroo kangaroos

NOUN a large, Australian marsupial with very strong back legs that it uses for jumping.

karate

NOUN a sport in which people fight each other using only their hands, elbows, feet and legs. [from Japanese **kara** + **te** meaning empty hand]

kayak kayaks

NOUN a covered canoe with a small opening for the person sitting in it, originally used by Inuit people.

kebab kebabs

NOUN pieces of meat or vegetable grilled on a stick. [from Arabic **kabab** meaning roast meat]

keen keener keenest

ADJECTIVE **1** If you are **keen** to do something, or for something to happen, you want very much to do it or for it to happen. *I was **keen** to meet my cousins from Australia.*
2 If you are **keen** on something or someone, you are fond of them or attracted to them.
3 If your senses are **keen**, you are able to see, hear, taste and smell things very clearly or strongly.

keep keeps keeping kept

VERB **1** If you **keep** something, you have it and don't give it away. *I will **keep** this book forever.*
2 If you **keep** an animal, you look after it. *He **keeps** rabbits.*
3 If you **keep** something somewhere, you store it there. *I **keep** my bicycle in the garage.*
4 If you **keep** doing something, you do it again and again.
5 If something **keeps** you a certain way, you stay that way because of it. *The duvet **keeps** me warm.*
6 If you **keep** a promise, you do what you have said you will do.
7 If you **keep** a secret, you do not tell it to anyone else.
NOUN **8** the main tower inside the walls of a castle.

keeper keepers

NOUN **1** a person whose job is to look after the animals in a zoo.
2 a goalkeeper in soccer or hockey. *The **keeper** managed to stop the ball and save the penalty.*

kennel kennels

NOUN **1** a small hut for a dog to sleep in.
2 A **kennels** is a place where dogs are bred and trained, or looked after when their owners are away.

kept

VERB the past tense and past participle of *keep*.

kerb kerbs

NOUN the raised edge of a pavement, that separates it from the road. *You must look both ways for traffic before stepping off the **kerb**.*

kernel kernels

NOUN the part of a nut that is inside the shell.

kestrel kestrels

NOUN a type of small hawk.

ketchup

NOUN a cold sauce, usually made from tomatoes.

kettle kettles

NOUN a covered container with a spout, in which you boil water.

key keys

NOUN **1** a specially shaped piece of metal that fits in a lock, and is turned in order to open the lock.

2 The **keys** on a piano or a computer are the buttons that you press in order to operate it.

ADJECTIVE **3** **Key** words or sentences are the important ones in a piece of text.

NOUN **4** information arranged in a way that can be used to identify animals, plants and materials. You can use a **key** to help you name an unknown animal, plant or material.

keyboard keyboards

NOUN a set of keys on a piano, typewriter or computer.

keyhole keyholes

NOUN the hole in a lock where you put a key.

khaki

NOUN OR ADJECTIVE yellowish-brown. Soldiers' uniforms are often made of **khaki** material. [from Urdu *kaki* meaning dusty]

kick kicks kicking kicked

VERB **1** If you **kick** someone or something, you hit them with your foot.

NOUN **2** If you give something a **kick**, you hit it with your foot.

3 INFORMAL If you get a **kick** out of something, you enjoy it very much.

kick off VERB **4** When a soccer or rugby team **kicks off**, they begin playing.

kid kids kidding kidded

NOUN **1** INFORMAL a child.

2 a young goat.

VERB **3** If you **kid** someone, you tease them and try to make them believe something that isn't true.

Synonym: (sense 3) tease

kidnap kidnaps kidnapping kidnapped

VERB If someone **kidnaps** someone else, they take them away by force and demand something in exchange for returning them. [from **kid** + **nap** meaning child stealing; in the 17th century children were kidnapped to work on American plantations]

kidney kidneys

NOUN one of the two organs in your body that remove waste products from your blood.

kill kills killing killed

VERB If someone **kills** a person, animal or plant, they make them die.

kiln kilns

NOUN an oven for baking china or pottery until it becomes hard and dry.

kilo kilos

NOUN a kilogram.

kilogram kilograms

NOUN a unit of mass and weight (kg) equal to 1000 grams.

kilohertz

NOUN a unit of measurement of radio waves (kHz) equal to 1000 hertz.

kilometre kilometres

NOUN a unit of distance (km) equal to 1000 metres.

kilowatt kilowatts

NOUN a unit of power (kW) equal to 1000 watts.

kilt kilts

NOUN a tartan skirt worn by men as part of Scottish Highland dress.

kimono kimonos

NOUN a long, loose garment with wide sleeves and a sash, worn in Japan.

kin

PLURAL NOUN Your **kin** are your relatives.

kind kinder kindest; kinds

ADJECTIVE **1** Someone who is **kind** behaves in a caring and helpful way towards other people.

NOUN **2** a particular thing of the same type as other things. *I do not like this **kind** of bread.*

kindly ADVERB   **kindness** NOUN

✔ When you use *kind* in its singular form, the adjective before it should also be singular: *that kind of dog.* When you use the plural form, *kinds*, the adjective before it should be plural: *those kinds of dog.*

Synonyms: (sense 1) considerate
(sense 2) sort, class

king kings

NOUN a man who is the head of state in a country, and who inherited his position from his parents.

a b c d e f g h i j k l m n o p q r s t u v w x y z

kingdom kingdoms

NOUN a country that is governed by a king or queen.

kingfisher kingfishers

NOUN a brightly-coloured bird that lives near water and feeds on fish.

kiosk kiosks

NOUN a small shop or hut where you can buy newspapers, snacks, and sweets.

kipper kippers

NOUN a herring that has been dried in smoke to preserve it and give it a special taste.

kiss kisses kissing kissed

VERB **1** When you **kiss** someone, you touch them with your lips in order to show your affection.

NOUN **2** When you give someone a **kiss**, you kiss them.

kit kits

NOUN **1** a collection of equipment and clothing that you use for a sport or other activity: *football kit*.

2 a set of parts that you fit together to make something. *I got a model aeroplane kit for my birthday*.

kitchen kitchens

NOUN a room used for cooking and preparing food.

kite kites

NOUN a light frame covered with paper or cloth, that you fly in the air at the end of a long string.

kitten kittens

NOUN a very young cat.

kiwi kiwi or kiwis

NOUN **1** a type of bird found in New Zealand. **Kiwis** cannot fly.

2 Someone who comes from New Zealand is called a **kiwi**.

[A Maori word]

kiwi fruit kiwi fruits

NOUN a fruit with a brown, hairy skin and green flesh.

knack

NOUN an ability to do something easily.

knead kneads kneading kneaded

VERB If you **knead** dough, you press it and squeeze it with your hands before baking it.

knee knees

NOUN the joint in your leg between your ankle and your hip.

kneel kneels kneeling knelt

VERB When you **kneel**, or **kneel down**, you bend your legs and lower your body so that one or both knees are touching the ground.

knew

VERB the past tense of *know*.

knickers

PLURAL NOUN underpants worn by women and girls.

knife knives

NOUN a sharp, metal tool used for cutting things.

knight knights knighting knighted

NOUN **1** In medieval times, a **knight** was a nobleman who served his king or lord in battle: *King Arthur and the Knights of the Round Table.*

VERB **2** If a king or queen **knights** a man, they give him the title "Sir" before his name.

[from Old English *cniht* meaning servant]

knit knits knitting knitted

VERB If you **knit** a piece of clothing, you make it from wool, using knitting needles or a knitting machine.

knob knobs

NOUN a round handle or switch on doors, furniture and machinery.

knock knocks knocking knocked

VERB **1** If you **knock** on something, you hit it hard with your hand to make a noise. *I knocked on the door when I arrived.*

2 If you **knock** against something, you bump into it.

knocker knockers

NOUN a metal lever attached to a door, that you use to knock on the door.

knot knots knotting knotted

NOUN **1** a fastening made by passing one end of a piece of string or fabric through a loop and pulling it tight. *The **knot** in my laces was so tight that I could not undo it.*

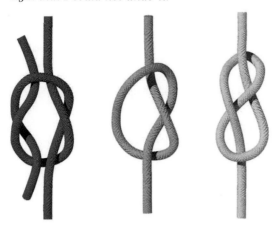

Square or   Overhand   Figure 8
reef knot   knot   knot

2 a hard, round spot on a piece of wood, where a branch grew on the tree.
3 a unit for measuring the speed of ships and aircraft.
VERB **4** If you **knot** a piece of string, you tie a knot in it.

know knows knowing knew known

VERB **1** If you **know** something, you have it clearly in your mind and you do not need to learn it. *I **know** how to swim.*
2 If you **know** a person, place or thing, you are familiar with it. *I've **known** him for five years.*

knowledge

NOUN all the information and facts that you know: *general **knowledge**.*

knuckle knuckles

NOUN one of the joints in your fingers.

koala koalas

NOUN an Australian marsupial with grey fur and small tufted ears. **Koalas** live in trees and eat eucalyptus leaves.

Koran or Qur'an

NOUN the holy book of Islam.
[from Arabic ***kara'a*** meaning to read]

kosher

ADJECTIVE **Kosher** food has been specially prepared to be eaten according to Jewish law.

a b c d e f g h i j **k** l m n o p q r s t u v w x y z

Ll

label labels labelling labelled

NOUN **1** a piece of paper or plastic attached to something and giving information about it. *The label on the bottle told him when to have his medicine.*

VERB **2** If you **label** something, you put a label on it.

laboratory laboratories

NOUN a place where scientific experiments are carried out.

labour

NOUN **1** hard work.

2 In Britain, **Labour** or the **Labour** Party is one of the main political parties.

Labrador Labradors

NOUN a large dog with short black or golden hair.

labyrinth labyrinths

NOUN a complicated series of paths or passages that are difficult to find your way around.

lace laces lacing laced

NOUN **1** a fine, decorated cloth, with a pattern of many holes in it.

2 one of the thin pieces of material that are used to fasten shoes.

VERB **3** When you **lace** something up, you fix it together by tying a lace.

lack lacks lacking lacked

NOUN **1** If there is a **lack** of something, there is not enough of it or there is none of it. *Despite his lack of training, he won the race.*

VERB **2** If someone or something **lacks** something, they do not have it.

lacquer lacquers

NOUN thin, clear paint that you put on wood to protect it and make it shiny.

ladder ladders

NOUN a wooden or metal frame consisting of two long poles with short bars in between. **Ladders** are used for climbing up and down things.

ladle ladles

NOUN a long-handled spoon with a deep, round bowl, which you use to serve soup.

lady ladies

NOUN **1** a polite word for woman.

2 In Britain, **Lady** is the title of the wife of a knight or a lord.

ladybird ladybirds

NOUN a small, flying beetle with a round body, usually red, patterned with black spots.

lag lags lagging lagged

VERB **1** If a person or a thing **lags** behind, they make slower progress than other people or other things and do not keep up. *Don't lag behind, or you'll get lost!*

2 If you **lag** pipes or water tanks, you cover them with insulating material to stop heat escaping and prevent freezing.

lager lagers

NOUN a kind of light beer.

lagoon lagoons

NOUN an area of water separated from the sea by reefs or sand.

laid

VERB the past tense of *lay*.

lain

VERB the past participle of some meanings of *lie*. *It must have lain there for days.*

lair lairs

NOUN a place where a wild animal lives.

lake lakes

NOUN a large area of fresh water surrounded by land.

lamb lambs
NOUN **1** a young sheep.
2 the meat from a lamb.

lame
ADJECTIVE **1** Someone who is **lame** has an injured leg and cannot walk easily.
2 A **lame** excuse is unconvincing.
lamely ADVERB **lameness** NOUN

lamp lamps
NOUN a device that produces light. *Please turn on the table **lamp** now that it is getting dark.*

lamppost lampposts
NOUN a tall column in a street, with a lamp at the top.

lance lances
NOUN a long spear that was used in the past by soldiers on horseback.

land lands landing landed
NOUN **1** an area of ground. *We camped on the **land** surrounding the castle.*
2 the parts of the earth's surface that are not covered by water.
VERB **3** When someone or something **lands** somewhere, they reach the ground after moving through the air.
4 When you **land** somewhere on a plane or a ship, you arrive there.

landing landings
NOUN the flat area at the top of a flight of stairs in a building.

landlady landladies
NOUN a woman who owns a house or small hotel and who lets rooms to people.

landlord landlords
NOUN **1** a man who owns a house or small hotel and who lets rooms to people.
2 a person who looks after a public house.
3 someone who owns a large amount of land or houses and lets some of it out in return for rent.

landmark landmarks
NOUN a noticeable feature in a landscape, that you can use to check your position. *The tower on the hill is a local **landmark**.*

landscape landscapes
NOUN everything you can see when you look across an area of land.

lane lanes
NOUN **1** a narrow road, especially in the country.
2 one of the parallel strips into which a road, a race track or a swimming pool is divided.

language languages
NOUN a system of words used by a particular group of people to communicate with each other.

lantern lanterns
NOUN a lamp in a metal frame with glass sides.

lap laps lapping lapped
NOUN **1** the flat area formed by your thighs when you are sitting down.
2 one circuit of a running track or racecourse.
VERB **3** When water **laps** against something, it gently moves against it in little waves.
4 When an animal **laps** a drink, it uses its tongue to flick the liquid into its mouth.

lapel lapels
NOUN the part of the collar that folds back over the front of a jacket or coat.

lapse lapses lapsing lapsed
NOUN **1** a moment of bad behaviour by someone who usually behaves well.
2 a period of time that has passed.
VERB **3** If you **lapse** into a different way of behaving, you start behaving that way. *The class **lapsed** into silence.*
4 If something such as a promise or an agreement **lapses**, it is no longer valid.

laptop laptops
NOUN a portable computer small enough to fit on your lap, which is especially useful if you are travelling.

lard
NOUN fat from a pig, used in cooking.

larder larders
NOUN a room in which you store food, often next to a kitchen.

large larger largest
ADJECTIVE bigger than usual.

largely
ADVERB to a great extent. *It was **largely** a party for his birthday, but we celebrated his sister's exam results too.*

lark larks larking larked

NOUN **1** a small, brown bird with a very pleasant song.

2 If you do something for a **lark**, you do it in a high-spirited or mischievous way for fun.

VERB **3** If you **lark** about, you enjoy yourself in a high-spirited way.

larva larvae

NOUN an insect after it has hatched from its egg, and before it becomes an adult. A caterpillar is the **larva** of a butterfly.

lasagne

NOUN an Italian dish made with wide, flat sheets of pasta, meat or vegetables and cheese sauce. [from Latin **lasanum** meaning cooking pot]

laser lasers

NOUN **1** a narrow beam of concentrated light produced by a special machine. It is used to cut very hard materials and in some kinds of surgery.

2 the machine that produces the beam of light. [from the first letters of *Light Amplification by Stimulated Emission of Radiation*]

lash lashes lashing lashed

NOUN **1** Your **lashes** are the hairs growing on the edge of your eyelids.

VERB **2** If rain **lashes** down, it beats down strongly.

3 If you **lash** things together, you tie them together firmly.

lash out VERB **4** If you **lash out** at someone you speak to them or strike them harshly.

lasso lassoes or lassos lassoing lassoed

NOUN **1** a length of rope looped at one end with a slip-knot, used by cowboys to catch cattle and horses.

VERB **2** If you **lasso** an animal you catch it by throwing the loop of a lasso around its neck.

last lasts lasting lasted

ADJECTIVE **1** The **last** person or thing is the one that comes after all the others of the same kind. *I was the **last** person to arrive.*

2 The **last** one of a group of things is the only one that remains after all the others have gone. *No one wanted the **last** piece of pizza.*

3 The **last** thing or event is the most recent one. *The **last** time we went to the beach it rained.*

VERB **4** If something **lasts**, it continues to exist or happen. *The sunny weather seems to have **lasted** for ages.*

5 If something **lasts** for a particular time, it remains in good condition for that time.

PHRASE **6** At **last** means after a long time. *The bus arrived **at last**.*

late later latest

ADVERB OR ADJECTIVE **1** If something or someone is **late**, they arrive after the time that was arranged or expected.

2 If something happens **late**, it happens near the end of something. *In the summer it doesn't get dark until **late** in the evening.*

lately

ADVERB If something happened **lately**, it happened recently. *We've had a lot of homework **lately**.*

lather

NOUN the frothy foam that you get when you rub soap in water.

Latin

NOUN **1** the language of ancient Rome.

ADJECTIVE **2** **Latin** peoples and cultures are those of countries such as France, Italy, Spain and Portugal, whose languages developed from Latin.

latitude latitudes

NOUN The **latitude** of a place is its distance north or south of the equator measured in degrees.

laugh laughs laughing laughed

VERB **1** When you **laugh**, you make a noise that shows that you are amused or happy.

NOUN **2** the sound you make when you laugh.

laughter

NOUN laughing or the sound of people laughing.

launch launches launching launched

VERB **1** When someone **launches** a ship, they put it into water for the first time.

2 When someone **launches** a rocket, they send it into space.

launderette launderettes

NOUN a shop with coin-operated washing machines and driers, where people can wash and dry their dirty clothes.

laundry laundries

NOUN **1** dirty clothes and sheets that are being washed or waiting to be washed.
2 a business that washes and irons clothes and sheets.

lava

NOUN the very hot liquid rock that shoots out of a volcano when it erupts, and becomes solid as it cools.

lavatory lavatories

NOUN a toilet.

lavender

NOUN a small bush with blue flowers that have a strong, pleasant scent.

lavish

ADJECTIVE If you are **lavish**, you are very generous with your time, money or gifts.

law laws

NOUN **1** the system of rules developed by the government of a country, that tells people what they are allowed to do.
2 one of the rules established by a government, that tells people what they are allowed to do.
lawful ADJECTIVE   **lawfully** ADVERB

lawn lawns

NOUN a piece of well-kept grass, usually in a park or garden.

lawnmower lawnmowers

NOUN a machine for cutting grass.

lawyer lawyers

NOUN someone who is trained in the law and who speaks for people in court.

lay lays laying laid

VERB **1** When you **lay** something somewhere, you place it there.
2 If you **lay** the table, you put things such as knives and forks on the table ready for a meal.
3 When a bird **lays** an egg, an egg comes out of its body.
✔ People often get confused about *lay* and *lie*. The verb *lay* takes an object: **lay** *the table please*. The verb *lie* does not take an object: *the book was **lying** on the table*.

layer layers

NOUN a single thickness of something underneath or above something else. *There was a thin **layer** of snow on the ground.*

layout layouts

NOUN the pattern in which something is arranged. *The clear **layout** of this book makes it a lot easier to use.*

lazy lazier laziest

ADJECTIVE If you are **lazy**, you are idle and are unwilling to work.
lazily ADVERB

lead leads leading led

*Said "**leed**"* VERB **1** If you **lead** someone somewhere, you go in front of them in order to show them the way.
2 If a road or door **leads** somewhere, you can get to that place by following the road or going through the door.
3 If you **lead** in a race or competition, you are at the front.
4 Someone who **leads** a group of people is in charge of them.
NOUN **5** If you take the **lead** in a race or competition, or if you are in the **lead**, you are winning.
6 a length of leather or chain attached to an animal's collar, used for controlling the animal. *Put the dog on the **lead** when you take him for a walk.*
7 an electric cable for connecting an electrical appliance to a battery or the mains.
*Said "**led**"* NOUN **8** a soft, grey, heavy metal.
9 the **lead** in a pencil is the part that makes marks on paper.

leader leaders

NOUN **1** If you are the **leader** of a group, you are in charge of it.
2 If you are the **leader** in a race or a competition, you are winning.

leaf leaves

NOUN **1** a flat structure growing from the stem of a plant. Most plants have green **leaves**.
2 one of the sheets of paper in a book.
leafy ADJECTIVE

leaflet leaflets

NOUN a piece of paper or thin booklet with information or advertisements.

league leagues

NOUN a group of people, clubs or countries that have joined together for a particular purpose or because they share a common interest.

leak leaks leaking leaked

VERB **1** If a container or other object **leaks**, it has a hole through which gas or liquid escapes.

NOUN **2** If a container or other object has a **leak**, it has a hole through which gas or liquid escapes.

lean leans leaning leant or leaned; leaner leanest

VERB **1** When you **lean** in a particular direction, you bend your body in that direction. *She leant out of the window.*

2 When you **lean** on something, you rest your body against it for support. *He was leaning on the railing.*

3 If you **lean** something somewhere, you place it there so that its weight is supported. *He leaned his bike against the wall.*

ADJECTIVE **4** If meat is **lean**, it does not have much fat.

leap leaps leaping leapt or leaped

VERB **1** If you **leap** somewhere, you jump a long distance or high in the air.

NOUN **2** a jump over a long distance or high in the air.

leap year leap years

NOUN A **leap year** has 366 days instead of 365, with an extra day in February. It occurs every four years.

learn learns learning learnt or learned

VERB When you **learn** something, you gain knowledge or a skill by practice or by being taught. *He's learning to play the piano.*

lease leases

NOUN A **lease** is an agreement that lets someone use a house or a flat in return for rent.

least

NOUN **1** the smallest possible amount of something.

ADJECTIVE OR ADVERB **2** a superlative form of *little. He ate the least amount of food because he felt ill.*

PHRASE **3** You use **at least** to show that you are referring to the minimum amount of something, and that the true amount may be greater. *There were at least 500 people at the concert.*

leather

NOUN animal skin that has been specially treated so that it can be used to make shoes, clothes, bags and other things.

leave leaves leaving left

VERB **1** When you **leave** a place or person, you go away from them.

2 If you **leave** something somewhere, you let it stay there, or put it there before you go away. *I left my bags in the car.*

3 If you **leave** a job or a school, you stop being a part of it.

4 In arithmetic, when you take one number from another, it **leaves** a third number. For example, if you take 2 from 12, it **leaves** 10.

NOUN **5** holiday time. *I'm going to use my leave to go abroad this year.*

lecture lectures

NOUN a formal talk intended to teach people about a particular subject.

led

VERB the past tense of *lead.*

ledge ledges

NOUN a narrow shelf on the side of a cliff or rock face, or on the outside of a building, directly under a window.

leek leeks

NOUN a long vegetable of the onion family, that is white at one end and has green leaves at the other.

left

VERB **1** the past tense of *leave.*

NOUN **2** one of the two opposite directions, sides or positions. The **left** is the side of a page that you begin reading on in English.

ADJECTIVE OR ADVERB **3** on or towards the **left** of something: *a cut over his left eye.*

ADJECTIVE **4** If a certain amount of something is **left** or **left over**, it remains when the rest has gone. *They have two games left to play.*

Antonym: (senses 2 and 3) right

leftovers

PLURAL NOUN the bits of uneaten food that are left at the end of a meal.

leg legs

NOUN **1** one of the long parts of a human or other animal's body that they stand on and walk with.

2 The **legs** of a pair of trousers are the parts that cover your legs.

3 The **legs** of a table or chair are the parts that rest on the floor and support it.

4 A **leg** of a journey or a sports match is one part of it. *The first **leg** of the race was very hard work.*

legacy legacies

NOUN property or money that is given to someone in the will of a person who has died.

legal

ADJECTIVE relating to the law.

legend legends

NOUN a very old and popular story.

legible

ADJECTIVE Writing that is **legible** is clear enough to be read.

legibly ADVERB   **legibility** NOUN

Antonym: illegible

legion legions

NOUN **1** In ancient Rome, a **legion** was a military unit of between 3000 and 6000 soldiers.

2 a large group of soldiers that form part of an army: *the French Foreign **Legion***.

3 **Legions** of people are very large numbers of them.

legislation

NOUN a law or group of laws made by a government.

legitimate

ADJECTIVE If something is **legitimate** it is allowed by law, or is accepted as fair by most people.

legitimately ADVERB

leisure

NOUN time when you do not have to work and can do things that you enjoy.

lemon lemons

NOUN a yellow citrus fruit with a sour taste.

lemonade

NOUN a clear, sweet drink made from lemons, water and sugar. **Lemonade** is often fizzy.

lend lends lending lent

VERB **1** If you **lend** something to someone, you let them have it for a period of time.

2 If a person or bank **lends** you money, they give you money and you agree to pay it back later, usually with interest.

length lengths

NOUN **1** The **length** of something is the distance from one end to the other. *We walked the **length** of the street.*

2 The **length** of an event or activity is the amount of time it continues. *The film is over two hours in **length**.*

lengthen lengthens lengthening lengthened

VERB If you **lengthen** something, you make it longer.

Antonym: shorten

lengthy lengthier lengthiest

ADJECTIVE Something that is **lengthy** lasts for a long time. *The speech was rather **lengthy**.*

lens lenses

NOUN a thin, curved piece of glass, plastic or other transparent material that makes things appear larger or clearer: *a camera **lens***.

lent

VERB the past tense and past participle of *lend*.

Lent

NOUN the forty-day period before Easter when some Christians fast or give up something that they enjoy.

lentil lentils

NOUN **Lentils** are small, dried, red or brown seeds that are cooked and eaten in soups, stews and curries.

leopard leopards

NOUN a large wild cat, with yellow fur and black or brown spots, found in Africa and Asia.

leotard leotards

Said "**lee-uh-tard**" NOUN a tight-fitting garment that covers the body rather like a swimming costume, which is worn for dancing or exercise.

lesbian lesbians

NOUN a homosexual woman.

less

ADJECTIVE OR ADVERB **1** a smaller amount of something, or to a smaller extent. *It is less than three weeks until we go back to school.* **2** a comparative form of *little*.

PREPOSITION **3** You use **less** to show that one number or amount is to be subtracted from another. *You can have your pocket money, less the money you borrowed last week.*

✔ You use *less* to talk about things that can't be counted: *less time*. When you are talking about amounts that can be counted you should use *fewer*: *there are fewer than ten children in that class.*

Antonym: (sense 1) more

lesson lessons

NOUN **1** a fixed period of time during which people are taught something by a teacher. **2** an experience that makes you understand something important.

let lets letting let

VERB **1** If you **let** someone do something, you allow them to do it. **2** If someone **lets** a house or flat that they own, they allow others to use it in return for payment.

lethal

ADJECTIVE Something that is **lethal** can kill you. *A gun is a lethal weapon.* [from Latin *letum* meaning death]

let's

VERB a contraction of *let us*, which is another way of saying *shall we*. *Let's go swimming.*

letter letters

NOUN **1** a message written on paper and sent to someone, usually through the post. **2** one of the written symbols that go together to make words.

letter box letter boxes; also spelt **letter-box**

NOUN **1** an oblong gap in a front door, through which letters are delivered. **2** a large metal container in the street or at a post office, for posting letters.

lettering

NOUN You use **lettering** to describe writing that is done in a certain way. *The poster had large black lettering.*

lettuce lettuces

NOUN a vegetable with large, green leaves that you eat in salads.

leukaemia or **leukemia**

Said "loo-**kee**-mee-a" NOUN a serious illness that affects the blood. [from Greek *leukos* meaning white and *haima* meaning blood]

level levels levelling levelled

NOUN **1** the height, position or amount of something. *This is the lowest level of rainfall for years.* **2** a standard or grade of achievement. *Now that I have passed this piano exam, I will move on to the next level.*

ADJECTIVE **3** A surface that is **level** is completely flat. **4** If one thing is **level** with another, it is at the same height or position.

VERB **5** If you **level** something, you make it flat.

Synonyms: (sense 2) grade, stage

level crossing level crossings

NOUN a place where traffic is allowed to drive across a railway track.

lever levers

NOUN **1** a handle on a machine that you pull in order to make the machine work. **2** a bar that you wedge underneath a heavy object and press down on to make the object move.

liable

ADJECTIVE **1** Something that is **liable** to happen will probably happen. *Britain is liable to be cold in January.* **2** If someone is **liable** for something such as a crime or a debt, they are legally responsible for it. **liability** NOUN

liar liars

NOUN a person who tells lies.

liberal

ADJECTIVE **1** If someone is **liberal**, they are tolerant of other people's behaviour and opinions.
2 If you are **liberal** with something, you are generous with it.
liberally ADVERB

liberty

NOUN the freedom to do what you want to do and go where you want to go.

librarian librarians

NOUN a person who works in, or is in charge of, a library.

library libraries

NOUN a building in which books are kept, especially a public building from which people can borrow books.

licence licences

NOUN an official document that gives you permission to do, use or own something. *You have to pass a test before you receive a full driving **licence**.*
✔ The noun *licence* ends in *ce*.

license licenses licensing licensed

VERB If someone **licenses** an activity, they give official permission for it to be carried out.
✔ The verb *license* ends in *se*.

lichen lichens

Said "**lie**-kun" NOUN a green or greeny-grey mossy growth, found on rocks, trees and walls.

lick licks licking licked

VERB If you **lick** something, you move your tongue over it. *I **licked** the stamp and stuck it to the envelope.*

lid lids

NOUN a cover for a box, jar or other container.

lie lies lying lay lain

VERB **1** If someone or something **lies** somewhere, they rest there in a flat position.
2 You use **lie** to say where something is or what its position is. *The village **lies** to the east of the river.*
✔ The past tense of this verb *lie* is *lay*. Do not confuse it with the verb *lay* meaning "put".

lie lies lying lied

VERB **1** If you **lie**, you say something that you know is not true. *He **lied** about his age.*
NOUN **2** something you say that you know is not true.

lieutenant lieutenants

Said "lef-**ten**-ant" NOUN a junior officer in the army or navy.
✔ In American English it is pronounced "loo-**ten**-ant".

life lives

NOUN **1** the state of being alive that makes people, animals and plants different from objects.
2 your existence from the time you are born until the time you die.

lifeboat lifeboats

NOUN a boat used for rescuing people who are in danger at sea.

life cycle life cycles

NOUN the series of changes and developments in the life of a living thing. *There are several stages in the **life cycle** of a butterfly.*

lifeguard lifeguards

NOUN a person whose job is to rescue people who are in difficulty in the sea or in a swimming pool.

life jacket life jackets

NOUN a sleeveless, inflatable jacket that keeps you afloat in water.

lifelike

ADJECTIVE A picture or a sculpture that is **lifelike** looks very real, almost as if it is alive.

Synonym: realistic

lifeline lifelines

NOUN something that helps you to survive or helps an activity to continue. *His help was a real **lifeline** to me after I had so many difficulties.*

lifetime lifetimes

NOUN the period of time during which you are alive.

lift lifts lifting lifted

VERB **1** If you **lift** something, you move it to a higher position.
NOUN **2** a device that carries people or goods from one floor to another in a building.

light lights lighting lighted or lit; lighter lightest

NOUN **1** the brightness from the sun, moon, fire or lamps, that lets you see things.
2 a lamp or other device that gives out brightness.
ADJECTIVE **3** If it is **light**, there is enough light from the sun to see things.
4 A **light** colour is pale.
5 A **light** object does not weigh much.
VERB **6** If you **light** a fire, you make it start burning.

Antonym: (sense 3) dark
(sense 5) heavy

lighten lightens lightening lightened

VERB **1** When something **lightens**, it becomes brighter and less dark. *After the storm the sky lightened*.
2 If you **lighten** a load, you make it less heavy. *My case was too heavy, so I lightened it by taking out three books.*

lighter lighters

NOUN a device for lighting something, such as a fire or a cigarette.

lighthouse lighthouses

NOUN a tower by the sea, that shines a powerful light to guide ships and warn them of danger.

lighting

NOUN The **lighting** in a room or building is the way it is lit.

lightning

NOUN very bright flashes of light you see in the sky, usually during a thunderstorm. **Lightning** is caused by electrical activity in the atmosphere.

light year light years

NOUN the distance that light travels in a year, which is about 6 million miles or 9·5 million kilometres.

like likes liking liked

VERB **1** If you **like** someone or something, you find them pleasing.
PREPOSITION **2** If one thing is **like** another, they are similar.

likeable or **likable**

ADJECTIVE A **likeable** person is pleasant and friendly.

likely likelier likeliest

ADJECTIVE If something is **likely**, it will probably happen or is probably true.

lilac lilacs

NOUN **1** a small tree with sweet-smelling clusters of mauve, pink or white flowers.
2 a pale mauve colour.

lily lilies

NOUN a plant with trumpet-shaped flowers of various colours.

limb limbs

NOUN Your **limbs** are your arms and legs.

lime limes

NOUN **1** a small, green, citrus fruit, rather like a lemon.
2 a bright green colour.
3 a chemical substance used in cement or as a fertiliser.

limerick limericks

NOUN an amusing nonsense poem of five lines.

limit limits limiting limited

NOUN **1** the largest or smallest amount of something that is possible or allowed. *The speed limit on this road is 30 mph.*
VERB **2** If you **limit** something, you restrict it to a certain amount or number. *The children were limited to two biscuits each.*
limited ADJECTIVE

limousine limousines

NOUN a large, luxurious car, usually driven by a chauffeur.

limp limps limping limped; limper limpest

VERB **1** If you **limp**, you walk in an uneven way because you have hurt your leg or foot.
NOUN **2** an uneven way of walking. *While her leg was in plaster she walked with a limp*.
ADJECTIVE **3** Something that is **limp** is soft or weak.

limpet limpets

NOUN a small shellfish with a pointed shell, that attaches itself very firmly to rocks.

line lines lining lined

NOUN **1** a long, thin mark.
2 a number of people or things that are arranged in a row.
3 a long piece of string or wire: *a washing* **line**.
4 a number of words together, for example the **lines** in a play are the words that an actor has to speak. *This is my favourite* **line** *in the poem.*
5 a railway or railway track.
VERB **6** If people or things **line** something, they make a border or edge along it. *Crowds* **lined** *the streets to see the Queen.*

linen

NOUN **1** a type of cloth made from a plant called flax.
2 household goods made of cloth, such as sheets and tablecloths.

liner liners

NOUN a large passenger ship that makes long sea journeys.

linesman linesmen

NOUN an official at a sports match who watches the lines of the field or court and decides if the ball has gone outside them.

linger lingers lingering lingered

VERB If someone or something **lingers**, they stay for a long time. *The smell* **lingered** *in the kitchen.*
lingering ADJECTIVE

linguist linguists

NOUN someone who studies foreign languages and can speak them well.

lining linings

NOUN any material that is used to line the inside of something. *There is a fleece* **lining** *in this jacket.*

link links linking linked

NOUN **1** one of the rings in a chain.
2 a relationship or connection between two things. *There is a* **link** *between the weather and the clothes we wear.*
3 a physical connection between two things or places. *There is a rail* **link** *between the two cities.*

VERB **4** If someone or something **links** people, places, or things, they join them together. *They want to* **link** *the village to the town with a better road.*

lion lions

NOUN a large member of the cat family that is found in Africa. Male **lions** have long hair on their head and neck, called a mane.

lioness lionesses

NOUN a female lion.

lip lips

NOUN Your **lips** are the two outer edges of your mouth.

lipstick lipsticks

NOUN a cosmetic for colouring the lips, usually in the form of a small stick.

liquid liquids

NOUN a substance such as water, which is neither a gas nor a solid and which can be poured. A **liquid** always takes the shape of the container it is in.

liquidizer liquidizers

NOUN an electric machine used for making food into liquid. *Dad put strawberries, bananas and milk in the* **liquidizer** *and mixed us a delicious milkshake.*

liquorice or **licorice**

NOUN **1** a root used to flavour sweets.
2 sweets flavoured with liquorice.

lisp lisps lisping lisped

NOUN **1** Someone who has a **lisp** pronounces the sounds *s* and *z* like *th*.
VERB **2** If someone **lisps**, they speak with a lisp.

list lists listing listed

NOUN **1** a set of words or items written one after the other: *a shopping* **list**.
VERB **2** If you **list** a number of things, you write them or say them one after another.

listen listens listening listened

VERB **1** If you **listen** to someone, you pay attention to what they are saying.
2 If you **listen** to something, you pay attention to its sound. *She enjoys listening to music.*

lit

VERB past tense and past participle of *light*.

literacy

NOUN the ability to read and write.

literally

ADVERB You use **literally** to emphasize that what you are saying is actually true, even though it seems unlikely. *We **literally** almost died of thirst.*

literate

ADJECTIVE If you are **literate**, you are able to read and write.
literacy NOUN

literature

NOUN Novels, plays and poetry are referred to as **literature**.
[from Latin ***litteratura*** meaning writing]

litre litres

NOUN a unit for measuring liquid (l) equal to 1000 millilitres or about 1·76 pints.

litter litters littering littered

NOUN **1** rubbish in the street and other public places.
2 baby animals born at the same time to the same mother.
VERB **3** If things **litter** a place, they are scattered all over it. *Paper **littered** the pavement.*

little less lesser least

ADJECTIVE **1** small in size or amount. *Stay a **little** longer.*
ADVERB OR PRONOUN **2** not much. *I had very **little** money left.*
NOUN **3** A **little** is a small amount or degree of something. *He showed me a **little** of his work.*

Antonyms: (sense 1) big, large

live lives living lived

*Rhymes with "**give**"* VERB **1** If someone or something **lives**, they are alive.
2 If you **live** in a place, that is where your home is. *He **lives** with his parents.*
3 The way someone **lives** is the kind of life they have. *We **live** quite simply.*
*Rhymes with "**five**"* ADJECTIVE **4 Live** television or radio is broadcast while the event is taking place.
5 Live animals or plants are alive, rather than dead or artificial.

lively livelier liveliest

ADJECTIVE full of energy and enthusiasm.

liver livers

NOUN a large organ in your body that cleans your blood and stores substances such as vitamins and minerals.

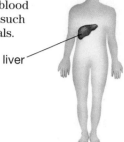

liver

living

ADJECTIVE **1** If someone or something is **living**, they are alive.
NOUN **2** Someone who works for a **living**, works to earn the money needed in order to live. *He makes a **living** by selling cars.*

living room living rooms

NOUN a room in a house where you sit and relax, doing such things as watching television and reading.

lizard lizards

NOUN a reptile with short legs and a tail.

llama llamas

NOUN a South American animal that looks rather like a small camel with thick hair and no hump.

load loads loading loaded

VERB **1** If you **load** a vehicle or container, you put things into it.
2 When you **load** a camera, you put film into it.
NOUN **3** something large or heavy that is being carried: *a tractor with a big **load** of hay.*
4 INFORMAL A **load** of something, or **loads** of something, means a lot of it. *He's got **loads** of CDs.*

loaf loaves

NOUN a large piece of bread in a shape that can be cut into slices.

loan loans loaning loaned

NOUN **1** a sum of money that you borrow.
VERB **2** If you **loan** something to someone, you lend it to them.

loathe loathes loathing loathed

VERB If you **loathe** someone or something, you feel a very strong dislike for them.
loathing NOUN   **loathsome** ADJECTIVE

lobster lobsters

NOUN an edible shellfish with two front claws and eight legs.

local locals

ADJECTIVE **1** existing in or belonging to the area where you live: *the **local** newspaper.*
NOUN **2** someone who lives in and comes from a particular area.

locality localities

NOUN a small area of a country or a city. *Golden eagles can be seen in certain **localities** in Scotland.*

locate locates locating located

VERB **1** If you **locate** someone or something, you find out where they are.
2 If something is **located** in a place, it is in that place.

location locations

NOUN the place where something is found or where something happens. *She couldn't remember the exact **location** of the church.*

loch lochs

NOUN In Scottish English, a **loch** is a lake. *They say there is a monster in **Loch** Ness.*

lock locks locking locked

VERB **1** If you **lock** something, you fasten it with a key.
2 If you **lock** something in a place, you put it there and fasten the lock. *They **locked** the money in the safe.*
NOUN **3** a device that prevents something from being opened except with a key. *He heard a key in the **lock**.*

locker lockers

NOUN a small cupboard for someone's personal belongings, for example in a changing room.

locket lockets

NOUN a small piece of jewellery worn on a chain around the neck, which opens so that you can put a small photograph inside.

locomotive locomotives

NOUN a railway engine.

locust locusts

NOUN an insect like a large grasshopper, that travels in huge swarms and eats crops.

loft lofts

NOUN the space immediately under the roof of a house, often used for storing things.

log logs

NOUN **1** a thick piece of wood from a branch or trunk of a tree, that has fallen or been cut off.
2 an official written account of what happens each day. *The captain wrote each day's events in the ship's **log**.*

logic

NOUN a way of reasoning that makes sense.
logical ADJECTIVE   **logically** ADVERB

logo logos

NOUN the special design that is put on all the products of an organization.

loiter loiters loitering loitered

VERB If you **loiter** in a place, you stand around without going very far or doing very much. *After school they **loitered** round the shops.*

lollipop lollipops

NOUN a hard sweet on the end of a stick.
[from Romani **lolli** meaning red and **pobbel** meaning apple]

lolly lollies

NOUN **1** a lollipop.
2 a flavoured ice or ice cream on a stick.

lonely lonelier loneliest

ADJECTIVE **1** If you are **lonely**, you are unhappy because you are alone.
2 A **lonely** place is one that very few people visit.

long longer longest; longs longing longed

ADJECTIVE **1** continuing for a great amount of time. *There had been no rain for a **long** time.*

ADVERB **2** You use **long** to talk about amounts of time. *How **long** is the film?*

ADJECTIVE **3** great in length or distance. *It's a **long** way home.*

4 You use **long** to talk about the distance that something measures from one end to the other.

PHRASE **5** If something **no longer** happens, it used to happen but does not happen now.

VERB **6** If you **long** for something to happen, or if you **long** to do it, you want it to happen very much.

long division long divisions

NOUN a method of dividing one large number by another one, where you write out all the stages instead of doing them in your head or on a calculator.

longitude longitudes

NOUN a position measured in degrees east or west of an imaginary line passing through Greenwich in London.

look looks looking looked

VERB **1** If you **look** at something, you turn your eyes towards it so that you can see it.

2 If you **look** for someone or something, you try to find them.

3 If you describe the way that something **looks**, you are describing its appearance. *He **looked** a bit pale.*

NOUN **4** If you take a **look** at something, you look at it. *Lucy took a last **look** in the mirror.*

5 The **look** on your face is the expression on it.

look after VERB **6** If you **look after** someone or something, you take care of them.

look forward VERB **7** If you **look forward** to something, you want it to happen because you think you will enjoy it.

PHRASE **8** You say **look out** to warn someone of danger. ***Look out!** There's a car coming.*

Synonym: (sense 4) glance

lookout lookouts

NOUN **1** someone who is watching for danger, or a place where someone watches for danger.

PHRASE **2** If you are **on the lookout** for something, you are watching or waiting for it to happen.

loom looms looming loomed

NOUN **1** a machine for weaving cloth.

VERB **2** If something **looms** in front of you, it suddenly appears as a tall, unclear and sometimes frightening shape. *A monster **loomed** out of the darkness.*

3 If a situation or event is **looming**, it is likely to happen soon and is rather worrying. *A storm is **looming** on the horizon.*

loop loops looping looped

NOUN **1** a curved or circular shape in something such as a piece of string or wire.

VERB **2** If you **loop** rope or string around an object, you place it in a loop around the object. *He **looped** the rope over the horse's neck.*

loose looser loosest

*Said "**looss**"* ADJECTIVE **1** not firmly held or fixed in place: *a **loose** tooth.*

2 not tight: *a **loose** jacket.*

ADVERB **3** If people or animals break **loose**, or are set **loose**, they are released after they have been held back or tied up.

✔ The adjective and adverb *loose* is spelt with two *o*s. Do not confuse it with the verb *lose*.

loot loots looting looted

VERB **1** If someone **loots** shops and houses, they steal goods from them, especially during a riot or war.

NOUN **2** stolen money or goods.

lopsided

ADJECTIVE Something that is **lopsided** is uneven because one side is different from the other, for example one side is heavier or larger.

lord lords

NOUN In Britain, **Lord** is a title used in front of the names of some men.

lorry lorries

NOUN a large vehicle for transporting goods by road.

lose loses losing lost

*Said "**looz**"* VERB **1** If you **lose** something, you cannot find it, or you no longer have it because it has been taken from you. *He **lost** his place in the team.*

2 If you **lose** a fight or an argument, you are beaten.

✔ The verb *lose* is spelt with one *o*. Do not confuse it with the adjective and adverb *loose*.

loss losses

NOUN The **loss** of something is the fact of having lost it or of having less of it.

lost

VERB **1** the past tense and past participle of *lose*.

ADJECTIVE **2** If you are **lost**, you do not know where you are.

3 If something is **lost**, you cannot find it.

lot lots

NOUN **1** a large amount of something: *a lot of children*.

2 very much or very often. *I miss him a lot*.

3 the whole of something. *He had a whole packet of biscuits and ate the lot*.

lotion lotions

NOUN a liquid that you put on your skin to protect or soften it: *suntan lotion*.

lottery lotteries

NOUN a way of raising money by selling tickets and giving prizes to people who have winning tickets, which are selected at random.

loud louder loudest

ADJECTIVE A **loud** noise produces a lot of sound.

loudly ADVERB

loudspeaker loudspeakers

NOUN a piece of electrical equipment that produces the sound in things such as radios, telephones and CD players.

lounge lounges lounging lounged

NOUN **1** a room in a house, hotel or airport where people can sit and relax.

VERB **2** If you **lounge** around, you lean against something or lie around in a lazy way.

louse lice

NOUN a small insect that lives on people's bodies.

lout louts

NOUN a young man who behaves in a rude or aggressive way.

loutish ADJECTIVE

love loves loving loved

VERB **1** If you **love** someone or something, you have strong feelings of affection for them.

2 If you would **love** to do something, you want very much to do it.

NOUN **3** a strong feeling of affection for someone or something.

lovely lovelier loveliest

ADJECTIVE very beautiful, attractive, pleasant or enjoyable. *We had a lovely day out*.

low lower lowest

ADJECTIVE OR ADVERB **1** Something that is **low** is close to the ground.

ADJECTIVE **2** below average in value or amount. *The temperature was low for the time of year*.

Antonym: high

lower lowers lowering lowered

VERB **1** If you **lower** something, you move it downwards. *She lowered the bucket into the well*.

ADJECTIVE **2** The **lower** of two things is the bottom one: *the lower deck of the bus*.

lower-case

ADJECTIVE **Lower-case** letters are small letters, not capital letters.

loyal

ADJECTIVE If you are **loyal**, you are firm in your friendship or support for someone or something.

lozenge lozenges

NOUN **1** a small sweet with medicine in it, that you can suck if you have a sore throat or a cough.

2 a diamond shape, like a rhombus. *See* **rhombus**.

lubricate lubricates lubricating lubricated

VERB If someone **lubricates** something like a machine, they put oil or grease on to it so that it moves smoothly.

lubrication NOUN **lubricant** NOUN

[from Latin *lubricus* meaning slippery]

luck

NOUN **1** something that happens by chance. *We had good luck with the weather. It was bad luck that I lost the game of Monopoly*.

PHRASE **2** You say **good luck** to someone when you are wishing them success.

lucky luckier luckiest

ADJECTIVE Someone who is **lucky** has a lot of good luck.

luckily ADVERB

luggage

NOUN Your **luggage** is the bags and suitcases that you take with you when you travel.

lukewarm

ADJECTIVE slightly warm.

lull lulls lulling lulled

NOUN **1** a pause in something, or a short time when it is quiet and calm.
VERB **2** If you **lull** someone, you calm them and make them feel safe.

lullaby lullabies

NOUN a song used for sending a baby or child to sleep.

lumber lumbers lumbering lumbered

NOUN **1** wood that has been roughly cut up.
VERB **2** If you **lumber** around, you move heavily and clumsily.

luminous

ADJECTIVE Something that is **luminous** glows in the dark without being hot.
luminously ADVERB   **luminosity** NOUN

lump lumps

NOUN a solid piece of something.

lunar

ADJECTIVE relating to the moon. *The lunar module landed safely on the moon.*
[from Latin *luna* meaning moon]

lunch lunches

NOUN a meal eaten in the middle of the day.

lung lungs

NOUN Your **lungs** are the two organs inside your chest that you breathe with.

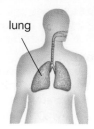

lung

lurch lurches lurching lurched

VERB **1** If someone or something **lurches**, they make a sudden, jerky movement.
PHRASE **2** If someone leaves you **in the lurch**, they leave you in a difficult or dangerous situation, instead of helping you.

lure lures luring lured

VERB If you **lure** someone or something, you tempt them into going somewhere or doing something. *He lured the cat back into the house with some milk.*

lurk lurks lurking lurked

VERB If someone **lurks** somewhere, they hide there and wait.

lush lusher lushest

ADJECTIVE In a **lush** field or garden, the grass or plants are healthy and growing thickly.

lute lutes

NOUN an old-fashioned, stringed musical instrument that is plucked like a guitar.

luxury luxuries

NOUN **1** great comfort, especially among expensive and beautiful surroundings.
2 A **luxury** is something that you would like to have but do not need, and is usually expensive.

lying

VERB the present participle of *lie*.

lyrics

PLURAL NOUN The **lyrics** of a song are the words.

Mm

macaroni
NOUN short, hollow tubes of pasta.
[an Italian word; from Greek *makaria* meaning food made from barley]

machine machines
NOUN a piece of equipment designed to do a particular job. It is usually powered by an engine or by electricity: *a washing machine*.

machine gun machine guns
NOUN a gun that works automatically, firing a continuous stream of bullets very quickly.

machinery
NOUN machines in general: *farm machinery*, *factory machinery*.

mackintosh mackintoshes
NOUN a raincoat made from waterproof cloth.

mad madder maddest
ADJECTIVE **1** Someone who is **mad** has a mental illness that causes them to behave in strange ways.
2 If you describe someone as **mad**, you mean that they are very foolish.
3 INFORMAL Someone who is **mad** is angry.
PHRASE **4** If you are **mad about** someone or something, you like them very much. *She had always been mad about football.*
madly ADVERB   **madness** NOUN

made
VERB past tense and past participle of *make*.

magazine magazines
NOUN a weekly or monthly publication containing articles and photographs.

maggot maggots
NOUN the larva of some kinds of fly. **Maggots** look like small, fat worms.
maggoty ADJECTIVE

magic
NOUN **1** In fairy stories, **magic** is a special power that can make impossible things happen.
2 the art of performing tricks to entertain people.
magical ADJECTIVE

magician magicians
NOUN **1** a person who performs tricks that seem like magic to entertain people.
2 In fairy stories, a **magician** is a man with magic powers.

magistrate magistrates
NOUN an official who acts as a judge in a law court that deals with less serious crimes.

magnet magnets
NOUN a piece of iron or steel that attracts other objects made of iron or steel towards it. **Magnets** can also push away, or repel, other **magnets**.

magnetic
ADJECTIVE Something that is **magnetic** is attracted towards a magnet. Only iron, steel, nickel and cobalt are **magnetic**.

magnificent
ADJECTIVE extremely beautiful or impressive.
[from Latin *magnificus* meaning great in deeds]

Synonyms: imposing, splendid

magnify magnifies magnifying magnified
VERB When a microscope or lens **magnifies** something, it makes it appear bigger than it actually is.
magnification NOUN

magnifying glass magnifying glasses
NOUN a glass lens that magnifies things, making them appear bigger than they really are.

magpie magpies
NOUN a large, black-and-white bird with a long tail.

mahogany
NOUN a hard, reddish-brown wood used for making furniture.

maid maids
NOUN a female servant.

maiden name maiden names
NOUN the surname a woman had before she married.

mail mails mailing mailed
NOUN **1** the letters and parcels delivered to you by the post office.
VERB **2** If you **mail** a letter, you send it by post.
[from Old French *male* meaning bag]

mail order

NOUN a system of buying goods by post.

maim maims maiming maimed

VERB **1** To **maim** someone is to injure them very badly for life.

ADJECTIVE **2** Somebody who is **maimed** is injured for life.

main mains

ADJECTIVE **1** most important or largest. *My main interest is music.*

NOUN **2** The **mains** are the large pipes or cables that carry gas, water or electricity to a building.

Synonyms: (sense 1) chief, major, principal

mainland

NOUN the main part of a country or continent, not including the islands around it.

mainly

ADVERB mostly, chiefly or usually. *We eat mainly vegetarian food.*

maintain maintains maintaining maintained

VERB **1** If you **maintain** something, you keep it going at a particular rate or level. *You will need to maintain this level of fitness if you want to take part in the finals.*

2 If you **maintain** a machine or a building, you keep it in good condition.

3 If you **maintain** a belief or an opinion, you have it and state it clearly.

maize

NOUN a tall plant that produces sweet corn.

majesty majesties

NOUN **1** You say **His Majesty** when you are talking about a king, and **Her Majesty** when you are talking about a queen.

2 the quality of being dignified and impressive.
majestic ADJECTIVE

major majors

ADJECTIVE **1** more important or more serious than other things. *She has a major role in the school play.*

NOUN **2** an army officer of the rank immediately above captain.

Antonym: (sense 1) minor

majority majorities

NOUN more than half of a group.

✔ You should use *majority* only to talk about things that can be counted: *the majority of schoolchildren like chocolate.* To talk about an amount that cannot be counted you should use *most*: *most of the harvest was saved.*

make makes making made

VERB **1** If you **make** something, you create or produce it. *This is the cake I made yesterday.*

2 If you **make** someone or something do something, you force them to do it or cause it to happen. *Her mother made her do her homework every night.*

3 If you **make** a promise to do something, you say you will definitely do it.

4 Two amounts added together **make** a sum: *3 and 5 make 8.*

5 If you **make** a phone call, you use the telephone to speak to someone.

NOUN **6** the name of the product of a particular manufacturer. *What make is your bicycle?*

make-believe

NOUN a fantasy of pretend or imaginary things.

make-up

NOUN coloured creams and powders that women and actors put on their faces.

malaria

NOUN a serious tropical disease, caught from mosquitoes, that causes fever and shivering.

male males

NOUN **1** a person or animal belonging to the sex that cannot have babies.

ADJECTIVE **2** concerning or affecting men rather than women.

Antonym: female

malevolent

Said "mal-**lev**-oh-lent" ADJECTIVE **1** **Malevolent** people want to cause harm or do evil things.

2 A **malevolent** act is cruel and spiteful.

malfunction malfunctions malfunctioning malfunctioned

VERB If a machine **malfunctions**, it fails to work properly.

malicious

ADJECTIVE **Malicious** talk or behaviour is intended to harm someone.

mall malls
NOUN a sheltered place with cafés, shops and restaurants: *a shopping **mall***.

mallet mallets
NOUN a wooden hammer with a square head.

malnutrition
NOUN a condition resulting from not eating enough healthy food or not having enough to eat.

mammal mammals
NOUN an animal that gives birth to live babies and feeds its young with milk from the mother's body. Human beings, dogs and whales are all **mammals**.
mammalian ADJECTIVE
[from Latin ***mamma*** meaning breast]

mammoth mammoths
ADJECTIVE **1** very large indeed.
NOUN **2** a huge animal that looked like a hairy elephant with long tusks. **Mammoths** became extinct a long time ago.

man men; mans manning manned
NOUN **1** an adult, male human being.
2 Human beings, both male and female, are sometimes referred to as **man**. *Primitive **man** lived in caves.*
VERB **3** If you **man** something, you are in charge of it or you operate it. *Can you **man** the bookstall?*

Antonym: (sense 1) woman

manage manages managing managed
VERB **1** If you **manage** to do something, you succeed in doing it even if it is difficult. *We **managed** to find somewhere to sit.*
2 If someone **manages** an organization or business, they are responsible for controlling it.

management
NOUN **1** the controlling and organizing of a business.
2 the people who control an organization.

manager managers
NOUN a man or woman who is responsible for running a business or organization.

mane manes
NOUN long hair growing from the neck of a lion or a horse.

manger mangers
NOUN a feeding box in a barn or stable.

mangle mangles mangling mangled
VERB **1** If you **mangle** something, you crush or twist it out of shape.
NOUN **2** an old-fashioned piece of equipment consisting of two large rollers, for squeezing water out of wet clothes.

mango mangoes or mangos
NOUN a sweet yellow fruit that grows in tropical climates.

mankind
NOUN used to refer to all human beings. *Pollution is a threat to **mankind**.*

manner manners
NOUN **1** the way you do something or behave.
PLURAL NOUN **2** If you have good **manners**, you behave very politely.

manoeuvre manoeuvres manoeuvring manoeuvred
Said "man-**noo**-ver" VERB **1** If you **manoeuvre** something into place, you move it there skilfully. *Mum **manoeuvred** the car into the small parking space.*
NOUN **2** A **manoeuvre** is a clever thing that you do or say in order to make something happen the way you want it to.

manor manors
NOUN a large country house with land, especially one that was built in the Middle Ages.

mansion mansions
NOUN a very large house.

manslaughter
NOUN; LEGAL the accidental killing of a person.

mantelpiece mantelpieces
NOUN a shelf over a fireplace.

manual manuals
ADJECTIVE **1 Manual** work involves physical strength or skill with your hands, rather than mental skill.
2 Manual equipment is operated by hand rather than being automatic or operated by electricity or a motor: *a **manual** whisk*.
NOUN **3** a book that tells you how to use a machine: *an instruction **manual***.
[from Latin ***manus*** meaning hand]
manually ADVERB

manufacture manufactures manufacturing manufactured

VERB **1** If someone **manufactures** goods, they make them in a factory.

NOUN **2** The **manufacture** of goods is the making of them in a factory.

manure

NOUN animal dung used to improve the soil.

manuscript manuscripts

NOUN a handwritten or typed copy of a book, play, or piece of music before it is printed. [from Latin **manus** meaning hand and **scribere** meaning to write]

many

ADJECTIVE OR PRONOUN **1** If there are **many** people or things, there are a large number of them.

2 You use **many** to talk about how great a number or quantity is. *How **many** tickets do you need?*

map maps

NOUN a detailed drawing of an area of land, showing its shape and features as it would appear if you saw it from above.

maple maples

NOUN a tree that has large leaves with five points.

marathon marathons

NOUN a race in which people run 26 miles along roads. [named after **Marathon**, a place from which a messenger ran more than 20 miles to Athens, bringing news of a victory in 490 BC]

marble

NOUN a very hard, cold stone that is often polished to show the coloured patterns in it.

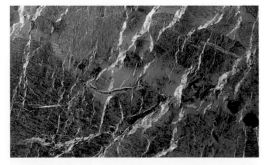

march marches marching marched

NOUN **1** an organized protest in which a large group of people walk somewhere together.

VERB **2** When soldiers **march**, they walk with quick regular steps as a group.

NOUN **3** music with a strong beat for marching to.

March

NOUN the third month of the year. **March** has 31 days. [from Latin **Martius** month of Mars, the Roman god of war]

mare mares

NOUN an adult female horse.

margarine

NOUN a soft substance made from vegetable oil and animal fats, and used like butter.

margin margins

NOUN **1** the blank space at the top and bottom and on each side of a written or printed page.

2 If you win a race or a competition by a large or small **margin**, you win it by a large or small amount.

marina marinas

NOUN a harbour for pleasure boats and yachts.

marine marines

NOUN **1** a soldier who is trained for duties at sea.

ADJECTIVE **2** relating to or involving the sea, and the animals and plants that live in the sea.

mark marks marking marked

NOUN **1** a small stain or damaged area on a surface.

2 a score given to a student for homework or for an exam.

3 a written or printed symbol.

VERB **4** If something **marks** a surface, it stains or damages it in some way.

5 When a teacher **marks** a student's work, they decide how good it is and give it a mark.

6 If you **mark** the opposing player in a team game such as hockey or netball, you stay close to them and prevent them from getting the ball.

market markets marketing marketed

NOUN **1** a place where goods are bought and sold, usually outdoors.

VERB **2** If someone **markets** a product, they sell it in an organized way.

marmalade

NOUN a type of jam made from oranges or lemons.

maroon

NOUN OR ADJECTIVE dark reddish-purple.

marquee marquees

NOUN a very large tent used at a fair, a wedding or other outdoor events.
[From French, meaning awning]

marriage marriages

NOUN **1** the relationship between a husband and wife.
2 a wedding ceremony.

married

VERB **1** past tense and past participle of *marry*.
ADJECTIVE **2** If someone is **married**, they have a husband or a wife.

marrow marrows

NOUN a long, thick green vegetable with cream-coloured flesh.

marry marries marrying married

VERB When a man and woman **marry**, they become husband and wife.

marsh marshes

NOUN an area of land that is permanently wet.

marshmallow marshmallows

NOUN a soft, spongy sweet, usually pink or white.

marsupial

marsupials
NOUN an animal that carries its young in a pouch. Koalas, kangaroos and wallabies are **marsupials**.
[from Greek *marsupion* meaning purse]

A kangaroo

martial

Said "**mar**-shul" ADJECTIVE **Martial** describes anything to do with military matters, war and soldiers.

martial arts

PLURAL NOUN The **martial arts** are techniques of self-defence, such as judo and karate, that come from the Far East.

martyr martyrs

NOUN someone who suffers or is killed for their beliefs.
martyrdom NOUN

marvel marvels marvelling marvelled

VERB **1** If you **marvel** at something, you are filled with amazement and admiration for it. *We marvelled at the sight of people swimming with the dolphins.*
NOUN **2** something that fills you with surprise and admiration.

marvellous

ADJECTIVE wonderful or excellent.

marzipan

NOUN a paste made of almonds, sugar and egg. It is put on top of cakes or used to make small sweets.

mascot mascots

NOUN a person, animal or toy that is thought to bring good luck.

masculine

ADJECTIVE typical of men, rather than women.

Antonym: feminine

mask masks masking masked

NOUN **1** something you wear over your face for protection or as a disguise.
VERB **2** If you **mask** something, you cover it so that it is protected or diguised.

mass masses

NOUN **1** a large amount or heap of something.
2 In science, **mass** is the amount of matter in an object. **Mass** is measured in grams (g).
3 A **Mass** is a communion service in a Roman Catholic church.
ADJECTIVE **4** involving or affecting a large number of people.

massacre massacres massacring massacred

NOUN **1** the killing of a very large number of people in a violent and cruel way.
VERB **2** To **massacre** a group of people means to kill them in large numbers in a violent and cruel way.

a b c d e f g h i j k l **m** n o p q r s t u v w x y z

massage massages massaging massaged
VERB **1** If you **massage** someone, you rub parts of their body in order to help them relax or to relieve pain.
NOUN **2** treatment that involves rubbing parts of the body.

massive
ADJECTIVE extremely large.

Synonyms: huge, vast, enormous

mast masts
NOUN the tall, upright pole that supports the sails of a boat.

master masters mastering mastered
VERB **1** If you **master** a skill, you learn how to do it well.
NOUN **2** someone who is very skilled at something: *a master baker.*
3 a male teacher.

masterpiece masterpieces
NOUN an excellent painting, novel, film or other work of art that has been made with great skill. *The 'Mona Lisa' is considered a masterpiece.*

mat mats
NOUN **1** a small piece of carpet or other material that is put on floors for protection or decoration.
2 a small piece of cloth or other material that is put on a table or other surface to protect it.

match matches matching matched
NOUN **1** an organized game of football, cricket, or some other sport.
2 a small, thin wooden stick tipped with a chemical that produces a flame when you strike it against a rough surface. **Matches** are used to light things.
VERB **3** If colours **match**, they go well together. *My dress matched my shoes.*
4 If you **match** one thing with another, you find the connection between them.

mate mates mating mated
NOUN **1** INFORMAL Your **mates** are your friends.
2 The first **mate** on a ship is second in importance after the captain.
VERB **3** When a pair of animals **mate**, they come together sexually in order to breed.

material materials
NOUN **1** cloth.
2 anything from which something else can be made: *artists' materials.*

maternal
ADJECTIVE **1** used to describe things relating to a mother. *My maternal grandfather was Welsh.*
2 A woman who is **maternal** has strong motherly feelings.

maternity
ADJECTIVE relating to or involving pregnant women and childbirth. *The baby was born in the maternity wing of the hospital.*

mathematics
NOUN the study of numbers, quantities and shapes.
mathematical ADJECTIVE
mathematically ADVERB
mathematician NOUN

maths
NOUN an abbreviation of *mathematics.*

matinee matinees
Said "**mat**-i-nay" NOUN an afternoon performance at a theatre or cinema.

matrix matrices
Said "**may**-trix, **may**-tri-sees" NOUN In maths, a **matrix** is a set of numbers or letters set out in rows and columns.

matt
ADJECTIVE dull rather than shiny. *Mum painted the front door matt green.*

matter matters mattering mattered
NOUN **1** a task or situation that you have to attend to. *We will have to discuss the matter with the head teacher.*
2 any substance. *The scientists explored how matter behaves at high temperatures.*
VERB **3** If something **matters**, it is important.
PHRASE **4** If you ask **What's the matter?**, you want to know what is wrong.

Synonyms: (sense 1) affair, business, subject

mattress mattresses
NOUN a large, flat, spongy pad that is put on a bed to make it comfortable to sleep on.

mature matures maturing matured

VERB **1** When a child or other young animal **matures**, it becomes an adult.
ADJECTIVE **2** fully grown or developed.
maturely ADVERB **maturity** NOUN

maul mauls mauling mauled

VERB If an animal **mauls** someone, they savagely attack and badly injure them.

mauve

Rhymes with "**stove**" NOUN OR ADJECTIVE a light purple colour.

maximum

ADJECTIVE **1** The **maximum** amount is the most that is possible or allowed. *The **maximum** score for this question is five marks.*
NOUN **2** the most that is possible or allowed. *Pupils are allowed a **maximum** of two pounds to spend on the school trip.*

Antonym: minimum

may

VERB **1** If something **may** happen, it is possible that it will happen.
2 If you **may** do something, you are allowed to do it.

May

NOUN the fifth month of the year. **May** has 31 days.
[probably from the Roman goddess *Maia*]

maybe

ADVERB If you think there is a possibility that something will happen, but you are not sure, you use **maybe**. *Maybe we will be allowed to go to the cinema tonight.*

mayonnaise

NOUN a thick salad dressing made with egg yolks and oil.

mayor mayors

NOUN someone who has been elected to represent the people of a town at official functions.

maze mazes

NOUN a system of complicated passages which it is difficult to find your way through.

me

PRONOUN A speaker or writer uses **me** to refer to himself or herself.

meadow meadows

NOUN a field of grass.

meagre

ADJECTIVE very small and poor: *meagre portions.*

meal meals

NOUN **1** an occasion when people eat.
2 the food people eat at meal times.

mean means meaning meant; meaner meanest

VERB **1** If you ask someone what something **means**, you want them to explain it to you.
2 If you **mean** to do something, you intend to do it.
3 If something **means** a lot to you, it is important to you.
ADJECTIVE **4** unkind.
5 Someone who is **mean** is unwilling to share with others.
NOUN **6** in mathematics, the **mean** is the average of a set of numbers.

Synonyms: (sense 2) aim, plan

meander meanders meandering meandered

VERB If a road or river **meanders**, it has a lot of bends in it.
[from *Maiandros*, the name of a Greek river]

meaning meanings

NOUN The **meaning** of a word, expression or gesture is what it refers to or expresses. *Do you know the **meaning** of the proverb "more haste, less speed"?*

meanwhile

ADVERB If something happens, and **meanwhile** something else is happening, the two things are happening at the same time.

measles

NOUN an infectious illness that causes a high temperature and red spots on the skin
[from Germanic *masele* meaning spot on the skin]

measure measures measuring measured

VERB **1** If you **measure** something, you find out the size or amount of it.
NOUN **2** a unit used to measure something.
3 a container or an instrument, such as a ruler or a measuring jug, that you use to measure something. *See page 444.*
4 an action that you take to achieve something.

a b c d e f g h i j k l **m** n o p q r s t u v w x y z

measurement measurements

NOUN the result you obtain when you measure something.

meat meats

NOUN the flesh of animals that people cook and eat.

mechanic mechanics

NOUN someone whose job is to repair and maintain machines and engines.

mechanical

ADJECTIVE **1** to do with machinery. Anything **mechanical** is worked by machinery.
2 If you do something in a **mechanical** way, you do it without thinking about it.
mechanically ADVERB

medal medals

NOUN a small piece of decorative metal, often shaped like a large coin and attached to a ribbon, given as an award for bravery or as a prize in sport.

meddle meddles meddling meddled

VERB If you **meddle**, you interfere and try to change things without being asked.

media

PLURAL NOUN You can refer to the television, radio and newspapers as the **media**.
✔ Although *media* is the plural of *medium*, it is becoming more common for it to be used as a singular. *The **media** is obsessed with the Royal Family.*

median medians

NOUN In mathematics, the **median** of a set of numbers is the middle number once the numbers have been arranged in order of size. *The **median** of 4, 0, 1, 2, 3 is 2, as 2 is in the middle once they are organized in order.*

medical

ADJECTIVE to do with the treatment of people who are ill.

medication medications

NOUN a substance that is used to treat illness.

medicine medicines

NOUN **1** a substance that you take to help cure an illness.
2 the care and treatment of ill people.

medieval or mediaeval

ADJECTIVE relating to the period between about 1100 AD and 1500 AD, especially in Europe.

mediocre

Said "mee-dee-**oh**-ker" ADJECTIVE Something that is **mediocre** is of average or poor quality or standard. *We were disappointed by the film – it was **mediocre**.*
mediocrity NOUN

Mediterranean

NOUN **1** the large sea between southern Europe and northern Africa.
ADJECTIVE **2** relating to the Mediterranean or the countries adjoining it.

medium mediums or media

ADJECTIVE **1** If something is of **medium** size, it is neither large nor small.
NOUN **2** a means of communicating or expressing something.

meek meeker meekest

ADJECTIVE A **meek** person is timid and does what other people say.
meekly ADVERB   **meekness** NOUN

meet meets meeting met

VERB **1** If you **meet** someone, you make an arrangement to go to the same place at the same time as they do. *Let's **meet** at your house before we go out.*
2 If you **meet** someone, you come face-to-face with them or are introduced to them for the first time. *We **met** on our first day at school.*

meeting meetings

NOUN **1** an event at which people discuss things or make decisions.
2 an occasion when you meet someone by arrangement.

melancholy

ADJECTIVE OR NOUN If you feel **melancholy**, you feel very sad.

melodramatic

ADJECTIVE behaving in an exaggerated, emotional way.

melody melodies

NOUN a tune.
[from Greek *meloidia* meaning singing]

melon melons
NOUN a large, juicy fruit with a green or yellow skin and many seeds inside.

melt melts melting melted
VERB When something **melts**, or when you **melt** it, it changes from a solid to a liquid because it has been heated.

member members
NOUN one of the people or things belonging to a group.

membrane membranes
NOUN a very thin skin.

memorable
ADJECTIVE **Memorable** things or people are likely to be remembered because they are special or unusual.

memorial memorials
NOUN a structure built to remind people of a famous person or event: *a war **memorial**.*

memorize memorizes memorizing memorized
VERB If you **memorize** something, you learn it so well that you remember it and can repeat it exactly. *She **memorized** all the times tables from 2 to 12 in one week.*

memory memories
NOUN **1** your ability to remember things.
2 A computer's **memory** is its capacity to store information.

men the plural of *man*.

menace menaces menacing menaced
NOUN **1** someone or something that is likely to cause harm. *That dog is a **menace**.*
VERB **2** If someone or something **menaces** you, they threaten to harm you.
menacing ADJECTIVE   **menacingly** ADVERB

mend mends mending mended
VERB If you **mend** something that is broken, you repair or fix it.

menstruation
NOUN the natural flow of blood from a woman's womb, which usually happens once a month.
menstruate VERB

mental
ADJECTIVE relating to the mind and the process of thinking: *mental arithmetic.*

mention mentions mentioning mentioned
VERB **1** If you **mention** something, you speak or write briefly about it.
NOUN **2** a brief comment about someone or something.

menu menus
NOUN **1** a list of the food and drink you can buy in a restaurant or café.
2 a list of options shown on a computer screen, which the user must choose from.

mercenary mercenaries
ADJECTIVE **1** Someone who is **mercenary** is mainly interested in getting money.
NOUN **2** a soldier who is paid to fight for a foreign country.

merchandise
NOUN goods for buying and selling. *The market stalls were full of all kinds of **merchandise**.*

merchant merchants
NOUN a trader who imports and exports goods.

mercury
NOUN a silver-coloured metallic element that is liquid at room temperature. **Mercury** is used in some thermometers.

mercy mercies
NOUN If you show **mercy**, you show kindness and forgiveness instead of punishing someone.

merge merges merging merged
VERB When two things **merge**, they combine or join together to make one thing. *The two roads **merged** at the junction.*

meridian meridians
NOUN one of the lines on maps or globes, drawn from the North Pole to the South Pole, that help to describe the position of a place.

merit merits meriting merited
NOUN **1** If something has **merit**, it is good or worthwhile.
2 The **merits** of something are its advantages or good qualities. *I can see now the **merits** of working hard.*
VERB **3** If something or someone **merits** a particular treatment, they deserve that treatment. *He **merits** a place in the team.*

mermaid mermaids
NOUN a creature in stories, with a woman's body and a fish's tail instead of legs.

merry merrier merriest
ADJECTIVE happy and cheerful.
merrily ADVERB

mesh
NOUN threads of wire, plastic or other material twisted together like a net.

mess messes messing messed
NOUN **1** something dirty or untidy.
2 something full of problems.
mess about or **mess around** VERB **3** If you **mess about** or **mess around**, you spend time doing silly or casual things. *Stop messing about and get on with your work.*
mess up VERB **4** If you **mess up** something, you make it untidy, spoil it or do it badly. *He'd already messed up one piece of paper.*

message messages
NOUN a piece of information or a request from one person to another.

messenger messengers
NOUN someone who takes a message.

messy messier messiest
ADJECTIVE **1** dirty or untidy.
2 complicated or confused. *He's got himself into a messy situation.*

met
VERB the past tense and past participle of *meet*.

metal metals
NOUN a hard substance such as iron, steel, copper or lead. **Metals** are good conductors of heat and electricity.
metallic ADJECTIVE

metaphor metaphors
NOUN an imaginative way of describing one thing as another thing. For example, if a person is shy and timid, you could describe them as a mouse.

meteor meteors
NOUN a piece of rock or metal moving rapidly through space, that burns very briefly and brightly when it enters the earth's atmosphere.

meteorite meteorites
NOUN a piece of rock from space that has landed on earth.

meteorology
NOUN the study of the weather.
meteorologist NOUN

meter meters
NOUN a device that measures and records something, such as a gas **meter** that records how much gas a household has used.

method methods
NOUN a particular way of doing something. *Use the method I showed you to work out the sum.*

methodical
ADJECTIVE **Methodical** people do things in a careful and organized way.
methodically ADVERB

metre metres
NOUN a unit of length (m) equal to 100 centimetres.

metric
ADJECTIVE relating to the system of measurement that uses metres, grams and litres.

mew mews mewing mewed
VERB When a cat **mews**, it makes a short, high-pitched noise.

miaow miaows miaowing miaowed
NOUN **1** the noise a cat makes.
VERB **2** When a cat **miaows**, it makes a crying sound.

mice
NOUN the plural of *mouse*.

micro-
PREFIX added to some words to mean very small. For example, a **micro**computer is a very small computer.

microbe microbes
NOUN a very small, living thing that can only be seen through a microscope. **Microbes** can feed, grow and reproduce.

microchip microchips
NOUN a small piece of silicon that has electronic circuits printed on it, and is used in computers and electronic equipment.

micro-organism micro-organisms
NOUN a very small organism that can only be seen under a powerful microscope. Some **micro-organisms** are harmful and cause disease. Others, such as yeast, are helpful. Microbes, germs and viruses are sometimes called **micro-organisms**.

microphone microphones

NOUN a device that is used to record sounds or make them louder.

microscope microscopes

NOUN a piece of equipment that magnifies very small objects so that you can study them. *When the class looked at a leaf through the* **microscope** *they could see the small veins that they had not been able to see before.*

microscopic

ADJECTIVE too small to be seen without using a microscope.

microwave microwaves

NOUN a type of oven that cooks food very quickly by radiation.

mid-

PREFIX used to form words that refer to the middle part of a place or a period of time. *We had a break* **mid***morning.*

midday

NOUN twelve o'clock in the middle of the day.

middle middles

NOUN 1 The **middle** of something is the part furthest from the edges, ends or surface. *He stood in the* **middle** *of the room.*
2 The **middle** of an event is the part that comes after the first part and before the last part. *There was an interval in the* **middle** *of the play.*
ADJECTIVE 3 The **middle** thing in a series is the one with an equal number of things on each side. *M and N are the* **middle** *letters in the alphabet.*

Middle Ages

NOUN In European history, the **Middle Ages** were the period between about 1100 AD and 1500 AD.

midnight

NOUN twelve o'clock at night.

midwife midwives

NOUN a nurse who is trained to help women during pregnancy and at the birth of their baby. **midwifery** NOUN

might

VERB 1 You use **might** to say that something will possibly happen or is possibly true. *I* **might** *not be back until tomorrow.*
NOUN 2 If you do something with all your **might**, you do it with all your strength and energy.

migraine migraines

NOUN a severe headache that makes you feel very ill.

migrant migrants

NOUN 1 a person who moves from one place to another, usually to find work. **Migrants** *arrived for the fruit-picking season.*
2 a bird, fish or animal that migrates from one part of the world to another. *The spotted flycatcher, a* **migrant** *bird from Africa, arrives in Britain in May.*

migrate migrates migrating migrated

VERB 1 If people **migrate**, they move from one place to another, especially to find work.
2 When birds or animals **migrate**, they move at a particular season to a different place, usually to breed or to find new feeding grounds.
migration NOUN   **migratory** ADJECTIVE

mild milder mildest

ADJECTIVE Something that is **mild** is gentle, and not very strong or severe: **mild** *weather.*
mildly ADVERB

mildew

NOUN a soft, white fungus that grows on things when they are warm and damp.
mildewed ADJECTIVE

mile miles

NOUN a unit of distance equal to about 1·6 kilometres.
[from Latin **milia passuum** meaning a thousand paces]

mileage mileages

NOUN the distance you have travelled, measured in miles. *The* **mileage** *from home to the hotel was 120 miles.*

military

ADJECTIVE to do with the armed forces of a country.

milk milks milking milked

NOUN **1** the white liquid produced by mammals to feed their young. People drink cows' and goats' milk and make it into butter, cheese and yogurt.

VERB **2** When someone **milks** a cow or other animal, they get milk from it by pulling its udders.

milkman milkmen

NOUN the man who delivers milk to your house.

mill mills

NOUN **1** a building where grain is crushed to make flour.

2 a factory for making materials such as steel, wool or cotton: *a cotton* **mill**.

3 a small device for grinding something. For example, a pepper **mill** grinds peppercorns.

millennium millennia or millenniums

NOUN a period of 1000 years.

milligram milligrams

NOUN a unit of weight (mg). There are 1000 **milligrams** in a gram.

millilitre millilitres

NOUN a unit for measuring liquid (ml). There are 1000 **millilitres** in a litre.

millimetre millimetres

NOUN a unit of length (mm). There are 10 **millimetres** in a centimetre.

million millions

NOUN the number 1, 000, 000.
millionth ADJECTIVE

millionaire millionaires

NOUN someone who has money or property worth at least a million pounds or dollars.

mime mimes miming mimed

NOUN **1** the use of movements and gestures to express something or to tell a story without using speech.

VERB **2** If you **mime** something, you describe or express it using mime.

mimic mimics mimicking mimicked

VERB **1** If you **mimic** someone's actions or voice, you imitate them in an amusing way.

NOUN **2** a person who can imitate other people.

minaret minarets

NOUN a tall, thin tower on a mosque.

minaret

mince minces mincing minced

NOUN **1** meat that has been ground into very small pieces.

VERB **2** If you **mince** meat, you grind it into very small pieces.

mincemeat

NOUN a sweet mixture of dried fruits used, for example, in mince pies.

mind minds minding minded

NOUN **1** Your **mind** is your ability to think, together with your memory and all the thoughts you have. *He could still see her face in his mind*.

PHRASE **2** If you **change your mind**, you change a decision that you have made or an opinion that you have.

VERB **3** If you do not **mind** what happens or what something is like, you do not have a strong preference about it. *I don't mind where we go.*

4 If you tell someone to **mind** something, you are warning them to be careful. *Mind that plate, it's hot.*

5 If you **mind** something for someone, you look after it for a while.

mindless

ADJECTIVE **1** **Mindless** behaviour is stupid and destructive.

2 A **mindless** job or activity is so simple, or repeated so often, that you do not need to think about it at all.

Synonym: (sense 2) repetitive

mine mines

PRONOUN **1** something belonging or relating to the person who is speaking or writing. *He's a good friend of* **mine**.
NOUN **2** a place where deep holes or tunnels are dug under the ground in order to extract minerals: *a coal* **mine**.
3 a bomb hidden in the ground or underwater, that explodes when people or things touch it.

minefield minefields

NOUN an area of land or water where explosive mines have been laid.

miner miners

NOUN a person who works underground in mines to find and dig out coal, diamonds, gold and other minerals: *a coal* **miner**.

mineral minerals

NOUN small particles that make up different rocks. For example, quartz and diamonds are **minerals**.

mineral water

NOUN water that comes from a natural spring.

mingle mingles mingling mingled

VERB If things **mingle**, they become mixed together.

mini-

PREFIX used with another word to describe something shorter or smaller than the usual size: *a* **mini**skirt.

miniature

ADJECTIVE a tiny copy of something much larger. *I bought a* **miniature** *version of the Eiffel Tower as a souvenir.*

minibeast minibeasts

NOUN an insect or other very small creature. *I found a snail for the lesson on* **minibeasts**.

minibus minibuses

NOUN a van with seats in the back, that is used as a small bus.

minimum

ADJECTIVE **1** A **minimum** amount of something is the smallest amount that is possible, allowed or needed.
NOUN **2** the smallest amount of something that is possible, allowed or needed.

Antonym: maximum

minister ministers

NOUN **1** a person who is in charge of a particular government department.
2 a member of the clergy, especially in a Protestant church.
[from Latin **minister** meaning servant]

ministry ministries

NOUN a government department that deals with a particular area of work: *the* **Ministry** *of Education.*

mink minks

NOUN an expensive fur used to make coats and hats.

minnow minnows

NOUN a very small, freshwater fish.

minor

ADJECTIVE less important or serious than other things. *He had a* **minor** *part in the play.*

Antonym: major

minority minorities

NOUN less than half of a group of people or things.

minstrel minstrels

NOUN a singer and entertainer in medieval times.

mint mints

NOUN **1** a plant with strong smelling leaves used as flavouring in cooking.
2 a sweet flavoured with these leaves.
3 the place where the official coins of a country are made.
ADJECTIVE **4** If something is in **mint** condition, it is like new.

minus

PREPOSITION **1** You use **minus** (−) to show that one number is being subtracted from another. *Ten* **minus** *six equals four* (10 − 6 = 4).
ADJECTIVE **2 Minus** before a number means that the number is less than zero. *There are sometimes temperatures of* **minus** 65 °C (−65 °C) *in the Arctic.*

minute minutes

Said "**min**-nit" NOUN **1** a unit of time equal to sixty seconds.
2 a short period of time. *See you in a* **minute**.
Said "my-**nyoot**" ADJECTIVE **3** extremely small: *a* **minute** *amount of milk is needed.*

miracle miracles

NOUN a surprising and wonderful event, especially one believed to have been caused by God.
[from Latin **mirari** meaning to wonder at]

mirage mirages

NOUN an image that you can see in the distance in very hot weather, but that does not actually exist.

mirror mirrors

NOUN an object made of glass in which you can see your reflection.

mis-

PREFIX added to some words to mean badly or wrongly. For example, **mis**behave means to behave badly, and **mis**calculate means to calculate wrongly.

misbehave misbehaves misbehaving misbehaved

VERB If someone **misbehaves**, they are naughty or behave badly.
misbehaviour NOUN

miscarriage miscarriages

NOUN 1 If a woman has a **miscarriage**, she gives birth to a baby too early, before it is able to survive in the outside world.
2 A **miscarriage** of justice is a wrong decision made by a court, which results in an innocent person being punished.

miscellaneous

Said "miss-uh-**lay**-nee-uss" ADJECTIVE A **miscellaneous** group is made up of a mixture of people or things that are different from each other.

mischief

NOUN naughty behaviour, teasing people or playing tricks.

mischievous

ADJECTIVE If you are **mischievous**, you enjoy being naughty by teasing or playing tricks on people.
mischievously ADVERB

miser misers

NOUN a mean person who enjoys hoarding money, but hates spending it.
miserly ADVERB

miserable

ADJECTIVE If you are **miserable**, you are very unhappy.

misery miseries

NOUN great unhappiness.

Synonym: grief

misfire misfires misfiring misfired

VERB If a plan **misfires**, it goes wrong.

misfit misfits

NOUN a person who cannot get on with other people or fit into a group.

misfortune misfortunes

NOUN an unpleasant occurrence that is regarded as bad luck. *I had the **misfortune** to fall off my bike.*

mishap mishaps

Said "**miss**-hap" NOUN an accidental or unfortunate happening that is not very serious. *Grandma had a small **mishap** when her hat blew away.*

misjudge misjudges misjudging misjudged

VERB If you **misjudge** someone or something, you form a wrong or unfair opinion of them.

mislay mislays mislaying mislaid

VERB If you **mislay** something, you cannot remember where you put it.

mislead misleads misleading misled

VERB If you **mislead** someone, you make them believe something that is not true.

misprint misprints

NOUN a mistake such as a spelling mistake in something that has been printed.

miss misses missing missed

VERB **1** If you **miss** someone or something, you feel sad because they are no longer with you.
2 If you **miss** a bus, plane or train, you arrive too late to catch it.
3 If you **miss** an event or activity, you fail to attend it. *I had to miss my piano lesson.*
4 If you **miss** something that you are aiming at, you fail to hit it. *The arrow missed the target.*
NOUN **5 Miss** is used before the name of a girl or unmarried woman. *My teacher this year is Miss Weston.*

missile missiles

NOUN **1** a weapon that moves long distances through the air and explodes when it reaches its target: *nuclear missiles.*
2 any object thrown to harm someone or something.

missing

ADJECTIVE Something that is **missing** is lost or not in its usual place. *One of my shoes is missing.*

mission missions

NOUN **1** a journey made by a military aeroplane or space rocket to carry out a task.
2 an important task that has to be done.

missionary missionaries

NOUN a Christian who has been sent to a foreign country to work for the Church.

misspell misspells misspelling misspelt or misspelled

VERB If you **misspell** a word, you spell it wrongly.

mist mists

NOUN many tiny drops of water in the air that make it hard to see clearly.

mistake mistakes mistaking mistook mistaken

NOUN **1** If you make a **mistake**, you do something wrong without intending to. *There are some spelling mistakes in your homework.*
VERB **2** If you **mistake** someone or something for another person or thing, you wrongly think that they are the other person or thing. *I mistook him for his brother.*

mistletoe

NOUN a plant that grows on trees and has white berries on it.

mistook

VERB the past tense of *mistake.*

mistreat mistreats mistreating mistreated

VERB If you **mistreat** a person or an animal, you treat them badly and make them suffer.

mistress mistresses

NOUN **1** a woman schoolteacher. *There is a new French mistress.*
2 a woman who is in charge of something or someone. *The dog had run away from its mistress.*

mistrust mistrusts mistrusting mistrusted

VERB **1** If you **mistrust** someone, you feel that that they are not to be trusted.
NOUN **2** the feeling of not being able to trust someone or something.

Antonym: trust

misunderstand misunderstands misunderstanding misunderstood

VERB **1** If you **misunderstand** someone, you do not properly understand what they say or do. *He misunderstood the instructions and took the wrong turning.*
NOUN **2** If people have a **misunderstanding**, they have a disagreement or a slight quarrel about something.

misuse misuses misusing misused

NOUN **1** The **misuse** of something is the incorrect or dishonest use of it.
VERB **2** If you **misuse** something, you use it wrongly or dishonestly.

mix mixes mixing mixed

VERB **1** If you **mix** things, you combine them.
mix up VERB **2** If you **mix up** things, you get confused.
mixed up ADJECTIVE

mixture mixtures

NOUN **1** two or more things mixed together. *They felt a mixture of fear and excitement as they climbed the wall.*
2 a substance consisting of two or more other substances that have been mixed together.

moan moans moaning moaned

VERB **1** If you **moan**, you make a low, miserable sound because you are in pain or unhappy.
2 If you **moan** about something, you complain about it.
NOUN **3** a low cry of pain or unhappiness.

moat moats

NOUN a wide, deep ditch around a castle, usually filled with water, to help defend the building.

mob mobs mobbing mobbed

NOUN **1** a large, disorganized crowd of people.
VERB **2** If a group **mobs** someone, they gather closely around them in a disorderly way. *The fans mobbed the band.*

mobile mobiles

ADJECTIVE **1** able to move or be moved easily. *He's much more mobile since getting his new wheelchair.*
NOUN **2** an ornament made up of several parts that hang from threads and move in the breeze.

mobile phone mobile phones

NOUN a small telephone that you can carry around with you.

mock mocks mocking mocked

VERB **1** If you **mock** someone, you tease them or try to make them look foolish.
ADJECTIVE **2** not genuine. *The ring is made of mock diamonds.*

Synonyms: (sense 1) laugh at, make fun of

mode modes

NOUN **1** a particular way of behaving or of doing something.
2 In mathematics, the mode is the most popular or most frequently occurring value. *Of the following numbers – 5, 5, 6, 7, 7, 7, 8 – 7 is the mode.*

model models modelling modelled

NOUN OR ADJECTIVE **1** a smaller copy of something that shows what it looks like or how it works in real life. *Mark has a model railway in his bedroom.*
NOUN **2** a type or version of a product. *Which model of computer did you choose?*
3 a person who wears clothes that are being displayed to possible buyers, or who poses for a photographer or artist.
ADJECTIVE **4** A **model** student is an excellent example of a student who is worth copying.

modem modems

NOUN a piece of equipment that links a computer to the telephone system so that data can be sent from one computer to another.

moderate moderates moderating moderated

Said "**mod**-er-ut" ADJECTIVE **1** A **moderate** amount of something is not too much or too little of it.
2 **Moderate** ideas and opinions are not extreme.
Said "**mod**-er-ayt" VERB **3** If something **moderates** or is **moderated**, it becomes less extreme. *He should moderate his temper.*
moderately ADVERB

modern

ADJECTIVE new and involving the latest ideas or equipment.
[from Latin *modo* meaning just recently]

modest

ADJECTIVE **1** quite small in size or amount. *He inherited a modest amount of money.*
2 **Modest** people do not boast about how clever or how rich they are.
modesty NOUN   **modestly** ADVERB

Antonym: (sense 2) boastful

modify modifies modifying modified

VERB If you **modify** something, you change it slightly to improve it. *When he had modified his bike, it went much faster.*

module modules

NOUN **1** one of the parts which, when put together, form a whole unit or object.
2 a part of a spacecraft that can do certain things away from the main body: *the lunar module.*

moist moister moistest

ADJECTIVE slightly wet, damp.

moisten moistens moistening moistened

VERB If you **moisten** something, you make it slightly wet.

moisture

NOUN tiny drops of water in the air or on the ground.

molar molars

NOUN Your **molars** are the large teeth at the back of your mouth.

mole moles

NOUN **1** a small animal with black fur. **Moles** live in tunnels underground.

2 a dark, slightly-raised spot on your skin.

molecule molecules

NOUN A **molecule** is made up of two or more atoms held together.

molecular ADJECTIVE

mollusc molluscs

NOUN an animal with a soft body and no backbone. Snails, slugs, clams and mussels are all **molluscs**.

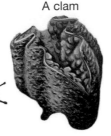

A clam

A slug

molten

ADJECTIVE **Molten** rock or metal has been heated to a very high temperature and has melted to become a thick liquid. *When the volcano erupted, **molten** lava flowed down the mountainside.*

moment moments

NOUN **1** a very short period of time. *I paused for a moment.*

2 the point at which something happens. *At that **moment**, the doorbell rang.*

PHRASE **3** If something is happening **at the moment**, it is happening now.

Synonyms: (sense 1) instant, second

momentum

NOUN the ability that an object has to continue moving as a result of its mass and the speed at which it is already moving.

monarchy monarchies

NOUN a system in which a queen or king reigns in a country.

monastery monasteries

NOUN a place where monks live and work.

monastic ADJECTIVE

[from Latin **monasterium** meaning to live alone]

Monday Mondays

NOUN the second day of the week, coming between Sunday and Tuesday.

[from Old English **monandoeg** meaning moon's day]

money

NOUN the coins and banknotes that you use to buy things.

mongrel mongrels

NOUN a dog with parents of different breeds.

monitor monitors monitoring monitored

VERB **1** If you **monitor** something, you regularly check its condition and progress.

NOUN **2** a machine used to check or record things.

3 the visual display unit of a computer.

4 a school pupil chosen to do special duties by the teacher.

monk monks

NOUN a member of a male religious community.

monkey monkeys

NOUN an agile animal that has a long tail and climbs trees.

mono-

PREFIX having one of something, for example a **mono**rail is a single rail, and a sound that is **mono**tone has only one tone.

monologue monologues

NOUN a long speech by one person during a play or conversation.

monotonous

ADJECTIVE having a regular pattern that is very dull and boring: *a **monotonous** voice.*

monotony NOUN **monotonously** ADVERB

monsoon monsoons

NOUN the season of very heavy rain in South-east Asia.

monster monsters

NOUN **1** a large, imaginary creature that looks very frightening.

2 a cruel and frightening person.

ADJECTIVE **3** extremely large. *She gave him a **monster** pack of CDs for his birthday.*

[from Latin **monstrum** meaning omen or warning]

a
b
c
d
e
f
g
h
i
j
k
l
m
n
o
p
q
r
s
t
u
v
w
x
y
z

month months

NOUN one of the twelve periods that a year is divided into.

monthly

ADJECTIVE If something happens or appears **monthly**, it takes place or appears once a month.

monument monuments

NOUN a large structure built to remind people of a famous person or event.
[from Latin *monere* meaning to remind]

moo moos mooing mooed

VERB 1 When cows **moo**, they make a long, deep sound.
NOUN 2 the long, deep sound that cows make.

mood moods

NOUN the way you are feeling at a particular time.
moody ADJECTIVE   **moodily** ADVERB

moody moodier moodiest

ADJECTIVE 1 **Moody** people change their mood often and very quickly, seemingly for no reason.
2 depressed and miserable.

moon moons

NOUN an object that moves round the earth once every four weeks. You see the **moon** as a shining circle or crescent in the sky at night. Some other planets have **moons**.

moonlight

NOUN the light that comes from the moon at night.

moor moors mooring moored

NOUN 1 a high area of open land. *The farmer had flocks of sheep grazing on the moors*.
VERB 2 If you **moor** a boat, you attach it to the land with a rope.

moose

NOUN a North American deer or elk, with large, flat antlers.
✔ *Moose* is spelt the same way for both the singular and the plural.

mop mops mopping mopped

NOUN 1 a tool for washing floors. It has a string or a sponge head at the end of a long handle.
VERB 2 If you **mop** something, you wipe it or clean it up with a mop or a cloth.

mope mopes moping moped

VERB If you **mope**, you feel miserable and sorry for yourself.

moral morals

PLURAL NOUN 1 **Morals** are values based on beliefs that are acceptable to a particular society.
ADJECTIVE 2 relating to beliefs about what is right and wrong: *moral values*.
NOUN 3 the lesson taught by a story, that usually tells you that good behaviour is best.
morality NOUN   **morally** ADVERB

morale

NOUN Your **morale** is the amount of confidence and optimism you feel. *The morale of the school was high*.

morbid

ADJECTIVE If you are **morbid**, you have a great interest in unpleasant things, especially death and illness.
[from Latin *morbus* meaning illness]

more

ADJECTIVE OR PRONOUN 1 a greater number or extent than something else. *More than 1500 schools took part in the event*.
2 an additional thing or amount of something. *I would like some more orange juice*.
ADVERB 3 **More** means to a greater degree or extent. *We can talk more later*.
4 You use **more** to show that something is repeated. *Repeat the exercise once more*.
5 You use **more** in front of adjectives and adverbs to form comparatives. *He did it more carefully the second time*.

Antonym: (sense 1) fewer, less

morning mornings

NOUN 1 the early part of the day, before noon.
2 the part of the day between midnight and midday.

Morse code

NOUN a code for sending messages by radio signals. Each letter is represented by a series of dots (short sounds) and dashes (longer sounds).

morsel morsels

NOUN a small piece of food.

mortal mortals
ADJECTIVE **1** a **mortal** wound causes death.
2 unable to live forever and certain to die.
NOUN **3** an ordinary person.

mortar mortars
NOUN **1** a mixture of sand, water and cement used to hold bricks firmly together.
2 a short cannon that fires missiles high into the air.

mortgage mortgages
NOUN a loan that people get from a bank or building society in order to buy a house.

mortuary mortuaries
NOUN a special room in a hospital where dead bodies are kept before being buried or cremated.

mosaic mosaics
NOUN a design made of small, coloured stones, tiles or pieces of coloured glass set into concrete or plaster.

Moslem
another spelling of *Muslim*.

mosque mosques
NOUN a building where Muslims go to worship.
[from Arabic ***masjid*** meaning temple]

mosquito mosquitoes or **mosquitos**
NOUN a small, flying insect that bites people and animals in order to suck their blood.

moss mosses
NOUN a soft, small, green plant that grows on damp soil or stone.
mossy ADJECTIVE

most
ADJECTIVE OR PRONOUN **1 Most** of a group of things or people means nearly all of them.
Most people prefer sunny weather.
2 a larger amount than anyone or anything else.
*She has the **most** points.*
ADVERB **3** You use **most** in front of adjectives or adverbs to form superlatives: *the **most** breathtaking scenery in the world.*

motel motels
NOUN a hotel for people who are travelling by car, with parking spaces close to the rooms.

moth moths
NOUN an insect like a butterfly that usually flies at night.

mother mothers
NOUN Your **mother** is your female parent.

mother-in-law mothers-in-law
NOUN the mother of someone's husband or wife.

motion motions
NOUN movement.

motionless
ADJECTIVE If someone or something is **motionless**, they are not moving at all.

motivate motivates motivating motivated
VERB If you **motivate** someone, you make them determined to do or achieve something.
motivated ADJECTIVE   **motivation** NOUN

motive motives
NOUN a reason or purpose for doing something.

motor motors
NOUN a part of a vehicle or machine. The **motor** uses fuel to make the vehicle or machine work.

Synonym: engine

motorbike motorbikes
NOUN a heavy two-wheeled vehicle that is driven by an engine.

motorcycle motorcyles
NOUN another word for a motorbike.

a b c d e f g h i j k l m n o p q r s t u v w x y z

motorist motorists

NOUN a person who drives a car or rides a motorbike.

motorway motorways

NOUN a wide road built for fast travel over long distances.

motto mottoes or mottos

NOUN a short sentence or phrase that is a rule for good or sensible behaviour. For example, "everything in moderation".

mould moulds moulding moulded

VERB **1** If you **mould** a substance, you make it into a particular shape. *Mould the dough into balls.*

NOUN **2** a container used to make something into a particular shape: *a jelly mould*.

3 a soft, grey or green growth that forms on old food or damp walls.

mouldy mouldier mouldiest

ADJECTIVE Something that is **mouldy** is covered with mould. *This old bread had gone mouldy.*

moult moults moulting moulted

VERB When an animal or bird **moults**, it loses its hair or feathers so that new ones can grow.

mound mounds

NOUN **1** a small, man-made hill.
2 a large, untidy pile.

mount mounts mounting mounted

VERB **1** If you **mount** a horse or bicycle, you climb on to it.
2 If something **mounts**, it increases in amount. *The contributions for the tombola were mounting.*
3 If you **mount** a picture or a photograph, you put it in a frame or an album to display it.
NOUN **4** a mountain, especially as part of the name. *Mount Everest is the highest mountain in the world.*

mountain mountains

NOUN a very high piece of land with steep sides.

mountaineer mountaineer

NOUN a person who climbs mountains.

mourn mourns mourning mourned

VERB If you **mourn** for someone who has died, you feel sad and think about them a lot.

mouse mice

NOUN **1** a small, furry rodent with a long tail.
2 a computer device that you move by hand to control the position of a cursor on the screen.

moustache moustaches

NOUN the hair that grows on a man's upper lip.

mouth mouths

NOUN **1** your lips, or the space behind them where your tongue and teeth are.
2 the entrance to a cave or a hole.
3 the place where a river flows into the sea.

mouthful mouthfuls

NOUN the amount of food you put in your mouth. *Don't take such huge mouthfuls!*

movable

ADJECTIVE Something that is **movable** can be moved from one place to another.

move moves moving moved

VERB **1** When you **move** something, or when it **moves**, its position changes. *The train began to move out of the station.*
2 If you **move** or **move house**, you go to live in a different place.
3 If something **moves** you, it causes you to feel a deep emotion. *The film moved us to tears.*
NOUN **4** a change from one place or position to another, especially in a game. *It's your move.*
moving ADJECTIVE

movement movements

NOUN **1** the action of changing position or moving from one place to another.
2 a group of people who act together to try and make something happen: *the animal rights movement*.
3 one of the main parts of a piece of classical music.

moving

ADJECTIVE Something that is **moving** makes you feel deep sadness or emotion: *a moving story*.

mow mows mowing mowed mown

VERB If you **mow** grass, you cut it with a lawnmower.

MP MPs

NOUN someone who has been elected by the people of an area to represent them in Parliament. **MP** is an abbreviation for *Member of Parliament*.

Mr

Said "**miss**-ter" NOUN **Mr** is used before a man's name when you are speaking to him or talking about him. *My teacher is called Mr Jones.*

Mrs

Said "**miss**-izz" NOUN **Mrs** is used before the name of a married woman when you are speaking or referring to her: *"Good morning, Mrs Green."*

Ms

Said "**miz**" NOUN **Ms** is used before a woman's name when you are speaking or referring to her. **Ms** does not show whether the woman is married or not.

much

ADVERB **1** You use **much** to indicate the great size, extent, or intensity of something. *He's much taller than you.*
2 If something does not happen **much**, it does not happen often. *He doesn't talk much.*
ADJECTIVE OR PRONOUN **3** You use **much** to talk about the size or amount of something. *There isn't much left.*

mud

NOUN wet, sticky earth.
muddy ADJECTIVE

muddle muddles muddling muddled

NOUN **1** a state of disorder or untidiness.
VERB **2** If you **muddle** things, you mix them up.
muddled ADJECTIVE
[from Dutch *moddelen* meaning to make muddy]

muesli

NOUN a mixture of cereal flakes, chopped nuts and dried fruit that you can eat with milk for breakfast.

muffled

ADJECTIVE A sound that is **muffled** is low or difficult to hear.

mug mugs mugging mugged

NOUN **1** a large, deep cup.
VERB **2** INFORMAL If someone **mugs** you, they attack you in the street in order to steal your money.

mule mules

NOUN the offspring of a female horse and a male donkey.

multiple multiples

ADJECTIVE **1** consisting of many parts or having many uses.
NOUN **2** a number that can be divided exactly by another number. *2, 4, 6, 8, 10, and 12 are all multiples of 2.*

multiplication

NOUN the process of multiplying one number by another.

multiply multiplies multiplying multiplied

VERB **1** When you **multiply** one number by another, you calculate the total you would get if you added the first number to itself the number of times shown by the second number. *Six multiplied by three is 18 ($6 \times 3 = 18$), because $6 + 6 + 6 = 18$.*
2 When something **multiplies**, it increases greatly in number or amount.

multitude multitudes

NOUN; FORMAL a very large number of people or things.

mum mums

NOUN; INFORMAL mother.

mumble mumbles mumbling mumbled

VERB If you **mumble**, you speak very quietly and indistinctly.

mummy mummies

NOUN **1** INFORMAL Your **mummy** is your mother.
2 a dead body that was preserved long ago by being rubbed with special oils and wrapped in cloth. *Mummies have been found in tombs in Egypt.*
[(sense 2) from Persian *mum* meaning wax]

A mummy's coffin from Ancient Egypt

mumps

NOUN a disease that causes painful swelling in the neck.

munch munches munching munched

VERB If you **munch** something, you chew it steadily and thoroughly.

mural murals

NOUN a picture painted on a wall.

a
b
c
d
e
f
g
h
i
j
k
l
m
n
o
p
q
r
s
t
u
v
w
x
y
z

A
B
C
D
E
F
G
H
I
J
K
L
M
N
O
P
Q
R
S
T
U
V
W
X
Y
Z

murder murders murdering murdered
NOUN **1** the deliberate killing of a person.
VERB **2** To **murder** someone means to kill them deliberately.
murderer NOUN

murky murkier murkiest
ADJECTIVE dark or dirty and hard to see through: *murky water*.
murk NOUN
[from Old Norse *myrkr* meaning darkness]

murmur murmurs murmuring murmured
VERB **1** If you **murmur** something, you say it very quietly.
NOUN **2** something someone says that can hardly be heard. *They spoke in low murmurs*.

muscle muscles
NOUN Your **muscles** are the bundles of fibres connected to your bones, that enable you to move. [from Latin *musculus* meaning little mouse, because muscles were thought to look like mice]

muscular
Said "**musk**-yoo-lar" ADJECTIVE **1 Muscular** people have strong, well-developed muscles.
2 involving or affecting your muscles: *muscular pain*.

museum museums
NOUN a public building where interesting or valuable objects are kept and displayed.

mushroom mushrooms
NOUN a fungus with a short stem and a round top. Some types of **mushroom** are edible.

music
NOUN **1** the pattern of sounds performed by people singing or playing instruments.
2 the written symbols that represent musical sounds.

musical musicals
ADJECTIVE **1** relating to playing or studying music. *She has considerable musical talent*.
NOUN **2** a play or a film that uses songs and dance to tell the story.
musically ADVERB

musician musicians
NOUN a person who plays a musical instrument well.

musket muskets
NOUN an old-fashioned gun with a long barrel.

Muslim Muslims; also spelt **Moslem**
NOUN **1** a person who believes in the Islamic religion and lives according to its rules.
ADJECTIVE **2** relating to Islam.

mussel mussels
NOUN a small, edible shellfish with a black shell.

must
VERB **1** If you tell someone that they **must** do something, you make them feel that they ought to do it. *You must try this pudding – it's delicious*.
2 If something **must** happen, it is very important or necessary that it happens. *You must be over 15 to see a film with a 15 certificate*.
3 If you think something is very likely, you think it **must** be so. *You must be Sam's brother*.

mustard
NOUN a spicy-tasting yellow or brown paste made from seeds.

mute
ADJECTIVE People or animals that are **mute** do not or cannot speak or make a sound.

mutilate mutilates mutilating mutilated
VERB **1** If you **mutilate** something, you damage or spoil it.
2 If someone is **mutilated**, they have been very badly cut and injured.

mutiny mutinies mutinying mutinied
VERB **1** If a group of sailors or soldiers **mutiny**, they rebel against their officers.
NOUN **2** a rebellion against someone in authority.
mutineer NOUN

mutter mutters muttering muttered
VERB If you **mutter**, or if you **mutter** something, you speak very quietly so that it is difficult for people to hear you.

mutton
NOUN the meat of an adult sheep.

mutual

Said "**mew**-choo-ul" ADJECTIVE **Mutual** is used to describe something that two or more people give to each other or share. *My dad and my brother have a **mutual** love of football.*

muzzle muzzles muzzling muzzled

NOUN **1** the nose and mouth of an animal.

2 a cover or a strap for a dog's nose and mouth to prevent it from biting.

3 the open end of a gun where the bullets come out.

VERB **4** If you **muzzle** a dog, you put a muzzle on it.

my

ADJECTIVE **My** refers to something belonging to the person who is speaking or writing. *I ride **my** bicycle to school every day.*

myself

PRONOUN You use **myself** when you are speaking about yourself. *I was cross with **myself** for being so mean.*

mysterious

ADJECTIVE **1** strange and puzzling. *They heard **mysterious** noises in the night.*

2 If someone is being **mysterious**, they are being secretive about something. *Mum is being very **mysterious** about my birthday present.*

mysteriously ADVERB

mystery mysteries

NOUN something that is not understood or known about. *The identity of the burglar remains a **mystery**.*

mystify mystifies mystifying mystified

VERB If something **mystifies** you, you find it impossible to understand. *I am **mystified** by the disappearance of my sweater.*

myth myths

NOUN a story that was made up long ago to explain natural events and people's religious beliefs.

a
b
c
d
e
f
g
h
i
j
k
l
m
n
o
p
q
r
s
t
u
v
w
x
y
z

Nn

nag nags nagging nagged
VERB If you **nag** someone, you keep complaining to them or pestering them about something.

nail nails nailing nailed
NOUN **1** Your **nails** are the thin, hard areas covering the ends of your fingers and toes.
2 a small piece of metal with a sharp point at one end, that you hammer into objects to hold them together.
VERB **3** If you **nail** something somewhere, you fix it there using a nail.

naïve
Said "ny-**eeve**" ADJECTIVE If you are **naïve**, you believe that things are easier or less complicated than they really are, usually because of your lack of experience.
naïvely ADVERB

naked
ADJECTIVE not wearing any clothes.

name names naming named
NOUN **1** a word that you use to identify a person, animal, place or thing.
VERB **2** When you **name** someone or something, you give them a name.

nameless
ADJECTIVE not having a name or not identified: *a nameless terror.*

nanny nannies
NOUN a person whose job is to look after young children.

nap naps napping napped
NOUN **1** a short sleep.
VERB **2** When you **nap**, you have a short sleep.

napkin napkins
NOUN a small piece of cloth or paper used to wipe your hands and mouth after eating.

nappy nappies
NOUN a piece of towelling or paper padding worn round a baby's bottom.

narrate narrates narrating narrated
VERB If you **narrate** a story, you tell it.

narrative narratives
NOUN a story or an account of events.

narrator narrators
NOUN the person in a book or a film or in a radio or television broadcast, who tells the story or explains what is happening.

narrow narrower narrowest; narrows narrowing narrowed
ADJECTIVE **1** Something that is **narrow** measures a small distance from one side to the other. *We walked down a **narrow** passageway.*
VERB **2** If something **narrows**, it becomes less wide. *The track **narrowed** ahead.*

nasty nastier nastiest
ADJECTIVE very unpleasant.

Synonyms: unkind, rude, disgusting

nation nations
NOUN a country and all the people who live there.

national
ADJECTIVE relating to a country or the whole country. *We all sang the **national** anthem.*

national anthem national anthems
NOUN the official song of a country.

nationality nationalities
NOUN the fact of being a citizen of a particular nation.

native natives
ADJECTIVE **1** Your **native** country is the country where you were born.
2 Your **native** language is the language that you first learned to speak.
NOUN **3** A **native** of a place is someone who was born there.

Nativity
NOUN In Christianity, the **Nativity** is the birth of Christ, or the festival celebrating this.

natural
ADJECTIVE **1** normal and to be expected. *It's **natural** to want to do well.*
2 existing or happening in nature, rather than caused or made by people. *Wool is a **natural** material.*
3 If you have a **natural** ability, you are born with it. *She has a **natural** flair for mathematics.*
naturally ADVERB

natural history

NOUN the study of animals and plants.

nature natures

NOUN **1** animals, plants, and all the other things in the world that are not made by people.
2 the basic quality or character of a person or thing. *They liked his warm, generous **nature**.*

naughty naughtier naughtiest

ADJECTIVE A child who is **naughty** behaves badly.
naughtiness NOUN

nausea

NOUN a feeling that you are going to be sick.
nauseous ADJECTIVE

nautical

ADJECTIVE relating to ships or navigation.

naval

ADJECTIVE relating to a navy.

navel navels

NOUN the small hollow on the front of your body, just below your waist.

navigate navigates navigating navigated

VERB When someone **navigates**, they work out the direction in which a ship, plane or car should go, using maps and sometimes instruments.
navigation NOUN   **navigator** NOUN

navy navies

NOUN the part of a country's armed forces that fights at sea.

near nearer nearest; nears nearing neared

PREPOSITION OR ADVERB **1** If something is **near** a place, it is a short distance from it. *They live in a cottage **near** the river.*
VERB **2** When you are **nearing** a particular place or time, you are approaching it and will soon reach it. *The dog began to bark as the visitor **neared** the door.*

nearby

ADJECTIVE OR ADVERB a short distance away.

nearly

ADVERB not completely, but almost. *I've **nearly** finished my homework.*

neat neater neatest

ADJECTIVE tidy and smart.
neatly ADVERB   **neatness** NOUN

necessary

ADJECTIVE Something that is **necessary** is needed or must be done. *It might be **necessary** to leave quickly.*

necessity necessities

NOUN **1** the need to do something.
2 something that is needed. *Water is a basic **necessity** of life.*

neck necks

NOUN **1** the part of your body that joins your head to the rest of your body.
2 the long, narrow part at one end of a bottle or guitar.

necklace necklaces

NOUN a piece of jewellery that a person wears around their neck.

nectar

NOUN a sweet liquid produced by flowers and collected by insects.

need needs needing needed

VERB **1** If you **need** something, you cannot achieve what you want without having it or doing it. *I **need** some help with my homework.*
PLURAL NOUN **2** Your **needs** are the things that you need to have.

Synonyms: (sense 2) necessities, requirements

needle needles

NOUN **1** a small, thin piece of metal with a hole at one end and a sharp point at the other, used for sewing.
2 long, thin pieces of steel or plastic, used for knitting.
3 the sharp part of a syringe that goes into your skin when you have an injection.
4 the thin pointer on a dial or compass that moves to show a measurement or bearing.
5 Pine **needles** are the sharp, pointed leaves of a pine tree.

needlework

NOUN sewing or embroidery that is done by hand.

negative negatives

ADJECTIVE **1** A **negative** answer means no.
2 A **negative** number is less than zero.
NOUN **3** the image that is first produced when you take a photograph.

Antonym: (senses 1 and 2) positive

a
b
c
d
e
f
g
h
i
j
k
l
m
n
o
p
q
r
s
t
u
v
w
x
y
z

neglect neglects neglecting neglected

VERB **1** If you **neglect** someone or something, you do not look after them properly. *Ben neglected his hamster.*

NOUN **2** failure to look after someone or something properly. *Most of her plants died from neglect.*

negotiate negotiates negotiating negotiated

VERB When people **negotiate**, they talk about a situation in order to reach an agreement about it.

neigh neighs neighing neighed

Said "**nay**" VERB **1** When a horse **neighs**, it makes a loud high-pitched sound through its nose.

NOUN **2** A **neigh** is a loud high-pitched sound made by a horse.

neighbour neighbours

NOUN someone who lives next door to you or near you.

neighbourhood neighbourhoods

NOUN Your **neighbourhood** is the area where you live.

neither

CONJUNCTION, ADJECTIVE, OR PRONOUN You use **neither** in front of two alternatives to mean not one and not the other. *He spoke neither English nor German.*

✔ When *neither* is followed by a plural noun, the verb can be plural too: *neither of these books are useful.* When you have two singular subjects, the verb should be singular too: *neither Alison nor Meera has done the work.*

neon

NOUN a gas used in glass tubes to make light sources and signs.

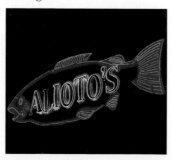

nephew nephews

NOUN Someone's **nephew** is the son of their sister or brother.

nerve nerves

NOUN **1** long, thin fibres that send messages between your brain and other parts of your body.

2 courage and calm in a difficult situation.

3 INFORMAL rudeness or cheek. *She had the nerve to answer back to the head teacher.*

nervous

ADJECTIVE easily worried and agitated.

nervously ADVERB

nest nests

NOUN a structure that birds, insects and other animals make, in which to lay eggs or rear their young.

 Wasp's nest Weaver bird's nest

nestle nestles nestling nestled

Said "**ness**-sl" VERB If you **nestle** somewhere, you settle there comfortably, often very close to someone or something else. *My kitten loves to nestle in my lap.*

net nets

NOUN **1** The **net** is the same as the Internet.

2 material made from threads woven together with small spaces in between.

3 a piece of this material used for a particular purpose, for example a fishing **net**.

netball

NOUN a game in which two teams of seven players each try to score goals by throwing a ball through a net at the top of a pole.

nettle nettles

NOUN a wild plant covered with little hairs that sting.

network networks

NOUN **1** a large number of lines or roads that cross each other at many points.

2 a group of computers connected to each other.

neutral

ADJECTIVE People who are **neutral** do not support either side in a disagreement or war.

never
ADVERB at no time in the past, present or future. *I've **never** met such a lovely person.*

nevertheless
ADVERB in spite of what has just been said. *I know you're home safely, but **nevertheless** I want you to ring for a lift in future.*

new newer newest
ADJECTIVE **1** recently made, created or discovered.
2 different. *We've got a **new** maths teacher.*

news
NOUN up-to-date information about things that have happened.

newsagent newsagents
NOUN a person or shop that sells newspapers and magazines.

newspaper newspapers
NOUN a publication, on large sheets of folded paper, that is produced regularly and contains news and articles.

newt newts
NOUN a small, amphibious creature with a moist skin, short legs and a long tail.

newton newtons
NOUN a unit for measuring force (N).
[named after Sir Isaac *Newton*]

New Year
NOUN the time when people celebrate the start of a year.

next
ADJECTIVE **1** The **next** thing, person or event is the one that comes immediately after the present one. *We'll catch the **next** train.*
ADVERB **2** You use **next** to refer to an action that follows immediately after the present one. *What shall we do **next**?*
3 The **next** place or person is the one nearest to you. *She lives in the **next** street.*
PHRASE **4** If one thing is **next to** another, it is at the side of it. *She sat down **next to** him.*

nib nibs
NOUN the pointed end of a pen, where the ink comes out.

nibble nibbles nibbling nibbled
VERB **1** When you **nibble** something, you take small bites of it.
NOUN **2** a small bite of something.

nice nicer nicest
ADJECTIVE pleasant or kind.
nicely ADVERB

nickname nicknames
NOUN an informal name for someone or something. *Red got his **nickname** because of his ginger hair.*
[from Middle English *an ekename* meaning an additional name]

nicotine
NOUN an addictive substance found in tobacco.
[named after Jacques *Nicot*, who first brought tobacco to France]

niece nieces
NOUN Someone's **niece** is the daughter of their sister or brother.

night nights
NOUN the time between sunset and sunrise, when it is dark.

nightdress nightdresses
NOUN a loose dress that a woman or girl wears to sleep in.

nightfall
NOUN the time of day when it starts to get dark.

nightingale nightingales
NOUN a small, brown European bird, the male of which sings very beautifully, especially at night.

nightmare nightmares

NOUN **1** a frightening dream.
2 an unpleasant or frightening situation. *The whole journey was a **nightmare**.*

nil

NOUN zero or nothing, especially in sports scores. *At half-time the score was still **nil–nil**.*

nimble nimbler nimblest

ADJECTIVE able to move quickly and easily.
nimbly ADVERB

nip nips nipping nipped

VERB **1** If you **nip** someone or something, you give them a slight pinch or bite.
2 If you **nip** somewhere, you go there quickly. *I have to **nip** to the shop for some milk.*
NOUN **3** A **nip** is small bite or pinch.

nitrogen

NOUN a chemical element, usually found as a colourless gas. **Nitrogen** makes up about 78% of the earth's atmosphere.

no

INTERJECTION **1** You say **no** when you do not want something or do not agree.
ADJECTIVE OR ADVERB **2** none at all or not at all. *He has **no** excuse for his behaviour.*

Antonym: (sense 1) yes

noble nobler noblest

ADJECTIVE If someone is **noble**, they are honest and brave, and deserve admiration.

nobody

PRONOUN not a single person. *For a long time **nobody** spoke.*
✔ *Nobody* and *no one* mean the same.

nocturnal

ADJECTIVE happening or active at night. *The hedgehog is a **nocturnal** animal.*

nod nods nodding nodded

VERB When you **nod** your head, you move it up and down, usually to say yes.

noise noises

NOUN a sound, especially one that is loud or unpleasant.

noisy noisier noisiest

ADJECTIVE making a lot of noise, or full of noise.

nomad nomads

NOUN a person who travels from place to place rather than staying in just one. *The Bedouin people in Arabia are **nomads**.*
nomadic ADJECTIVE
[from Latin ***nomas*** meaning wandering shepherd]

nominate nominates nominating nominated

VERB If a person **nominates** someone for a job or position, they formally suggest that they have it.
nomination NOUN

non-

PREFIX not, for example something that is **non**existent does not exist.

none

PRONOUN not a single thing or person, or not even a small amount of something. *They asked me for my ideas, but I had **none**.*

non-fiction

NOUN writing dealing with facts and events rather than imaginative storytelling.

Antonym: fiction

nonsense

NOUN foolish or meaningless words or behaviour.

nonsmoking

ADJECTIVE a **nonsmoking** area is a place where smoking is forbidden.

nonstop

ADJECTIVE OR ADVERB continuing without any pauses or breaks.

Synonym: continuous

noodle noodles

NOUN a kind of pasta shaped into long, thin pieces.

noon

NOUN midday.

no one or no-one

PRONOUN not a single person. *No one goes to that play park any more.*

Synonym: nobody

noose nooses

NOUN a loop at the end of a piece of rope, with a knot that tightens when the rope is pulled.

nor

CONJUNCTION used after "neither", or to add emphasis. *Neither you nor I know the answer. I couldn't afford to go to the fair, and nor could my friends.*

normal

ADJECTIVE usual and ordinary.

north

NOUN one of the four main points of the compass. If you face the point where the sun rises, **north** is on your left. The abbreviation is N.

north-east

NOUN, ADVERB OR ADJECTIVE halfway between north and east.

northern

ADJECTIVE in or from the north. *The mountains of **northern** Spain are very beautiful.*

north-west

NOUN, ADVERB OR ADJECTIVE halfway between north and west.

nose noses

NOUN the part of your face above your mouth, that you use for smelling and breathing.

nostalgia

NOUN a feeling of affection for the past, and sadness that things have changed.
nostalgic ADJECTIVE   **nostalgically** ADVERB

nostril nostrils

NOUN Your **nostrils** are the two openings in your nose that you breathe through.

nosy nosier nosiest; also spelt **nosey**

ADJECTIVE **Nosy** people always want to know about other people's business, and like to interfere where they are not wanted.

not

ADVERB used to make a sentence mean the opposite. *I am **not** very happy.*

note notes

NOUN **1** a short letter.
2 You take **notes** to help you remember what has been said.
3 In music, a **note** is a musical sound of a particular pitch, or a written symbol that represents this sound.
4 a piece of paper money: *a ten-pound **note**.*

notebook notebooks

NOUN a small book for writing notes in.

nothing

PRONOUN not a single thing, or not a single part of something.

notice notices noticing noticed

VERB **1** If you **notice** something, you become aware of it. *She **noticed** a bird sitting on the fence.*
NOUN **2** a written announcement.
VERB **3** If you **take notice of** something, you pay attention to it.

noticeable

ADJECTIVE obvious and easy to see.

notify notifies notifying notified

VERB If you **notify** someone of something, you officially inform them of it. *You must **notify** us of any change of address.*
notification NOUN

notorious

ADJECTIVE well known for something bad: *a **notorious** criminal.*

nought noughts

NOUN the number 0, zero.

noun nouns

NOUN a word that refers to a person, thing or idea. Examples of **nouns** are "table", "happiness" and "John".

nourish nourishes nourishing nourished

VERB If you **nourish** people or animals, you give them plenty of food.
nourishing ADJECTIVE

nourishment

NOUN the food that your body needs to grow and stay healthy, including vitamins and minerals: *"Eat your vegetables, they're full of nourishment."*

novel novels

NOUN **1** a book that tells a long story about imaginary people and events.
ADJECTIVE **2** new and interesting. *This whole trip has been a **novel** experience.*

novelty novelties

NOUN **1** the quality of being new and interesting.
2 something new and interesting.
3 a small object sold as a gift or souvenir.

a
b
c
d
e
f
g
h
i
j
k
l
m
n
o
p
q
r
s
t
u
v
w
x
y

A
B
C
D
E
F
G
H
I
J
K
L
M
N
O
P
Q
R
S
T
U
V

November

NOUN the eleventh month of the year. **November** has 30 days.
[from Latin **November** meaning the ninth month]

novice novices

NOUN someone who is not yet experienced at something. *Most of the group are **novices** at horse riding.*

now

ADVERB **1** at the present time or moment.
CONJUNCTION **2** as a result or consequence of a particular fact. *Your writing will improve **now** you have a new pen.*

nowhere

ADVERB not anywhere. *There was **nowhere** to hide.*

nozzle nozzles

NOUN a spout fitted on to the end of a pipe or hose to control the flow of liquid or gas.

nuclear

ADJECTIVE relating to the energy produced when atoms are split. *We live near a **nuclear** power station.*

nucleus nuclei

*Said "**nyoo**-clee-us" and "**nyoo**-clee-eye"* NOUN **1** the central part of an atom or a cell.

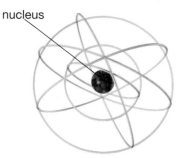

nucleus

An atom

rtant or central part of something.
? the **nucleus** of the team.

?one is **nude**, they are naked.
?icture or statue of a naked

nudge nudges nudging nudged

VERB **1** If you **nudge** someone, you push them gently with your elbow to get their attention or to make them move.
NOUN **2** a gentle push with your elbow.

nugget nuggets

NOUN a small rough lump of something, especially gold.

nuisance nuisances

NOUN someone or something that is annoying or causing problems.

numb

ADJECTIVE unable to feel anything. *I was so cold my hands and feet felt **numb**.*
[from Middle English **nomen** meaning paralysed]

number numbers numbering numbered

NOUN **1** a word or symbol used for counting or calculating. *See page 448.*
2 the series of numbers that you dial when you telephone someone.
VERB **3** If you **number** something, you give it a number, usually in a sequence. *Please **number** each page you write on.*

numeracy

NOUN the ability to do arithmetic.

numeral numerals

NOUN a symbol that is used to represent a number.

numerator numerators

NOUN the top number of a fraction. It tells you the number of pieces or parts you are dealing with.

numerical

ADJECTIVE expressed in numbers or relating to numbers. *Please put these pages in **numerical** order.*

numerous

ADJECTIVE Things that are **numerous** exist or happen in large numbers. *There are **numerous** things to do in a large city.*

nun nuns

NOUN a woman who has taken religious vows and is a member of a religious community.

nurse nurses nursing nursed

NOUN **1** a person whose job is to look after people who are ill.

VERB **2** If you **nurse** someone, you look after them when they are ill. *I helped dad to **nurse** mum when she had flu.*

nursery nurseries

NOUN **1** a place where young children are looked after when their parents are working.
2 a place where plants are grown and sold.

nursery rhyme nursery rhymes

NOUN a short poem or song for young children, such as *Little Miss Muffet* and *Jack and Jill*.

nursery school nursery schools

NOUN a school for children aged three to five years old.

nut nuts

NOUN **1** a fruit with a hard shell that grows on certain trees and bushes.

2 a piece of metal with a hole in the middle that a bolt screws into.

nutrient nutrients

Said "**new**-tree-unt" NOUN one of the substances that help plants and animals to grow. *Very heavy rainfall washes valuable **nutrients** from the soil.*

nutrition

Said "new-**trish**-un" NOUN the food that you eat that helps you to grow and keeps you healthy. *Good **nutrition** is vital for healthy development.*

nutritious

ADJECTIVE If food is **nutritious** it helps you to grow and remain healthy. *Spinach is a very **nutritious** vegetable.*

nylon

NOUN a type of strong, artificial fibre used for making, for example, clothes, ropes and brushes. *The rock climbers used brightly coloured ropes made of **nylon** to abseil down the rock face.*

Oo

A B C D E F G H I J K L M N O P Q R S T U V W X Y Z

oak oaks
NOUN a large tree that produces acorns. The **oak** has a hard wood that is often used to make furniture.

oar oars
NOUN a pole with a flat end used to row a boat through water.

oasis oases
NOUN a small area in a desert where water and plants are found.

oath oaths
NOUN a formal promise, especially a promise to tell the truth in a court of law.

oats
PLURAL NOUN a type of grain.

obedient
ADJECTIVE If you are **obedient,** you do as you are told.
obediently ADVERB   **obedience** NOUN

Antonym: disobedient

obey obeys obeying obeyed
VERB If you **obey** a person or an order, you do what you are told to do.

obituary obituaries
NOUN a piece of writing about the life and achievements of someone who has just died.

object objects objecting objected
Said "ob-jekt" NOUN **1** anything solid that you can touch or see, and that is not alive. *This painting is an **object** of beauty.*
2 an aim or purpose. *The **object** of the marathon is to raise money.*
Said "ob-**jekt**" VERB **3** If you **object** to something, you dislike it, disagree with it or disapprove of it.

objection objections
NOUN If you have an **objection** to something, you dislike it or disagree with it.

oblige obliges obliging obliged
VERB **1** If you are **obliged** to do something, you have to do it.
2 If you **oblige** someone, you help them. *He **obliged** us by showing the way.*

ADJECTIVE **3** If you are **obliged** to someone, you are grateful to them. *I would be much **obliged** if you could show me where this street is.*
obliging ADJECTIVE

oblique
ADJECTIVE An **oblique** line slopes at an angle.

oblong oblongs
NOUN **1** a four-sided shape with four right angles, similar to a square but with two sides longer than the other two.
ADJECTIVE **2** shaped like an oblong.

obnoxious
ADJECTIVE extremely unpleasant.

Synonyms: hateful, odious

oboe oboes
NOUN a woodwind instrument that makes a high-pitched sound.
oboist NOUN
[from French **haut bois** meaning literally high wood, a reference to the instrument's pitch]

obscene
ADJECTIVE very rude and likely to upset people.
obscenely ADVERB   **obscenity** NOUN

obscure obscures obscuring obscured
ADJECTIVE **1** Something **obscure** is difficult to see or to understand.
VERB **2** If something **obscures** something else, it makes it difficult to see or understand. *The moon **obscured** the sun during the eclipse.*

Antonyms: (sense 1) obvious, clear

observant
ADJECTIVE An **observant** person notices things that are not usually noticed.

observation observations
NOUN the act of watching something closely. *You will need to make careful **observations** of the experiment before you do the writing.*
[from Latin **observare** meaning to watch]

observe observes observing observed
VERB If you **observe** someone or something, you watch them carefully.
observant ADJECTIVE   **observer** NOUN

obsession obsessions

NOUN If someone has an **obsession** about something or someone, they cannot stop thinking about them.
obsessional ADJECTIVE **obsessed** ADJECTIVE
obsessive ADJECTIVE

obsolete

ADJECTIVE out of date and no longer used.

obstacle obstacles

NOUN something that is in your way and makes it difficult for you to do something.

obstinate

ADJECTIVE Someone who is **obstinate** is stubborn and unwilling to change their mind.

obstruct obstructs obstructing obstructed

VERB If something **obstructs** a road or path, it blocks it.

obtain obtains obtaining obtained

VERB If you **obtain** something, you get it.

obtuse

ADJECTIVE An **obtuse** angle is an angle between 90° and 180°.

115°

obvious

ADJECTIVE easy to see or understand. *It was obvious that he didn't know the answer.*
obviously ADVERB

occasion occasions

NOUN a time when something happens. *I met her on several occasions.*

occasional

ADJECTIVE happening sometimes, but not often. *We go for an occasional walk in the woods.*
occasionally ADVERB

occupant occupants

NOUN the people who live or work in a building.

occupation occupations

NOUN a job or profession.

occupy occupies occupying occupied

VERB **1** The people who **occupy** a building are the people who live or work there.
2 If something **occupies** you, you spend your time doing it or thinking about it.

occur occurs occurring occurred

VERB **1** If something **occurs**, it happens.
occur to VERB **2** If something **occurs to** you, you suddenly think of it or realize it.

ocean oceans

NOUN one of the five very large areas of sea in the world.

o'clock

ADVERB You use **o'clock** after the number of the hour to say what the time is. *We have to be at school by eight o'clock.*

octagon octagons

NOUN a flat shape with eight straight sides.
octagonal ADJECTIVE

octahedron octahedrons

NOUN a solid figure with eight identical flat surfaces.

octave octaves

NOUN the difference in pitch between the first note and the eighth note of a musical scale.

October

NOUN the tenth month of the year. **October** has 31 days.
[from Latin *october* meaning the eighth month, as it was the eighth month in the Roman calendar]

octopus octopuses

NOUN a sea creature with eight long tentacles that it uses to catch food.

odd odder oddest

ADJECTIVE **1** strange or unusual.
2 Odd things do not match each other. *She always ended up with odd socks.*
3 Odd numbers cannot be divided exactly by two. Three and seven are examples of **odd** numbers.

Antonym: (sense 3) even

odour odours

NOUN; FORMAL a strong smell.

off

PREPOSITION OR ADVERB **1** used to show movement away from or out of a place. *They got **off** the bus.*

2 used to show separation or distance from a place. *There are several islands **off** the coast of Britain.*

ADVERB **3** not at work. *He took a day **off**.*

ADVERB OR ADJECTIVE **4** not switched on. *The television was **off**.*

ADJECTIVE **5** cancelled or postponed. *The match is **off**.*

6 Food that is **off** is no longer fresh enough to eat, usually tastes unpleasant, and may make you ill.

✔ Do not use *of* after *off*. You should say "I got *off* the bus", not "I got *off of* the bus". In informal speech, people sometimes say *off* when they mean from: "We bought eggs *off* a farmer" instead of "from a farmer". Always use *from* in written work.

offence offences

NOUN **1** a crime. *Burglary is a serious **offence**.*

PHRASE **2** If you **cause offence**, you embarrass or upset someone.

3 If you **take offence**, you feel that someone has been rude or hurtful to you.

offend offends offending offended

VERB **1** If you **offend** someone, you upset them.

2 If someone **offends**, they break the law.

offender NOUN

offensive

ADJECTIVE If something is **offensive**, it is rude and upsetting.

offer offers offering offered

VERB **1** If you **offer** something to someone, you ask them if they would like it, or say that you are willing to do it. *I **offered** to wash the car.*

NOUN **2** something that someone says they will give you or do for you.

office offices

NOUN **1** a room where people work at desks.

2 a place where people can go for information, tickets or other services.

officer officers

NOUN a person with a position of authority in the armed forces, the police or a government organization.

official

ADJECTIVE approved by the government or by someone in authority.

officially ADVERB

often

ADVERB happening many times or a lot of the time. *He **often** goes swimming on Sunday.*

ogre ogres

NOUN a cruel, frightening giant in fairy stories.

oil oils oiling oiled

NOUN **1** a thick, sticky liquid found under rocks that is used for fuel, lubrication and for making plastics and chemicals.

2 a thick, greasy liquid made from plants or animal fat: *cooking **oil**.*

VERB **3** If you **oil** something, you put oil in it or on it to make it work better. *This squeaky hinge needs to be **oiled**.*

oily

ADJECTIVE Something that is **oily** is covered with or contains oil.

ointment ointments

NOUN a smooth, thick substance that you put on sore skin to heal it.

old older oldest

ADJECTIVE **1** having lived or existed for a long time.

2 **Old** is used to give the age of someone or something. *The baby is six months **old**.*

3 You can use **old** to talk about something that is no longer used or has been replaced by something else. *I bumped into my teacher from my **old** primary school.*

old-fashioned

ADJECTIVE **1** Something **old-fashioned** is out of date and no longer fashionable.

2 If someone is **old-fashioned**, they believe in the values and standards of the past.

Antonym: (sense 1) fashionable

---

olive olives

NOUN **1** a small green or black fruit containing a stone. **Olives** are usually pickled and eaten as a snack, or crushed to produce oil for cooking.

ADJECTIVE OR NOUN **2** dark yellowish-green.

Olympic Games

Said "ul-**lim**-pic games" NOUN a series of international sporting contests held in a different country every four years. [The word *Olympic* comes from *Olympia* in Greece, where games were held in ancient times]

omelette omelettes

NOUN a dish made by beating eggs together and cooking them in a flat pan.

omit omits omitting omitted

VERB If you **omit** something, you do not include it. *She **omitted** to mention that her mother could not come.*

omni-

PREFIX added to some words to mean all or everywhere, for example **omni**potent means all-powerful, and **omni**present means present everywhere.

omnibus omnibuses

NOUN 1 a book containing a collection of stories or articles by the same author or about the same subject.
ADJECTIVE 2 An **omnibus** edition of a radio or television series contains two or more episodes that were originally shown separately.
3 **Omnibus** is an old-fashioned word for bus.

omnivore omnivores

NOUN an animal that eats all kinds of food, including meat and plants.
omnivorous ADJECTIVE

on

PREPOSITION 1 touching something or attached to it. *We sat **on** the seat.*
2 If you are **on** a bus, a plane or a train, you are inside it.
3 If something happens **on** a particular day, that is when it happens.
4 If something is done **on** an instrument or a machine, it is done using it.
5 A book or a talk **on** a particular subject is about that subject.
ADVERB 6 If someone has a piece of clothing **on**, they are wearing it.
ADJECTIVE 7 If a machine or a switch is **on**, it is working or is in action: *"Please would you switch the radio **on**?"*

once

ADVERB 1 If something happens **once**, it happens one time only.
2 If something was **once** true, it was true in the past, but is no longer true. *That ground was **once** covered by trees.*
CONJUNCTION 3 If something happens **once** another thing has happened, it happens immediately afterwards. *I'll do my homework **once** I've finished my tea.*
PHRASE 4 If you do something **at once**, you do it immediately. *We must go home **at once**.*
5 If several things happen **at once**, they all happen at the same time. *He tried to hold three glasses **at once**.*

one

NOUN 1 the number 1.
ADJECTIVE 2 When you refer to **one** person or **one** thing, you mean a single person or thing. *We have **one** main holiday a year.*
PRONOUN 3 **One** refers to a particular person or thing. *This book was the best **one** she had read for ages.*

onion onions

NOUN a small, round vegetable with a very strong taste.

only

ADVERB 1 You use **only** to show the one thing or person involved: ***Only** one girl was able to complete the race.*
2 You use **only** to make a condition that must happen before something else can happen. *You will be allowed in **only** if you have a ticket.*
3 You use **only** to emphasize that something is unimportant or small. *He's **only** very young.*
ADJECTIVE 4 If you talk about the **only** thing or person, you mean that there are no others. For example, if you are an **only** child, you have no brothers or sisters.
CONJUNCTION 5 You can use **only** to mean but or except. *He was very much like you, **only** with blond hair.*

onomatopoeia

Said "on-uh-mat-uh-**pee**-a" NOUN the use of words that sound like the thing that they represent. "Hiss" and "buzz" are examples of **onomatopoeia**.

ooze oozes oozing oozed

VERB When a thick liquid **ooze**, it flows slowly. *The cold mud **oozed** over her toes.*
[from Old English **wos** meaning juice]

opaque

ADJECTIVE If something is **opaque**, it does not let light through, so you cannot see through it: *opaque glass windows.*

Antonym: clear

open opens opening opened

ADJECTIVE **1** Something that is **open** is not closed or fastened, allowing things to pass through. *A light breeze came through the **open** window.*
2 not enclosed or covered. *At last we were out in the **open** countryside.*
VERB **3** When you **open** something, or when it **opens**, it is moved so that it is no longer closed. *She **opened** the box of chocolates.*
4 When a shop or office **opens**, people are allowed to go in to do business.
5 If you **open** a book, you turn back the cover so that you can read it.
6 If something **opens**, it starts or begins.
ADJECTIVE **7** Someone who is **open** is honest and not secretive.
openly ADVERB

opening openings

NOUN **1** a hole or gap. *There was a small **opening** in the fence.*
ADJECTIVE **2** coming first. *He sang the **opening** song in the concert.*
NOUN **3** the first part of a book or film. *I love the **opening** of that book.*

opera operas

NOUN a play in which the words are sung rather than spoken.

operate operates operating operated

VERB **1** When you **operate** a machine, you make it work. *I know how to **operate** the computer.*
2 When surgeons **operate**, they cut open a person's body to remove or repair a damaged part.

operation operations

NOUN **1** a form of medical treatment in which a surgeon cuts open a patient's body to remove or repair a damaged part.

2 a complex, planned event. *Moving house is going to be quite a difficult **operation**.*

opinion opinions

NOUN a belief or view.

opponent opponents

NOUN someone who is against you in an argument or a contest.

opportunity opportunities

NOUN a chance to do something.

oppose opposes opposing opposed

VERB **1** If you **oppose** something or someone, you disagree with them and are against them.
ADJECTIVE **2** **Opposing** means opposite or very different. *We managed to be friends even though we had **opposing** points of view.*

opposite opposites

PREPOSITION OR ADVERB **1** If one thing is **opposite** another, it is facing it. *Our house is **opposite** the park.*
NOUN **2** If people or things are **opposites**, they are completely different from each other.

opposition

NOUN **1** If there is **opposition** to something, there is resistance to it and people oppose it. *There is a lot of **opposition** to the building of a new road.*
2 In a games or sports event, the **opposition** is the person or team that you are competing against.

opt opts opting opted

VERB **1** If you **opt** for something, you choose to do it. *I **opted** to go to the Gym Club.*
2 If you **opt** out of something, you choose not to do it or be involved with it. *I **opted** out of football practice.*

optical

ADJECTIVE concerned with vision, light, or images.

optician opticians

NOUN someone who tests people's eyesight, and makes and sells glasses and contact lenses.

optimist optimists

NOUN An **optimist** is a person who is always hopeful that everything will turn out well in the future.
optimism NOUN   **optimistic** ADJECTIVE

Antonym: pessimist

option options
NOUN a choice between two or more things.

optional
ADJECTIVE If something is **optional**, you can choose whether to do it or not. *Tennis is optional at our school.*

Antonym: compulsory

or
CONJUNCTION used to link two alternatives or choices. *You need to decide whether to stay or leave.*

oral
ADJECTIVE **1** spoken rather than written. *Tomorrow we have our French oral examination.*
2 to do with your mouth or using your mouth. *Oral hygiene is vital for healthy teeth.*
orally ADVERB

orange oranges
NOUN **1** a round citrus fruit that is juicy and sweet and has a thick reddish-yellow skin.
ADJECTIVE OR NOUN **2** reddish-yellow.
[from Sanskrit **naranga** meaning orange]

orang-utan orang-utans; also spelt orang-utang
NOUN a large ape with reddish-brown hair.

orbit orbits orbiting orbited
NOUN **1** the curved path followed by an object going round a planet or the sun.
VERB **2** If something **orbits** a planet or the sun, it goes round and round it. *Our moon orbits the earth.*

orchard orchards
NOUN a piece of land where fruit trees are grown.

orchestra orchestras
NOUN a large group of musicians who play musical instruments together.

orchid orchids
NOUN a type of plant with beautiful and unusual flowers.

ordeal ordeals
NOUN a very difficult and unpleasant experience.

order orders ordering ordered
NOUN **1** a command given by someone in authority.
2 If things are arranged or done in a particular **order**, they are arranged or done in that sequence: *alphabetical order.*
VERB **3** If you **order** someone to do something, you tell them firmly to do it.
4 When you **order** something, you ask for it to be brought or sent to you.

ordinary
ADJECTIVE not special or different in any way.

ore ores
NOUN rock or earth from which metal can be obtained.

organ organs
NOUN **1** Your **organs** are parts of your body that have a particular purpose, for example your lungs are the **organs** with which you breathe.
2 a large musical instrument with a keyboard and windpipes through which air is forced to produce a sound.

organic
ADJECTIVE **1** **Organic** food is produced without the use of artificial fertilizers or pesticides.
2 produced or found in living things.
organically ADVERB

organism organisms
NOUN any living animal or plant.

organization organizations; also spelt organisation
NOUN **1** any business or group of people working together for a purpose.
2 the act of planning and arranging something.

organize organizes organizing organized; also spelt organise
VERB If you **organize** something, you plan and arrange it.

oriental
ADJECTIVE Something that is **oriental** comes from the Far East, which includes countries such as India, China and Japan. *I like oriental food.*

orienteering
NOUN a sport in which people find their way from one place to another in the countryside, using a map and compass.

origin origins

NOUN the beginning or cause of something. *The origins of man have been written about in many books.*

original originals

ADJECTIVE **1** the first or earliest. *The original owner of this house made lots of alterations.*
2 imaginative and clever. *His paintings are highly original.*
NOUN **3** a work of art or a document that is the one that was produced first, and is not a copy.
originally ADVERB

ornament ornaments

NOUN a small, attractive object that you display in your home or that you wear in order to look attractive.

ornithology

NOUN the study of birds.
ornithologist NOUN

orphan orphans

NOUN a child whose parents are dead.

orphanage orphanages

NOUN a place where orphans are looked after.

ostrich ostriches

NOUN the largest bird in the world. **Ostriches** can run fast but cannot fly.

other others

PRONOUN **1** The **other** can mean the second of two things. *One of the rooms is empty, but the other is not.*
ADJECTIVE **2 Other** people or things are different from those already mentioned.
3 The **other** day means a few days ago.

otherwise

ADVERB **1** or else.
2 apart from the thing mentioned. *The food was good, but otherwise the party was awful.*

otter otters

NOUN a small, furry animal with a long tail, that lives near water. **Otters** swim well and eat fish.

ought

VERB **1** If you say that someone **ought** to do something, you mean they should do it.
2 If you say that something **ought** to be the case, you mean that you expect it to be the case. *He ought to be here by now.*

ounce ounces

NOUN a unit of weight equal to one-sixteenth of a pound or about 28·35 grams.

our

ADJECTIVE belonging to us. *Our cat is black.*

ours

PRONOUN belonging to us. *That cat is ours.*

ourselves

PRONOUN **Ourselves** is used when talking about a group of people that includes the speaker or writer. *We didn't hurt ourselves too badly.*

out

ADVERB **1** towards the outside of a place or thing. *Take the ice cream out of the freezer.*
ADJECTIVE **2** not at home.

outbreak outbreaks

NOUN If there is an **outbreak** of something unpleasant, such as war, it suddenly occurs. *The outbreak of the disease made many people unwell.*

outburst outbursts

NOUN a sudden strong expression of emotion, especially anger or violent action. *He apologized for his angry outburst.*

outcome outcomes

NOUN a result.

outdoor

ADJECTIVE happening or used outside.

outer

ADJECTIVE The **outer** parts of something are the parts furthest from the centre: *the outer doors.*

outer space

NOUN everything beyond the earth's atmosphere.

outfit outfits

NOUN a set of clothes. *I bought a new outfit for the party.*

outgoing

ADJECTIVE Someone who is **outgoing** is friendly and not shy. *She is always fun to be with as she has such an outgoing personality.*

outgrow outgrows outgrowing outgrew outgrown

VERB **1** If you **outgrow** a piece of clothing, you grow too big to wear it. *I've already outgrown my best jeans.*

2 If you **outgrow** a way of behaving, you stop behaving that way because you are older and more mature.

outing outings

NOUN a trip made for pleasure.

outlaw outlaws outlawing outlawed

VERB **1** If someone **outlaws** something, they ban it.

NOUN **2** In the past, an **outlaw** was a criminal.

outlet outlets

NOUN **1** a hole or pipe through which water or air can flow away.

2 a shop that sells goods made by a particular manufacturer.

outline outlines outlining outlined

NOUN **1** The **outline** of something is its shape.

VERB **2** If you **outline** a plan or idea, you give brief details of it.

outlook outlooks

NOUN **1** Your **outlook** is your general attitude towards life. *His outlook on life is always positive.*

2 The **outlook** of a situation is the way it is likely to develop. *The outlook for the weather over the next few days is not very good.*

outnumber outnumbers outnumbering outnumbered

VERB If there are more of one group than of another, the first group **outnumbers** the second. *Boys outnumber girls in our class.*

outpatient outpatients

NOUN someone who receives treatment in hospital without staying overnight.

output outputs

NOUN **1** the amount of something produced by a person or organization.

2 The **output** of a computer is the information that it produces.

outrage outrages outraging outraged

VERB **1** If something **outrages** you, it angers and shocks you.

NOUN **2** a feeling of anger and shock.

3 something very shocking or violent.

outrageous ADJECTIVE   **outrageously** ADVERB

outright

ADJECTIVE **1** total and complete. *She made an outright refusal to come with us.*

ADVERB **2** completely, totally. *Smoking in the building has been banned outright.*

outside

NOUN **1** The **outside** of something is the part that surrounds or encloses the rest of it. *We wandered around the outside of the house.*

ADVERB, ADJECTIVE, OR PREPOSITION **2** not inside.

NOUN **3** not included in something. *The building will be closed outside school hours.*

✔ Do not use *of* after *outside*. You should say "I will meet you *outside* the school", not "*outside of* the school".

outskirts

PLURAL NOUN the parts around the edge of a city or town. *Our home is on the outskirts of a large town.*

outspoken

ADJECTIVE **Outspoken** people give their opinions openly, even if they shock other people.

outstanding

ADJECTIVE extremely good.

outwit outwits outwitting outwitted

VERB If you **outwit** someone, you use your intelligence or a clever trick to defeat them or get the better of them.

oval ovals

NOUN **1** a shape similar to a circle, but wider in one direction than the other.

ADJECTIVE **2** shaped like an oval.

[from Latin *ovalis* meaning egg-shaped]

ovary ovaries

Said "**oh**-var-ree" NOUN one of the two organs that produce eggs in the body of a woman or other female animal.

oven ovens

NOUN the part of a cooker that you use for baking or roasting food.

over overs

PREPOSITION **1** directly above something or covering it. *She hung the picture* **over** *the fireplace. He put his hands* **over** *his eyes.*
2 A view **over** an area is a view across it. *I love the view* **over** *the lake to the mountains.*
3 If something happens **over** a period of time, it happens during that period. *I went to New Zealand* **over** *Christmas.*
4 If an amount of something is left **over**, that amount remains.
ADVERB OR PREPOSITION **5** If you lean **over,** you bend your body in a particular direction. *He leant* **over** *to open the door of the car.*
ADVERB **6** If something rolls or turns **over**, it moves so that its other side is facing upwards.
ADJECTIVE **7** Something that is **over** is completely finished.
NOUN **8** In cricket, an **over** is a series of six balls bowled by one bowler.

over-

PREFIX too much, or to too great an extent. For example, if fruit is **over**ripe, it is too ripe, and if someone **over**eats, they eat too much.

overall

ADJECTIVE OR ADVERB taking into account all the parts or aspects of something. ***Overall***, *the project has been a success.*

overalls

PLURAL NOUN a piece of clothing that you wear to protect your other clothes when you are working.

overboard

ADVERB If you fall **overboard**, you fall over the side of a ship into the water.

overcast

ADJECTIVE When the sky is **overcast**, it is covered by thick cloud.

overcoat overcoats

NOUN a thick, warm coat.

overcome overcomes overcoming overcame overcome

VERB **1** If you **overcome** a problem or a feeling, you manage to deal with it or control it.
2 If you are **overcome**, you are affected by strong emotions. *They were* **overcome** *with happiness.*

3 If you are **overcome** by fumes, gas or smoke, for example, you are made unconscious by them.

overcrowded

ADJECTIVE If a place is **overcrowded,** there are too many things or people in it**.**

overdue

ADJECTIVE If someone or something is **overdue**, they are late. *The train is now* **overdue**.

overflow overflows overflowing overflowed

VERB If a liquid **overflows**, it spills over the edge of its container. If a river **overflows**, it flows over its banks.

overgrown

ADJECTIVE If a place is **overgrown**, it is thickly covered with plants and weeds.

overhaul overhauls overhauling overhauled

VERB **1** If you **overhaul** something, you examine and check it carefully, and repair any faults.
NOUN **2** An **overhaul** is a careful and detailed examination of something in order to repair its faults.

overhead

ADVERB OR ADJECTIVE above your head, or in the sky. *Seagulls flew* **overhead**. *The* **overhead** *wires were being repaired.*

overhear overhears overhearing overheard

VERB If you **overhear** someone's conversation, you hear what they are saying to someone else.

overlap overlaps overlapping overlapped

VERB If one thing **overlaps** another, it covers part of the other thing.

overload overloads overloading overloaded

VERB If you **overload** someone or something, you give them too much to do or to carry.

overlook overlooks overlooking overlooked

VERB **1** If a building or window **overlooks** a place, it has a view of it from above.
2 If you **overlook** something, you ignore it or do not notice it.

overnight

ADVERB OR ADJECTIVE **1** during the night. *We took an* **overnight** *flight.*
2 sudden or suddenly. *He seemed to become such a good player* **overnight**.

overseas
ADJECTIVE OR ADVERB abroad. *We have some* ***overseas*** *students visiting the school. My brother is going* ***overseas*** *for a year.*

oversleep oversleeps oversleeping overslept
VERB If you **oversleep**, you sleep on past the time you intended to wake up.

overtake overtakes overtaking overtook overtaken
VERB If you **overtake** someone or something, you pass them because you are moving faster than they are.

overtime
NOUN time that someone works in addition to their normal working hours.

overture overtures
NOUN the opening piece of music at a concert, show or ballet.

overweight
ADJECTIVE People or animals that are **overweight** are too heavy for their size.

overwhelm overwhelms overwhelming overwhelmed
VERB 1 If something **overwhelms** you, it affects you very strongly.
2 If one group of people **overwhelms** another, they completely defeat them.
3 If you **overwhelm** someone with something, you load them with too much of it. *He was* ***overwhelmed*** *with work.*

owe owes owing owed
VERB 1 If you **owe** someone money, they have lent it to you and you have not yet paid it back.
2 If you **owe** a quality or skill to someone, you only have it because of them. *He* ***owes*** *his success as a tennis player to his coach.*

owl owls
NOUN a bird of prey that hunts at night. **Owls** have large eyes and short, hooked beaks.

own owns owning owned
ADJECTIVE OR PRONOUN 1 If something is your **own**, it belongs to you or is associated with you. *She now has her* ***own*** *bedroom.*
VERB 2 If you **own** something, it belongs to you.
PHRASE 3 **On your own** means alone.

owner owners
NOUN the person to whom something belongs.

ox oxen
NOUN **Oxen** are cattle used for carrying or pulling things.

oxygen
NOUN a colourless gas that makes up about 21% of the earth's atmosphere. All animals and plants need **oxygen** to live, and fires need it to burn.

oyster oysters
NOUN a large, flat shellfish. Some **oysters** can be eaten, and others produce pearls.

ozone
NOUN a form of oxygen that is poisonous and has a strong smell.
[from Greek *ozein* meaning smell]

ozone layer
NOUN a layer of the earth's atmosphere that protects living things from the harmful radiation of the sun.

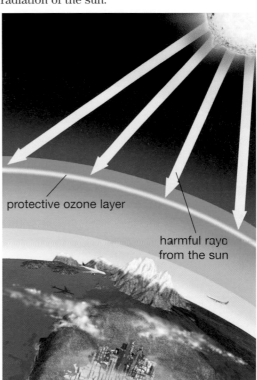

protective ozone layer

harmful rays from the sun

a b c d e f g h i j k l m n o p q r s t u v w x y z

Pp

pace paces pacing paced
NOUN **1** the distance you move when you take one step.
2 Your **pace** is the speed at which you are walking or running.
VERB **3** If you **pace**, you walk up and down, usually because you are anxious or impatient.

Pacific
NOUN the ocean separating North and South America from Asia and Australia.

pacifist pacifists
NOUN someone who is opposed to all violence and war.
pacifism NOUN

pacify pacifies pacifying pacified
VERB If you **pacify** someone who is angry, you calm them.
pacifier NOUN

pack packs packing packed
VERB **1** If you **pack** things, you put them neatly into a container, bag or box.
NOUN **2** a complete set of playing cards.
3 a group of wolves or dogs.

package packages
NOUN a small parcel.

packet packets
NOUN a small box or bag in which something is sold.

pact pacts
NOUN a formal agreement or treaty.

pad pads
NOUN **1** a set of sheets of paper glued together at one end.
2 a thick, soft piece of material.
3 one of the soft parts under an animal's paws.

paddle paddles paddling paddled
NOUN **1** a short pole with a broad blade at one or both ends, used to move a small boat or a canoe.
VERB **2** If someone **paddles** a boat, they move it using a paddle.
3 If you **paddle**, you walk in shallow water with bare feet.

paddock paddocks
NOUN a small field where horses are kept.

padlock padlocks padlocking padlocked
NOUN **1** a special kind of metal lock used to fasten two things together.
VERB **2** If you **padlock** something, you lock it with a padlock.

pagan pagans
NOUN **1** someone who does not believe in any of the main religions of the world.
ADJECTIVE **2** involving beliefs and worship outside the main religions of the world: *pagan myths and cults*.
paganism NOUN

page pages
NOUN **1** one side of a sheet of paper in a book or magazine. *Turn to **page** four.*
2 a single sheet of paper.

pageant pageants
NOUN a grand, colourful show or parade.
pageantry NOUN
[from Latin *pagina* meaning a scene of a play]

pagoda pagodas
NOUN a tall, elaborately decorated Buddhist or Hindu temple.

paid
VERB past tense and past participle of *pay*.

pail pails
NOUN a bucket.

pain pains
NOUN **1** a feeling of discomfort and hurt in your body, caused by an illness or injury.
PHRASE **2** If you are **in pain** you are hurting.
[from Latin *poena* meaning punishment]

painful
ADJECTIVE causing emotional or physical pain.

painkiller painkillers
NOUN a drug that reduces or stops pain.

painless

ADJECTIVE Something that is **painless** causes no pain.

paint paints painting painted

NOUN **1** a coloured liquid used to decorate buildings and make pictures.
VERB **2** If you **paint** a picture of something, you make a picture of it using paint.
3 If you **paint** something such as a wall, you cover it with paint.

painting paintings

NOUN **1** a picture that someone has created using paints.
2 the activity of painting pictures.

pair pairs

NOUN **1** two things of the same type that are meant to be used together: *a **pair** of socks*.
2 objects that have two main parts of the same size and shape: *a **pair** of scissors*.

pal pals

NOUN; INFORMAL a friend.
[from the Romani for brother]

palace palaces

NOUN a large, grand house, especially the home of a king or queen.

pale paler palest

ADJECTIVE not strong or bright in colour.

palette palettes

NOUN a board on which an artist mixes colours.

palm palms

NOUN **1** a tropical tree with no branches and broad, long leaves at the top of its trunk. **Palm** trees often produce fruit, such as coconuts or dates.
2 the flat area on the inside of your hand.

pamper pampers pampering pampered

VERB If you **pamper** someone, you give them a lot of kindness and comfort.

pamphlet pamphlets

NOUN a very thin book in paper covers, giving information about something.

pan pans

NOUN a round metal container with a long handle, used for cooking things.

pancake pancakes

NOUN a thin, flat piece of fried batter that can be served with savoury or sweet fillings.

panda pandas

NOUN a large animal, rather like a bear, that lives in China. A giant **panda** has black fur with large patches of white.

pane panes

NOUN a sheet of glass in a window or door.

panel panels

NOUN **1** a group of people who are chosen to discuss or decide something.
2 a flat piece of wood, metal or other material that is part of a larger object, such as a door or a wall.

panic panics panicking panicked

NOUN **1** a sudden strong feeling of fear or anxiety.
VERB **2** If you **panic**, you become so afraid or anxious that you cannot act sensibly.

panorama panoramas

NOUN an extensive view over a wide area of land.
panoramic ADJECTIVE

pant pants panting panted

VERB If you **pant**, you take short, quick breaths through your mouth.

panther panthers

NOUN a large wild animal belonging to the cat family, especially the black leopard.

pantomime pantomimes

NOUN a funny musical play, usually based on a fairy story and performed at Christmas.

pants

PLURAL NOUN **1** underpants or knickers.
2 another name for trousers.

paper papers

NOUN **1** a material that you write on or wrap things with.
2 a newspaper.
[from *papyrus*, the plant from which paper was made in ancient Egypt, Greece and Rome]

paperback paperbacks

NOUN a book with a thin cardboard cover.

papier-mâché

Said "pap-yey **mash**-ay" NOUN a mixture of mashed wet paper and glue that can be moulded into shapes, then dried and decorated to make bowls, ornaments and other objects.
[from French, meaning chewed paper]

A B C D E F G H I J K L M N O **P** Q R S T U V W X Y Z

parable parables
NOUN a short story that makes a moral or religious point.

parachute parachutes
NOUN a large umbrella-like piece of fabric attached by lines to a person or package so that it can fall safely to the ground from an aircraft.
parachuting NOUN

parade parades parading paraded
NOUN **1** a line of people or vehicles moving together through a public place in order to celebrate something.
VERB **2** When people **parade**, they walk together in a group, usually in front of spectators.
3 When soldiers **parade**, they gather together for inspection.

paradise
NOUN **1** According to some religions, **paradise** is a wonderful place where good people go when they die.
2 Somewhere very beautiful and wonderful in real life can be called **paradise**. *Some of the beaches we went to on holiday were **paradise**.*

paraffin
NOUN a strong-smelling liquid used as a fuel.

paragraph paragraphs
NOUN a section of a piece of writing. **Paragraphs** begin on a new line.

parallel
ADJECTIVE If two lines or objects are **parallel**, they are the same distance apart along the whole of their length.

parallelogram parallelograms
NOUN a four-sided shape, each side of which is parallel to the opposite side.

paralysed
ADJECTIVE If a part of your body is **paralysed**, you cannot move it. *Since the accident my uncle has been **paralysed** from the waist down.*
paralyse VERB   **paralysis** NOUN

paramedic paramedics
NOUN a person who does some types of medical work, for example for the ambulance service.

parasite parasites
NOUN a small animal or plant that lives on or inside a larger animal or plant.
parasitic ADJECTIVE
[from Greek ***parasitos*** meaning someone who eats at someone else's table]

paratroops or **paratroopers**
PLURAL NOUN soldiers trained to be dropped from aircraft by parachute.

parcel parcels
NOUN something wrapped up in paper.

parched
ADJECTIVE **1** very dry and in need of water. *The earth was **parched** during the drought.*
2 very thirsty. *I was **parched** after the race.*

pardon pardons pardoning pardoned
PHRASE **1** You say **pardon** or **I beg your pardon** when you want someone to repeat something they have said.
VERB **2** If you **pardon** someone, you forgive or excuse them for something they have done wrong.

parent parents
NOUN Your **parents** are your father and mother.

parish parishes
NOUN an area with its own church and clergyman.

park parks parking parked
VERB **1** When someone **parks** a vehicle, they drive it into a position where it can be left.
NOUN **2** a public area with grass and trees.

parliament parliaments
NOUN the group of people who make or change the laws of a country.

parole
NOUN When prisoners are given **parole**, they are released early on condition that they behave well.

parrot parrots
NOUN a brightly coloured tropical bird with a curved beak.

parsley
NOUN a herb with curly leaves used for flavouring in cooking.

parsnip parsnips
NOUN a long, pointed, cream-coloured root vegetable.

part parts parting parted
NOUN **1** a piece of something, and not all of it.
2 If you have a **part** in a play, you have a role in it.
VERB **3** If you **part** people or things, you separate them.

partial
ADJECTIVE **1** not complete or whole.
PHRASE **2** If you are **partial to** someone or something, you like them.
partially ADVERB

participate participates participating participated
VERB If you **participate** in an activity, you take part in it or join in with other people.

participle participles
NOUN a word that is formed from a verb and used as part of the verb or as an adjective. For example, eating is the present **participle** of eat, and loaded is the past **participle** of load.

particle particles
NOUN a very small piece of something. *There were **particles** of dust floating in the air.*

particular
ADJECTIVE **1** to do with only one person or thing. *That **particular** recipe is very easy to make.*
2 If you are **particular**, you are fussy and pay attention to detail.
particularly ADVERB

partition partitions
NOUN a screen separating one part of a room or vehicle from another.

partly
ADVERB to some extent, but not completely. *It's **partly** my fault.*

partner partners
NOUN **1** Someone's **partner** is the person they are married to or living with.
2 one of two people who do something together, such as dancing or running a business.

part of speech parts of speech
NOUN one of the groups that words are divided into in grammar, such as a noun or an adjective.

partridge partridges
NOUN a brown game bird with a round body and a short tail.

part-time
ADJECTIVE OR ADVERB involving work for only a part of each normal working day or week.

party parties
NOUN **1** a social occasion when people meet to enjoy themselves, often in order to celebrate something.
2 a group of people who are doing something together. *A **party** of school children visited the museum.*

pass passes passing passed
VERB **1** If you **pass** someone or something, you go past them without stopping.
2 If you **pass** something to someone, you give it to them.
3 If you **pass** an examination, you are successful in it.

passage passages
NOUN **1** a long, narrow corridor or space that connects two places. *There was a **passage** from the front garden through to the back garden.*
2 a section of a book or piece of music.

passenger passengers
NOUN a person travelling in a vehicle, aircraft or ship.

passion passions
NOUN a very strong feeling.

passive
ADJECTIVE **1** Someone who is **passive** does not take action or react strongly to things.
2 In grammar, the **passive**, or **passive** voice, is the form of the verb in which the person or thing to which an action is being done is the subject of the sentence. For example, the sentence "The burglar was seen by the police" is in the **passive**. For the active, or active voice, the subject of the sentence is the person or thing doing the activity: "The police saw the burglar".

Passover
NOUN an eight-day Jewish festival held in spring.

passport passports

NOUN an official document showing your identity and nationality, that you need to show when you enter or leave a country.

password passwords

NOUN **1** a secret word known to only a few people. It allows people on the same side to recognize a friend.

2 a word you need to know to get into some computer files.

past

NOUN **1** the period of time before the present.

ADJECTIVE **2 Past** events are ones that happened or existed before the present.

PREPOSITION OR ADVERB **3** You use **past** to tell the time when it is thirty minutes or less after a particular hour. *It's ten **past** eleven.*

4 If you go **past** something, you move towards it and continue until you are on the other side. *An ambulance drove **past**.*

PREPOSITION **5** Something that is **past** a place is situated on the other side of it. *The farm is just **past** the next village.*

pasta

NOUN a dried mixture of flour, eggs and water, formed into different shapes.

[an Italian word meaning flour mixture]

paste pastes pasting pasted

NOUN **1** a soft, sticky mixture that can be spread easily.

VERB **2** If you **paste** something somewhere, you stick it there with glue.

pasteurized or pasteurised

*Said "**past**-yoor-ized"* ADJECTIVE **Pasteurized** milk has been heated by a special process to kill bacteria.

[after the French chemist Louis *Pasteur* who invented the process]

pastime pastimes

NOUN something that you enjoy doing in your spare time.

pastry pastries

NOUN **1** a mixture of flour, fat and water that is used for making pies.

2 a small cake. *There is a selection of **pastries** for tea.*

pasture pastures

NOUN an area of grass where cows, horses and sheep can graze.

pasty pasties; pastier pastiest

*Rhymes with "**nasty**"* NOUN **1** a small pie containing meat and vegetables

*Rhymes with "**tasty**"* ADJECTIVE **2** Someone who is **pasty** looks pale and unhealthy.

pat pats patting patted

VERB If you **pat** someone or something, you tap it lightly with an open hand.

patch patches patching patched

NOUN **1** a piece of material used to cover a hole in something. *She put a **patch** over the hole in her jeans.*

2 an area of a surface that is different in appearance from the rest. *We want to grow vegetables on that **patch** of ground.*

VERB **3** If you **patch** something that has a hole in it, you mend it by fixing something over the hole.

patchy patchier patchiest

ADJECTIVE uneven in quantity, quality or both. *We drove through **patchy** fog.*

pâté pâtés

*Said "**pa**-tay"* NOUN a paste made from meat, fish or vegetables, and spread on toast or biscuits.

[from the French word for paste]

patent patents

NOUN the official right given to someone to make something they have invented. It stops others from copying it.

paternal

ADJECTIVE relating to or like a father.

[from Latin *pater* meaning father]

path paths

NOUN **1** a strip of ground for people to walk or ride along.

2 the direction in which something travels. *The trail of smoke showed the **path** of the plane.*

pathetic

ADJECTIVE **1** If something is **pathetic**, it makes you feel pity.

2 very poor or unsuccessful. *He made a **pathetic** attempt to swim.*

pathetically ADVERB

[from Greek *pathetikos* meaning sensitive]

patience

NOUN the ability to stay calm in a difficult or irritating situation.

patient patients

ADJECTIVE **1** If you are **patient**, you stay calm in a difficult or irritating situation.
NOUN **2** a person receiving treatment from a doctor.
patiently ADVERB

patio patios

NOUN a paved area close to a house.

patriot patriots

NOUN someone who loves their own country and is very loyal to it.
patriotic ADJECTIVE   **patriotism** NOUN

patrol patrols patrolling patrolled

VERB **1** When soldiers, police or guards **patrol** an area, they walk or drive around it to make sure there is no trouble.
NOUN **2** a group of people patrolling an area.

patter patters pattering pattered

VERB **1** If something **patters** on a surface, it makes quick, light, tapping sounds. *The rain pattered against the window.*
NOUN **2** a series of light tapping sounds. *We could hear the patter of light rain.*

pattern patterns

NOUN **1** a design of shapes repeated at regular intervals.
2 a drawing that can be copied to make something else, such as clothes.

pause pauses pausing paused

VERB **1** If you **pause**, you stop speaking or doing something for a short time.
NOUN **2** a period when something stops for a short time before continuing.

pavement pavements

NOUN a raised pathway with a hard surface along the side of a road.
[from Latin *pavimentum* meaning hard floor]

pavilion pavilions

NOUN a building at a sports ground, especially a cricket pitch, where players can change.

paw paws

NOUN the foot of an animal that has claws and pads.

pawn pawns pawning pawned

VERB **1** If you **pawn** something, you leave it with someone called a pawnbroker who lends you money. When you repay the money, the pawnbroker will give back the item you **pawned**.
NOUN **2** the smallest and least valuable piece in the game of chess.

pay pays paying paid

VERB **1** If you **pay** someone, you give them money in exchange for something.
2 If you **pay attention**, you listen carefully to what is being said.

payment payments

NOUN If you make a **payment** for something, you give someone money in exchange for goods or a service.

PC PCs

NOUN **1** the abbreviation of *personal computer*.
2 In Britain, **PC** is also the abbreviation of *police constable*.

PE

NOUN an abbreviation of *physical education*, which is the sports that you do at school.

pea peas

NOUN a small, round green seed that is eaten as a vegetable.

peace

Said "*peess*" NOUN **1** a state of undisturbed calm and quiet.
2 If a country is at **peace**, it is not at war.
✔ Another word that sounds like *peace* is *piece*.

peaceful

ADJECTIVE quiet and calm.

peach peaches

NOUN a soft, round fruit with yellow flesh and a yellow and red skin.

peacock peacocks

NOUN a large male bird with very long green and blue tail feathers that it can spread out in a fan. The female is called a peahen.

peak peaks

NOUN **1** the highest point of a mountain.
2 The **peak** of an activity or process is the point at which it is strongest or most successful.
3 the part of a cap that sticks out over your eyes.

peal peals

NOUN the loud musical sound made by bells ringing one after another.

peanut peanuts

NOUN a small nut that grows under the ground.

pear pears

NOUN a green or yellow fruit that is narrow at the top and wider at the bottom.

pearl pearls

NOUN a hard, round, creamy-white ball used in jewellery. **Pearls** grow inside the shell of an oyster.

peasant peasants

NOUN a person who works on the land, earning little money.

peat

NOUN dark-brown decaying plant material found in cool, wet regions. Dried **peat** can be used as fuel or fertilizer.

pebble pebbles

NOUN a smooth, round stone often found on the beach.

peck pecks pecking pecked

VERB If a bird **pecks** something, it bites at it quickly with its beak. *The birds pecked at the seeds on the ground.*

peculiar

ADJECTIVE strange and unusual. *She thought the food tasted peculiar.*
peculiarly ADVERB   **peculiarity** NOUN

pedal pedals pedalling pedalled

VERB 1 When you **pedal** a bicycle, you push the pedals around with your feet to make it move.
NOUN 2 a control lever that you press with your foot to make a machine or vehicle work.

pedestrian pedestrians

NOUN someone who is walking. *Only pedestrians are allowed down this street.*

pedigree pedigrees

ADJECTIVE 1 A **pedigree** animal is bred from a single breed and its ancestors are known and recorded.
NOUN 2 a list of a person's or an animal's ancestors.

peek peeks peeking peeked

VERB 1 If you **peek** at something, you have a quick look at it.
NOUN 2 a quick look at something.

peel peels peeling peeled

NOUN 1 the skin of a fruit or vegetable.
VERB 2 When you **peel** fruit or vegetables, you remove the skin.
3 If a layer of something **peels**, it comes off a surface. *Paint was peeling off the walls.*

peep peeps peeping peeped

VERB 1 If you **peep** at something, you have a quick, secretive look at it, or you look at it through a small opening.
NOUN 2 a quick look at something.

peer peers peering peered

VERB 1 If you **peer** at something, you look at it very hard. *He peered into the dark room.*
NOUN 2 Your **peers** are your equals in age, interests and background.

peg pegs

NOUN 1 a plastic or wooden clip for attaching clothes to a washing line.
2 a hook where you can hang things.

pelican pelicans

NOUN a large water bird with a pouch beneath its beak in which it stores fish.

pellet pellets

NOUN a small ball of food, paper, lead or other material.

pelt pelts pelting pelted

NOUN 1 the skin and fur of an animal, especially when it is used for making clothes.
VERB 2 If you **pelt** someone with something, you throw it at them very hard.
3 If rain **pelts** down, it rains very hard.

pen pens

NOUN 1 an instrument with a pointed end used for writing with ink.
2 a small, fenced area where farm animals are kept: *a sheep pen.*

penalty penalties

NOUN 1 a punishment.
2 In sport, a **penalty** is an advantage or point given to one team when their opponents break the rules.

pence

NOUN a plural form of *penny*.

pencil pencils

NOUN a small stick of wood with a type of soft mineral called graphite in the centre, used for drawing or writing.
[from Latin *pencillus* meaning painter's brush]

pendant pendants

NOUN a piece of jewellery attached to a chain and worn round the neck.

pendulum pendulums

NOUN a rod with a weight at one end that swings regularly from side to side. A **pendulum** can be used to control a clock.

penetrate penetrates penetrating penetrated

VERB If someone or something **penetrates** an object or area, they succeed in getting into or through it. *Eventually they **penetrated** the forest and found the cabin.*

pen friend pen friends

NOUN someone living in a different place or country whom you write to regularly, although you may never have met each other.

penguin penguins

NOUN a black and white bird with webbed feet and small wings like flippers. **Penguins** are found mainly in the Antarctic.

penicillin

NOUN a powerful antibiotic obtained from fungus and used to treat infections.

peninsula peninsulas

NOUN an area of land almost surrounded by water.
[from Latin *paene* + *insula* meaning almost an island]

penis penises

NOUN the part of the body that male humans or other animals use when urinating or having sexual intercourse.

penknife penknives

NOUN a small folding knife.

penny pennies or pence

NOUN a unit of currency in Britain and some other countries. In Britain there are 100 **pennies** in a pound.

pension pensions

NOUN a regular sum of money paid to a retired, widowed or disabled person.

pentagon pentagons

NOUN a flat shape with five straight sides.
pentagonal ADJECTIVE

pentathlon pentathlons

NOUN a sports contest in which athletes compete in five different events.
[from Greek *pente* meaning five and *athlon* meaning contest]

people

PLURAL NOUN human beings – men, women and children.

pepper peppers

NOUN 1 a hot-tasting powdered spice used for flavouring in cooking.
2 a hollow green, red or yellow vegetable, with sweet-flavoured flesh.

peppermint peppermints

NOUN 1 a plant with a strong taste. It is used for making sweets and in medicine.
2 a sweet flavoured with peppermint.

per

PREPOSITION **Per** means "for each" and is used when speaking about prices, measurements, rates and ratios: *60 kilometres **per** hour, three times **per** year, 90p **per** kilo.*

perceive perceives perceiving perceived

VERB If you **perceive** something, you see, notice or understand it.

per cent

PHRASE You use **per cent** to show amounts out of a hundred. The symbol for per cent is %. *She got 98 **per cent** (98%) for her maths test.*
[from Latin *per* meaning each and *centum* meaning hundred]

percentage percentages

NOUN an amount or rate expressed as a number of hundredths.

perceptive

ADJECTIVE Someone who is **perceptive** notices and understands things more quickly than other people.
perceptively ADVERB

Synonyms: observant, sharp

a b c d e f g h i j k l m n o p q r s t u v w x y z

perch perches perching perched

VERB **1** If you **perch** on something, you sit on the edge of it.

2 When a bird **perches** on something, it stands on it.

NOUN **3** a short rod for a bird to stand on.

4 an edible freshwater fish.

percolator percolators

NOUN a special pot for making and serving coffee.

percussion

NOUN OR ADJECTIVE musical instruments that you hit or shake to produce sounds, such as drums and tambourines.

percussionist NOUN

drum

tambourine

cymbal

triangle

perennial

ADJECTIVE occurring or lasting for many years.

perfect perfects perfecting perfected

Said "**pur**-fikt" ADJECTIVE **1** Something that is **perfect** is as good as it possibly can be.

Said "pur-**fekt**" VERB **2** If you **perfect** something, you make it as good as it possibly can be.

perform performs performing performed

VERB **1** If you **perform** a play or piece of music, you do a show of it in front of an audience.

2 If you **perform** a task or action, you do it.

performer NOUN

performance performances

NOUN an entertainment provided for an audience. *The orchestra gave an excellent* ***performance***.

perfume perfumes

NOUN **1** a pleasant-smelling liquid that people put on their skin.

2 a pleasant smell. *These roses have a lovely* ***perfume***.

perhaps

ADVERB You use **perhaps** when you are not sure if something is true or possible. ***Perhaps** we could see you tomorrow?*

peril perils

NOUN; FORMAL great danger.

perilous ADJECTIVE   **perilously** ADVERB

perimeter perimeters

NOUN **1** the distance all the way round the edge of an area.

2 the edge or boundary of something.

period periods

NOUN **1** a particular length of time. *We will be away for a **period** of a few months.*

2 When a woman or girl has a **period,** she bleeds from her womb, usually once a month.

3 In American English, a **period** is a full stop.

periodical periodicals

NOUN a magazine that is published regularly.

periscope periscopes

NOUN a tube with mirrors placed in it so that you can see things that are otherwise out of sight. **Periscopes** are used for seeing out of submarines.

perish perishes perishing perished

VERB **1** If fruit, rubber or fabric **perishes**, it rots.

2 FORMAL If someone or something **perishes**, they die or are destroyed.

perishable ADJECTIVE

perm perms

NOUN If someone has a **perm,** their hair is curled and treated with chemicals to keep the curls for several months.

permanent

ADJECTIVE lasting forever or present all the time.

permission

NOUN If you have **permission** to do something, you are allowed to do it.

permit permits permitting permitted

Said "pur-**mit**" VERB **1** If someone or something **permits** you to do something, they allow it or make it possible: *we **permit** children to ride bicycles to school.*

Said "**pur**-mit" NOUN **2** an official document that says that you are allowed to do something.

Synonym: (sense 1) give permission

perpendicular

ADJECTIVE A line that is **perpendicular** to another one meets it at a right angle (90°).

perpetual

ADJECTIVE never ending.
perpetually ADVERB

perplexed

ADJECTIVE If you are **perplexed**, you are puzzled and do not know what to do.

Synonym: confused

persecute persecutes persecuting persecuted

VERB If someone **persecutes** another person, they continually treat them with cruelty and unfairness, often because of their religious beliefs.
persecution NOUN   **persecutor** NOUN

persevere perseveres persevering persevered

VERB If you **persevere**, you keep trying to do something and do not give up.
perseverance NOUN

persist persists persisting persisted

VERB **1** If something **persists**, it continues and will not stop. *The rain **persisted** all day.*
2 If you **persist** in doing something, you continue with it in spite of difficulties or opposition.

person people or persons

NOUN **1** a man, woman or child.
2 In grammar, the first **person** is the speaker (I), the second **person** is the person being spoken to (you), and the third **person** is anyone else being referred to (he, she, they).
PHRASE **3** If you do something **in person**, you do it yourself rather than letting someone else do it for you.
[from Latin **persona** meaning actor's mask]
✔ The usual plural of *person* is *people*. *Persons* is much less common, and is used only in formal or official English.

Synonyms: (sense 1) human being, individual

personal

ADJECTIVE **1** belonging or relating to a particular person.
2 Personal matters are personal things that you may not wish to discuss with other people. *I cannot tell you for **personal** reasons.*

Synonyms: (sense 1) individual, own

personality personalities

NOUN Your **personality** is your character and nature. *She's got a very lively **personality**.*

personally

ADVERB **1** in person. *He came to school to thank us **personally** for the money we raised for the charity.*
2 You use **personally** to express your own opinion of something. ***Personally**, I don't mind where we go.*

personnel

Said "per-son-**nell**" PLURAL NOUN the people who work for an organization.

perspective perspectives

NOUN **1** the impression of distance and depth in a picture or a drawing.
2 a particular way of thinking about something or looking at something. *What is your perspective on discipline?*

perspire perspires perspiring perspired

VERB When people **perspire**, they sweat.
perspiration NOUN

persuade persuades persuading persuaded

VERB If you **persuade** someone to do something, or **persuade** them that something is true, you make them to do it or believe it by giving them good reasons.
persuasion NOUN   **persuasive** ADJECTIVE

pessimism
NOUN the feeling that bad things will always happen.

pessimist pessimists
NOUN If you are a **pessimist**, you expect the worst to happen.
pessimistic ADJECTIVE   **pessimistically** ADVERB

Antonym: optimist

pest pests
NOUN **1** an insect or other small animal that damages plants or food supplies.
2 someone who keeps bothering or annoying you.

pester pesters pestering pestered
VERB If you **pester** someone, you keep bothering them or asking them to do something.

pesticide pesticides
NOUN a chemical sprayed on to plants to kill insects and grubs.

pet pets
NOUN **1** a tame animal kept at home.
2 a person who is treated as a favourite.

petal petals
NOUN one of the coloured outer parts of a flower that attract insects. Some **petals** are perfumed.

petition petitions
NOUN a written document, signed by a lot of people, requesting official action be taken on something.

petrified
ADJECTIVE If you are **petrified**, you are very frightened.

Synonym: terrified

petrol
NOUN a liquid that is used as a fuel for motor vehicles.

petty pettier pettiest
ADJECTIVE trivial and unimportant. *We should not argue over **petty** things.*

pew pews
NOUN a long wooden seat with a back, that people sit in church.

pH
NOUN The **pH** of a solution or of the soil is a measurement of how acid or alkaline it is. Substances with a **pH** above 7 are alkaline and substances with a **pH** below 7 are acid.

phantom phantoms
NOUN **1** a ghost.
ADJECTIVE **2** imagined or unreal.

pharmacy pharmacies
NOUN a shop where medicines are sold.

Synonym: chemists

phase phases
NOUN a particular stage in the development of something.

pheasant pheasants
NOUN a large, long-tailed game bird.

phenomenon phenomena
ADJECTIVE something that happens or exists, especially something extraordinary or remarkable. *The eclipse was a fascinating **phenomenon**.*
phenomenal ADJECTIVE   **phenomenally** ADVERB

philosophy philosophies
NOUN **1** the study or creation of ideas about humans, their relationship to the universe and beliefs.
2 a set of beliefs a person has.

phobia phobias
NOUN a deep fear or dislike of something.
phobic ADJECTIVE

phoenix phoenixes
*Said "**fee**-niks"* NOUN an imaginary bird that, according to myth, sets fire to itself every five hundred years, and rises from the ashes.

phone phones phoning phoned
NOUN OR VERB an abbreviation of *telephone*.

phoney phonier phoniest; also spelt **phony**
ADJECTIVE false, not genuine and meant to trick. *He had a **phoney** passport.*

Antonym: genuine

photo photos
NOUN an abbreviation of *photograph*.

photocopier photocopiers
NOUN a machine that makes instant copies of documents.

photocopy photocopies photocopying photocopied
VERB **1** If you **photocopy** a document you make a copy of it using a photocopier.
NOUN **2** a copy of a document made using a photocopier.

photograph photographs photographing photographed
NOUN **1** a picture taken with a camera and then printed on special paper.
VERB **2** If you **photograph** someone or something, you use a camera to take a picture of them.

photography
Said "fo-**tog**-raff-ee" NOUN the job or hobby of taking photographs.
photographer NOUN

photosynthesis
Said "fo-toh-**sin**-th-sis" NOUN the process by which green plants make their own food from carbon dioxide and water in the presence of sunlight.

phrase phrases
NOUN a short group of words or musical notes.

physical
ADJECTIVE concerning the body rather than the mind.
[from Greek *phusis* meaning nature]

physical education
NOUN physical exercise and sports that you do at school.

physics
NOUN the scientific study of the forces and properties of matter, such as heat, light, sound and electricity.

pianist pianists
NOUN someone who plays the piano.

piano pianos
NOUN a large musical instrument with a row of black and white keys. When the keys are pressed, little hammers hit wires to produce different notes.

piccolo piccolos
NOUN a high-pitched wind instrument like a small flute.

pick picks picking picked
VERB **1** If you **pick** someone or something, you choose them. *I picked Hannah for my partner.*
2 If you **pick** a flower or a fruit, you break it off from where it is growing.
3 If someone **picks** a lock, they open it with a piece of wire instead of a key.
pick on VERB **4** If you **pick on** someone, you treat them unkindly and unfairly.
pick up VERB **5** If you **pick up** someone or something, you lift them.
6 If you **pick up** someone or something from a place, you collect them from there.

picket pickets picketing picketed
VERB **1** When a group of people **picket** a place of work during a strike, they stand outside and try to persuade other workers not to go in to work.
NOUN **2** someone who is picketing a place.

pickle pickles
NOUN vegetables or fruit preserved in vinegar or salt water.

pickpocket pickpockets
NOUN a thief who steals things from pockets or bags.

picnic picnics
NOUN a meal eaten out of doors.

pictogram pictograms
NOUN a type of graph that uses small pictures to show information.

pictorial
ADJECTIVE relating to or using pictures.

picture pictures
NOUN a drawing, painting, photograph or television image of someone or something.

picturesque
ADJECTIVE A place that is **picturesque** is very attractive and unspoiled.
[from Italian *pittoresco* meaning in the style of a painter]

pie pies
NOUN a dish of meat, vegetables or fruit covered with pastry.

piece pieces

Said "**peess**" NOUN **1** a portion or part of something.

2 an individual thing of a particular kind. *This is a good piece of work.*

3 a coin: *a 50 pence piece.*

✔ another word that sounds like *piece* is *peace.*

pie chart pie charts

NOUN a circular diagram that is divided into segments to show how a quantity or an amount of something is shared.

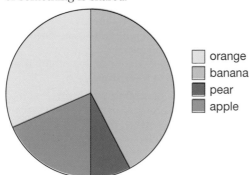

orange
banana
pear
apple

Fruit in the lunchboxes of Room 5

pier piers

NOUN a large structure at the seaside, with a platform built from the shore out into the sea, that people can walk along.

pierce pierces piercing pierced

VERB If a sharp object **pierces** something, it goes through it, making a hole.

piercing

ADJECTIVE **1** a **piercing** sound is high pitched and sharp, and it hurts your ears.

2 Someone with **piercing** eyes seems to stare at you intensely.

Synonym: (sense 1) shrill

pig pigs

NOUN a farm animal with pink or black skin, a curly tail and a snout, that is kept for its meat. Pork, ham and bacon all come from **pigs**.

pigeon pigeons

NOUN a grey bird with a small head and large chest, often found in towns and cities.

piglet piglets

NOUN a young pig.

pigsty pigsties

NOUN **1** a small shelter with an enclosed area where pigs are kept.

2 If you say a place is like a **pigsty**, you mean that it is very dirty and untidy.

pigtail pigtails

NOUN a plait of hair. *She wore her hair in pigtails.*

pike pikes

NOUN **1** a large freshwater fish with strong, sharp teeth.

2 a weapon used in medieval times. A **pike** was a long pole with a spike on the end.

pile piles piling piled

NOUN **1** a quantity of things lying on top of one another.

VERB **2** If you **pile** things somewhere, you put them on top of one another.

pilgrim pilgrims

NOUN a person who goes on a journey to a holy place for religious reasons.

pilgrimage pilgrimages

NOUN a journey to a holy place, for religious reasons.

pill pills

NOUN a small, round tablet of medicine that you swallow.

pillar pillars

NOUN a tall, solid structure like a large post, often made of stone and usually supporting part of a building.

pillow pillows

NOUN a large cushion that you rest your head on when you are in bed.

pilot pilots

NOUN **1** a person who is trained to fly an aircraft.

2 the person who guides a ship into port.

pimple pimples

NOUN a small spot on the skin.

pimply ADJECTIVE

pin pins pinning pinned

NOUN **1** a thin, pointed piece of metal, used to fasten things like paper or cloth together.

VERB **2** If you **pin** something, you attach it with a pin.

pincers
PLURAL NOUN **1** The **pincers** of a crab or a lobster are its large front claws.
2 a tool consisting of two pieces of metal hinged in the middle, used for gripping and pulling things.

pinch pinches pinching pinched
VERB **1** If you **pinch** something, you squeeze it between your thumb and first finger.
2 INFORMAL If someone **pinches** something, they steal it.
NOUN **3** A **pinch** of something is the amount that you can hold between your thumb and first finger. *Add a **pinch** of salt to the soup.*

pine pines pining pined
NOUN **1** an evergreen tree with very thin leaves called needles.
VERB **2** If you **pine** for something or someone, you feel sad because they are not there.

pineapple pineapples
NOUN a large, oval tropical fruit with sweet, yellow flesh and thick, woody skin.

pink pinker pinkest
ADJECTIVE pale reddish-white.

pint pints
NOUN a unit of measurement for liquids equal to about 0·568 litres.

pioneer pioneers
NOUN one of the first people to go to a place or to do something new.

pip pips
NOUN **1** the hard seeds in a fruit.
2 a short, high-pitched sound.

pipe pipes piping piped
NOUN **1** a long, hollow tube through which liquid or gas can flow.
2 an object that is used for smoking tobacco, consisting of a small hollow bowl attached to a thin tube.
3 a musical instrument.
VERB **4** If liquid or gas is **piped** somewhere, it is transferred there through a pipe.

pipeline pipelines
NOUN **1** a large underground pipe that carries oil or gas over a long distance.
PHRASE **2** If something is **in the pipeline**, it is already planned or has begun.

pirate pirates
NOUN a sailor who attacks and robs other ships.

pistol pistols
NOUN a small gun held in the hand.

pit pits
NOUN **1** a large hole in the ground.
2 a coal mine.

pitch pitches pitching pitched
NOUN **1** an area of ground marked out for playing a game such as football or cricket.
2 The **pitch** of a sound is how high or low it is.
3 a black substance painted on to roofs and boat bottoms to make them waterproof.
VERB **4** If you **pitch** something somewhere, you throw it there with a lot of force.
5 If you **pitch** a tent, you put it up.

pitcher pitchers
NOUN a large jug.

pitchfork pitchforks
NOUN a long-handled fork with two large prongs, used for lifting and moving hay.

pitfall pitfalls
NOUN one of the difficulties or dangers of a situation.

pitta pittas
NOUN a flat disc of bread with a hollow inside, that can be filled with food.
[from Greek, meaning a cake]

pity pities pitying pitied
VERB **1** If you **pity** someone, you feel sorry for them.
NOUN **2** a feeling of sadness and concern for someone.
3 If you say that something is a **pity**, you mean it is disappointing. *It's a **pity** we couldn't play tennis.*

pivot pivots pivoting pivoted
VERB **1** If something **pivots**, it balances or turns on a central point.
NOUN **2** the central point on which something balances or turns.
pivotal ADJECTIVE

pizza pizzas
Said "**peet**-sa" NOUN a flat piece of dough usually covered with cheese, tomato and other savoury food and baked in an oven.
[an Italian word]

placard placards
NOUN a large notice carried at a demonstration or displayed in a public place. *The man carried a **placard** advertising the furniture sale.*

place places placing placed
NOUN **1** a particular point, position, building, or area. *They found a good **place** to camp.*
2 a particular position in a race, competition, or series. *Last year she finished in third **place**.*
3 If you have a **place** in a team or on a course, you are allowed to join the team or course. *I eventually got a **place** at the new school.*
VERB **4** If you **place** something somewhere, you put it there. *She **placed** her hand gently on my shoulder.*
PHRASE **5** When something **takes place**, it happens. *The competition will **take place** next month.*

placid
ADJECTIVE calm and not easily excited or upset.
placidly ADVERB

Synonyms: even-tempered, unexcitable

plague plagues plaguing plagued
Said "**playg**" NOUN **1** a very infectious disease that kills large numbers of people.
2 A **plague** of unpleasant things is a large number of them occurring at the same time.
VERB **3** If you **plague** someone, you keep pestering them.
4 If problems **plague** you, they keep causing you trouble.

plaice
NOUN an edible European flat fish.

plaid plaids
Said "**plad**" NOUN woven material with a tartan design.

plain plainer plainest; plains
ADJECTIVE **1** very simple in style, with no pattern or decoration.
2 obvious or easy to understand.
NOUN **3** a large, flat area of land with very few trees.
✔ Another word that sounds like *plain* is *plane*.

plait plaits plaiting plaited
Said "**plat**" VERB **1** If you **plait** hair or rope, you twist three lengths together in turn to make one thick length.

NOUN **2** a length of hair that has been plaited.

plan plans planning planned
NOUN **1** a method of achieving something that has been worked out beforehand.
VERB **2** If you **plan** something, you decide in detail what you are going to do.
3 If you **plan** to do something, you intend to do it.

plane planes
NOUN **1** an abbreviation of *aeroplane*.
2 a tool for smoothing wood.
ADJECTIVE **3** A **plane** shape has a flat, level surface. A **plane** mirror is flat and not curved.
✔ Another word that sounds like *plane* is *plain*.

planet planets
NOUN a large sphere in space that orbits a sun. The earth and Mars are both **planets** that revolve around our sun.

plank planks
NOUN a long rectangular piece of wood.

plankton
NOUN a layer of tiny plants and animals that live just below the surface of a sea or lake.

plant plants planting planted
NOUN **1** a living thing that grows in the earth and has a stem, leaves, and roots. *See page 434.*
VERB **2** If you **plant** things such as flowers or trees, you put them in the ground so that they will grow.

plantation plantations

NOUN **1** a large area of land where crops such as tea, cotton or sugar are grown.
2 a large number of trees planted together.

plaque plaques

Said "**plak**" NOUN **1** a flat piece of metal or porcelain, fixed to a wall, with an inscription on it in memory of a famous person or event.
2 a substance that forms around your teeth. It is made up of bacteria, saliva and food.

plaster plasters

NOUN **1** a paste made of sand, lime and water, that is used to form a smooth surface for inside walls and ceilings.
2 a strip of sticky material with a small pad, used for covering cuts on your body.
3 Plaster of Paris is a white powder mixed with water, that becomes hard when it dries. It is used for making moulds and for holding broken bones in place while they heal.
plasterer NOUN

plastic plastics

NOUN **1** a light synthetic material made from oil by a chemical process. **Plastics** can be moulded into different shapes for many different uses.
ADJECTIVE **2** made of plastic.

Plasticine

NOUN; TRADEMARK a soft, coloured material like clay, used for making models.

plate plates

NOUN **1** a flat dish used to hold food.
2 a flat piece of hard material such as glass or metal.

plateau plateaus or plateaux

NOUN a large area of high and fairly flat land.
[from Old French *platel* meaning a flat piece of metal]

platform platforms

NOUN **1** a raised structure on which someone or something can stand.
2 the raised area in a railway station where passengers get on and off trains.

platinum

NOUN a valuable silver-coloured metal.

platypus platypuses

NOUN an Australian mammal that lives in rivers. It has brown fur, webbed feet, and a beak like a duck.
[from Greek *platus* meaning flat and *pous* meaning foot]

play plays playing played

VERB **1** When children **play**, they take part in games or use toys for fun.
2 When you **play** a sport or game, you take part in it.
3 If an actor **plays** a character in a play or film, they perform that role.
4 If you **play** a musical instrument, you produce music from it.
5 If you **play** a CD or tape, you listen to it.
NOUN **6 Play** is the activity of playing a game or sport.
7 a story acted out in the theatre, on the radio or on television.

playground playgrounds

NOUN a special area for children to play in.

playgroup playgroups

NOUN an informal group of very young children who play together, supervised by adults.

playscript playscripts

NOUN the written version of a play. *See* **script**.

playtime playtimes

NOUN the time in a school day when children go out to play.

playwright playwrights

NOUN a person who writes plays.

plea pleas

Said "**plee**" NOUN **1** If you make a **plea**, you make an urgent request or an appeal for something.
2 In a law court, a **plea** is someone's statement that they are guilty or not guilty.

plead pleads pleading pleaded

VERB **1** If you **plead** with someone, you beg them for something. *She came to* **plead** *for help.*
2 In a law court, when a person **pleads** guilty or not guilty, they state that they are guilty or not guilty.

pleasant
ADJECTIVE nice, pleasing, enjoyable or attractive in some way.

please pleases pleasing pleased
1 You say **please** when you are asking someone politely to do something. *Can you help me, please?*
VERB **2** If something **pleases** you, it makes you feel happy and satisfied.

pleasure pleasures
NOUN a feeling of happiness, satisfaction or enjoyment.

pleat pleats
NOUN a permanent fold in fabric, made by folding one part over another.

pledge pledges pledging pledged
NOUN **1** a solemn promise.
VERB **2** If you **pledge** something, you promise that you will do it or give it.

plenty
NOUN OR PRONOUN If you have **plenty** of something, you have more than enough for your needs. *We've got **plenty** of time.*

pliable
ADJECTIVE If something is **pliable,** you can bend it without breaking it. *This **pliable** material will be easier to work with.*

Synonym: flexible

pliers
PLURAL NOUN a small tool with metal jaws for gripping small objects such as nails and bending wire.

plight plights
NOUN a difficult or dangerous situation: *the **plight** of the homeless.*

plod plods plodding plodded
VERB If you **plod**, you walk slowly and heavily. *We **plodded** home through the mud.*

plop plops plopping plopped
NOUN **1** a gentle sound of something lightweight dropping into a liquid.
VERB **2** If something **plops** into a liquid, it drops into it with a gentle sound.

plot plots plotting plotted
NOUN **1** a secret plan made by a group of people.
2 The **plot** of a film, novel or play is the story.
VERB **3** If people **plot** to do something, they plan it secretly.

plough ploughs ploughing ploughed
NOUN **1** a large farming tool that is pulled across a field to turn the soil over before planting seeds.
VERB **2** When farmers **plough** land, they use a plough to turn over the soil.

pluck plucks plucking plucked
VERB **1** If you **pluck** a fruit or flower, you remove it with a sharp pull.
2 If you **pluck** a dead bird, such as a chicken or a turkey, you pull the feathers off it before cooking it.
3 When you **pluck** a stringed instrument, you pull the strings and let them go.

plug plugs plugging plugged
NOUN **1** a device that connects a piece of electrical equipment to an electric socket.
2 a thick circular piece of rubber or plastic that you use to block the hole in a sink or bath.
plug in VERB **3** If you **plug in** a piece of electrical equipment, you push its plug into an electric socket.

plum plums
NOUN a small fruit with a smooth red or yellow skin and a stone in the middle.

plumage
NOUN a bird's feathers.

plumber plumbers
NOUN a person who connects and repairs water pipes.

plump plumper plumpest
ADJECTIVE rounded, or slightly fat.

plunge plunges plunging plunged
VERB If you **plunge** somewhere, especially into water, you fall or rush there.

Synonyms: dive, drop, fall

plural plurals
NOUN the form of a word that is used when referring to more than one person or thing. *The usual **plural** of person is people.*

plus

PREPOSITION **1** You use **plus** to show that one number is being added to another. *Two **plus** two equals four.*
2 You can use **plus** when you mention an additional item. *She gave us our coats, **plus** a blanket.*

plywood

NOUN wooden board made from several thin sheets of wood glued together under pressure.

p.m.

ADJECTIVE used to show times between 12 noon and 12 midnight. *I go to bed at 8 **p.m.** on schooldays and 9 **p.m.** at weekends.* [from Latin ***post meridiem*** meaning after noon]

pneumatic

ADJECTIVE operated by or filled with compressed air: *a **pneumatic** drill.*

pneumonia

NOUN a serious disease that affects a person's lungs and makes breathing difficult.

poach poaches poaching poached

VERB **1** If someone **poaches** animals, they hunt them illegally on someone else's land.
2 When you **poach** food, especially fish, or an egg taken out of its shell, you cook it gently in hot liquid.
poacher NOUN

pocket pockets

NOUN a small pouch for keeping things in, that forms part of a piece of clothing.

pocket money

NOUN an amount of money given regularly to children by their parents.

pod pods

NOUN a long, narrow seed container that grows on plants such as peas or beans.

poem poems

NOUN a piece of writing, usually arranged in short rhythmic lines, with words chosen for their sound or impact.

poet poets

NOUN a person who writes poems.

poetry

NOUN poems, considered a form of literature.

point points pointing pointed

VERB **1** If you **point** at or to something, you hold out your finger towards it to show where it is.
NOUN **2** the thin, sharp end of something such as a needle or knife.
3 a particular place or time. *At some **point** during the night, the storm began.*
4 a single mark in a competition. *They won by 21 **points** to 18.*
5 the purpose or the most important part of something. *What do you think is the **point** of this exercise?*
6 an opinion or fact expressed by someone. *That's a very good **point**.*
7 In mathematics, the decimal **point** in a number is marked by a dot: $5 \cdot 2$.
8 one of the 32 marks on the circumference of a compass to show direction.

pointed

ADJECTIVE A **pointed** object has a thin, sharp end.

pointless

ADJECTIVE Something that is **pointless** has no purpose.

point of view points of view

NOUN Your **point of view** is your opinion about something or your attitude towards it.

poised

ADJECTIVE If you are **poised** to do something, you are ready to do it at any moment.

poison poisons poisoning poisoned

NOUN **1** a substance that harms or kills you if you swallow it or absorb it.
VERB **2** to **poison** someone means to harm them by giving them poison.

poke pokes poking poked

VERB **1** If you **poke** someone or something, you give them a push with your finger or a sharp object.
poke out VERB **2** If something **pokes out** from behind or from underneath another thing, it shows. *The label **poked out** from the back of his anorak.*

polar

ADJECTIVE relating to the area around the North Pole or the South Pole: *the **polar** regions.*

polar bear polar bears

NOUN a large white bear that lives in the area around the North Pole.

pole poles

NOUN **1** a long, slender, rounded piece of wood or metal.

2 The earth has two **poles** at the opposite ends of its imaginary axis: the North and South **Pole**.

pole vault

NOUN an athletics event in which contestants jump over a high bar using a long, flexible pole to lift themselves into the air.

police

PLURAL NOUN the official organization responsible for making sure that people obey the law.

police officer police officers

NOUN a member of the police force.

policy policies

NOUN a set of plans and ideas, especially in politics or business. *What is their **policy** on education?*

polish polishes polishing polished

NOUN **1** a substance that you put on an object to clean it and make it shine.

VERB **2** If you **polish** something, you put polish on it or rub it with a cloth to make it shine.

polite

ADJECTIVE Someone who is **polite** has good manners and is not rude to other people.

Synonym: courteous

political

ADJECTIVE to do with politics and politicians.

politician politicians

NOUN a person who is involved in the government of a country.

politics

NOUN the activity of governing a country.

poll polls

NOUN a survey in which people are asked their opinions about something.

pollen

NOUN a fine yellow or orange powder produced by the male part of a flowering plant.

pollinate pollinates pollinating pollinated

VERB A plant is **pollinated** when pollen from the male part of another plant lands on its female part. This leads to fertilization and the formation of seeds.

pollination

NOUN the process by which plants are fertilized with pollen.

pollute pollutes polluting polluted

VERB If water, air or land is **polluted**, it is dirty and dangerous to use or live in.

polo

NOUN a game played between two teams of players on horseback. The players use wooden hammers with long handles to hit a ball.

poltergeist poltergeists

NOUN a noisy, mischievous ghost that moves or throws things around in a house.

poly-

PREFIX added to some words to mean many, for example **poly**gons and **poly**hedrons are many-sided shapes.

polyester

NOUN a man-made fibre, especially used to make clothes.

polygon polygons

NOUN any two-dimensional shape whose sides are all straight.

polyhedron polyhedra

NOUN a solid shape with many faces.

polystyrene

NOUN a very light plastic, especially used as insulating material or to make containers.

polythene

NOUN a type of plastic that is used to make thin sheets or bags.

pompous

ADJECTIVE Someone who is **pompous** behaves in a way that is too serious and self-important. **pomposity** NOUN

pond ponds

NOUN a small area of water enclosed by land.

ponder ponders pondering pondered

VERB If you **ponder**, you think carefully and seriously about something.

pony ponies
NOUN a small horse.

ponytail ponytails
NOUN a hairstyle in which long hair is scooped up and tied at the back of the head so that it hangs down like a tail.

pool pools
NOUN **1** a small area of still water, such as a pond or a puddle.
2 an abbreviation of *swimming pool*.

poor poorer poorest
ADJECTIVE **1** having very little money.
2 of a low quality or standard.

poorly
ADJECTIVE **1** If you are **poorly**, you feel ill.
ADVERB **2** If something is done **poorly**, it is not done well.

pop pops popping popped
NOUN **1** modern music, played and enjoyed especially by young people.
2 a short, sharp, explosive sound.
3 a fizzy, non-alcoholic drink.
VERB **4** If you **pop** somewhere, you go there quickly for a short while. *I will **pop** in to see you before tea.*

popcorn
NOUN a snack food made from grains of maize that are heated until they puff up and burst.

Pope Popes
NOUN the head of the Roman Catholic Church.

poplar poplars
NOUN a type of tall, slender tree.

poppadom poppadoms
NOUN thin, round, crisp bread, fried or roasted and served with Indian food.
[from Tamil ***pappadam*** meaning lentil cake]

poppy poppies
NOUN a plant with a large red flower on a hairy stem, that often grows in cornfields and meadows.

popular
ADJECTIVE liked or approved of by a lot of people.

populated
ADJECTIVE If a place is **populated**, people or animals live there.

population populations
NOUN **1** the people who live in a place.
2 the number of people living in a place.

porch porches
NOUN a covered area at the entrance to a building.

porcupine porcupines
NOUN a large rodent with long spines covering its body.
[from Old French ***porc d'espins*** meaning pig with spines]

pore pores poring pored
NOUN **1** The **pores** in your skin or on the surface of a plant are very small holes that allow moisture to pass through.
VERB **2** If you **pore** over a piece of writing or a diagram, you study it carefully.

pork
NOUN meat from a pig.

porous
ADJECTIVE If something is **porous**, it lets water through.

porpoise porpoises
NOUN a sea mammal related to the dolphin.
[from Latin ***porcus*** meaning pig and ***piscis*** meaning fish]

porridge
NOUN a thick, sticky food made from oats cooked in water or milk.

port ports
NOUN **1** a town or area that has a harbour or docks.
ADJECTIVE **2** The **port** side of a ship is the left side when you are facing the front.

portable
ADJECTIVE designed to be easily carried.

portcullis portcullises
NOUN a large gate made of strong bars, that can be lowered to defend a castle or a fort.

porter

A B C D E F G H I J K L M N O P Q R S T U V W X Y Z

porter porters
NOUN a person employed to carry luggage and other goods at a railway station or in a hotel.

porthole portholes
NOUN a small window in the side of a ship or aircraft.

portion portions
NOUN **1** a part of something.
2 an amount of food sufficient for one person.

Synonyms: (sense 1) bit, piece

portrait portraits
NOUN a picture or photograph of someone, often of only their head and shoulders.

pose poses posing posed
NOUN **1** a way of standing, sitting or lying for a photograph to be taken, or a drawing or painting to be made of you. *Try to hold this pose while the others draw it.*
VERB **2** If you **pose** for a photograph or painting, you stay in a particular position so that someone can photograph or paint you.
3 If you **pose** as someone or something, you pretend to be someone or something you are not.
4 If something **poses** a problem or danger, it causes it. *This polluted water could pose a threat to their health.*

position positions positioning positioned
NOUN **1** When someone or something is in a particular **position**, they are sitting or lying in that way. *I raised myself to a sitting position.*
2 The **position** that you are in is the situation that you are in. *Your request puts me in a difficult position.*
PHRASE **3** If you are **in position** at the beginning of a race, you are ready to start.
VERB **4** If you **position** something, you put it in place.

positive
ADJECTIVE **1** If something is **positive**, it is certain.
2 If someone is **positive**, they are confident and hopeful.

possession possessions
NOUN a thing that you own, or that you have with you.

possessive
ADJECTIVE **1** A **possessive** person wants to keep things for themselves.
NOUN **2** In grammar, the **possessive** is the form of a noun or pronoun used to show possession, for example, "my", "his", "theirs", "Harry's".

possible
ADJECTIVE If something is **possible**, it can be done or can happen.
possibility NOUN

possum possums
NOUN a nocturnal marsupial with thick fur and a long tail that lives in trees.

post posts posting posted
NOUN **1** the system by which letters and parcels are collected and delivered.
2 letters and parcels that are delivered to you.
3 an upright pole fixed into the ground.
VERB **4** If you **post** a letter, you send it to someone through the post.

postage
NOUN the money that you pay to send letters and parcels by post. *You will need to send extra money for postage and packing.*

post box post boxes
NOUN a box into which you put letters that are to be sent by post.

postcard postcards
NOUN a card, often with a picture on one side, that you write on and send to someone without an envelope.

postcode postcodes
NOUN a short sequence of letters and numbers at the end of an address.

poster posters
NOUN a large notice, picture or advertisement that you stick on a wall.

postman or **postwoman**
NOUN someone who collects and delivers parcels and letters.

post office post offices

NOUN a building where you can buy stamps and post letters and parcels.

postpone postpones postponing postponed

VERB If you **postpone** an event, you arrange for it to take place at a later time than was originally planned.

potato potatoes

NOUN a round, white, root vegetable that has a brown or red skin and grows beneath the ground.

potential

ADJECTIVE **1** capable of happening or of becoming a particular kind of person or thing. *He's a potential world champion.*
NOUN **2** If someone or something has **potential**, they are capable of being successful or useful in the future.

pothole potholes

NOUN **1** a hole in the surface of a road caused by bad weather or traffic.
2 a deep, natural hole in the ground that often leads to an underground cavern.

potion potions

NOUN a drink containing medicine, poison or supposed magical powers.
[from Latin *potio* meaning a drink]

potter potters pottering pottered

NOUN **1** a person who makes pottery.
VERB **2** If you **potter** about, you pass the time doing pleasant, unimportant things.

pottery potteries

NOUN **1** pots, dishes and other items made from clay and fired in a kiln.
2 the craft of making pottery. *Mum made a lovely bowl in her pottery class.*

pouch pouches

NOUN **1** a small, soft container with a fold-over top, like a bag or a pocket.
2 a pocket of skin in which marsupials carry their young.

poultry

NOUN chicken, turkeys and other birds that are kept for their meat or eggs.

pounce pounces pouncing pounced

VERB If a person or other animal **pounces** on something, they jump on it suddenly.

pound pounds pounding pounded

NOUN **1** the main unit of currency in Britain.
2 a unit of weight equal to 16 ounces, or about 0·454 kilograms.
VERB **3** If you **pound** something, or **pound** on it, you hit it repeatedly or crush it.
4 If your heart **pounds**, it beats very fast and strongly.
5 If you **pound** somewhere, you run there with loud, heavy footsteps.

pour pours pouring poured

VERB **1** If you **pour** liquid out of a container, you tip the container until the liquid flows out.
2 If something **pours** somewhere, it flows there quickly and in large quantities.
3 If it is **pouring** with rain, it is raining very heavily.

pout pouts pouting pouted

VERB If you **pout**, you stick out your lips, or your bottom lip, because you are cross or annoyed.

poverty

NOUN the state of being very poor.

powder powders

NOUN many tiny particles of a solid, dry substance, such as flour.

power powers

NOUN **1** control over people and events.
2 physical strength.
3 the rate at which energy is changed from one form to another, such as electrical energy changed into light or heat.

powerful

ADJECTIVE **Powerful** people or organizations have a great deal of power or influence.
powerfully ADVERB

powerless

ADJECTIVE If you are **powerless,** you are unable to control or influence events.
powerlessly ADVERB

power station power stations

NOUN a building where electricity is produced.

practical

ADJECTIVE **1** Someone who is **practical** is efficient and sensible, and good at getting things done.
2 Something that is **practical** is sensible and useful.
3 involving real situations and doing things, rather than ideas or theories. *We will do some* ***practical*** *experiments in Science today.*
[from Greek ***praktikos*** meaning concerned with action]

practical joke practical jokes

NOUN a trick you play on someone.

practice practices

NOUN **1** regular training or exercise that you do to improve your skill at something.
2 A doctor's or lawyer's **practice** is their business.
✔ The noun *practice* ends in *ice*.

practise practises practising practised

VERB **1** If you **practise** something, you do it regularly in order to do it better. *She* ***practises*** *every day on the piano.*
2 When people **practise** a religion, custom or craft, they regularly take part in the activities associated with it: *a custom still* ***practised*** *in some areas.*
3 If you **practise** medicine or law, you work as a doctor or lawyer.
✔ The verb *practise* ends in *ise*.

prairie prairies

NOUN a large area of flat, grassy land in North America.

praise praises praising praised

VERB **1** If you **praise** someone or something, you say good things about them, or tell them they have done well.
NOUN **2** what you say or write when you praise someone or something.

pram prams

NOUN a small carriage, like a baby's cot on wheels, for pushing a baby around in.

prank pranks

NOUN a childish trick.

prawn prawns

NOUN a small, edible shellfish with a long tail.

pray prays praying prayed

VERB When someone **prays**, they speak to God, to give thanks or to ask for help.

prayer prayers

NOUN the activity of praying or the words said when someone prays.

pre-

PREFIX added to some words to mean before a particular time or event, for example **pre**school, **pre**war, **pre**history.

preach preaches preaching preached

VERB When someone **preaches**, they give a short talk on a religious or moral subject.
preacher NOUN

precarious

ADJECTIVE **1** Someone or something in a **precarious** position is not very safe or secure, and they may fall or fail at any time. *Her position was* ***precarious*** *because she needed only one point to win.*
2 Something that is **precarious** is likely to fall because it is not well balanced or secured.
precariously ADVERB

precaution precautions

NOUN an action that is intended to prevent something unwanted or unpleasant from happening.

precede precedes preceding preceded

VERB **1** If one event **precedes** another, it happens before it. *A short film* ***preceded*** *the talk about elephants.*
2 If you **precede** someone, you go in front of them.

precinct precincts

NOUN a pedestrian shopping area.

precious

ADJECTIVE Something that is **precious** is valuable or important and should be looked after or used carefully.
[from Latin ***pretiosus*** meaning valuable]

precipice precipices

NOUN a very steep rock face or sheer cliff.

precise

ADJECTIVE very accurate. *We will never know the* ***precise*** *details of what happened.*

Synonym: exact

predator predators

NOUN an animal that kills and eats other animals.

predatory ADJECTIVE

predecessor predecessors

NOUN Someone's **predecessor** is the person who used to do their job before them.

predicament predicaments

NOUN a difficult or awkward situation.

predict predicts predicting predicted

VERB If you **predict** something, you say what you think will happen in the future.

preen preens preening preened

VERB When a bird **preens**, it cleans and tidies its feathers using its beak.

preface prefaces

NOUN an introduction at the beginning of a book, explaining what it is about or why it was written.

prefect prefects

NOUN a pupil who has special duties at a school. [from Latin *praefectus* meaning someone put in charge]

prefer prefers preferring preferred

VERB If you **prefer** one thing to another, you like it better than the other thing.

preferable

ADJECTIVE Something that is **preferable** to something else, is more suitable or you like it better than the other thing. *We thought that going to the cinema was* **preferable** *to watching TV.*

prefix prefixes

NOUN a letter or group of letters added to the beginning of a word to make a new word, for example *dis-*, *pre-*, and *un-*.

pregnant

ADJECTIVE A woman or other female animal who is **pregnant** has a baby developing in their womb.

prehistoric

ADJECTIVE existing at a time in the past before anything was written down.

prejudice prejudices

NOUN an unreasonable and unfair dislike of or preference for a particular person or thing.

prejudiced ADJECTIVE

preliminary

ADJECTIVE **Preliminary** activities take place before something starts and in preparation for it. *They lost in the* **preliminary** *rounds of the competition.*

prelude preludes

NOUN **1** something that happens before an event and prepares you for it.

2 a short piece of music.

premature

ADJECTIVE happening too early, or earlier than expected. *The* **premature** *baby had to spend time in hospital to gain weight.*

prematurely ADVERB

premier premiers

Said "**prem**-mee-uh" NOUN **1** The leader of a government is sometimes referred to as the **premier**.

2 In Australia, the leader of a State government is called the **Premier**.

ADJECTIVE **3** considered to be the best or most important: *the* **premier** *department store.* [from Latin *primarius* meaning principal]

premiere premieres

Said "**prem**-mee-er" NOUN the first public performance of a new play or film. *The* **premiere** *of the new film is in London next week.* [from French *premier* meaning first]

premises

Said "**prem**-is-iz" PLURAL NOUN buildings and land belonging to an organization.

premium premiums

Said "**pree**-mee-um" NOUN **1** an extra sum of money that has to be paid for something.

2 money paid regularly to an insurance company.

premonition premonitions

NOUN a feeling that something unpleasant is going to happen.

preoccupied

ADJECTIVE If you are **preoccupied**, you are deep in thought or totally involved with something, and you do not notice anything else. *It is difficult to talk to him as he seems so* **preoccupied**.

a b c d e f g h i j k l m n o p q r s t u v w x y z

preparation preparations

NOUN **1 Preparation** is the act of getting things ready.

2 Preparations are all the things you do and the arrangements you make before an event can happen. *We started making preparations for the party by buying some decorations.*

prepare prepares preparing prepared

VERB If you **prepare** something, or **prepare** for something, you get it ready or get ready for it.

preposition prepositions

NOUN a word that is used before a noun or pronoun to show how it is connected to other words. For example, in the sentence "I put the book on the table", the word "on" is the **preposition**. *See pages 438–9.*

Some other prepositions are:

about	around	beside	in	through
above	at	between	like	towards
across	before	beyond	near	under
after	behind	by	off	until
against	below	except	over	up
along	beneath	from	since	with

prescribe prescribes prescribing prescribed

VERB If a doctor **prescribes** a medicine for a patient, he or she tells the patient what medicine they need and gives them a prescription.

prescription prescriptions

NOUN a written instruction from a doctor to a chemist, to provide a person with a particular medicine.

presence

NOUN the **presence** of a person in a place is the fact that they are there.

present presents presenting presented

Said "**prez**-ent" ADJECTIVE **1** If someone is **present** at a place or an event, they are there.
2 happening now.
NOUN **3** the period of time that is taking place now.

4 something that you give to someone for them to keep, especially on their birthday or at Christmas, or on some other special occasion *Said* "pri-**zent**" VERB **5** If you **present** someone with something, or if you **present** it to them, you formally give it to them.

Synonyms: (sense 2) contemporary, current
(sense 4) gift

---

presentation presentations

NOUN **1** a talk or a lecture showing or describing something.
2 a ceremony where awards or prizes are given.
3 The **presentation** of something is the way it looks. *My teacher was pleased with the presentation of my project.*

presently

ADVERB If something will happen **presently**, it will happen soon. *I'll finish the job presently.*

preservative preservatives

NOUN a substance or a chemical that stops things such as food from going bad.

preserve preserves preserving preserved

VERB If you **preserve** something, you make sure that it stays as it is and does not change or end.

president presidents

NOUN The **president** of a country that has no king or queen is the leader of the country: *the President of the United States.*

press presses pressing pressed

VERB **1** If you **press** something, you push it or hold it firmly against something else.
2 If you **press** clothes, you iron them.
3 If you **press** someone to do something, you try to make them do it.
NOUN **4** a machine for printing.
5 The **press** is a term used for all the newspapers and the journalists who work for them.

pressure pressures

NOUN **1** the amount of force that is pushing on a particular area.
2 If there is **pressure** on you to do something, someone is trying to persuade or force you do it.

presume presumes presuming presumed

VERB If you **presume** something, you think that it is probably true without knowing for certain. **presumption** NOUN

Synonyms: believe, suppose

pretend pretends pretending pretended

VERB If you **pretend** that something is the case, you try to make people believe that it is true when it is not.

pretty prettier prettiest

ADJECTIVE **1** attractive and pleasant.
ADVERB **2** INFORMAL quite or rather. *He spoke pretty good English.*

prevent prevents preventing prevented

VERB If you **prevent** something, you stop it happening.

preview previews

NOUN a showing of something like a film, play or exhibition before it is shown to the general public.

previous

ADJECTIVE A **previous** time or thing is one that occurred before the present one. *I'm happier in this class than I was in the previous one.*
previously ADVERB

prey preys preying preyed

NOUN **1** an animal that is hunted and eaten by another animal.
VERB **2** An animal that **preys** on another animal lives by hunting and eating it.

price prices

NOUN the amount of money that you pay to buy something. *The price of bread has increased significantly.*

priceless

ADJECTIVE Something that is **priceless** is so valuable that it is difficult to work out how much it is worth.

prick pricks pricking pricked

VERB If you **prick** something, you stick a sharp object into it.

prickle prickles prickling prickled

NOUN **1** a small sharp point or thorn growing on a plant.
VERB **2** If your skin **prickles**, it feels as if a lot of sharp points are being stuck into it.
prickly ADJECTIVE

pride prides

NOUN **1** a feeling of satisfaction and pleasure you have when you, or people close to you, have done something well.
2 a feeling of dignity and self-respect.
3 a group of lions that live together.

priest priests

NOUN **1** a member of the clergy in some Christian Churches.
2 someone who performs religious ceremonies in non-Christian religions.

prim primmer primmest

ADJECTIVE Someone who is **prim** always behaves very correctly and is easily shocked by anything rude.

primary

ADJECTIVE extremely important or most important.

primary colour primary colours

NOUN The **primary colours** are red, yellow and blue. From these all the other colours can be made.

primary school primary schools

NOUN a school for children between the ages of 5 and 11.

prime

ADJECTIVE **1** main or most important.
2 of the best quality.
[from Latin *primus* meaning first]

prime minister prime ministers

NOUN the leader of the government.

primitive

ADJECTIVE **1** connected with a society in which people live very simply.
2 very simple, basic or old-fashioned. *Their accommodation was primitive, but they still enjoyed their trip.*

primrose primroses

NOUN a small plant that has pale yellow flowers in spring.
[from Latin *prima rosa* meaning first rose]

prince princes

NOUN a male member of a royal family, especially the son of a king or queen.

princess princesses

NOUN a female member of a royal family, especially the daughter of a king or queen, or the wife of a prince.

principal principals

ADJECTIVE **1** main or most important. *He had the **principal** role in the play.*
NOUN **2** the person in charge of a school or college.
✔ Do not confuse *principal* with *principle*.

principle principles

NOUN **1** a general rule or law about how something works.
2 a belief that you have about the way you should behave. *I try to help others as a matter of **principle**.*
✔ Do not confuse *principle* with *principal*.

print prints printing printed

VERB **1** When words or pictures are **printed**, they are put on to paper in large numbers by a printing machine, for example to make books or newspapers.
2 If you **print** your name, or some other writing, you write letters that are not joined up.
NOUN **3** The letters and numbers on the pages of a book or newspaper are referred to as the **print**. *The columns of tiny **print** were difficult to read.*

printer printers

NOUN **1** a person who prints books and newspapers.
2 a machine that prints the data from a computer on to paper.

print-out print-outs

NOUN a printed copy of information from a computer.

priority priorities

NOUN something that needs to be dealt with first because it is more urgent or important than others. *He needed to make his homework a **priority**.*

prism prisms

NOUN **1** In maths, a **prism** is any three-dimensional shape that has the same size and shape of face at each end. A **prism** is the same size and shape along its length.

2 a solid piece of clear glass or plastic with flat sides, that can be used to separate light passing through it into the colours of the rainbow.

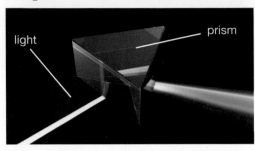

prison prisons

NOUN a building where people who have broken the law are locked up as a punishment.

prisoner prisoners

NOUN someone who is kept in prison or held in captivity.

privacy

NOUN If you have **privacy**, you have somewhere private where you can be alone without being disturbed.

private privates

ADJECTIVE **1** for the use of only one person or group of people, rather than for the general public. *The hotel had a **private** beach.*
2 meant to be kept secret.
NOUN **3** a soldier of the lowest rank.

privilege privileges

NOUN a special right or advantage that is given to a person or group.

prize prizes

NOUN a reward given to the winner of a competition or game.

pro-

PREFIX supporting or being in favour of: *a **pro**-animal rights march.*

Antonym: anti-

probability

NOUN the measure of how likely an event is.

probable

ADJECTIVE likely to happen or likely to be true.

probably

ADVERB likely but not certain. *I am **probably** having a party for my birthday.*

probation

NOUN **1** a period of time during which a person convicted of a crime is supervised by a social worker called a **probation** officer, instead of being sent to prison.
2 a period of time when someone is tried out to see if they are suitable for a particular job.

probe probes probing probed

VERB **1** If you **probe**, you investigate something, often by asking a lot of questions to discover the facts about it.
2 If you **probe** something, you gently push a long, thin instrument into it, usually to find something.
NOUN **3** a long, thin instrument used to look closely at something.
[from Latin ***probare*** meaning to test]

problem problems

NOUN **1** an unsatisfactory situation that causes difficulties.
2 a puzzle or question that you solve using logical thought or mathematics.

Synonyms: (sense 1) difficulty, predicament

procedure procedures

NOUN a way of doing something, especially the correct or usual way. *The entire **procedure** takes about 15 minutes.*

proceed proceeds proceeding proceeded

Said "pro-**seed**" VERB **1** If you **proceed** to do something, you do it after doing something else. *He then **proceeded** to tell us the story.*
2 If you **proceed**, you move in a particular direction. *We **proceeded** along the corridor.*
Said "pro-seedz" PLURAL NOUN **3** The **proceeds** of an event are the money that is obtained from it. *The **proceeds** from the concert will go towards famine relief.*
[from Latin ***pro*** + ***cedere*** meaning to go onward]

process processes processing processed

NOUN **1** a series of actions or events that have a particular result.
PHRASE **2** If you are **in the process** of doing something, you have started doing it but have not yet finished.

VERB **3** You **process** something when you put it through a series of actions in order to have a particular result. For example, you **process** milk to pasteurize it.

procession processions

NOUN a group of people or vehicles moving together in a line, often as part of a ceremony. *There was a **procession** of musicians along the high street on Sunday.*

proclaim proclaims proclaiming proclaimed

VERB If someone **proclaims** something, they announce it or make it known publicly.
proclamation NOUN

prod prods prodding prodded

VERB If you **prod** something or somebody, you give them a poke with your finger.

produce produces producing produced

Said "pro-**dewss**" VERB **1** If someone or something **produces** something, they make it or cause it to happen.
2 If you **produce** something from somewhere, you bring it out so that it can be seen. *The magician **produced** a rabbit out of the hat.*
3 If you **produce** a film, play or other form of entertainment, you are in charge of organizing it.
Said "**prod**-yooss" NOUN **4** food that is grown to be sold.

producer producers

NOUN The **producer** of a record, film, play or programme is the person in charge of making it or putting it on: *a television **producer**.*

product products

NOUN **1** something that is made or produced to be sold.
2 The **product** is the answer to a multiplication sum. *The **product** of 4 and 6 is 24.*

production productions

NOUN **1** the process of manufacturing or growing something in large quantities.
2 a version of something such as a play or a film.

profession professions

NOUN a job for which you need special training and education: *the medical **profession**, the teaching **profession**.*

professional professionals

ADJECTIVE **1 Professional** is used to describe activities that are done to earn money rather than as a hobby. *He earns a lot of money as a **professional** footballer.*

2 You can use **professional** to describe work that is of a very high standard.

NOUN **3** someone who does a particular type of work to earn money.

professor professors

NOUN the most senior teacher in a department of a British university, or a teacher at an American college or university.

proficient

ADJECTIVE If you are **proficient** at something, you can do it well. *I am pleased to see how **proficient** you are in reading.*

proficiency NOUN

profile profiles

NOUN the outline of a face seen from the side. [from Italian ***profilare*** meaning to sketch lightly]

profit profits profiting profited

NOUN **1** an amount of money that you gain when you are paid more for something than it cost to buy or make.

VERB **2** If you **profit** from something, you gain or benefit from it. *I think you will **profit** from some extra lessons.*

profound

ADJECTIVE **1** very deep or intense: *discoveries that have a **profound** effect on life today.*

2 showing or needing deep thought or understanding. *He asked a **profound** question for someone of his age.*

program programs programming programmed

NOUN **1** a set of instructions that a computer follows in order to perform particular tasks.

VERB **2** When someone **programs** a computer, they prepare a program and put it into the computer.

programme programmes

NOUN **1** something that is broadcast on television or radio.

2 a planned series of events.

3 a booklet giving information about a play, concert or show.

progress progresses progressing progressed

Said "**proh**-gress" NOUN **1** the process of gradually improving or getting near to achieving something.

Said "pro-**gress**" VERB **2** If you **progress,** you become more advanced or skilful at something.

3 to continue or move forward. *As the trip **progressed**, I began to feel sick.*

prohibit prohibits prohibiting prohibited

VERB If someone **prohibits** something, they forbid it or make it illegal.

✔ You *prohibit* a person *from* doing something.

project projects projecting projected

Said "**proj**-ekt" NOUN **1** a carefully planned task that requires a lot of time or effort.

Said "pro-**jekt**" VERB **2** If you **project** an image on to a screen, you make it appear there using a projector.

3 If something **projects**, it sticks out.

projector projectors

NOUN a piece of equipment that produces a large image on a screen by shining light through a photographic slide or film strip.

prologue prologues

Said "**pro**-log" NOUN a short piece of writing at the beginning of a book, or a speech that introduces a play.

prolong prolongs prolonging prolonged

VERB If you **prolong** something, you make it last longer. *We **prolonged** the holiday.*

promenade promenades

Said "prom-un-**ahd**" NOUN a path or road by the sea for walking along.

prominent

ADJECTIVE **1** A **prominent** person is important or well known.

2 very noticeable. *The church is a **prominent** landmark.*

[from Latin ***prominere*** meaning to stick out]

promise promises promising promised

VERB **1** If you **promise** to do something, you say that you will definitely do it.

NOUN **2** a statement made by someone that they will definitely do something.

3 Someone or something that shows **promise** seems likely to be successful in the future.

promising

ADJECTIVE likely to be successful or good.

promote promotes promoting promoted

VERB **1** If someone **promotes** something, they try to make it happen, or become more popular or successful.

2 If someone is **promoted,** they are given a more important job at work.

prompt prompts prompting prompted

VERB **1** If something or someone **prompts** you to do something, they encourage you or make you decide to do it.

2 If you **prompt** an actor, you remind them of their lines in a play if they forget them.

ADJECTIVE **3** A **prompt** action is done immediately, without any delay.

prone

ADJECTIVE **1** If you are **prone** to something, you have a tendency to be affected by it or to do it. *I am **prone** to catching colds in the winter.*

2 If you are **prone**, you are lying flat and face downwards.

prong prongs

NOUN The **prongs** of a fork are the long pointed parts.

pronoun pronouns

NOUN a word that is used to replace a noun. **Pronouns** are used instead of naming a person or a thing. "He", "she" and "them" are all examples of **pronouns**.

pronounce pronounces pronouncing pronounced

VERB **1** When you **pronounce** a word, you say it.

2 When someone **pronounces** something, they state or announce it formally.

pronunciation pronunciations

NOUN the way a word is usually said.

proof

NOUN If you have **proof** of something, you have evidence which shows that it is true or exists.

Synonym: confirmation

prop props propping propped

VERB **1** If you **prop** an object somewhere, you lean it against something for support.

NOUN **2** an object, such as a piece of wood or metal, used to support something.

3 an object or piece of furniture used on stage in the theatre, or on a film set.

propaganda

NOUN information, sometimes untrue and often exaggerated, that is used by political groups to influence people.

propel propels propelling propelled

VERB To **propel** something is to push it forward.

propeller propellers

NOUN a device on a boat or aircraft with rotating blades, that makes the boat or aircraft move.

proper

ADJECTIVE If you do something in the **proper** way, you do it correctly.

properly

ADVERB If something is done **properly**, it is done correctly and to the right standard.

proper noun proper nouns

NOUN A proper noun is the name of a person, place or institution, and usually starts with a capital letter. For example, "Mary", "London" and the "Statue of Liberty" are all **proper nouns**. *See* **noun**.

property properties

NOUN **1** A person's **property** is something, or all the things, that belong to them.

2 A **property** is a building and the land around it.

3 a characteristic that something has. *A **property** of mint is its strong smell.* [from Latin ***proprietas*** meaning something personal]

prophet prophets

NOUN a person who predicts what will happen in the future.

proportion proportions

NOUN **1** part of an amount or group.

2 The **proportion** of one amount to another is its size in relation to the whole amount, usually expressed as a fraction or percentage. *The **proportion** of boys in the school is 58%.*

propose proposes proposing proposed

VERB **1** If you **propose** a plan or idea, you suggest it.

2 If you **propose** to someone, you ask them to marry you.

proprietor proprietors

NOUN the owner of a shop or business.

prose

NOUN ordinary written language, rather than poetry.

prosecute prosecutes prosecuting prosecuted

VERB If someone is **prosecuted**, they are charged with a crime and put on trial.

prospect prospects prospecting prospected

NOUN **1** something that may happen in the future.

2 Your **prospects** are your chances of being successful in the future. *If she works hard at school, her prospects are good.*

VERB **3** When people **prospect** for gold, oil or other minerals, they search for them.
prospector NOUN

prosper prospers prospering prospered

VERB When people or businesses **prosper**, they are successful and make money.
prosperous ADJECTIVE   **prosperity** NOUN

protect protects protecting protected

VERB If you **protect** someone or something, you prevent them from being harmed.

protein proteins

NOUN a substance that is found in meat, eggs and milk. It is needed by your body to make you grow and keep you healthy.

protest protests protesting protested

Said "pro-test" VERB **1** If you **protest**, you say or do something to show that you strongly disapprove of something.

Said "**pro**-test" NOUN **2** a demonstration or statement to show that you strongly disapprove of something.

Protestant Protestants

NOUN someone who belongs to the branch of the Christian Church that separated from the Catholic Church in the sixteenth century.

protractor protractors

NOUN a flat, semicircular instrument used for measuring angles.

protrude protrudes protruding protruded

VERB; FORMAL If something **protrudes** from a surface or edge, it sticks out. *The handle of his racquet protruded from his sports bag.*
protrusion NOUN

proud prouder proudest

ADJECTIVE **1** If you are **proud** of something, you feel satisfaction and pleasure because of something you own or have achieved.

2 Someone who is **proud** has a lot of dignity and self-respect.

prove proves proving proved or proven

VERB If you **prove** that something is true, you show by means of argument or evidence that it is definitely true.

Synonyms: confirm, verify

proverb proverbs

NOUN a short, well-known saying that gives advice or makes a comment about life. For example, "a stitch in time saves nine".
proverbial ADJECTIVE

provide provides providing provided

VERB If you **provide** something for someone, you give it to them or make it available to them.

province provinces

NOUN one of the areas into which some large countries are divided. *Each province has its own administration.*

provision provisions

NOUN the act of supplying or making something available to people.

provisional

ADJECTIVE A **provisional** arrangement is one that has been agreed on for the time being, but has not yet been made definite.

provisions

PLURAL NOUN supplies of food and drink.

provoke provokes provoking provoked

VERB **1** If you **provoke** someone, you deliberately try to make them angry.

2 If something **provokes** a reaction or feeling, it causes it.
provocation NOUN   **provocative** ADJECTIVE

prow prows

NOUN the front part of a boat or ship.

prowl prowls prowling prowled

VERB If a person or animal **prowls** around, they move around quietly and secretly, as if hunting.

proximity

NOUN; FORMAL nearness to someone or something. *I lost my bag in the proximity of the swimming pool.*

prune prunes pruning pruned

NOUN 1 a dried plum.

VERB 2 When someone **prunes** a tree or shrub, they cut back some of the branches to make it grow well.

pry pries prying pried

VERB If someone **pries**, they try to find out about something secret or private.

PS

PS is written at the end of a letter to give an extra message. It is an abbreviation of *postscript*.
[from Latin *postscribere* meaning to write (*scribere*) after (*post*)]

psalm psalms

NOUN one of the 150 songs, poems and prayers that form the Book of **Psalms** in the Bible.
[from Greek *psalmos* meaning song accompanied on the harp]

pseudonym pseudonyms

NOUN a false name an author uses rather than using their real name.

psychiatry

Said "sy-**ky**-a-tree" NOUN the branch of medicine concerned with mental illness.
psychiatrist NOUN **psychiatric** ADJECTIVE
[from Greek *psukhmacron* meaning mind and *iatros* meaning healer]

psychic

ADJECTIVE having unusual mental powers, such as the ability to read people's minds or predict the future.

psychology

NOUN the scientific study of the mind and of the reasons for people's behaviour.

PTO

an abbreviation of *please turn over*. **PTO** is written at the bottom of a page to show that there is more writing on the other side.

pub pubs

NOUN a place where people go to buy and drink alcoholic and other drinks, and to talk to their friends. **Pub** is an abbreviation of *public house*.

puberty

NOUN the stage when a person's body changes from that of a child into that of an adult.

public

NOUN 1 You can refer to people in general as the **public**. *The castle is open to the public on Sundays.*

ADJECTIVE 2 relating to people in general: *public opinion.*

3 provided for everyone to use. *We try to use public transport whenever possible.*

publication publications

NOUN 1 The **publication** of a book is the act of printing it and making it available.

2 a book, newspaper or magazine.

publicity

NOUN information or advertisements about an item or event to attract attention to it.

public school public schools

NOUN 1 In England and Wales, a **public school** is a private secondary school that charges fees.

2 In Scotland and America, a **public school** is a state school.

publish publishes publishing published

VERB 1 When a company **publishes** a book, newspaper or magazine, they print copies of it and distribute it.

2 When a newspaper or magazine **publishes** an article or photograph, they print it.

pudding puddings

NOUN 1 a cooked sweet food, often made with flour and eggs, and usually served hot.

2 You can refer to the sweet course of a meal as the **pudding**.

puddle puddles

NOUN a small shallow pool of rain water or other liquid.

puff puffs puffing puffed

VERB **1** If you are **puffing,** you are breathing loudly and quickly with your mouth open.
2 If something **puffs out** or **puffs up**, it swells and becomes larger and rounder.
NOUN **3** a small blast of air, smoke or steam. *The car let out a **puff** of smoke before it sped away.*

pull pulls pulling pulled

VERB **1** If you **pull** something, you get hold of it and move it towards you with force.
2 If a vehicle or an animal **pulls** something, they move it along behind them.
3 When you **pull** the curtains, you move them across a window.
4 If you **pull** a muscle, you damage it temporarily by stretching it too much.
5 If someone **pulls down** a building, they demolish it.
6 If you **pull out** of an activity, you decide not to do it.

pulley pulleys

NOUN a piece of machinery with a wheel and chain or rope over it, used for lifting heavy things.

pullover pullovers

NOUN a knitted piece of clothing, put on over your head, that covers the top part of your body.

pulpit pulpits

NOUN the small raised platform in a church or cathedral where a member of the clergy stands to preach.

pulse pulses

NOUN **1** the regular beating of your heart as it pumps blood through your body. You can feel your **pulse** at your wrists and some other places on your body.
2 Your **pulse** rate is a measure of how fast your heart is beating.

pump pumps pumping pumped

NOUN **1** a machine that is used to force a liquid or gas to move in a particular direction.
VERB **2** If someone or something **pumps** a liquid or gas somewhere, they force it to flow in that direction, using a pump.

pumpkin pumpkins

NOUN a very large, round, orange vegetable.

pun puns

NOUN a clever and amusing use of words so that what you say has two different meanings.

punch punches punching punched

VERB **1** If you **punch** someone or something, you hit them hard with your fist.
NOUN **2** a hard blow with the fist.

punchline punchlines

NOUN The **punchline** of a joke or a story is the last part, that makes it funny.

punctual

ADJECTIVE arriving at the correct time.
punctually ADVERB   **punctuality** NOUN

Synonyms: on time, prompt

punctuation

NOUN the marks in writing that make it easier to understand, such as full stops, question marks and commas.

puncture punctures

NOUN a small hole in a car or bicycle tyre, made by a sharp object.

pungent

ADJECTIVE having a strong, unpleasant smell or taste.
pungency NOUN

punish punishes punishing punished

VERB To **punish** someone means to make them suffer for doing wrong.
punishment NOUN

puny punier puniest

ADJECTIVE very small and weak.

pupa pupae

NOUN an insect at the stage of development between a larva and a fully grown adult.

Synonym: chrysalis

pupil pupils

NOUN **1** The **pupils** at a school are the children who attend it.
2 Your **pupils** are the small, round, black holes in the centre of your eyes.

puppet puppets

NOUN a doll that can be moved by pulling strings or by putting your hand inside its body.

puppy puppies

NOUN a young dog.

purchase purchases purchasing purchased
VERB **1** When you **purchase** something, you buy it.
NOUN **2** something that you have bought.

pure purer purest
ADJECTIVE **1** Something that is **pure** is not mixed with anything else.
2 clean and free from harmful substances.

purify purifies purifying purified
VERB If someone **purifies** something, they remove all dirty or harmful substances from it.
purification NOUN

purple
ADJECTIVE OR NOUN reddish-blue.

purpose purposes
NOUN **1** the reason for something.
2 the thing that you want to achieve.
PHRASE **3** If you do something **on purpose**, you do it deliberately.

purr purrs purring purred
VERB When a cat **purrs**, it makes a low vibrating sound because it is contented.

purse purses
NOUN **1** a container, usually made of leather, plastic or fabric and like a very small bag, for carrying money and credit cards.
2 In American English, a **purse** is a handbag.

pursue pursues pursuing pursued
VERB **1** If you **pursue** someone, you follow them in order to catch them.
2 If you **pursue** an activity or plan, you try to achieve it.

pus
NOUN a thick yellowish liquid that forms in an infected wound or a boil.

push pushes pushing pushed
VERB If you **push** someone or something, you use force to move them away from you.

pushchair pushchairs
NOUN a small folding chair on wheels in which a baby or a toddler can be pushed along.

put puts putting put
VERB **1** If you **put** something somewhere, you move it into that position.
2 If you **put** an idea in a particular way, you express it.

PHRASE **3** If you **put off** doing something, you delay it.
4 If you **put out** the light, you switch it off.
5 If you **put up** with something, you let it happen without complaining.

putt putts
NOUN In golf, a **putt** is a gentle stroke made when the ball is near the hole.

putty
NOUN a paste used to fix panes of glass into frames.

puzzle puzzles puzzling puzzled
VERB **1** If something **puzzles** you, it confuses you and you do not understand it.
NOUN **2** a game or question that requires a lot of thought to complete or solve.

PVC
NOUN a plastic material used for making various things, including clothing, drainpipes and tiles. **PVC** is an abbreviation of *polyvinylchloride*.

pyjamas
PLURAL NOUN loose trousers and a loose jacket that you wear in bed.
[from Persian ***pay jama*** meaning leg clothing]

pylon pylons
NOUN a tall metal structure that carries overhead electricity cables.

pyramid pyramids
NOUN **1** a three-dimensional shape with a flat base and flat triangular sides sloping upwards to a point.
2 an ancient stone structure in this shape, built over the tombs of Egyptian kings and queens.

python pythons
NOUN a large snake that kills other animals by squeezing them with its body.
[from Greek ***Puthon,*** a huge mythical serpent]

Qq

quack quacks quacking quacked

VERB **1** When a duck **quacks**, it makes a loud harsh sound.

NOUN **2** A **quack** is the sound made by a duck.

quadrangle quadrangles

NOUN **1** a courtyard with buildings all round it.

2 In geometry, a **quadrangle** is a four-sided shape.

quadrant quadrants

NOUN a quarter of a circle.

quadrilateral quadrilaterals

NOUN a plane shape with four straight sides.

quadruplet quadruplets

NOUN one of four children born at the same time to the same mother.

quail quails

NOUN a type of small game bird with a round body and a short tail.

quaint quainter quaintest

ADJECTIVE If something is **quaint**, it is attractive and charming in an old-fashioned or unusual way. *The **quaint** little village was filled with thatched cottages.*

quake quakes quaking quaked

VERB **1** If you **quake**, you tremble because you are very frightened.

2 If the ground **quakes**, it moves, usually because of an earthquake.

NOUN **3** an abbreviation of *earthquake*.

Quaker Quakers

NOUN a member of a Christian group called the Society of Friends, that gathers together for peaceful thought and prayer.

qualification qualifications

NOUN Your **qualifications** are your skills and achievements. You gain **qualifications** by passing tests and examinations.

qualify qualifies qualifying qualified

VERB If you **qualify**, you pass examinations and gain qualifications, often for a particular job. *After many years of study and training she **qualified** as a doctor.*

quality

NOUN The **quality** of something is how good it is.

quantity quantities

NOUN an amount that you can measure or count.

quarantine

Said "**kwo**-ran-teen" NOUN a period of time that a person or animal has to spend apart from others to prevent the possible spread of disease.

[from Italian *quarantina* meaning forty days]

quarrel quarrels quarrelling quarrelled

NOUN **1** an angry argument.

VERB **2** If people **quarrel**, they have an angry argument.

quarry quarries

NOUN a place where stone is removed from the ground by digging or blasting.

quart quarts

Said "**kwort**" NOUN a unit of liquid volume equal to two pints or about 1·136 litres.

quarter quarters

NOUN **1** one of four equal parts of something.

2 When you are telling the time, **quarter** means fifteen minutes before or after the hour. *The programme starts at a **quarter** to six, and finishes at a **quarter** past.*

3 an American or Canadian coin worth 25 cents, which is a **quarter** of a dollar.

quartet quartets

NOUN **1** a group of four musicians who sing or play together.

2 a piece of music written for four instruments or singers.

quartz

NOUN a type of hard, shiny crystal used in making very accurate watches and clocks.

quay quays

NOUN a place where boats are tied up and loaded or unloaded.

queasy queasier queasiest

ADJECTIVE If you feel **queasy**, you feel slightly sick.

queen queens

NOUN a female monarch or a woman married to a king.

queer queerer queerest
ADJECTIVE very strange.

quench quenches quenching quenched
VERB If you **quench** your thirst, you have a drink so that you are no longer thirsty.

query queries
NOUN a question. *I cannot answer your* **query**.

quest quests
NOUN a long search for something.

question questions questioning questioned
NOUN **1** a sentence that asks for information.
VERB **2** If you **question** someone, you ask them questions.
PHRASE **3** If something is **out of the question**, it is impossible and not worth considering.

question mark question marks
NOUN a punctuation mark (?) used at the end of a question.

questionnaire questionnaires
NOUN a list of questions that people fill in as part of a survey.

queue queues queuing or queueing queued
NOUN **1** a line of people or vehicles that are waiting for something.
VERB **2** When people **queue**, or **queue up**, they stand in a line waiting for something.

quibble quibbles quibbling quibbled
VERB If you **quibble** about something, you argue about something that is not very important.

quiche quiches
Said "**keesh**" NOUN a tart with a savoury filling made of eggs.

quick quicker quickest
ADJECTIVE If you are **quick**, you move or do things with great speed.

quicksand quicksands
NOUN an area of deep, wet sand that you sink into if you walk on it.

quid
NOUN; INFORMAL In British English, a **quid** is a pound in money.

quiet quieter quietest
ADJECTIVE **1** If someone or something is **quiet**, they are not making much noise, or they are not making any noise at all.

2 A **quiet** place, time or situation is calm and peaceful.
NOUN **3** silence.

quill quills
NOUN **1** a pen made from a feather.
2 A bird's **quills** are the large feathers on its wings and tail.
3 A porcupine's **quills** are its spines.

quilt quilts
NOUN a thick, soft, warm cover for a bed, usually padded.

quit quits quitting quit
VERB If you **quit** something, you leave it or stop doing it.

quite
ADVERB fairly but not very. *She's* **quite** *old, but not as old as my grandma.*

quiver quivers quivering quivered
VERB **1** If something **quivers,** it trembles. *The leaves on the trees* **quivered** *in the breeze.*
NOUN **2** a container for carrying arrows.

quiz quizzes
NOUN a game in which someone tests your knowledge by asking you questions.

quota quotas
NOUN a number or quantity of something that is allowed by the rules. *We have already had our* **quota** *of class outings for this term.*
[from Latin **quot** meaning how many]

quotation quotations
NOUN a small part of a piece of writing taken from a book or speech.

quotation marks
PLURAL NOUN the punctuation marks (" " ' ') that show where written speech or quotations begin and end.

quote quotes quoting quoted
VERB If you **quote** something that someone has written or said, you repeat their words.

quotient quotients
NOUN the number of times one number can be divided into another. For example, in $42 \div 6 = 7$, 7 is the **quotient**.

Qur'an
NOUN another spelling of Koran.

Rr

rabbi rabbis
NOUN a Jewish religious leader.

rabbit rabbits
NOUN a small furry rodent with long ears.

rabies
NOUN a disease that causes humans and some other animals, especially dogs, to go mad and die.

race races racing raced
NOUN **1** a competition to see who is fastest at something.
2 a large group of people who look alike in some way. Different **races** have, for example, different skin colour or differently shaped eyes.
VERB **3** If you **race**, you take part in a race. *She has **raced** against some of the best in the world.*
4 If you **race** somewhere, you go there as quickly as possible. *He **raced** after the others.*

racecourse racecourses
NOUN a place where horse races are run.

racehorse racehorses
NOUN a horse that is trained to run fast for races.

racial
ADJECTIVE to do with the different races that people belong to.
racially ADVERB

racism
Said "**ray**-sizm" NOUN **1** hostility shown by one race of people to another.
2 believing that one race of people is better than all others.
racist NOUN OR ADJECTIVE

rack racks
NOUN a piece of equipment for holding things or hanging things on.

racket rackets
NOUN **1** a bat with an oval frame and strings across and down it, used in games like tennis.
2 If someone is making a **racket**, they are making a lot of noise.

radar
NOUN a way of discovering the position or speed of objects, such as ships or aircraft, by using radio signals. *They could see the ship on the **radar** screen.*
[an abbreviation for ***radio detecting and ranging***]

radiant
ADJECTIVE **1** shining or sparkling.
2 Someone who is **radiant** looks beautiful because they are so happy.

radiate radiates radiating radiated
VERB **1** Things that **radiate** from something come out in lines from a central point, like the spokes of a wheel or the sun's rays.
2 When a fire or a light **radiates** heat or light, it gives them out.

radiation
NOUN **1** very small particles given out by radioactive substances.
2 the heat and light energy given out from a source such as the sun.

radiator radiators
NOUN **1** a hollow metal device filled with hot water for heating a room.
2 the part of a car that is filled with water to cool the engine.

radio radios
NOUN **1** a system of sending sound over a distance by transmitting electrical signals.
2 the broadcasting of programmes for the public to listen to by radio.
3 a piece of equipment for listening to radio programmes. *They are in daily **radio** contact with the expedition.*
4 a piece of equipment for sending and receiving **radio** messages. *A policeman raised the alarm on his **radio**.*

radioactive
ADJECTIVE **Radioactive** substances give out energy in the form of powerful and harmful rays.

radish radishes
NOUN a small salad vegetable with a red skin and white flesh, and with a hot taste.

radius radii

NOUN **1** a straight line going from the centre of a circle to the outside edge.
2 the length of a straight line going from the centre of a circle to the outside edge.

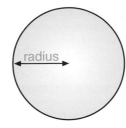
radius

raffle raffles raffling raffled

NOUN **1** a competition in which people buy numbered tickets and win a prize if their ticket is chosen.
VERB **2** If you **raffle** something, you give it as a prize in a raffle.

raft rafts

NOUN a floating platform made from long pieces of wood tied together.

rafter rafters

NOUN the sloping pieces of wood that support a roof.

rag rags

NOUN **1** a piece of old cloth used to wipe or clean things.
2 If someone is dressed in **rags**, they are wearing very old, torn clothes.

rage rages raging raged

NOUN **1** strong, uncontrollable anger.
VERB **2** If something such as a storm or battle **rages**, it continues with great force or violence.

Synonyms: (sense 1) anger, fury, wrath

ragged

ADJECTIVE torn or frayed, with rough edges.

raid raids raiding raided

VERB **1** When people **raid** a place, they enter it by force in order to attack it or to look for something or someone.
NOUN **2** a sudden, surprise attack.

rail rails

NOUN **1** a fixed bar that you can hang things on.
2 one of the heavy metal bars that trains run along.

railings

PLURAL NOUN a series of metal bars that make up a fence.

railway railways

NOUN a route along which trains travel on metal tracks.

rain rains raining rained

NOUN **1** water falling from the clouds in small drops.
VERB **2** When it **rains**, small drops of water fall from clouds in the sky.
✔ Other words that sound like *rain* are *rein* and *reign*.

rainbow rainbows

NOUN an arch of different colours that sometimes appears in the sky after it has been raining.

raincoat raincoats

NOUN a waterproof coat.

rainfall

NOUN the amount of rain that falls in one place during a particular period of time.

rainforest rainforests

NOUN a dense forest of tall trees that grows in a tropical area where there is a lot of rain.

raise raises raising raised

VERB **1** If you **raise** something, you make it higher. *He raised his hand.*
2 If you **raise** your voice, you speak more loudly.
3 If you **raise** money for something, you get people to give money towards it.

raisin raisins

NOUN a dried grape.

rake rakes

NOUN a garden tool with a row of metal teeth and a long handle, for collecting together dead leaves or cut grass.

rally rallies

NOUN **1** a competition in which vehicles race along public roads.
2 a large public meeting.
3 In tennis or squash, a **rally** is a continuous series of shots exchanged by the players.

ram rams ramming rammed

VERB **1** If you **ram** something somewhere, you push it there firmly. *She rammed her purse into her bag as she ran for the bus.*
2 If one vehicle **rams** another, it crashes into it.
NOUN **3** an adult male sheep.

a b c d e f g h i j k l m n o p q **r** s t u v w x y z

Ramadan

NOUN the ninth month of the Muslim year, during which Muslims eat and drink nothing during daylight.

[from Arabic *Ramadan* meaning "be hot", as the fasting takes place during a hot month]

ramble rambles rambling rambled

NOUN **1** a long walk in the countryside.

VERB **2** to go for a ramble.

3 If you **ramble**, you talk in a confused way. **rambler** NOUN

ramp ramps

NOUN a sloping surface linking two places that are at different levels.

rampage rampages rampaging rampaged

VERB If you **rampage**, you rush about wildly, causing damage.

rampart ramparts

NOUN an earth bank, often with a wall on top, built to protect a castle or city.

ramshackle

ADJECTIVE A **ramshackle** building is in very poor condition.

ran

VERB the past tense of *run*.

ranch ranches

NOUN a large farm where cattle or horses are reared, especially in the USA.

random

ADJECTIVE OR NOUN Something that is done in a **random** way, or at **random**, is done by chance or without a definite plan.

Synonyms: chance, haphazard

rang

VERB the past tense of *ring*.

range ranges ranging ranged

NOUN **1** a selection or choice of different things of the same kind. *This top is available in a wide **range** of colours.*

2 a set of values on a scale.

3 the maximum distance over which something can reach things or detect things.

4 a long line of hills or mountains.

VERB **5** When a set of things **ranges** between two points, they vary within these points on a scale.

ranger rangers

NOUN someone whose job is to look after a forest or park.

rank ranks

NOUN **1** a position or grade that someone holds in an organization.

2 a row of people or things. *We went to the taxi **rank** outside the station to catch a taxi home.*

ransack ransacks ransacking ransacked

VERB If you **ransack** a place, you disturb everything in order to search for or steal something, and leave it in a mess.

ransom ransoms

NOUN money that is demanded by kidnappers to free someone they have taken hostage.

rap raps rapping rapped

NOUN **1** a quick knock or blow on something. *There was a sharp **rap** on the door.*

2 a type of music in which the words are spoken in a rapid, rhythmic way.

VERB **3** If you **rap** something, or **rap** on it, you hit it with a series of quick blows.

rape rapes raping raped

VERB If a man **rapes** someone, he forces them to have sex with him against their will.

rapid

ADJECTIVE happening or moving very quickly.

rapier rapiers

NOUN a long thin sword with a sharp point.

rare rarer rarest

ADJECTIVE **1** Something that is **rare** is not common or does not often happen.

2 Meat that is **rare** is cooked very lightly.

rascal rascals

NOUN someone who does naughty or mischievous things.

rash rashes

NOUN **1** an area of red spots that appear on your skin when you are ill or have an allergy.

ADJECTIVE **2** If you are **rash**, you do something without thinking properly about it.

rasher rashers

NOUN a thin slice of bacon.

raspberry raspberries

NOUN a small soft red fruit that grows on a bush.

rat rats

NOUN a rodent with a long tail, that looks like a large mouse.

rate rates

NOUN how quickly or slowly, or how often something happens.

rather

ADVERB **1** fairly, or to a certain extent: *rather large*.

2 If you would **rather** do one thing than another, you would prefer to do it. *I don't want to go out. I'd* **rather** *stay here.*

ratio ratios

NOUN The **ratio** between two things shows how many times one is bigger than another. A **ratio** is used to compare two or more quantities, for example, if a class has 15 boys and 10 girls, the **ratio** of boys to girls is 15 to 10.

ration rations rationing rationed

NOUN **1** the amount of something you are allowed to have.

VERB **2** When something is **rationed**, you are only allowed a limited amount of it because there is a shortage.

rationing NOUN

rational

Said "**rash**-un-ul" ADJECTIVE well thought out, sensible and reasonable. *It was a* **rational** *decision.*

Antonym: irrational

---

rattle rattles rattling rattled

VERB When something **rattles**, or when you **rattle** it, it makes short, regular knocking sounds, for example because it is shaking.

rattlesnake rattlesnakes

NOUN a poisonous American snake that can rattle its tail.

rave raves raving raved

VERB **1** If someone **raves**, they talk in an excited and uncontrolled way.

2 INFORMAL If you **rave** about something, you talk about it very enthusiastically.

NOUN **3** INFORMAL a large dance event with electronic music.

raven ravens

NOUN **1** a large black bird with a deep, harsh call.

ADJECTIVE **2 Raven** hair is black and shiny.

ravenous

ADJECTIVE very hungry.

ravenously ADVERB

ravine ravines

NOUN a deep, narrow valley with steep sides.

ravioli

NOUN an Italian dish made of small squares of pasta filled with meat or vegetable paste and served with sauce.

raw

ADJECTIVE **1 Raw** food is uncooked.

2 If part of your body is **raw**, the skin has been rubbed or scraped away.

3 A **raw** substance is in its natural state before being processed.

raw material raw materials

NOUN natural substances used to make things.

ray rays

NOUN a beam of light: *the sun's* **rays**.

razor razors

NOUN an instrument that people use for shaving.

re-

PREFIX used to form words that show something is being done again. For example, if you **re**use something you use it again, if you read something again you **re**read it, and if you marry for a second time you **re**marry.

reach reaches reaching reached

VERB **1** When you **reach** a place, you arrive there.

2 When you **reach** for something, you stretch out your arm to touch or get hold of it. *I can't* **reach** *that shelf.*

react reacts reacting reacted

VERB When you **react** to something, you behave in a particular way because of it.

reaction reactions

NOUN Your **reaction** to something is what you say, do or feel because of it.

reactor reactors

NOUN a device used to produce nuclear energy.

read reads reading read

VERB When you **read** something that is written, you look at it and understand or say aloud the words that are there.

reader readers

NOUN The **readers** of a newspaper or magazine are the people who read it regularly.

readily

Said "**red**-ily" ADVERB **1** willingly or eagerly. *They **readily** tidied their bedrooms.* **2** easily done or easy to get. *Help was **readily** available.*

reading readings

NOUN **1** the act of reading books, newspapers or magazines. **2** The **reading** on a meter, gauge or other measuring instrument is the amount it shows.

ready

ADJECTIVE If someone or something is **ready**, they are prepared for doing something. *Your glasses will be **ready** in a fortnight.*

real

ADJECTIVE **1** actually true and not imagined. **2** genuine and not artificial.

realistic

ADJECTIVE **1** A **realistic** painting, story or film shows things in a way that is like real life. **2** If you are **realistic** about a situation, you recognize and accept that it is true.

reality

NOUN **1** what is real, and not imagined or invented. **2** If something has become a **reality**, it has happened. *Her dream of being a dancer had become a **reality**.*

Synonyms: (sense 1) fact, truth

realize realizes realizing realized; also spelt **realise**

VERB If you **realize** something, you become aware of it or understand it.

really

ADVERB **1** You use **really** to emphasize a point. *It is a **really** good film.* **2** You use **really** when you are talking about the true facts about something. *What was **really** going on?*

reap reaps reaping reaped

VERB When someone **reaps** a crop, such as corn, they cut and gather it. **reaper** NOUN

reappear reappears reappearing reappeared

VERB When people or things **reappear**, they can be seen again after they have been out of sight.

rear rears rearing reared

NOUN **1** The **rear** of something is the part at the back. VERB **2** To **rear** children or other young animals means to bring them up until they are able to look after themselves. **3** When a horse **rears**, it raises the front part of its body, so that its front legs are in the air.

rearrange rearranges rearranging rearranged

VERB If you **rearrange** something, you organize it or arrange it in a different way.

reason reasons reasoning reasoned

NOUN **1** the fact that explains why something happens. VERB **2** to think in a logical way and draw conclusions. **3** If you **reason** with someone, you discuss something with them in a sensible way.

reasonable

ADJECTIVE **1** fair and sensible. **2** A **reasonable** amount is a fairly large amount.

reassure reassures reassuring reassured

VERB If you **reassure** someone, you say or do things to calm their fears or stop them from worrying.

recoil

rebel rebels rebelling rebelled
Said "**reb**-el" NOUN **1** someone who does not agree with rules, and behaves differently from other people.
2 one of a group of people who are fighting against their own country's army in order to change how it is ruled.
Said "rib-**el**" VERB **3** When someone **rebels**, they refuse to obey rules, and they behave differently from other people.

rebellious
ADJECTIVE Someone who is **rebellious** breaks rules and refuses to obey orders.
rebellion NOUN

rebound rebounds rebounding rebounded
VERB If something **rebounds**, it bounces back after hitting something.

rebuild rebuilds rebuilding rebuilt
VERB When something is **rebuilt**, it is built again after being damaged or destroyed.

rebuke rebukes rebuking rebuked
VERB If you **rebuke** someone, you tell them off for something wrong that they have done.

recall recalls recalling recalled
VERB When you **recall** something, you remember it.

recede recedes receding receded
VERB **1** When something **recedes**, it moves away into the distance. *We watched the tide receding*.
2 When a man's hair **recedes**, he starts to go bald from the front of his head.

receipt receipts
NOUN a piece of paper given to you as proof that you have paid for something or delivered something.

receive receives receiving received
VERB When you **receive** something, you get it after someone has given or sent it to you.

receiver receivers
NOUN the part of a telephone that you hold near to your ear and your mouth.

recent
ADJECTIVE A **recent** event is something that happened a short time ago.

reception receptions
NOUN **1** the place near the entrance of a hotel or office where appointments and enquiries are dealt with.
2 a formal party.

receptionist receptionists
NOUN In a hotel or office, the **receptionist** is the person who receives and welcomes visitors as they arrive, answers the telephone and arranges appointments.

recipe recipes
NOUN a list of ingredients and instructions for cooking or preparing a particular dish. *My grandma gave me her recipe for Yorkshire pudding.*

recital recitals
NOUN a performance of poetry or music, usually by one person.

recite recites reciting recited
VERB If you **recite** something such as a poem, you say it aloud.
recitation NOUN

reckless
ADJECTIVE If you are **reckless**, you do not care about any danger or damage you cause.

reckon reckons reckoning reckoned
VERB **1** If you **reckon** an amount, you calculate it.
2 If you **reckon** something is true, you think it is true.

reclaim reclaims reclaiming reclaimed
VERB **1** When you **reclaim** something, you fetch it after losing it or leaving it somewhere.
2 If land is **reclaimed**, it is made useable again, for example by draining water from it.

recline reclines reclining reclined
VERB to lean or lie back. *We reclined on deckchairs in the sun.*

recognize recognizes recognizing recognized; also spelt recognise
VERB When you **recognize** someone or something, you realize you know who or what they are.

recoil recoils recoiling recoiled
VERB If you **recoil**, you suddenly back away from something, usually because it shocks or horrifies you. *I recoiled from the huge spider.*

recollect recollects recollecting recollected
VERB If you **recollect** something, you remember it.
recollection NOUN

recommend recommends recommending recommended
VERB If you **recommend** something to someone, you suggest that they try it because you think it is good.

reconcile reconciles reconciling reconciled
VERB When people are **reconciled**, they become friendly again after a quarrel.
reconciliation NOUN

reconstruct reconstructs reconstructing reconstructed
VERB To **reconstruct** something that has been damaged means to build it again.
reconstruction NOUN

record records recording recorded
Said "**rek**-ord" NOUN **1** a written account of something.
2 a round, flat piece of plastic on which music has been recorded.
3 an achievement that is the best of its type. *He holds the world* **record** *for the high jump.*
Said "ri-**kord**" VERB **4** If you **record** information, you write it down so that it can be referred to later.
5 If you **record** sounds and pictures, you copy them on to a tape or disc so that they can be listened to or watched again.

recorder recorders
NOUN **1** a small woodwind instrument.
2 a machine for copying sounds and pictures, such as a tape **recorder** or a video **recorder**.

recount recounts recounting recounted
Said "ri-**count**" VERB **1** If you **recount** a story, you tell it.
Said "**ree**-count" **2** If you **recount** something such as votes, you count them for a second time.

recover recovers recovering recovered
VERB **1** When you **recover**, you get better after being ill.
2 If you **recover** something that has been lost or stolen, you get it back.

recreation recreations
NOUN the things you do for enjoyment in your spare time.

recruit recruits recruiting recruited
VERB **1** If you **recruit** people, you persuade them to join a group or help with something.
NOUN **2** someone who has joined the army or some other organization.
recruitment NOUN

rectangle rectangles
NOUN a four-sided shape with four right angles.
rectangular ADJECTIVE

recuperate recuperates recuperating recuperated
VERB When you **recuperate**, you gradually recover after being ill or injured.
recuperation NOUN

recur recurs recurring recurred
VERB If something **recurs**, it happens again.

recycle recycles recycling recycled
VERB When you **recycle** something, you use it again for a different purpose.

red redder reddest; reds
NOUN OR ADJECTIVE **1** the colour of blood or of a ripe tomato.
ADJECTIVE **2** **Red** hair is between orange and brown in colour.

redden reddens reddening reddened
VERB If something **reddens**, it becomes red. *His face* **reddened** *with embarrassment.*

red-handed
PHRASE If you catch someone **red-handed**, you catch them while they are doing something wrong.

redraft redrafts redrafting redrafted
VERB If you **redraft** a piece of writing, you rewrite it to improve or change it.

red tape
NOUN official rules that make things take longer than they need to.

reduce reduces reducing reduced
VERB If you **reduce** something, you make it smaller in size or amount.

Synonyms: cut, decrease

reduction reductions
NOUN If there is a **reduction** in something, it becomes smaller or less. *There are great reductions in prices during the sales.*

redundant
ADJECTIVE **1** When people are made **redundant**, they lose their jobs because there is no more work for them.
2 If something becomes **redundant**, it is no longer needed or useful.

reed reeds
NOUN **1** a hollow-stemmed plant that grows in shallow water or on wet ground.
2 a thin piece of cane or metal inside some wind instruments, that vibrates and makes a sound when air is blown over it.

reef reefs
NOUN a long line of rocks or coral close to the surface of the sea.

rook rooks rooking rooked
VERB **1** If something **reeks**, it has a strong, unpleasant smell.
NOUN **2** a strong, unpleasant smell.

reel reels reeling reeled
NOUN **1** a cylindrical object around which you wrap something such as a fishing line, a film or thread.
2 a fast Scottish dance.
VERB **3** If you **reel**, you stagger and look as if you will fall.

refer refers referring referred
VERB **1** If you **refer** to someone or something, you mention them when you are speaking or writing.
2 If you **refer** to a book or other source of information, you look at it in order to find something out.
3 If someone **refers** a problem or a question to someone else, they pass it on to them to deal with.

referee referees
NOUN the official who controls a sports match and makes sure that the rules are not broken.

reference references
NOUN **1** a mention of someone or something in a speech or a piece of writing.
2 a document written by someone who knows you, that describes your character and abilities, usually when you are applying for a job.

reference book reference books
NOUN a book that you use to get information.

referendum referendums or referenda
NOUN a vote in which all the people of voting age in a country are asked to say if they agree with a particular government policy or not.

refill refills refilling refilled
VERB **1** If you **refill** something, you fill it again.
NOUN **2** a container of something to replace something that is used up. *I need a refill for my pen.*

refine refines refining refined
VERB If substances such as oil or sugar are **refined**, all the impurities are taken out of them.

refined
ADJECTIVE Someone who is **refined** is very polite and well mannered.

refinery refineries
NOUN a factory where sugar or oil are refined.

reflect reflects reflecting reflected
VERB **1** When rays of heat or light **reflect** off something, they bounce back from it.
2 When something smooth and shiny, such as a mirror, **reflects** something, it shows an image of it.
3 When you **reflect** on something, you think about it carefully.

reflection reflections
NOUN the image you see when you look in a mirror or in very clear, still water.

reflex reflexes
NOUN **1** a sudden uncontrollable movement that you make as a result of pressure or a blow to a particular nerve.
2 If you have good **reflexes**, you respond very quickly when something unexpected happens.

reform reforms reforming reformed
VERB **1** When organizations or laws are **reformed**, changes are made to them to improve them.
2 When people **reform**, they stop doing bad things such as committing crimes.

refrain refrains refraining refrained
VERB **1** FORMAL If you **refrain** from doing something, you do not do it.
NOUN **2** a short, simple part of a song that is repeated.

Synonym: (sense 2) chorus

refresh refreshes refreshing refreshed
VERB If something **refreshes** you, it makes you feel less tired or less thirsty.

refreshing
ADJECTIVE If something is **refreshing**, it makes you cool or less tired after you have been hot or busy. *We went for a **refreshing** swim after walking along the beach.*

refreshments
PLURAL NOUN drinks and snacks.

refrigerator refrigerators
NOUN an electrically cooled container for putting food in to keep it fresh.

refuel refuels refuelling refuelled
VERB When an aircraft or vehicle is **refuelled**, it is filled with more fuel.

refuge refuges
NOUN a place where you go for safety and protection.
[from Latin ***refugere*** meaning to flee]

Synonyms: haven, sanctuary, shelter

refugee refugees
NOUN a person who has been forced to leave their country and live elsewhere, for example because of war, famine or persecution.

refund refunds refunding refunded
NOUN **1** a sum of money that is paid back to you, for example because you have returned goods to a shop.
VERB **2** If someone **refunds** your money, they pay it back to you.

refuse refuses refusing refused
Said "ri-**fyooz**" VERB **1** If you **refuse** something, you say no to it, or decide firmly that you will not do it or do not accept it
Said "**ref**-yooss" NOUN **2** rubbish or waste.

regal
ADJECTIVE very grand and suitable for a king or queen.

regard regards regarding regarded
VERB **1** To **regard** someone or something in a certain way is to think of them in that way. *We **regarded** him as a friend.*
2 to look closely at someone or something.
NOUN **3** If you have a high **regard** for someone, you have a very good opinion of them.

regarding
PREPOSITION on the subject of: *"I will now answer any questions **regarding** your homework," said the teacher.*

regardless
PREPOSITION OR ADVERB If you do something **regardless** of what may happen as a result, you do it anyway.

regards
PLURAL NOUN kind wishes or friendly feelings for someone, usually sent in a message. *Give him my **regards** when you see him.*

regatta regattas
NOUN a race meeting for sailing or rowing boats.

reggae
NOUN a type of music with a strong beat, originally from the West Indies.

regiment regiments
NOUN a large group of soldiers commanded by a colonel.
regimental ADJECTIVE

region regions
NOUN a large area of a country or of the world.

register registers registering registered

NOUN **1** an official list that is used to keep a record of things that happen or people who attend an event.

VERB **2** When something is **registered**, it is recorded on an official list.

regret regrets regretting regretted

VERB **1** If you **regret** something, you wish that it had not happened or you had not done it.

2 You can use **regret** to say you are sorry about something. *We* **regret** *any inconvenience caused to passengers by the delay.*

regretful

ADJECTIVE If you are **regretful**, you are sorry or sad about something.

regular

ADJECTIVE **1 Regular** events happen at equal or frequent intervals.

2 If you are a **regular** visitor somewhere, you go there often.

regulate regulates regulating regulated

VERB If someone or something **regulates** something, they control it. *My grandad takes tablets to* **regulate** *his blood pressure.*

regulation regulations

NOUN an official rule.

rehearse rehearses rehearsing rehearsed

VERB When people **rehearse** a performance, they practise it in preparation for the actual event.

reign reigns reigning reigned

VERB **1** When a king or queen **reigns**, he or she is the leader of the country.

NOUN **2** The **reign** of a king or queen is the period when they reign

✔ Other words that sound like *reign* are *rain* and *rein*.

rein reins

NOUN one of the thin leather straps that you hold when you are riding a horse.

✔ Other words that sound like *rein* are *rain* and *reign*.

reindeer

NOUN a deer with large antlers, that lives in northern regions of the world.

reinforce reinforces reinforcing reinforced

VERB If you **reinforce** something, you strengthen it.

reject rejects rejecting rejected

VERB If you **reject** something, you throw it away or refuse to accept it.

rejoice rejoices rejoicing rejoiced

VERB If you **rejoice**, you celebrate because you are very pleased about something.

relate relates relating related

VERB **1** If one thing **relates** to another, it is concerned or connected with it in some way, or can be compared with it.

2 If you **relate** a story, you tell it.

related

ADJECTIVE If people, animals or plants are **related**, they belong to the same family groups or species.

relation relations

NOUN **1** one of the people who are related to you, such as aunts, uncles and grandparents.

2 the way that one thing is connected or compared with another.

relationship relationships

NOUN The **relationship** between two people or groups is the way they feel and behave towards each other.

relative relatives

ADJECTIVE **1** compared with other things or people of the same kind.

NOUN **2** a member of your family.

relax relaxes relaxing relaxed

VERB **1** When you **relax**, or when something **relaxes** you, you become calm and less worried or tense. *Massage is used to* **relax** *muscles.*

2 If you **relax**, you stop work and rest or enjoy your free time.

Synonyms: take it easy, unwind

relay relays relaying relayed

VERB **1** If you **relay** something, such as a message, you pass it from one person to the next.

NOUN **2** a race between teams, in which each team member runs one part of the race.

a
b
c
d
e
f
g
h
i
j
k
l
m
n
o
p
q
r
s
t
u
v
w
x
y
z

release releases releasing released

VERB If you **release** someone or something, you set them free or unfasten them.

relent relents relenting relented

VERB If someone **relents**, they give in and allow something that they refused to allow before. *Dad relented and allowed us to stay up late.*

relevant

ADJECTIVE connected with what is being discussed or dealt with.

reliable

ADJECTIVE **Reliable** people and things can be trusted and depended upon.

relic relics

NOUN 1 an object or custom that has survived from an earlier time.
2 an object regarded as holy because it is thought to be connected with a saint.

relief

NOUN If you feel **relief**, you feel glad because something unpleasant is over or has been avoided.

relieve relieves relieving relieved

VERB If something **relieves** an unpleasant feeling, it makes it less unpleasant.

relieved

ADJECTIVE If you are **relieved**, you are thankful that something worrying or unpleasant has stopped. *I was relieved when the exams were over.*

religion religions

NOUN 1 belief in a god or gods.
2 a particular set of religious beliefs: *the Christian religion.*

religious

ADJECTIVE to do with religion.

relish relishes relishing relished

VERB 1 If you **relish** something, you enjoy it very much. *He relished the thought of chocolate cake for tea.*
NOUN 2 enjoyment: *"I'm allowed to stay up as long as like," she said with relish.*
3 a savoury pickle.

reluctant

ADJECTIVE If you are **reluctant** to do something, you do not want to do it.

rely relies relying relied

VERB If you **rely** on someone or something, you trust and depend on them. *I relied on my friends to help me.*

remain remains remaining remained

VERB 1 If you **remain** in a particular place, you stay there.
PLURAL NOUN 2 The **remains** of something are the parts that are left after most of it has been destroyed or used.

remainder

NOUN 1 the part of something that is left.
2 In arithmetic, the **remainder** is the amount left over when one number cannot be divided exactly by another.

remark remarks remarking remarked

VERB 1 If you **remark** on something, you mention it or comment on it.
NOUN 2 a comment you make or something you say.

remarkable

ADJECTIVE impressive and noticeable. *Her tennis skills were remarkable.*

remedy remedies remedying remedied

NOUN 1 a cure for something.
2 a way of dealing with a problem.
VERB 3 If you **remedy** a problem, you put it right.

remember remembers remembering remembered

VERB 1 If you **remember** someone or something from the past, you still have an idea of them and you are able to think about them.
2 If you **remember** to do something, you do it when you intended to.
3 If you **remember** something, it suddenly comes into your mind again.

remind reminds reminding reminded

VERB 1 If someone **reminds** you of something, they help you remember it.
2 If someone or something **reminds** you of another person or thing, they are similar to the other person or thing and make you think of them.

remnant remnants

NOUN a small part of something that is left after the rest has been used or destroyed.

remorse

NOUN; FORMAL a strong feeling of guilt and regret.
remorseful ADJECTIVE

remote remoter remotest

ADJECTIVE **1** far away from where most people live.
2 far away in time.

remote control

NOUN a system of controlling a machine or vehicle from a distance, using radio or electronic signals.

removal removals

NOUN **1** the act of taking something away. *The house felt very bare after the removal of the furniture.*
ADJECTIVE **2** A **removal** company moves furniture from one building to another.

remove removes removing removed

VERB If you **remove** something, you take it away.

rendezvous

Said "**ron**-day-voo" NOUN a meeting or meeting place.
[a French word, meaning "present yourselves!"]

renew renews renewing renewed

VERB **1** If you **renew** something such as a piece of equipment, you replace it or parts of it with a new one or new parts.
2 If you **renew** an activity or relationship, you begin it again.

renovate renovates renovating renovated

VERB If you **renovate** something old, you repair it and restore it to good condition.
renovation NOUN

renowned

ADJECTIVE well known, especially for something good. *She's renowned for her kindness.*

rent rents renting rented

VERB **1** If you **rent** something, you pay the owner a regular sum of money to use it.
NOUN **2** the amount of money you pay regularly to use something that belongs to someone else.

rental rentals

NOUN **1** the amount paid as rent.
ADJECTIVE **2** to do with rent.

repair repairs repairing repaired

NOUN **1** something that you do to mend something that is damaged.
VERB **2** If you **repair** something that is damaged, you mend it.

repay repays repaying repaid

VERB **1** When you **repay** money, you give it back to the person who lent it to you.
2 If you **repay** a favour, you do something to help the person who helped you.
repayment NOUN

repeat repeats repeating repeated

VERB **1** If you **repeat** something, you say, write or do it again.
NOUN **2** something that is done again or happens again.

repeatedly

ADVERB again and again, several times. *He knocked repeatedly on the door, but nobody answered.*

repel repels repelling repelled

VERB **1** If something **repels** you, it disgusts you.
2 If someone **repels** an attack, they defend themselves successfully against it.
3 If someone or something **repels** something, they push it away. *True magnets can repel other magnets.*
repellent ADJECTIVE

repetition

NOUN If there is a **repetition** of something, it happens again or is repeated.

repetitive

ADJECTIVE Something that is **repetitive** is repeated over and over again, and can be extremely boring. *Fruit picking is a repetitive job.*

replace replaces replacing replaced

VERB **1** If you **replace** something, you put it back.
2 If you **replace** something old, broken or missing, you put another one or a new one in its place. *Ben replaced Tina in the team.*

replay replays replaying replayed

VERB **1** If you **replay** a tape or a film, you play it again.
NOUN **2** a sports match that is played for a second time.

replica replicas

NOUN an accurate copy of something.

reply replies replying replied

VERB **1** If you **reply** to something, you say or write something as an answer to it.

NOUN **2** what you say or write when you answer someone.

report reports reporting reported

VERB **1** If you **report** that something has happened, you inform someone about it.

NOUN **2** an account of an event or situation.

reporter reporters

NOUN someone who writes news articles or broadcasts news reports.

represent represents representing represented

VERB If someone **represents** you, they act on your behalf.

representative representatives

NOUN a person who acts on behalf of another person or group of people.

reprieve reprieves

NOUN a cancellation or postponement of a punishment, especially the death penalty.

reprimand reprimands reprimanding reprimanded

VERB If you **reprimand** someone, you officially tell them that they should not have done something.

reproach reproaches reproaching reproached

VERB **1** If you **reproach** someone, you blame them for something, or criticize them.

NOUN **2** the act of reproaching someone.

reproduce reproduces reproducing reproduced

VERB **1** If you **reproduce** something, you make a copy of it.

2 When living things **reproduce**, they produce more of their own kind. *Rats* **reproduce** *up to five times every year.*

reproduction

NOUN the process by which each living thing produces young.

reptile reptiles

NOUN an animal such as a snake, turtle or lizard that has scales on its skin, lays eggs, and is cold-blooded.

[from Latin *reptilis* meaning creeping]

lizard   turtle

republic republics

NOUN a country that has a president rather than a king or queen.

repulsion

NOUN the force pushing two magnets away from each other.

repulsive

ADJECTIVE horrible and disgusting.

reputation reputations

NOUN the opinion that people have of someone or something.

request requests requesting requested

VERB **1** If you **request** something, you ask for it politely or formally.

NOUN **2** If you make a **request** for something, you ask for it.

require requires requiring required

VERB **1** If you **require** something, you need it.

2 If you are **required** to do something, you have to do it. *You are* **required** *to report to the office at 9 a.m.*

requirement requirements

NOUN something you must have or must do.

rescue rescues rescuing rescued

VERB **1** If you **rescue** someone, you save them from a dangerous or unpleasant situation.

NOUN **2** an attempt to save someone from a dangerous or unpleasant situation.

research researches researching researched

NOUN **1** detailed study to discover facts about something.

VERB **2** If you **research** something, you study it carefully to discover facts about it.

resemble resembles resembling resembled

VERB If one thing or person **resembles** another, they are similar to each other.

resent resents resenting resented
VERB If you **resent** something, you feel bitter and angry about it.

reserve reserves reserving reserved
VERB 1 If you **reserve** something, you ask for it to be kept aside or ordered for you, or you keep it for a particular purpose. *We have reserved this table for someone else.*
NOUN 2 an area of land where animals, birds or plants are officially protected and can safely breed.
3 If you are a **reserve** in a team, you play if one of the other team members cannot.

reserved
ADJECTIVE 1 kept for someone. *We have reserved a table at the restaurant.*
2 People who are **reserved** are quiet and shy.

reservoir reservoirs
Said "**rez**-uh-vwar" NOUN a lake, often artificial, used for storing water before it is supplied to people.

residence residences
NOUN; FORMAL Your **residence** is your home.

resident residents
NOUN A **resident** of a house or area is someone who lives there.

resign resigns resigning resigned
VERB 1 If you **resign** from your job, you give it up.
2 If you **resign** yourself to an unpleasant situation, you accept it without complaining.
resignation NOUN

resist resists resisting resisted
VERB 1 If you **resist** something, you refuse to accept it and try to stop it happening.
2 If you **resist** an attack, you fight back.

resistance
NOUN fighting or taking action against something or someone. *Her body's resistance to disease helped her to get well.*

resolute
Said "**rez**-ul-loot" ADJECTIVE If you are **resolute**, you are determined not to change your mind.
resolutely ADVERB

resolution resolutions
Said "rez-ul-**loo**-shun" NOUN 1 determination.
2 If you make a **resolution**, you promise yourself that you will do something.
3 A decision made at a meeting. *The resolution to improve the play area was agreed.*

resolve resolves resolving resolved
VERB 1 If you **resolve** a problem, you find a way of sorting it out.
2 If you **resolve** to do something, you make up your mind firmly to do it.
NOUN 3 determination to do something.

resort resorts resorting resorted
NOUN 1 a place where a lot of people spend their holidays, especially by the sea.
VERB 2 If you **resort** to doing something, you do it because everything else has failed and you have no alternative.
PHRASE 3 If you do something **as a last resort**, you do it because you can find no other way of solving a problem.

resource resources
NOUN The **resources** of a country, organization or person are the materials, money or skills they have and can use.

resourceful
ADJECTIVE A **resourceful** person is good at solving problems and finding ways to do things.

respect respects respecting respected
VERB 1 If you **respect** someone, you admire and like them.
2 If you **respect** someone's feelings or wishes, you treat them with consideration.
NOUN 3 a feeling of admiration for someone's good qualities or achievements.
4 consideration for other people.

a b c d e f g h i j k l m n o p q **r** s t u v w x y z

respectable

respectable

ADJECTIVE Someone who is **respectable** behaves in a way that is approved of in the society where they live.

respiration

NOUN breathing. *His respiration was affected by his cold.*

respond responds responding responded

VERB If you **respond** to someone or something, you react to them by doing or saying something.

response responses

NOUN a reply or a reaction to something.

responsible

ADJECTIVE 1 If you are **responsible** for something, you are in charge of it and must take the blame if it goes wrong. *If we get a pet, you will be responsible for looking after it.*

2 A **responsible** person is sensible, trustworthy and reliable.

3 If you are **responsible** for something, you are the cause of it. *She was responsible for the accident.*

responsibility NOUN

rest rests resting rested

VERB 1 If you **rest**, you take a break from what you are doing and relax for a while.

2 If you **rest** something against something else, you lean it there.

NOUN 3 The **rest** of something is all the parts that are left or have not been mentioned.

4 If you have a **rest**, you do not do anything active for a while.

5 an object that supports something else, such as a head**rest** or a foot**rest**.

restaurant restaurants

NOUN a place where you can buy and eat a meal: *an Italian restaurant.*

restless

ADJECTIVE If you are **restless**, you find it hard to stay still or relaxed because you are bored or impatient.

restlessness NOUN   **restlessly** ADVERB

restore restores restoring restored

VERB If you **restore** something, you get it back to its original state.

restrain restrains restraining restrained

VERB If you **restrain** someone or something, you hold them back or stop them from doing what they want to.

restrict restricts restricting restricted

VERB To **restrict** someone or something means to set limits on them. *The police restricted parking outside the school.*

result results resulting resulted

NOUN 1 The **result** of an action or situation is what happens because of it.

2 The **result** of a contest, calculation or exam is the final score, figure or mark at the end of it.

VERB 3 If something **results** from a particular event, it is caused by that event.

resume resumes resuming resumed

VERB If you **resume** something, you start doing it again after a break. *After dinner, Dad resumed his work on the car.*

retail

NOUN the activity of selling goods to the public, usually in small amounts.

retailer NOUN

Antonym: wholesale

retain retains retaining retained

VERB If you **retain** something, you keep it.

retaliate retaliates retaliating retaliated

VERB If you **retaliate**, you do something to harm or upset someone because they have harmed or upset you.

retaliation NOUN

retire retires retiring retired

VERB 1 When older people **retire**, they leave their job and stop working.

2 If you **retire** from a race, you withdraw from it.

retort retorts retorting retorted

VERB 1 If you **retort**, you reply angrily.

NOUN 2 a short, angry reply.

retrace retraces retracing retraced

VERB If you **retrace** your steps, you go back exactly the same way you came.

retreat retreats retreating retreated

VERB If you **retreat** from someone or something unpleasant or dangerous, you move away from them.

retrieve retrieves retrieving retrieved
VERB If you **retrieve** something, you get it back or find it again.

return returns returning returned
VERB **1** If you **return** to a place, you go back there.
2 If you **return** something to someone, you give it back to them.
NOUN **3** the act of giving or putting something back.
4 a ticket for a journey to a place and back again.

reunion reunions
NOUN a meeting or a party at which people who have not seen each other for a long time get together.
reunite VERB

rev revs revving revved
VERB **1** When someone **revs** an engine, they press the accelerator to increase its speed.
NOUN **2** The speed of an engine is measured in **revs**, which is an abbreviation of *revolutions per minute*.

reveal reveals revealing revealed
VERB **1** If you **reveal** something, you tell people about it.
2 If you **reveal** something that has been hidden, you uncover it.

revel revels revelling revelled
VERB If you **revel** in a situation, you enjoy it very much.
reveller NOUN   **revelry** NOUN

revenge
NOUN the act of hurting someone who has hurt you.

revenue revenues
NOUN money that a government, company or organization receives.

Reverend
NOUN a title used before the name of a member of the clergy.

reverse reverses reversing reversed
VERB **1** If you **reverse** the order of things, you arrange them in the opposite order.
2 When someone **reverses** a car, they drive it backwards.

reversible
ADJECTIVE **Reversible** clothing can be worn with either side on the outside.

review reviews reviewing reviewed
NOUN **1** an article in a magazine or newspaper, or a talk on television or radio, giving an opinion of a new book, play, or film.
VERB **2** When someone **reviews** a book, play or film, they write an account or have a discussion expressing their opinion of it.

revise revises revising revised
VERB If you **revise** for an exam, you go over your work to make sure you know it properly.

revive revives reviving revived
VERB When you **revive** someone who has fainted, they become conscious again.

revolt revolts revolting revolted
NOUN **1** a violent uprising or rebellion against authority.
VERB **2** When people **revolt**, they rebel against the system that governs them.
3 If something **revolts** you, it disgusts you.

revolting
ADJECTIVE horrible and disgusting.

revolution revolutions
NOUN a violent attempt by a large number of people to change the way their country is run.

revolutionize revolutionizes revolutionizing revolutionized
VERB If something is **revolutionized**, it is changed completely, usually for the better.
*Science and technology have **revolutionized** the way we live.*

revolve revolves revolving revolved
VERB When something **revolves**, it turns in a circle around a central point.
revolving ADJECTIVE

revolver revolvers
NOUN a small gun held in the hand.

reward rewards rewarding rewarded
NOUN **1** something you are given because you have done something good.
VERB **2** If you **reward** someone, you give them a reward.

a
b
c
d
e
f
g
h
i
j
k
l
m
n
o
p
q
r
s
t
u
v
w
x
y
z

rewarding

ADJECTIVE Something that is **rewarding** gives you a lot of satisfaction. *Nursing is a* **rewarding** *job.*

rewind rewinds rewinding rewound

VERB If you **rewind** a cassette or video tape, you wind it back to the beginning.

rewrite rewrites rewriting rewrote rewritten

VERB If you **rewrite** something you have written, you write it again to make changes to it and improve it.

Synonym: redraft

rhetorical

ADJECTIVE A question that is **rhetorical** is asked in order to make a statement, rather than to get an answer. For example, "What's the world coming to?"

rheumatism

NOUN an illness that makes your joints and muscles stiff and painful.
rheumatic ADJECTIVE

rhinoceros rhinoceroses

NOUN a large African or Asian mammal with one or two horns on its nose.
[from Greek *rhin* meaning of the nose and *keras* meaning horn]

rhombus rhombuses or rhombi

NOUN a plane shape like a diamond, with four equal sides and no right angles.

rhubarb

NOUN a plant with long red stems that can be cooked with sugar and eaten.

rhyme rhymes rhyming rhymed

VERB **1** If one word **rhymes** with another, both words have a very similar sound in their final syllable. For example, "Sally" rhymes with "valley".
NOUN **2** a word that rhymes with another. *He couldn't find a* **rhyme** *for "orange".*

rhythm rhythms

NOUN a regular series of sounds, movements or actions. *The poem was easy to learn because it had a strong* **rhythm***.*

rib ribs

NOUN the curved bones that go from your spine to your chest.

ribbon ribbons

NOUN a long, narrow piece of cloth used as a fastening or decoration.

rice

NOUN white or brown grains taken from a cereal plant and used for food.

rich richer richest; riches

ADJECTIVE **1** Someone who is **rich** has a lot of money or possessions.
2 Something that is **rich** in something contains a large amount of it. *Fruit is* **rich** *in vitamins.*
3 Rich food contains a large amount of fat, oil or sugar.
PLURAL NOUN **4 Riches** are valuable possessions or large amounts of money.

rickshaw rickshaws

NOUN a two-wheeled, hand-pulled cart used in Asia for carrying passengers.

ricochet ricochets ricocheting or ricochetting ricocheted or ricochetted

Said "**rik**-oh-shay" VERB When an object **ricochets**, it hits a surface and then bounces away from it.

rid

PHRASE When you **get rid of** something you do not want, you throw it away.

riddle riddles

NOUN an amusing or puzzling question, sometimes in rhyme, to which you must find an answer.

ride rides riding rode ridden

VERB **1** When you **ride** a horse or a bicycle, you sit on it and control it as it moves along.
2 When you **ride** in a car, you travel in it.
NOUN **3** a journey on a horse or bicycle or in a vehicle.

ridge ridges

NOUN a long, narrow piece of high land.

ridicule ridicules ridiculing ridiculed

VERB **1** If you **ridicule** someone, you make fun of them in an unkind way.
NOUN **2** unkind laughter or teasing.

ridiculous

ADJECTIVE very foolish.

rifle rifles

NOUN a gun with a long barrel.

rig rigs rigging rigged

NOUN 1 a large structure used for taking oil or gas from the ground or the sea bed: *an oil rig*.

VERB 2 When someone **rigs** a boat, they fit it with ropes and sails.

right rights

NOUN 1 correct behaviour. *At least he knew right from wrong.*

2 If you have a **right** to do something, you are allowed to do it.

3 one of two opposite directions, sides or positions. If you are facing north and you turn to the **right**, you will be facing east.

ADJECTIVE OR ADVERB 4 If something is **right**, it is correct.

5 on or towards the right of something.

Antonym: (senses 1 and 4) wrong
(senses 3 and 5) left

right angle right angles

NOUN an angle of 90°.

rigid

ADJECTIVE A **rigid** object is stiff and does not bend easily.

rigidly ADVERB

rim rims

NOUN the outer edge of something such as a bowl or wheel.

rind rinds

NOUN the skin on bacon, cheese and some fruits.

ring rings ringing rang rung

VERB 1 If you **ring** someone, you phone them.

2 When a telephone or bell **rings**, it makes a clear, loud sound.

NOUN 3 a small circle of metal that you wear on your finger.

ringleader ringleaders

NOUN the leader of a group, who leads the others into mischief or crime.

rink rinks

NOUN a large indoor area for ice skating or roller skating.

rinse rinses rinsing rinsed

VERB When you **rinse** something, you wash it in clean water, without soap.

riot riots rioting rioted

NOUN 1 When there is a **riot**, a crowd of people behave violently in a public place.

VERB 2 When people **riot**, they behave violently in a public place.

rip rips ripping ripped

VERB If you **rip** something, you tear it.

ripe riper ripest

ADJECTIVE **Ripe** fruit or grain is fully developed and ready to be eaten.

ripple ripples rippling rippled

NOUN 1 a little wave on the surface of calm water.

2 If there is a **ripple** of laughter or applause, people laugh or clap their hands gently for a short time.

VERB 3 When the surface of water **ripples**, little waves appear on it.

rise rises rising rose risen

VERB 1 If something **rises**, it moves upwards. *Wilson watched the smoke rise from the fire.*

2 When the sun or moon **rises**, it appears from below the horizon.

NOUN 3 When something goes up, it is called a **rise**, for example a **rise** in the land or a **rise** in prices.

VERB 4 When you **rise**, you get out of bed.

5 If something such as a sound, or the level of a liquid or prices **rise**, they become higher.

risk risks risking risked

NOUN 1 If there is a **risk** of something unpleasant, it might happen.

2 Someone or something that is a **risk** is likely to cause harm or have bad results.

VERB 3 If you **risk** something, you do something knowing that an unpleasant thing might happen as a result. *If he doesn't play, he risks losing his place in the team.*

ritual rituals

NOUN 1 a traditional ceremony.

ADJECTIVE 2 **Ritual** activities happen as part of a tradition or ritual.

rival rivals

NOUN Someone's **rival** is the person they are competing with.

river rivers

NOUN a large, continuous stretch of fresh water flowing in a channel across land, to a larger **river**, a lake or the sea.

road roads

NOUN a long stretch of hard ground built between two places so that people can travel along it easily.

roam roams roaming roamed

VERB If you **roam** around, you wander around without any particular reason.

roar roars roaring roared

VERB 1 If something **roars**, it makes a very loud noise.

NOUN 2 a very loud noise.

roast roasts roasting roasted

VERB 1 When you **roast** meat or other food, you cook it in an oven or over a fire.

ADJECTIVE 2 **Roast** meat or vegetables have been roasted.

rob robs robbing robbed

VERB If someone **robs** a person or place, they steal money or property from them.

robe robes

NOUN a long, loose piece of clothing that covers the body.

robin robins

NOUN a small bird with a red breast.

robot robots

NOUN a machine that moves and does things automatically.

[from Czech *robota* meaning work]

rock rocks rocking rocked

NOUN 1 **Rock** is made up of small pieces of one or more minerals. The earth's surface is made up of **rock**.

2 A **rock** is a piece of **rock**.

3 music with a strong beat, usually involving electric guitars and drums.

4 a hard sweet, usually brightly coloured and shaped like a long stick.

VERB 5 When something **rocks**, or when you **rock** it, it moves regularly backwards and forwards or from side to side.

rocket rockets

NOUN 1 a space vehicle, usually shaped like a long pointed tube.

2 an explosive missile.

rod rods

NOUN a long, thin pole or bar.

rode

VERB the past tense of *ride*.

rodent rodents

NOUN a small mammal with sharp front teeth that it uses for gnawing. Rabbits and mice are **rodents**.

[from Latin *rodere* meaning to gnaw]

rogue rogues

NOUN a dishonest or mischievous person.

role roles

NOUN An actor's **role** is the character that he or she plays in a play or film.

roll rolls rolling rolled

VERB 1 If something **rolls**, or if you **roll** it, it moves along a surface, turning over many times.

2 If you **roll** something, or **roll it up**, you wrap it around itself so that it has a rounded shape.

NOUN 3 A **roll** of paper or cloth is a long piece of it that has been rolled into a tube.

4 a small, circular loaf of bread.

Rollerblade Rollerblades

NOUN; TRADEMARK **Rollerblades** are special roller skates that have the wheels set in one straight line on the bottom of the boot.

roller coaster roller coasters

NOUN a pleasure ride at a fun fair, consisting of a small railway that goes up and down steep slopes and around bends.

roller skate roller skates

NOUN **Roller skates** are shoes or boots with four small wheels underneath.

roller-skate VERB

Roman Catholic Roman Catholics

NOUN someone who belongs to the branch of the Christian Church that has the Pope in Rome as its leader.

romance romances

NOUN **1** a love story.

2 If two people have a **romance**, they have a romantic relationship.

Roman numerals

PLURAL NOUN numbers written in the form of letters and used by ancient Romans. For example, I = 1, V = 5, X = 10, L = 50, C = 100, D = 500, M = 1000.

romantic

ADJECTIVE **1** to do with romance and love.

2 A **romantic** person is rather emotional and not very realistic about life and love.

Romani; also spelt **Romany**

NOUN the language of the Gypsies.

roof roofs

NOUN the covering on top of a building or vehicle.

rook rooks

NOUN **1** a large black bird.

2 a chess piece that can move any number of squares in a straight but not diagonal line. It is also called a castle.

room rooms

NOUN **1** a separate section in a building, divided from other **rooms** by walls.

2 If there is **room** for something, there is enough space for it.

roost roosts roosting roosted

NOUN **1** a place where birds rest or build their nests.

VERB **2** When birds **roost**, they settle somewhere for the night.

root roots

NOUN **Roots** are the parts of a plant that usually grow underground. They anchor the plant and carry water from the soil. *See* page 434.

root word root words

NOUN a word that you can add a prefix or a suffix to in order to make other words. For example, in the words "unclear", "clearly" and "cleared", the **root word** is "clear".

rope ropes roping roped

NOUN **1** a thick, strong cord made by twisting together several thinner cords.

VERB **2** If you **rope** one thing to another, you tie them together with rope.

rosary rosaries

NOUN a string of beads that Catholics use for counting prayers.

rose roses

NOUN **1** a flower that has a pleasant smell and grows on a bush with thorns.

VERB **2** the past tense of **rise**.

rosette rosettes

NOUN a large circular badge of coloured ribbons worn as a prize in a competition or to support a political party.

Rosh Hashanah; also spelt **Rosh Hashana**

NOUN the festival celebrating the Jewish New Year.

rosy rosier rosiest

ADJECTIVE **1** reddish-pink. *Our cheeks were **rosy** after our walk on the windy beach.*

2 hopeful and positive. *He always has a **rosy** outlook on life.*

rot rots rotting rotted

VERB When food, wood or other substances **rot**, or when something **rots** them, they decay and fall apart.

Synonym: decompose

rotary

ADJECTIVE moving or able to move in a circular direction around a fixed point.

rotate rotates rotating rotated

VERB When something **rotates**, it turns with a circular movement, like a wheel.

rotation rotations

NOUN **1** a complete circular movement: *the **rotation** of a wheel, the **rotation** of the earth.*

PHRASE **2** If you do things **in rotation**, you do them one after the other, and when you finish you start all over again.

rotor rotors

NOUN **1** the part of a machine that turns.
2 The **rotors**, or **rotor** blades, of a helicopter are the four long, flat pieces of metal on top of it, that rotate and lift it off the ground.

rotten

ADJECTIVE **1** Something that is **rotten** has decayed.
2 INFORMAL bad, unpleasant or unfair. *I think it's a rotten idea.*

rough rougher roughest

ADJECTIVE **1** uneven and not smooth. *His hands were hard and rough.*
2 using too much force. *Don't be so rough with that toy or you'll break it.*
3 approximate. *At a rough guess, it is five o'clock.*

Antonyms: (sense 1) smooth
(sense 2) gentle
(sense 3) exact, precise

roughly

ADVERB **1** almost or approximately. *There are roughly 100 marbles in that box.*
2 If you treat someone or something **roughly**, you treat them clumsily or violently.

round rounder roundest; rounds

ADJECTIVE **1** Something **round** is shaped like a ball or a circle.
PREPOSITION OR ADVERB **2** If something is **round** something else, it surrounds it.
3 If something goes **round**, it moves in a circle. *The sails of the windmill went round.*
PREPOSITION **4** If you go **round** something, you go to the other side of it. *Suddenly a car came round the corner.*
ADVERB **5** If you turn or look **round**, you turn or look in a different direction.
6 If you move things **round**, you move them so that they are in different places.
7 If you go **round** to someone's house, you visit them.
NOUN **8** one of a series of events, especially in a competition.
9 a series of calls or deliveries. *Our house is the last one on the milkman's round.*
10 a whole slice of bread, or a sandwich made of two slices.

11 a type of song in which people sing the same words but start at different times.
rounded ADJECTIVE

roundabout roundabouts

NOUN **1** a meeting point of several roads with a circle in the centre that vehicles have to travel around.
2 a circular platform that goes round and that children can ride on in a playground.
3 a large, circular platform with horses or cars on it, for children to ride on as it goes round and round.

Synonym: (sense 3) merry-go-round

rounders

NOUN a team game in which players hit a ball with a bat and run round a circuit.

rouse rouses rousing roused

VERB **1** If you **rouse** someone, you wake them up.
2 If you **rouse** yourself, you make yourself get up and do something.
3 If something **rouses** your emotions, it makes you feel those emotions.
ADJECTIVE **4** Something that is **rousing**, such as a game, speech or song, makes you feel excited and emotional.

route routes

NOUN a way from one place to another: *the most direct route to the town centre.*

routine routines

ADJECTIVE **1** **Routine** activities are done regularly.
NOUN **2** the usual way or order in which you do things.

row rows rowing rowed

Rhymes with "snow" VERB **1** When you **row** a boat, you use oars to make it move through the water.
NOUN **2** several objects or people in a line
Rhymes with "cow" NOUN **3** an argument.
4 a lot of noise.

rowdy rowdier rowdiest

ADJECTIVE rough and noisy.
rowdily ADVERB

royal

ADJECTIVE belonging to or involving a queen, a king, or a member of their family.

RSVP

RSVP written at the end of a letter or an invitation means please reply.
[an abbreviation for the French expression *Répondez s'il vous plaît* meaning please reply]

rub rubs rubbing rubbed

VERB If you **rub** something, you move your hand, or a cloth, very firmly backwards and forwards over it.

rubber rubbers

NOUN **1** a strong, elastic substance used for making tyres, boots and other products.
2 a small piece of rubber or plastic that you use to remove mistakes when writing or drawing with a pencil.

rubbish

NOUN **1** unwanted things or waste material.
2 something foolish.
3 something of very poor quality.

Synonyms: (sense 1) garbage, refuse, trash

rubble

NOUN bits of old brick and stone.

ruby rubies

NOUN a type of red jewel.

rucksack rucksacks

NOUN a bag with shoulder straps for carrying things on your back.

rudder rudders

NOUN a piece of wood or metal at the back of a boat or plane that is moved to make the boat or plane turn.

rude ruder rudest

ADJECTIVE **1** not polite.
2 indecent or offensive.

ruff ruffs

NOUN a stiff circular collar with many pleats in it. These collars were very popular in the 16th century.

ruffle ruffles ruffling ruffled

VERB **1** If you **ruffle** someone's hair, you move your hand quickly backwards and forwards over their head.
2 If something **ruffles** you, it makes you annoyed or upset.

NOUN **3 Ruffles** are small folds made in a piece of material for decoration.

rug rugs

NOUN **1** a small thick carpet.
2 a warm covering for your knees or for sitting on outdoors.

rugby

NOUN a game played by two teams, who try to kick or throw an oval ball past a line at their opponents' end of the pitch.
[named after *Rugby* School where it was first played]

A rugby ball

rugged

ADJECTIVE **1** Somewhere **rugged** is rocky, wild and unsheltered.
2 Someone **rugged** is strong and tough.

ruin ruins ruining ruined

VERB **1** If you **ruin** something, you destroy or spoil it completely.
NOUN **2** the part that is left after something has been severely damaged.

rule rules ruling ruled

NOUN **1 Rules** are instructions that tell you what you must do.
VERB **2** When someone **rules** a country or a group of people, they govern it and are in charge of its affairs.

ruler rulers

NOUN **1** a person who rules a country.
2 a long, flat object with straight edges, marked with a scale, used for measuring things or drawing straight lines.

rum rums

NOUN a strong alcoholic drink made from sugar cane juice.

rumble rumbles rumbling rumbles

VERB **1** If something **rumbles**, it makes a continuous low sound. *My stomach is rumbling because I am hungry.*
NOUN **2** a continuous deep sound. *There was a rumble of thunder.*

rumour rumours

NOUN a piece of information or a story that people are talking about, but which may not be true.

a
b
c
d
e
f
g
h
i
j
k
l
m
n
o
p
q
r
s
t
u
v
w
x
y
z

run runs running ran

VERB **1** When you **run**, you move quickly, with both feet leaving the ground at each stride.

2 If you **run** water, you turn on the tap to let the water flow out.

3 If your nose is **running**, a lot of liquid is coming out of it.

4 If you **run** an activity or a place such as a school or shop, you are in charge of it.

5 If you **run away** from a place, you leave it suddenly and secretly.

run out VERB **6** If you **run out** of something, you have no more left.

rung rungs

NOUN one of the bars that form the steps of a ladder.

runner runners

NOUN **1** a person who runs as a sport, especially in competitions.

2 a person who takes messages or runs errands.

3 A **runner** on a plant such as a strawberry is a long shoot from which a new plant develops.

runny runnier runniest

ADJECTIVE flowing or moving like liquid.

runway runways

NOUN a long strip of ground used by aeroplanes for taking off and landing.

rural

ADJECTIVE to do with the countryside.

rush rushes rushing rushed

VERB **1** If you **rush** somewhere, or if you are **rushed** there, you go there quickly.

2 If you **rush** something, or if you are **rushed** into something, you do it too quickly.

NOUN **3** a type of plant that grows in or beside fresh water, such as rivers, ponds and lakes.

rust rusts rusting rusted

NOUN **1** a reddish-brown substance that forms on metal when it is exposed to water and the oxygen in the air.

VERB **2** When metal **rusts**, it corrodes and a reddish-brown substance is formed. **Rusting** occurs when iron or steel is exposed to water and the oxygen in the air.

rustle rustles rustling rustled

VERB If something **rustles**, it makes a soft, crisp sound as it moves, like the sound of dry leaves moving.

rusty rustier rustiest

ADJECTIVE **1** covered with rust. *The old bicycle was rusty*.

2 not as good as it once was because of lack of practice. *Dad's maths is a bit rusty*.

rut ruts

NOUN a deep, narrow groove in the ground made by the wheels of a vehicle.

ruthless

ADJECTIVE very harsh or cruel, and without any pity.

rye

NOUN a cereal crop that produces light-brown grain used to make flour.

Ss

Sabbath Sabbaths
NOUN the day of the week that some religious groups, such as Jews and Christians, use for rest and prayer.
[from Hebrew *shabbath* meaning to rest]

sabotage sabotages sabotaging sabotaged
NOUN **1** the deliberate damaging of machinery and equipment such as railway lines.
VERB **2** If something is **sabotaged**, it is deliberately damaged.
saboteur NOUN

sabre sabres
NOUN **1** a heavy curved sword.
2 a light sword used in fencing.

sachet sachets
NOUN a small packet containing something like sugar or shampoo.

sack sacks
NOUN **1** a large bag made of rough material, for carrying such things as potatoes and grain: *a sack of potatoes*.
PHRASE **2** INFORMAL If someone **gets the sack**, they are dismissed from their job by their employer.

sacred
ADJECTIVE holy, or connected with religion or religious ceremonies.

sacrifice sacrifices sacrificing sacrificed
VERB If you **sacrifice** something valuable or important, you give it up.

sad sadder saddest
ADJECTIVE If you are **sad**, you feel unhappy.

sadden saddens saddening saddened
VERB If something **saddens** you, it makes you feel sad.
saddening ADJECTIVE

saddle saddles saddling saddled
NOUN **1** a leather seat strapped to an animal's back, for the rider to sit on.
2 the seat on a bicycle.
VERB **3** If you **saddle** a horse, you put a saddle on it.

safari safaris
NOUN an expedition for hunting or observing wild animals.
[from Swahili *safari* meaning journey]

safari park safari parks
NOUN a large park where wild animals such as lions, giraffes and elephants are free to roam.

safe safer safest; safes
ADJECTIVE **1** If you are **safe**, you are not in any danger.
2 Something that is **safe** does not cause harm or danger.
NOUN **3** a strong metal box with special locks, in which you can keep valuable things.

safeguard safeguards safeguarding safeguarded
VERB **1** If you **safeguard** something, you protect it.
NOUN **2** a law or a rule to help protect people or things from harm.

safety
NOUN protection, being safe: *child safety. We should have safety in our homes*.

saga sagas
NOUN a very long story, usually telling of many different adventures.

said
VERB the past tense and past participle of *say*.

sail sails sailing sailed
VERB **1** When a ship **sails**, it moves across water.
2 If you **sail** somewhere, you go there by ship.
NOUN **3** one of the large pieces of material attached to a ship's mast. The wind blows against the **sail** and moves the ship.
4 The arm of a windmill is called a **sail**.

sailor sailors
NOUN **1** a member of a ship's crew.
2 someone who sails.

saint saints
NOUN a person who is given a special honour by a Christian Church, after they have died, because they lived a very holy life.

sake sakes
PHRASE If you do something for someone's **sake**, you do it to help or please them.

salad salads
NOUN a mixture of foods eaten cold or warm, and often raw.

salami
NOUN a kind of spicy sausage.
[Italian plural of *salame*, from *salare* meaning to salt]

salary salaries
NOUN a payment made each month to an employee.

sale sales
NOUN **1** The **sale** of goods is the selling of them.
2 an occasion when a shop sells things at reduced prices.

saliva
NOUN the watery liquid in your mouth that softens food, which helps you chew and digest it.

salmon salmons or salmon
NOUN a large, edible, silver-coloured fish with pink flesh.

salt
NOUN a white substance used to flavour and preserve food.

salute salutes saluting saluted
NOUN **1** a formal sign of respect. Soldiers give a **salute** by raising their right hand to their forehead.
VERB **2** If you **salute** someone, you give them a salute.

salvage salvages salvaging salvaged
VERB If you **salvage** things, you save them from, for example, a wrecked ship or a destroyed building.

same
ADJECTIVE **1** If two things are the **same**, they are like one another.
2 just one thing and not two different ones. *They were born in the **same** town.*

sample samples sampling sampled
NOUN **1** a small amount of something that you can try or test, for example for quality or to find out more about it.
VERB **2** If you **sample** something, you try it. *I sampled his cooking.*

sanctuary sanctuaries
NOUN **1** a place where you are safe from harm or danger.
2 a place where wildlife is protected.

sand sands
NOUN a substance consisting of tiny pieces of stone. Beaches are made of **sand**.

sandal sandals
NOUN light shoes with straps, worn in warm weather.

sandstone
NOUN a type of rock formed from sand, often used for building.

sandwich sandwiches
NOUN two slices of bread with a filling between them.

sandy sandier sandiest
ADJECTIVE **1** A **sandy** area is covered with sand.
2 Sandy hair is a light orange-brown colour.

sane saner sanest
ADJECTIVE If someone is **sane**, they have a healthy mind.

sang
VERB the past tense of *sing*.

sank
VERB the past tense of *sink*.

sap saps sapping sapped
NOUN **1** the juice found in the stems of plants.
VERB **2** If something such as an illness **saps** your energy or your strength, it gradually weakens you.

sapling saplings
NOUN a young tree.

sapphire sapphires
NOUN a blue precious stone.

sarcastic
ADJECTIVE If someone is **sarcastic**, they say the opposite of what they really mean in order to mock or insult someone.

sardine sardines
NOUN a small edible sea fish.

sari saris
NOUN a piece of clothing consisting of a long piece of material folded around the body, worn especially by Indian women.
[a Hindi word]

sash sashes

NOUN a long piece of cloth worn round the waist or over one shoulder.

sat

VERB the past tense and past participle of *sit*.

satchel satchels

NOUN a leather or cloth bag with a long strap, especially used for carrying books to and from school.

satellite satellites

NOUN **1** a spacecraft sent into space to orbit the earth, to collect information, or as part of a communications system.

2 a natural object in space that moves round another, larger object, such as a planet or star.

satellite dish satellite dishes

NOUN a dish-shaped aerial that receives television signals sent by satellite.

satellite television

NOUN television programmes received by signals from artificial satellites.

satin satins

NOUN a kind of smooth, shiny fabric often made from silk.

satisfactory

ADJECTIVE acceptable or adequate.
satisfactorily ADVERB

satisfy satisfies satisfying satisfied

VERB If you **satisfy** someone, you do something or give them something to make them pleased or contented.

saturated

ADJECTIVE soaking wet.

Saturday Saturdays

NOUN the seventh day of the week, coming between Friday and Sunday.

sauce sauces

NOUN a liquid eaten with food to add flavour. *It's pasta with tomato **sauce** for dinner.*

saucepan saucepans

NOUN a deep metal pan with a handle and a lid used for cooking.

saucer saucers

NOUN a small curved plate for a cup to stand on.

sauna saunas

Said "**saw**-nah" NOUN If you have a **sauna**, you go into a very hot room in order to sweat, then have a cold bath or shower.
[a Finnish word]

saunter saunters sauntering sauntered

VERB If you **saunter** somewhere, you walk there slowly and casually.

sausage sausages

NOUN a mixture of minced meat and herbs formed into a tubular shape and served cooked.

savage savages savaging savaged

ADJECTIVE **1** cruel and violent.
NOUN **2** If you call someone a **savage**, you mean that they are violent and uncivilized.
VERB **3** If an animal **savages** you, it attacks you and bites you.

Synonyms: (sense 1) brutal, vicious

savannah savannahs

NOUN a grassy plain with few trees in a hot country.

save saves saving saved

VERB **1** If you **save** someone, you rescue them or help to keep them safe.
2 If you **save** something, you keep it so that you can use it later.
3 If you **save** time, money or effort, you stop it from being wasted.

savings

PLURAL NOUN Your **savings** are money you have saved.

saviour saviours

NOUN 1 a person who saves others from danger or loss.
PROPER NOUN 2 In Christianity, the **Saviour** is Jesus Christ.

savoury

ADJECTIVE salty or spicy. *Salt and vinegar crisps are my favourite **savoury** snack.*

saw saws sawing sawed

NOUN 1 a tool that has a blade with sharp teeth along one edge for cutting wood.
VERB 2 If you **saw** something, you cut it with a saw.
3 the past tense of *see*.

sawdust

NOUN the fine powder produced when you saw wood.

saxophone saxophones

NOUN a curved metal wind instrument often played in jazz bands.
[named after Adolphe *Sax* (1814–1894), who invented the instrument]

say says saying said

VERB If you **say** something, you speak words.

saying sayings

NOUN a well-known sentence or phrase that tells you something about life.

scab scabs

NOUN a hard, dry covering that forms over a wound while it is healing.

scaffolding

NOUN a framework of poles and boards that is used by workmen to stand on while they are working on the outside of a building.

scald scalds scalding scalded

VERB 1 If you **scald** yourself, you burn yourself with very hot liquid or steam.
NOUN 2 a burn caused by very hot liquid or steam.

scale scales

NOUN 1 the size or extent of something. *The scale of the building was enormous.*
2 a set of marks or numbers used for measuring something.
3 The **scale** of something like a map, a plan or a model shows the relationship between the measurements represented and those in the real world. For example, a **scale** of 1:10 tells you that one centimetre on a model represents 10 centimetres in real life.
4 one of the small, hard pieces of skin covering the body of a fish or a reptile.
5 a series of musical notes going upwards or downwards in a particular order.
PLURAL NOUN 6 **Scales** are a piece of equipment used for weighing things or people.

scalene

ADJECTVE A **scalene** triangle has sides of different lengths.

scalp scalps

NOUN the skin under the hair on your head.

scamper scampers scampering scampered

VERB If you **scamper**, you run quickly and lightly.

scampi

PLURAL NOUN large prawns, often eaten fried in breadcrumbs.

scan scans scanning scanned

VERB 1 If you **scan** something, you look at every part of it carefully.
2 If you **scan** a piece of writing, you look at it quickly but not in detail.
3 If a machine **scans** something, it examines it with a beam of light or X-rays.
NOUN 4 an examination of part of the body with X-ray or laser equipment.

scandal scandals

NOUN 1 a situation or event that people think is shocking and immoral.
2 gossip about bad things that can ruin a person's reputation.
scandalous ADJECTIVE

scanner scanners

NOUN a machine that is used to examine, identify or record things by using a beam of light or an X-ray.

scapegoat scapegoats
NOUN If someone is made a **scapegoat**, they are blamed for something, although it may not be their fault.

scar scars scarring scarred
NOUN 1 a mark left on your skin after a wound has healed.
VERB 2 If an injury **scars** you, it leaves a mark on your skin for ever.

scarce scarcer scarcest
ADJECTIVE If something is **scarce**, there is not very much of it.

scare scares scaring scared
VERB 1 If something **scares** you, it frightens you.
NOUN 2 something that gives you a fright.

scarecrow scarecrows
NOUN an object shaped like a person and put in a field to scare birds away from the crops.

scarf scarfs or scarves
NOUN a piece of cloth worn round your neck or head to keep you warm.

scarlet
NOUN OR ADJECTIVE bright red.

scary scarier scariest
ADJECTIVE; INFORMAL frightening. *The film was so scary I hid behind the sofa.*

scatter scatters scattering scattered
VERB 1 When you **scatter** things, you throw or drop them so they spread over a large area.
2 If a group of people or animals **scatter**, they suddenly move off in different directions.

scavenge scavenges scavenging scavenged
VERB If a human or other animal **scavenges** for things, they search for them among waste and rubbish.
scavenger NOUN

scene scenes
NOUN part of a play or film in which a series of events happen in one place.

scenery
NOUN 1 In the countryside, you can refer to everything you see as the **scenery**.
2 In a theatre, the **scenery** is the painted cloth on the stage that makes it seem like a particular place.

scent scents
NOUN a smell, especially a pleasant one.

sceptic sceptics
NOUN someone who does not believe things easily.

schedule schedules
NOUN a list of events or things you have to do, and the times at which each thing should be done or will happen.

scheme schemes scheming schemed
NOUN 1 a plan or arrangement.
VERB 2 When people **scheme**, they make secret plans.

scholar scholars
NOUN 1 a person who studies an academic subject and knows a lot about it.
2 In South African English, a **scholar** is a school pupil.

scholarship scholarships
NOUN If you win a **scholarship** to a school or university, your studies are paid for by the school or university, or by some other organization.

school schools
NOUN a place where children are educated.

schooner schooners
NOUN a type of sailing ship with more than one mast.

science sciences
NOUN the study of living things, materials and physical processes such as forces, electricity, sound and light.

science fiction
NOUN stories about travelling through space, and imaginary events happening in the future or in other worlds.

scientist scientists
NOUN someone who studies science or is an expert in science.

scissors
PLURAL NOUN a cutting tool with two sharp blades.

scold scolds scolding scolded
VERB If you **scold** someone, you tell them off.

a
b
c
d
e
f
g
h
i
j
k
l
m
n
o
p
q
r
s
t
u
v
w
x
y
z

scone scones

NOUN a small cake made from flour and fat, and usually eaten with cream and jam.

scoop scoops scooping scooped

VERB **1** If you **scoop** something up, you pick it up using a spoon or the palm of your hand.
NOUN **2** an object like a large spoon that is used for picking up food such as ice cream.

scooter scooters

NOUN **1** a small, light motorcycle.
2 a simple cycle that a child rides, with two wheels and a narrow platform for standing on while pushing the ground with one foot.

scope

NOUN **1** the opportunity or freedom to do something.
2 the extent of something. *That subject is beyond the scope of this lesson.*

scorch scorches scorching scorched

VERB If you **scorch** something, you burn it slightly.

score scores scoring scored

VERB **1** If you **score** in a game, you get a goal, a run or a point.
NOUN **2** the number of goals, runs or points obtained by the two opponents in a game.

scornful

ADJECTIVE If you are **scornful** of something or someone, you think very little of them and show very little respect for them.

scorpion scorpions

NOUN an animal that looks like a small lobster. It has a long tail with a poisonous sting on the end.

scoundrel scoundrels

NOUN; OLD-FASHIONED a man who cheats and deceives people.

scour scours scouring scoured

VERB **1** If you **scour** a place, you look all over it in order to find something.
2 If you **scour** something like a pan, you clean it by rubbing it hard with something rough.

scout scouts scouting scouted

NOUN **1** A **Scout** is a boy who is a member of the **Scout** Association, an organization for boys that aims to develop character and responsibility.

2 someone who is sent on ahead to get information about something.
VERB **3** If you **scout** around for something, you look around for it.

scowl scowls scowling scowled

VERB **1** If you **scowl**, you frown because you are angry.
NOUN **2** an angry expression.

scrabble scrabbles scrabbling scrabbled

VERB If you **scrabble** at something, you scrape at it with your hands.

scramble scrambles scrambling scrambled

VERB **1** If you **scramble** over something, you climb over it using your hands to help you.
2 When you **scramble** eggs, you mix them up and cook them in a pan.
NOUN **3** a motorcycle race over rough ground.

scrap scraps scrapping scrapped

NOUN **1** a very small piece of something.
2 unwanted or waste material.
3 INFORMAL If you get into a **scrap**, you get into a fight.
VERB **4** If you **scrap** something, you get rid of it.

scrapbook scrapbooks

NOUN a book with blank pages that you can fill with photographs or cuttings that interest you.

scrape scrapes scraping scraped

VERB **1** If you **scrape** something off a surface, you remove it by pulling a rough or sharp object over it.
2 If you **scrape** past something, you pass very close to it.

scratch scratches scratching scratched

VERB **1** If you **scratch** something, you make a small cut or mark on it with something sharp.
2 If you **scratch**, you rub your skin with your nails because it is itching.
NOUN **3** a small cut or mark on the surface of something.

scrawl scrawls scrawling scrawled

VERB **1** If you **scrawl** something, you write it in a careless and untidy way.
NOUN **2** careless and untidy writing.

scream screams screaming screamed

VERB **1** If you **scream**, you shout or cry in a loud, high-pitched voice.
NOUN **2** a loud, high-pitched cry.

screech screeches screeching screeched

VERB **1** If a person, animal or machine **screeches**, they make an unpleasant, high-pitched noise.

NOUN **2** an unpleasant high-pitched noise.

screen screens screening screened

NOUN **1** a vertical surface on which a picture can be shown, such as a television **screen**. **2** a panel used to separate different parts of a room, or to protect or hide something.

VERB **3** If a doctor **screens** you for a disease, they test to see if you have it.

screenplay screenplays

NOUN the script of a film.

screw screws screwing screwed

NOUN **1** a small, sharp piece of metal with a spiral groove cut into it, used for fixing things together or for fixing something to a wall using a twisting action.

VERB **2** If you **screw** something on to something else, you fix it there by twisting it round and round, or by using a screw. *He screwed the top on the ink bottle.*

screw up VERB **3** If you **screw up** paper or cloth, you twist it or squeeze it into a tight ball.

screwdriver screwdrivers

NOUN a tool for putting in or taking out screws.

scribble scribbles scribbling scribbled

VERB **1** If you **scribble** something, you write it quickly and untidily. **2** To **scribble** also means to make meaningless marks. *When Caroline was three she scribbled on a wall.*

script scripts

NOUN the written version of a play or film.

scripture scriptures

NOUN sacred writings, especially the Bible.

scroll scrolls

NOUN a long roll of paper or parchment with writing on it.

scrounge scrounges scrounging scrounged

VERB; INFORMAL If you **scrounge** something, you get it by asking for it rather than by earning or buying it.

scrub scrubs scrubbing scrubbed

VERB **1** If you **scrub** something, you clean it by rubbing it very hard, especially with a brush and water.

NOUN **2** ground covered with bushes and small trees.

scruffy scruffier scruffiest

ADJECTIVE untidy.

scrum scrums

NOUN When rugby players form a **scrum**, they form a group and push against each other with their heads down in an attempt to get the ball.

scuba diving

NOUN the sport of swimming underwater with special breathing equipment. [an abbreviation for *self-contained underwater breathing apparatus*]

scuffle scuffles scuffling scuffled

VERB **1** When people **scuffle**, they have a short, rough fight.

NOUN **2** a short, rough fight.

sculptor sculptors

NOUN someone who makes sculptures.

sculpture sculptures

NOUN a work of art made by shaping or carving stone, clay or wood.

scum

NOUN a layer of dirty froth on the surface of a liquid.

scurry scurries scurrying scurried

VERB If you **scurry**, you run with quick short steps.

scuttle scuttles scuttling scuttled

VERB **1** If a person or an animal **scuttles**, they run with short, quick steps. **2** To **scuttle** a ship means to sink it deliberately by making holes in the bottom.

NOUN **3** a container for coal.

scythe scythes

NOUN a tool with a long handle and a curved blade used for cutting grass or grain.

sea seas

NOUN one of the areas of salty water that cover much of the earth's surface.

seafood

PLURAL NOUN fish or shellfish from the sea eaten as food.

A B C D E F G H I J K L M N O P Q R **S** T U V W X Y Z

seagull seagulls

NOUN a common, white, grey and black bird that lives near the sea.

seahorse seahorses

NOUN a small fish that swims upright, with a head that looks rather like a horse's head.

seal seals sealing sealed

NOUN **1** a fish-eating mammal with flippers, that lives partly on land and partly in the sea.
2 something fixed over the opening of a container that prevents anything getting in or out, and which must be broken before the container can be opened.
VERB **3** If you **seal** an envelope, you stick down the flap.

seam seams

NOUN **1** a line of stitches joining two pieces of cloth.
2 a long, narrow layer of coal beneath the ground.

search searches searching searched

VERB **1** If you **search** for something, you look for it very thoroughly.
2 If a person is **searched**, their body and clothing are examined to see if they are hiding anything.
NOUN **3** an attempt to find something. *I found my purse after a long search*.

searchlight searchlights

NOUN a light with a powerful beam that can be turned in different directions.

seashore

NOUN the land along the edge of the sea.

seasick

ADJECTIVE feeling sick because of the movement of a boat.
seasickness NOUN

seaside

NOUN a place by the sea, especially where people go on holiday.

season seasons seasoning seasoned

NOUN **1** one of the periods into which a year is divided and which have their own typical weather conditions. The **seasons** are spring, summer, autumn and winter.

2 a period of the year when something usually happens.
VERB **3** If you **season** food, you add salt, pepper, herbs or spices to it.

seasoning seasonings

NOUN something with a strong taste, like salt, pepper or spices used to add flavour to food.

seat seats

NOUN something you can sit on.

seat belt seat belts

NOUN a strap that you put around your body for safety when you are travelling in a car, coach or aircraft.

seaweed

NOUN plants that grow in the sea.

secluded

ADJECTIVE quiet and hidden from view. *We found a lovely secluded beach*.

second seconds

ADJECTIVE **1** The **second** item in a series is the one that comes after the first, counted as number two.
NOUN **2** one of the sixty parts that a minute is divided into.

secondary

ADJECTIVE **1** Something **secondary** is less important than something else.
2 Secondary education is education for pupils between the ages of 11 and 18.

secondary school secondary schools

NOUN a school for pupils aged between 11 and 18.

second-hand

ADJECTIVE OR ADVERB Something that is **second-hand** has already been owned by someone else. *My brother has a second-hand car*.

second person

NOUN In grammar, you use the **second person** "you" when you speak or write to someone directly, for example, "you said", "you are".

secret secrets

ADJECTIVE **1** Something that is **secret** is known to only a small number of people and hidden from everyone else: *a secret meeting*.
NOUN **2** something known to only a small number of people and hidden from everyone else.

secretary secretaries

NOUN a person employed by an organization to keep records, write letters and do office work.

secretive

ADJECTIVE **Secretive** people tend to hide their feelings and intentions, and like to keep things secret.

sect sects

NOUN a group of people who have special or unusual religious beliefs.

section sections

NOUN one of the parts that something is divided into.

secure secures securing secured

VERB **1** If you **secure** something, you make it safe or fix it firmly.

ADJECTIVE **2** If something is **secure**, it is safe from harm.

security

NOUN OR ADJECTIVE all the things you do to make sure that you and your property are safe.

see sees seeing saw

VERB **1** If you **see** something, you look at it or notice it with your eyes.

2 If you **see** something, you understand it or realize what it means. *I **see** what you mean.*

3 If you **see** that something happens, you make sure that it is done.

seed seeds

NOUN the part of a plant that can grow into a new plant of the same type.

seek seeks seeking sought

VERB; FORMAL If you **seek** something, you try and find it.

seem seems seeming seemed

VERB If something **seems** to be the case, it appears to be the case, or you think it is the case.

seen

VERB the past participle of *see*.

seep seeps seeping seeped

VERB If a liquid or gas **seeps**, it flows very slowly.

seesaw seesaws

NOUN a long plank supported in the middle, so that one person can sit on at either end and each can move up and down.

seethe seethes seething seethed

VERB **1** When a liquid **seethes**, it boils or bubbles.

ADJECTIVE **2** If you are **seething**, you are very angry.

segment segments

NOUN **1** one part of something. **2** The **segments** of an orange or grapefruit are the sections you can divide it into.

segregate segregates segregating segregated

VERB To **segregate** two groups of people means to keep them apart from each other.

seize seizes seizing seized

VERB If you **seize** something, you grab it firmly.

seldom

ADVERB not very often. *They **seldom** watch television.*

select selects selecting selected

VERB If you **select** something, you choose it.

self selves

NOUN your own personality or nature that makes you different from anyone else.

self-conscious

ADJECTIVE Someone who is **self-conscious** is easily embarrassed, and worried about what other people think of them. *She was **self-conscious** when the teacher asked her to read her poem.*

self-defence

NOUN the use of special physical techniques to protect yourself when someone attacks you.

selfish

ADJECTIVE caring only about yourself, and not about other people.

self-service

ADJECTIVE A **self-service** shop or restaurant is one where you serve yourself.

sell sells selling sold

VERB If you **sell** something, you let someone have it in return for money.

Sellotape

NOUN; TRADEMARK a transparent sticky tape.

semaphore

NOUN a system of signalling by holding flags out with your arms in different positions to show letters of the alphabet.

semi-

PREFIX You add **semi-** to the beginning of a word to mean half or partly. For example, a **semi**circle is half of a circle.

semicircle semicircles

NOUN a half of a circle, or something with this shape.
semicircular ADJECTIVE

semicolon semicolons

NOUN the punctuation mark (;) is used to separate different parts of a sentence or to show a pause.

semidetached

ADJECTIVE A **semidetached** house is joined to another house on one side.

semifinal semifinals

NOUN one of the two matches or races in a competition that are held to decide who will compete in the final.

send sends sending sent

VERB **1** When you **send** something to someone, you arrange for it to be delivered to them.
2 If a person **sends** someone somewhere, they tell them to go there.

senile

ADJECTIVE If old people become **senile**, they become confused and cannot look after themselves.

senior seniors

ADJECTIVE **1** A **senior** official or employee has one of the highest and most important jobs in an organization.
NOUN **2** If you are someone's **senior**, you are older than they are, or in a more important position.

senior citizen senior citizens

NOUN an elderly person, especially one receiving a pension.

sensation sensations

NOUN **1** a feeling that you have.
2 If something causes a **sensation**, it causes great interest and excitement.

sensational

ADJECTIVE **1** INFORMAL extremely good. *The concert was **sensational**.*
2 causing great excitement or interest.

sense senses

NOUN **1** the physical abilities of sight, hearing, smell, touch and taste. *I have a good **sense** of smell.*
2 a feeling: *a **sense** of guilt.*
3 the ability to think and behave sensibly.
PHRASE **4** If something **makes sense**, you can understand it or it seems sensible.

senseless

ADJECTIVE **1** Something **senseless** has no reason to it. *The violence of the hooligans was **senseless**.*
2 If someone is **senseless**, they are unconscious.

sensible

ADJECTIVE showing good sense and judgment.

sensitive

ADJECTIVE **1** If you are **sensitive**, you understand other people's feelings.
2 If you are **sensitive** about something, you are easily worried or upset about it.
3 easily affected or harmed by something. *My skin is **sensitive** to the sun.*

Synonym: (sense 1) perceptive
(sense 2) touchy

sent

VERB the past tense and past participle of *send*.

sentence sentences sentencing sentenced

NOUN **1** a group of words that make a statement, question or command. When written down, a **sentence** begins with a capital letter and ends with a full stop.
2 In a law court, a **sentence** is a punishment given to someone who has been found guilty.
VERB **3** When a guilty person is **sentenced**, they are told officially what their punishment will be.

sentimental
ADJECTIVE **1** having an exaggerated feeling of tenderness or sadness.
2 having something to do with a person's feelings.

sentry sentries
NOUN a soldier who keeps watch and guards a camp or building.

separate separates separating separated
ADJECTIVE **1** If something is **separate** from something else, the two things are not connected.
VERB **2** If you **separate** people or things, you cause them to be apart from each other.
3 If people or things **separate**, they move away from each other.

September
NOUN the ninth month of the year. **September** has 30 days.
[from the Latin word *septem* meaning seven, because it was the seventh month of the Roman calendar]

septic
ADJECTIVE If a wound becomes **septic**, it becomes infected by harmful bacteria.

sequel sequels
NOUN A **sequel** to a book or film is another book or film that continues the story.

sequence sequences
NOUN **1** a number of events coming one after the other.
2 the order in which things are arranged or happen. *Put the pictures in* **sequence** *to tell the story.*

serene
ADJECTIVE peaceful and calm.

sergeant sergeants
NOUN a rank in the police force, the army or the air force.

serial serials
NOUN a story that is broadcast or published in a number of parts over a period of time.

series
NOUN **1** a number of things coming one after the other.

2 A radio or television **series** is a set of programmes with the same title.

serious
ADJECTIVE **1** A **serious** problem or situation is very bad and worrying.
2 **Serious** matters are important and should be thought about carefully.
3 If you are **serious** about something, you really mean it.
4 People who are **serious** are thoughtful, quiet and do not laugh much.

sermon sermons
NOUN a talk on a religious or moral subject given as part of a church service.

serpent serpents
NOUN; LITERARY a snake.

servant servants
NOUN someone who is employed to work in another person's house.

serve serves serving served
VERB **1** If you **serve** food or drink to people, you give it to them.
2 When someone **serves** customers in a shop, bar or restaurant, they help them and supply them with what they want. *The shop was very busy so we had to wait for the assistant to* **serve** *us.*
3 In some games, such as tennis, when you **serve** you start the game by hitting the ball to your opponent.

service services
NOUN **1** a system organized to provide something for the public. *The bus* **service** *from our village into town is very good.*
2 Motorway **services** consist of a petrol station, toilets, a shop and a restaurant.
3 If your car has a **service**, it is checked over and repaired if it is broken or damaged.
4 a religious ceremony.

serviette serviettes
NOUN a square of cloth or paper used when you are eating to protect your clothes or to wipe your mouth.

session sessions
NOUN the period during which an activity takes place.

set sets setting set

VERB **1** When something such as jelly or concrete **sets**, it changes from a liquid into a solid.

NOUN **2** a group of things that go together.

3 In maths, a **set** is a collection of numbers that are treated as a group.

4 In tennis, a **set** is a group of six or more games.

VERB **5** If you **set** your watch or clock, you adjust it for a particular time.

ADJECTIVE **6** If you do something at a **set** time, it is fixed at that time and does not change.

settee settees

NOUN a long comfortable seat for two or three people to sit on.

Synonym: sofa

setting settings

NOUN The **setting** of something like a play or a story is its surroundings, and where it happens.

settle settles settling settled

VERB **1** If you **settle** something, you decide on it or sort it out. *Let's settle this argument as quickly as possible.*

2 If you **settle** in a place, you make it your home.

3 If you **settle**, or **settle** down, you relax and make yourself comfortable.

4 If snow or dust **settles**, it sinks slowly down and comes to rest.

settlement settlements

NOUN a place where people have settled and made their homes.

sever severs severing severed

Rhymes with "never" VERB If you **sever** something, you cut it off or cut right through it.

several

ADJECTIVE OR PRONOUN a small number of people or things.

severe

Said "suh-veer" ADJECTIVE **1** extremely bad or serious.

2 strict or harsh.

sew sews sewing sewed sewn

VERB When you **sew** something, you use a needle and thread to make or mend it.

sewage

NOUN dirty water and waste that is carried away in drains from buildings.

sewer sewers

NOUN a series of pipes and drains that carries away dirty water and waste from buildings.

sex sexes

NOUN **1** one of the two groups, male and female, into which animals, including humans, are divided.

2 the physical activity by which people and animals produce young.

sexual ADJECTIVE

sexism

NOUN the belief that one sex is less intelligent or less able than the other, or in some way not as good as the other.

sexist ADJECTIVE OR NOUN

sexual intercourse

NOUN the physical act of sex between two people.

shabby shabbier shabbiest

ADJECTIVE Something or someone who is **shabby** looks old and ragged.

shack shacks

NOUN a small, roughly built hut.

shade shades shading shaded

NOUN **1** an area of darkness and coolness that sunshine does not reach.

2 the different forms of a colour. For example, olive green is a **shade** of green.

3 an object that decreases or shuts out light, such as a lampshade.

VERB **4** If you **shade** a person or a thing, you protect them from the sun's heat or light.

shadow shadows shadowing shadowed

NOUN **1** the dark shape formed when an opaque object stops light from reaching a surface.

VERB **2** When you **shadow** someone, you follow them and watch them closely.

shady shadier shadiest

ADJECTIVE A **shady** place is sheltered from the sunlight by trees or buildings.

shaft shafts

NOUN **1** A **shaft** in a mine or for a lift is a passage that goes straight down.

2 a beam of light.

3 In a machine, the **shaft** is a rod that turns in order to transmit power or movement.

shaggy shaggier shaggiest

ADJECTIVE covered with thick, long, untidy hair.

shake shakes shaking shook shaken

VERB **1** If you **shake** something, you move it quickly from side to side or up and down.
2 If something **shakes**, it moves from side to side or up and down with small, quick movements.
3 When you **shake** your head, you move it from side to side in order to say no.
NOUN **4** If you give something a **shake**, you shake it.
PHRASE **5** When you **shake hands** with someone, you grasp their hand in yours as a way of greeting them.

shaky shakier shakiest

ADJECTIVE rather weak and shaking and unsteady. *The foal got up on **shaky** legs.*

shall should

VERB used with "I" and "we" to refer to the future. *I **shall** go shopping tomorrow. I **should** wait till next week to open my birthday present.*

shallow shallower shallowest

ADJECTIVE not deep. *The water here is quite **shallow**.*

shame

NOUN **1** the feeling of guilt or embarrassment you get when you know you have done something wrong or foolish.
2 If you say something is a **shame**, you mean you are sorry about it. *It's a **shame** you can't come round to tea.*

shampoo shampoos

NOUN a soapy liquid used for washing your hair.

shamrock shamrocks

NOUN a plant with three round leaves on each stem, which is the national emblem of Ireland. [from Irish Gaelic **seamrog** meaning little clover]

shanty shanties

NOUN **1** a small, rough hut.
2 A sea **shanty** is a song sailors used to sing.

shape shapes

NOUN **1** The **shape** of something is the form or pattern of its outline, for example whether it is round or square. *The chocolates came in a box in the **shape** of a heart.*
2 something with a definite form, for example a circle or square. *See pages 446–7.*

share shares sharing shared

VERB **1** If two people **share** something, they both use it, do it, or have it. *We **shared** a bar of chocolate.*
NOUN **2** A **share** of something is a portion of it. *I want a fair **share** of the cake.*
share out VERB **3** If you **share out** something, you give it out equally among a group of people. *They **shared out** the food between them.*

shark sharks

NOUN a large, powerful fish, usually with two fins on its back and rows of sharp teeth.

sharp sharper sharpest

ADJECTIVE **1** A **sharp** object has an edge or point that is good for cutting or piercing things.
2 A **sharp** change is sudden and noticeable. *There was a **sharp** rise in temperature after the sun came up.*
3 A **sharp** taste is sour.
4 Someone who is **sharp** can pick up ideas very quickly.
5 A **sharp** pain is strong and sudden.

sharpen sharpens sharpening sharpened

VERB If you **sharpen** an object such as a knife, you make its edge or point sharper.

shatter shatters shattering shattered

VERB If something **shatters**, it breaks into a lot of small pieces. *The windows **shattered** in the explosion.*

shave shaves shaving shaved

VERB When someone **shaves**, they remove hair with a razor from part of their body.

shavings

PLURAL NOUN small, fine pieces of wood that have been cut off a larger piece.

shawl shawls

NOUN a large piece of cloth worn round a woman's head or shoulders, or used to wrap a baby in.

she
PRONOUN **She** is used to refer to a woman or girl who has already been mentioned.

sheaf sheaves
NOUN **1** a bundle of papers.
2 a bundle of ripe corn.

shear shears shearing sheared shorn
VERB When someone **shears** a sheep, they cut the wool off it.

shears
PLURAL NOUN **Shears** are a tool like a large pair of scissors, used especially for cutting hedges.

sheath sheaths
NOUN a cover for the blade of a knife or a sword.

shed sheds shedding shed
NOUN **1** a small building used for storing things, especially in a garden.
VERB **2** When an animal **sheds** hair or skin, some of it comes off.
3 If you **shed** tears, you cry.

she'd
a contraction of *she had*.

sheen
NOUN a gentle shine on the surface of something.

sheep
NOUN a mammal kept on farms for its meat and wool.
✔ The plural of *sheep* is *sheep*.

sheepdog sheepdogs
NOUN a breed of dog often used for controlling sheep.

sheepish
ADJECTIVE If you look **sheepish**, you look shy or embarrassed.

sheer sheerer sheerest
ADJECTIVE **1** A **sheer** cliff or drop is vertical.
2 complete and total: *sheer exhaustion*.
3 **Sheer** fabrics are very light and delicate.

sheet sheets
NOUN **1** a large rectangular piece of cloth used to cover a bed.
2 a rectangular piece of paper.

sheikh sheikhs
Rhymes with "**make**" NOUN an Arab chief or ruler.
[from Arabic *shaykh* meaning old man]

shelf shelves
NOUN a flat piece of wood, metal or glass fixed to a wall or a cabinet or cupboard and used for putting things on.

shell shells
NOUN **1** the hard covering of an egg or nut.
2 the hard, protective covering on the back of a tortoise, snail or crab.

she'll
a contraction of *she will*.

shellfish shellfish or shellfishes
NOUN a small sea creature with a shell.

shelter shelters sheltering sheltered
NOUN **1** a small building made to protect people from bad weather or danger. *We waited in the bus shelter.*
2 If a place gives **shelter**, it protects you from bad weather or danger.
VERB **3** If you **shelter** in a place, you stay there and are safe and protected.
4 To **shelter** someone or something means to protect them from bad weather or danger.

shepherd shepherds
NOUN a person who looks after sheep.

sheriff sheriffs
NOUN **1** in America, a person elected to enforce the law in a county.
2 in Scotland, the senior judge of a county or district.
3 in Australia, an officer of the Supreme Court who does certain paperwork.

sherry sherries
NOUN a kind of strong wine.

she's
a contraction of *she is* or (before a verb in the past tense) *she has*.

shield shields shielding shielded
NOUN **1** a large piece of a strong material like metal or plastic that soldiers or policeman carry to protect themselves.
VERB **2** If you **shield** someone or something, you protect them from something. *He shielded his eyes from the sun with his hand.*

shift shifts shifting shifted

VERB **1** If you **shift** something, you move it.
2 If something **shifts**, it moves.
NOUN **3** a set period during which people work: *the night shift*.

shilling shillings

NOUN a coin that was once used in Britain, Australia and New Zealand. There were 20 **shillings** in a pound.

shimmer shimmers shimmering shimmered

VERB **1** If something **shimmers**, it shines with a faint, flickering light.
NOUN **2** a faint, flickering light.

shin shins

NOUN the front part of your leg between your knee and your ankle.

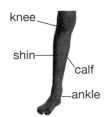

knee
shin
calf
ankle

shine shines shining shone or shined

VERB **1** When something **shines**, it is bright because it gives out or reflects light.
2 If you **shine** a torch or lamp somewhere, you point it there so that it becomes light.
3 If you **shine** your shoes, you polish them.

shingle

NOUN small pebbles on the seashore.

shingles

PLURAL NOUN a disease that causes a painful red rash, especially around the waist.

shiny shinier shiniest

ADJECTIVE **Shiny** things are bright and look as if they have been polished.

ship ships shipping shipped

NOUN **1** a large boat that carries passengers or cargo.
VERB **2** If people or things are **shipped** somewhere, they are transported there by ship.

shipwreck shipwrecks; shipwrecked

NOUN **1** When there is a **shipwreck**, a ship is destroyed in a storm or an accident at sea.
2 the remains of a ship that has been damaged or sunk.
ADJECTIVE **3** If someone is **shipwrecked**, they survive a shipwreck and manage to reach land.

shipyard shipyards

NOUN a place where ships are built and repaired.

shirk shirks shirking shirked

VERB If you **shirk** a task, you try to avoid doing it.

shirt shirts

NOUN a piece of clothing with a collar, sleeves and buttons down the front, worn on the upper part of the body.

shiver shivers shivering shivered

VERB When you **shiver**, you tremble slightly because you are cold or scared.

shoal shoals

NOUN a large group of fish swimming together.

shock shocks shocking shocked

NOUN **1** a sudden upsetting experience.
VERB **2** If something **shocks** you, it upsets you because it is unpleasant and unexpected.

shocking

ADJECTIVE **1** Something that shocks people is **shocking**.
2 INFORMAL very bad. *The weather has been shocking*.

shoddy shoddier shoddiest

ADJECTIVE badly made or done.

shoe shoes

NOUN a strong covering for each of your feet. **Shoes** cover most of your foot, but not your ankle.

shoelace shoelaces

NOUN a cord for fastening a shoe.

shone

VERB the past tense and past participle of *shine*.

shook

VERB the past tense of *shake*.

shoot shoots shooting shot

VERB **1** If someone **shoots** a person or an animal, they injure or kill them by firing a gun at them.
2 When a film is **shot**, it is filmed.

shooting star shooting stars

NOUN a meteor.

shop shops shopping shopped

NOUN **1** a place where things are sold.
2 a place where a particular type of work is done: *a bicycle repair* **shop**.
VERB **3** When you **shop**, you go to the shops to buy things.

shopkeeper shopkeepers

NOUN someone who owns or manages a small shop.

shopping

NOUN Your **shopping** is the goods you have bought in a shop.

shore shores

NOUN the land along the edge of a sea, lake or wide river.

short shorter shortest

ADJECTIVE **1** not lasting very long.
2 small in length, distance or height.
3 If you are **short** of something, you do not have enough of it.
4 If a name is **short** for another name, it is a quick way of saying it: *her friend Kes (***short*** for Kesewa).*

shortage shortages

NOUN If there is a **shortage** of something, there is not enough of it.

shortcut shortcuts

NOUN **1** a quicker way of getting somewhere than the usual route.
2 a quicker way of doing something than the usual way.

shorten shortens shortening shortened

VERB If you **shorten** something, you make it shorter.

shorthand

NOUN a way of writing in which signs represent words or syllables. It is used to write down quickly what someone is saying.

shortly

ADVERB soon. *I'll be there* **shortly**.

shorts

PLURAL NOUN trousers with legs that stop at or above the knee.

short-sighted

ADJECTIVE If you are **short-sighted**, you cannot see things clearly when they are far away.

shot shots

VERB **1** the past tense of *shoot*.
NOUN **2** the act of firing a gun.
3 In football, golf, tennis and other ball games, a **shot** is the act of kicking or hitting the ball.
4 a photograph or short film sequence.

should

VERB **1** You use **should** to say that something ought to happen. *Kylie* **should** *have done better.*
2 You also use **should** to say that you expect something to happen. *We* **should** *have heard by now.*
3 **Should** is used in questions where you are asking someone for advice about what to do: **Should** *we tell her about it?*

shoulder shoulders

NOUN Your **shoulders** are the parts of your body between your neck and the tops of your arms.

shouldn't

a contraction of *should not*.

shout shouts shouting shouted

NOUN **1** a loud call or cry.
VERB **2** If you **shout** something, you say it very loudly.

shove shoves shoving shoved

VERB **1** If you **shove** someone or something, you push them roughly.
NOUN **2** a rough push.

shovel shovels shovelling shovelled

NOUN **1** a tool like a spade, with the sides curved up, used for moving earth or snow.
VERB **2** If you **shovel** earth or snow, you move it with a shovel.

show shows showing showed shown

VERB **1** If you **show** someone something, you let them see it.
2 If you **show** someone how to do something, you demonstrate it to them. *Jake* **showed** *me how to make a chocolate cake.*
3 If something **shows**, you can see it.
4 If you **show** someone to a room or seat, you lead them there.
NOUN **5** a form of entertainment at the theatre or on television. *My favourite talk* **show** *is on TV tonight.*
6 a display or exhibition: *a flower* **show**.
show off VERB **7** INFORMAL If someone is **showing off**, they are trying to impress people.

shower showers showering showered

NOUN **1** a device that sprays you with water so that you can wash yourself.

2 If you have a **shower**, you wash yourself by standing under a **shower**.

3 a short period of rain.

VERB **4** If you are **showered** with a lot of things, they fall on you like rain.

showroom showrooms

NOUN a shop where goods such as cars or electrical items are displayed for customers to look at.

shrank

VERB the past tense of *shrink*.

shrapnel

NOUN small pieces of metal scattered from an exploding shell.

[named after General Henry *Shrapnel* (1761–1842), who invented it]

shred shreds shredding shredded

VERB **1** If you **shred** something, you cut or tear it into very small pieces.

NOUN **2** a small, narrow piece of paper or material.

shrew shrews

NOUN a small mouse-like mammal with a long pointed nose.

shrewd shrewder shrewdest

ADJECTIVE Someone who is **shrewd** makes good judgments and uses their common sense.

shriek shrieks shrieking shrieked

NOUN **1** a high-pitched cry or scream.

VERB **2** If you **shriek**, you make a high-pitched cry or scream.

shrill shriller shrillest

ADJECTIVE A **shrill** sound is unpleasantly high-pitched and piercing.

shrilly ADVERB

shrimp shrimps

NOUN a small edible shellfish with a long tail and many legs.

shrine shrines

NOUN a place of worship connected with a sacred person or object.

shrink shrinks shrinking shrank shrunk

VERB If something **shrinks**, it becomes smaller.

shrinkage

NOUN the amount by which something shrinks.

shrivel shrivels shrivelling shrivelled

VERB When something **shrivels**, it becomes dry and withered.

shrub shrubs

NOUN a bushy plant with woody stems.

shrug shrugs shrugging shrugged

VERB If you **shrug** your shoulders, you raise them slightly as a sign that you do not know or do not care about something.

shrunk

VERB the past participle of *shrink*.

shudder shudders shuddering shuddered

VERB **1** If you **shudder**, you tremble with fear or horror.

2 If a machine or vehicle **shudders**, it shakes violently.

NOUN **3** a shiver of fear or horror.

shuffle shuffles shuffling shuffled

VERB **1** If you **shuffle**, you walk without lifting your feet off the ground properly, so that they drag.

2 If you **shuffle** a pack of cards, you mix them up before you begin a game.

shut shuts shutting shut

VERB **1** If you **shut** something, you close it.

ADJECTIVE **2** If something is **shut**, it is closed.

shutter shutters

NOUN **1** a screen that can be closed over windows.

2 the device in a camera that opens and closes to let light on to the film.

shuttle shuttles

ADJECTIVE **1** A **shuttle** service is an air, bus or train service that makes frequent journeys between two places.

NOUN **2** a type of American spacecraft.

shuttlecock shuttlecocks

NOUN the feathered object that players hit over the net in the game of badminton.

shy shyer shyest

ADJECTIVE A **shy** person is quiet and uncomfortable in the company of other people.

sibling siblings

NOUN; FORMAL Your **siblings** are your brothers and sisters.

[from Old English *sibling* meaning relative]

sick sicker sickest

ADJECTIVE **1** If you are **sick**, you are ill.

2 If you feel **sick**, you feel as if you are going to vomit.

3 If you are **sick**, you vomit.

sickness sicknesses

NOUN an illness or disease.

side sides siding sided

NOUN **1** a position to the left or right of something. *There were trees on both* **sides** *of the road.*

2 The **sides** of something are its outside surfaces, or edges, that are not at the top, bottom, front or back. *There is a label on the* **side** *of the box.*

3 The **sides** of an area, surface or object are its different surfaces or edges. *Write on one* **side** *of the paper.*

4 Your **sides** are the parts of your body from your armpits down to your hips.

5 The two **sides** in a war, argument or relationship are the two people or groups involved. *Whose* **side** *are you on?*

ADJECTIVE **6** situated on a side of a building or vehicle: *the* **side** *door.*

VERB **7** If you side with someone, you support them in a quarrel or an argument.

sideways

ADVERB moving or facing towards one side. *I took a step* **sideways**.

siding sidings

NOUN a short railway track beside the main tracks, where engines and carriages are left when not in use.

siege sieges

NOUN a military operation in which an army surrounds a place to stop food or help from reaching the people inside.

sieve sieves sieving sieved

NOUN **1** a tool made of mesh, used for sifting or straining things.

VERB **2** If you **sieve** a powder or liquid, you pass it through a sieve to get rid of lumps and make it smooth.

sift sifts sifting sifted

VERB If you **sift** a powdery substance like flower or sugar, you pass it through a sieve to remove lumps.

sigh sighs sighing sighed

VERB When you **sigh**, you let out a deep breath, usually because you are tired, sad or relieved.

sight sights

NOUN **1** being able to see.

2 something you see. *The sunset was a beautiful* **sight**.

PLURAL NOUN **3 Sights** are interesting places that tourists visit.

sightseeing

NOUN visiting the interesting places that tourists usually visit.

sign signs signing signed

NOUN **1** a mark or symbol that always has a particular meaning, for example in mathematics or music: *a plus* **sign**.

2 a board or notice with words, a picture or a symbol on it, giving information or a warning: *a stop* **sign**.

VERB **3** If you **sign** a document, you write your name on it by hand, in the way you usually write it.

signal signals

NOUN **1** a gesture, sound or action that is meant to give a message to someone.

2 A railway **signal** is a piece of equipment beside the track that tells train drivers whether or not to stop.

signature signatures

NOUN If you write your **signature**, you write your name by hand in the way you usually write it.

significant

ADJECTIVE **1** A **significant** amount is large enough to be noticed and to matter. *A* **significant** *number of people can't read.*

2 Something that is **significant** is important and means something.

sign language

NOUN a way of communicating using your hands, used especially by deaf people.

signpost signposts

NOUN a road sign with information on it, such as the name of a town and how far away it is.

Sikh Sikhs

NOUN a person who believes in Sikhism, an Indian religion that separated from Hinduism in the 16th century and which teaches that there is only one God called Nam.

silence

NOUN When there is **silence** there is no sound.

Synonym: quietness

silent

ADJECTIVE **1** If you are **silent**, you are not saying anything.
2 When something is **silent**, it makes no noise.

silhouette silhouettes

NOUN the dark outline of a shape against a light background.
silhouetted ADJECTIVE

silicon

NOUN an element found in sand, clay and stone. It is used to make glass and parts of computers.

silk silks

NOUN fine, soft cloth made from threads produced from silkworm cocoons.

sill sills

NOUN a strip of stone, wood or metal underneath a window or a door.

silly sillier silliest

ADJECTIVE foolish or childish.

silver

NOUN a valuable greyish-white metal used for making jewellery and ornaments.

similar

ADJECTIVE If one thing is **similar** to another, they are quite like each other.

simile similes

NOUN an expression in which a person or thing is described as being similar to someone or something else. Examples of **similes** are *she runs like a deer* and *he's as white as a sheet*.

simmer simmers simmering simmered

VERB When food **simmers**, it cooks gently, just below boiling point.

simple simpler simplest

ADJECTIVE **1** Something that is **simple** is easy to understand or do.
2 plain in style.

simplify simplifies simplifying simplified

VERB If you **simplify** something, you make it simple or easy to understand.

simply

ADVERB in a simple way.

simultaneous

ADJECTIVE Things that are **simultaneous** happen at the same time.
simultaneously ADVERB

sin sins sinning sinned

NOUN **1** wicked behaviour, particularly if it breaks a religious or moral law.
VERB **2** To **sin** means to do something wicked.

since

PREPOSITION, CONJUNCTION, OR ADVERB **1** from a particular time until now. *I've been waiting* **since** *half past three.*
2 because. *I had a drink,* **since** *I was feeling thirsty.*

sincere

ADJECTIVE If you are **sincere**, you are genuine and truly mean what you say.

sing sings singing sang sung

VERB **1** When you **sing**, you make musical sounds with your voice, usually with words that fit a tune.
2 When birds or insects **sing**, they make pleasant and tuneful sounds.

singe singes singeing singed

VERB If you **singe** something, you burn it slightly so that it goes brown but does not catch fire.

single singles

ADJECTIVE **1** only one and not more. *A **single** shot was fired.*

2 People who are **single** are not married.

3 A **single** bed or bedroom is for one person.

NOUN **4** A **single**, or a **single** ticket, is a ticket for a journey to a place but not back again.

5 a recording of one or two short pieces of music on a small record, CD or cassette.

singular

NOUN In grammar, the **singular** is the form of a word that means just one person or thing.

Antonym: plural

---

sinister

ADJECTIVE Something or someone **sinister** seems harmful or evil.

[from Latin **sinister** meaning left-hand side, because the left side was considered unlucky]

sink sinks sinking sank sunk

NOUN **1** a fixed basin with taps supplying water, usually in a kitchen or bathroom.

VERB **2** If something **sinks**, it moves downwards, especially through water.

sip sips sipping sipped

VERB If you **sip** a drink, you take small mouthfuls.

sir

NOUN **1** FORMAL a polite way to address a man.

2 **Sir** is the title of a knight or baronet.

siren sirens

NOUN a warning device, for example on an ambulance, that makes a loud, wailing noise. *The fire engines switched on their **sirens** as they raced to the fire.*

sister sisters

NOUN Your **sister** is a girl or woman who has the same parents as you.

sister-in-law sisters-in-law

NOUN Someone's **sister-in-law** is the wife of their brother, the sister of their husband or wife, or the woman married to their wife's or husband's brother.

sit sits sitting sat

VERB When you **sit**, you rest your bottom on something such as a chair or the floor. *We **sat** on the bench at the bus stop.*

site sites

NOUN a piece of ground where something happens or will happen: *the **site** for the fairground.*

sitting room sitting rooms

NOUN a room with comfortable chairs for relaxing in.

situated

ADJECTIVE in a particular place. *The cottage was **situated** on the edge of a forest.*

situation situations

NOUN **1** what is happening in a particular place at a particular time.

2 The **situation** of a town or a building is its surroundings and its position.

size sizes

NOUN **1** The **size** of something is how big it is.

2 a standard measurement for clothes, shoes and other objects.

sizzle sizzles sizzling sizzled

VERB If something **sizzles**, it makes a hissing sound. *The sausages **sizzled** in the frying pan.*

skate skates skating skated

NOUN **1** **Skates** are ice **skates** or roller **skates**.

VERB **2** If you **skate**, you move about wearing skates.

skateboard skateboards

NOUN a narrow board on wheels, that you stand on and ride for fun.

skateboarder NOUN **skateboarding** NOUN

skeleton skeletons

NOUN the framework of bones in your body.

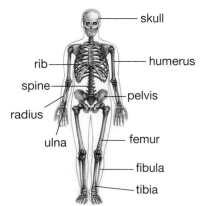

skull
rib
spine
radius
humerus
pelvis
ulna
femur
fibula
tibia

sketch sketches sketching sketched
NOUN **1** a quick, rough drawing.
VERB **2** If you **sketch** something, you draw it quickly and roughly.

sketchy sketchier sketchiest
ADJECTIVE If something is **sketchy**, it has little detail. *The map showing how to get to the new house was sketchy.*

ski skis skiing skied
NOUN **1** **Skis** are long pieces of wood, metal or plastic that you fasten to special boots so you can move easily on snow.
VERB **2** When you **ski**, you move on snow wearing skis, especially as a sport.
[from Old Norse *skith* meaning snowshoes]

skid skids skidding skidded
VERB **1** If someone or something **skids,** they slide accidentally.
NOUN **2** a skidding movement.

skilful
ADJECTIVE having a lot of skill.
skilfully ADVERB

skill skills
NOUN **1** the knowledge and ability that enable you to do something well.
2 a type of work or technique that needs special training and knowledge. *I would like to learn some new skills.*

skim skims skimming skimmed
VERB **1** If you **skim** something from the surface of a liquid, you remove it.
2 If something **skims** a surface, it moves lightly, smoothly and quickly over it: *seagulls skimming the waves.*

skin skins
NOUN **1** the natural covering of a person or animal
2 the outer covering a fruit or vegetable.

skinny skinnier skinniest
ADJECTIVE thin.

skip skips skipping skipped
VERB **1** When you **skip**, you jump lightly from one foot to the other, often over a rope.
2 If you **skip** something, you miss it out. *Amy skipped the part with the long words.*

skipper skippers
NOUN; INFORMAL the captain of a ship or boat.

skirt skirts
NOUN a piece of clothing that fastens at a woman's or girl's waist and hangs down over her legs.

skittle skittles
NOUN **1** a wooden or plastic object, shaped like a bottle, that people try to knock down with a ball.
2 **Skittles** is a game in which players roll a ball and try to knock down objects called skittles.

skull skulls
NOUN the bony part of your head that surrounds your brain.

skunk skunks
NOUN a small black and white animal from North America that gives off an unpleasant smell if it is frightened.

sky skies
NOUN the space around the earth that you can see when you look upwards.

skyscraper skyscrapers
NOUN a very tall building.

slab slabs
NOUN a thick, flat piece of something, such as stone.

slack slacker slackest
ADJECTIVE Something that is **slack** is loose and not firmly stretched or pulled tight.

slam slams slamming slammed
VERB If you **slam** something, such as a door, or if it **slams**, it shuts with a loud bang.

slang
NOUN very informal words and expressions.

slant slants slanting slanted
VERB **1** If something **slants**, it slopes.
NOUN **2** a slope or a leaning position.

a b c d e f g h i j k l m n o p q r **s** t u v w x y z

slap slaps slapping slapped
VERB **1** If you **slap** someone, you hit them with the palm of your hand.
NOUN **2** If you give someone a **slap**, you slap them.

slash slashes slashing slashed
VERB **1** If someone **slashes** something, they make a long, deep cut in it.
NOUN **2** a long, deep cut.

slate slates
NOUN **1** a dark grey rock that splits easily into thin layers.
2 Slates are small, flat pieces of slate used for covering roofs.

slaughter slaughters slaughtering slaughtered
VERB **1** To **slaughter** farm animals means to kill them for meat.
2 To **slaughter** animals or people means to kill a large number of them unjustly or cruelly.
NOUN **3** the killing of many people or animals.

slave slaves slaving slaved
NOUN **1** someone who is owned by another person and must work for them.
VERB **2** If you **slave** over something, you work very hard at it.

slay slays slaying slew slain
VERB; LITERARY To **slay** someone means to kill them.

sledge sledges
NOUN a vehicle on runners used for travelling over snow.

sledgehammer sledgehammers
NOUN a large, heavy hammer.

sleek sleeker sleekest
ADJECTIVE If something such as hair is **sleek**, it is smooth and shiny.

sleep sleeps sleeping slept
VERB When you **sleep**, you close your eyes and your whole body rests.

sleepless
ADJECTIVE unable to sleep or without sleep. *I had a sleepless night last night.*

sleepy sleepier sleepiest
ADJECTIVE tired and feeling like sleeping.
sleepily ADVERB   **sleepiness** NOUN

sleet
NOUN a mixture of rain and snow.

sleeve sleeves
NOUN The **sleeves** of a piece of clothing are the parts that cover your arms: *a shirt with long sleeves.*

sleigh sleighs
NOUN a sledge pulled by animals.

slender
ADJECTIVE slim.

slept
VERB the past tense and past participle of *sleep.*

slice slices slicing sliced
NOUN **1** A **slice** of cake, bread or other food is a piece of it cut from a larger piece.
VERB **2** If you **slice** food, you cut it into thin pieces.
3 To **slice** through something means to cut or move through it quickly, like a knife. *The ship sliced through the water.*

slick slicker slickest; slicks
ADJECTIVE **1** A **slick** action is done quickly and smoothly.
NOUN **2** An oil **slick** is a layer of oil floating on the surface of the sea or a lake.

slide slides sliding slid
VERB When something **slides**, it moves smoothly over or against something else. *She slid the door open.*

slight slighter slightest
ADJECTIVE **1** small in amount: *a slight dent in the car.*
2 A **slight** person has a slim, small body.

slim slimmer slimmest

ADJECTIVE **1** A **slim** person is thin.
2 A **slim** object is fairly thin: *a **slim** book*.
3 If there is only a **slim** chance that something will happen, there is only a small chance that it will happen.

slime

NOUN an unpleasant, thick, slippery substance.

sling slings slinging slung

VERB **1** INFORMAL If you **sling** something somewhere, you throw it there.
2 If you **sling** a rope between two points, you attach it so that it hangs loosely between them.
NOUN **3** a piece of cloth tied round a person's neck to support a broken or injured arm.

slip slips slipping slipped

VERB **1** If you **slip**, you accidentally lose your balance.
2 If you **slip** somewhere, you go there quickly and quietly.
NOUN **3** a small mistake.
4 a small piece of paper.

slipper slippers

NOUN **Slippers** are loose, soft shoes that you wear indoors.

slippery

ADJECTIVE smooth, wet or greasy, and difficult to hold or walk on.

slit slits

NOUN a long cut or narrow opening.

slither slithers slithering slithered

VERB To **slither** somewhere means to move there by sliding along the ground in an uneven way. *The snake **slithered** into the water.*

sliver slivers

NOUN a small, thin piece of something.

slog slogs slogging slogged

VERB **1** If you **slog** at something, you work hard at it.
NOUN **2** a piece of hard work or effort.

slogan slogans

NOUN a short, easily-remembered phrase used in advertising or by a political party.

Synonyms: catch phrase, motto

slope slopes sloping sloped

NOUN **1** a flat surface that is at an angle, so that one end is higher than the other.
VERB **2** If a surface **slopes**, it is at an angle.

sloppy sloppier sloppiest

ADJECTIVE **1** liquid and spilling easily.
2 careless or badly done.
3 sentimental.
sloppily ADVERB   **sloppiness** NOUN

slot slots

NOUN a narrow opening in a machine or container for pushing something into. *She put the coin in the **slot**.*

sloth sloths

NOUN **1** a South and Central American animal that moves very slowly and hangs upside down from the branches of trees.
2 FORMAL laziness.
slothful ADJECTIVE

slouch slouches slouching slouched

VERB If you **slouch**, you stand or sit with your shoulders and head drooping forwards.

slow slower slowest; slows slowing slowed

ADJECTIVE **1** moving, happening or doing something with very little speed.
2 If a clock or watch is **slow**, it shows a time earlier than the correct one.
VERB **3** If something **slows**, or you **slow** it, it moves or happens more slowly.
slow down VERB **4** If something **slows down** or something **slows** it **down,** it moves or happens more slowly.

slug slugs

NOUN a small, slow-moving animal with a slimy body, like a snail without an outer shell.

sluggish

ADJECTIVE moving slowly and without much energy.

slum slums

NOUN a poor, run-down area of a city or town.

slumber slumbers slumbering slumbered

NOUN **1** LITERARY sleep.
VERB **2** LITERARY When you **slumber**, you sleep.

slump slumps slumping slumped

VERB If you **slump** somewhere, you fall or sit down heavily.

slush
NOUN melting snow.

sly slyer or **slier** slyest or **sliest**
ADJECTIVE **1** A **sly** person is cunning and good at deceiving people.
2 A **sly** expression or remark shows that you know something other people do not know.

smack smacks smacking smacked
VERB **1** If you **smack** someone, you hit them with your open hand.
NOUN **2** If you give someone a **smack**, you smack them.

small smaller smallest
ADJECTIVE not large in size, number or amount.

smart smarter smartest
ADJECTIVE **1** A **smart** person is clean and neatly dressed.
2 clever. *That's a **smart** idea.*

smash smashes smashing smashed
VERB **1** If you **smash** something, you break it into a lot of pieces by hitting it or dropping it.
2 If someone or something **smashes** through something, such as a fence, they go through it by breaking it.
3 To **smash** against something means to hit it with great force. *A huge wave **smashed** against the boat.*

smear smears smearing smeared
NOUN **1** a dirty, greasy mark on a surface.
VERB **2** If something **smears** something else, it leaves a dirty or greasy mark by rubbing against it.

smell smells smelling smelled or **smelt**
VERB **1** When you **smell** something, you notice it with your nose.
2 If something **smells**, it gives out an odour that people notice.
NOUN **3** Your sense of **smell** is your ability to smell things.
4 an odour or scent, especially an unpleasant one.

smile smiles smiling smiled
VERB When you **smile**, you are happy. Your lips curve upwards at the edges and open a little.

smirk smirks smirking smirked
VERB When you **smirk**, you smile in a sneering, unpleasant way.

smog
NOUN a mixture of smoke and fog that occurs in some industrial cities.
[from a combination of *smoke* and *fog*]

smoke smokes smoking smoked
NOUN **1** a mixture of gases and small bits of solid material sent into the air when something burns.
VERB **2** If something is **smoking**, smoke is coming from it.
3 When someone **smokes** a cigarette, cigar or pipe, they suck smoke from it into their mouth and blow it out again.

smooth smoother smoothest; smooths smoothing smoothed
ADJECTIVE **1** A **smooth** surface has no roughness and no holes in it.
2 A **smooth** liquid or mixture has no lumps in it.
VERB **3** If you **smooth** something, you move your hands over it to make it smooth and flat.

smother smothers smothering smothered
VERB **1** If you **smother** a fire, you cover it with something to put it out.
2 To **smother** a person means to cover their face with something so that they cannot breathe.

smoulder smoulders smouldering smouldered
VERB When something **smoulders**, it burns slowly, producing smoke but no flames.

smudge smudges smudging smudged
NOUN **1** a dirty or blurred mark or a smear on something.
VERB **2** If you **smudge** something, you make it dirty or messy by touching it or rubbing it.

smug smugger smuggest
ADJECTIVE Someone who is **smug** is very pleased with how good or clever they are, and is self-satisfied in an unpleasant way.
smugly ADVERB

smuggle smuggles smuggling smuggled
VERB To **smuggle** goods means to take them in or out of a country secretly and against the law.

snack snacks
NOUN **1** a small, quick meal.
2 something eaten between meals.

snag snags snagging snagged
NOUN **1** a small problem.
VERB **2** If you **snag** your clothes, you catch them on something sharp.

snake snakes
NOUN a long, thin reptile with scales and no legs.

snap snaps snapping snapped
VERB **1** If something **snaps**, it breaks suddenly with a sharp noise.
2 If an animal **snaps** at you, it shuts its jaws together quickly as if it is going to bite you.
NOUN **3** an informal photograph.

snare snares snaring snared
NOUN **1** a trap for catching birds or small animals.
VERB **2** To **snare** an animal or bird means to catch it using a snare.

snarl snarls snarling snarled
VERB **1** When an animal **snarls**, it bares its teeth and makes a fierce growling noise.
2 If you **snarl**, you say something in a fierce, angry way.
NOUN **3** the noise an animal makes when it snarls.

snatch snatches snatching snatched
VERB **1** If you **snatch** something, you reach out for it quickly and grab it.
NOUN **2** A **snatch** of conversation or song is a very small piece of it.

sneak sneaks sneaking sneaked
VERB If you **sneak** somewhere, you go there quietly, trying not to be seen or heard.

sneaky sneakier sneakiest
ADJECTIVE dishonest or deceitful.

sneer sneers sneering sneered
VERB If you **sneer** at someone or something, you show by what you say that you think they are stupid or inferior.

sneeze sneezes sneezing sneezed
VERB **1** When you **sneeze**, you suddenly take a breath and blow it noisily down your nose, because there is a tickle in your nose or you have a cold.
NOUN **2** the action or sound of sneezing.

sniff sniffs sniffing sniffed
VERB When you **sniff**, you breathe in air through your nose hard enough to make a sound.

snigger sniggers sniggering sniggered
VERB If you **snigger**, you laugh quietly and disrespectfully.

snip snips snipping snipped
VERB If you **snip** something, you make small quick cuts in it or through it.

sniper snipers
NOUN a person who shoots at people from a hiding place.

snivel snivels snivelling snivelled
VERB When someone **snivels**, they cry and sniff in an irritating way.

snob snobs
NOUN **1** someone who admires people considered to be socially superior and looks down on people considered to be socially inferior.
2 someone who believes that they are better than other people.
snobbery NOUN

snooker
NOUN a game played on a large table covered with smooth green cloth. Players score points by hitting differently coloured balls into pockets using a long stick called a cue.

snoop snoops snooping snooped
VERB; INFORMAL If you **snoop**, you secretly look round a place to find out things.

snooze snoozes snoozing snoozed
VERB **1** INFORMAL If you **snooze**, you sleep lightly for a short time, especially during the day.
NOUN **2** INFORMAL a short, light sleep.

snore snores snoring snored
VERB When a sleeping person **snores**, they make a loud noise each time they breathe.

snorkel snorkels snorkelling snorkelled
NOUN **1** a tube you can breat through when you are swimming jus under the sur of the sea.
VERB **2** If you **snorkel,** you swim underw using a snork
snorkelling NOUN

snorkel

snout snouts

NOUN An animal's **snout** is its nose.

snow snows snowing snowed

NOUN **1** soft white flakes of ice that fall from the sky in cold weather.

VERB **2** When it **snows**, snow falls from the sky.

snowball snowballs

NOUN a ball of snow for throwing.

snowflake snowflakes

NOUN a flake of snow.

snowman snowmen

NOUN a pile of snow shaped like a person.

snowstorm snowstorms

NOUN a storm with snow falling.

snub snubs snubbing snubbed

VERB **1** If you **snub** someone, you behave rudely towards them, especially by making an insulting remark or ignoring them.

ADJECTIVE **2** A **snub** nose is short and turned-up.

snug

ADJECTIVE **1** A **snug** place is warm and comfortable.

2 If you are **snug**, you are warm and comfortable.

3 If something is a **snug** fit, it fits very closely.

snugly ADVERB

snuggle snuggles snuggling snuggled

VERB If you **snuggle** somewhere, you cuddle up more closely to something or someone.

so

ADVERB **1** also. *She laughed, and* **so** *did the teacher.*

2 very. *You are* **so** *funny.*

CONJUNCTION **3** therefore, for that reason. *I was cold,* **so** *I put on a coat.*

soak soaks soaking soaked

VERB **1** If you **soak** something, or leave it to **soak**, you put it in a liquid and leave it there for some time.

2 When a liquid **soaks** something, it makes it very wet.

3 When something **soaks** up a liquid, the liquid is drawn up into it. *The cloth* **soaked** *up the spilt milk.*

soap soaps

NOUN a substance used with water for washing yourself: *a bar of* **soap**.

soap opera soap operas

NOUN a popular television drama serial about people's daily lives.

[so called because soap manufacturers used to be typical sponsors]

soar soars soaring soared

VERB If something **soars** into the air, it rises high into it.

soaring ADJECTIVE

sob sobs sobbing sobbed

VERB When someone **sobs**, they cry noisily, gulping in short breaths.

sober soberer soberest

ADJECTIVE **1** not drunk.

2 serious and thoughtful.

soccer

NOUN a game played by two teams of eleven players kicking a ball in an attempt to score goals.

sociable

ADJECTIVE **Sociable** people are friendly and enjoy talking to other people.

Synonym: friendly

social

ADJECTIVE **1** to do with society or life within a society: *women from similar* **social** *backgrounds.*

2 to do with leisure activities that involve meeting other people. *We should organize more* **social** *events.*

society societies

NOUN **1** the community of people in a particular country or region.

2 an organization for people who have the same interests.

sock socks

NOUN a piece of clothing that covers your foot and ankle.

socket sockets

NOUN **1** a place on a wall or on a piece of electrical equipment into which you can put a plug or bulb.

2 any hollow part of something, or an opening into which another part fits: *eye* **sockets**.

sofa sofas

NOUN a long comfortable seat, with a back and arms, for two or more people. [from Arabic **suffah** meaning an upholstered raised platform]

soft softer softest

ADJECTIVE **1** not hard, stiff or firm: *a **soft** towel*. **2** very gentle: *a **soft** breeze*.

soften softens softening softened

VERB When you **soften** something, you make it softer.

software

NOUN computer programs.

soggy soggier soggiest

ADJECTIVE unpleasantly wet.

soil soils soiling soiled

NOUN **1** the top layer of the land surface of the earth, in which plants can grow. VERB **2** If you **soil** something, you make it dirty.

solar

ADJECTIVE to do with the sun: *solar energy*.

solar system

NOUN the sun and all the planets, comets and asteroids that orbit round it. *See* pages 426–7.

sold

VERB the past tense and past participle of *sell*.

soldier soldiers

NOUN a person in an army.

sole soles

NOUN The **sole** of your foot or shoe is the underneath part.

solemn

ADJECTIVE serious rather than cheerful.

solicitor solicitors

NOUN a lawyer who gives legal advice and prepares legal documents and cases.

solid solids

NOUN **1** a substance that is not a liquid or gas. **2** an object that is hard or firm. ADJECTIVE **3** You say that something is **solid** when it does not have any space in it: *a **solid** steel bar*. **4** A **solid** shape is a three-dimensional shape such as a cylinder or a cone.

solidify solidifies solidifying solidified

VERB If something **solidifies**, it changes from a liquid into a solid.

solitary

ADJECTIVE alone.

Mercury   Venus   Moon   Earth   Mars   Jupiter   Saturn   Uranus   Neptune   Pluto

Sun

The solar system

solo solos

NOUN **1** a piece of music played or sung by one person alone.

ADJECTIVE **2** A **solo** performance or activity is done by one person alone.

ADVERB **3** alone: *to sail **solo** around the world.*

solstice solstices

NOUN one of two times in the year when the sun is at its furthest point south or north of the equator.

soluble

ADJECTIVE able to be dissolved in a liquid: *soluble aspirin.*

solution solutions

NOUN **1** a way of dealing with a problem or difficult situation.

2 the answer to a riddle or a puzzle.

3 a liquid in which a solid substance has been dissolved.

solve solves solving solved

VERB If you **solve** a problem or a question, you find a solution or answer to it.

Synonym: work out

sombre

ADJECTIVE **1 Sombre** colours are dark and dull.

2 A **sombre** person is serious, sad or gloomy.

some

ADJECTIVE OR PRONOUN You use **some** to refer to a quantity or number when you are not stating the exact quantity or number. *There's **some** money on the table.*

somebody

PRONOUN some person. *See **someone**.*

somehow

ADVERB **1** You use **somehow** to say that you do not know how something was done or will be done. *You'll find a way of doing it **somehow**.*

2 You use **somehow** to say that you do not know the reason for something: ***Somehow** it didn't feel quite right.*

someone

PRONOUN You use **someone** to refer to a person without saying exactly who you mean. *I need **someone** to help me.*

somersault somersaults somersaulting somersaulted

NOUN **1** a forwards or backwards roll in which the head is placed on the ground and the body is brought over it.

VERB **2** If you **somersault**, you perform a somersault.

something

PRONOUN You use **something** to refer to anything that is not a person, without saying exactly what it is. *There was **something** wrong.*

sometimes

ADVERB occasionally, rather than always or never.

somewhere

ADVERB **1 Somewhere** is used to refer to a place without stating exactly where it is: *a flat **somewhere** in the city.*

2 Somewhere is used when giving an approximate amount, number or time. *It was **somewhere** between four and five o'clock.*

son sons

NOUN a person's male child.

song songs

NOUN **1** a piece of music with words that are sung to the music.

2 singing. *I was woken by the bird **song** early in the morning.*

sonnet sonnets

NOUN a poem with 14 lines that rhyme according to fixed patterns.

soon sooner soonest

ADVERB If something is going to happen **soon**, it will happen in a very short time.

soot

NOUN black powder that rises in the smoke from a fire.

sooty ADJECTIVE

soothe soothes soothing soothed

VERB **1** If you **soothe** someone who is angry or upset, you make them calmer.

2 Something that **soothes** pain makes the pain less severe.

sophisticated

ADJECTIVE **1** A **sophisticated** person is experienced in social situations and able to talk easily about anything.

2 Something **sophisticated** is made using advanced and complicated methods, or is able to do advanced and complicated things: *a sophisticated new telescope.*

Synonyms: (sense 1) cultured, urbane
(sense 2) highly developed

sorcerer sorcerers

NOUN someone in stories who performs magic by using the power of evil spirits.

sore sorer sorest; sores

ADJECTIVE **1** If part of your body is **sore**, it causes you pain and is uncomfortable. *I have a cough and a sore throat.*

NOUN **2** a painful place where your skin has become infected.

Synonyms: (sense 1) painful, sensitive, tender

sorrow sorrows

NOUN deep sadness or regret.

sorry sorrier sorriest

ADJECTIVE If you are **sorry** about something, you feel sadness, regret, or sympathy because of it.

sort sorts sorting sorted

NOUN **1** Different **sorts** of something are different types of it.

VERB **2** If you **sort** things, you arrange them into different groups.

sort out VERB **3** If you **sort out** a problem or misunderstanding, you find a solution to it.

Synonym: (sense 1) kind

SOS

NOUN a signal appealing urgently for help from someone whose life is in danger. **SOS** stands for Save Our Souls.

sought

VERB the past tense and past participle of *seek*.

soul souls

NOUN the spiritual part of a person that some people think continues after the body is dead.

sound sounds sounding sounded

NOUN **1** **Sound** is everything that can be heard.
2 something particular that you hear: *the sound of a door opening.*

VERB **3** If something **sounds**, or if you **sound** it, it makes a noise. *He sounded his horn to warn them.*

sound effect sound effects

NOUN **Sound effects** are added to films or plays to make them sound more life-like.

soundproof soundproofs soundproofing soundproofed

ADJECTIVE **1** If a room is **soundproof**, sound cannot get into it or out of it.

VERB **2** To **soundproof** something means to make it soundproof.

soup soups

NOUN liquid food made by boiling meat, fish or vegetables in water.

sour

ADJECTIVE **1** If something is **sour**, it has a sharp, acid taste like lemons or vinegar.
2 If milk is **sour**, it is no longer fresh.

source sources

NOUN The **source** of something is the person, place or thing that it originally comes from: *the source of the river.*

south

NOUN one of the four main points of the compass. If you face the point where the sun rises, **south** is on your right. The abbreviation for **south** is S.
southern ADJECTIVE

south-east

NOUN, ADJECTIVE AND ADVERB midway between south and east. The abbreviation for **south-east** is SE.

southern

ADJECTIVE from or to do with the south.

south-west

NOUN, ADJECTIVE AND ADVERB midway between south and west. The abbreviation for **south-west** is SW.

souvenir souvenirs

NOUN something you keep to remind you of a holiday, place or event.

sovereign sovereigns

NOUN **1** a king, queen or royal ruler of a country.
2 In the past, a **sovereign** was a British gold coin worth one pound.

a
b
c
d
e
f
g
h
i
j
k
l
m
n
o
p
q
r
s
t
u
v
w
x
y
z

sow sows sowing sowed sown

Rhymes with "**cow**" NOUN **1** a female pig.
Rhymes with "**go**" VERB **2** If you **sow** seeds, you put them in the ground so they can grow.

soya

NOUN a protein derived from **soya** beans. **Soya** beans are used to make **soya** flour, margarine, oil and milk.

space spaces

NOUN **1** the area that is empty or available in a place, building or container.
2 the area beyond the earth's atmosphere surrounding the stars and planets.
3 a gap between two things.

spacecraft spacecraft

NOUN a vehicle for travelling in outer space.

spaceship spaceships

NOUN a spacecraft.

spacesuit spacesuits

NOUN protective clothing that astronauts wear in outer space.

spacious

ADJECTIVE having or providing a lot of space.

spade spades

NOUN **1** a tool with a flat metal blade and a long handle used for digging.
2 **Spades** is one of the four suits in a pack of playing cards. It is marked by a black symbol in the shape of a heart-shaped leaf with a stem.

spaghetti

NOUN long, thin pieces of pasta.
[the plural of the Italian word *spaghetto* meaning string]

span spans spanning spanned

NOUN **1** a period of time: *looking back over a span of 40 years*.
2 the total length of something from one end to the other. *Seagulls have a large wing span*.
3 Your **span** is the distance from the top of your thumb to the top of your little finger when your hand is stretched.
VERB **4** If something **spans** a particular length of time, a distance or a gap, it stretches across it. *The bridge spanned the width of the river*.

spaniel spaniels

NOUN a breed of dog with long ears and silky fur.

spank spanks spanking spanked

VERB If a child is **spanked**, it is punished by being slapped, usually on the leg or bottom.

spanner spanners

NOUN a tool with a specially shaped end that fits round a nut to turn it.

spare spares sparing spared

ADJECTIVE **1** extra, or kept to be used when it is needed. *There is a spare tyre in the boot of the car.*
VERB **2** If you **spare** something for a particular purpose, you make it available. *Can you spare the time to help me later?*
3 If someone is **spared** an unpleasant experience, they are prevented from suffering it.

spark sparks

NOUN a tiny, bright piece of burning material thrown up by a fire.

sparkle sparkles sparkling sparkled

VERB If something **sparkles**, it shines with a lot of small, bright points of light.

Synonyms: glitter, twinkle

sparrow sparrows

NOUN a common, small bird with brown and grey feathers.

sparse sparser sparsest

ADJECTIVE small in number or amount and spread out over an area.

spatter spatters spattering spattered

VERB If something **spatters** a surface, it covers it with small drops of liquid.

spawn spawns spawning spawned

NOUN **1** a jelly-like substance containing the eggs of fish or amphibians.
VERB **2** When fish or amphibians **spawn**, they lay their eggs.

speak speaks speaking spoke spoken

VERB **1** When you **speak**, you use your voice to say words.
2 If you **speak** a foreign language, you know it and can use it.

Synonyms: (sense 1) say, talk, utter

speaker speakers

NOUN **1** a person who is speaking or making a speech.
2 the part of a radio or stereo system from which the sound comes.

spear spears spearing speared

NOUN **1** a weapon consisting of a long pole with a sharp point.
VERB **2** To **spear** something means to pierce it with a spear or other pointed object.

special

ADJECTIVE Someone or something **special** is different from other people or things, often in a way that makes it more important or better than others.

specialist specialists

NOUN an expert in a particular subject.

species

NOUN a group of plants or animals that have the same main features and are able to breed with each other.
✔ The plural of *species* is *species*.

specimen specimens

NOUN an example or small amount of something that gives an idea of what the whole is like: *a specimen of your writing*.

speck specks

NOUN **1** a very small stain.
2 a very small amount of something.

speckled

ADJECTIVE Something that is **speckled** is covered in small marks or spots.

spectacle spectacles

1 NOUN a grand and impressive event or performance.
PLURAL NOUN **2** Someone's **spectacles** are their glasses.

spectacular

ADJECTIVE very impressive or dramatic.

spectator spectators

NOUN a person who watches an event or a show.

spectrum spectra or spectrums

NOUN the range of different colours produced when light passes through a prism or a drop of water. A rainbow shows the colours in a **spectrum**.

speech speeches

NOUN **1** the ability to speak or the act of speaking.
2 a formal talk given to an audience.

speech bubble speech bubbles

NOUN a line around words, used in comic strips or cartoons to show what characters are saying.

speechless

ADJECTIVE unable to speak.

speech marks

PLURAL NOUN punctuation marks (" " ' ') used in written texts to show when someone is speaking.

speed speeds speeding sped or speeded

NOUN **1** the rate at which something moves or happens.
2 very fast movement or travel.
VERB **3** If you **speed** somewhere, you move or travel there quickly.
4 Someone who is **speeding** is driving a vehicle faster than the legal speed limit.

speedboat speedboats

NOUN a fast motorboat.

speedway speedways

NOUN the sport of racing lightweight motorcycles round a track.

spell spells spelling spelt or spelled

VERB **1** When you **spell** a word, you name or write its letters in order.
NOUN **2** a short period of something. *We expect a spell of good weather.*
3 words or rhymes used to perform magic.

spellbound

ADJECTIVE If you are **spellbound**, you are so fascinated by something that you cannot think of anything else.

spelling spellings

NOUN the correct order of letters in a word.

spend spends spending spent

VERB **1** When you **spend** money, you buy things with it.
2 If you **spend** time or energy, you use it.

sperm sperms

NOUN a cell produced in the sex organ of a male animal that can enter a female animal's egg and fertilize it.

a b c d e f g h i j k l m n o p q r **s** t u v w x y z

sphere spheres
NOUN a perfectly round object, such as a ball.

sphinx sphinxes
NOUN In mythology, the **sphinx** was a monster with a person's head and a lion's body.

spice spices
NOUN a substance obtained from a plant, often in the form of a powder or a seed, and added to food to give it flavour.

spicy spicier spiciest
ADJECTIVE strongly flavoured with spices.

spider spiders
NOUN a small animal with eight legs. Some **spiders** spin webs to catch insects for food, others hunt.

spike spikes
NOUN something long and sharply pointed. Runners often have **spikes** on the soles of their shoes to stop them slipping.

spill spills spilling spilled or spilt
VERB If you **spill** something, or if it **spills**, it accidentally falls or runs out of a container.

spin spins spinning spun
VERB 1 If someone or something **spins**, it turns quickly around a central point. *The earth spins on its own axis.*
NOUN 2 a rapid turn around a central point.

spinach
NOUN a vegetable with large green leaves.

spine spines
NOUN 1 the row of bones down the middle of your back.
2 a spike on a plant or an animal. *Porcupines are covered in spines.*
3 the part of a book where the pages are joined together.

Synonym: (sense 1) backbone

spiral spirals
NOUN 1 a continuous curve that winds round and round, with each curve moving further out or further up.
ADJECTIVE 2 in the shape of a spiral.

spire spires
NOUN the pointed structure on top of a steeple.

spirit spirits
NOUN 1 the part of you that is not physical and that is connected with the way you are.
2 a ghost or supernatural being.
3 liveliness, energy and self-confidence.

spiritual
ADJECTIVE 1 to do with people's thoughts and beliefs, rather than their bodies and physical surroundings.
2 to do with people's religious beliefs.

spit spits spitting spat
VERB 1 If you **spit**, you forcefully send saliva out of your mouth.
NOUN 2 saliva.
3 a long piece of metal or wood that you push through meat so that it can be hung over a fire to cook.
4 a long, flat, narrow piece of land sticking out into the sea.

spite
NOUN 1 the desire to deliberately hurt or upset somebody.
PHRASE 2 **In spite of** is used to begin a statement that makes the rest of what you are saying seem surprising. *In spite of the rain, they watched the fireworks outside.*

spiteful
ADJECTIVE A **spiteful** person does or says nasty things to people to hurt them.
spitefully ADVERB

splash splashes splashing splashed
VERB 1 If you **splash** around in water, you make the water fly around in a noisy way.
NOUN 2 the sound made when something hits or falls into water.

splendid
ADJECTIVE very good or very impressive.

splint splints
NOUN a straight piece of metal or wood that is tied to a broken arm or leg to stop it moving.

splinter splinters splintering splintered
NOUN 1 a thin, sharp piece of wood or glass that has broken off a larger piece.
VERB 2 If something **splinters**, it breaks into thin, sharp pieces.

split splits splitting split
VERB If something **splits**, or if you **split** it, it divides into two or more parts.

split second split seconds
NOUN an extremely short period of time.

splutter splutters spluttering spluttered
VERB **1** If you **splutter**, you speak in a confused way because you are embarrassed or angry.
2 If someone or something **splutters**, they make a series of short, coughing, spitting noises.

spoil spoils spoiling spoiled or **spoilt**
VERB **1** To **spoil** something means to damage it or stop it being successful or satisfactory. *My holiday was* **spoiled** *by rain.*
2 To **spoil** children means to give them everything they want, making them selfish.

spoilsport spoilsports
NOUN someone who spoils other people's fun.

spoke spokes
NOUN **1** The **spokes** of a wheel are the bars that connect the hub to the rim.
VERB **2** the past tense of *speak*.

spoken
VERB the past participle of *speak*.

sponge sponges
NOUN **1** a soft, natural or man-made material with lots of small holes, used for washing yourself.
2 an animal found in the sea that has a body made up of many cells.
3 a soft, light cake or pudding.
spongy ADJECTIVE

sponsor sponsors sponsoring sponsored
VERB **1** If an organization **sponsors** something, such as an event or someone's training, it gives money to pay for it.
2 If you **sponsor** someone who is doing something for charity, you agree to give them a sum of money for the charity if they manage to do it.
NOUN **3** a person or organization that sponsors something or someone.

spontaneous
ADJECTIVE something that is not planned or arranged.
spontaneously ADVERB

spooky spookier spookiest
ADJECTIVE frightening and creepy.

spoon spoons
NOUN an object shaped like a small shallow bowl with a long handle, used for eating, stirring and serving food.

sport sports
NOUN games and other enjoyable activities that need physical effort and skill.

spot spots spotting spotted
NOUN **1** a small, round coloured area on a surface.
2 a pimple on a person's skin.
3 a small amount of something.
4 a particular place.
VERB **5** If you **spot** something, you suddenly see it.
PHRASE **6** If you do something **on the spot**, you do it immediately.

spotless
ADJECTIVE perfectly clean.

spotlight spotlights
NOUN a powerful light that can be directed to light up a small area: *stage* **spotlights**.

spotty spottier spottiest
ADJECTIVE marked with spots.

spouse spouses
NOUN Someone's **spouse** is the person they are married to.

spout spouts spouting spouted
VERB **1** When liquid or flame **spouts** out of something, it shoots out in a long stream.
NOUN **2** a tube or opening from which liquid can pour.
VERB **3** When someone **spouts** what they have learned, they say it in a boring way.

sprain sprains spraining sprained
VERB **1** If you **sprain** a joint, you accidentally damage it by twisting it violently.
NOUN **2** the injury caused by spraining a joint.

sprang
VERB the past tense of *spring*.

sprawl sprawls sprawling sprawled
VERB **1** If you **sprawl** somewhere, you sit or lie there with your legs and arms spread out. *She* **sprawled** *on the bed reading her book.*
2 A place that **sprawls** is spread out over a large area.

spray sprays spraying sprayed

NOUN **1** many small drops of liquid splashed or forced into the air.
2 a liquid kept under pressure in a container.
VERB **3** If you **spray** a liquid over something, you cover it with drops of the liquid. *We sprayed the dry lawn with water from the hose pipe.*

spread spreads spreading spread

VERB **1** If you **spread** a substance on a surface, you put a thin layer of it on the surface. *Spread the butter on the bread before you make the sandwich.*
2 If you **spread** something out, you open it out or arrange it so that it can be seen or used easily. *He spread the map out on his knees.*
3 If something **spreads**, it gradually reaches more people. *The news spread quickly.*

sprightly sprightlier sprightliest

ADJECTIVE lively and active.

spring springs springing sprang sprung

NOUN **1** the season between winter and summer, when most plants start to grow.
2 a coil of wire that returns to its original shape after being pressed or pulled.
3 a place where water naturally comes up through the ground.
VERB **4** If you **spring**, you jump upwards or forwards.

springboard springboards

NOUN a springy board on which a gymnast or diver jumps to gain height.

springbok springboks

NOUN a small South African antelope that moves in leaps.

sprinkle sprinkles sprinkling sprinkled

VERB If you **sprinkle** a liquid or powder over something, you scatter it over it.

sprint sprints sprinting sprinted

NOUN **1** a short, fast race.
VERB **2** If you **sprint**, you run fast over a short distance.

sprout sprouts sprouting sprouted

VERB **1** When something **sprouts**, it starts to grow.
2 If things **sprout** up, they appear very quickly.
NOUN **3** an abbreviation of *Brussels sprouts*.

sprung

VERB the past participle of *spring*.

spun

VERB the past tense and past participle of *spin*.

spur spurs spurring spurred

VERB **1** If you **spur** someone on, you encourage them.
NOUN **2** a sharp device worn on the heel of a rider's boot to urge the horse to go faster.

spurt spurts spurting spurted

NOUN **1** a jet of liquid or flame.
2 a sudden increase in speed.
VERB **3** If a liquid **spurts**, it gushes in a sudden stream. *Water spurted out of the hose.*

spy spies spying spied

NOUN **1** a person sent to find out secret information about a country or organization.
VERB **2** Someone who **spies** tries to find out secret information about another country or organization.
3 If you **spy** on someone, you watch them secretly.

squabble squabbles squabbling squabbled

VERB **1** When people **squabble**, they quarrel about something unimportant.
NOUN **2** a quarrel.

squad squads

NOUN a small group of people chosen to do a particular activity.

squadron squadrons

NOUN a section of one of the armed forces, especially the air force.
[from Italian *squadrone* meaning soldiers drawn up in a square formation]

squalid

ADJECTIVE dirty, untidy and in bad condition.

squander squanders squandering squandered

VERB If you **squander** money or resources, you waste them.

square squares

NOUN **1** a plane shape with four equal sides and four right angles.
2 In a town or city, a **square** is a flat, open area with buildings or streets around the edge.
ADJECTIVE **3** shaped like a **square**.
[from Latin *quadra* meaning square]

squash squashes squashing squashed
VERB If you **squash** something, you press it so that it becomes flat or loses its shape.

squat squats squatting squatted; squatter, squattest
VERB **1** If you **squat** down, you crouch, balancing on your feet with your legs bent.
2 A person who **squats** in an unused building lives there without permission and without paying.
ADJECTIVE **3** short and thick.

squawk squawks squawking squawked
VERB **1** When a bird **squawks**, it makes a loud, harsh noise.
NOUN **2** a loud, harsh noise made by a bird.

squeak squeaks squeaking squeaked
VERB **1** If something or someone **squeaks**, they make a short, high-pitched sound.
NOUN **2** a short, high-pitched sound.

squeal squeals squealing squealed
VERB **1** When things or people **squeal**, they make long, high-pitched sounds.
NOUN **2** a long, high-pitched sound.

squeamish
ADJECTIVE easily upset by unpleasant sights or situations.

squeeze squeezes squeezing squeezed
VERB **1** When you **squeeze** something, you press it firmly from two sides.
2 If you **squeeze** somewhere, you force yourself into a small space or through a gap.
3 If you **squeeze** something somewhere, you force it into a small space.

squelch squelches squelching squelched
VERB If something **squelches**, it makes a wet sucking sound.

squid squids
NOUN an animal that lives in the sea, with a long soft body and ten limbs.

squiggle squiggles
NOUN a wiggly line.

squint squints squinting squinted
VERB **1** If you **squint**, you screw up your eyes to look at something.
NOUN **2** If someone has a **squint**, their eyes look in different directions from each other.

squirm squirms squirming squirmed
VERB If you **squirm**, you wriggle and twist your body about, usually because you are nervous or embarrassed.

squirrel squirrels
NOUN a small furry rodent with a long bushy tail.

squirt squirts squirting squirted
VERB **1** If a liquid **squirts**, or you **squirt** it, it comes out of a narrow opening in a thin, fast stream.
NOUN **2** a thin, fast stream of liquid.

stab stabs stabbing stabbed
VERB To **stab** someone means to wound them by pushing a knife into their body.

stable stables
NOUN **1** a building in which horses are kept.
ADJECTIVE **2** Something that is **stable** cannot be moved or shaken.
3 If someone is **stable**, they are level-headed and dependable.

stack stacks stacking stacked
NOUN **1** a pile of things, one on top of the other.
VERB **2** If you **stack** items, you pile them up neatly.

stadium stadiums
NOUN a sports ground with rows of seats around it for spectators.

staff staffs
NOUN the people who work for an organization.

stag stags
NOUN an adult male deer.

stage stages staging staged
NOUN **1** In a theatre, the **stage** is the raised platform where the actors or entertainers perform.
VERB **2** If someone **stages** a play or event, they organize it or present it.

stagger staggers staggering staggered
VERB **1** If someone **staggers**, they walk unsteadily because they are ill or drunk.
2 If something **staggers** you, it amazes you.
3 If events are **staggered**, they are arranged so that they do not all happen at the same time.

stagnant

ADJECTIVE **Stagnant** water is still rather than flowing, and is often smelly and dirty.

stain stains

NOUN a mark on something that is difficult or impossible to clean off.

stair stairs

NOUN one of a set of steps, usually inside a building going from one floor to another.

staircase staircases

NOUN a set of stairs.

stake stakes staking staked

PHRASE **1** If something is **at stake**, it might be lost or damaged if something else is not successful. *The cup was **at stake** if he missed the goal.*
VERB **2** If you say you would **stake** your money, life or reputation on the result of something, you mean you would risk it.
✔ Do not confuse *stake* with *steak*.

stalactite stalactites

NOUN a stony spike hanging down like an icicle from the ceiling of a cave.

stalactite

stalagmite

stalagmite stalagmites

NOUN a pointed piece of rock standing on the floor of a cave.

stale staler stalest

ADJECTIVE **Stale** food or air is no longer fresh.

Synonyms: fusty, musty, old

stalk stalks stalking stalked

NOUN **1** The **stalk** of a flower or leaf is its stem.
VERB **2** To **stalk** a person or an animal means to follow them quietly in order to catch, kill or observe them. *The cat is **stalking** the bird in the garden.*

stall stalls stalling stalled

NOUN **1** a large table displaying goods for sale or information.
PLURAL NOUN **2** In a theatre, the **stalls** are the seats at the lowest level, in front of the stage.
VERB **3** When a vehicle **stalls**, the engine suddenly stops.

stallion stallions

NOUN an adult male horse that can be used for breeding.

stamen stamens

NOUN the part of a flower that produces pollen. *See page 434.*

stamina

NOUN the physical or mental energy needed to do something for a very long time. *Running a marathon takes determination and **stamina**.*

stammer stammers stammering stammered

VERB **1** When someone **stammers**, they speak with difficulty, repeating words and sounds and hesitating.
NOUN **2** Someone who has a **stammer** tends to stammer when they speak.

stamp stamps stamping stamped

NOUN **1** a small piece of paper that you stick on a letter or parcel before posting it, to prove that you have paid the postage.
VERB **2** To **stamp** a piece of paper means to make a mark on it using a small block with a pattern cut into it. *He **stamped** her passport.*
3 If you **stamp**, you lift your foot and put it down hard on the ground.
stamp out VERB **4** To **stamp out** something means to put an end to it. *We must try to **stamp out** this kind of behaviour.*

stampede stampedes stampeding stampeded

VERB **1** When a group of animals **stampede**, they rush forward in a wild, uncontrolled way.
NOUN **2** a group of animals stampeding.

stand stands standing stood

VERB **1** If you are **standing**, you are upright with your weight on your feet.
2 If something **stands** somewhere, that is where it is. *The house stands on top of a hill.*
3 If you cannot **stand** someone or something, you do not like them at all.
4 If you **stand** in an election, you are a candidate.
stand up VERB **5** When you **stand up**, you get into a standing position.
NOUN **6** A **stand** at a sports ground is a building where people can watch what is happening.

standard standards

NOUN **1** how good something is.
2 an officially agreed level against which things can be measured or judged.

standstill

NOUN a complete stop.

stank

VERB the past tense of *stink*.

stanza stanzas

NOUN a verse of a poem.

staple staples stapling stapled

NOUN **1** a small piece of wire that holds sheets of paper firmly together. You insert it with a device called a stapler.
VERB **2** If you **staple** sheets of paper, you fasten them together with staples.

star stars

NOUN **1** a large ball of burning gases in space that appears as a point of light in the sky at night. Our sun is a **star**.
2 a shape with several points, usually five or six, sticking out in a regular pattern.
3 a famous actor, sports player or musician.

starboard

ADJECTIVE OR NOUN The **starboard** side of a ship is the right-hand side when you are facing the front.

starch starches

NOUN **1** a substance found in foods such as bread, rice, pasta and potatoes that gives you energy.
2 a substance used for stiffening fabric.

stare stares staring stared

VERB **1** If you **stare** at something, you look at it for a long time.
NOUN **2** a long fixed look at something.

starfish starfishes or starfish

NOUN a star-shaped animal found in the sea that has five pointed limbs.

starling starlings

NOUN a common European bird with shiny dark feathers.

start starts starting started

VERB **1** If you **start** something, you begin it.
NOUN **2** The **start** of something is the point or time at which it begins.

startle startles startling startled

VERB If something sudden and unexpected **startles** you, it surprises you and give you a slight fright.

starve starves starving starved

VERB If people are **starving**, they are suffering from a serious lack of food and are likely to die.

state states stating stated

NOUN **1** The **state** of something or someone is their condition, or how they are.
2 Some countries are divided into regions called **states** that make some of their own laws.
3 You can call the government and the officials of a country the **state**. *Carmen received a pension from the state.*
VERB **4** If you **state** something, you say it or write it clearly, especially in a formal way. *Please state your name and address.*

statement statements

NOUN something you say or write that gives information in a formal way.

static

ADJECTIVE **1** never moving or changing. *The temperature is fairly static.*
NOUN **2** an electrical charge caused by friction.

station stations

NOUN **1** a building where trains or buses stop to let passengers on and off.
2 A building that is used by people such as the police and fire brigade: *police station.*

stationary

ADJECTIVE not moving: *a **stationary** car*.

✔ Do not confuse *stationary* with *stationery*.

Synonym: motionless

stationery

NOUN paper, pens and other writing equipment.

✔ Do not confuse *stationery* with *stationary*

statistics

PLURAL NOUN facts worked out by looking at information that is given in numbers. *They gathered **statistics** about journeys to school.*

statue statues

NOUN a sculpture, often of a person.

stay stays staying stayed

VERB **1** If you **stay** in one place, you do not move away from it.

2 If you **stay** with a friend, you spend time with them as a visitor.

steady steadier steadiest

ADJECTIVE firm and not moving about. *She made sure the ladder was **steady** before she climbed up it.*

Synonyms: firm, secure, stable

steak steaks

NOUN a large, good-quality piece of beef or fish.

✔ Do not confuse *steak* with *stake*.

steal steals stealing stole stolen

VERB If someone **steals** something, they take it without permission and without meaning to return it.

steam

NOUN the hot vapour formed when water boils.

steam-engine steam-engines

NOUN any engine that is powered by steam.

steel

NOUN a very strong metal made mainly from iron.

steel band steel bands

NOUN a group of people who play music on special metal drums.

steep steeper steepest

ADJECTIVE A **steep** slope rises sharply and is difficult to go up.

steeple steeples

NOUN a tall pointed structure above a church roof.

steer steers steering steered

VERB When someone **steers** a vehicle or boat, they control it so that it goes in the direction they want.

stem stems

NOUN the thin, usually upright, part of a plant that grows above the ground and on which the leaves and flowers grow. *See page 434.*

stencil stencils stencilling stencilled

NOUN **1** a thin sheet of card, metal or plastic with a pattern cut out of it. The pattern can be copied on to another surface by painting over the **stencil**.

VERB **2** If you **stencil** a design on to a surface, you create it using a stencil.

step steps stepping stepped

NOUN **1** the movement of lifting your foot and putting it down again when you are walking, running or dancing.

2 one of the places at different levels that you put your feet on when you go up and down a ladder or stairs.

VERB **3** If you **step** in a particular direction, you take a step there.

stepbrother stepbrothers

NOUN Someone's **stepbrother** is the son of their stepmother or stepfather.

stepchild stepchildren

NOUN a stepdaughter or stepson.

stepdaughter stepdaughters

NOUN someone's daughter by their wife's or husband's previous marriage.

stepfather stepfathers

NOUN a man who is married to your mother but who is not your natural father.

stepmother stepmothers

NOUN a woman who is married to your father but who is not your natural mother.

stepsister stepsisters

NOUN the daughter of someone's stepmother or stepfather.

stepson stepsons

NOUN someone's son by their wife's or husband's previous marriage.

stereo stereos

NOUN a piece of equipment that reproduces sound from records, tapes or CDs, directing the sound through two speakers.

stereotype stereotypes

NOUN a simplified way people think of a particular type of person or thing: *the **stereotype** of the polite, industrious Japanese.*

sterile

ADJECTIVE **1** clean and free from germs.
2 unable to have children or reproduce.
sterility NOUN

sterling

NOUN the money system of Great Britain.

stern sterner sternest

ADJECTIVE very serious and strict.

stethoscope stethoscopes

NOUN a device used by doctors to listen to a patient's heart and breathing, made of earpieces connected to a hollow tube and a small disc.

stew stews stewing stewed

NOUN **1** a dish of small pieces of savoury food cooked together slowly in a liquid.
VERB **2** If you **stew** meat, vegetables or fruit, you cook them slowly in a liquid.
[from Middle English *stuen* meaning to take a very hot bath]

steward stewards

NOUN **1** a person who works on a ship or plane looking after passengers and serving meals.
2 a person who helps to direct the public at events such as a race or a concert.

stick sticks sticking stuck

NOUN **1** a long, thin piece of wood.
VERB **2** If you **stick** a long or pointed object into something, you push it in.
3 If you **stick** one thing to another, you attach it with glue or tape.
4 If something **sticks**, it becomes fixed or jammed.
stick out VERB **5** If something **sticks out**, it projects from something else.
stick up for VERB **6** INFORMAL If you **stick up for** someone or something, you support or defend them.

sticker stickers

NOUN a label with words or pictures on it for sticking on something.

sticky stickier stickiest

ADJECTIVE If something is **sticky**, it is covered with a substance that can stick to other things.

stiff stiffer stiffest

ADJECTIVE **1** Something that is **stiff** is firm and not easily bent: *a **stiff** piece of card.*
2 If you feel **stiff**, your muscles or joints ache when you move.
3 **Stiff** behaviour is formal, and not friendly or relaxed.
4 difficult or severe. *It was a **stiff** competition.*

stifle stifles stifling stifled

VERB **1** If you feel **stifled**, you feel you cannot breathe properly.
2 If you **stifle** something, you stop it happening. *She **stifled** a yawn.*
ADJECTIVE **3** **Stifling** heat is very hot and makes it difficult to breathe. *The atmosphere in the greenhouse was **stifling**.*

stile stiles

NOUN a step built in a hedge or wall so that people can climb over or through it.

still stiller stillest

ADVERB OR ADJECTIVE **1** If someone or something is **still**, they stay in the same position without moving.
2 You say **still** when something is the same as it was before. *I've **still** got a headache.*
3 When the air is **still**, there is no wind.
4 A **still** drink is not fizzy.
5 even then. *I've worked all day and there's **still** more to do.*

stilts

PLURAL NOUN **1** long poles on which people balance or walk.
2 long poles on which houses are sometimes built.

stimulate stimulates stimulating stimulated

VERB **1** To **stimulate** something means to encourage it to begin or develop: *to stimulate interest*.

2 If something **stimulates** you, it interests and excites you.

Synonym: inspire

sting stings stinging stung

VERB **1** If an animal or plant **stings** you, it pricks your skin and hurts.

2 If a part of your body **stings**, you feel a sharp tingling pain there.

stink stinks stinking stank stunk

VERB **1** Something that **stinks** smells very unpleasant.

NOUN **2** a very unpleasant smell.

stir stirs stirring stirred

VERB **1** When you **stir** a liquid, you move it around using a spoon or a stick.

2 If someone **stirs**, they move slightly, or start to move after sleeping or being still. *It was very noisy but the baby didn't **stir***.

stirrup stirrups

NOUN one of the two metal loops hanging by leather straps from a horse's saddle, that you put your feet in when riding.

stitch stitches stitching stitched

VERB **1** When you **stitch** pieces of material together, you use a needle and thread to sew them together.

NOUN **2** one of the pieces of thread that can be seen where material has been sewn.

3 one of the pieces of thread that can be seen where skin has been sewn together to heal a wound. *He had eleven **stitches** in his lip*.

4 a sharp pain you feel in your side after running.

stoat stoats

NOUN a small wild mammal with a long body, brown fur and a black-tipped tail.

stock stocks

NOUN **1** the total amount of goods a shop has for sale.

2 If you have a **stock** of things, you have a supply ready for use.

stocking stockings

NOUN one of a pair of long pieces of fine, stretchy fabric that cover a woman's leg and foot.

stole stoles

VERB **1** the past tense of *steal*.

NOUN **2** a shawl to cover a woman's shoulders.

stolen

VERB the past participle of *steal*.

stomach stomachs

NOUN **1** the organ inside your body where food is digested.

2 the front part of your body below your waist.

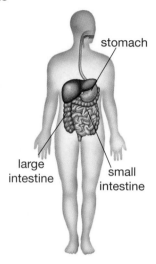

stomach

large intestine

small intestine

stone stones

NOUN **1** the hard solid substance found in the ground and used for building.

2 a small piece of rock.

3 a unit of weight equal to 14 pounds or about 6·35 kilograms.

stony stonier stoniest

ADJECTIVE **Stony** ground has many stones in it.

stood

VERB the past tense and past participle of *stand*.

stool stooles

NOUN a seat with legs but no back or arms.

stoop stoops stooping stooped

VERB **1** If you **stoop**, you bend your body forwards.

2 If you would not **stoop** to something, you would not disgrace yourself by doing it.

stop stops stopping stopped

VERB **1** If you **stop** doing something, you no longer do it.

2 If an activity **stops**, it comes to an end.

3 If you **stop** something, you prevent it from happening or continuing.

4 If people or things that are moving **stop**, they no longer move.

NOUN **5** a place where a bus, train or other vehicle stops to let passengers on and off.

stopwatch stopwatches

NOUN a watch that can be started and stopped, that is used to time things such as races.

storage

NOUN the keeping of something somewhere until it is needed.

store stores storing stored

NOUN **1** a shop.

2 a supply of something that is kept until it is needed.

3 a place where things are kept while they are not used.

VERB **4** When you **store** something somewhere, you keep it there until it is needed.

storey storeys

NOUN one of the floors or levels of a building.

stork storks

NOUN a very large white and black bird with long red legs and a long bill. **Storks** live mainly near water in Eastern Europe and Africa.

storm storms storming stormed

NOUN **1** a period of bad weather, when there is heavy rain, a strong wind, and often thunder and lightning.

VERB **2** If soldiers **storm** a defended place, they make a surprise attack in it.

NOUN **3** If there is a **storm** of protest, many people complain loudly.

story stories

NOUN a telling of events, real or imaginary, spoken or written.

stout stouter stoutest

ADJECTIVE **1** rather fat.

2 thick, strong and sturdy: *stout walking shoes*.

stove stoves

NOUN a piece of equipment for heating a room or for cooking. *She warmed the milk on the stove*.

straddle straddles straddling straddled

VERB If you **straddle** something, you stand or sit with your legs either side of it.

straight straighter straightest

ADJECTIVE OR ADVERB **1** continuing in the same direction without curving or bending.

2 honest and direct: *a straight answer*.

ADVERB **3** immediately and directly. *We will go straight to school*.

4 If you stand up **straight**, you stand upright.

straighten straightens straightening straightened

VERB If you **straighten** something, you make it straight.

straightforward

ADJECTIVE **1** easy to understand.

2 honest and truthful.

strain strains straining strained

ADJECTIVE **1** If you feel **strained**, you feel tense and anxious.

NOUN **2** If a **strain** is put on something, it is affected by a strong force that may damage it.

VERB **3** If you **strain** a muscle, you use it too much and injure it so that it is painful.

4 If you **strain** food or a mixture, you separate the solid parts from the liquid parts, for example by putting it through a sieve.

strait straits

NOUN a narrow strip of sea between two pieces of land, that connects two larger areas of sea.

stranded

ADJECTIVE If someone or something is **stranded**, they are stuck somewhere and cannot leave: *stranded on the rocks*.

strange stranger strangest

ADJECTIVE **1** unusual or unexpected: *a strange dream*.

2 not known, seen or experienced before. *She was all alone in a strange country*.

stranger strangers

NOUN someone you have never met before.

strangle

strangle strangles strangling strangled
VERB To **strangle** someone means to kill them by squeezing their throat to stop them breathing.

strap straps
NOUN a narrow piece of leather or cloth, used to fasten or hold things together.

strategy strategies
NOUN a plan for achieving something.

straw straws
NOUN 1 a hollow tube of paper or plastic that you use to suck a drink into your mouth.
2 the dry, yellowish stalks of some crops.

strawberry strawberries
NOUN a small red fruit with tiny seeds in its skin.

stray strays straying strayed
VERB 1 When people or animals **stray**, they wander away from where they should be.
2 If your thoughts **stray**, you stop concentrating.
ADJECTIVE 3 A **stray** dog or cat is one that has wandered away from its home.
NOUN 4 a stray dog or cat.

streak streaks
NOUN a long, narrow mark or stain.

stream streams streaming streamed
NOUN 1 a small river.
2 You can refer to a steady flow of something as a **stream**: *a constant **stream** of children.*
VERB 3 If something **streams**, it flows fast, without stopping. *Rain **streamed** down the windscreen.*

streamer streamers
NOUN a long piece of paper or ribbon used as a decoration.

street streets
NOUN a road in a town or village, usually with buildings along it.

strength
NOUN how strong or powerful someone or something is.

Synonyms: might, force, power

strenuous
ADJECTIVE involving a lot of effort or energy.

stress stresses stressing stressed
NOUN 1 worry and nervous tension.
VERB 2 If you **stress** a point, you emphasize it and draw attention to how important it is.

Synonyms: (sense 1) anxiety, pressure, strain

stretch stretches stretching stretched
VERB 1 If you **stretch** something soft or elastic, you pull it to make it longer or bigger.
2 Something that **stretches** over an area covers the whole of that area. *Forests **stretched** the length of the valley.*
3 When you **stretch**, you move part of your body as far away from you as you can.
NOUN 4 an area of something. *This is a quiet **stretch** of beach.*

stretcher stretchers
NOUN a long piece of material with a pole along each side, used to carry an injured person.

strict stricter strictest
ADJECTIVE 1 Someone who is **strict** controls other people very firmly.
2 exact or complete. *We were given **strict** instructions.*

stride strides striding strode stridden
VERB 1 If you **stride** along, you walk quickly with long steps.
NOUN 2 a long step.

strike strikes striking struck
VERB 1 If you **strike** something, you hit it with a lot of force.
2 If workers **strike**, they refuse to work because they want better working conditions or more money.
3 If you **strike** a match, you make a flame by rubbing it against something rough.

striking
ADJECTIVE very noticeable because of being unusual or attractive.

string strings
NOUN 1 thin rope made of twisted threads.
2 a row or series of similar things: *a **string** of islands.*

strip strips stripping stripped
NOUN 1 a long, narrow piece of something.
VERB 2 If you **strip**, you take off all your clothes.

stripe stripes

NOUN a long, thin line of colour.

strode

VERB the past tense of *stride*.

stroke strokes stroking stroked

VERB **1** If you **stroke** something, you move your hand smoothly and gently over it.
NOUN **2** The **strokes** of a brush or pen are the movements that you make with it.
3 If someone has a **stroke**, a blood vessel in the brain bursts or gets blocked, possibly causing death or paralysis.
4 a style of swimming. *My best **stroke** is the front crawl.*

stroll strolls strolling strolled

VERB **1** If you **stroll** along, you walk slowly in a relaxed way.
NOUN **2** a slow, pleasurable walk.

Synonyms: amble, saunter

strong stronger strongest

ADJECTIVE **1** Someone who is **strong** has a lot of physical power.
2 You also say that someone is **strong** when they are confident and have courage.
3 Strong objects are able to withstand rough treatment, and are not easily damaged.
4 great or intense: *a **strong** wind.*

struck

VERB the past tense and past participle of *strike*.

structure structures

NOUN **1** The **structure** of something is the way it is made, built or organized.
2 something that has been built or put together.

struggle struggles struggling struggled

VERB **1** If you **struggle** to do something difficult, you try hard to do it.
2 When people **struggle**, they twist and move violently to get free of something or someone.
NOUN **3** Something that is a **struggle** is difficult to achieve and takes a lot of effort.

stubble

NOUN **1** the short stalks remaining in the ground after a crop is harvested.
2 If a man has **stubble** on his face, he has very short hair growing there because he has not shaved recently.

stubborn

ADJECTIVE Someone who is **stubborn** is determined not to change the way they think or how they do things.

Synonym: obstinate

stuck

ADJECTIVE **1** If something or someone is **stuck**, they cannot be moved.
2 If you are **stuck**, you cannot go on with your work because you are finding it too difficult.
VERB **3** past tense and past participle of *stick*.

stud studs

NOUN **1** a small piece of metal, or other material, fixed into something. *Rachel wore gold **studs** in her ears.*
2 A male horse or other animal that is kept for **stud** is kept for breeding purposes.
3 a place where horses are kept and bred.

student students

NOUN a person studying at a university, college or school.

studio studios

NOUN **1** a room where an artist works.
2 a room containing special equipment where records, films, or radio or television programmes are made.

studious

ADJECTIVE Someone who is **studious** studies hard or is fond of studying.

study studies studying studied

VERB **1** If you **study** a particular subject, you spend time learning about it.
2 If you **study** something, you look at it carefully.
NOUN **3** a room for studying or working in.

stuff stuffs stuffing stuffed

NOUN **1** You can refer to a substance or a group of things as **stuff**. *She spread out her **stuff** on top of the table.*
VERB **2** If you **stuff** something somewhere, you push it there quickly and carelessly.
3 If you **stuff** something, you fill it with something else. *Mum **stuffed** the turkey.*

stuffy stuffier stuffiest

ADJECTIVE **1** If it is **stuffy** in a room there is not enough fresh air.
2 boring and old-fashioned.

stumble stumbles stumbling stumbled

VERB **1** If you **stumble** while you are walking or running, you trip and nearly fall.

2 If you **stumble** when you are speaking, you hesitate or make mistakes.

stump stumps stumping stumped

NOUN **1** a small part of something that is left when the rest has gone: *a tree **stump***.

2 In cricket, the **stumps** are the three upright wooden sticks that support the bails, forming the wicket.

VERB **3** If a question or problem **stumps** you, you cannot think of an answer or solution.

stun stuns stunning stunned

VERB **1** If you are **stunned**, or something **stuns** you, you are very shocked by it.

2 If something **stuns** a person or an animal, it knocks them unconscious.

stung

VERB the past tense and past participle of *sting*.

stunk

VERB the past participle of *stink*.

stunt stunts

NOUN an unusual or dangerous and exciting thing that someone does to get publicity or as part of a performance.

stupid stupider stupidest

ADJECTIVE If you are **stupid**, you are not sensible and do not make wise decisions.

sturdy sturdier sturdiest

ADJECTIVE strong, firm and well built.

stutter stutters stuttering stuttered

NOUN **1** Someone who has a **stutter** finds it difficult to speak smoothly and often repeats the beginning of words.

VERB **2** When someone **stutters**, they hesitate or repeat sounds when speaking.

sty sties

NOUN a hut with a yard where pigs are kept on a farm.

style styles

NOUN **1** how something is done, made, said or written. *The food was cooked in Cantonese **style***.

2 A person or place that has **style** is smart, elegant and fashionable.

sub-

PREFIX You add **sub-** to the beginning of a word to mean below or beneath. For example something that is **sub**standard is below the required standard, and a **sub**heading comes somewhere below a main heading.

subheading subheadings

NOUN a title to a part of a larger section of a book. A chapter may have several sections in it, each with a **subheading**.

subject subjects subjecting subjected

Said "**sub**-jekt" NOUN **1** The **subject** of a book, programme or conversation is the thing or person it is about. *Horses are the **subject** of this book.*

2 something that you learn about. *Maths is my favourite **subject**.*

3 The **subjects** of a country are the people who live there.

4 In grammar, the **subject** is the word or words representing the person or thing doing the action. For example, in the sentence "My cat keeps catching birds", "my cat" is the **subject**. *Said* "**sub**-jekt" VERB **5** If you **subject** someone to something, you make them experience it.

submarine submarines

NOUN a type of ship that can travel beneath the surface of the sea.

submerge submerges submerging submerged

VERB To **submerge** means to go beneath the surface of a liquid, or to push something beneath the surface of a liquid.

submit submits submitting submitted

VERB **1** If you **submit** to something or someone, you give in to them.

2 If you **submit** something like a report or an essay, you hand it in.

subscribe subscribes subscribing subscribed
VERB If you **subscribe** to something, you regularly pay a sum of money to be a member of something or to receive a magazine.

subside subsides subsiding subsided
VERB 1 If something **subsides**, it sinks.
2 To **subside** is to become quiet or back to normal after a fuss.

substance substances
NOUN anything that is a solid, a powder, a liquid or a paste.

Synonym: material

substantial
ADJECTIVE 1 very large in degree or amount.
2 large and strongly built.

substitute substitutes substituting substituted
VERB 1 If you **substitute** one thing for another, you use it instead of the other thing.
NOUN 2 If one thing is a **substitute** for another, it is used instead of it or put in its place.

Synonyms: (sense 2) alternative, replacement

subtitle subtitles
NOUN A film or television programme with **subtitles** has the speech, or a translation of it, printed at the bottom of the screen.

subtle subtler subtlest
ADJECTIVE very fine, delicate or small in degree.

subtract subtracts subtracting subtracted
VERB If you **subtract** one number from another, you take away the first number from the second.

suburban
ADJECTIVE to do with the outskirts of a town or city.

subway subways
NOUN 1 a footpath that goes underneath a road.
2 an underground railway.

succeed succeeds succeeding succeeded
VERB 1 If you **succeed**, you manage to do what you are trying to do.
2 If one person **succeeds** another, they come after them and take their place.

success successes
NOUN the achievement of something you have been trying to do.

successful
ADJECTIVE having success.

succession successions
NOUN 1 a number of things happening one after the other.
2 When someone becomes the next person to have an important position, you can call this event their **succession**.

such
ADVERB 1 You can use **such** to emphasize something. *He's such a nice boy.*
ADJECTIVE 2 the same kind or similar. *I have never seen such flowers.*
PHRASE 3 You can use **such as** to introduce examples of something. *There were trees such as oak, ash and elm.*

suck sucks sucking sucked
VERB If you **suck** something, you hold it in your mouth and pull at it with your cheeks and tongue, usually to get liquid out of it.

sudden
ADJECTIVE happening quickly and unexpectedly. *We heard a sudden cry.*

sue sues suing sued
VERB To **sue** someone means to start a legal case against them, usually to claim money from them.

suede
NOUN a thin, soft leather with a velvety surface.

suffer suffers suffering suffered
VERB If you **suffer**, you feel pain or sadness.

sufficient
ADJECTIVE If an amount is **sufficient**, there is enough of it available.

suffix suffixes
NOUN a group of letters that is added to the end of a word to form a new word, for example -*ness* or -*ship*, which would make "good" into "goodness" and "friend" into "friendship".

suffocate suffocates suffocating suffocated
VERB If someone **suffocates**, they die because they have no air to breathe.

A B C D E F G H I J K L M N O P Q R S T U V W X Y Z

sugar

NOUN a sweet substance obtained from some plants and used to sweeten food and drinks.

icing sugar

brown sugar lumps

caster sugar

suggest suggests suggesting suggested

VERB When you **suggest** something, you offer it as an idea.

suicide

NOUN People who commit **suicide** deliberately kill themselves.

suit suits suiting suited

NOUN **1** a matching jacket and trousers or skirt.
VERB **2** If an arrangement **suits** you, it is convenient and suitable for you.
3 If a piece of clothing or a colour **suits** you, you look good when you are wearing it.
NOUN **4** A **suit** in a pack of cards is one of the sets of diamonds, clubs, hearts or spades.

suitable

ADJECTIVE right or acceptable for a certain person, occasion, time or place. *Many roads are not* **suitable** *for cycling.*

suitcase suitcases

NOUN a case in which you carry your belongings when you are travelling.

suite suites

NOUN **1** a set of rooms in a hotel.
2 a set of matching furniture or bathroom fittings.

sulk sulks sulking sulked

VERB If you **sulk**, you show your annoyance by being silent and moody.

sullen

ADJECTIVE behaving in a bad-tempered and disagreeably silent way.

sulphur

NOUN a yellow chemical used in industry and medicine. **Sulphur** burns with a very unpleasant smell.

sultana sultanas

NOUN a dried, seedless grape.

sum sums

NOUN **1** an amount of money.
2 the total of numbers added together.

summarize summarizes summarizing summarized; also spelt summarise

VERB If you **summarize** something, you give a short account of its main points.

summary summaries

NOUN a short account of the main points of something said or written.

summer summers

NOUN the warmest season of the year, between spring and autumn.

summit summits

NOUN the top of a mountain. *The view from the* **summit** *was spectacular.*

summon summons summoning summoned

VERB If someone **summons** you, they order you to go to them.

sun

NOUN **1** the star in our solar system around which the earth and other planets travel, and that gives us heat and light.
2 the heat and light from the sun.

sunbathe sunbathes sunbathing sunbathed

VERB When you **sunbathe**, you sit in the sun to get brown.

sunburn

NOUN sore red skin due to being in the sun for too long.

Sunday Sundays

NOUN the first day of the week, coming before Monday.

sundial sundials

NOUN an object for telling the time, made with a pointer that casts a shadow from the sun on to a flat base marked with hours.

sunflower sunflowers
NOUN a tall flower with a very large, round yellow head.

sung
VERB the past participle of *sing*.

sunglasses
PLURAL NOUN dark glasses worn to protect your eyes from the sun.

sunk
VERB the past participle of *sink*.

sunlight
NOUN the light from the sun.

sunny sunnier sunniest
ADJECTIVE having lots of sunshine.

sunrise sunrises
NOUN the time in the day when the sun first appears.

sunset sunsets
NOUN the time when the sun goes down.

sunshine
NOUN warmth and light that come from the sun.

super
ADJECTIVE excellent, very good.

superb
ADJECTIVE very good indeed.

superficial
ADJECTIVE only on the surface.

superior
ADJECTIVE **1** better or of higher quality than other similar things.
2 in a more important position than another person.

superlative superlatives
ADJECTIVE **1** of the highest quality, the best.
2 the form of an adverb or adjective that expresses "most". For example, the superlative of "hot" is "hottest", and the superlative of "easy" is "easiest".

supermarket supermarkets
NOUN a very large self-service shop that sells food and household goods.

supernatural
ADJECTIVE Something that is **supernatural**, such as ghosts or witchcraft, cannot be explained by natural, scientific laws.

supersonic
ADJECTIVE faster than the speed of sound. [from Latin *super* + *sonus* meaning above sound]

superstar superstars
NOUN a very famous entertainer or sportsperson.

superstitious
ADJECTIVE People who are **superstitious** believe in things like magic and powers that bring good or bad luck.

supervise supervises supervising supervised
VERB If you **supervise** someone, you check what they are doing to make sure that they do it correctly.

supper suppers
NOUN a meal eaten in the evening or a snack eaten before you go to bed.

supple
ADJECTIVE able to bend and move easily. *Gymnasts are usually very supple.*

supplement supplements supplementing supplemented
VERB **1** To **supplement** something means to add something to it to improve it. *Many villagers supplemented their food supply by fishing for salmon.*
NOUN **2** something that is added to something else to improve it.

supply supplies supplying supplied
VERB **1** If you **supply** someone with something, you provide them with it.
PLURAL NOUN **2** **Supplies** are food and equipment for a special purpose. *His medical supplies were running low.*

support supports supporting supported
VERB **1** If something **supports** an object, it is underneath it and holding it up.
2 If you **support** a sports team, you are a fan.
3 If you **support** someone, you give them money, help or encouragement.
NOUN **4** If you give **support** to someone, you are kind, encouraging and helpful to them.
5 something that supports an object.

suppose supposes supposing supposed
VERB If you **suppose** that something is so, you think that it is likely.

suppress suppresses suppressing suppressed

VERB If an army or government **suppresses** something, it stops people doing it.

supreme

ADJECTIVE greatest, best or most important.

sure surer surest

ADJECTIVE **1** If you are **sure** about something, you know you are right.
2 If something is **sure** to happen, it will definitely happen.

surf surfs surfing surfed

NOUN **1** the white foam that forms on the top of waves when they break near the shore.
VERB **2** When you **surf**, you ride towards the shore on top of a wave, on a special board called a surfboard.

3 When you **surf** the Internet, you go from website to website reading the information.

surface surfaces

NOUN the top or outside area of something. *The wind ruffled the **surface** of the lake.*

surge surges surging surged

NOUN **1** a sudden great increase in the amount of something. *After the rain there was a **surge** of water down the river.*
VERB **2** If someone or something **surges**, they move suddenly and powerfully. *The crowd **surged** forward.*

surgeon surgeons

NOUN a doctor who performs operations.

surgery surgeries

NOUN **1** medical treatment in which part of the patient's body is cut open. *He had to have **surgery** to repair his knee.*
2 a room where doctors or dentists see their patients.

surname surnames

NOUN your last name. Members of the same family usually have the same **surname**.

surplus surpluses

NOUN If there is a **surplus** of something, there is more of it than is needed.

surprise surprises surprising surprised

NOUN **1** an unexpected event.
2 the feeling caused when something unexpected happens.
VERB **3** If something **surprises** you, it gives you a feeling of surprise.

surrender surrenders surrendering surrendered

VERB If someone **surrenders**, they admit that they are defeated.

surround surrounds surrounding surrounded

VERB To **surround** someone or something means to be situated all around them. *The house is **surrounded** by a high fence.*

surroundings

PLURAL NOUN the things and conditions around a person or place.

survey surveys surveying surveyed

Said "sur-**vey**" VERB **1** If you **survey** something, you look carefully at the whole of it. *They stood back and **surveyed** the scene.*
2 to make a detailed inspection of something.
Said "**sur**-vey" NOUN **3** A **survey** of something, such as people's habits, is a detailed examination of it, often in a report.

survive survives surviving survived

VERB To **survive** means to continue to live or exist in spite of danger or difficulties.

suspect suspects suspecting suspected

Said "sus-**spekt**" VERB **1** If you **suspect** something, you think that it might be true.
2 If you **suspect** someone of doing something wrong, you think that they have done it.
Said "**suss**-pekt" NOUN **3** someone who is thought to be guilty of a crime.

suspend suspends suspending suspended

VERB **1** to hang something up.
2 to delay something for a time.

suspense

NOUN the feeling of excitement or fear when you are waiting for something to happen.

suspicion suspicions

NOUN the feeling of not trusting someone or that something is wrong.

suspicious

ADJECTIVE **1** If you are **suspicious** of someone, you do not trust them.
2 If something is **suspicious**, it causes suspicion.

swallow swallows swallowing swallowed

VERB If you **swallow** something, you make it go down your throat and into your stomach.

swam

VERB the past tense of *swim*.

swamp swamps swamping swamped

NOUN **1** an area of permanently wet land.
VERB **2** If something is **swamped**, it is covered or filled with water.
3 If you are **swamped** by things, you have more than you can manage.

swan swans

NOUN a large, usually white, bird with a long neck that lives on rivers or lakes.

swap swaps swapping swapped

Rhymes with "**stop**" VERB If you **swap** one thing for another, you replace the first thing with the second.

Synonym: exchange

swarm swarms swarming swarmed

NOUN **1** a large group of insects flying together.
VERB **2** When bees or other insects **swarm**, they fly together in a large group.
3 If a place is **swarming** with people, it is crowded with people.

swat swats swatting swatted

VERB If you **swat** an insect, you hit it quickly to kill it.

sway sways swaying swayed

VERB If something or someone **sways**, they lean or swing slowly from side to side.

swear swears swearing swore sworn

VERB **1** If you **swear**, you use very rude words.
2 If you **swear** to do something, you promise that you will do it.

sweat sweats sweating sweated

NOUN **1** the salty liquid that comes through your skin when you are hot or afraid.
VERB **2** When you **sweat**, sweat comes through your skin.

sweater sweaters

NOUN a knitted piece of clothing covering your upper body and arms.

sweatshirt sweatshirts

NOUN a piece of clothing made of thick cotton, covering your upper body and arms.

swede swedes

NOUN a large round root vegetable with yellow flesh and a brownish-purple skin.

sweep sweeps sweeping swept

VERB **1** If you **sweep** the floor, you use a brush to gather up dust or rubbish from it.
2 If you **sweep** things off a surface, you push them all off with a quick, smooth movement.
3 If something **sweeps** from one place to another, it moves there very quickly. *The boat swept down the river with the outgoing tide.*

sweet sweeter sweetest; sweets

ADJECTIVE **1** tasting of sugar or honey.
2 A **sweet** sound is gentle and tuneful.
3 attractive and delightful. *He's such a sweet little baby.*
NOUN **4** small pieces of sweet food, such as toffees, chocolates and mints.
5 something sweet that you eat at the end of a meal.

Synonym: (sense 5) dessert

sweet corn

NOUN a long stalk covered with juicy yellow seeds that can be eaten as a vegetable.

sweetheart sweethearts

NOUN You can call someone you are very fond of **sweetheart**.

swell swells swelling swelled swollen

VERB If something **swells**, it becomes larger and rounder.

sweltering

ADJECTIVE If the weather is **sweltering**, it is very hot.

swept

VERB the past tense and past participle of *sweep*.

a b c d e f g h i j k l m n o p q r **s** t u v w x y z

swerve swerves swerving swerved
VERB If someone or something **swerves**, they suddenly change direction to avoid colliding with something.

swift swifter swiftest; swifts
ADJECTIVE **1** happening or moving very quickly.
NOUN **2** a bird with narrow crescent-shaped wings.

swim swims swimming swam swum
VERB When you **swim**, you move through water by making movements with your arms and legs.

swimming
NOUN the act of moving through water using your arms and legs.

swimming costume swimming costumes
NOUN a garment you wear while swimming.

swimming pool swimming pools
NOUN an area of water made for swimming, usually a large hole that has been tiled and filled with water.

swimsuit swimsuits
NOUN a one-piece swimming costume.

swindle swindles swindling swindled
VERB **1** If someone **swindles** someone else, they trick them to obtain money or property.
NOUN **2** a trick in which someone is cheated out of money or property.

swine swine
NOUN; OLD-FASHIONED a pig. The plural of **swine** is swine.

swing swings swinging swung
VERB **1** If something **swings**, or if you **swing** it, it moves repeatedly from side to side or backwards and forwards from a fixed point.
NOUN **2** a seat hanging from a frame or a branch, that moves backwards and forwards when you sit on it.

swipe swipes swiping swiped
VERB **1** If you **swipe** at something, you try to hit it with a curved swinging movement.
2 If a credit card is **swiped**, it is put though an electronic machine to read it when paying.
3 INFORMAL If someone **swipes** something, they steal it.

switch switches switching switched
NOUN **1** a device used to control an electrical device or machine. When the **switch** is on, or closed, it completes the circuit and electricity can flow.
2 a change.
VERB **3** To **switch** to a different task or topic means to change to it.
switch off VERB **4** If you **switch off** a light or a machine, you stop it working by pressing a switch.
switch on VERB **5** If you **switch on** a light or a machine, you start it working by pressing a switch.

switchboard switchboards
NOUN a panel with switches on for connecting telephone lines.

swivel swivels swivelling swivelled
VERB **1** to turn round on a central point.
ADJECTIVE **2** A **swivel** chair or lamp is made so that you can move the main part of it while the base remains in a fixed position.

swollen
ADJECTIVE **1** Something that is **swollen** has swelled up.
VERB **2** the past participle of *swell*.

Synonyms: (sense 1) enlarged, puffed up

swoop swoops swooping swooped
VERB To **swoop** is to move downwards through the air in a fast curving movement.

swop swops swopping swopped
VERB to swap.

sword swords
NOUN a weapon consisting of a very long blade with a short handle.

swum
VERB the past participle of *swim*.

swung
VERB the past tense and past participle of *swing*.

sycamore sycamores
NOUN a tree that has large leaves with five points, and winged seed cases.

syllable syllables
NOUN a part of a word that contains a single vowel sound and is said as one unit: *"Book" has one **syllable** and "reading" has two.*

syllabus syllabuses or syllabi
NOUN the subjects that are studied for a particular course or examination.

symbol symbols
NOUN a shape, design or idea that is used to represent something. *Apple blossom is a Chinese **symbol** of peace and beauty.*

symmetrical
ADJECTIVE **Symmetrical** objects can be divided in half so that both halves match, with one half like a reflection of the other.

symmetry
NOUN If something has **symmetry,** it is the same in both halves.

sympathetic
ADJECTIVE feeling sympathy or understanding for someone.

sympathy
NOUN an understanding of people's feelings and opinions, especially someone who is in difficulties.

Synonym: compassion

symphony symphonies
NOUN a piece of music for an orchestra, usually in four parts called movements.

symptom symptoms
NOUN something wrong with your body that is a sign of illness.

synagogue synagogues
NOUN a building where Jewish people meet for worship and religious instruction.

synonym synonyms
NOUN two words that have the same or a very similar meaning. *Speak is a **synonym** for talk.* See page 442.

synthetic
ADJECTIVE made from artificial substances rather than natural ones.

syringe syringes
NOUN a hollow tube with a plunger, used for drawing up or pushing out liquids. Doctors and vets use them to give injections.

syrup syrups
NOUN a thick sweet liquid made by boiling sugar with water.
[from Arabic ***sharab*** meaning drink]

system systems
NOUN an organized way of doing or arranging something according to a fixed plan or set of rules.

a
b
c
d
e
f
g
h
i
j
k
l
m
n
o
p
q
r
s
t
u
v
w
x
y
z

Tt

tab tabs
NOUN a small extra piece that is attached to something and sticks out, for example a sticky marker that you put in a book to mark your place.

table tables
NOUN **1** a piece of furniture with a flat top supported by one or more legs.
2 a set of facts or figures arranged in rows or columns.

tablecloth tablecloths
NOUN a cloth used to cover a table and to keep it clean.

tablespoon tablespoons
NOUN **1** a large spoon used for serving food.
2 the amount that a **tablespoon** contains. *For this recipe you need two **tablespoons** of caster sugar.*

tablet tablets
NOUN **1** medicine in a small, solid lump that you swallow.
2 a flat piece of stone with words carved on it.
3 a small block of soap.

Synonym: (sense 1) pill

table tennis
NOUN a game for two or four people who use bats to hit a small ball over a net across the middle of the table.

tabloid tabloids
NOUN a newspaper with small pages, short news stories, and lots of photographs.

tack tacks tacking tacked
NOUN **1** a short nail with a flat top.
2 If you change **tack**, you find a different way of doing something.
VERB **3** If you **tack** something to a surface, you fix it there with a tack.
4 If you **tack** in a boat, you sail in a zigzag course to catch the wind.
5 If you **tack** a piece of fabric, you sew it with long, loose stitches.
NOUN **6** equipment for horses, such as bridles, saddles and harnesses.

tackle tackles tackling tackled
VERB **1** If you **tackle** a difficult task, you start dealing with it.
2 If you **tackle** someone in a game such as hockey or soccer, you try to get the ball away from them.
NOUN **3** an attempt to get the ball away from your opponent in certain sports.

tact
NOUN the ability to deal with people without upsetting or offending them.
tactless ADJECTIVE   **tactlessly** ADVERB

tactful
ADJECTIVE Someone who is **tactful** has the ability to deal with people without upsetting or offending them.
tactfully ADVERB

tactic tactics
NOUN one of the methods you use in order to achieve what you want.

tadpole tadpoles
NOUN a young frog or toad. **Tadpoles** are black with round heads and long tails, and live in water. [Middle English *tadde* meaning toad and *pol* meaning head]

tag tags tagging tagged
NOUN **1** a small label made of cloth.
2 a game in which one person chases the other people who are playing.
VERB **3** If you **tag along** behind someone, you follow and try to keep up.

tail tails
NOUN **1** The **tail** of an animal is the part extending beyond the end of its body. For example, a fox has a bushy **tail.**
2 the end part of something.
ADJECTIVE OR ADVERB **3** When you toss a coin, the **tails** side is the one that does not have a person's head on it.

tailor tailors
NOUN a person who makes, alters and repairs clothes, especially for men.

take takes taking took taken

VERB **1** If you **take** someone or something to a place, you get them there. *She **took** the cat to the vet.*

2 Take is used to show what activity is being done. *Sam **took** a shower.*

3 If you **take** a pill or some medicine, you swallow it.

4 When you **take** one number from another, you subtract it.

5 If you **take** a photograph, you use a camera to produce it.

take after VERB **6** If you **take after** a member of your family, you are like them in some way.

take off VERB **7** When a plane **takes off,** it goes into the air.

takeaway takeaways

NOUN **1** a shop or restaurant that sells hot, cooked food to be taken away and eaten elsewhere.

2 a hot cooked meal bought from a takeaway restaurant.

talcum powder

NOUN a soft, perfumed powder to put on the skin to dry it.

tale tales

NOUN a story.

talent talents

NOUN the ability to do something very well.

talk talks talking talked

VERB **1** When you **talk,** you say things to someone.

NOUN **2** a conversation or discussion.

3 an informal speech about something.

talkative

ADJECTIVE If you are **talkative**, you talk a lot.

Synonym: chatty

tall taller tallest

ADJECTIVE **1** If you are **tall**, you are more than the average height.

2 having a particular height. *How **tall** are you?*

tally tallies

NOUN an informal record that you keep as you count objects.

Talmud

NOUN a collection of books of the ancient Jewish ceremonies and laws.

talon talons

NOUN a sharp, hooked claw, especially of a bird of prey.

tambourine tambourines

NOUN a percussion instrument made of a skin stretched tightly over a circular frame. It has small round pieces of metal around the edge that jangle when the **tambourine** is beaten or shaken.

[from Old French *tambourin* meaning little drum]

tame tamer tamest; tames taming tamed

ADJECTIVE **1** A **tame** animal is not afraid of people.

VERB **2** If you **tame** a wild animal, you train it not to be afraid of humans.

tamper tampers tampering tampered

VERB If you **tamper** with something, you interfere with it.

tan tans tanning tanned

NOUN **1** a suntan.

2 a yellowish-brown colour.

VERB **3** If your skin **tans**, it goes brown in the sun.

4 When an animal's skin is **tanned**, it is turned into leather by treating it with chemicals.

tang tangs

NOUN a strong flavour or smell.

tangerine tangerines

NOUN **1** a type of small sweet orange that is easy to peel.

NOUN OR ADJECTIVE **2** reddish-orange.

tangle tangles tangling tangled

NOUN **1** a mass of things, such as hairs or fibres, that are twisted together and difficult to separate.

VERB **2** If you **tangle** something, you twist it into knots.

tank tanks

NOUN **1** a large container for storing liquid or gas.

2 an armoured military vehicle that moves on tracks and has guns or rockets.

tanker tankers

NOUN a ship or lorry designed to carry large quantities of gas or liquid.

a
b
c
d
e
f
g
h
i
j
k
l
m
n
o
p
q
r
s
t
u
v
w
x
y
z

A B C D E F G H I J K L M N O P Q R S **T** U V W X Y Z

tantrum tantrums
NOUN a noisy and sometimes violent outburst of bad temper, especially by a child.

tap taps tapping tapped
NOUN **1** a device for controlling the flow of gas or liquid from a pipe.
VERB **2** If you **tap** something, you hit it lightly and quickly.
NOUN **3** a light hit, or its sound.

tape tapes taping taped
NOUN **1** a long plastic ribbon covered with a magnetic substance and used to record sounds, pictures and computer information.
2 a cassette with magnetic **tape** wound round it: *video tape*.
3 a strip of sticky plastic used for sticking things together.
VERB **4** If you **tape** sounds or television pictures, you record them using a tape recorder or a video recorder.

tape measure tape measures
NOUN a long, narrow tape marked with centimetres or inches, and used for measuring.

taper tapers tapering tapered
VERB Something that **tapers** becomes thinner towards one end.

tape recorder tape recorders
NOUN a machine that records sounds on to a special magnetic tape that can be played back later.

tapestry tapestries
NOUN a piece of heavy cloth with designs embroidered on it.
[from Old French *tapisserie* meaning carpeting]

Part of the Bayeaux Tapestry

tar
NOUN a thick, black, sticky substance that is used in making roads.

tarantula tarantulas
NOUN a large, hairy, poisonous spider.

target targets
NOUN something you aim at when firing a weapon.

tarmac
NOUN a mixture of tar and crushed stones, used for making road surfaces.
[short for *tarmacadam*, from the name of John *McAdam*, the Scottish engineer who invented it]

tarnish tarnishes tarnishing tarnished
VERB If metal **tarnishes**, it becomes stained and loses its shine.
tarnished ADJECTIVE

tarpaulin tarpaulins
NOUN a sheet of heavy waterproof material used as a protective covering.

tart tarts
NOUN **1** a pastry case, usually filled with something sweet such as fruit or jam.
ADJECTIVE **2** Something **tart** has a sharp or sour taste.

tartan tartans
NOUN a coloured, woollen fabric from Scotland, with a special pattern of checks and stripes, depending on which clan it belongs to.

task tasks
NOUN any piece of work that has to be done.

Synonyms: chore, duty, job

tassel tassels
NOUN a tuft of loose threads tied by a knot and used for decoration.

taste tastes tasting tasted
NOUN **1** Your sense of **taste** is your ability to recognize the flavour of things in your mouth.
2 The **taste** of something is its flavour.
3 your own particular choice of things such as clothes, music and food. *Jenny and I have the same taste in music.*
VERB **4** When you can **taste** something in your mouth, you know what its flavour is like.
5 If food or drink **tastes** of something, it has that flavour.

tasty tastier tastiest

ADJECTIVE Something that is **tasty** has a pleasant flavour.

tattered

ADJECTIVE ragged and torn.

tattoo tattoos tattooing tattooed

VERB **1** If someone is **tattooed**, they have a design drawn on their skin by pricking little holes and filling them with coloured dye. NOUN **2** a picture or design tattooed on someone's body.

taught

VERB the past tense and past participle of *teach*.

taunt taunts taunting taunted

VERB If you **taunt** someone, you tease them about their weaknesses or failures in order to make them angry or upset.

taut

ADJECTIVE Something that is **taut** is stretched very tight.

tawny

ADJECTIVE brownish-yellow.

tax taxes taxing taxed

NOUN **1** an amount of money that people have to pay to the government so that it can provide public services such as health care and education.
VERB **2** If a sum of money is **taxed**, a certain amount of it is paid to the government.
3 If something **taxes** you, it exhausts you and drains your energy.

taxi taxis

NOUN a car with a driver that you hire, usually for a short journey.

tea teas

NOUN **1** the dried leaves of a shrub found in Asia.
2 a drink made by soaking the leaves of the tea plant in hot water.
3 a meal taken in the late afternoon or early evening.

tea bag tea bags

NOUN a small paper packet with tea leaves in it, that you use to make a drink of tea.

teach teaches teaching taught

VERB If someone **teaches** you something, they help you learn about it or show you how to do it.

Synonyms: educate, instruct, train

teacher teachers

NOUN someone who teaches at a school or college.

teak

NOUN a hard wood that comes from a large Asian tree.

team teams

NOUN a group of people who play together against another group in a sport or game.

teapot teapots

NOUN a container in which tea is made. It has a handle, a spout and a lid.

tear tears tearing tore torn

Rhymes with **"fear"** NOUN **1** a drop of liquid that comes out of your eyes when you cry.
Rhymes with **"hair"** **2** a hole or rip that has been made in something. *There was a tear in the curtain.*
VERB **3** If you **tear** something, you damage it by pulling so that a hole or rip appears in it.

tearful

ADJECTIVE If you are **tearful**, you cry easily or you are crying.

tease teases teasing teased

VERB If someone **teases** you, they deliberately make fun of you or embarrass you.

teaspoon teaspoons

NOUN **1** a small spoon used for stirring drinks.
2 the amount that a **teaspoon** holds. *I have two teaspoons of sugar in my coffee.*

teat teats

NOUN **1** a nipple on a female animal.
2 a piece of rubber or plastic that is shaped like a nipple and fitted to a baby's feeding bottle.

technical

ADJECTIVE If something is **technical**, it is to do with machines, the way things work, and materials used in industry, transport and communications.

a b c d e f g h i j k l m n o p q r s **t** u v w x y z

technique techniques
Said "tek-**neek**" NOUN a particular way of doing something.

technology
NOUN practical things that have come about because of a greater understanding of science. *New **technology** has helped us develop faster computers.*

teddy bear teddy bears
NOUN a soft, furry toy bear.

tedious
ADJECTIVE boring and lasting for a long time.

teenager teenagers
NOUN a person aged between 13 and 19 years old.

teeth
NOUN the plural of *tooth*.

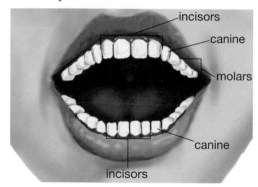

incisors
canine
molars
canine
incisors

tele-
PREFIX You add **tele-** to the beginning of a word to mean at or over a distance: ***tele**phone*. [from the Greek *tele* meaning far]

telecommunications
NOUN the science and activity of sending signals and messages over long distances, for example by radio and telephone.

telegram telegrams
NOUN a message sent by telegraph to an office, and then delivered by hand to a person's home. *He received many letters and **telegrams** of congratulations when he won the race.*

telegraph
NOUN a system of sending messages over long distances using electrical or radio signals.

telephone telephones telephoning telephoned
NOUN **1** a piece of electrical equipment for talking directly to someone who is in a different place.
VERB **2** If you **telephone** someone, you speak to them using a telephone.

telescope telescopes
NOUN a long instrument, shaped like a tube, that contains lenses. When you look through it with one eye, distant objects appear larger and nearer.

teletext
NOUN a system for displaying pages of news and information on a television screen.

televise televises televising televised
VERB If an event is **televised**, it is filmed and shown on television.

television televisions
NOUN a piece of electronic equipment that receives pictures and sounds transmitted over a distance.

tell tells telling told
VERB **1** If you **tell** someone something, you let them know about it.
2 If you **tell** someone to do something, you order them to do it.

telly tellies
NOUN an abbreviation of *television*.

temper
NOUN **1** Your **temper** is the mood you are in and the way you are feeling, whether you are irritable and angry or calm and peaceful. *I started the day in a bad **temper**.*
PHRASE **2** If you **lose your temper**, you become very angry.

temperamental
ADJECTIVE Someone who is **temperamental** changes their mood often and suddenly.

temperature temperatures
NOUN **1** how hot or cold something is. *There was a sudden drop in **temperature** once the sun had gone down.*
2 Your **temperature** is the temperature of your body. The normal body **temperature** for humans is 37 °C. *His **temperature** continued to rise.*

temple temples

NOUN **1** a building used for the worship of a god in various religions.
2 the part on either side of your head between your forehead and your ear.

tempo tempos or tempi

NOUN; TECHNICAL The **tempo** of a piece of music is its speed.

temporary

ADJECTIVE lasting for only a short time.

tempt tempts tempting tempted

VERB **1** If you **tempt** someone, you try to persuade them to do something by offering them something they want.
ADJECTIVE **2** If something is **tempting**, it is attractive and difficult to resist.

tenant tenants

NOUN someone who pays rent for the place they live in, or for land or buildings that they use.
tenancy NOUN

tend tending tended

VERB **1** If something **tends** to happen, it usually happens.
2 If you **tend** something or someone, you look after them. *Bob tended the plants.*

tendency tendencies

NOUN the way a person or a thing is likely to behave or has a habit of behaving. *She has a tendency to write messily.*

tender tenderer tenderest

ADJECTIVE **1** Someone who is **tender** is gentle and caring.
2 Tender food is easy to cut and chew.
3 If a part of your body is **tender**, it is painful and sore.

Synonyms: (sense 1) affectionate, gentle, loving

tendon tendons

NOUN **Tendons** are like strong cords. They hold your muscles and bones together.

tennis

NOUN a game played by two or four players on a rectangular court. The players hit a ball over a central net.

tense tenser tensest; tenses tensing tensed

ADJECTIVE **1** If you are **tense**, you feel worried and unable to relax.
NOUN **2** The **tense** of a verb shows whether it is in the past, present or future.
VERB **3** If you **tense** your muscles, you tighten them up.

tension tensions

NOUN the feeling of nervousness or worry that you have when something dangerous or important is happening.

tent tents

NOUN a shelter made of fabric held up by poles and pinned down at the bottom with pegs and ropes.

tentacle tentacles

NOUN the long, bending parts of an animal, such as an octopus, that it uses to feel and hold things.

tepid

ADJECTIVE **Tepid** liquid is only slightly warm.

term terms

NOUN **1** one of the periods of time that each year is divided into at a school or college.
2 Terms are words that relate to a particular subject, for example, medical **terms**, legal **terms** and scientific **terms**.
3 Terms are the conditions of an agreement. *He made a list of terms for doing the job.*
4 If you are on good **terms** with someone, you get on well with them.

terminal terminals

NOUN **1** a place where vehicles, passengers or goods begin or end a journey.
2 a keyboard and screen connected to a main computer.
ADJECTIVE **3** A **terminal** illness or disease cannot be cured and gradually causes death.
[from Latin *terminus* meaning end]

terminate terminates terminating terminated

VERB When you **terminate** something, or it **terminates**, it stops or ends.

terrace terraces

NOUN **1** a row of houses joined together.
2 a flat area of stone next to a building, where people can sit.

terrapin terrapins

NOUN a small North American freshwater turtle. [an American Indian word]

terrible

ADJECTIVE **1** serious and unpleasant. *He had a terrible illness.*

2 very bad or of poor quality. *That is a terrible haircut.*

terrier terriers

NOUN a breed of small dog. [from Old French *chien terrier* meaning earth dog, because they were originally bred to hunt animals living in holes in the ground, such as rabbits and badgers]

terrific

ADJECTIVE **1** very pleasing or impressive. *That was a terrific film.*

2 very great or strong. *There is a terrific wind blowing down on the beach.*

terrify terrifies terrifying terrified

VERB If something **terrifies** you, it makes you feel extremely frightened.

territory territories

NOUN The **territory** of a country is the land that it controls.

terror terrors

NOUN great fear or panic.

terrorism

NOUN the use of violence for political purposes.

test tests testing tested

VERB **1** When you **test** something, you try it to find out what it is, what condition it is in, or how well it works.

2 To **test** someone means to ask them questions to find out how much they know.

NOUN **3** a set of questions or tasks given to someone to find out what they know or can do.

testicle testicles

NOUN one of the parts of a man's body that make sperm.

test tube test tubes

NOUN a small cylindrical glass container that is used in chemical experiments.

tetanus

NOUN a painful infectious disease caused by germs getting into wounds.

tether tethers tethering tethered

VERB **1** If you **tether** an animal, you tie it to something such as a post.

NOUN **2** a rope for tying an animal to something such as a post.

tetrahedron tetrahedrons or tetrahedra

NOUN a solid shape with four triangular faces.

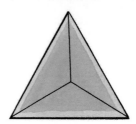

text texts

NOUN the written part of a book, rather than the pictures or the index.

textbook textbooks

NOUN a book about a particular subject for students to use.

textile textiles

NOUN a woven cloth or fabric.

texture textures

NOUN the way something feels when you touch it. *Silk has a very smooth, soft texture.*

than

CONJUNCTION OR PREPOSITION You use **than** when you compare one thing with another. *She is bigger than her sister.*

thank thanks thanking thanked

VERB When you **thank** someone, you show that you are pleased or grateful for something that they have done for you.

that those

ADJECTIVE OR PRONOUN **1 That** is used when you are referring to someone or something you have already mentioned. *That is the film I want to see.*

CONJUNCTION **2 That** is used to introduce a fact, a statement or a result. *His writing was so bad that nobody could read it.*

thatched

ADJECTIVE If a house has a **thatched** roof, it is made of straw or reeds.

thaw thaws thawing thawed

VERB **1** When snow or ice **thaws**, it melts.
2 When you **thaw** frozen food, or when it **thaws**, it defrosts.

the

ADJECTIVE called the definite article. You use **the** in front of a noun when you are referring to something in particular. *That's* ***the*** *chair I bought yesterday.*

theatre theatres

NOUN **1** a building where plays and other shows are performed on a stage.
2 a room in a hospital where operations are carried out.

theft thefts

NOUN the crime of stealing.

Synonym: robbery

their

ADJECTIVE **Their** refers to something belonging to people or things, other than yourself or the person you are talking to, that have already been mentioned. *The children had been playing football, and* ***their*** *shirts were dirty.*
✔ Other words that sound like *their* are *there* and *they're*.

theirs

PRONOUN **Theirs** refers to something belonging to people or things, other than yourself or the person you are talking to, that have already been mentioned. *The children said that the ball that came over the wall was* ***theirs***.

them

PRONOUN **Them** refers to things or people, other than yourself or the person you are talking to, that have already been mentioned. *She took her gloves off and put* ***them*** *in a drawer.*

theme themes

NOUN a main idea in a piece of writing, painting, film or music. *The main* ***theme*** *of the book is growing up.*

themselves

PRONOUN **Themselves** is used when people, other than yourself or the person you are talking to, do an action and are affected by it. *They enjoyed* ***themselves*** *at the fair.*

then

ADVERB after that; next. *He put on his shoes and* ***then*** *went for a walk.*

theology

NOUN the study of religion and God.

theory theories

NOUN an idea or set of ideas that is meant to explain something.

therapy

NOUN the treatment of a mental or physical illness.
therapist NOUN

there

ADVERB in that place or to that place. *He's sitting over* ***there***.
✔ Other words that sound like *there* are *their* and *they're*.

therefore

ADVERB as a result. *I worked hard and* ***therefore*** *I won a prize.*

thermal

ADJECTIVE **1** to do with or caused by heat.
2 Thermal clothing is specially designed to keep you warm in cold weather.

thermometer thermometers

NOUN an instrument for measuring the temperature of a room or a person's body.

Thermos

NOUN; TRADEMARK a container used to keep drinks hot or cold.

thermostat thermostats

NOUN a device used to control temperature, for example on a central heating system.

thesaurus thesauruses

NOUN a reference book in which words with similar meanings are grouped together.

these

ADJECTIVE OR PRONOUN the plural of *this*.

they

PRONOUN **They** refers to people or things that have already been mentioned. *I saw Tom and Ben.* ***They*** *were looking in a shop window.*

they'd

a contraction of *they had*.

they'll

a contraction of *they will*.

they're

a contraction of *they are*.

✔ Other words that sound like *they're* are *their* and *there*.

they've

a contraction of *they have*.

thick thicker thickest

ADJECTIVE **1** Something **thick** has a large distance between its two sides. *I'd like a **thick** slice of bread and butter.*
2 If you want to know how **thick** something is, you want to know the measurement between its two sides. *How **thick** is this wall?*
3 close together and in a large number. *She has **thick**, dark hair.*
4 **Thick** liquids contain little water and do not flow easily. *The **thick** soup was very filling.*

Antonyms: (senses 1, 2 and 4) thin

thicken thickens thickening thickened

VERB If you **thicken** something, or if it **thickens**, it becomes thicker. *Stir the custard in the pan until it **thickens**.*

thickness thicknesses

NOUN how thick something is.

thief thieves

NOUN a person who steals.

thigh thighs

NOUN the top part of your leg, between your knee and your hip.

thimble thimbles

NOUN a small metal or plastic cap that you put on the end of your finger to protect it from the needle when you are sewing.

thin thinner thinnest

ADJECTIVE **1** Something that is **thin** is much narrower than it is long.
2 A **thin** person or animal has very little fat on their body.
3 **Thin** liquids contain a lot of water and flow easily.

Antonym: (senses 1 and 3) thick

thing things

NOUN an object rather than a plant, animal or person.

think thinks thinking thought

VERB **1** When you **think** about ideas or problems, you use your mind to sort them out.
2 If you **think** something, you believe it is true. *I **think** she's got a bike for her birthday.*
3 If you **think** of something, you remember it or it comes into your mind.
4 If you are **thinking** of doing something, you might do it.

third thirds

ADJECTIVE **1** The **third** thing in a series is the one after the second, counted as number three.
NOUN **2** one of three equal parts into which something can be divided.

third person

NOUN In grammar, the **third person** is "he", "she", "it" or "they".

thirst

NOUN If you have a **thirst**, you feel the need to drink something.

thirsty thirstier thirstiest

ADJECTIVE If you are **thirsty**, you feel as if you need to drink something.
thirstily ADVERB

this those

ADJECTIVE OR PRONOUN **This** means the one here, not a different one: ***This** food looks nice.*

thistle thistles

NOUN a wild plant with prickly-edged leaves and purple flowers.

thorn thorns

NOUN one of many sharp points growing on the stems of some plants. For example, brambles have many **thorns**.

thorough

ADJECTIVE done very carefully and completely.
thoroughly ADVERB

those
ADJECTIVE OR PRONOUN the plural of *that*.

though
Rhymes with "**show**" CONJUNCTION **1** despite the fact that. *She felt better, **though** her cough was still bad.*
2 You can use **though** to mean if. *Try to look as **though** you're working.*

thought thoughts
VERB **1** the past tense and past participle of *think*.
NOUN **2** the activity of thinking. *She was lost in **thought**.*

thoughtful
ADJECTIVE **1** If you are **thoughtful**, you are quiet and serious.
2 A **thoughtful** person thinks of what other people need and what they would like.
thoughtfully ADVERB

thoughtless
ADJECTIVE A **thoughtless** person does not care or think about other people's needs.
thoughtlessness NOUN   **thoughtlessly** ADVERB

thousand thousands
NOUN the number 1000.
thousandth ADJECTIVE

thrash thrashes thrashing thrashed
VERB **1** To **thrash** someone is to beat them by hitting them with something like a stick or a whip.
2 If you **thrash** someone in a contest or fight, you defeat them completely.
3 If you **thrash**, or **thrash** about, you move about wildly and violently.

thread threads
NOUN a long, fine piece of cotton, silk, nylon or wool.

threadbare
ADJECTIVE Fabric or clothes that are **threadbare** are old and worn thin.

threat threats
NOUN **1** a warning that someone will harm you if you do not do what they want.
2 a danger or something that might cause harm.

threaten threatens threatening threatened
VERB If you **threaten** someone, you tell them that you intend to harm them in some way.

three-dimensional
ADJECTIVE A **three-dimensional** object or shape is not flat, but has height or depth as well as length and width.

threw
VERB the past tense of *throw*.

thrill thrills thrilling thrilled
NOUN **1** a sudden feeling of great excitement, pleasure or fear.
VERB **2** If something **thrills** you, it gives you a feeling of great pleasure and excitement.
thrilled ADJECTIVE   **thrilling** ADJECTIVE

thriller thrillers
NOUN a book, film or play that tells an exciting story about dangerous or mysterious events.

thrive thrives thriving throve thrived
VERB to grow strongly and healthily, or to prosper.

throat throats
NOUN **1** the back of your mouth and the top part of the tubes inside your neck that lead to your stomach and lungs.
2 the front part of your neck.

throb throbs throbbing throbbed
VERB If something **throbs**, it beats or vibrates with a strong, regular rhythm. *My finger **throbbed** after I trapped it in the door.*

throne thrones
NOUN a ceremonial chair used by a king or queen on important official occasions.

throng throngs thronging thronged
NOUN **1** a large crowd of people. *There was a **throng** of fans waiting at the stage door.*
VERB **2** If people **throng** somewhere, or **throng** a place, they go there in great numbers. *Hundreds of royal admirers **thronged** to see the procession.*

throttle throttles throttling throttled
VERB If a person **throttles** someone, they kill or injure them by squeezing their throat.

Synonym: strangle

a
b
c
d
e
f
g
h
i
j
k
l
m
n
o
p
q
r
s
t
u
v
w
x
y
z

through

PREPOSITION If you move **through** something, you go from one side of it to the other. *We followed the path **through** the woods.*

throughout

PREPOSITION AND ADVERB all the way through.

throw throws throwing threw thrown

VERB **1** When you **throw** something you let it go with a quick movement of your arm, so that it moves through the air.

throw away VERB **2** If you **throw away** something that you do not want, you get rid of it, usually by putting it in the rubbish bin.

Synonyms: (sense 1) chuck, fling, toss

thrush thrushes

NOUN a small brown songbird.

thrust thrusts thrusting thrust

VERB If you **thrust** something somewhere, you move or push it there quickly and with a lot of force.

thud thuds thudding thudded

VERB **1** to fall heavily.
NOUN **2** the dull sound of something heavy falling.

thug thugs

NOUN a very rough and violent person.
[from Hindi *thag* meaning thief]

thumb thumbs

NOUN the short, thick, jointed part on the side of your hand, similar to a finger but lower down.

thump thumps thumping thumped

VERB **1** If you **thump** someone or something, you hit them hard with your fist.
2 When your heart **thumps**, it beats strongly and quickly.
NOUN **3** a hard hit.
4 a fairly loud, dull sound.

thunder

NOUN the loud rumbling noise that you hear from the sky during some storms, often after a flash of lightning.

thunderstorm thunderstorms

NOUN a storm with thunder and lightning.

Thursday

NOUN the fifth day of the week, coming between Wednesday and Friday.
[from Old English **Thursdœg** meaning "Thor's day"; Thor was the Norse god of thunder]

tick ticks ticking ticked

NOUN **1** a written mark to show that something is correct.
VERB **2** If you **tick** something written on a piece of paper, you put a tick next to it.
3 When a clock **ticks**, it makes a regular clicking noise as it works.

ticket tickets

NOUN a piece of paper or card which shows that you have paid for a journey or have paid to go into a place. *Don't lose your bus **ticket**.*

tickle tickles tickling tickled

VERB When you **tickle** someone, you move your fingers lightly over their body in order to make them laugh.

tide tides

NOUN the regular change in the level of the sea on the shore.

tidy tidier tidiest; tidies tidying tidied

ADJECTIVE **1** Something that is **tidy** is neat and arranged in an orderly way.
2 Someone who is **tidy** always keeps their things neat.
VERB **3** If you **tidy** a place, you make it neat by putting things in their proper place.

tie ties tying tied

VERB **1** If you **tie** one thing to another, you fasten it using cord of some kind.
2 If you **tie** a piece of cord or cloth, you fasten the ends together in a knot or bow.
NOUN **3** a long, narrow piece of cloth worn around the neck under a shirt collar, and tied in a knot at the front.

tiger tigers

NOUN a large wild cat that has an orange-coloured coat with black stripes.

tight tighter tightest

ADJECTIVE **1** If clothes are **tight**, they fit you very closely.
ADVERB **2** If you hold **tight**, you hold on very firmly.

tighten tightens tightening tightened

VERB **1** If you **tighten** something like a rope or a chain, you pull it until it is straight and firmly stretched.
2 If you **tighten** something like a screw or a knot, you fasten or fix it more firmly.

tightrope tightropes

NOUN a tightly-stretched rope on which an acrobat balances and performs tricks.

tights

PLURAL NOUN a piece of clothing made of thin stretchy material that fits closely round a person's hips, legs and feet.

tile tiles tiling tiled

NOUN **1** a flat, rectangular piece of something, such as slate, carpet or baked clay, that is used to cover surfaces.
VERB **2** If you **tile** a surface, you fix tiles to it.

till tills tilling tilled

NOUN **1** a drawer or box in a shop where money is kept, usually in a cash register.
PREPOSITION OR CONJUNCTION **2** up to a certain time. *You can stay up **till** nine o'clock.*
VERB **3** If someone **tills** the soil, they plough it.

tiller tillers

NOUN a handle fixed to the top of the rudder on a boat. It turns the rudder and steers the boat.

tilt tilts tilting tilted

VERB If you **tilt** an object, you move it so that one end or side is higher than the other.

timber timbers

NOUN **1** wood that has been cut and prepared ready for building and making furniture.
2 The **timbers** of a ship or house are the large pieces of wood that have been used to build it.

time times timing timed

NOUN **1** what we measure in minutes, hours, days, weeks and years.
2 a particular point in the day. *What **time** is it?*
3 a particular period in history.
VERB **4** If you **time** something like a race, you measure how long it takes.

times

PLURAL NOUN multiplied by. *Two **times** three is six* $(2 \times 3 = 6)$.

timetable timetables

NOUN **1** a plan of the times when particular activities or jobs should be done.
2 a list of the times when particular trains, boats, buses or aircraft arrive and depart.

timid

ADJECTIVE If you are **timid**, you are shy and lacking in confidence.
timidly ADVERB

Antonym: bold

tin tins

NOUN **1** a soft, silvery-white metal.
2 a metal container that is filled with food and then sealed in order to keep the food fresh.
3 a small metal container that may have a lid.

tingle tingles tingling tingled

VERB When a part of your body **tingles**, you feel a slight prickling sensation there.
tingling NOUN OR ADJECTIVE

tinkle tinkles tinkling tinkled

VERB Something that **tinkles** makes a light, ringing sound.

tinsel

NOUN long threads with strips of shiny paper attached, used as a decoration at Christmas.

tint tints

NOUN a shade of a particular colour, particularly a pale one.

tiny tinier tiniest

ADJECTIVE extremely small.

tip tips tipping tipped

NOUN **1** the point or the very end of something.
2 a small gift of money given to someone like a waiter, who has done a service for you.
3 a place where rubbish is left.
4 a piece of useful information or advice.
VERB **5** If you **tip** something, you tilt or overturn it. *When he jumped up he **tipped** the chair over.*
6 If you **tip** something somewhere, you pour it quickly and carelessly, or you empty it from a container. *When they had finished the washing up, they **tipped** the water out of the bowl.*

tiptoe tiptoes tiptoeing tiptoed

VERB If you **tiptoe** somewhere, you walk there very quietly on your toes.

tire tires tiring tired

VERB **1** If something **tires** you, it makes you use a lot of energy so that you want to rest or sleep afterwards.

2 If you **tire** of something, you become bored with it.

tired ADJECTIVE   **tiredness** NOUN

tired

VERB the past tense and past participle of *tire*.

tissue tissues

NOUN a small piece of soft paper that you use as a handkerchief.

title titles

NOUN the name of something such as a book, play, film or piece of music.

to

PREPOSITION **1** towards.

2 used to compare units. *There are 100 centimetres* **to** *a metre.*

3 compared with or rather than. *I prefer fruit* **to** *chocolate.*

4 used to indicate the limit of something. *I am allowed to spend up* **to** *an hour watching television each night.*

ADVERB **5** if you push something like a door **to**, you close it but do not shut it completely.

✔ Other words that sound like *to* are *too* and *two*.

toad toads

NOUN an animal similar to a frog, but with drier skin and living more on land and less in the water.

toadstool toadstools

NOUN a type of fungus similar to a mushroom and often poisonous.

toast toasts toasting toasted

NOUN **1** slices of bread made brown and crisp by cooking them at a high temperature.

VERB **2** If you **toast** bread, you cook it at a high temperature so that it becomes brown and crisp.

toaster toasters

NOUN an electrical device for toasting bread.

tobacco

NOUN the dried leaves of a plant called tobacco. People smoke it in pipes, cigarettes and cigars.

toboggan toboggans tobogganing tobogganed

NOUN **1** a flat seat with two wooden or metal runners, used for sliding over the snow.

VERB **2** If you **toboggan**, you use a toboggan to slide over the snow.

Synonym: sledge

today

NOUN the day that is happening now.

toddler toddlers

NOUN a small child who has just learned to walk.

toe toes

NOUN **1** one of the five movable parts at the end of your foot.

2 the part of a shoe or sock that covers the end of your foot.

toffee toffees

NOUN a sticky, chewy sweet made by boiling sugar and butter together with water.

toga togas

NOUN a long, loose robe worn in ancient Rome.

together

ADVERB **1** If people do something **together**, they do it with each other.

2 If two things happen **together**, they happen at the same time.

3 If things are joined, mixed or fixed **together**, they are put with each other.

toil toils toiling toiled

VERB **1** If you **toil**, you work very hard.

NOUN **2** very hard work.

toilet toilets

NOUN **1** a large bowl, connected to the drains, which you use to get rid of waste from your body.

2 a small room containing a toilet.

Synonym: lavatory

token tokens
NOUN **1** a piece of paper or card that is worth a particular amount of money and can be exchanged for goods. *I got a book **token** for my birthday.*
2 a flat round piece of metal or plastic that can sometimes be used instead of money. *Some of the telephones only take **tokens**.*
3 a sign or symbol of something. *We bought her some flowers as a **token** of our thanks.*

told
VERB the past tense and past participle of *tell*.

tolerate tolerates tolerating tolerated
VERB If you **tolerate** something, you put up with it even though you do not like it.

tomato tomatoes
NOUN a small, round, red fruit used as a vegetable and eaten cooked or raw.

tomb tombs
NOUN a large grave where one or more people are buried.

tomorrow
NOUN OR ADVERB the day after today.

ton tons
NOUN a unit of weight equal to 2240 pounds or about 1016 kilograms.

tone tones
NOUN **1** a particular quality that a sound has: *the clear **tone** of the bell.*
2 a shade of a colour.

tongs
PLURAL NOUN two long narrow pieces of metal joined together at one end. You press the pieces together to pick up objects.

tongue tongues
NOUN the soft part in your mouth that you can move and use for tasting, licking and speaking.

tongue twister tongue twisters
NOUN a sentence or a rhyme that is very difficult to say.

tonight
ADVERB OR NOUN the evening or night that will come at the end of today.

tonne tonnes
NOUN a unit of weight equal to 1000 kilograms.

tonsil tonsils
NOUN one of the two small, soft lumps at the back of your throat.

tonsillitis
NOUN a painful swelling of your tonsils caused by an infection.

too
ADVERB **1** also or as well. *She was there **too**.*
2 Too shows that there is more of something than you want. *I've had **too** much to eat.*
✔ Other words that sound like *too* are *to* and *two*.

took
VERB the past tense of *take*.

tool tools
NOUN any hand-held piece of equipment that you use to help you do a particular kind of work.

tooth teeth
NOUN one of the hard, white bony parts in your mouth that you use for biting and chewing food. *See **teeth**.*

toothache
NOUN a pain in one of your teeth.

toothbrush toothbrushes
NOUN a brush for cleaning your teeth.

toothpaste
NOUN the substance that you use with a toothbrush to clean your teeth.

top tops
NOUN **1** the highest point of something. *There was snow on the mountain **top**.*
2 the upper side of something. *There was a vase of flowers on the table **top**.*
3 a piece of clothing that you wear on the top half of your body.
4 a toy that can be made to spin.
ADJECTIVE **5** The **top** thing of a series of things is the highest one: *the **top** floor of the building.*

topic topics
NOUN a particular subject that you write about or discuss.

topical
ADJECTIVE to do with things that are happening now.

Torah
NOUN Jewish law and teaching.

torch torches

NOUN a small electric light carried in the hand and powered by batteries.

[from Old French **torche** meaning "handful of twisted straw", which was set on fire and held up to provide light]

tore

VERB the past tense of *tear*.

torment torments tormenting tormented

NOUN **1** great pain or unhappiness.

VERB **2** If something **torments** you, it causes you great unhappiness.

3 If someone **torments** you, they keep deliberately annoying you.

torn

VERB the past participle of *tear*.

tornado tornadoes or tornados

NOUN a violent storm with strong circular winds around a funnel-shaped cloud.

torpedo torpedoes torpedoing torpedoed

NOUN **1** a tube-shaped bomb that travels underwater and explodes when it hits a target.

VERB **2** If a ship is **torpedoed**, it is hit, and usually sunk, by a torpedo.

torrent torrents

NOUN a very strong stream or fall of water. *The rain fell in a torrent*.

torrential

ADJECTIVE **Torrential** rain pours down very fast and in great quantities.

tortoise tortoises

NOUN a slow-moving reptile with a hard shell over its body into which it can pull its head and legs for protection.

torture tortures torturing tortured

VERB If someone **tortures** another person, they deliberately cause them great pain, usually as a punishment or to get information from them.

toss tosses tossing tossed

VERB **1** If you **toss** something somewhere, you throw it there lightly and carelessly.

2 If you **toss** a coin, you decide something by throwing a coin into the air and guessing which side will face upwards when it lands.

total totals totalling totalled

NOUN **1** the number you get when you add several numbers together.

VERB **2** If you **total** amounts, you add them together to find the total.

ADJECTIVE **3** complete.

toucan toucans

NOUN a large tropical bird with a large, colourful beak.

touch touches touching touched

VERB **1** If you **touch** something, you put your fingers or hand on it.

2 When two things **touch**, they come into contact.

3 If something **touches** you, it affects your emotions. *The sad story touched us all*.

NOUN **4** Your sense of **touch** is your ability to feel things by touching them.

touchdown touchdowns

NOUN the landing of an aircraft or spacecraft.

touchy touchier touchiest

ADJECTIVE sensitive and easily offended.

tough tougher toughest

ADJECTIVE **1** A **tough** person is strong and able to put up with things that are difficult.

2 Something that is **tough** is strong and difficult to break or damage.

3 **Tough** food is difficult to cut and chew.

Antonym: (sense 3) tender

tour tours touring toured

NOUN **1** a long journey during which you visit several places.

2 a short trip round a place such as a city or a famous building.

VERB **3** If you **tour** a place, you go on a journey or a trip round it.

tourist tourists

NOUN someone who is travelling on holiday.

tournament tournaments

NOUN a competition in which many players or teams compete in a series of games or contests.

tow tows towing towed
VERB **1** If a vehicle **tows** another vehicle, it pulls it along behind it.
NOUN **2** To give a vehicle a **tow** is to pull it along behind.

towards
PREPOSITION If you go **towards** something, you move in its direction.

towel towels
NOUN a piece of thick, soft cloth that you use to dry yourself with.

tower towers
NOUN a tall, narrow building, sometimes attached to a larger building such as a castle or church.

town towns
NOUN a place with many streets and buildings where people live and work.

toxic
ADJECTIVE poisonous.

toy toys
NOUN something to play with.

trace traces tracing traced
VERB **1** If you **trace** something like a drawing, you copy it by drawing on thin paper over the top, which you can see through.
2 If you **trace** something, you find it after looking for it. *Scientists **traced** the origin of the disease.*
NOUN **3** a tiny amount of something or a small mark.

track tracks tracking tracked
NOUN **1** a narrow road or path.
2 a strip of ground with rails on it that a train travels along.
3 a piece of ground, shaped like a ring, that horses, cars or athletes race around.
VERB **4** If you **track** someone or something, you follow them by following the marks they leave as they pass.

tracksuit tracksuits
NOUN a loose, warm suit of trousers and a top, worn for outdoor sports.

tractor tractors
NOUN a vehicle with large rear wheels, that is used on farms for pulling machinery and other heavy loads.

trade trades
NOUN the activity of buying, selling or exchanging goods or services between people or countries.

Synonym: business

trademark trademarks
NOUN a name or symbol that a manufacturer always uses on its products. **Trademarks** are usually protected by law so that no one else can use them.

trade union trade unions
NOUN an organization of workers that tries to improve the pay and conditions of its members.

tradition traditions
NOUN a custom or belief that has existed for a long time and been passed down through the generations without changing.
[from Latin ***traditio*** meaning a handing down]

traditional
ADJECTIVE **1** passed down from one generation to the next.
2 having existed or gone on for a long time.

traffic
NOUN all the vehicles, ships, aircraft or people moving along a route at a particular time.

traffic lights
PLURAL NOUN a set of lights used to control traffic at road junctions.

traffic warden traffic wardens
NOUN an official whose job is to make sure that vehicles are not parked in the wrong place or for longer than is allowed.

tragedy tragedies
NOUN **1** a very sad or disastrous event or situation, especially one in which people are killed.
2 a serious story or play that usually ends with the death of the main character.

tragic
ADJECTIVE very sad and distressing, usually involving death, destruction or disaster.

trail trails
NOUN **1** a rough path across open country or through forests.
2 a series of marks or other signs left by someone or something as they move along. *He left a **trail** of mud behind him.*

trailer trailers

NOUN **1** a small vehicle that can be loaded with things and pulled behind a car or lorry.
2 a series of short pieces taken from a film or television programme in order to advertise it.

train trains training trained

NOUN **1** a number of carriages or trucks that are pulled by a railway engine along railway lines.
VERB **2** If you **train**, you learn how to do a particular job.
3 If you **train**, or someone **trains** you, for a sports match or a race, you prepare for it by doing exercises.

trainers

PLURAL NOUN special shoes worn for running and other sports.

traitor traitors

NOUN someone who betrays their country or the group that they belong to.

tram trams

NOUN a passenger vehicle that runs on rails along the street and is powered by electricity from an overhead wire.

tramp tramps tramping tramped

NOUN **1** a person who has no home, no job, and very little money.
2 a long country walk.
VERB **3** If you **tramp** from one place to another, you walk with slow, heavy footsteps.

trample tramples trampling trampled

VERB If you **trample** on something, you tread heavily on it so that it is damaged.

trampoline trampolines

NOUN a piece of gymnastic equipment made of a large piece of strong cloth held tight by springs in a frame, on which a gymnast bounces.

trance trances

NOUN If someone is in a **trance**, they seem to be asleep, but they can still see, hear, answer questions and obey orders.

trans-

PREFIX You add **trans-** to a word to mean across, through or beyond. For example, **trans**atlantic means across or beyond the Atlantic Ocean.

transaction transactions

NOUN a business deal that involves buying and selling something.

transatlantic

ADJECTIVE used to describe something that crosses the Atlantic Ocean or is on the other side of it.

transfer transfers transferring transferred

VERB **1** If you **transfer** something from one place to another, you move it there.
NOUN **2** a piece of paper with a design or drawing on one side that can be ironed or pressed on to another surface, such as cloth, paper or china.

transform transforms transforming transformed

VERB If you **transform** something, or it **transforms,** it changes completely.

transfusion transfusions

NOUN a process in which blood donated by a healthy person is injected into the body of another person who needs it because they are badly injured or ill.

transistor transistors

NOUN **1** a small electrical device in something such as a television or radio, which is used to control electric currents.
2 a small portable radio.

translate translates translating translated

VERB If you **translate** something that someone has said or written, you say it or write it in a different language.

translucent

ADJECTIVE If something is **translucent**, it allows the light to shine through and appears to glow.

transmit transmits transmitting transmitted

VERB **1** When a message or an electronic signal is **transmitted**, it is sent by radio waves.
2 If you **transmit** something, you send it to a different place.
3 If you **transmit** a disease, you pass it on to other people.

A B C D E F G H I J K L M N O P Q R S T U V W X Y Z

transmitter transmitters

NOUN a device for sending radio messages.

transparent

ADJECTIVE If an object or substance is **transparent**, you can see through it.

Synonyms: clear, see-through

transplant transplants transplanting transplanted

VERB **1** To **transplant** something living, like a plant or an organ, means to remove it from one place and put it in another.

NOUN **2** an operation where an organ, such as a heart or a kidney, is taken from one person and put into another.

transport transports transporting transported

VERB **1** If you **transport** someone or something, you take them from one place to another.

NOUN **2** the name for vehicles you travel in. *Cars and planes are forms of **transport**.*

trap traps trapping trapped

NOUN **1** a piece of equipment or a hole that is dug to catch animals.

2 a plan to trick, capture or cheat a person.

VERB **3** If you **trap** animals, you catch them using a trap.

4 If you **trap** someone, you trick, capture or cheat them.

trap door trap doors

NOUN a small door in a floor or ceiling.

trapeze trapezes

NOUN a bar hanging from two ropes on which acrobats and gymnasts swing and perform skilful movements.

trash

NOUN rubbish.

traumatic

ADJECTIVE A **traumatic** experience is very upsetting and causes great stress.

travel travels travelling travelled

VERB **1** If you **travel,** you go from one place to another.

NOUN **2** the journeys that people make.

trawler trawlers

NOUN a fishing boat that pulls a wide net behind it to catch fish.

tray trays

NOUN a flat piece of wood, metal or plastic used for carrying things on.

treacherous

ADJECTIVE **1** disloyal and untrustworthy. **2** dangerous or unreliable.

treacle

NOUN a thick, sweet syrup used to make cakes and toffee.

tread treads treading trod trodden

VERB **1** If you **tread** on something, you walk on it or step on it.

NOUN **2** The **tread** of a tyre or shoe is the pattern of ridges on it that stops it slipping.

3 the part of a staircase or ladder that you put your foot on.

treason

NOUN the crime of betraying your country, for example by helping its enemies.

treasure treasures treasuring treasured

NOUN **1** a collection of gold, silver, jewels or other precious objects, especially one that has been hidden.

2 a valuable object, such as a work of art.

VERB **3** If you **treasure** something, you look after it carefully because it is important to you. *She **treasured** the shells she had collected on her holiday.*

treasury treasuries

NOUN **1** a place where treasure is stored.

2 The **Treasury** is the government department that looks after a country's finances.

treat treats treating treated

NOUN **1** If you give someone a **treat**, you buy or arrange something special for them that they will enjoy.

VERB **2** When a doctor **treats** a patient or an illness, he or she gives them medical care and attention.

3 If you **treat** someone or something in a particular way, you behave that way towards them.

treaty treaties

NOUN a written agreement between countries, in which they agree to do something or to help each other.

treble trebles trebling trebled

VERB **1** If something **trebles**, or is **trebled**, it becomes three times greater in number or amount.

NOUN **2 Treble** the amount of something is three times the amount.

tree trees

NOUN a large plant with a hard trunk, branches and leaves.

trek treks trekking trekked

VERB **1** If you **trek** somewhere, you go on a long and difficult journey to get there.

NOUN **2** a long and difficult journey, especially one made on foot.

[an Afrikaans word]

tremble trembles trembling trembled

VERB If you **tremble**, you shake slightly, usually because you are frightened or cold.

tremendous

ADJECTIVE **1** large or impressive. *It was a* **tremendous** *performance.*

2 INFORMAL very good or pleasing. *The game was* **tremendous** *fun.*

tremor tremors

NOUN **1** a small earthquake.

2 a slight, uncontrollable shaking movement.

trench trenches

NOUN a long narrow channel or ditch dug into the ground.

trend trends

NOUN **1** a general direction in which something is moving.

2 a fashion.

trendy trendier trendiest

ADJECTIVE; INFORMAL fashionable.

trespass trespasses trespassing trespassed

VERB If you **trespass** on someone's land or property, you go on to it without their permission.

trial trials

NOUN **1** a legal process in which a court listens to evidence to decide whether a person is innocent or guilty of a crime.

2 a type of experiment in which someone or something is tested to see how well they perform.

triangle triangles

NOUN **1** a plane shape with three straight sides.

2 a percussion instrument consisting of a thin steel bar bent in the shape of a triangle. It produces a note when struck with a small metal rod.

triangular ADJECTIVE

tribe tribes

NOUN a group of people of the same race, who have the same customs, religion, beliefs, language or land.

tribal ADJECTIVE

tributary tributaries

NOUN a stream or river that flows into a larger river.

tribute tributes

NOUN something said or done to show admiration and respect for someone.

trick tricks tricking tricked

VERB **1** If someone **tricks** you, they deceive you.

NOUN **2** an action done to deceive someone.

3 a clever or skilful action that is done in order to entertain people: *a card* **trick**.

trickle trickles trickling trickled

VERB When a liquid **trickles**, it flows slowly in a thin stream.

tricky trickier trickiest

ADJECTIVE difficult to do or deal with.

tricycle tricycles

NOUN a vehicle similar to a bicycle but with three wheels, two at the back and one at the front.

tried

VERB the past tense and past participle of *try*.

trifle trifles

NOUN **1** a cold pudding made of layers of sponge cake, fruit, jelly and custard.

2 something unimportant or of little value.

trigger triggers

NOUN the small lever on a gun that is pulled in order to fire it.

trim trims trimming trimmed; trimmer trimmest

VERB **1** If you **trim** something, you cut small amounts off it to make it more tidy.

ADJECTIVE **2** neat and tidy.

NOUN **3** If something is given a **trim**, it is cut a little.

4 a decoration along the edges of something: *a coat with a velvet **trim***.

trinket trinkets

NOUN a cheap ornament or piece of jewellery.

trio trios

NOUN **1** a group of three musicians who sing or play together.

2 a piece of music written for three instruments or singers.

trip trips tripping tripped

NOUN **1** a journey made to a place.

VERB **2** If you **trip**, or **trip over**, you catch your foot on something and fall over.

3 If you **trip** someone, or **trip** them up, you make them fall over by making them catch their foot on something.

triple triples tripling tripled

ADJECTIVE **1** made of three things or three parts.

VERB **2** If you **triple** something, or if it **triples**, it becomes three times greater in number or size.

triplet triplets

NOUN one of three children born at the same time to the same mother.

tripod tripods

NOUN a stand with three legs used to support something like a camera or telescope.

triumph triumphs triumphing triumphed

NOUN **1** a great success or achievement.

2 a feeling of great satisfaction when you win or achieve something.

VERB **3** If you **triumph**, you win a victory or succeed in overcoming something.

triumphant

ADJECTIVE If you are **triumphant**, you feel very happy because you have won a victory or achieved something.

trivial

ADJECTIVE unimportant.

trod

VERB the past tense of *tread*.

trodden

VERB the past participle of *tread*.

troll trolls

NOUN an imaginary creature in Scandinavian mythology, that is either a dwarf or a giant and lives in caves or mountains.

trolley trolleys

NOUN **1** a basket or cart on wheels, in which you can carry your shopping or luggage.

2 a small table on wheels, used to serve food and drink.

trombone trombones

NOUN a brass wind instrument with a U-shaped tube that you slide to produce different notes.

troop troops trooping trooped

PLURAL NOUN **1** **Troops** are soldiers.

NOUN **2** A **troop** of people or animals is a group of them.

VERB **3** If people **troop** somewhere, they go there in a group.

trophy trophies

NOUN a cup or shield given as a prize to the winner of a competition.

tropic tropics

NOUN The **tropics** are the hottest regions of the world, that lie on either side of the equator.

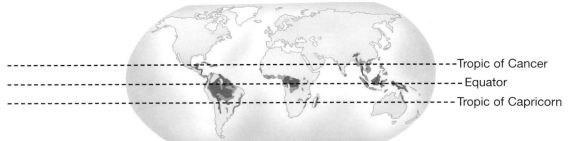

Tropic of Cancer

Equator

Tropic of Capricorn

tropical

ADJECTIVE belonging to or typical of the tropics.

trot trots trotting trotted

VERB **1** When a horse **trots**, it runs with short steps, lifting its feet quite high off the ground. **2** If you **trot**, you run slowly with small steps.

trouble troubles troubling troubled

NOUN **1** a difficulty or problem.
PHRASE **2** If you are **in trouble**, someone is angry with you because of something you have done wrong.
VERB **3** If something **troubles** you, it worries or bothers you.
4 If you **trouble** someone, you worry or bother them.

Synonym: (sense 1) worry

trough troughs

NOUN a long, narrow container from which animals drink or feed.

trousers

PLURAL NOUN a piece of clothing for the lower half of your body, from the waist down, covering each leg separately.

trout

NOUN a type of edible freshwater fish.

trowel trowels

NOUN **1** a garden tool like a small spade, used for planting or weeding.
2 a small, flat spade used by builders for spreading cement and mortar.

truant truants

NOUN a child who stays away from school without permission.

truce truces

NOUN an agreement between two people or groups to stop fighting for a short time.

truck trucks

NOUN a large motor vehicle used for carrying heavy loads.

trudge trudges trudging trudged

VERB **1** If you **trudge**, you walk with slow, heavy steps.
NOUN **2** a slow tiring walk.

true truer truest

ADJECTIVE **1** A **true** story or statement is based on facts and is not invented.
PHRASE **2** If something **comes true** it actually happens. *I hope your wish comes true.*

Synonyms: (sense 1) accurate, correct, factual

trumpet trumpets

NOUN a wind instrument made of a narrow brass tube that widens at the end into a bell-like shape.

truncheon truncheons

NOUN a short, thick stick that policemen carry as a weapon.

trunk trunks

NOUN **1** the main stem of a tree from which the branches and roots grow.
2 the long flexible nose of an elephant.
3 a large, strong case or box with a hinged lid, used for storing things.
4 In American English, the **trunk** of a car is the boot, a covered space at the back or front that is used for luggage.
5 the main part of your body, excluding your arms, legs and head.
PLURAL NOUN **6** A man's **trunks** are his bathing pants or shorts.

trust trusts trusting trusted

VERB **1** If you **trust** someone, you believe that they are honest and reliable, and will treat you fairly.
2 If you **trust** someone to do something, you believe they will do it.
NOUN **3** the feeling that someone can be trusted.
4 the responsibility you have to people who trust you.

trustworthy

ADJECTIVE A **trustworthy** person is responsible and reliable, and you know that they will do what they say they will do.

truth truths

NOUN the facts about something, rather than things that are imagined or invented.

truthful

ADJECTIVE A **truthful** person is honest and tells the truth.

try tries trying tried

VERB **1** If you **try** to do something, you make an effort to do it.
2 If you **try** something, you use it, taste it or experiment with it to see how good or suitable it is.
3 When a court **tries** a person, they listen to evidence to decide if that person is guilty of a crime.
4 A person who **tries** your patience is extremely irritating and difficult.
NOUN **5** an attempt to do something.
6 A **try** in rugby is when a player scores by carrying the ball over the opponents' goal line and putting it on the ground.

try on VERB **7** If you **try on** a piece of clothing, you wear it to see if it fits you or if it looks nice.

T-shirt T-shirts; also spelt **tee shirt**

NOUN a simple short-sleeved cotton shirt with no collar.

tub tubs

NOUN a wide, circular container.

tuba tubas

NOUN a large brass musical instrument that can produce very low notes.

tube tubes

NOUN **1** a hollow cylinder made of metal, plastic, rubber or other material.
2 The **Tube** is another name for the London Underground train system.

tuck tucks tucking tucked

VERB **1** If you **tuck** a piece of fabric into or under something, you push the loose ends inside or under it to make it tidy.
2 If you **tuck** into a meal, you eat eagerly and with pleasure.
3 If you **tuck** someone up in bed, you put the bedclothes snugly round them.

Tuesday

NOUN the third day of the week, coming between Monday and Wednesday.
[an Anglo-Saxon name honouring the god of war called **Tiw**, said **tue**]

tuft tufts

NOUN A **tuft** of something, such as hair or grass, is a bunch of it growing closely together.

tug tugs tugging tugged

VERB **1** If you **tug** something, you give it a quick hard pull.
NOUN **2** a small powerful boat that tows large ships.

tug-of-war

NOUN a contest between two teams pulling a rope from opposite ends.

tulip tulips

NOUN a brightly coloured spring flower.
[from Turkish **tulbend** meaning turban, because of the flower's shape]

tumble tumbles tumbling tumbled

VERB If you **tumble**, you fall with a rolling or bouncing movement.

tumbler tumblers

NOUN **1** a drinking glass with no handle or stem.
2 an acrobat.

tumour tumours

NOUN an abnormal growth in the body.

tuna

NOUN a large edible fish that lives in warm seas.

tune tunes

NOUN a series of musical notes arranged in a particular way.

tunnel tunnels tunnelling tunnelled

NOUN a long underground passage: *a railway tunnel*.

turban turbans

NOUN a long piece of cloth worn wound round the head, especially by a Hindu, Muslim or Sikh man.

turbine turbines

NOUN a machine or engine powered by a stream of air, gas, water or steam.
[from Latin **turbo** meaning whirlwind]

turf

NOUN short, thick, even grass and the layer of soil beneath it.

turkey turkeys

NOUN a large bird kept for its meat.

turn turns turning turned

VERB **1** When you **turn**, you move so that you are facing or going in a different direction.

2 When you **turn** something, or when it **turns**, it moves so that it faces in a different direction or is in a different position. *She **turned** the key in the lock.*

3 When something **turns**, or **turns into** something else, it becomes something different, or has a different appearance or quality. *The leaves **turned** brown in autumn.*

NOUN **4** If it is your **turn** to do something, you do it next.

VERB **5** If you **turn down** something, you refuse it. *I was not hungry, so I **turned down** the chips.*

6 If you **turn up** the television, for example, you increase the volume.

7 If someone **turns up**, they arrive.

turnip turnips

NOUN a round root vegetable with a white or yellow skin.

turquoise

NOUN **1** light bluish-green.

2 A light bluish-green stone used in jewellery.

turret turrets

NOUN a small narrow tower on top of a larger tower or other building, such as a castle.

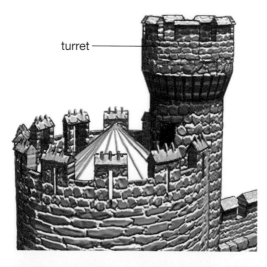

turret

turtle turtles

NOUN a large reptile with flippers for swimming and a thick shell covering its body. It lays its eggs on land but lives the rest of its life in the sea. *See **reptile**.*

tusk tusks

NOUN one of the pair of long, curving, pointed teeth of an elephant, wild boar or walrus.

tutor tutors

NOUN a private teacher or a teacher at a college or university.

TV

NOUN an abbreviation of *television*.

tweed tweeds

NOUN a thick woollen cloth. Someone wearing **tweeds** is wearing a **tweed** suit.

tweezers

PLURAL NOUN a small tool with two arms that can be closed together to grip something. **Tweezers** are used for pulling out hairs or picking up small objects.

twice

ADVERB two times.

twiddle twiddles twiddling twiddled

VERB If you **twiddle** something, you turn it quickly round and round or over and over.

twig twigs

NOUN a small branch on a tree or bush.

twilight

NOUN the time after sunset when it is just getting dark.

twin twins

NOUN If two people are **twins**, they have the same mother and were born on the same day.

twinkle twinkles twinkling twinkled

VERB Something that **twinkles** shines with little flashes of light.

Synonym: glitter, sparkle

twirl twirls twirling twirled

VERB If you **twirl** something, you make it spin round quickly.

twist twists twisting twisted

VERB **1** When you **twist** something, you turn the two ends in opposite directions.

2 If you **twist** part of your body, you injure it by turning it too sharply or in an odd direction.

two-dimensional
  ADJECTIVE a flat or plane shape.

tying
  VERB the present participle of *tie*.

type types typing typed
  NOUN **1** If something is the same **type** as something else, they belong to the same group and have many things in common.
  VERB **2** If you **type** something, you use a typewriter or word processor to write it.

  Synonyms: (sense 1) kind, sort

typewriter typewriters
  NOUN a machine with keys that are pressed to write numbers and letters on a page.

typhoon typhoons
  NOUN a very violent tropical storm.
  [from Chinese *tai fung* meaning great wind]

typical
  ADJECTIVE Something that is **typical** of a person or animal is usual and what is to be expected of them.

tyrannosaurus tyrannosauruses
  NOUN a very large meat-eating dinosaur that walked upright on its back legs.

tyrant tyrants
  NOUN a person who treats the people they have power over with cruelty.

tyre tyres
  NOUN a thick ring of rubber fitted round each wheel of a vehicle and filled with air.

a b c d e f g h i j k l m n o p q r s t u v w x y z

Uu

udder udders
NOUN the bag-like part of a cow, goat or ewe from which milk comes.

UFO UFOs
NOUN an abbreviation of *unidentified flying object*. **UFOs** are objects seen in the skies, which some people believe come from other planets because they cannot be identified.

ugly uglier ugliest
ADJECTIVE very unattractive or unpleasant.

ulcer ulcers
NOUN a sore area on the skin or inside the body, that can take a long time to heal.

ultimate
ADJECTIVE **1** final.
NOUN **2** the best example of something.

ultraviolet light
NOUN **Ultraviolet light** is not visible to the human eye. It is a form of radiation that causes your skin to tan in sunlight.

umbrella umbrellas
NOUN a folding frame covered in fabric and attached to a long stick, which you can open over you to protect you from the rain.

umpire umpires umpiring umpired
NOUN **1** The **umpire** in a cricket or tennis match is the person who makes sure that the game is played fairly and the rules are not broken.
VERB **2** If a person **umpires** a game, they are the umpire.

un-
PREFIX You add **un-** to the beginning of a word to mean not. For example, **un**common means not common, and **un**likely means not likely.

unable
ADJECTIVE If you are **unable** to do something, you cannot do it.

unanimous
Said "yoo-**nan**-nim-mus" ADJECTIVE A **unanimous** decision or vote has the agreement of everyone involved.

unaware
ADJECTIVE not aware.

unbearable
ADJECTIVE Something **unbearable** is so painful or upsetting that you feel that you cannot bear or endure it.

unbelievable
ADJECTIVE **1** very surprising or wonderful.
2 so unlikely that it is hard to believe.

uncanny
ADJECTIVE strange and mysterious.

uncertain
ADJECTIVE If you are **uncertain** about something, you are not sure about it.
uncertainty NOUN

Synonym: doubtful

uncle uncles
NOUN the brother of your mother or father, or the husband of your aunt.
[from Latin ***avunculus*** meaning mother's brother]

uncomfortable
ADJECTIVE **1** If you are **uncomfortable**, your body is not relaxed or comfortable.
2 If something like a chair or a piece of clothing is **uncomfortable**, it is not comfortable to sit in or to wear.
3 If you feel **uncomfortable** in a situation, you feel worried or nervous.

uncommon
ADJECTIVE not common.

unconscious
ADJECTIVE If someone is **unconscious**, they are unable to see, feel or hear anything that is going on. This is usually because they have fainted or been badly injured.

uncover uncovers uncovering uncovered
VERB **1** to take the cover off something.
2 to find out a secret or discover something.

under
PREPOSITION **1** below or beneath.
2 less than: *children **under** the age of 14.*
3 controlled or ruled by. *The soldiers were **under** his command.*
4 If something like a building is **under** construction, or **under** repair, it is in the process of being built or repaired.

under-

PREFIX You add **under-** at the beginning of a word to mean beneath or below. For example, if you **under**estimate an amount, you estimate it below what it really is.

undercarriage undercarriages

NOUN the part of an aircraft, including the wheels, that supports the aircraft when it is on the ground.

underestimate underestimates underestimating underestimated

VERB **1** If you **underestimate** someone, you do not realize how much they can do.
2 If you **underestimate** something, you do not realize how big it is or how long it will take.

undergo undergoes undergoing underwent undergone

VERB If you **undergo** something, you experience it or are subjected to it. *She **underwent** an operation to remove her tonsils.*

underground

ADJECTIVE **1** below the surface of the ground.
NOUN **2** a railway system in which trains travel in tunnels below the ground.

undergrowth

NOUN small plants growing under trees.

underline underlines underlining underlined

VERB If you **underline** a word or sentence, you draw a line under it.

undermine undermines undermining undermined

VERB **1** If you **undermine** a person's efforts or plans, you weaken them.
2 To **undermine** something is to make a hollow or tunnel beneath it. When the sea **undermines** a cliff, for example, it gradually wears away the base and weakens it.

underneath

PREPOSITION AND ADVERB below or beneath.

underpants

PLURAL NOUN a piece of men's underwear worn under trousers.

underpass underpasses

NOUN a place where one road or path goes under another.

underprivileged

ADJECTIVE **Underprivileged** people have less money and fewer opportunities than other people.

understand understands understanding understood

VERB **1** If you **understand** what someone says, or what you read, you know it means.
2 If you **understand** how something works, you know how it works.
3 If you **understand** someone, you know them well and think you know why they behave the way they do.

understudy understudies

NOUN someone who has learnt the lines of a part in a play, and plays the part when the main actor or actress cannot perform.

undertake undertakes undertaking undertook undertaken

VERB If you **undertake** to do something, you agree to do it.

undertaker undertakers

NOUN someone whose job is to prepare bodies for burial and arrange funerals.

underwater

ADVERB OR ADJECTIVE below the surface of the water.

underwear

NOUN Your **underwear** is the clothing you wear next to your skin under your other clothes.

undo undoes undoing undid undone

VERB **1** If you **undo** something like a knot, you loosen or unfasten it.
2 If you **undo** something that has been done, you reverse or remove the effects of it.

undress undresses undressing undressed

VERB If you **undress**, you take your clothes off.

unearth unearths unearthing unearthed

VERB If you **unearth** something, you dig it up or discover it.

uneasy uneasier uneasiest

ADJECTIVE anxious or worried.

unemployed

ADJECTIVE An **unemployed** person has no job.

uneven

ADJECTIVE An **uneven** surface is not level or smooth.

unexpected

ADJECTIVE Something **unexpected** is surprising because it was not thought likely to happen.

unfair

ADJECTIVE Something **unfair** does not seem right, reasonable or fair.

unfold unfolds unfolding unfolded

VERB **1** If you **unfold** something that is folded, such as a map, you open it out.
2 When a story **unfolds**, it gradually becomes clear.

unfortunate

ADJECTIVE unlucky.

unfriendly

ADJECTIVE not friendly.

ungrateful

ADJECTIVE not grateful.

unhappy unhappier unhappiest

ADJECTIVE sad, not happy.

unhealthy

ADJECTIVE not healthy.

unicorn unicorns

NOUN an imaginary animal that looks like a white horse with a straight horn growing from its forehead.
[from Latin ***unicornis*** meaning having one horn]

uniform uniforms

NOUN a special set of clothes worn by people at work or school.
[from Latin ***uniformis*** meaning of one kind]

unify unifies unifying unified

VERB If several things, especially countries, are **unified**, they join together to make one.

uninhabited

ADJECTIVE An **uninhabited** place is a place where nobody lives.

union unions

NOUN an organization of workers that aims to improve the working conditions, pay and benefits of its members.

unique

ADJECTIVE Something that is **unique** is the only one of its kind.
[from Latin ***unicus*** meaning one and only]

unisex

ADJECTIVE designed to suit either men or women.

unison

NOUN If a group of people does something in **unison**, they all do it together at the same time.
[from Latin ***unisonus*** meaning making the same musical sound]

unit units

NOUN **1** one single, complete thing.
2 a term used to describe a fixed quantity or measurement. *A centimetre is a **unit** of length.*

unite unites uniting united

VERB If a number of people **unite**, they join together and act as a group.

universal

ADJECTIVE concerning or relating to everyone and everything.

universe universes

NOUN everything that exists, including the whole of space, all the stars and the planets.
[from Latin ***universum*** meaning whole world]

university universities

NOUN a place where students study for degrees.

unkempt

ADJECTIVE untidy and not looked after properly.
[from Old English ***uncembed*** meaning not combed]

unkind

ADJECTIVE rather cruel, not kind.

unknown
> ADJECTIVE If someone or something is **unknown**, people do not know about them or have not heard of them.

unleaded
> ADJECTIVE **Unleaded** petrol does not contain any lead, and is less harmful to the atmosphere than petrol that does contain lead.

unless
> CONJUNCTION You use **unless** to introduce the only circumstances in which something may or may not happen or is not true. *The team will play tomorrow* **unless** *it is raining. I won't go* **unless** *you ask me.*

unlike
> ADJECTIVE **1** If one thing is **unlike** another, the two things are different.
> PREPOSITION **2** not like. *Unlike me, she hates chocolate.*

unlikely unlikelier unlikeliest
> ADJECTIVE not likely to happen or be true.

unload unloads unloading unloaded
> VERB to take things out of or off a container, a vehicle or a trailer.

unlock unlocks unlocking unlocked
> VERB When you **unlock** something, you open it by turning a key in the lock.

unlucky unluckier unluckiest
> ADJECTIVE If you are **unlucky**, you are unfortunate and have bad luck.

> **Antonyms:** fortunate, lucky

unnatural
> ADJECTIVE not natural or normal.

unnecessary
> ADJECTIVE not necessary.

unoccupied
> ADJECTIVE A house that is **unoccupied** has no one living in it.

unpack unpacks unpacking unpacked
> VERB When you **unpack**, you take everything out of a suitcase, bag or box.

unpleasant
> ADJECTIVE **1** Something **unpleasant** is not enjoyable and may make you uncomfortable or upset.
> **2** An **unpleasant** person is unfriendly or rude.

unplug unplugs unplugging unplugged
> VERB If you **unplug** something, you take the plug out of the socket to disconnect it from the electricity supply.

unpopular
> ADJECTIVE not liked very much.

unravel unravels unravelling unravelled
> VERB **1** If you **unravel** threads that are knitted or tangled, you undo or untangle them.
> **2** If you **unravel** a mystery, you solve it.

unreal
> ADJECTIVE existing only in the imagination, not real.

unreasonable
> ADJECTIVE not reasonable or fair.

unroll unrolls unrolling unrolled
> VERB If you **unroll** something that has been rolled up, you open it and make it flat.

unruly
> ADJECTIVE badly behaved and difficult to control.

unsafe
> ADJECTIVE not safe.

unscrew unscrews unscrewing unscrewed
> VERB If you **unscrew** something, you remove it by turning it or by removing the screws that are holding it.

unselfish
> ADJECTIVE An **unselfish** person is not selfish and is concerned about other people's needs.

unsteady
> ADJECTIVE If you are **unsteady**, you are not steady and have difficulty balancing.

unsuccessful
> ADJECTIVE If you are **unsuccessful**, you do not manage to succeed in what you are trying to do.

unsuitable
> ADJECTIVE Things that are **unsuitable** are not right or suitable for a particular purpose.

untidy untidier untidiest
> ADJECTIVE not tidy.

untie unties untying untied
> VERB If you **untie** something that has been tied, you unfasten or undo it.

A
B
C
D
E
F
G
H
I
J
K
L
M
N
O
P
Q
R
S
T
U
V
W
X
Y
Z

until

PREPOSITION OR CONJUNCTION **1** If something happens **until** a particular time, it happens before that time and stops at that time. *The shops stay open **until** eight o'clock on Thursdays.*
2 If something does not happen **until** a particular time, it does not happen before that time and only starts happening at that time. *It didn't rain **until** the middle of the afternoon.*

untrue

ADJECTIVE not true.

unusual

ADJECTIVE Something that is **unusual** is not usual and does not happen very often.

unwell

ADJECTIVE If you are **unwell**, you are ill.

unwilling

ADJECTIVE If you are **unwilling** to do something, you do not want to do it.
unwillingly ADVERB

unwind unwinds unwinding unwound

VERB **1** If you **unwind** something that was wound into a ball or around something else, you undo it.
2 If you **unwind** after working hard, you relax.

unwrap unwraps unwrapping unwrapped

VERB If you **unwrap** something, you take off the paper or other wrapping that is around it.

up

ADVERB OR PREPOSITION **1** towards or in a higher place. *They went **up** the stairs to bed.*
ADVERB **2** If an amount of something goes **up**, it increases.
PREPOSITION **3** If you go **up** the road, you go along it.
ADJECTIVE **4** If you are **up**, you are not in bed.

upbringing

NOUN the way you have been brought up, and how your parents have taught you to behave.

upheaval upheavals

NOUN a sudden big change that causes a lot of disturbance.

uphill

ADVERB If you go **uphill**, you go up a hill or a slope.

upholstery

NOUN the soft covering on chairs and sofas that makes them comfortable.
upholstered ADJECTIVE

upon

PREPOSITION on or on top of.

upper

ADJECTIVE refers to something that is above something else, or is the higher part of something.

upper-case

ADJECTIVE letters that are written as capitals. For example, A, H, L and P are all **upper-case** letters.

upright

ADJECTIVE OR ADVERB **1** Something or someone that is **upright**, is standing up straight or vertically, rather than bending or lying down.
2 An **upright** person is decent and honest.

uproar

NOUN a lot of shouting and noise, often because people are angry.
[from Dutch *oproer* meaning revolt]

Synonyms: commotion, pandemonium

upset upsets upsetting upset

ADJECTIVE **1** unhappy and disappointed.
VERB **2** If something **upsets** you, it makes you feel worried or unhappy.
3 If you **upset** something, you knock it over or spill it accidentally.
NOUN **4** A stomach **upset** is a slight stomach illness.

upside down

ADJECTIVE **1** the wrong way up. *Bats hang upside down*.

2 If a place is **upside down** it is very untidy.

upstairs
ADVERB OR ADJECTIVE up to or on a higher floor.

up-to-date
ADJECTIVE If something is **up-to-date**, it is modern or is the newest thing of its kind.

upwards
ADVERB going towards a higher place.

uranium
NOUN a radioactive metallic element used to make nuclear energy and weapons.

urban
ADJECTIVE to do with towns or cities rather than the country.
[from Latin **urbs** meaning city]

urge urges urging urged
NOUN **1** If you have an **urge** to do something, you very much want to do it.
VERB **2** If you **urge** someone to do something, you try to persuade and encourage them to do it.

urgent
ADJECTIVE If something is **urgent**, it needs to be dealt with immediately.

urine
NOUN the waste liquid that you get rid of from your body when you go to the toilet.

us
PRONOUN A speaker or writer uses **us** to mean himself or herself and one or more other people.

use uses using used
Said "**yooz**" VERB **1** If you **use** something, you do something with it that helps you to do a job or sort out a problem
Said "**yooss**" NOUN **2** the purpose or value of something, and the way it is used.

used
Said "**yoosst**" VERB **1** something that happened before but does not happen now. *We **used** to fish in this stream.*
ADJECTIVE **2** If you are **used to** something, you are familiar with it and have often experienced it.
Said "**yoozd**" VERB **3** the past tense and past participle of *use*.
ADJECTIVE **4** A **used** item has already belonged to someone else.

useful
ADJECTIVE If something is **useful**, you can use it to help you in some way.

useless
ADJECTIVE Something that is **useless** is no good for anything.

usher ushers
NOUN a person who shows people where to sit at the theatre or cinema.

usual
ADJECTIVE **1** Something **usual** is expected and happens often.
PHRASE **2** If something happens **as usual**, it happens as you would expect, and is not surprising because it often happens that way.

utensil utensils
NOUN a tool. *A whisk is a kitchen **utensil**.*

utility utilities
NOUN a service that is useful for everyone, such as water and gas supplies.

utter utters uttering uttered
VERB **1** When you **utter** sounds, you make or say them.
ADJECTIVE **2** complete or total. *This is **utter** nonsense.*

a b c d e f g h i j k l m n o p q r s t **u** v w x y z

A
B
C
D
E
F
G
H
I
J
K
L
M
N
O
P
Q
R
S
T
U
V
W
X
Y
Z

Vv

vacant
ADJECTIVE If something is **vacant**, it is not being used or no-one is in it. *I couldn't find a **vacant** seat on the train.*

vacation vacations
NOUN a holiday.

vaccinate vaccinates vaccinating vaccinated
Said "**vak**-si-nayt" VERB If someone **vaccinates** you, they give you an injection to protect you against a disease.

vacuum vacuums vacuuming vacuumed
NOUN **1** a completely empty space containing no matter, solid, liquid or gas.
VERB **2** If you **vacuum** something, you clean it using a vacuum cleaner.
[from Latin ***vacuum*** meaning empty space]

vacuum cleaner vacuum cleaners
NOUN an electrical device that sucks up dust and dirt from the floor.

vagina vaginas
NOUN A woman's **vagina** is the passage that leads to her womb.

vague vaguer vaguest
Said "**vayg**" ADJECTIVE not clear, definite or certain. *They could see the **vague** outline of the mountains in the distance.*
vaguely ADVERB   **vagueness** NOUN

Synonym: unclear

vain vainer vainest
ADJECTIVE **1** A **vain** person is too proud of their looks, intelligence or other good qualities.
2 A **vain** attempt to do something is an unsuccessful attempt.

valentine valentines
NOUN **1** someone you love and send a card to on Saint **Valentine's** Day, February 14th.
2 a card you send to someone you love on Saint **Valentine's** Day.
[Saint ***Valentine*** was a third-century martyr]

valiant
ADJECTIVE brave and courageous.

valid
ADJECTIVE A **valid** ticket or document is legal and accepted by people in authority.

valley valleys
NOUN a long stretch of land between hills, often with a river flowing through it.

valuable
ADJECTIVE of great worth or very important. *The diamond ring was very **valuable**.*

value values valuing valued
NOUN **1** the importance or usefulness of something.
2 the amount of money that something is worth.
VERB **3** If you **value** something, you think it is important and valuable.

valve valves
NOUN **1** a device attached to a pipe or tube that controls the flow of gas or liquid.
2 a small flap in your heart or in a vein that controls the flow and direction of blood.

vampire vampires
NOUN In horror stories, **vampires** come out of graves at night and suck people's blood.

van vans
NOUN a vehicle for carrying goods.

vandal vandals
NOUN someone who deliberately damages or destroys things, particularly public property.
vandalize or **vandalise** VERB
vandalism NOUN

vanilla
NOUN a flavouring used in food such as ice cream. It comes from the pod of a tropical plant.

vanish vanishes vanishing vanished
VERB If something **vanishes**, it disappears or does not exist any more.

vapour

NOUN a mass of tiny drops of water or other liquids in the air, which looks like mist. [from Latin **vapor** meaning steam]

variety varieties

NOUN a number of different kinds of similar things: *There was a **variety** of food from different countries on the menu.*

Synonyms: assortment, range

various

ADJECTIVE of several different types: *trees of **various** sorts.*

Synonyms: different, miscellaneous

varnish varnishes varnishing varnished

NOUN **1** a liquid which, when painted on to a surface such as wood, gives it a hard, clear, shiny finish.
VERB **2** If you **varnish** something, you paint it with varnish.

vary varies varying varied

VERB If something **varies**, it changes and is not always the same.

vase vases

NOUN a jar or other container for putting cut flowers in.

vast

ADJECTIVE extremely large.
vastly ADVERB   **vastness** NOUN

vat vats

NOUN a large container used for storing liquids.

VAT

NOUN an abbreviation of *value-added tax*, which is a tax you pay on things you buy.

vault vaults vaulting vaulted

NOUN **1** a strong secure room where valuables are stored, often underneath a building, or where people are buried underneath a church. **2** an arched roof, often found in churches.
VERB **3** If you **vault** over something, you jump over it using your hands or a pole to help.

VCR

NOUN an abbreviation of *video cassette recorder*.

VDU

NOUN an abbreviation of *visual display unit*, which is a monitor screen for computers.

veal

NOUN the meat from a calf.

Veda

NOUN the collection of ancient sacred writings of the Hindu religion.

vegetable vegetables

NOUN **Vegetables** are plants or parts of plants that can be eaten. Peas, carrots, cabbage and potatoes are **vegetables**.

vegetarian vegetarians

NOUN a person who does not eat meat, poultry or fish.

vegetation

NOUN the plants growing in a particular area.

vehicle vehicles

NOUN a machine, often with an engine, such as a car, bus or lorry, used for moving people or goods from one place to another.

veil veils

NOUN a piece of thin, soft cloth that women sometimes wear over their heads and faces.

vein veins

NOUN Your **veins** are the tubes in your body through which your blood flows to your heart. *See **artery**.*

velvet

NOUN a very soft material that has a thick layer of short threads on one side.

vengeance

NOUN the act of harming someone because they have harmed you.

venison

NOUN the meat from a deer.

Venn diagram Venn diagrams

NOUN a diagram using circles to show how sets of things relate to each other. **Venn diagrams** are used in mathematics.

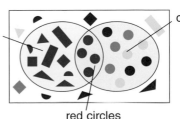

red shapes

circles

red circles

venom

NOUN the poison of a snake, scorpion or spider. [from Latin **venenum** meaning love potion or poison]

venomous ADJECTIVE   **venomously** ADVERB

vent vents

NOUN an opening in something, especially to let out smoke or gas.

ventilate ventilates ventilating ventilated

VERB If you **ventilate** a place, you allow fresh air to move freely through it.

venture ventures venturing ventured

NOUN **1** something new that you do which involves some sort of risk.

VERB **2** If you **venture** somewhere that might be dangerous, you go there.

veranda verandas; also spelt verandah

NOUN a platform with a roof that is fixed to the outside wall of a house at ground level. It is often made of wood.

verb verbs

NOUN In grammar, a **verb** is a word that expresses actions and states, for example "be", "become", "take" and "run".

verbal

ADJECTIVE things that are spoken rather than written.

verbally ADVERB

verdict verdicts

NOUN In a law court, a **verdict** is the decision reached by the judge or jury about whether a prisoner is guilty or not guilty.

verge verges

NOUN the narrow strip of grassy ground at the side of a road. *We walked along the verge.*

verify verifies verifying verified

VERB If you **verify** something, you check that it is true or correct.

verifiable ADJECTIVE   **verification** NOUN

verruca verrucas

NOUN a small, hard, infectious growth that you can get on the sole of your foot.

versatile

ADJECTIVE If someone or something is **versatile**, they have many different skills or uses.

versatility NOUN

verse verses

NOUN **1** another word for poetry.

2 one part of a poem, song or chapter of the Bible.

version versions

NOUN A **version** of something is a form of it that is different in some way from earlier or later forms.

versus

PREPOSITION **Versus** means against, and is used to show that two people or teams are competing against each other.

vertebra vertebrae

NOUN one of the bones that make up your backbone.

vertebrate vertebrates

NOUN an animal with a backbone.

vertex vertices

NOUN the highest point of a hill, or a corner of a two-dimensional or three-dimensional shape. *See* **apex**.

vertical

ADJECTIVE Something that is **vertical** is in an upright position or points straight up.

very

ADJECTIVE OR ADVERB **Very** is used before words to emphasize them. *I had a very bad dream.*

Synonyms: extremely, greatly, really

vessel vessels

NOUN **1** a ship or large boat.

2 a container for liquids.

3 one of the tubes in an animal or a plant that carries blood or other liquid around the body.

vest vests

NOUN a piece of underwear worn on the top half of the body for warmth. [from Latin **vestis** meaning clothing]

vet vets

NOUN a doctor for animals. **Vet** is an abbreviation of *veterinary surgeon.*

veteran veterans

NOUN **1** a person with a lot of experience of something, or who has been involved in something for a long time.

2 someone who has served in the armed forces, particularly during a war. *My uncle is a Gulf War veteran.*

via

PREPOSITION If you go to one place **via** another, you travel through that other place to get to your destination.
[from Latin *via* meaning way or road]

viaduct viaducts

NOUN a high bridge that carries a road or railway across a valley.

vibrate vibrates vibrating vibrated

VERB If something **vibrates**, it moves a tiny amount backwards and forwards very quickly.
vibration NOUN

vicar vicars

NOUN a priest in the Church of England.

vice vices

NOUN a bad habit, such as being greedy or smoking.

vice versa

ADVERB the other way around.

vicinity vicinities

NOUN an area round something. *She was seen in the vicinity of the school.*

vicious

ADJECTIVE cruel and violent.

victim victims

NOUN someone who has been harmed or injured by someone or something.

victor victors

NOUN the winner of a contest or battle.

victory victories

NOUN a success in a battle or competition.

Synonyms: conquest, triumph, win

video videos videoing videoed

NOUN **1** a sound and picture recording that can be played back on a television set.
2 the recording and showing of films and events using a **video** recorder, tape and a television set.
3 a video recorder. *Set the video to record a programme at eight o'clock.*
VERB **4** If you **video** something, you record it on video tape to watch later.
[from Latin *videre* meaning to see]

view views

NOUN everything you can see from a particular place.

viewer viewers

NOUN one of the people who watch something, especially a television programme.

viewpoint viewpoints

NOUN Your **viewpoint** is your attitude towards something

vigilant

ADJECTIVE careful and alert to danger or trouble.
vigilance NOUN   **vigilantly** ADVERB

vigorous

ADJECTIVE energetic or enthusiastic.
vigorously ADVERB

villa villas

NOUN a house, especially a pleasant holiday home in a country with a warm climate.

village villages

NOUN a collection of houses and other buildings in the countryside.
[from Old French *ville* meaning farm]

villain villains

NOUN someone who harms others or breaks the law.

Synonyms: criminal, rogue

vine vines

NOUN a climbing plant, especially one that produces grapes.

vinegar

NOUN a sharp-tasting liquid made from sour wine and used for flavouring food.
[from French *vin aigre* meaning sour wine]

vineyard vineyards

NOUN an area of land where grapes are grown for making wine.

vintage

ADJECTIVE **1** A **vintage** wine is a good quality wine made in a particular year.
2 A **vintage** car is one made between 1918 and 1930.

vinyl

NOUN a strong plastic used to make things such as furniture and floor coverings..

viola violas

NOUN a musical instrument like a violin, but larger and with a lower pitch.

A
B
C
D
E
F
G
H
I
J
K
L
M
N
O
P
Q
R
S
T
U
V
W
X
Y
Z

violence

NOUN **1** behaviour that is intended to hurt or kill.

2 force that does harm or damage. *The violence of the storm did a lot of damage.*
violent ADJECTIVE   **violently** ADVERB

violet violets

NOUN **1** a plant with dark purple flowers.
NOUN OR ADJECTIVE **2** bluish purple.

violin violins

NOUN a musical instrument with four strings that is held under the chin and played with a bow.

VIP

NOUN an abbreviation of *very important person. The **VIPs** had the best seats at the concert.*

viper vipers

NOUN a type of poisonous snake.

virgin virgins

NOUN **1** someone who has never had sexual intercourse.
PROPER NOUN **2** In the Christian religion, the **Virgin**, or the Blessed **Virgin**, is a name given to Mary, the mother of Jesus Christ.

virtual

ADJECTIVE almost exactly the same as the real thing.

virtual reality

NOUN an environment or image that has been created by a computer and looks real to the person using it.

virtue virtues

NOUN **1** moral goodness.
2 a good quality in someone's character.

virus viruses

NOUN **1** a tiny organism that can cause disease.
2 a disease caused by a virus can be called a **virus**.
3 a program that damages the information stored in a computer system.

visible

ADJECTIVE able to be seen.

vision visions

NOUN **1** the ability to see.
2 a picture of something in your mind or imagination.

visit visits visiting visited

VERB **1** If you **visit** someone, you go to see them and spend time with them.
2 If you **visit** a place, you go to see it.
NOUN **3** a trip to see a person or place.

visor visors

NOUN **1** a transparent, movable shield attached to a helmet, which can be pulled down to protect the eyes or face.
2 a shade to protect your eyes from the sun.

visual

ADJECTIVE to do with sight and seeing.

vital

ADJECTIVE necessary or very important.

Synonym: essential

vitality

NOUN People who have **vitality** are energetic and lively.

vitamin vitamins

NOUN one of a group of substances you need to have in your diet in order to stay healthy. For example, **vitamin** C is found in oranges.

vivid

ADJECTIVE very bright in colour or clear in detail.

vivisection

NOUN the use of living animals for medical research.

vixen vixens

NOUN a female fox.

vocabulary vocabularies

NOUN **1** the total number of words someone knows in a particular language.
2 all the words in a language.

vocal

ADJECTIVE to do with or involving the use of the human voice.
vocalist NOUN   **vocally** ADVERB

vocation vocations

NOUN **1** If you have a **vocation**, you want very much to do a particular job, especially one that involves helping other people.
2 a profession or career.

voice voices

NOUN Your **voice** is what you hear when you speak or sing.

void voids

NOUN a very large empty space or deep hole.

volcano volcanoes

NOUN a mountain with an opening at the top called a crater, from which lava, gas and ash sometimes erupt.

[named after *Vulcan*, the Roman god of fire]

vole voles

NOUN a small mammal like a mouse with a short tail, which lives in fields and near rivers.

volley volleys

NOUN **1** A **volley** of shots or missiles is a lot of them fired or thrown at the same time.

2 In tennis, a **volley** is a stroke in which the player hits the ball before it bounces.

volleyball

NOUN a game in which two teams hit a ball back and forth over a high net with their hands. The ball is not allowed to bounce on the ground.

volt volts

NOUN the unit used to measure the voltage of a battery.

[named after Alessandro *Volta* who invented the electric battery]

voltage voltages

NOUN the measure of how much electrical current a battery can push through an electric circuit.

volume volumes

NOUN **1** the amount of space something contains or occupies.

2 The **volume** of a radio, TV or record player is how loud it is.

3 a book, or one of a series of books.

voluntary

ADJECTIVE Something **voluntary** is done because you want to do it, not because you are paid or told to do it.

voluntarily ADVERB

volunteer volunteers volunteering volunteered

NOUN **1** someone who does work that they are not paid for.

VERB **2** If you **volunteer** to do something, you offer to do it without expecting any reward.

vomit vomits vomiting vomited

VERB If you **vomit**, food and drink comes back up from your stomach and out through your mouth.

vote votes voting voted

NOUN **1** Someone's **vote** is their choice in an election, or at a meeting where decisions are taken.

VERB **2** When people **vote**, they show their choice or opinion, usually by writing on a piece of paper or by raising their hand.

voucher vouchers

NOUN a piece of paper that can be used instead of money to pay for something.

vow vows vowing vowed

VERB **1** If you **vow** to do something, you make a promise to do it.

NOUN **2** a promise.

vowel vowels

NOUN **1** a sound made without your tongue touching the roof of your mouth or your teeth.

2 In the English language the letters a, e, i, o and u are **vowels**.

voyage voyages

NOUN a long journey on a ship or in a spacecraft.

vulgar

ADJECTIVE rude or offensive.

vulnerable

ADJECTIVE without protection and easily hurt or damaged.

Synonym: defenceless

vulture vultures

NOUN a large bird that lives in hot countries and eats the flesh of dead animals.

a
b
c
d
e
f
g
h
i
j
k
l
m
n
o
p
q
r
s
t
u
v
w
x
y
z

Ww

waddle waddles waddling waddled
VERB to walk with short, quick steps, swaying slightly from side to side. *A duck* **waddled** *past.*

wade wades wading waded
VERB If you **wade**, you walk through water or mud.

wafer wafers
NOUN a thin, crisp biscuit, often eaten with ice cream.

waffle waffles waffling waffled
VERB **1** When someone **waffles**, they talk or write a lot without being clear or without saying anything of importance.
NOUN **2** a thick, crisp pancake with squares marked on it, often eaten with syrup poured over it.

wag wags wagging wagged
VERB **1** When a dog **wags** its tail, it shakes it repeatedly from side to side.
2 If you **wag** your finger, you move it repeatedly up and down.

wage wages
NOUN the regular payment made to someone each week for the work they do.

wagon wagons; also spelt **waggon**
NOUN a strong four-wheeled cart for carrying heavy loads. **Wagons** are usually pulled by horses or tractors.

wail wails wailing wailed
VERB If a person or an animal **wails**, they cry or moan loudly.

waist waists
NOUN the middle part of your body where it narrows slightly above your hips.

waistcoat waistcoats
NOUN a sleeveless piece of clothing, usually worn over a shirt and under a jacket.

wait waits waiting waited
VERB **1** If you **wait**, you spend time in a place or a situation, usually doing little or nothing, before something happens.
2 to serve people food and drinks as a waiter or waitress.

NOUN **3** A **wait** is a period of time before something happens.

waiter waiters
NOUN a man who works in a restaurant, serving people with food and drink.

waitress waitresses
NOUN a woman who works in a restaurant, serving people with food and drink.

wake wakes waking woke woken
VERB When you **wake**, or when something **wakes** you, you become conscious again after being asleep.

walk walks walking walked
VERB **1** When you **walk**, you move along by putting one foot in front of the other on the ground.
NOUN **2** If you go for a **walk**, you go from one place to another on foot.

wall walls
NOUN **1** a narrow structure of brick or stone built round a garden or building.
2 one of the four sides of a room.

wallaby wallabies
NOUN a marsupial that looks like a small kangaroo.
[from *wolaba*, an Australian Aboriginal word]

wallet wallets
NOUN a small, flat, folding case made of leather or plastic, used for holding paper money and sometimes credit cards.

wallpaper wallpapers
NOUN thick coloured or patterned paper that comes in rolls, for pasting on to the walls of rooms to decorate them.

walnut walnuts
NOUN **1** a nut that you can eat. It has a wrinkled shape and a hard, round, light-brown shell.
2 the tree on which walnuts grow. The wood from these trees is often used for making expensive furniture.

A B C D E F G H I J K L M N O P Q R S T U V **W** X Y Z

walrus walruses

NOUN an animal that lives in the sea. It looks like a large seal with a tough skin, coarse whiskers, and two tusks.

waltz waltzes waltzing waltzed

NOUN **1** a dance that has a rhythm of three beats to the bar.

VERB **2** If you **waltz** with someone, you dance a waltz with them.

wand wands

NOUN a long, thin rod used by magicians when they perform magic tricks, and by fairies in stories.

wander wanders wandering wandered

VERB If you **wander** in a place, you walk around in a casual way.

want wants wanting wanted

VERB **1** If you **want** something, you feel that you would like to have it or do it.

2 to need something.

wanted

ADJECTIVE being looked for, especially by the police as a suspected criminal.

war wars

NOUN a period of fighting between countries or states, when weapons are used and many people may be killed.

ward wards

NOUN **1** a long room with beds in for patients in a hospital.

2 a child who is looked after by a guardian rather than their parents.

warden wardens

NOUN **1** a person in charge of a place like a park or a block of flats, or an institution like a prison or a hostel.

2 an official who makes sure that certain laws or rules are obeyed.

wardrobe wardrobes

NOUN a tall cupboard in which you can hang your clothes.

[from Old French *warder* meaning to guard robes and *robes* meaning clothing]

warehouse warehouses

NOUN a large building where goods are stored.

warm warmer warmest; warms warming warmed

ADJECTIVE **1** Something that is **warm** has some heat, but not enough to be hot.

2 **Warm** clothes or blankets are made of material that protects you from the cold.

VERB **3** If you **warm** something, you heat it up gently so that it stops being cold.

warn warns warning warned

VERB If you **warn** someone, you tell them that they may be in danger or in trouble.

warning warnings

NOUN something said or written to warn someone of a possible danger or problem.

warp warps warping warped

VERB If something **warps**, or is **warped**, it becomes bent and twisted, usually because of heat or dampness.

warrant warrants

NOUN a special document that gives someone permission to do something. *The police had a* ***warrant*** *to search the house for evidence.*

warren warrens

NOUN an area of ground where there are many rabbit burrows.

warrior warriors

NOUN a fighting man or soldier.

wart warts

NOUN a small, hard growth on the skin.

wary warier wariest

ADJECTIVE If you are **wary** of something or someone, you are not sure about them, so you are cautious.

was

VERB a past tense of *be*.

wash washes washing washed

VERB **1** If you **wash** something, you clean it with water and soap.

2 If you **wash**, you clean yourself using soap and water.

wash up VERB **3** If you **wash up**, you wash the dishes, pans and cutlery used in preparing and eating a meal.

washable

ADJECTIVE able to be washed without being damaged.

washing
NOUN clothes that need to be washed or that have been washed.

washing machine washing machines
NOUN a machine for washing clothes.

washing-up
NOUN the task of washing plates, cutlery and pots after a meal.

wasp wasps
NOUN a flying insect with yellow and black stripes across its body, which can sting.

waste wastes wasting wasted
VERB 1 If you **waste** time, money or energy, you use too much of it on something that is not important or that you do not need.
NOUN 2 using more money or some other resource than you need to.
3 rubbish or other material that is no longer wanted, or that is left over.

watch watches watching watched
NOUN 1 a small clock, usually worn on a strap on a person's wrist.
VERB 2 If you **watch** something, you look at it for some time and pay attention to what is happening.
watch out VERB 3 If you **watch out** for something or someone, you keep alert to see if they are near you.
4 If you tell someone to **watch out**, you are warning them to be careful.

water waters watering watered
NOUN 1 a clear, colourless, tasteless liquid that falls from clouds as rain.
VERB 2 If you **water** a plant, you pour water into the soil around it.
3 If your eyes or mouth **water**, they produce tears or saliva. *My mouth started watering when I smelled Mum's baking.*

watercolour watercolours
NOUN 1 a type of paint that is mixed with water and used for painting pictures.
2 a picture that has been painted using watercolours.

watercress
NOUN a small plant that grows in streams and pools. It is often eaten in salads.

waterfall waterfalls
NOUN water from a stream or river as it flows over rocks or the edge of a steep cliff and falls to the ground below.

Victoria Falls, Zimbabwe

waterlogged
ADJECTIVE Something that is **waterlogged** is so wet that it cannot soak up any more water.

watermark watermarks
NOUN 1 a mark showing the level of water.
2 a faint design in some types of paper which you can see if you hold it up to the light.

waterproof
ADJECTIVE Something that is **waterproof** does not let water pass through it. *We put on our waterproof jackets as it was raining.*

watertight
ADJECTIVE Something that is **watertight** does not allow water to pass in or out.

waterworks
NOUN the place where the public supply of water is stored and cleaned, and from where it is supplied to our homes.

watt watts
*Said "**wot**"* NOUN a unit of measurement of electrical power.
[Named after James **Watt** (1736–1819) who invented the steam engine]

wave waves waving waved
VERB 1 If you **wave** your hand, you move it from side to side, usually to say hello or goodbye.
2 If you **wave** something, you hold it up and move it from side to side. *People in the crowd were waving flags.*
NOUN 3 a ridge of water on the surface of the sea caused by wind or by tides.
4 the form in which some types of energy, such as heat, light or sound travel.

wax waxes
NOUN **1** a solid, slightly shiny substance made of fat or oil, that melts easily and is used to make candles and polish.
2 the sticky yellow substance in your ears.

way ways
NOUN **1** The **way** of doing something is how you do it.
2 The **way** to a place is how you get there.

WC WCs
NOUN an abbreviation of *water closet*. It is used on plans and signs to show where the toilet is located.

we
PRONOUN **We** refers to the person writing or talking and one or more other people.

weak weaker weakest
ADJECTIVE If someone is **weak**, they do not have much strength or energy.

wealth
NOUN a large amount of money or property that someone owns.

wealthy wealthier wealthiest
ADJECTIVE Someone who is **wealthy** has a lot of money.

weapon weapons
NOUN an object used to hurt or kill people in a fight or war.

wear wears wearing wore worn
VERB **1** When you **wear** something, such as clothes, make-up or jewellery, you have them on your body or face.
wear out VERB **2** When something **wears out**, or when you **wear** it **out**, it is used so much that it becomes thin, weak, and no longer usable.

weary wearier weariest
ADJECTIVE If you are **weary**, you are very tired.
wearily ADVERB   **weariness** NOUN

weasel weasels
NOUN a small wild mammal with a long, thin body and short legs.

weather
NOUN the conditions of sunshine, rain, wind or snow at a particular time in a particular place.

weave weaves weaving wove woven
VERB **1** If you **weave** something like cloth or a basket, you make it by crossing threads or grasses over and under each other. Cloth is often **woven** using a machine called a loom.
2 If you **weave** your way, you move from side to side past people and other obstacles.

web webs
NOUN a fine net of threads that a spider makes from a sticky substance that it produces in its body.

webbed
ADJECTIVE **Webbed** feet have skin joining the toes together, like ducks' feet.

website websites
NOUN a place on the Internet where you can find out about a particular subject or person.

we'd
a contraction of *we had* or *we would*.

wedding weddings
NOUN a marriage ceremony.

wedge wedges wedging wedged
VERB **1** If you **wedge** something somewhere, you make it stay there by holding it tightly, or by fixing something next to it to stop it from moving.
NOUN **2** a piece of something such as wood, metal or rubber with one thin edge and one thick edge, used to hold something still. *I put a **wedge** under the door to keep it open.*
3 a piece of something that has a thick triangular shape. *I cut a **wedge** of cheese.*

Wednesday
NOUN the fourth day of the week, coming between Tuesday and Thursday.
[Wednesday was the day the Anglo-Saxons honoured their god *Odin* or *Woden*]

a
b
c
d
e
f
g
h
i
j
k
l
m
n
o
p
q
r
s
t
u
v
w
x
y
z

weed weeds weeding weeded

NOUN **1** a wild plant growing somewhere it is not wanted.

VERB **2** If you **weed** an area of ground, you remove the weeds from it.

week weeks

NOUN **1** a period of seven days, especially one beginning on a Sunday and ending on a Saturday.

2 the part of a week that does not include Saturday and Sunday.

weekday weekdays

NOUN any day except Saturday and Sunday.

weekend weekends

NOUN Saturday and Sunday.

weekly

ADJECTIVE AND ADVERB happening or appearing once every week.

weep weeps weeping wept

VERB If someone **weeps**, they cry.

weigh weighs weighing weighs

VERB **1** If something **weighs** a particular amount, that is how heavy it is.

2 If you **weigh** something, you find out how heavy it is by using scales.

weight weights

NOUN the heaviness of something.

weir weirs

NOUN a low dam built across a river to raise the water level, control the flow of water, or change the direction of the water.

[from Old English *wer* meaning river-dam or enclosure for fish]

weird weirder weirdest

ADJECTIVE strange or odd.

welcome welcomes welcoming welcomed

VERB **1** If you **welcome** a visitor, you greet them in a friendly way when they arrive.

2 **Welcome** can be said as a greeting to a visitor who has just arrived.

ADJECTIVE **3** If someone is **welcome** at a place, they will be accepted there in a friendly way.

[from Old English *wilcuma* meaning welcome guest]

weld welds welding welded

VERB If you **weld** two pieces of metal together, you join them by heating their edges and pressing them together so that when they cool they harden into one piece.

welder NOUN

welfare

NOUN The **welfare** of a person or group is their health, comfort and happiness.

welfare state

NOUN a system in which the government uses money from taxes to provide health care and education services, and to give benefits to people who are old, unemployed or sick.

well better best; wells

ADJECTIVE **1** If you are **well**, you are healthy.

ADVERB **2** If you do something **well**, you do it to a high standard.

NOUN **3** a hole in the ground with water or oil at the bottom.

we'll

a contraction of *we will* or *we shall*.

wellington wellingtons

NOUN long waterproof rubber boots.

[named after the Duke of *Wellington*]

went

VERB the past tense of *go*.

wept

VERB the past tense and past participle of *weep*.

were

VERB a past tense of *be*.

we're

a contraction of *we are*.

west

NOUN one of the four main points of the compass. It is the direction in which you look to see the sun set. The abbreviation for **west** is W.

western westerns

ADJECTIVE **1** in or from the west.

NOUN **2** a film or book about the west of America in the nineteenth and early twentieth centuries.

wet wetter wettest; wets wetting wet or wetted
ADJECTIVE **1** covered or soaked with water or other liquid.
2 Wet weather is rainy.
VERB **3** If you **wet** something, you make it wet.

we've
a contraction of *we have.*

whale whales
NOUN a very large sea mammal that breathes out water through a hole on the top of its head.

wharf wharves or **wharfs**
NOUN a platform beside a river or the sea, where ships load and unload.

what
ADJECTIVE **1 What** is used in questions. *What time is it?*
2 You use **what** to emphasize a comment. *What excellent work!*
PHRASE **3** You use **what about** to show that you are making a suggestion or a question. *What about the homework from last night?*
PRONOUN **4** refers to information about something. *I really have no idea what you mean.*

whatever
PRONOUN **1** anything or everything of a particular type.
CONJUNCTION **2** You use **whatever** to mean no matter what. *I will go whatever happens.*

wheat
NOUN a cereal plant grown for its grain that is used to make flour.

wheel wheels wheeling wheeled
NOUN **1** a circular object that turns on a rod attached to its centre. **Wheels** are fixed underneath vehicles so that they can move along.
VERB **2** If you **wheel** something somewhere, you push it along on wheels.

wheelbarrow wheelbarrows
NOUN a small cart with a single wheel at the front, pushed along by two handles at the back. It is used by people such as gardeners and builders.

wheelchair wheelchairs
NOUN a chair with large wheels, for use by people who find walking difficult or impossible.

wheeze wheezes wheezing wheezed
VERB If someone **wheezes**, they breathe with difficulty, making a whistling sound.

when
ADVERB **1** You use **when** to ask at what time something will happen or how long ago it has happened. *When shall I see you?*
CONJUNCTION **2** You use **when** to refer to a certain time. *I had fun when I was on holiday.*

whenever
CONJUNCTION at any time, or every time that something happens. *I go to the park whenever I can.*

where
ADVERB **1** You use **where** to ask which place something is in, is from, or is going to. *Where are we?*
CONJUNCTION **2** You use **where** to refer to a place in which something or someone is. *You do not know where we live.*

wherever
CONJUNCTION in, at or to any place or situation. *Alex heard the same thing wherever he went.*

whether
CONJUNCTION You use **whether** when you are talking about two or more things to choose from. *I don't know whether that's true or false.*

which
ADJECTIVE OR PRONOUN **1** You use **which** to ask about alternatives. *Which girl is your sister?*
2 Which shows the thing you are talking about or gives more detail about it. *The book which is on the table is mine.*

whichever
PRONOUN AND ADJECTIVE You use **whichever** when talking about different possibilities. *You can have cake or chocolate, whichever you prefer.*

whiff whiffs
NOUN a slight smell of something. *I caught a whiff of her perfume as she passed.*

while

CONJUNCTION **1** If something happens **while** something else is happening, the two things happen at the same time. *Mum went to the café* ***while*** *I had my lesson.*
2 While can be used to mean but or although. *I like dogs,* ***while*** *my brother prefers cats.*
NOUN **3** a period of time: *a little* ***while*** *earlier.*

whim whims

NOUN a sudden wish or desire.

Synonym: impulse

---

whimper whimpers whimpering whimpered

VERB When children or animals **whimper**, they make soft, low, unhappy sounds.

whine whines whining whined

VERB **1** If a person or an animal **whines**, they make a long, high-pitched noise, especially one that sounds sad or unpleasant.
2 If someone **whines** about something, they complain about it in an annoying way.

whip whips whipping whipped

NOUN **1** a long, thin piece of leather or rope attached to a handle, which is used for hitting people or animals.
VERB **2** To **whip** a person or animal means to hit them with a whip.

whirl whirls whirling whirled

VERB When something **whirls**, or when you **whirl** it round, it turns or spins round very fast.

whirlpool whirlpools

NOUN a small area in a river or the sea where the water is moving quickly round and round in a circle so that objects floating near it are pulled into its centre.

whirlwind whirlwinds

NOUN a tall column of air that spins round and round very fast.

whirr whirrs whirring whirred

VERB When something like a machine **whirrs**, it makes a continuous buzzing sound.

whisk whisks whisking whisked

VERB **1** If you **whisk** eggs or cream, you stir air into them quickly.
2 If you **whisk** something somewhere, you move it there quickly.
NOUN **3** a kitchen utensil for whisking things.

whisker whiskers

NOUN **1** The **whiskers** of an animal such as a cat are the long, stiff hairs near its mouth.
2 You can refer to the hair on a man's face, especially on his cheeks, as his **whiskers**.

whisky whiskies; also spelt whiskey

NOUN a strong alcoholic drink made from grain such as barley.

whisper whispers whispering whispered

VERB When you **whisper**, you talk very quietly and softly.

whistle whistles whistling whistled

VERB **1** When you **whistle**, you make a high-pitched sound by forcing your breath out between your lips. *He* ***whistled*** *a tune.*
2 If something **whistles**, it makes a loud, high sound. *The kettle* ***whistled***.
NOUN **3** a small metal tube that you blow into to produce a whistling sound.

white whiter whitest; whites

NOUN OR ADJECTIVE **1** the lightest possible colour, like milk or fresh snow.
2 White coffee contains milk or cream.
NOUN **3** The **white** of an egg is the clear liquid around the yolk.

who

PRONOUN **1** You use **who** when you are asking about someone's identity. ***Who*** *are you?*
2 You use **who** to refer to the person you are talking about. *I know you are the one* ***who*** *was in trouble yesterday.*

whoever

PRONOUN **Whoever** means the person who. ***Whoever*** *wants to can go on the excursion.*

whole wholes

NOUN OR ADJECTIVE **1** The **whole** of something is all of it.
ADVERB **2** in one piece. *He swallowed the sweet* ***whole***.

wholemeal

ADJECTIVE **Wholemeal** flour is made from the whole grain of the wheat plant, including the husk.

wholemeal bread

wholesale

ADJECTIVE OR ADVERB If a shopkeeper buys his goods **wholesale**, he buys large amounts of them cheaply before selling them on to his customers.

Antonym: retail

wholesome

ADJECTIVE healthy or good for you.

whose

PRONOUN **1** You use **whose** to ask who something belongs to. *Whose shoe is this?*
2 Whose gives information about something belonging to the person or things just mentioned. *She is the pupil whose poem won the prize.*
✔ Many people are confused about the difference between **whose** and **who's**. **Whose** shows who the thing being described belongs to. *Whose bag is this?* **Who's**, with the apostrophe, is a contraction of **who is** or **who has**. *Who's that girl? Who's got my ruler?*

why

ADVERB OR PRONOUN You use **why** when you are talking about the reason for something. *Why did you do that? I wondered why he did that.*

wick wicks

NOUN the cord that burns in the middle of a candle.

wicked

ADJECTIVE **1** very bad.
2 mischievous in an amusing or attractive way.
wickedly ADVERB   **wickedness** NOUN
[from Old English *wicca* meaning witch]

Synonyms: (sense 1) evil, sinful

wicker

NOUN things made of reed or cane woven together, such as baskets or furniture.

wicket wickets

NOUN **1** one of the two sets of stumps and bails at which the bowler aims the ball in cricket.
NOUN **2** The grass between the **wickets** in cricket is also called the **wicket**.

wide wider widest

ADJECTIVE **1** measuring a large distance from one side to the other.
2 measuring a certain amount from one side to the other. *The pool is 10 metres wide.*
3 If there is a **wide** variety, range or selection of something, there are many different kinds of it.
ADVERB **4** If you open or spread something **wide**, you open it as far as you can. *Open your mouth wide.*

widow widows

NOUN a woman whose husband has died.

widower widowers

NOUN a man whose wife has died.

width widths

NOUN The **width** of something is how wide it is from one side to the other.

wife wives

NOUN A man's **wife** is the woman he is married to.

wig wigs

NOUN a covering of artificial hair worn over someone's own hair to change their appearance or to hide their baldness.
[short for *periwig*, from Italian *perrucca* meaning wig]

wiggle wiggles wiggling wiggled

VERB If you **wiggle** something, you move it up and down or from side to side with small jerky movements.
wiggly ADJECTIVE

wigwam wigwams

NOUN a kind of tent used by Native Americans.
[from American Indian *wikwam* meaning their house]

wild wilder wildest; wilds

ADJECTIVE **1 Wild** animals and plants live and grow in natural surroundings and are not looked after by people.
2 Wild land is natural and not used for farming.
3 Wild behaviour is excited and uncontrolled.
NOUN **4** a free and natural state of living. *There are very few tigers left in the wild.*

wilderness wildernesses

NOUN an area of natural land that is not cultivated.

wildlife

NOUN wild animals and plants.

a
b
c
d
e
f
g
h
i
j
k
l
m
n
o
p
q
r
s
t
u
v
w
x
y
z

wilful

ADJECTIVE **1** Someone who is **wilful** is determined to get their own way.
2 Something that is **wilful** is done or said deliberately: *wilful damage*.
wilfully ADVERB

Synonyms: (sense 1) headstrong, stubborn

will wills

VERB **1** You use **will** to form the future tense. *I will do the washing up after dinner*.
NOUN **2** the determination to do something.
3 a legal document in which people say what they want to happen to their money and property when they die.
4 what you choose or want to do. *Don't make them do it against their will*.

willing

ADJECTIVE If you are **willing**, you are glad and ready to do what is wanted or needed.

willow willows

NOUN a tree with long, thin branches and narrow leaves that often grows near water.

wilt wilts wilting wilted

VERB If a plant **wilts**, it droops because it needs more water or is dying.

wily wilier wiliest

ADJECTIVE clever and cunning.

wimp wimps

NOUN; INFORMAL someone who is feeble and timid.

win wins winning won

VERB **1** If you **win** a fight, game or argument, you defeat your opponent.
2 If you **win** a prize, you receive it as a reward for succeeding in something.

winch winches winching winched

NOUN **1** a machine used to lift or pull heavy objects. It consists of a cylinder or wheel around which a rope or cable is wound.
VERB **2** If you **winch** an object or person somewhere, you lift, lower or pull them using a winch.

wind winds winding wound

Rhymes with "**mind**" VERB **1** If a road or river **winds**, it is not straight, but twists and turns.
2 When you **wind** something round something else, you wrap it round it several times.

3 When you **wind** a clock or machine, or **wind** it up, you turn a key or handle several times to make it work
Rhymes with "**tinned**" NOUN **4** a current of air that moves across the land and sea.
5 The **wind** section of an orchestra is the group of musicians who play **wind** instruments.

windmill windmills

NOUN a machine in a special building, for generating electricity, grinding grain or pumping water. It is powered by long arms called sails that are turned by the wind.

window windows

NOUN a space in a wall or roof or in the side of a vehicle, usually with glass in it so that light can pass through and people can see in or out.

windpipe windpipes

NOUN the tube through which air travels in and out of your lungs when you breathe.

windscreen windscreens

NOUN the glass at the front of a vehicle through which the driver looks.

windsurfing

NOUN the sport of moving over the surface of the sea or a lake on a board with a sail fixed to it.
windsurfer NOUN

windy windier windiest

ADJECTIVE If it is **windy**, there is a lot of wind.

wine wines

NOUN an alcoholic drink usually made from grapes.

wing wings

NOUN **1** A bird's or insect's **wings** are the parts of its body that it uses for flying.
2 An aeroplane's **wings** are the long, flat parts on each side that support it while it is in the air.

wink winks winking winked

VERB When you **wink**, you close and open one eye very quickly, often to show that something is a joke or a secret.

winner winners

NOUN someone who wins something.

winter winters

NOUN the coldest season of the year, between autumn and spring.

wipe wipes wiping wiped

VERB If you **wipe** something, you rub its surface lightly with a cloth or your hand to clear off dirt or liquid.

wire wires wiring wired

NOUN **1** long, thin, bendy metal that can be used to make or fasten things, or to conduct an electric current.

VERB **2** If someone **wires** something, or **wires** it up, they connect it so that electricity can pass through it.

wisdom

NOUN a person's ability to use the things they have done and learned to give good advice or make good decisions.

wise wiser wisest

ADJECTIVE Someone who is **wise** can use their experience and knowledge to make sensible decisions and judgements.

wish wishes wishing wished

NOUN **1** something that you want very much.
2 the act of wishing for something.
VERB **3** If you **wish** something for someone, you hope that they will have it. *I **wished** her good luck in her exams.*
4 If you **wish** to do something, you want to do it.
5 If you **wish** something was true, you would like it to be, but know it is not very likely.

wisp wisps

NOUN A **wisp** of something such as smoke or hair is a small, thin, streak or bunch of it. *A **wisp** of hair fell over her eyes.*
wispy ADJECTIVE

wit wits

NOUN the ability to use words or ideas in an amusing and clever way.

witch witches

NOUN a woman who claims to have magic powers and to be able to use them for good or evil. **Witches** are often characters in fairy stories.
[from Old English *wicca* meaning witch]

witchcraft

NOUN the skill or art of using magic powers, especially evil ones.

with

PREPOSITION If you are **with** someone you are in their company. *We went **with** Mum to the shops.*

withdraw withdraws withdrawing withdrew withdrawn

VERB **1** If you **withdraw** something, you take it out. *He **withdrew** the money from his bank.*
2 If you **withdraw** from something, you do not continue with it. *She **withdrew** from the race because of injury.*

wither withers withering withered

VERB If a plant **withers**, it wilts or shrivels up and dies.

within

PREPOSITION OR ADVERB **1** inside, not going outside certain limits. *Stay **within** the school grounds.*
2 before a period of time has passed. *Bring back the book **within** three weeks.*

without

PREPOSITION **1** not having, not feeling, or not showing something. *They went out **without** coats as it was a warm, dry day.*
2 If you do something **without** someone else, they are not with you when you do it. *He went **without** me.*

witness witnesses

NOUN **1** someone who has seen an event, such as an accident, and can describe what happened.
2 someone who appears in a court of law to say what they know about a crime or other event.

witty wittier wittiest

ADJECTIVE amusing in a clever way.

wizard wizards

NOUN a man in a fairy story who has magic powers.

wobble wobbles wobbling wobbled

VERB If something **wobbles**, it shakes or moves from side to side because it is loose or unsteady.

wok woks

NOUN a large bowl-shaped pan used for Chinese cooking.

woke

VERB the past tense of *wake*.

woken

VERB the past participle of *wake*.

wolf wolves; wolfs wolfing wolfed

NOUN **1** a wild animal related to the dog. **Wolves** hunt in packs and kill other animals for food.

VERB **2** INFORMAL If you **wolf** food, or **wolf** it down, you eat it up quickly and greedily.

woman women

NOUN an adult female human being.

womb wombs

NOUN A woman's **womb** is the part inside her body where her unborn baby grows.

won

VERB the past tense and past participle of *win*.

wonder wonders wondering wondered

VERB **1** If you **wonder** about something, you think about it and try to guess or understand more about it.

2 If you **wonder** at something, you are amazed by it.

NOUN **3** a feeling of amazement and admiration.

wonderful

ADJECTIVE marvellous or impressive.

won't

a contraction of *will not*.

wood woods

NOUN **1** the substance that forms the trunks and branches of trees.

2 a large area of trees growing near each other.

wooden

ADJECTIVE Something **wooden** is made of wood.

woodland woodlands

NOUN land that is mostly covered with trees.

woodlouse woodlice

NOUN a small animal with seven pairs of legs, that lives in damp soil and rotten wood.

woodpecker woodpeckers

NOUN a climbing bird with a long, sharp beak that it uses to drill holes in trees to find the insects that live in the bark.

woodwind

ADJECTIVE **Woodwind** instruments are musical instruments such as flutes, oboes, clarinets and bassoons, made of wood or metal. They are played by being blown into.

woodwork

NOUN **1** the activity of making things out of wood.

2 the parts of a building that are made of wood.

woof woofs

NOUN the sound a dog makes.

wool wools

NOUN **1** the hair that grows on sheep and some other animals.

2 thread or cloth made from the wool of animals, and used to make clothes, blankets and carpets.

woollen

ADJECTIVE made of wool.

woolly

ADJECTIVE made of wool, or looking like wool.

word words

NOUN **1** a single unit of language in speech or writing which has a meaning. "Bird", "hot" and "sing" are all **words**.

PLURAL NOUN **2** The **words** of a play or song are the words you say or sing.

NOUN **3** If you give someone your **word** about something, you promise to do it.

4 If you ask for a **word** with someone, you want to say something briefly to them.

word processor word processors

NOUN a computer used for writing, editing and storing letters and documents.

wore

VERB the past tense of *wear*.

work works working worked

VERB **1** People who **work** have a job that they are paid to do.

2 When you **work**, you spend time and energy doing something useful.

3 If something **works**, it does what it is supposed to do.

PHRASE **4** If something **works its way** into a certain position, it moves itself there gradually.

5 If you **work out** an answer to a problem, you solve it.

workout workouts

NOUN a session of exercise or training for the body.

workshop workshops

NOUN a room or building that has tools or machinery in it that are used for making or repairing things.

world worlds

NOUN **1** the planet we live on.
2 A person's **world** is the life they lead and the people they know.
3 a particular field of activity. *He is a top player in the rugby world.*
PHRASE **4** If you **think the world** of someone, you like or admire them very much.

worm worms

NOUN a small, thin animal without bones or legs, especially an earthworm.

worn

VERB **1** past participle of *wear*.
ADJECTIVE **2** looking old or exhausted.

worry worries worrying worried

VERB **1** If you **worry**, you feel anxious about a problem or about something that might happen.
NOUN **2** a problem, or something that makes you worry.

worse

ADJECTIVE OR ADVERB less good or less well. The comparative form of bad and badly. *The team's results are worse this year than they were last year.*

Antonym: better

worship worships worshipping worshipped

VERB If you **worship** a god, you show your love and respect by praying or singing hymns.

worst

ADJECTIVE the least well or the least good. The superlative form of bad and badly. *It was the worst meal I have ever eaten.*

Antonym: best

worth

PREPOSITION **1** If something is **worth** a sum of money, it has that value.
2 If something is **worth** doing, it deserves to be done.

worthless

ADJECTIVE Something that is **worthless** has no use or no value.

worthwhile

ADJECTIVE If something is **worthwhile**, it is important enough to spend time or effort doing it.

would

VERB **1** the past tense of *will*. You use **would** to talk about something that was in the future the last time you were talking about it. *We were sure it would be a success.*
2 You use **would** in polite questions. *Would you like some lunch?*

wouldn't

a contraction of *would not*.

wound wounds wounding wounded

Rhymes with "sound" VERB **1** the past tense and past participle of *wind*.
Said "woond" NOUN **2** an injury to part of a person's or an animal's body, especially a cut.
VERB **3** If someone or something **wounds** a person or an animal, they injure them, especially with a cut.

wove

VERB the past tense of *weave*.

woven

VERB the past participle of *weave*.

wrap wraps wrapping wrapped

VERB If you **wrap** something, you fold cloth or paper around it.

wrapping wrappings

NOUN material used to wrap something, such as a present.

wrath

NOUN great anger.

wreath wreaths

NOUN an arrangement of flowers and leaves, often in the shape of a circle, which is put on a grave to remember someone who has died.

wreck wrecks wrecking wrecked

VERB **1** To **wreck** something means to break it, destroy it, or spoil it completely.
NOUN **2** a vehicle or ship that has been badly damaged, usually in an accident.
wreckage NOUN

wren wrens
NOUN a small brown songbird.

wrench wrenches wrenching wrenched
VERB **1** If you **wrench** something, you give it a sudden and violent twist or pull.
2 If you **wrench** a limb or a joint, you twist and injure it.
NOUN **3** a **wrenching** movement.
4 a tool for gripping or tightening nuts and bolts.

wrestle wrestles wrestling wrestled
VERB If you **wrestle** someone, or **wrestle** with them, you fight them by holding or throwing them, but not hitting them.
wrestler NOUN

wretched
ADJECTIVE very unhappy or unfortunate.

wriggle wriggles wriggling wriggled
VERB **1** If a person or an animal **wriggles**, they twist and turn their body in a lively and excited way.
2 If you **wriggle** out of doing something that you do not want to do, you manage to avoid doing it.

wring wrings wringing wrung
VERB When you **wring** a wet cloth, or **wring** it out, you squeeze the water out of it by twisting it.

wrinkle wrinkles wrinkling wrinkled
NOUN **1** a soft fold or crease in something, especially a person's skin as they grow older.
VERB **2** If something **wrinkles**, folds or creases develop on it.

wrinkled
ADJECTIVE Something that is **wrinkled** has wrinkles in it.

wrist wrists
NOUN the part of your body between your hand and your arm, which bends when you move your hand.

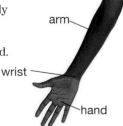
arm
wrist
hand

wristwatch wristwatches
NOUN a watch you wear on your wrist.

write writes writing wrote written
VERB **1** When you **write**, you use a pen or pencil to form letters, words or numbers on a surface. *I have **written** my name in the front of my book.*
2 If you **write** something such as a poem, a book or a piece of music, you think of the words or notes for yourself.
3 When you **write** to someone, you send them a letter.

writer writers
NOUN **1** a person who writes books, stories or articles as a job.
2 The **writer** of something is the person who wrote it.

writhe writhes writhing writhed
VERB If you **writhe**, you twist and turn your body, often because you are in pain.

writing writings
NOUN **1** something that has been written or printed.
2 Your **writing** is the way you write with a pen or pencil.

written
VERB the past participle of *write*.

wrong
ADJECTIVE **1** If there is something **wrong** with an object, it is not working properly or has a fault. *There must be something **wrong** with the car as it will not start.*
2 If something is **wrong**, it is not correct or truthful.
3 An action that is **wrong** is bad or against the law.

wrote
VERB the past tense of *write*.

wrung
VERB the past tense and past participle of *wring*.

Xx

X-ray X-rays X-raying X-rayed

NOUN **1** a type of radiation that can pass through some solid materials. **X-rays** are used by doctors to examine the bones or organs inside a person's body.

2 a picture made by sending X-rays through someone's body in order to examine the inside of it.

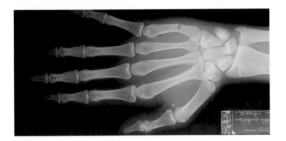

VERB **3** If someone **X-rays** something, they make a picture of the inside of it by passing X-rays through it.

xylophone xylophones

Said "**ziy**-lu-fohn" NOUN a musical instrument made of a row of wooden bars of different lengths. It is played by hitting the bars with special hammers.

Yy

yacht yachts

NOUN a boat with sails or an engine, used for racing or for pleasure trips.

yak yaks

NOUN a type of long-haired ox with long horns, found mainly in the mountains of Tibet.

yam yams

NOUN a root vegetable that grows in tropical regions.

yard yards

NOUN **1** a unit of length equal to 36 inches or about 91·4 centimetres.

2 a paved space with walls around it, next to a building.

3 a place where certain types of work are carried out, such as a ship**yard** or a builder's **yard**.

yarn yarns

NOUN **1** thread used for knitting or making cloth.

2 INFORMAL a story that someone tells, often with invented details to make it more interesting or exciting.

yashmak yashmaks

NOUN a veil that some Muslim women wear over their faces when they are in public.

[an Arabic word]

yawn yawns yawning yawned

VERB When you **yawn**, you open your mouth wide and take in more air than usual, often when you are tired or bored.

year years

NOUN **1** a period of twelve months or 365 days (366 days in a leap year), usually measured from the first of January to the thirty-first of December. It takes a **year** for the earth to orbit the sun.

2 the part of a year during which something happens or is organized: *the school year*.

yeast yeasts

NOUN a type of fungus used in baking and in making beer.

A B C D E F G H I J K L M N O P Q R S T U V W X **Y** Z

yell yells yelling yelled
VERB **1** If you **yell**, you shout loudly, usually because you are angry, excited, or in pain.
NOUN **2** a loud shout.

yellow yellower yellowest
NOUN OR ADJECTIVE the colour of buttercups, egg yolks or lemons.

yelp yelps yelping yelped
VERB **1** When people or animals **yelp**, they give a sudden cry.
NOUN **2** a sudden cry.

yes
INTERJECTION You say **yes** to agree with someone, to say that something is true, or to accept something.

Antonym: no

yesterday
NOUN OR ADVERB the day before today.

yet
ADVERB **1** If something has not happened **yet**, you expect it to happen in the future.
2 If something should not be done **yet**, it should be done later. *Don't switch it off **yet**.*
CONJUNCTION **3** You use **yet** to introduce something that is rather surprising. *He doesn't like maths, **yet** he always does well.*

yew yews
NOUN an evergreen tree with bright red berries.

yodel yodels yodelling yodelled
VERB When someone **yodels**, they sing normal notes with high quick notes in between. You can hear this style of singing in the Swiss and Austrian Alps.

yoga
NOUN a Hindu form of exercise that develops the body and the mind, making you relaxed and fit.

yogurt yogurts; also spelt **yoghurt**
NOUN a slightly sour, thick, liquid food made from milk that has had bacteria added to it.

yoke yokes
NOUN a wooden bar laid across the necks of animals such as oxen to hold them together when they pull a plough or a cart.

yolk yolks
NOUN the yellow part in the middle of an egg.

Yom Kippur
NOUN an annual Jewish religious holiday, which is a day of fasting and prayers. It is also called the Day of Atonement.
[from Hebrew **yom** meaning day and **kippur** meaning atonement]

you
PRONOUN **You** refers to the person or people you are talking or writing to.

you'd
a contraction of *you had* or *you would*.

you'll
a contraction of *you will* or *you shall*.

young younger youngest
ADJECTIVE **1** A **young** person, animal or plant has not lived very long and is not yet mature.
NOUN **2** The **young** of an animal are its babies.

your
ADJECTIVE belonging to you.

you're
a contraction of *you are*.

yours
PRONOUN belonging to you.

yourself yourselves
PRONOUN you and only you. *Have you hurt **yourself**?*

youth youths
NOUN **1** Someone's **youth** is the time of their life before they are a fully mature adult.
2 a boy or young man.
3 young people in general.

you've
a contraction of *you have*.

yo-yo yo-yos
NOUN a round wooden or plastic toy attached to a string. You play by making the **yo-yo** move up and down the string.

Zz

zany zanier zaniest
ADJECTIVE odd in a funny way.
[from Italian *zanni* meaning clown]

zap zaps zapping zapped
VERB; INFORMAL If you **zap** someone or
something in a computer game, you get rid of
them.

zeal
NOUN eagerness and enthusiasm.

zebra zebras
NOUN a type of African wild horse with black
and white stripes.

zebra crossing zebra crossings
NOUN part of a road marked with broad black
and white stripes, where pedestrians can cross.

zero
NOUN nought. The sign for zero is 0.

zest
NOUN **1** a feeling of great enjoyment and
enthusiasm.
2 The **zest** of a citrus fruit such as an orange or
lemon is the outside of the peel, used to flavour
food and drinks.
zestful ADJECTIVE   **zestfully** ADVERB

zigzag zigzags zigzagging zigzagged
NOUN **1** a line that has a series of sharp, angular
bends to the right and left.

VERB **2** If you **zigzag**, you move forward in a
series of sharp turns to the left and right.

zinc
NOUN a bluish-white metal used to coat other
metals to stop them rusting.

zip zips zipping zipped
NOUN **1** a fastener used on clothes and bags,
with two rows of metal or plastic interlocking
teeth that separate or fasten together as you
pull a small tag along them.
VERB **2** When you **zip** something, or **zip** it up,
you fasten it using a zip.

zodiac
NOUN a diagram used by astrologers to
represent the movement of the stars. It is
divided into 12 sections, each with a special
name and symbol. *"Capricorn"*, *"Gemini"*,
"Taurus" and *"Pisces"* are all signs of the
zodiac.
See pages 426–7.
[from the Greek *zōidiakos kuklos* meaning
"circle of signs"]

zone zones
NOUN an area of land or sea that is considered
different from the areas around it, or is
separated from the areas around it in some
way.

zoo zoos
NOUN a place where live animals are kept so
that people can look at them.

zoology
NOUN the scientific study of animals.
zoological ADJECTIVE   **zoologist** NOUN

zoom lens zoom lenses
NOUN A **zoom lens** on a camera helps the
photographer to take close-up pictures from far
away.

zucchini
PLURAL NOUN small vegetable marrows with dark
green skin. They are also called courgettes.
[from Italian plural of *zucchino* meaning
gourd]

The solar system

Earth, our planet, is one of nine planets that travel around the sun. These planets make up the solar system. The path that a planet follows around the sun is called its orbit, and the sun's gravity keeps the planets in their orbits. The planets are all at different distances from the sun and take different lengths of time to orbit it.

① The **sun** is the fiery centre of our solar system.

② **Mercury** is a small, hot, rocky planet with a very thin atmosphere. It takes 88 days to orbit the sun.

③ **Venus** is the same size as the earth, but is extremely hot and covered in thick clouds of acid. It takes 225 days to orbit the sun.

④ **Earth** has air in its atmosphere, temperatures that are not too extreme, and plenty of water, all of which mean that we can live here. It takes just over 365 days (one year) to orbit the sun.

⑤ The **moon** is dry and dusty, and the surface is covered with craters. It orbits the earth every 27·3 days and stays with the earth in its orbit around the sun.

⑨ **Uranus** is an enormous ball of gas covered in blue-green clouds. It has rings around it that may be made of pieces of ice. It takes 84 years to orbit the sun.

⑩ **Neptune** is a huge, bluish ball of gas with two rings around it. It takes 165 days to orbit the sun.

⑪ **Pluto** is the smallest and coldest planet in the solar system. It is not made of gas like some of the distant planets, but is made of rock and ice. It takes 248 years to orbit the sun.

⑥ **Mars** is a rocky planet, sometimes called the Red Planet because it is covered in iron oxide dust. It takes two years to orbit the sun.

⑧ **Saturn** is a large, bright planet surrounded by rings made up of small pieces of ice. It takes nearly 30 years to orbit the sun.

⑦ **Jupiter** is the largest of the planets. It is a huge ball of gases that takes 12 years to orbit the sun.

The sky at night

People have always been fascinated by the stars. The stars that we can see in the night sky depend on the time of year and whether we are in the northern hemisphere or the southern hemisphere. Patterns formed by groups of bright stars are called constellations, many of which were given names by ancient astronomers which we still know them by today. Twelve of the constellations are called the signs of the zodiac.

Northern hemisphere

1	Pisces	**5**	Orion
2	Aries	**6**	Gemini
3	Cancer	**7**	Virgo
4	Polaris	**8**	Leo
	(the North Pole Star)	**9**	Taurus

The sky at night

As the earth turns on its axis, the constellations move across the sky through the year, but the North Pole Star, which is in line with the axis, remains in the same place. Because of this, the North Pole Star has been used for centuries to help with navigation.

Southern hemisphere

1	Aquarius	**5**	Virgo
2	Capricornus	**6**	Sagittarius
3	Crux (Southern Cross)	**7**	Scorpius
4	Libra	**8**	Orion

Continents

Continents

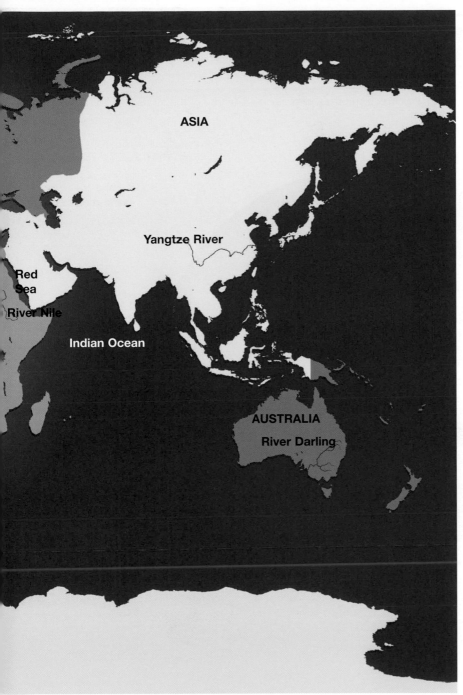

ASIA

Yangtze River

Red Sea

River Nile

Indian Ocean

AUSTRALIA

River Darling

Continents
Africa
Antarctica
Asia
Australia
Europe
North America
South America

Oceans and seas
Antarctic Ocean
Arctic Ocean
Atlantic Ocean
Indian Ocean
Mediterranean Sea
North Sea
Pacific Ocean
Red Sea

Rivers
Amazon (South America)
Danube (Europe)
Mississippi (North America)
Nile (Africa)
Yangtze (Asia)
Darling (Australia)

A cross-section of the earth

The earth was formed around 4600 million years ago. In the beginning it was not solid, but molten. Over time the outside has cooled to form a hard, rock **crust**.

Beneath the crust is another layer of rock called the **mantle**. The mantle is very hot but does not melt completely due to great pressure.

At the centre of the earth is the **core**. The **outer core** is liquid, but it is thought that the **inner core** is solid.

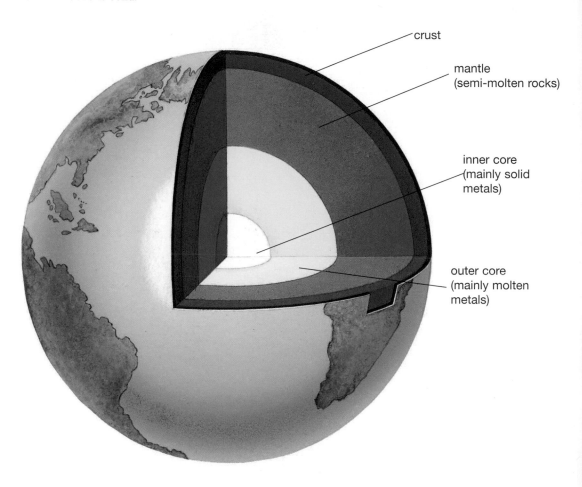

crust

mantle
(semi-molten rocks)

inner core
(mainly solid
metals)

outer core
(mainly molten
metals)

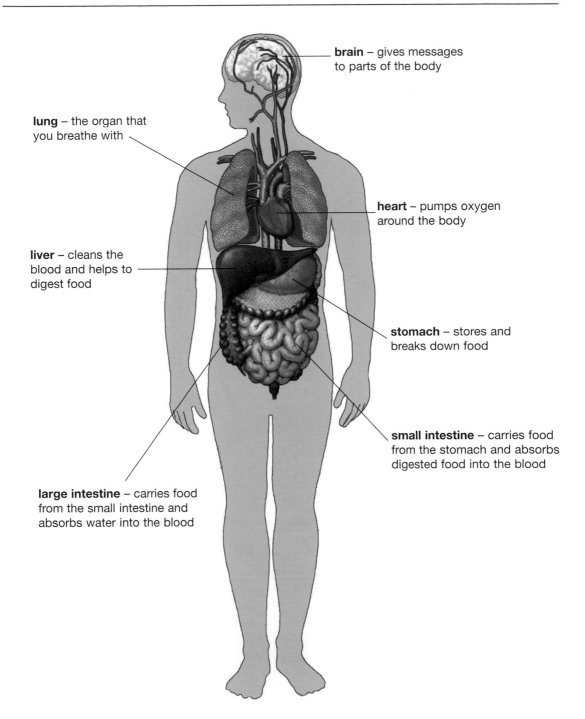

brain – gives messages to parts of the body

lung – the organ that you breathe with

heart – pumps oxygen around the body

liver – cleans the blood and helps to digest food

stomach – stores and breaks down food

small intestine – carries food from the stomach and absorbs digested food into the blood

large intestine – carries food from the small intestine and absorbs water into the blood

Parts of a plant

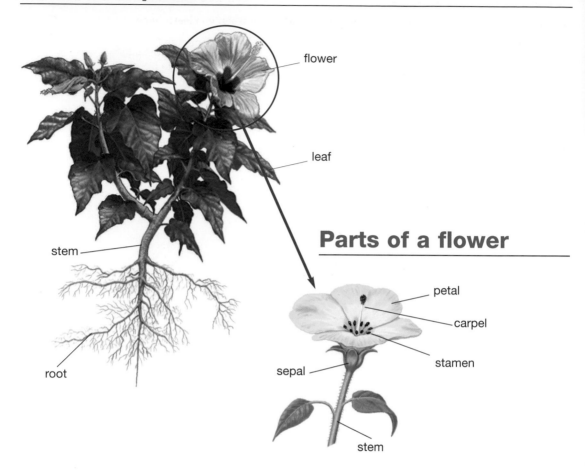

flower

leaf

stem

root

Parts of a flower

petal

carpel

stamen

sepal

stem

Parts of an insect

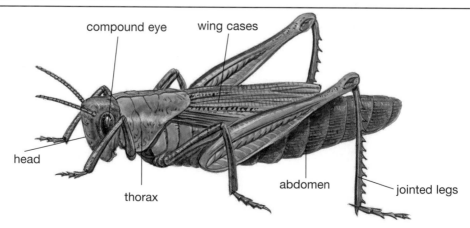

compound eye

wing cases

head

thorax

abdomen

jointed legs

Tricky words to spell

These words are often misspelled and need special attention when you learn them.

accessible
accommodation
address
all right
amateur
arguing
awful
awkward
balance
balloon
because
believe
beautiful
camouflage
catastrophe
committee
conscience
despair
develop
diesel
efficient
eighth
embarrass
exercise
fascinate
February
forecast
gardener
guard

guide
hiccup
imaginary
immediately
interrupt
its (belongs to it)
it's (short for *it is*)
jealous
jewellery
judgment
knowledge
library
lightning (flash of)
manoeuvre
medieval
Mediterranean
miniature
mischievous
misspell
mysterious
necessary
neighbour
occasion
occurred
operate
ought
paraffin
parallel
paralyse

people
pronunciation
quarrelling
queue
quiet
quite
receipt
religious
rhythm
ridiculous
schedule
seize
separate
sincere
strength
succeed
successful
suddenly
technique
temperature
tomatoes
twelfth
typical
Wednesday
weird
whether
writing
written
xylophone

Words from other languages

Many words we use today come from other languages. Here are some examples.

Latin: adolescent, adverb, benefit, calculate, castle, evaporate, human, industry, literature, manual, observe, square, video.

Greek: acrobat, autograph, colossal, history, hour, ozone, pathetic, telephone.

French: banquet, café, chef, oboe, tapestry, torch, vinegar.

Old English: barn, beetle, bless, cluster, daisy, Easter, ooze, sibling, Thursday, welcome.

Arabic: genie, kebab, sofa, syrup.

Hindi: bungalow, juggernaut, jungle, thug, yoga.

Spanish: alligator, crusade, cockroach, grenade.

Italian: ballet, brave, macaroni, pasta, picturesque, profile, quarantine, spaghetti, squadron, zany.

Parts of speech

Nouns

Nouns are naming words. They can be the names of people, places, things, groups, qualities or ideas. There are four types of noun. Many nouns have two forms, the **singular** form, which is used to refer to one person or thing, and the **plural** form, which is used to describe more than one person or thing. (*See* page 437.)

- **Proper nouns** name particular people, things or places, such as "Queen Elizabeth", "China", "Divali", "Glasgow". Proper nouns always begin with a capital letter.

- **Common nouns** name people, things, places and ideas in general, for example, "dog", "foot", "town" and "bacon". Common nouns do not start with a capital letter unless they begin a sentence. There are two types of common noun:

  - **concrete nouns** which name objects, such as "table", "chair" and "horse";

  - **abstract nouns** which name ideas, such as "happiness", "fear", "wonder" and "sorrow".

- **Collective nouns** name a group of people or things. A *crew* is a group of sailors, a *team* is a group of sports players, a *pack* is a collection of cards.

- **Compound nouns** Sometimes one word is not enough to name something accurately, so two or more words are used, for example "ozone layer", "department store" and "horse chestnut".

Pronouns

Pronouns are words you use instead of a noun.

- **Personal pronouns** are used instead of naming people: "I", "you", "he", "she", "it", "they", "them", "him", "we", "us".

- **Possessive pronouns** show who or what owns them: "yours", "his", "hers", "its", "ours", "their", "theirs", "mine".

Verbs

A sentence must contain a verb. **Verbs** can describe an action: "I *sing*"; "he is *running*", "they are *playing*". Verbs can also describe how something or someone is: "he *is* ill"; "his tyres *are* flat"; "the teacher will *be* late".

Verbs have three main tenses:

Past	Present	Future
I *danced*	I *dance*	I *shall dance*
I *was dancing*	I *am dancing*	I *am going to dance*
I *did dance*	I *do dance*	I *am about to dance*
I *had danced*		I *shall be dancing*

Adjectives

Adjectives are words that tell us more about nouns or pronouns. They are usually put in front of the word they are describing: a *big* dog; a *silly* game; a *beautiful* day; and a *brilliant* match.

- **Comparative adjectives** tell you more about the noun. You form a comparative by adding *-er* to the adjective: "a *bigger* dog"; "a *sillier* game".

  Some adjectives have the word *more* in front of them to make them comparative: "a *more beautiful* day"; "a *more brilliant* match".

- **Superlative adjectives** express the idea of most. You form a superlative by adding *-est* to the adjective: "the *biggest* dog"; "the *silliest* game".

  Some adjectives have the word *most* in front of them to make them superlative: "the *most beautiful* day"; "the *most brilliant* match".

Adjective	Comparative	Superlative
high	higher	highest
funny	funnier	funniest
beautiful	more beautiful	most beautiful
brilliant	more brilliant	most brilliant

Adverbs

Adverbs tell us more about verbs. Usually an adverb is found very close to its verb: "he rode *furiously*"; "she played *happily*"; "they sang *quietly*". Many adverbs end in the suffix *–ly*. Adverbs can be *phrases* as well as individual words: *out of tune, for several hours, by mistake, earlier than expected.*

Parts of speech

Adverbs often answer the following questions.
How? ... *slowly, happily, frantically*
Where? ... *outside, inside, above, below*
When? ... *today, yesterday, tomorrow, annually*
Why? ... *because of, due to*
How many? ... *once, again*
How much? ... *very, extremely, completely*
How often? ... *frequently, often, rarely*

Prepositions

Prepositions link two nouns or pronouns. They often indicate place, movement or time:

"they ran *around* the tree". *See* pages 438–9.

Conjunctions

Conjunctions are the words that connect parts of a sentence, such as "and", "because", "but", "for", "however", "since" and "yet".

Interjections

Interjections are usually words on their own that express strong feelings, such as "Hi!" "Hello!" "Never!" "Phew!" "Oh!" and "EEEK!" They usually end with an exclamation mark.

Singular and plural

Singular means one of something and plural means more than one. The usual way to show a noun in the plural is to add an -s: pen – pens; cat – cats; candle – candles. This table will help you with the exceptions.

Noun ending	Plural	Examples	
-ch, -s, -sh, -ss or **-x**	add **-es**	stitch – stitches gash – gashes dress – dresses	bus – buses fox – foxes
-y with a consonant in front	change **-y to –ies**	party – parties	
-y with a vowel in front	add **-s**	donkey – donkeys	
-f or **-fe**	change **-f** or **fe** to **-ves**	loaf – loaves wife – wives	
	there are some exceptions	roof – roofs safes – safe	
-o	add **-es**	hero – heroes	
Some nouns are the same in both the singular and the plural		sheep – sheep deer – deer	fish – fish

Question words

When you are asking about a person you use **who?**
When you want to know about something happening or something that has happened you use **what?**
When you want to know information you use **why?**
When your question is about time you use **when?**
When you want to know about the way something is done you use **how?**
When you want to know about two different possibilities you use **which?**
When you want to find out about a place you use **where?**

Prepositions

Prepositions link two nouns or pronouns, to show how they are connected to each other.

- Prepositions may tell you the **place** of something in relation to another thing:
  *She found the book **on** the table.*
  *We saw the ball **beneath** the bush.*

- Prepositions may indicate **movement**:
  *The dog ran **towards** us.*
  *They walked **along** the beach.*

- Prepositions may indicate **time**:
  *I cannot go out **until** I have had my tea.*
  *We went on holiday **for** a week.*

for

about

at

amid

through

over

down   up   like   against   off   on

behind   around

beneath

by

from

beyond

in front   beside

438

Prepositions

in

of

towards

to

across

inside

between

near   far

above   below

since

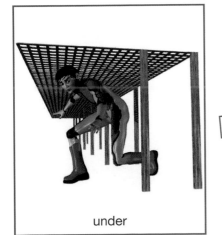

under

upon

till

until

with

439

Prefixes

Root words

A **root word** is a basic word from which other words are made. For example, the root word 'cover' can change to **un**cover, **dis**cover, **re**cover, cover**ing**, **redis**cover**y** and so on. The new parts of the word, such as "un-", "dis-" and "-ing", are **prefixes** and **suffixes**.

Prefixes

The **prefix** is a group of letters added to the beginning of a word. It changes or adds to the meaning of the root: **tele**scope, **mis**understand, **semi**circle. Some common prefixes are listed below.

Prefix	Meaning	Example
anti-	opposite of, against	anticlockwise
arch-	chief	archbishop
auto-	self	autobiography
co-	together	cooperate
com-	together	compare
contra-	against	contradict
de-	take away	defrost
dis-	opposite of	disappear
em-	in	embark
ex-	former	ex-partner
extra-	more	extraordinary
fore-	before, in front of	forecast
il-; im-; in-; ir-	not	illegal; impossible; inaccurate; irrational
inter-	between	international
micro-	very small	microscope
mid-	middle	midday
mini-	smaller	minibus
mis-	wrong	misspell
mono-	one	monologue
multi-	many	multitude
non-	not	non-fiction
over-	too much	overgrown
poly-	many	polygon
post-	after	post-war
pre-	before	prehistoric
pro-	supporting	pro-European
re-	again	reappear
semi-	half	semicircle
sub-	below	submarine
super-	over, more than	supersonic
tele-	at a distance	telephone
trans-	across	transport
ultra-	beyond	ultraviolet
un-	not	unkind
under-	under, not enough	underestimate

Suffixes

The **suffix** is a letter or group of letters added to the end of a word. It can change the tense of the word from present to past, as in *talk* to *talked*. It can also change the class of the word.

Suffixes can:

- change nouns into other nouns: good – good**ness**; friend – friend**ship**; art – art**ist**.
- change nouns into verbs: length – length**en**; fright – fright**en**.
- change nouns or verbs into adjectives: drink – drink**able**; use – use**ful**; harm – harm**less**.
- change adjectives into adverbs: slow – slow**ly**; happy – happ**ily**; quick – quick**ly**.
- change verbs or adjectives into nouns: happy – happi**ness**; enjoy – enjoy**ment**; invite – invita**tion**.
- change nouns to be feminine: lion – lion**ess**; prince – princ**ess**.
- change a noun to a diminutive (a word that shows something is small): kitchen – kitchen**ette**; pig – pig**let**.

Suffixes	Meaning	Example
-able, -ible, -uble	able to be	edible, soluble
-ant, -ent	a doer	attendant
-dom	condition, rank, territory	freedom, kingdom
-ee	one who is	employee
-er	a doer	farmer, miner, teacher
-er	more	higher, lower
-ess	to make the feminine	goddess, princess
-est	most	hardest, lightest
-ful	full of	truthful
-hood	state of	childhood
-ic	belonging to	prehistoric
-ize	used to make verbs	advertize
-ish	like	boyish
-ism	belief	Judaism, Buddhism
-ist	a doer	artist
-itis	inflammation of	appendicitis
-less	free from	thoughtless, smokeless
-let	small	booklet, piglet
-ly	used to make adverbs	hotly, sleepily
-ment	used to make nouns	pavement
-ness	state of being	kindness
-oid	like	cuboid
-ology	study of	biology
-or	a doer	sailor, actor
-ous	used to make adjectives	dangerous
-ship	state of being	friendship
-some	tending to	tiresome
-ty	showing condition	cruelty
-wards	in a direction	southwards

Synonyms, antonyms and homonyms

Synonyms

A **synonym** is a word meaning the same, or almost the same, as another word.
Here are some useful synonyms for some everyday words.

angry   annoyed, cross, furious, mad

good   enjoyable, well-behaved, clever, fine, tasty

big   huge, large, enormous, vast, colossal

small   little, tiny, young, unimportant, trivial

say   announce, complain, declare, exclaim, mention, remark, state, utter, whisper, shout, mumble

Some words have a different meaning depending on how they are used, for example,
look at these ways of using the word **nice**.

a nice man   pleasant, charming, good, kind, helpful, sweet, friendly

a nice outing   enjoyable, lovely, agreeable, delightful

a nice meal   tasty, delicious

Antonyms

An **antonym** is a word meaning the opposite of another word. For example, *exciting* is an
antonym for *boring*. Antonyms are often formed by adding prefixes to root words:

im + possible = impossible   non + sense = nonsense
un + usual = unusual   il + legal = illegal
dis + honest = dishonest   in + complete = incomplete

The suffix *-less* is also used to form antonyms:
worth + less = worthless
harm + less = harmless
pain + less = painless

Homonyms

Homonyms are words that sound the same but have a different meaning and spelling. Common
nouns that are often confused are **passed** and **past**, **piece** and **peace**, **stationery** and **stationary**.
Look these up in the dictionary to find out the different meanings.

Watch out for these homonyms:

their (belonging to them)   They took their coats off.
they're (a contraction of *they are*)   They're going to go swimming.
there   Put your shoes over there.

too   I liked the film too.
to   Can we go to the fair?
two   There were two apples left.

whose (belonging to whom)   Whose bag is this?
who's (a contraction of *who is* or *who has*)   Who's the best at running?

Punctuation

Starting a sentence

A **capital letter** is used to start a sentence.

It is time for us to leave.

Capital letters are also used for proper nouns.

My friend Nancy is coming to visit.

Ending a sentence

You can end a sentence with:

- a **full stop** (.):

I have finished my homework.

- a **question mark** (?) if it is a question:

Can I go round to Danny's after tea?

- an **exclamation mark** (!) to show strong feeling:

The party was excellent!

In a sentence

A **dash** (–) is used when there is an interruption of some sort.

Jeremy – my brother – is a teacher.

Commas (,) are used whenever the reader ought to pause.

You must use a comma:

- to separate words in a list:

eggs, bacon, mushrooms, sausages and beans.

- to separate words or phrases in a sentence:

The dog, Ellie May, barked loudly.

- in direct speech:

"No," I said, "I can't sing that song!"

Brackets ( ) can be used to enclose any word or words that you put into a sentence as an afterthought:

The cook (my mum) dropped the cake on the floor (she had forgotten to use her oven glove).

Apostrophes (') are used:

- to show omitted letters:

can't (cannot), *won't* (will not), *shan't* (shall not)

- to show possession:

The cat's bowl (if there is only one cat); *the cats' bowl* (if there is more than one cat)

When adding 's to a noun looks ugly or makes it difficult to say, the *s* is dropped:

Nicholas' scooter (*Nicholas's* looks ugly).

You use a **colon** (:) in front of a list:

She packed all her summer clothes: a swimsuit, two dresses, jeans, T-shirts and a pair of sandals.

A **semicolon** (;) is used to separate different parts of a sentence or list, or to show a pause:

There was a choice of sandwiches: cheese, ham and pineapple; prawn, cucumber and mayonnaise; beef and horseradish sauce; or cheese and tomato.

Quotation or speech marks (" " or ' ') show where speech begins and ends. If a sentence ends with the actual words somebody speaks, the quotation marks end the sentence:

"It's freezing today," said Joey.

Joey said, "It's freezing today."

Measures

Length

millimetre (mm)
centimetre (cm)
metre (m)
kilometre (km)
mile

Mass or weight

gram (g)
half-kilogram
kilogram (kg)
pint (pt)

Capacity

millilitre (ml)
half-litre
litre (l)

Time

Telling the time
a.m.
p.m.
o'clock
half past
quarter past
quarter to
analogue
digital
clock
watch
timer

eight thirty-five

twenty-five to nine

More time words

yesterday
today
tomorrow

calendar
date
weekend
holiday
birthday
term

second
minute
hour
day
week
fortnight
month
year
leap year
decade
century
millennium

dawn
sunrise
morning
midday
noon
afternoon
dusk
twilight
sunset
evening
night
midnight

breakfast time
break time
playtime
lunch time
dinner time
bedtime

Time

When/how often?	Days	Months	Seasons
never	Monday	January	spring
once	Tuesday	February	summer
twice	Wednesday	March	autumn
rarely	Thursday	April	winter
occasionally	Friday	May	
from time to time	Saturday	June	
sometimes	Sunday	July	
often		August	
soon		September	
frequently		October	
usually		November	
always		December	

Words to use when talking or writing about time

If events happen **simultaneously**, they happen at the same time.

Contemporary events are those which are happening now.

The time or distance between two events is a **span**.
>   *The time **span** was three months.*

Things that happen **consecutively** happen one after the other.

A particular length of time can be called a **period**.

An uninterrupted time period is a **duration**.
>   *The **duration** of my project was one week.*

Time in music is **tempo**.
>   *The **tempo** made me tap my feet.*

If you arrange things in slightly different time periods, you **stagger** them.
>   *I **staggered** my tasks so I did not get too tired.*

If time **elapses**, it passes.

If you talk about time going back into the distant past, you talk about time **immemorial**.

A very long time, specifically a thousand million years, is an **aeon**.

If you talk about time going on for ever, you talk about **eternity**.
>   *The lesson seemed to last an **eternity**.*

A particular period in history can be called an **age**.

A particular period in history can also be called an **era**.
>   *Women wore long dresses during the Elizabethan **era**.*

A period of the year when something usually happens is called a **season**.
>   *I'm looking forward to the cricket **season**.*

2D shapes

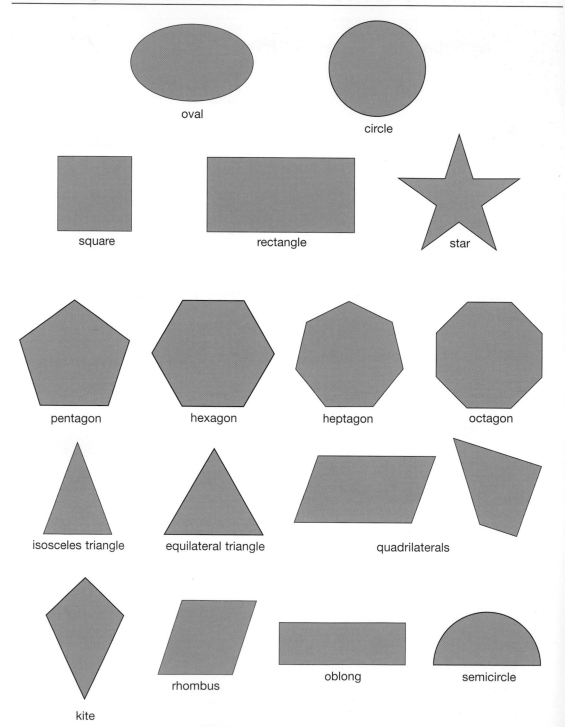

oval

circle

square

rectangle

star

pentagon

hexagon

heptagon

octagon

isosceles triangle

equilateral triangle

quadrilaterals

kite

rhombus

oblong

semicircle

3D shapes

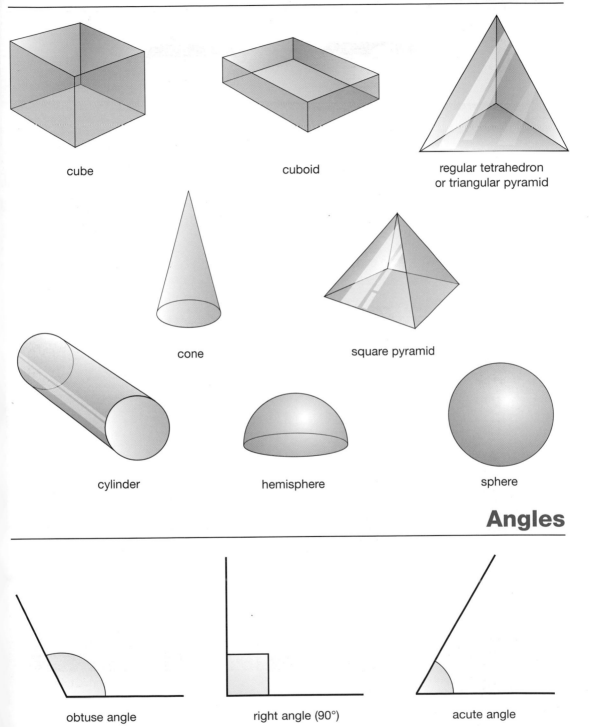

cube

cuboid

regular tetrahedron
or triangular pyramid

cone

square pyramid

cylinder

hemisphere

sphere

Angles

obtuse angle

right angle (90°)

acute angle

Number bank

Cardinal numbers

1 one	17 seventeen
2 two	18 eighteen
3 three	19 nineteen
4 four	20 twenty
5 five	30 thirty
6 six	40 forty
7 seven	50 fifty
8 eight	60 sixty
9 nine	70 seventy
10 ten	80 eighty
11 eleven	90 ninety
12 twelve	100 one hundred
13 thirteen	1000 one thousand
14 fourteen	10 000 ten thousand
15 fifteen	1 000 000 one million
16 sixteen	10 000 000 ten million

Ordinal Numbers

1st	first	12th	twelfth
2nd	second	13th	thirteenth
3rd	third	14th	fourteenth
4th	fourth	15th	fifteenth
5th	fifth	16th	sixteenth
6th	sixth	17th	seventeenth
7th	seventh	18th	eighteenth
8th	eighth	19th	nineteenth
9th	ninth	20th	twentieth
10th	tenth	21st	twenty-first
11th	eleventh	22nd	twenty-second

Roman numerals

I	1	IX	9
II	2	X	10
III	3	L	50
IV	4	C	100
V	5	D	500
VI	6	M	1000
VII	7	MCMXCVI	1996
VIII	8	MM	2000

Fractions

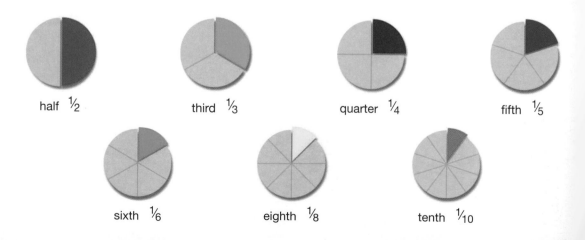

half ½   third ⅓   quarter ¼   fifth ⅕

sixth ⅙   eighth ⅛   tenth ¹⁄₁₀